WITHDRAWN
UTSA LIBRARIES

RENEWALS 458-4574

Adolf Hitler

A Biographical Companion

Adolf Hitler
A Biographical Companion

David Nicholls

ABC-CLIO

Santa Barbara, California
Denver, Colorado
Oxford, England

Frontispiece photograph: Hulton-Deutsch Collection/Corbis

Copyright © 2000 by David Nicholls

All rights reserved. No part of this publication may be reproduced, stored in a retrieval system, or transmitted, in any form or by any means, electronic, mechanical, photocopying, recording, or otherwise, except for the inclusion of brief quotations in a review, without prior permission in writing from the publishers.

Library of Congress Cataloging-in-Publication Data
Nicholls, David, 1949–
Adolf Hitler : a biographical companion / David Nicholls.
    p.   cm.
Includes bibliographical references and index.
  ISBN 0-87436-965-7 (alk. paper)
  1. Hitler, Adolf, 1869–1945. 2. Heads of state—Germany—Biography.
3. National socialism. 4. Germany—Politics and government—1939–1945.
I. Title.
DD247.H5 N53 2000
943.086'092—dc21
                                                   00-010198
                                                      CIP

05 04 03 02 01 00   10 9 8 7 6 5 4 3 2 1

ABC-CLIO, Inc.
130 Cremona Drive, P.O. Box 1911
Santa Barbara, California 93116–1911

Typesetting by Letra Libre, Inc.

This book is printed on acid-free paper ∞.
Manufactured in the United States of America

Library
University of Texas
at San Antonio

ABC-CLIO BIOGRAPHICAL COMPANIONS

Benjamin Franklin, by Jennifer L. Durham
Thomas Jefferson, by David S. Brown
Susan B. Anthony, by Judith E. Harper
Napoleon, by David Nicholls
Joseph Stalin, by Helen Rappaport
Adolf Hitler, by David Nicholls

ABC-CLIO Biographical Companions are encyclopedic guides to the lives of men and women who have had a significant impact on the social, political, and cultural development of the Western world. Each volume presents complete biographical information in an easily accessible format. An introduction and a chronology provide an overview, while the A-to-Z entries amplify a myriad of topics related to the person. A collection of documents and extensive illustrations give the reader an acute sense of the individual's life and times.

CONTENTS

INTRODUCTION

Studying Adolf Hitler raises peculiar problems. Writing about a man responsible for such overwhelming evil inevitably has a moral as well as a normal historical or philosophical dimension. Hitler turned his crazy pipe dreams into the deaths of millions of people and a living nightmare for millions more. Should we even attempt to explain him? And if we do, is there not a danger of personalizing evil, easily placing the blame on the peculiarities of one individual when in reality, responsibility was more broadly spread? What of those who supported him, kept silent, or remained indifferent? Can Hitler be held responsible for the moral shortcomings or the mere human limitations of so many others, especially those who felt genuinely powerless in the face of Nazi tyranny? Raising these very questions provides one good reason for studying Hitler: he forces us to ask questions about ourselves.

But for many people any attempt to explain Hitler is in itself obscene. The endeavor to get at the roots of Hitler's psychology and worldview risks the creation of a "Hitler without victims," while at the same time to ascribe any real meaning to his actions is to play his own game. The only people for whom the Holocaust had a purpose were the Nazis. And referring to the Holocaust, the historian Eberhard Jäckel writes: "The rational power of language becomes paralyzed in the face of that event" (Jäckel 1984, p. 106). But to attempt historical explanation is not to ascribe a higher meaning or purpose, certainly not to the actions of Hitler. It is both historically and humanly necessary to come to terms with Hitler and his career of destruction.

Hitler is one of the rare individuals about whom it may be said incontrovertibly that without him, history would have been very different. His twelve-year rule in Germany left a legacy that lasted for more than half a century, in the Cold War, the shape of Europe, and as a moral trauma that will never and should never be surmounted. He permanently changed the world. In one sense he embodies the twentieth century: "The century which, in a sense, his name has dominated has gained much of its character by war and genocide—Hitler's hallmarks" (Kershaw 1998, p. xx). Hitler's person and his actions incarnate what the critic and historian Peter Conrad has placed among "the abiding concerns of our century": "the competition between humanity and inhuman mechanism, or between human values and subhuman behavior" (Conrad 1998, p. 8). The nature of his barbarity and that of his followers, the forces that made him possible, are still matters calling urgently for assessment and judgment.

Hitler's story is the history of his rise to power and how he used that power. At the center stands a kind of nonperson, a man with a giant ego but little or no discernible personality, certainly not a very interesting one. Even his strongest opinions, which filled the hole where a personality should have been, were secondhand. He was a man without friends, only accomplices. In 1930 the satirist Kurt Tucholsky said of Hitler: "The man doesn't exist. . . . He is only the noise he makes" (Bullock 1991, p. 191). The saying of Petrarch, quoted by a recent biographer of Joseph Stalin, could apply equally to Hitler: "When destiny raises a base character by acts of great importance, it reveals his lack of substance" (Volkogonov 1995, p. xxviii).

The main component of Hitler's "personality" was his ideological obsession, his weltanschauung (worldview). As General Heinz Guderian wrote, with hindsight: "He had a special picture of the world, and every fact had to be fitted into that fancied world. As he believed, so the world must be; but, in fact it was the picture of another world" (Bullock 1991, p. 958). But even this was secondhand, a grab bag of racist and nationalist ideas, many of them widely influential not only in Germany but throughout Europe. Reacting against the defeat of Germany in World War I and the left-wing revolution that followed it, Hitler, like many others, looked for scapegoats and found them in the "November criminals," that is the politicians who had signed the armistice and went on to create a new democratic republic, and above all in the Jews.

At the heart of Hitler's worldview was a crude racial interpretation of history. The story of humankind was driven and dominated by the competition between "races." In his crude form of Social Darwinism, history was a struggle for the "survival of the fittest" between the superior Aryan race and the inferior races seeking constantly to weaken and dilute pure Aryan blood and the rightfully dominant position of the Aryan race. Hitler found this nonsense in a succession of writers, most of whom he probably never read in any depth, and in simpler terms in the *völkisch* press of Vienna and Munich before 1914. Thanks to him, the malevolent craziness of racial thought moved from the margins of society to the center of politics. And if he played it down for electoral purposes before 1933, it was always inherent in the way he talked of Germany and the Germans.

Too many politicians and ordinary voters did not realize until it was too late that for Hitler a "strong Germany" did not mean merely a revived German state, ready to take its rightful place among the nations, but a mighty German race expanding aggressively to a position of world power. This meant the subjugation of "inferior" races and ultimately the extermination of the most vile and insidious of all races, the Jews. In Hitler's fantastic vision, the "eternal Jew" and his materialist values had been responsible for the evils afflicting not only the German but the human race. The international leveling creed of Marxism, the brainchild of "the Jew Karl Marx," as he always called him, was merely the latest manifestation of "Jewish materialism." It was Hitler's mission to wipe it from the face of the earth, starting with Germany. The internationalist delusions of both social democracy and bolshevism had weakened the national spirit and were to be destroyed.

Hitler pursued his goals with a highly effective blend of cold calculation and a gambler's instinct, always betting on the weakness of his opponents. During his assumption of power in the international politics of the 1930s and the early stages of World War II, Hitler would hesitate, worry, and then finally take decisive action or raise the stakes, hoping that the others would back down. As a "conviction politician" par excellence, Hitler would pour scorn on the advice of more cautious professionals, whether diplomats, soldiers, or even other leading Nazis, and so long as this tactic worked from 1933 to 1941, it helped him build both reputation and popularity. As General Alfred Jodl noted during his trial at Nuremberg: "The Führer regarded it as proper in his military leadership, as he had in his political activity, to establish goals which were so far-reaching that the objective professionals would declare them impossible. But he did this deliberately, convinced that the actual course of events would leave these more modest calculations behind" (Bullock 1991, p. 745).

All objections, all difficulties would crumble before the Führer's mighty will, and when he began to fail from 1942 onward it was because he had been let down by his subordinates. Hitler was always prone to outbursts of blind fury, and those on the receiving end could never be sure whether these were genuine or based on cool calculation. A personality built on hatred could always find new objects for his anger. Hermann Rauschning, not always a reliable witness in detail, was right in general when he wrote: "Hatred is like wine to him, it intoxicates him. One must have heard his tirades of denunciation to realise how he can revel in hate" (Bullock 1991, p.395). Hitler, the vegetarian, nondrinker, and nonsmoker, found sustenance and intoxication in execration and misanthropy. The only human beings for whom he showed any genuine affection were his mother and possibly his niece, Geli Raubal.

Ambition, racial obsession, hatred, scorn for humanity: these traits of Hitler's character, when blended with a dose of paranoia and a growing messianic complex, made a deadly cocktail. Once Hitler had decided that he was not merely the "drummer" announcing the new great leader for Germany but was himself that leader, then the people became nothing more than the mass whose purpose was to support him in a spirit of blind obedience. Hitler, the self-styled disciple of Richard Wagner, believed in his mission either to succeed totally or to go down in a blaze of operatic glory. Toward the end, in Hitler's increasingly deranged mind, the German people had proved unworthy of him. The "degenerate" Germans withdrew their support and deserved their fate. As in Wagner's *Rienzi,* the people were not worthy of their tribune. All the facets of Hitler's character, such as it was, amount together to an all-embracing egomania, which meant that ultimately he would bring everyone and everything down with him.

A major part of Hitler's continuing fascination lies in his success in harnessing the dynamic, irrational elements in politics against the inevitable but often shabby compromises inherent in democracy. He exploited the deep emotions of fear, resentment, and despair to create a new hope and launched a new crusade through a movement filled with apparently unstoppable dynamism. The unhappy individual was to be subsumed into a revivified, cleansed, and pure new community—the *Volksgemeinschaft.* The Nazi movement was young, forceful, and idealistic, in contrast to the dull and compromised democratic politicians of the Weimar Republic. Almost anything was achievable if only the will was there to carry it through.

Hitler's real talent lay in demagogy—the whipping up and channeling of the emotions of his audience. He represents the most extreme example of a phenomenon often seen in a age of mass politics. In his own eyes and those of his followers he was the "little man" risen from nowhere to become the leader of a great nation, partly through his own willpower and partly by articulating the hopes, fears, and aspirations of other "little people." Rejecting economics as the basis of his appeal, he concentrated on the psychological effects of economic and political events, inciting anger and resentment against ready-made scapegoats: "bourgeois" politicians, big business, Marxists, foreigners, and Jews. And his demagogy could be so successful because it appealed simultaneously to idealism and base instinct: on the one hand, the utopian vision of a *völkisch* national community; on the other hand, the thuggery of the Sturmabteilung (SA) and other Nazi minions, intimidating and eliminating all real and imagined enemies.

Like other demagogic leaders before and after him, Hitler rose from nowhere. Born in 1889 in the small town of Braunau-am-Inn on the German-Austrian border where his father was a customs official, his family origins were obscure, but his own immediate background was impeccably respectable and lower middle class. Attempts to "explain" Hitler psychologically through his childhood and early years are unconvincing, ranging from the speculative to the outlandish. Resentful of his distant father, Alois, who died in 1903, but doting on his mother, Klara, probably the only human being he truly loved, he was not so different from many thousands of boys from a similar milieu. There was nothing remarkable about the young Hitler.

The family moved to Linz, which Hitler always looked upon as his home town, in 1905. Here until his mother's death in 1907 he lived a life of indolence and daydreaming. Consistently mediocre at school, he indulged idle pretensions to be an artist or an architect. To do this he had to move to Vienna. In the autobiographical sections of *Mein Kampf* Hitler was deliberately misleading about his years in Vienna from 1908 to 1913. Rejected twice for entry into the Vienna Academy of Fine Arts, Hitler scraped a living selling his pictures, sometimes sinking into extreme penury and residing mostly in a men's hostel. In his account Hitler did not seek to hide his poverty, but his claims to have been a "worker" laboring on a building site and converting his fellow workers from the evils of social democracy were grossly exaggerated.

Nor is it true to say that Hitler was "made" by his years in Vienna. There is no evidence to suggest that he was as yet anti-Semitic: he dealt amicably with Jewish art dealers and even attended the salons of Jewish connoisseurs. But he did immerse himself in racist newspapers and pamphlet literature, and he observed with enthusiasm the success of Vienna's anti-Semitic mayor, Karl Lueger, and with distaste the turbulent multiethnic politics of the Habsburg Empire. The "Viennese" Hitler was an argumentative young man whose tirades had little effect on his fellow hostel dwellers and whose principal enthusiasms were architecture and the operas of Richard Wagner.

Hitler the politician was created not in Vienna but during World War I. He moved from Vienna to Munich in 1913, partly to avoid conscription into the Austro-Hungarian army, partly to try his artistic chances in a "truly German" city. When war broke out in August 1914 Hitler welcomed it enthusiastically and volunteered for the "List Regiment" (Reserve Infantry Regiment 16). Apart from brief periods of leave (which he did not appreciate) he spent the next four years in the trenches of the Western Front in Flanders. His war service in the hazardous role of a dispatch runner was exemplary, earning him the Iron Cross, First Class. He would constantly refer to his experience as an "ordinary soldier" with much more justification than his pretense to having been a worker.

Temporarily blinded in a gas attack, Hitler was convalescing in Pasewalk, Pomerania, when he heard of the abdication of Kaiser Wilhelm II on 9 November 1918, the proclamation of the German republic, and the armistice of 11 November. Hitler showed no understanding of what had led to the dramatic events of 1918–1919, the sufferings of the German people caused by the Allied blockade, and the drain of blood in a war on two fronts. As he learned of communist uprisings in Berlin and Munich and the difficult creation of the Weimar Republic by Social Democratic and centrist politicians, all he could see was capitulation to the enemy, embodied in the Treaty of Versailles, signed on 28 June 1919. The German army had not been defeated; everything was ascribed to treachery by the "November criminals" (the politicians who had sued for peace), Marxists (including socialists of every stripe), and, incredibly, the Jews. In the years to come, Hitler was to make great use of the "stab in the back" legend and dedicate himself to the destruction of the Versailles peace and the republic born in revolution.

Hitler did not leave the army until March 1920. In June 1919 he attended a "political education" course run by the Reichswehr at Munich University and was subsequently stationed at a camp at Lechfeld, charged with indoctrinating soldiers awaiting demobilization against the growing extremism of Left and Right. Informants from the army were sent to observe meetings of extremist groups, and on 12 September 1919, acting in such a capacity, Hitler attended a meeting in Munich of the German Workers' Party (DAP), one of several nationalist and *völkisch* groups founded in the wake of defeat and revolution. Hitler joined the party a few days later. He later described this as the most important decision in his life: "From here there was and could be no turning back" (Hitler 1992, p. 204).

The twenty-five-point program of the DAP, drafted by Hitler and Anton Drexler, one of the founders of the party, was proclaimed at a meeting on 24 February 1920. It would in due course be declared "unalterable," but in practice large sections of it were ignored. It consisted mainly of the commonplaces of the anti-Semitic, *völkisch,* and nationalist Right, with populist elements such as the breaking of "interest slavery," confiscation of war profits, and protection of the middle class. Unobjectionable banalities such as "common good before individual good" and vague calls for land reform sat alongside the demand for a "strong central power" implying authoritarian government and showing that Hitler was already imagining himself at the head of a personalized autocratic regime. A week after the proclamation of its program the DAP changed its name to National Socialist German Workers' Party (NSDAP), or Nazi Party for short.

Hitler now found his true vocation as a beer hall orator and agitator, one of many such in Munich but more effective than most. He soon learned all the tricks of the trade: how to gauge the mood of an audience, cajole them, win them over, and rise to a suitable climax. Set down in cold print, his words may look banal and unimpressive, but the careful staging, the sense of anticipation in hearing Hitler speak, and the building up of a hysterical atmosphere all served to underline Hitler's abilities in his chosen calling. He was soon the indispensable dominant figure in the as yet insignificant NSDAP.

The next step was for Hitler to become the unquestioned leader of the NSDAP. After quitting the party briefly in July 1921, on 29 July he was elected party chairman with dictatorial powers. Hitler was now the Führer (leader) of the Nazi movement, a title that in itself was not unusual among nationalist groups devoted to the cult of the providential leader. Indeed, Drexler had previously been the Führer of the NSDAP. Hitler, however, was to turn the "Führer principle" into the fundamental dogma of his power, first in the Nazi movement and then in Germany. August 1921 saw the foundation of the Sturmabteilung (SA, or Stormtroopers). Initially intended to guard Nazi meetings against left-wing disruption, the SA quickly became the NSDAP's paramilitary organization, brawling and imposing itself in the beer halls and the streets.

Hitler's reputation grew rapidly. A three-day sojourn in prison in July 1922 helped to make his name known in *völkisch* circles outside Munich. In October 1922 Julius Streicher, the racist nationalist leader in Nuremberg, merged his *völkisch* group into the NSDAP and accepted Hitler's supremacy. In Munich itself, one newspaper declared in June 1923 that alongside the Hofbräuhaus, Hitler was the city's one notable curiosity. As his dubious standing increased, people outside and above Hitler's normal milieu of squabbling beer hall fanatics began to take notice. Through the good offices of Ernst "Putzi" Hanfstaengl, who became a sort of "social secretary," Hitler gained access to the salons of Munich society. Hanfstaengl was fascinated by this "virtuoso on the keyboard of the mass psyche" (Kershaw 1998, p. 187), even if he was contemptuous of Hitler's half-baked notions about art.

The most important contact made by Hitler was with Erich Ludendorff, the former war hero who had taken up residence in Munich in 1919 and was widely regarded as the symbolic leader of the radical nationalist Right. This connection was crucial to Hitler during 1923, the year of national emergency and crisis in Bavaria that would make his name known for the first time throughout Germany. As the NSDAP grew in numbers and notoriety, it held its first "Reich Party Rally" in Munich from 27 to 29 January. Two weeks earlier, the Ruhr region had been occupied by French and Belgian troops to enforce the payment of the war reparations imposed by the Treaty of Versailles. The German government proclaimed a policy of "passive resistance," much to the impotent fury of the nationalists. At the same time, hyperinflation, which caused the value of the German mark collapse to almost nothing, sparked unrest on both Left and Right, ripe for exploitation by the Nazis and those who thought like they did. The Bavarian government assumed emergency powers in response, but rumors of a putsch circulated from February onward.

The "Beer Hall Putsch" or "Hitler Putsch" of 8–9 November 1923 came to play a central role in Nazi mythology. The Nazi "martyrs" who died were revered as heroes, and the "blood flag," a swastika banner supposedly stained with their blood, would be paraded reverently at the Nuremberg rallies. The reality was confused, bloody, but absurd. It should also have meant the end of Hitler as a serious political figure. The proclamation of nationalist revolution and the deposition of the Bavarian and national governments, instead of culminating in a German version of Benito Mussolini's "March on Rome," ended in a brief shootout that left fourteen Nazis dead. Among the wounded were Hitler himself and Hermann Goering, a World War I fighter ace with useful aristocratic connections who had recently become commander of the SA.

The result of Hitler's first bid for power was that he found himself, along with the other putsch leaders, on trial for high treason. Hitler turned the courtroom into a public platform for his views, making his name known to the German public outside the *völkisch* circles where he had been a big fish in a small pond. He became and was to remain a celebrity. Thanks to the compliance of sympathetic judges, Hitler received the minimum sentence of five years imprisonment and a fine of 200 gold marks. In fact, he served only eight months in comfortable confinement in the fortress of Landsberg-am-Lech. Here he claimed to have read a lot, probably very superficially, and composed *Mein Kampf*, a mixture of distorted autobiography and political manifesto, which he dictated to the devoted Rudolf Hess, the future deputy Führer of the Third Reich. It was to become the Bible of Nazism, owned if not necessarily read by all Germans who wanted an untroubled life.

Hitler was released from Landsberg on 20 December 1924, unburdened by anything more troublesome than a growing sense of his own importance. Up to this time Hitler had seen himself as the "drummer" of the national cause, preparing the ground for the leader or leaders to come. The aim of the putsch had been to install a national government, to include Hitler but in which Ludendorff would inevitably be the leading figure. And to carry it out, the SA had temporarily merged with other paramilitary groups. According to this plan, Hitler was to be not the leader who would "save the Fatherland that was sinking into chaos" but "the agitator who understood how to mobilize the masses" (Kershaw 1998, p. 170). Then, either in Landsberg or over a longer period of time, Hitler became convinced that he was himself the leader for whom his benighted countrymen were waiting.

In 1925, however, the Fatherland was no longer in chaos. The Weimar Republic was entering its "golden age" of economic and relative political stability. A message like

Hitler's could only truly flourish in an atmosphere of crisis, and the future Führer would have to await his opportunity. In the meantime the banned NSDAP would have to be recreated and rebuilt and, the time for putsches having passed, follow a road to power based as far as possible on legality, exploiting the freedom granted by the detested democratic republic. It would have to be a dynamic movement, not a political party like the others or a *völkisch* debating society, and it was prepared to bolster legal actions with menace, bullying, and hoodlum tactics.

The Nazi Party was refounded in February 1925, but Hitler would have to wait until 1929 before the right conditions arose for its great leap forward: "For that, Hitler's only hope was a massive and comprehensive crisis of the state" (Kershaw 1998, p. 311). In the meantime, he had to affirm his own ascendancy over the Nazi movement, eliminate or assimilate any potential rivals, keep hammering home his message, and exploit any opportunities for agitation. He was banned from speaking in Bavaria until March 1927. Other states had also imposed such bans: that in Prussia was only lifted in September 1928. And in the more stable political conditions prevailing in the late 1920s, his meetings in Munich no longer attracted the same huge numbers and fervent enthusiasm.

Nevertheless, these were years of steady progress for the Nazis. Party membership slowly increased. On the eve of the crisis of 1929 it was three times larger that at the time of the putsch, and more importantly, it had spread throughout Germany, setting down roots, however feeble, in regions where it had been unknown. *Mein Kampf* was published in two volumes in 1925 and 1926. And Hitler outmaneuvered his potential rivals. The most serious threat, from those who took seriously the "socialist" elements in the Nazi program, was effectively eliminated. The hopes of Gregor Strasser and others of the Nazi "Left" were dashed by Hitler at a meeting of party leaders at Bamberg on 14 February 1926. In fact, the most important constituent of the Nazi program was Hitler itself. For people newly attracted to Nazism, like the young Josef Goebbels, it was the Führer's intransigence and his providential role, his idealistic appeal and call to power, that formed the real attraction of the movement. Here was a man who would rid Germany of her internal enemies and brook no compromise with her international rivals.

In 1928, however, prospects for the NSDAP remained limited at best. In the Reichstag elections of 28 May the Nazis gained only 2.6 percent of the vote and twelve seats. But they fared better in state elections in early 1929: 5 percent in Saxony; 4 percent in Mecklenburg, enough to hold the balance between Left and Right; and 7 percent in Baden in October. On 23 June the northern Bavarian town of Coburg became the first to elect a Nazi town council. But this was as yet of no great consequence. Then on 24 October, Wall Street, New York, the largest stock market in the world, crashed. The crisis Hitler needed had arrived, in Germany and the world. His rise to power was never inevitable, but now his seeming weaknesses, his extremism and refusal to compromise, could become his strengths. The idea of the providential leader moved from the realm of nationalist fantasy into the sphere of possibility.

A first chance to test public opinion was provided by the Young Plan, a new scheme for the payment of reparations, signed on 7 June 1929. Hitler joined with other extreme nationalist groups in calling for a plebiscite and rejection of the plan. The results of the plebiscite, held on 22 December, were disappointing: the Nazis and their allies secured only 13.8 percent support. But the propaganda value of the campaign had been immense. The "Hitler movement" was a force to be reckoned with, and unlike the "bourgeois" politicians it seemed to know where it was going.

On 27 March 1930 the Reich government, a "grand coalition" led by the Social Democrats, resigned. Amid much confusion and wheeling and dealing, the president, Field Marshal Paul von Hindenburg, a conservative whose political sympathies and instincts were more monarchist than republican, appointed the centrist Heinrich Brüning as chancellor at the head of a minority government. Brüning introduced a deflationary program to deal with the economic crisis, but the Nazis joined with the Social Democrats and others in rejecting it, leading to the dissolution of the Reichstag and new elections. With the benefit of hindsight, this can be seen as a disaster for democracy in Germany. In the elections of 14 September the NSDAP gained 18.3 percent of the vote and became the second-largest party in the Reichstag, with 107 seats. The legal road to power was opening for Hitler, if he knew how to take it and if other politicians did not take him seriously enough. Accordingly, on 25 September 1930 Hitler swore an oath before the Reich Court in Leipzig that his party would not attempt to gain power by illegal means. This was a legalistic half-truth. The Nazis would use their strength in the Reichstag to disrupt the parliamentary process while spreading their influence in society by all means possible.

The SA, with Hitler's longtime crony Ernst Röhm as chief of staff, fought with Communist and Socialist paramilitaries in working-class areas, while Hitler himself created a more respectable and responsible image for consumption by middle-class voters and business people. Even the suicide of his niece, Geli Raubal, in his Munich apartment did Hitler no permanent damage. In an important speech to industrialists at Düsseldorf on 26 January 1932, Hitler assured them that they had nothing to fear from the Nazis as long as they worked in the "national interest." The residual radicalism in the NSDAP was finally broken in December 1932 when Gregor Strasser resigned all his party offices. Although still professing a sort of racially based egalitarianism, Hitler's path to power lay in promising all things to all people. In this he was greatly helped by the frock-coated "bourgeois" politicians he so despised.

The notional offer of a ministerial post in the state of Braunschweig allowed Hitler finally to acquire German citizenship in February 1932. After his oath of allegiance to the state, he could stand against Hindenburg in the presidential election of 13 March, gaining a remarkable 30.1 percent of the vote. A second election of 10 April, necessary because Hindenburg had just failed to gain an absolute majority, saw Hitler's support rise to 36.8 percent, against Hindenburg's 53 percent. The continuing violence in the streets caused the SA to be banned between 13 April and 16 June, but this did not halt the seemingly inexorable progress of the Nazis. State elections on 24 April left the NSDAP as the largest party in Prussia (the largest state in the Reich), Württemberg, Anhalt, and Hamburg, and the second-largest in Bavaria.

Political machinations at the top continued to help Hitler. Brüning resigned as chancellor on 30 May and was succeeded by Franz von Papen. For President Hindenburg and the other conservative politicians, the principal enemy was still the Left. As an indication of their attitude, on 20 July the government of Prussia, headed by the Social Democrat Otto Braun, was deposed; Social Democrats in the civil service and the police were removed from office; and Papen took over direct responsibility for Prussia as Reich commissar. While the Right and Center maneuvered and the Left committed suicide by squabbling within itself and refusing to defend the republic, new Reichstag elections on 31 July 1932 saw the Nazis become the largest party, with 37.3 percent of the vote and 230 seats.

Hitler now held the key to the political situation, but it soon became clear that he could not be bought off, though the illusion persisted that he could be controlled. In an audience with Hindenburg on 13 August, Hitler rejected an offer of the post of vice chancellor, insisting that he be given full responsibility for government. He was betting, not for the last time, on his gambler's instinct. Papen dissolved the Reichstag on 12 September, but the new elections of 6 November still left the Nazis as the largest party, even though their support fell to 33.1 percent. After Papen dissolved the Reichstag, a number of businessmen, led by Hjalmar Schacht, appealed to Hindenburg to appoint Hitler as chancellor, but instead he turned in desperation to the veteran soldier Kurt von Schleicher as an obvious stopgap. It was Papen who was to act as kingmaker for Hitler.

On 4 January 1933 Papen met with Hitler in the house of the Cologne banker Kurt von Schröder. But it was in the second half of this fateful month that the complex intrigues by conservative politicians around Hitler, as self-serving as they were self-defeating, reached their climax. Despite warnings from Ludendorff and others who knew Hitler rather better than they did, Papen and the circle around Hindenburg forged an agreement to make Hitler chancellor with Papen as vice chancellor, heading a cabinet made up mainly of non-Nazi conservatives. Schleicher resigned on 28 January. On 30 January Hitler was appointed Reich chancellor of a "national government" containing only two other Nazis (Goering and Wilhelm Frick). "We've hired him," declared Papen, while the general view was that Hitler could be boxed in and controlled. They could not have been more wrong. Within a few months a new dictatorial regime would rule Germany.

The Nazis consolidated their power with remarkable speed and ease. The *Gleichschaltung* or "coordination" of German society was completed for practical purposes in less than a year, and by August 1934 Hitler's position as Führer of the German Reich was officially secured. But to what extent was this the consecration of Hitler's personal power and how much that of his party? Contrary to the projected image of ruthless efficiency and unanimity, the vaunted Third Reich was run in a manner that verged on the anarchic. The various party and state organs and bodies contended for influence and power in what has been termed a "polycracy," as did the Nazi leaders. Goering, Heinrich Himmler, Goebbels, and the rest of the "party comrades" fought to extend their personal fiefdoms at each other's expense. Such was the confusion, empire building, and lack of clarity involved in the running of Germany, brutal and gruesome though it was, that Hitler himself, the godlike but lazy figure presiding over this organized chaos, has been characterized as a "weak dictator," little involved personally, but merely laying down the broad outlines of what was done in his name and to his glory.

Like all "strong leaders," Hitler thrived on the mutual distrust and rivalry of his subordinates. Unlike Stalin, for example, he was bored with details, the everyday minutiae of tyranny. He preferred to hold forth at length, dropping hints or making suggestions but making his wishes and intentions clear to those whose job it was to carry them out. This does not necessarily make him a "weak dictator"; in fact, it may equally be seen as the source of his strength. Ian Kershaw has characterized the process as "working towards the Führer." Everyone in the Reich, at all levels, was required to carry out the policies of which Hitler approved or was thought to approve. As Hans Frank told an audience of civil servants: "Act in such a way that if the Führer knew of your action, he would approve the action."

If such a system and such a mentality meant that the actions of local Nazis could run ahead of what Hitler would ideally have wanted, it had more advantages than disadvantages from the Führer's point of view. While the "little Hitlers" in the towns and villages often made themselves extremely unpopular, Hitler himself seemed to stand above it all. "If only the Führer knew," things would not be so bad, people said, but he was concerning himself with the grand idea of making Germany great again. Hitler's popularity and the "Hitler myth" could survive both the brutality of detested petty party officials and the tasteless junketing and corruption of Nazi bigwigs. But none of this detracts from Hitler's personal responsibility and culpability. The seeming paradox has been summarized expertly by Eberhard Jäckel: "There is abundant evidence that all the major decisions in the Third Reich were made by Hitler, and there is equally abundant evidence that the regime was largely anarchic and this can be described as a polycracy. The misunderstanding is to suppose that the two observations are contradictory and that only one of them can be true" (Jäckel 1984, p. 30).

The rise of the "Hitler myth" and the rapid success of *Gleichschaltung* was based on the widespread feeling that his accession to power represented a new beginning for Germany. The country had been saved from confusion, mediocrity, or even complete collapse by the providential and unforeseen advent of a leader who brought new hope and a fresh future. The majority of people may have been skeptical or hostile at first, but a run of political successes and economic improvement seemed for several years to confirm the optimistic view. Those who continued to disagree soon learned to keep quiet. And the small minority who saw clearly that Hitler was leading Germany to disaster seemed to be flying in the face of evident reality, at least until 1939, if not 1942.

Hitler was also lucky. Within a month of his becoming chancellor, on 27 February 1933 the Reichstag building in Berlin burned down. Portraying the fire as the signal for a Communist uprising, the next day the government issued the "Reichstag Fire Decree" suspending civil rights. Mass arrests of Communists and other left-wingers followed. Once again, Hitler had saved Germany from Marxist conspiracy. In Reichstag elections on 5 March the Nazis won 43.9 percent of the vote, the highest support they ever received under reasonably free conditions and the signal for the start of outright repression. With his nationalist allies Hitler enjoyed a parliamentary majority and could therefore turn the Reichstag proceedings into a brutish farce and destroy the remaining vestiges of democracy.

"Coordination" now proceeded apace. In March and April the Nazis seized power in those federal states not previously under their control; the first concentration camp was established at Dachau; an Enabling Act was passed, giving Hitler comprehensive legislative powers; and a nationwide boycott of Jewish shops was announced for 1 April but produced lukewarm public response. Approval of Hitler did not extend to the brutishness of the SA. Yet with widespread public approval and even wider passive acquiescence for Hitler and the Nazis, Germany was turned into a one-party state in less than six months. Trade unions were forcibly destroyed, and political parties were either banned or voluntarily dissolved themselves. And on 10 May the infamous burning of the books of "non-German" authors in university cities dramatically signaled the end of intellectual freedom, again voluntarily on the part of many academics and students.

More than 1.5 million people rushed to join the Nazi Party, either through genuine enthusiasm or opportunism, between 30 January and 1 May 1933. A ban was placed on new recruitment, which was to be lifted temporarily in 1937 and permanently in 1939. The party remained a political and racial elite, but the precise relationship between the party, its various organizations, and the state was to remain unclear, allowing the Schutzstaffel (SS) to develop into a state within a state. Hitler as the embodiment of the nation and in accordance with the Führer principle was seen as above such mundane matters. For ordinary Germans, their allegiance was to be to Hitler rather than to an impersonal party or state. He made this easier for many people and increased his popularity considerably when he solved the problem of the SA in typical fashion with the "Night of the Long Knives" on 30 June 1934. Röhm, despite being one of Hitler's oldest political "comrades," was arrested and shot along with other SA leaders. It meant the end of the SA as a political force.

The death of Hindenburg on 2 August 1934 allowed the offices of president and chancellor to be amalgamated in Hitler's person. The armed forces, the Reichswehr, now willingly swore a personal oath of allegiance to Hitler as "Führer and Reich chancellor." Hitler now was the state, and party and people were to "work towards" him. The process of *Gleichschaltung* had been completed in early 1934 with the abolition of the sovereignty of the individual German states or *Länder,* and a new labor law weighted heavily in favor of management against workers. Even if the results of plebiscites and pseudoelections cannot be taken literally, Hitler's overwhelming popularity is nonetheless unmistakable. Future generations were taken care of when the Hitler Youth, affiliated to the NSDAP, was declared to be the state youth organization in December 1936.

Hitler's rapid consolidation of power was based on decisive action and the ruthless elimination of opponents. It appeared irresistible and had been accepted by the overwhelming majority of the people. But when it came to his own major obsessions—making Germany great again and solving the "Jewish problem"—he would have to employ both boldness and caution, be pragmatic and opportunist in the pursuit of long-term goals that were conceived in terms at once grandiose and ill-defined.

The process of making the various areas of public life *Judenrein,* or "Jew-free," was drawn out, creating doubt and uncertainty but also maintaining the illusion among many German Jews that Hitler's ideas were so fantastic that they could never be fully realized. Profession after profession, as they became "coordinated," adopted rules either banning or restricting Jewish participation. Then the "Nuremberg Laws," hastily concocted but announced with great fanfare at the party rally of September 1935, denied citizenship of the Reich to Jews, banned marriage and sexual relations between Jews and non-Jews, and provided the basis for further and more wide-ranging discriminatory measures during the following four years.

Hitler had played down his anti-Semitism when campaigning in free elections, and it was a minor or even negligible factor in his rise to popular acclaim. The first boycott of Jewish shops and its attendant SA gangsterism caused disquiet. But the Night of the Long Knives made it appear that Hitler was getting rid of his most extreme and loutish followers, and his successes in foreign policy caused adulation of the Führer to reach new heights. Following Germany's withdrawal from the League of Nations and the Geneva Disarmament Conference in October 1933, Hitler embarked on a program of rearmament and a series of bloodless foreign policy coups. Playing skillfully on the widespread feeling in Europe that his criticisms of the Treaty of Versailles were largely understandable and partly justified, Hitler kept his promise of restoring German power and prestige.

Hitler played pragmatically but decisively on European memories of World War I and fears of a new conflict. He signed a nonaggression pact with Poland in January 1934, but only when the troubles of that year were overcome and Hitler firmly ensconced as Führer could he move into top gear. He exploited the terms of the hated Versailles settlement to obtain the reincorporation of the Saarland into the Reich on 1 March 1935 and immediately introduced conscription, effectively proclaiming German rearmament to the world. The Anglo-German Naval Agreement of June 1935 validated the revival of Germany as a recognized naval power. The impotence of French protests showed that there was no real possibility of united international resistance to Hitler's plans. The creation of the "Stresa Front" by France, Italy, and Great Britain in April 1935 in an attempt to bind Germany to its treaty obligations barely survived the naval treaty and was effectively destroyed by Fascist Italy's attack on Abyssinia in October. The aggressive imperial ambitions of Benito Mussolini, Hitler's fellow dictator and early inspiration, widened Hitler's freedom of action. On 7 March 1936 German troops marched into the demilitarized Rhineland in direct breach of the Locarno Pact of 1925. Hitler had unilaterally expanded the frontiers of Germany laid down at Versailles and confirmed at Locarno. The postwar settlement was dead.

The reaction in Germany was ecstatic. In three years Hitler had achieved what the politicians of the Weimar Republic had failed to accomplish in fourteen and without spilling a drop of German blood. Luise Solmitz, a middle-class housewife in Hamburg whose part-Jewish husband and their daughter had been robbed of German citizenship by the Nuremberg Laws, recorded her gushing enthusiasm for the Führer: "I was totally overwhelmed by the events of this hour . . . overjoyed at the entry march of our soldiers, at the greatness of Hitler and the power of his speech, the force of this man" (Kershaw 1998, p. 590). She spoke for many. A Reichstag "election" held on 29 March recorded 99 percent support for Hitler. When he opened the Olympic Games in Berlin on 1 August, proudly flaunting the achievements of his regime to the world while removing the signs banning Jews from most public places, Hitler had reached his first apotheosis.

But those who deluded themselves that Hitler's aims were restricted to the restoration of Germany would soon be disillusioned. Hitler never followed any ready-made blueprint, either domestically or internationally, but beneath the inevitable compromises, hesitations, and bluffing, the depth of his hatreds and the megalomaniac self-belief remained constant. While clinging to vague plans for war, he had to take advantage of whatever opportunities presented themselves. The announcement of the "Four-Year Plan" in September 1936 was meant to place the German economy as far as possible on an autarchic (self-sufficient) basis in anticipation of a war economy. But despite difficulties in the agrarian sector and the choice of "guns or butter," Hitler could not as yet impose too many sacrifices on a German people eager for bloodless victories but, especially among the working class, less willing to swallow in its entirety the fantasy vision of a racially pure and united national community, or *Volksgemeinschaft,* from which sectional interests and class conflict had been banished. The police organs of the dictatorship—the Gestapo and Sicherheitsdienst (SD)—kept a close eye on public opinion while eliminating any overt dissent in the most brutal manner.

On the international front Hitler sealed his uneasy alliance with the other militaristic powers with the "Berlin-Rome Axis," proclaimed by Mussolini on 1 November 1936 and the Anti-Comintern Pact with Japan, signed on 25 November 1936 and joined by Italy in November 1937. Behind the scenes Hitler was rambling in typical fashion about Czechoslovakia and Austria as the next targets in the struggle for "living space" and the uniting of the Germanic peoples. His skill lay in always appearing strong and decisive in public while allowing Nazi satraps like Goering and Himmler to build up their personal empires, despite the administrative disorder and economic inefficiency that resulted. The only potentially independent force of any significance in the state was the army, the high command of which had happily sworn an oath of personal loyalty to the Führer but was still full of the kind of cautious professionals whom Hitler disdained. The "Blomberg-Fritsch Crisis" of January–February 1938 brought them to heel. War Minister Werner von Blomberg and head of the army Werner Fritsch were dismissed on trumped-up pretexts. The conservative Konstantin von Neurath was replaced as foreign minister by the sycophantic Joachim von Ribbentrop, and Hitler himself took over as supreme commander of the Wehrmacht.

With hindsight, the road to war now seems to have been open if not inevitable. The real purposes of Hitler's regime could not be seen as anything but aggression and racism. The former outcast of Vienna reached his second apotheosis in March 1938 with the Anschluss, the incorporation of his Austrian homeland into what was now the Greater German Reich. This was one of Hitler's most cherished ambitions, but conditions and diplomatic necessity had forced him to wait until 1938. Now he bullied the Austrian Chancellor Kurt von Schuschnigg into appointing the Austrian Nazi Arthur Seyss-Inquart as minister of the interior and using his call for help as an excuse for sending German troops into Austria, where they received an enthusiastic welcome. Hitler's own reception from the crowd in Vienna was equally fervent. He had finally gained revenge for the supposed humiliations of his youth, and the last vestige of the ethnically mixed Habsburg Empire had been absorbed into a greater "Germandom."

It is tempting to speculate on how Hitler would have been viewed by history if he had been assassinated or otherwise removed in April 1938. Using conventional criteria, he might well have gone down as a great statesman, a new Bismarck. He had restored German power and prestige, buried the Versailles settlement, and united the two German-speaking states, and all by peaceful means. In 1938 the persecution of the Jews and other minorities was not yet irreversible. If his personal regime had been replaced by a less repressive government, Hitler may indeed have been seen as a "great man." Unfortunately, he still had seven years to live. The "good years" were coming to an end for Germans, and the worst years were about to begin for the Jews. And the whole world would pay an enormous price for Hitler's dreams.

Considering the war that broke out in 1939, the historian Richard Overy writes: "It was not the war Hitler had expected, but he fought it willingly enough. It was the war the western allies expected, but they fought it with great reluctance" (Overy 1996, p. 12). Opinions differ as to when Hitler would ideally have wished to go to war. On the one hand, he was undoubtedly aware of Germany's relative economic weakness (his planned "military-industrial complex" was still stumbling to its feet) and would have wanted more time to build up his armed forces, especially the air force. On the other hand, it is clear that he felt cheated of the chance to unleash his new military machine in 1938. The Führer's opportunism, love of brinkmanship, and disdainful attitude toward the British and French leaders were in the end more significant than any long-term schemes on either side.

Hitler's next target after Austria was Czechoslovakia, the hated Slav country and democratic creation of the Treaty of Versailles. Using the real and imagined grievances of the ethnic German population of the Sudetenland as a pretext, on 30 May 1938 Hitler issued an directive to the Wehrmacht declaring his intention of destroying the Czechoslovak state. The crisis of September 1938 was defused by the Munich Agreement, which handed the Sudetenland to Germany but to the great relief of the peoples of Europe appeared to have preserved the peace. But Hitler was not to be thwarted in his plans to destroy what remained of Czechoslovakia. On 14–15 March 1939 German troops marched into the rump state. A "Reich Protectorate of Bohemia and Moravia" was set up, and Slovakia became an "independent" state as a puppet of Hitler.

The next, decisive crisis came over Poland. On 21 March 1939 Hitler demanded the return to Germany of the contentious city of Danzig (Gdansk), since Versailles a "free city" at the head of the "Polish corridor" separating East Prussia from the rest of the Reich. On 31 March Poland rejected Hitler's demands, and Britain and France guaranteed their support for Polish independence. But would the British and French be prepared to "die for Danzig"? In case they were, Hitler had to prepare the diplomatic ground. After giving a secret directive to prepare the attack on Poland, he formed the "Pact of Steel" military alliance with Mussolini on 22 May, and on 23 August produced the diplomatic bombshell of a nonaggression treaty with the Soviet Union, the Nazi-Soviet Pact. A secret clause in the pact arranged for the division of Poland between the Third Reich and the Soviet Union. The attack on Poland began on 1 September 1939, and on 3 September Great Britain and France declared war on Germany.

Hitler conceived of war as a struggle between peoples and races, to be decided by the survival of the fittest. The intensification of persecution of the supposed "enemy within," the Jews, went hand in hand with the drift to war. Between June and September 1938, as the Sudeten crisis deepened, synagogues in Munich and Nuremberg were demolished, Jewish doctors and lawyers were banned from practicing, and Jews were forced to add the forenames "Sara" or "Israel" to their existing names. Then on 7 November an official of the German embassy in Paris, Ernst vom Rath, was shot by a young Jew named Herschel Grynszpan and died two days later. This provided the excuse for Reichskristallnacht ("Crystal Night," or the night of broken glass) unleashed by the SA and local Nazis throughout Germany. More than ninety

Jews were murdered, countless others injured or maltreated, 191 synagogues burned, and Jewish shops and property destroyed and looted in an orgy of destruction.

The devastation unsettled public opinion, but Hitler and the Nazis managed to blame the victims and rushed through further anti-Jewish measures, using the danger of further disorder as a transparent excuse. About 30,000 Jews were arrested and sent to concentration camps, and a series of new laws forced Jews out of the economy as their businesses were "Aryanized" and pushed on to the fringes of society. In a speech to the Reichstag on 30 January 1939, as his troops prepared to march into Czechoslovakia, Hitler "prophesied" the destruction of the Jews in the event of a new European war. Almost 80,000 Jews managed to leave Germany in 1939, compared with around 40,000 in 1938 and 23,000 in 1937.

The months between the declaration of war and Hitler's launching of his western offensive in May 1940 were dubbed the "phony war" by the populations of Britain, France, and Germany, but for Jews in Austria and Czechoslovakia they brought the first deportations to the ghettos of Poland. Hitler had wished to attack in the west as early as possible, but the offensive was repeatedly postponed. In April 1940 he invaded Denmark and Norway and then violated the neutrality of the Netherlands, Belgium, and Luxemburg as his blitzkrieg swept into France in May and June. On 22 June 1940 the armistice with France was signed in the forest of Compiègne in the same railway carriage in which Marshal Ferdinand Foch had accepted the German surrender in 1918. Hitler's victory over the country he had called "the inexorable mortal enemy of the German people" (Hitler 1992, p. 565) was complete. Preparations for invasion of Britain, however, were finally abandoned by September.

Hitler was now at the height of his power: only Great Britain still stood out against him. But any hopes he might have had for making peace with the British turned out to be illusory. Britain would not be defeated by invasion or air power or accept Hitler's domination of the continent. Indeed, the war would not be won by the kind of warfare Hitler understood—the lightning offensive, fight to the death, no retreat—which has been described as "more Custer than Clausewitz" (Overy 1996, p. 275). When he launched his greatest blitzkrieg against the Soviet Union in June 1941, Hitler expected the war to last a matter of weeks. In fact, it lasted four years and became a major factor in his downfall. In planning Operation Barbarossa against his Soviet ally, Hitler knew he could face a war on two fronts, but his belief in his own will and the racial inferiority of the Russian enemy created the illusion that they would be swiftly defeated.

Hitler told his military commanders that the war in the east would be a new type of conflict, a "war of annihilation." In this he was proved right as a struggle of unparalleled savagery engulfed a vast region from the Baltic to the Caucasus. The battle for Moscow between October and December 1941 marked the first failure of the blitzkrieg and left a German army unprepared for a winter war in Russia. The first crisis for Hitler's war leadership coincided with the order on 14 October 1941 to deport Jews from Reich territory to the eastern ghettos and the first killings by poison gas in Chelmno, Poland, in December. Hitler declared war on the United States on 11 December, following the Japanese attack on Pearl Harbor. Though he was allied with Japan by the Tripartite Pact of September 1940, Hitler did not need to declare war on the United States, but he had as low an opinion of Americans as he did of Russians. As his forces faced a Soviet counteroffensive at Moscow, Hitler as always blamed his generals and took over personally as head of the army.

Hitler's "will" in the military field would soon be exposed as bad leadership in all but

the most favorable circumstances. The system he had created or that had come into being for his glorification and the war he had started found their logical conclusions in genocide, atrocity, and ultimately the annihilation of Hitler's Reich. The Wannsee Conference, held in Berlin on 20 January 1942, coordinated the measures for a "Final Solution of the Jewish Question," and in March the first mass killings of Jews from southern Poland marked the beginning of "Aktion Reinhard": the systematic killing in the extermination camps of Belzec, Sobibor, and Treblinka. At the end of March the first transports of Jews from Germany and western Europe arrived at Auschwitz, where systematic mass gassing began in June. The central anti-Semitic aspect of Hitler's ideological "crusade" was reaching its atrocious consummation. But as Himmler ordered the deportation of all Jews from concentration camps in the Reich to Auschwitz, the tide of war was beginning to turn against Hitler.

The German drive toward the oil-producing regions of the Caucasus was ended by the defeat at Stalingrad, where the 6th Army surrendered at the beginning of February 1943. The army chief of staff, Franz Halder, sacked in September 1942, described Hitler's war leadership as "a pathological reaction to the impressions of the moment" (Overy 1996, p. 277). In the decisive theaters of eastern Europe and the Atlantic, where the attempt to starve Great Britain into submission finally failed, the inadequacies of Hitler's style of victory through megalomaniac willpower were at last exposed. The fighting on the Eastern Front had been the kind of war decreed by Hitler in accordance with his worldview, but in the struggle for survival the enemy proved to be the fittest. The long-drawn-out Battle of the Atlantic, however, was won by painstaking hard work, adaptability, intelligence work, innovation based on seemingly dull technical advances, and the mundane heroism of merchant seamen and their escorts. Largely unknown or incomprehensible to the public, this was a kind of warfare about which Hitler knew nothing and cared little.

Nor could Hitler understand the peculiar nature of the alliance against him. The coalition of democracy with Stalinist communism was indeed unnatural, as Hitler understood, but he could not comprehend that, for all the divisions and difficulties between the Allies, they were united in their desire to destroy *him*. His only explanation for the unity against him was the ubiquitous "Jewish conspiracy," his eternal substitute for explanation. The effort to exterminate the Jews went on regardless of the diversion of resources from the war effort. Most of the ghettos of the east were closed in March 1943 and the survivors taken to the extermination camps. Even in April–June 1944, by which time Mussolini had fallen and the Allies in conference at Teheran had agreed in principle on a postwar division of Germany, Greek and Hungarian Jews were deported en masse to Auschwitz.

In Hitler's increasingly deranged mind, if Germany was heading for defeat it was because the German people had proved unworthy of him and the mission he had bestowed upon them. The "Hitler myth" still retained a considerable hold over the public until the end, but the Führer himself fell almost completely out of view. The Allies landed in Sicily in July 1943 and in Normandy in June 1944. But to those Germans who were not fanatical Nazis, it was the enemy in the east who caused most concern. In a speech on 18 February 1943 Goebbels had proclaimed "total war," a completely self-sacrificing national effort for victory. Allied bombing, an extensive propaganda campaign, and Speer's organizational effort as minister for armaments and munitions brought the war home to the Reich.

Hitler had broken his promise to spare the German people from the effects of his imperial schemes. But he and Goebbels largely succeeded in persuading the people that the war against the Soviets was about survival or annihilation, not winners or losers. And he kept promising an increasingly skeptical population that "wonder weapons" would soon be produced to snatch victory at the last moment. The first V1 missiles were fired on British targets in June 1944 and the first V2 rockets against London and Antwerp in September, but it was already too late. The Red Army launched its major offensive against Germany itself on 22 June 1944, and, despite stubborn resistance, news of German defeats and the stream of refugees from the east ensured that the reality of the catastrophe stared the German people in the face.

Hitler's colossal self-assurance remained intact almost to the end. On 20 July 1944 he survived the most serious attempt on his life, when a bomb planted in his East Prussian headquarters by Claus von Stauffenberg injured him only slightly. His rage against the army officers behind the plot resulted in a bloody revenge. But the Führer had survived, seemingly miraculously. On 25 July, the day after the extermination camp of Majdanek had been liberated by the Red Army, Hitler gave Goebbels sweeping powers to mobilize what was left of Germany's resources. Hitler was clinging desperately to every last hope. As Allied armies swept through France and liberated Paris, he called up all able-bodied German men between the ages of sixteen and sixty to form the Volkssturm, an ill-equipped and untrained "people's army." The last photograph of Hitler shows a strained and ailing Führer inspecting an almost comically inadequate looking band of Volkssturm members.

Hitler's last desperate attempt to stem the Allied advance in the west, the Ardennes offensive of December 1944, known as the "Battle of the Bulge," enjoyed initial success but soon petered out. At the same time, in November 1944, Himmler ordered the end of gassings at Auschwitz and the removal of all traces of the killings. The rats were preparing to abandon the sinking ship. Perhaps surprisingly, among the leading Nazis only the cynical Goebbels remained with Hitler to the end and voluntarily shared his fate. As the men of the Red Army discovered the remnants of Hitler's "masterpiece," liberating the remaining 5,000 inmates of Auschwitz on 27 January 1945, the Führer retreated into a fantasy world, ordering nonexistent troops around like the military genius he thought he was, but he was increasingly ignored even by the most sycophantic of his entourage.

Hitler made his last broadcast speech on 30 January 1945. U.S. troops crossed the Rhine at Remagen on 7 March. Determined to bring his unworthy countrymen down with him, on 19 March Hitler issued his "Nero order" for the destruction of all industrial plants to prevent them from falling into enemy hands, but fortunately for Germany Speer managed over the following weeks to block, for the most part, its implementation. Speer's testimony and that of the last photographs show Hitler as a physical wreck who shuffled instead of walking, with trembling limbs and a face yellow and swollen. Physical and nervous exhaustion, not helped by years of addiction to quack medicine, had taken their final toll.

The battle for Berlin began on 16 April 1945, and on 25 April U.S. and Soviet troops met up at Torgau on the Elbe. Mussolini, seeking a final refuge in Germany, was captured by Italian partisans and shot on 28 April. The death of Roosevelt brought Hitler a brief moment of joy, but any hope he clung to was now merely hysterical. On 29 April Hitler made his will, naming Admiral Karl Doenitz as his successor as head of state. He was still lucid enough to ignore the claims of his one-time Nazi "comrades," most of whom were now trying desperately to come to personal terms with the victorious western Allies. But Hitler had not changed: he still ex-

horted the German people to continue its "merciless opposition" to "international Jewry." The Führer committed suicide in the bunker of the Reich Chancellery in Berlin on 30 April 1945, two days before the Red Army finally conquered the German capital. The Third Reich ended with the burning of Hitler's body, along with that of his mistress Eva Braun, whom he had finally married just before their deaths. Germany surrendered at the U.S. headquarters in Reims on 7 May, and the ceremony was repeated at the Soviet headquarters in Berlin on 9 May.

The rise and fall of a great political figure usually possesses, to a greater or lesser degree, a tragic dimension in the Shakespearean sense, an element of greatness brought low by overweening ambition or a tragic flaw. In Hitler's case his career was so unrelentingly destructive and sordid that no such dimension exists. His legacy, however, was profound, long-lasting, and multifaceted. His mad dreams eventually crumbled to nothing, but he left Europe transformed and stands forever as a warning and a reminder of human degradation.

Hitler had set himself the task of destroying his three great enemies: democracy, communism, and the Jews. The horrors of the Holocaust need no underlining. Jewish communities throughout Europe, especially in Germany itself and in eastern Europe, were destroyed permanently or reduced to a handful of survivors, a shadow of their former selves. But the Jews were not wiped out, and Hitler's fantasy of a racial empire in central and eastern Europe collapsed amid unheard-of brutality and terror. The racial dream of Nazism was ultimately revealed to have been as futile as it was stupid and vicious.

Hitler's ideological bugbears proved as resilient as his "racial" enemies. Democracy not only survived in its heartlands of Great Britain and the United States but after Hitler's defeat was restored in the countries of western Europe he had conquered and in

Italy. Only Spain and Portugal retained dictatorial regimes. Not least, democracy returned to the larger part of Hitler's now divided Reich, in Austria and the Federal Republic of Germany. Communism, the "Jewish bolshevism" he had vowed to destroy, extended its power enormously as a result of Hitler's war. In the years after the Führer's fall Stalin, bathing in the prestige conferred by victory over Hitler, imposed his grip over eastern Europe. Communist regimes were installed in Poland, Czechoslovakia, Hungary, Romania, Bulgaria, and under different circumstances in Yugoslavia and Albania. Thanks to Hitler, "Bolshevik" power was also installed in the eastern part of Germany in the Soviet occupation zone, later the German Democratic Republic. The division of Germany was to last for forty years.

This schism across Europe, solidified in the Cold War, was Hitler's true political legacy. He had driven the two systems he detested into a convergence of interests to rid the world of him, and his fall created the conditions under which the Cold War between those two systems could develop in the years following his death. The confrontation lasted for more than forty years. But the deeper legacy of moral trauma will take longer to overcome, if it ever is. It should certainly never be forgotten. The direct political consequences of his actions may at last have faded away, but Jäckel's words that Hitler remains as "an eternal monument to what is humanly possible" (Jäckel 1984, p. 106) still ring sadly true.

References

Bullock, Alan. 1991. *Hitler and Stalin: Parallel Lives.* London: HarperCollins.

Conrad, Peter. 1998. *Modern Times, Modern Places.* London: Thames and Hudson.

Hitler, Adolf. 1992. *Mein Kampf.* Trans. Ralph Manheim. Intro. by D. C. Watt. London: Pimlico.

Jäckel, Eberhard. 1984. *Hitler in History.* Hanover: University Press of New England.

Kershaw, Ian. 1998. *Hitler 1889–1936: Hubris.* New York: Allen Lane The Penguin Press.

Overy, Richard. 1996. *Why the Allies Won.* London: Norton.

Volkogonov, Dmitri. 1991. *Stalin: Triumph and Tragedy.* Paperback ed., 1995. London: Weidenfeld and Nicolson.

Adolf Hitler

A Biographical Companion

Afrika Korps

When in January 1941 Hitler decided to send German troops to support the Italians in Libya, the 5th Light Division and 15th Panzer Division were hastily organized into the Deutsches Afrika Korps (DAF), under the command of Erwin Rommel. Although the term was often used inaccurately to refer to all the German forces in North Africa, the DAF proper was the spearhead of Rommel's larger forces operational between August 1941 and May 1943. The prowess and self-confidence of the Afrika Korps became legendary, a remarkable tribute to Rommel's powers of leadership, and it remained a formidable force throughout the North African campaign.

Related entries: North Africa; Rommel, Erwin

Suggestions for further reading:
Lewin, Ronald. 1977. *The Life and Death of the Afrika Korps.* London: Batsford.

Agriculture

The idealization of rural life, the corrupting effect of "cosmopolitan" cities on the healthy instincts of the German Volk, and the ideology of "Blood and Soil" were all central to Hitler's worldview

and his vision of the Germany of the future. He opined in *Mein Kampf* that "the possibility of preserving a healthy peasant class as a foundation for the whole nation can never be valued highly enough" (Hitler 1992, p. 126). His policies were to have the opposite effect. The rural theme was plugged incessantly by Nazi propaganda, in which the Aryan farmer and his patriarchal family were held up as the ideals toward which Germans should aspire. Underpinning the fantasy was the reality that the Nazis had always received relatively strong support in the countryside, especially in Protestant regions. The agricultural community looked forward to a bright future under the Third Reich, but it proved to be short-lived, and many were to vote with their feet by moving to the accursed cities or else were absorbed into Hitler's new armed legions.

The ideology of *Blut und Boden* inspired reforms of the entailment of peasant holdings, designed to preserve the bonds between people and land. By the Reich Entailment Law of September 1933, holdings of between 7.5 and 125 hectares were tied in perpetuity to active farmers of proven German blood and their direct descendants. These farms were known as *Erbhöfe* and their proprietors as *Bauer,* the normal German term for "farmer" or "peasant" now applied to them exclusively. These *Bauer* were encouraged to wear folkloric costumes, and the regime organized its own harvest festival symbolizing the fruits of the soil and the union of the sexes. Inevitably, the sunny vision did not coincide with reality. Never more than one-third of farms became *Erbhöfe;* they did nothing to improve agricultural efficiency, and farmers themselves proved less than enthusiastic, viewing the new law as a restriction of their freedom to dispose of their land as they wished. The mass of smallholdings and the huge Junker estates in eastern Germany both remained exempt from the legislation. The reform was a typical example of promised change carried out halfheartedly and subordinated to the immediate needs of the regime. The *Erbhöfe* formed part of the myth of *völkisch* revival, but not much else.

The Nazi regime declared a policy of agricultural self-sufficiency, determined not only by ideology but also by Germany's shortage of foreign currency and the desire to use it for imports connected with rearmament. The policy did lead to a growth in farm incomes during the early years of the Reich, but this was not sustained. A disastrous harvest in 1934 led to the declaration of a "Battle for Production" involving a reduction of the acreage under grain while maintaining the quantity of grain produced, with the land so released to be converted to fodder production. Another bad harvest in 1935 only made things worse, but new measures to stimulate production were introduced under the Four-Year Plan. Fertilizer prices were reduced and grants given to aid mechanization and for bringing new land under cultivation.

Helped by good harvests in 1938 and 1939, on the eve of the war farm production was some 20 percent higher than in 1928–1929, and food consumption per head increased by between 4 and 5 percent. But the heavy bias toward arable farming rather than livestock in the Four-Year Plan created the so-called fats crisis, which produced Josef Goebbels's famous plea to the German people to choose "guns or butter."

Livestock farms, less well subsidized than their arable counterparts, had to pay rising prices for farm housing and machinery, while their prices were effectively frozen by the Reich Food Estate. Behind it all lay the problem of flight from the land. Between 1933 and 1939 agriculture lost possibly up to half a million people. "The problem of the flight from the land," a Sicherheitsdienst report said in 1938, "has been recognized . . . as a problem of enormous significance for the whole nation" (Kershaw 1983, p. 57).

The problems of agriculture were aggravated from 1939 onward by war conditions, especially the trade blockade of fodder imports and fertilizers. The labor loss accelerated as young men called up for the army had to be replaced by women, youths, and foreign workers, principally Poles and Italians. Rationing was introduced on the outbreak of war, but the bad winter of 1941–1942 destroyed much winter grain, potato crops, and stores. By 1943 rationing had broken down and been replaced by a burgeoning black market. Grain and other food supplies were taken from the occupied territories, but those in Russia and the Ukraine were used mostly to supply the armed forces. In 1944–1945 food supplies were reduced to a critical level. Hitler bequeathed to his conquerors an agriculture in ruins.

Related entries: *Blut und Boden;* Darré, Richard Walther; Economic Policy; Four-Year Plan; Propaganda; Reich Food Estate; Social Policy; Trade Policy; *Volksgemeinschaft*

Suggestions for further reading:
Corni, Gustavo. 1990. *Hitler and the Peasants.* New York, Oxford, and Munich: Berg.
Farquharson, John E. 1976. *The Plough and the Swastika: The NSDAP and Agriculture, 1928–45.* Bloomington: Indiana University Press.
Hitler, Adolf. 1992. *Mein Kampf.* Trans. Ralph Manheim. Intro. by D. C. Watt. London: Pimlico.
Kershaw, Ian. 1983. *Popular Opinion and Political Dissent in the Third Reich: Bavaria 1933–1945.* Oxford: Clarendon Press.

Wunderlich, Frieda. 1961. *Farm Labour in Germany, 1810–1945.* Princeton: Princeton University Press.

Alsace-Lorraine

*T*he return of the contentious provinces of Alsace and Lorraine on the left bank of the Rhine between Luxemburg and Switzerland was a primary aim of all German nationalists. Alsace-Lorraine was returned to France by the Treaty of Versailles and officially renounced by Germany in the Locarno Pact of 1925. In the 1930s Hitler repeatedly assured the world that he had no interest in this "centuries-old bone of contention," but after the defeat of France in 1940 the region was annexed to the German Reich, despite the protests of the Vichy government. Alsace was joined to Baden, and Lorraine became part of the Westmark *Gau.* The provinces were returned to France in 1945.

Related entries: Foreign Policy; France

Anschluss

*A*t the very beginning of *Mein Kampf,* Hitler wrote: "German Austria must return to the great German mother country, and not because of any economic considerations. No, and again no: even if such a vision were unimportant from an economic point of view; yes, even if it were harmful, it must nevertheless take place. One blood demands one Reich" (Hitler 1992, p. 3). Union, or Anschluss, with his homeland was one of Hitler's most cherished goals, but the failure of the Austrian Nazis' attempted coup in 1934 and Hitler's opportunistic approach in foreign policy meant that he had to wait until 1938. The regime of Kurt von Schuschnigg, although it had banned the Nazi Party, was in a weak position when faced with Nazi-inspired demonstrations and disturbances. The crushing of the Social Democrats and liberals in 1934 had left little basis for Schuschnigg's rule.

On 12 February 1938 Hitler summoned Schuschnigg to Berchtesgarden for a meeting at which the Austrian chancellor, hoping to preserve Austrian independence, agreed to Hitler's demands for the lifting of the ban on the Austrian Nazi Party; the appointment of the Nazi Arthur Seyss-Inquart as minister of the interior; and the absorption of Austria into the German economic system. Seyss-Inquart, now with complete control over the police, did nothing to counter a rising wave of Nazi demonstrations and violence in Vienna and other Austrian cities, possibly running ahead of Hitler's personal wishes.

Schuschnigg made one final effort to prevent the Anschluss by calling a referendum on independence. To forestall this measure Hitler decided to intervene, using as a pretext a call from Seyss-Inquart for help in controlling the disorder. German troops crossed the border on 12 March 1938 and received an enthusiastic welcome. On 14 March Hitler made a triumphant entry into Vienna, the city that had seen his poverty and failure as a young man. Speaking to a cheering crowd, he declared: "I believe it was God's will to send a youth from here into the Reich, to let him grow up, to raise him to be the leader of the nation so as to enable him to lead back his homeland into the Reich" (Bullock 1991, p. 629).

The Greater German Reich was proclaimed, with Austria rebaptized as the Ostmark. For many Germans and Austrians it was the long overdue consummation of German unity. Hitler had once again secured a massive achievement without firing a shot, and his popularity soared to new heights. Those who took a different view, including Schuschnigg, were rounded up for dispatch to concentration camps. The persecution and humiliation of Austrian Jews began immediately, to the acclamation of a population probably more deeply imbued with anti-Semitism than that of Germany itself. A plebiscite held throughout the new expanded Reich approved the Anschluss by 99 percent. Although the result is obviously not to be taken literally, there can be no doubt that the Anschluss enjoyed overwhelming popular support in both Germany and Austria.

Related entries: Austria; Foreign Policy; Pan-Germanism; Schuschnigg, Kurt von

Suggestions for further reading:
Bullock, Alan. 1991. *Hitler and Stalin: Parallel Lives.* London: HarperCollins.
Gehl, Jürgen. 1963. *Austria, Germany and the Anschluss.* Oxford: Oxford University Press.
Hitler, Adolf. 1992. *Mein Kampf.* Trans. Ralph Manheim. Intro. by D. C. Watt. London: Pimlico.

Anti-Comintern Pact

Signed on 25 November 1936, the Anti-Comintern Pact provided for cooperation between Germany and Japan in opposing the Communist International and was left open for other powers to join. Benito Mussolini signed up Italy in November 1937, creating what Count Galeazzo Ciano, with typical hyperbole, called "the most formidable political and military combination that has ever existed" (Mack Smith 1981, p. 217). Signatories promised not to assist the Soviet Union if it attacked or threatened another partner or to sign any treaty with that country without the consent of the others, but both these provisions were hedged about with possible exceptions. The pact alarmed the rest of the world, since it allowed each signatory the freedom to go its own way, as Japan did in China, though it did not foresee any joint action. But the propaganda image was more powerful than the reality: the alliance of the victors of World War I was finally buried, and Germany and Japan

were associated with Italy in a pact spanning the globe. It served to reinforce the impression that Hitler had in less than five years in power become the most successful leader in Europe.

Related entries: Axis; Foreign Policy; Italy; Japan; Soviet Union

Suggestions for further reading:
Mack Smith, Denis. 1981. *Mussolini.* London: Weidenfeld and Nicolson.
Weinberg, Gerhard L. 1970. *The Foreign Policy of Hitler's Germany: Diplomatic Revolution in Europe 1933–36.* Chicago: University of Chicago Press.

Anti-Semitism

Anti-Semitism lay at the center of Hitler's worldview. It was not a secondary element to be exploited opportunistically, nor was it mere prejudice based on thoughtless stereotyping. It was the very core of his interpretation of history and the present. Nothing in his ideas was original, certainly not the wildly ludicrous assertions about "the Jew" being behind bolshevism and capitalism, Germany's defeat in World War I, liberalism, democracy, and anything else that in Hitler's crazed vision had over the centuries opposed or oppressed the Aryan German *Volk.* "The Jew" (like most overt anti-Semites Hitler used the singular) was responsible for all the ills of the modern world, from materialism to modern art, and the coming struggle of which Hitler always talked would one way or another see the elimination of "the Jew" from German and later European life.

Psychological explanations of Hitler's anti-Semitism are unconvincing or simply wrong. They also trivialize the question. The notion spread by his political opponents on the Right that he may have had Jewish ancestors has been disproved. Similarly, the idea that he blamed the Jewish physician, Dr. Eduard Bloch, for his mother's death from cancer is the opposite of the truth: in fact, Hitler praised Dr. Bloch for his work and gave him presents in gratitude. None of the professors who refused Hitler entry to the Vienna Academy of Arts was Jewish, though this did not prevent him from blaming "the Jews" in retrospect. The story that Hitler contracted syphilis from a Jewish prostitute was the post-1945 invention of a certain Josef Greiner. Hitler's own explanations are, as always, untrustworthy. His claims to have been physically disgusted by the eastern European Jews in Vienna and then to have made a study of the "Jewish question" before seeing the light were made in retrospect. There is no direct evidence for Hitler being virulently anti-Semitic during his years in Vienna.

Anti-Semitism is the oldest prejudice of Christian civilization throughout Europe. Of its several variations—religious, economic, racial—it was the latter that led to Hitler and Auschwitz. For the racial anti-Semite there is no escape for Jews through conversion to Christianity: there can never be any such thing as a "good Jew." In the years before 1914 anti-Semitism was probably more influential in Hitler's native Austria than in Germany. German Jews had been legally emancipated in 1869; they did not suffer the pogroms inflicted on their fellows in Russia and Poland; nor was there any German equivalent to the Dreyfus case in France. But both before and after World War I, state governments, the army, the judiciary, and the universities all widely evaded their obligations to treat Jews as equal citizens. They also faced difficulties in entering politics, except in the Social Democratic Party and later the extreme Left.

It was in Vienna, however, that Hitler, whatever the exact evolution of his views (which is unlikely to have followed any normal logical trail), observed the political effectiveness of anti-Semitism and read and absorbed racist literature. At a time when anti-Semitic parties in Germany were in decline, Hitler could observe how Karl Lueger, mayor of Vienna, had used anti-Semitism to discredit liberalism and socialism. He also admired the anti-Semitic pan-German leader Georg von Schönerer and devoured the *völkisch* pamphlets of such writers as Guido von List and Jörg Lanz von Liebenfels, creators of esoteric Germanic nonsense exalting the purity and superiority of the race and the glory of its struggle for survival. Hitler soaked himself in anti-Semitism, and some time, in some way it became his central obsession.

By the time Hitler emerged from World War I, "the Jew" had become for him the universal scapegoat. He had decided to his own bizarre satisfaction that Marxists and Jews, often one and the same, were responsible for Germany's defeat. While the Nazi movement may have had no coherent economic or social ideas, anti-Semitism provided it with one consistent theme and object of hatred. The historian Saul Friedländer refers usefully to the "redemptive" anti-Semitism of Hitler and his core followers, a messianic belief that salvation for Germany could only come through the elimination of Jews and Jewish influence from national life, as distinguished from the vague anti-Jewish prejudices or indifference of the bulk of the population.

It is generally accepted by historians that anti-Semitism played only a small part in Hitler's gaining of popular support during his rise to power. They would agree with William S. Allen's conclusion in his study of a small town in Lower Saxony that the people "were drawn to anti-Semitism because they were drawn to Nazism, not the other way around" (Allen 1984, p. 77). Insofar as popular attitudes can be generalized, they are best characterized as indifference toward or passive approval of anti-Jewish propaganda and measures. The thesis of Daniel J. Goldhagen (1996) that the German people as a whole were "eliminationist anti-Semites," though it performed a valuable service in forcing a serious look at popular participation in the Holocaust, has not been defended by other historians. But the German people were willing to tolerate the isolation of their Jewish co-citizens within Germany and to remain silent. Enough of them were also willing to act as informers for the Gestapo and other authorities of the Nazi regime. Above all, perhaps, it was the capitulation to anti-Semitic prejudices of educated Germans, including academics, teachers, lawyers, doctors, and other professionals, that helped pave the road to Auschwitz with bigotry, pseudoscientific rubbish, and indifference. In Ian Kershaw's words: "The road to Auschwitz was built by hate, but paved with indifference" (Kershaw 1983, p. 277).

Related entries: Holocaust; Jews and Jewish Policy; Lueger, Karl; *Mein Kampf;* Nazi Movement; Nuremberg Laws; Public Opinion; Racial Theory; Rosenberg, Alfred; Schönerer, Georg Ritter von; *Stürmer, Der;* Universities; Wagner, Richard

Suggestions for further reading:

Allen, William Sheridan. 1984. *The Nazi Seizure of Power: The Experience of a Single German Town.* Rev. ed. New York: Franklin, Watts.
Finkelstein, Norman G., and Ruth Bettina Birn, eds. 1998. *A Nation on Trial: The Goldhagen Thesis and Historical Truth.* New York: Henry Holt.
Friedländer, Saul. 1997. *Nazi Germany and the Jews. Vol. 1: The Years of Persecution, 1933–1939.* New York: HarperCollins.
Goldhagen, Daniel Jonah. 1996. *Hitler's Willing Executioners: Ordinary Germans and the Holocaust.* New York: Alfred A. Knopf.
Gordon, Sarah. 1984. *Hitler, Germans and the "Jewish Question."* Princeton: Princeton University Press.
Graml, Hermann. 1992. *Anti-Semitism in the Third Reich.* Oxford: Blackwell.
Kauders, Anthony. 1996. *German Politics and the Jews: Düsseldorf and Nuremberg, 1910–1933.* Oxford: Clarendon Press.
Kershaw, Ian. 1983. *Popular Opinion and Political Dissent in the Third Reich: Bavaria 1933–1945.* Oxford: Clarendon Press.
Niewyk, Donald L. 1980. *The Jews in Weimar Germany.* Baton Rouge: Louisiana State University Press.
Pauley, Bruce F. 1992. *From Prejudice to Persecution: A History of Austrian Anti-Semitism.* Chapel Hill: University of North Carolina Press.
Pulzer, Peter. 1988. *The Rise of Political Anti-Semitism in Germany and Austria.* Rev. ed. Cambridge, MA: Harvard University Press.

Antonescu, Ion (1880–1946)

Named prime minister of Romania on 4 September 1940 following the collapse of France and the Soviet annexation of Bessarabia and Bukovina, Antonescu established a pro-German dictatorship with himself as "Conducator" of the "National Legionary State." Long associated with the extreme right Iron Guard, he modeled his regime on Mussolini's Italy and forced Romanian participation in Hitler's invasion of Russia. Antonescu met Hitler several times after November 1940 and contributed thirty Romanian divisions to the invasion force, and when the Romanians captured Odessa, the Russian port was renamed in his honor. Antonescu's position weakened as German fortunes waned. By April 1944 the Red Army stood on the Romanian frontier, and the Allies were bombing Bucharest. On 23 August Prince Michael led a coup, imprisoning Antonescu and his henchmen, and Romania changed sides. Antonescu was sentenced to death by the victorious Soviets and executed on 1 June 1946.

Related entries: Michael, King of Romania; Romania

Appeasement

Thanks to Hitler and the British and French statesmen of the 1930s, the word "appeasement," which should be a positive one involving making peace and settling conflict, has come to mean the making of ultimately futile concessions to a potential aggressor. "Appeasement" and "appeaser" have become insults to be hurled at political opponents deemed to be "soft" on any dictatorial regime. Yet British and French appeasement policy toward Hitler cannot be dismissed as cowardice or mere passivity. It was aimed at preventing

Neville Chamberlain, on his return from meeting Hitler, brandishes the famous "piece of paper" containing the Munich Agreement before the press and public at Croydon Airport, London. The prime minister's gesture came to symbolize the policy of appeasement, but his promise of "peace in our time" proved to be short-lived. (Archive Photos)

war in a Europe still haunted by the blood-bath of World War I and was based on the sincere conviction that differences between nations should be settled by negotiation, not armed conflict. The tragedy was that Hitler believed in and wanted armed conflict. For him, as for Mussolini, war was natural and good.

Appeasement was also motivated by a growing sense in Britain and to a lesser extent in France that the Treaty of Versailles had been unjust to Germany. Some observers such as John Maynard Keynes had predicted from early days that it would lead to further conflict within twenty years, and by the late 1920s the feeling had grown in Britain that Germany should not be made to shoulder all the "war-guilt" for 1914–

1918. The French, who had suffered more than any other nation during the war, were less likely to accept this, but many British people had come to see Versailles as an instrument of French vengeance and ambitions. More than this, Versailles was held to be responsible for Hitler's rise to power. Nazism was a disease caused by the injustice of the peace settlement, and it was assumed that radical German nationalism would abate if legitimate national grievances and aspirations were satisfied. It was, therefore, worth making concessions to avoid any hostile response from Germany.

A final motivating force for appeasement among British and French conservatives was the fear of communism. In this way of thinking, fascism may have been contemptible, but Germany and Italy stood as guarantees against Soviet expansionism, and Hitler was in his own way a bulwark against communism in central and eastern Europe. Fighting against him unless forced to might aid the spread of communism into Germany and further westward.

None of these reasons, taken separately or together, can be said to justify appeasement of Hitler, but they serve to make it comprehensible. The policies of Stanley Baldwin, Neville Chamberlain, and Edouard Daladier enjoyed strong, probably overwhelming popular support in Britain and France. But they allowed Hitler to achieve the string of bloodless foreign policy successes that increased his own popularity among the German people. The appeasers were not contemptible, but like so many people they failed to appreciate how different Hitler was from a "normal" statesman. Those who did, like Winston Churchill or Anthony Eden, were in a definite minority.

Related entries: Chamberlain, Neville; Czechoslovakia; Daladier, Edouard; Foreign Policy; France; Great Britain; Munich Agreement; Poland; Rhineland; Soviet Union; Sudetenland; Versailles, Treaty of

Suggestions for further reading:
Bell, P. H. M. 1997. *The Origins of the Second World War in Europe.* 2nd ed. London and New York: Longman.
Parker, R. A. C. 1993. *Chamberlain and Appeasement: British Policy and the Coming of the Second World War.* New York: St. Martin's Press.

Architecture

Hitler always claimed that as a youth his overwhelming desire was to be an architect. However, his failure to get into the Vienna Academy of Fine Arts to study painting may have had much to do with this. He later wrote that he first went to Munich with the aim of one day becoming a famous architect, but his conflicting accounts of the steps he took to get training and work seem to indicate that, in reality, he drifted as indolently and aimlessly as he had in Vienna. Only the coming of World War I was to reveal Hitler's true vocation. Yet architecture was to remain an obsession with Hitler, and one that as Führer of the Third Reich he could indulge on a megalomaniac scale, in theory if less in practice. He would cut short important meetings to pore over architectural models and plans with Albert Speer and up to the end in his bunker would chatter enthusiastically about his plans for Berlin and Linz.

Hitler's tastes in building were predictably conservative, confined mostly to the neobaroque and neoclassical. He admired the neoclassical facades and wide boulevards of Vienna's famous Ringstrasse and the similarly monumental constructions of the Munich of the Wittelsbach kings and, according to Speer, also rhapsodized about Charles Garnier's Paris Opera House. The avant-garde and all forms of modernism, as in every other branch of the arts, completely passed him by. Under the aegis of the young and ambitious Speer and in full accord with Hitler's ideas, a crude and grandiose neoclassicism became the dominant style for the public buildings of the Third Reich. Above all it was scale that appealed to Hitler: the constructions of the Reich were to be monumental, conveying an impression of solidity, power, and permanence. The viewer or visitor was to be overwhelmed rather than merely impressed. Hitler's and Speer's plans for "Germania," the new Berlin, were meant to put the Paris of Baron Georges-Eugène Haussmann in the shade.

Supporters of modernism in architecture had initially hoped that Hitler's Reich, like Mussolini's Italy, would seek to present a dynamic and progressive image and encourage innovation, at least up to a point. But they were rapidly disillusioned. Hitler personally ordered the removal of modernist elements from the stadium designed by Speer for the 1936 Olympics. Functionalist architecture in Hitler's Germany was largely reserved for industrial buildings, such as power stations or the Heinkel aircraft factory at Oranienburg, whereas for popular housing, schools, Hitler Youth hostels, and other "vernacular" projects the regime adopted a "Blood and Soil" regionalism. But the "regional" elements were largely decorative, grafted on to a standardized design. The docile inhabitants of the fantasy world of Hitler, the failed architect, were meant to dwell happily in a world of kitsch, leaving their quaint and caricatured versions of Bavarian or Tyrolean farmhouses for work in their techno-functionalist factories and gaping in awe at the herculean constructions of the state, the party, and the Führer's ego.

Related entries: Art; Berlin; Cultural Policy; Linz; Nuremberg Rallies; Speer, Albert; Vienna

Suggestions for further reading:
Art and Power. 1995. *Art and Power: Europe under the Dictators 1930–45.* London: Hayward Gallery.
Scobie, Alex. 1990. *Hitler's State Architecture: The Impact of Classical Antiquity.* University Park: Pennsylvania State University Press.
Speer, Albert. 1970. *Inside the Third Reich.* New York: Macmillan.

Arnhem, Battle of

Operation Market Garden, a combined ground and airborne attack launched on 17 September 1944 on the initiative of Field Marshal Bernard Montgomery, was designed to secure control of the Dutch river crossings of the Maas, Waal, and Rhine before the winter halted operations. However, while successful American landings at Nijmegen and Eindhoven secured the bridges there, the British and Polish forces at Arnhem encountered a German counterattack from two SS Panzer Divisions and were pinned down. The survivors were forced to retreat across the Rhine on 25 September. The failure at Arnhem showed that Hitler's forces could still respond with flexibility and finesse and ended the Allied hopes for victory before the end of 1944.

Related entries: Montgomery, Bernard Law; Panzer Divisions

Art

The adolescent Adolf Hitler dreamed of becoming a great artist. In reality, this was not so easy, and following rejection by the Vienna Academy of Fine Arts, he was reduced to selling his mediocre watercolors in Vienna and then Munich merely to survive. This did not prevent him from being as big an expert on art as he was on everything else or from holding the most consistent and dogmatic views. Hitler viewed himself as an "artist-politician," leading the crusade for idealistic, Germanic art against the spiritual degeneration and "art bolshevism" represented by modern movements in art.

His own tastes were rooted in nineteenth-century naturalism and German Romanticism. Hitler's personal art collection, discovered by American soldiers in an Austrian railway tunnel in 1949, was put on public display for the first time in Weimar in 1999. It shows a preference for vast mountain scenes, caricature versions of German Romantic art, for mythological paintings featuring lots of nude women, and for rustic scenes of happy German peasant families and jolly shepherds. He was indeed the "Führer of Kitsch."

Any nonnaturalistic art was a result of mental and physical defects in the artist, a sign of moral decadence and primitive degeneration, for which, inevitably, the Jew and the Bolshevik were ultimately responsible. Cubism, futurism, and dadaism, he wrote in *Mein Kampf,* were "the morbid excrescences of insane and degenerate men" and "the symptoms of the decay of a slowly rotting world" (Hitler 1992, p. 235). "For if the age of Pericles seems embodied in the Parthenon, the Bolshevistic present is embodied in a cubist monstrosity" (Hitler 1992, p. 238).

Under the Third Reich, therefore, nonobjective, nonnaturalistic art was banned. Josef Goebbels's initial enthusiasm for expressionism was quickly terminated by Hitler. *Gleichschaltung* was applied through the Reich Chamber of Culture, and more than 40,000 artists and graphic designers were approved for membership in its subchamber, the Reich Chamber of Visual Art. But this did not compensate for the loss of talent. Those failing to adhere to Nazi artistic and political standards had their right to paint withdrawn, and many of the most renowned German artists went into exile or ceased work. Others conformed and remained silent, but the most favored artists were those who clearly expressed their adherence to Hitlerian ideas in their works.

In July 1937 a new House of German Art was opened by Hitler in Munich, the "artistic capital of the Reich." While its Great German Art Exhibition showed "authentic" German art, an exhibition of "Degenerate Art" *(Entartete Kunst),* the first of several in Germany, that attracted far more visitors opened in the gallery wing of the Hofarkaden. A selection of the thousands of "degenerate" paintings that had been purged from German museums, including works by Paul Klee, Emil Nolde, Max Beckmann, and Oskar Kokoschka, were held up for public disapproval before being sold to collectors abroad or destroyed.

With the temple of art cleansed of degeneracy, the purpose of Nazi art was to celebrate the new age and in particular the new human type: sportsman, hero, worker, warrior, mother. Opening the exhibition of 1937, Hitler declared: "Never was Mankind closer than now to Antiquity in its appearance and its sensibilities. Sport, contests and competition are hardening millions of youthful bodies, displaying them to us more and more in a form and temper that they have neither manifested nor been thought to possess for perhaps a thousand years. A radiantly beautiful type is growing up" (*Art and Power* 1995, p. 338). Nazi painting and sculpture was to celebrate this beauty, formed on classical Greek models, which may account for the curious absence of monumental figures of Hitler himself. The Führer's image was everywhere, but only in paintings or as a portrait bust.

The new art was to be clear, direct, and heroic, with no room for pessimism or complexity, and free from the neuroses of the modern. It was clean, pure, and simple. The favorite subject was the naked human body: Hitler's favorite painter, Adolf Ziegler, painted nothing but female nudes and was known as the "master of German pubic hair." Sportsmen and women, the heroes and heroines of classical myth, and allegorical figures were especially well regarded. But the Teutonic myths so important in Nazi ideology, music, and nationalist literature are almost completely absent from the visual arts.

The most visible and representative Nazi artists were sculptors like Arno Breker, who became Hitler's favorite, and Josef Thorak. Both specialized in huge heroic naked figures, classically based but rigid, with chests like armored breastplates and often given allegorical titles that were in fact virtually interchangeable. Gigantic and pompous, such figures provided a suitable setting for ceremony and ritual or could adorn monumental party and state buildings with suitable power and seriousness. They are works of reverence rather than living art. And in their grandiose vacuity they seem to personify Hitler's artistic pretensions: vast and ambitious but unimaginative, narrow, unoriginal, and bland.

Related entries: Architecture; Cultural Policy; Propaganda

Suggestions for further reading:

Art and Power. 1995. *Art and Power: Europe under the Dictators 1930–45.* London: Hayward Gallery.

Barron, Stephanie, ed. 1991. *"Degenerate Art": The Fate of the Avant-Garde in Nazi Germany.* Los Angeles: Los Angeles County Museum of Art.

Hinz, Berthold. 1979. *Art in the Third Reich.* New York: Pantheon.

Hitler, Adolf. 1992. *Mein Kampf.* Trans. Ralph Manheim. Intro. by D. C. Watt. London: Pimlico.

Petropolous, Jonathan. 1996. *Art as Politics in the Third Reich.* Chapel Hill: University of North Carolina Press.

Atlantic, Battle of the

The long, bitter, and bloody struggle for control of the maritime trade routes on which Britain depended for vital supplies was one of the decisive battles of the war, but fortunately Hitler seems never to have fully appreciated its importance. The German navy used every means at its disposal, surface vessels and U-boats, to destroy enough merchant shipping to force Britain out of the conflict, but the Führer never fully complied with the requests of Admiral Karl Doenitz for full commitment to the Atlantic.

The British introduced a convoy system, using escort vessels equipped with the latest Allied Submarine Detection Investigation Committee submarine detection system, as soon as war broke out but were desperately short of both escort ships and coastal aircraft. At the same time both sides began extensive minelaying operations. British losses in the first year of the war were serious but not catastrophic. The fall of Norway and France in 1940 provided the Germans with new bases from which to threaten all shipping passing south of Ireland. The British had to withdraw resources for defense against anticipated invasion, and losses soared. Between June and December 1940 almost 3 million tons of shipping was destroyed, mostly by U-boats. Doenitz ur-gently pressed Hitler for greater commitment to construction of submarines and more cooperation from the Luftwaffe, but with only partial success.

By the summer of 1941 the U-boats had perfected their new "wolfpack" tactics, and Allied losses were still dangerously high. But the British were now fighting back: the threat of surface raiders was greatly reduced during 1941, the menace of mines was reduced by effective sweeping, aircraft were deployed more effectively under the control of the Admiralty, and a new generation of purpose-built destroyer escorts came into service. The greater involvement of the United States and Canada in convoy protection countered the greater geographical spread of U-boat attacks, but the lack of adequate air cover still made convoys vulnerable.

The pressure was further eased by the British decipherment of the German "Enigma" code and experiments in integrated defense using escort carriers. Again Hitler damaged the German response by ordering the transfer of submarines to the Mediterranean. But the Allies also had to make difficult decisions. All Royal Air Force heavy bombers were transferred to the bombing offensive over Germany, and the U.S. entry into the war forced the transfer of ships to the Pacific and the Atlantic seaboard. Doenitz moved the main focus of his attacks to the mid-Atlantic, with remarkable results. In November 1942 losses peaked at 729,000 tons. In all, the Allies lost 1,664 ships during 1942. By the end of the year British oil supplies were dangerously low, and Doenitz had, despite Hitler's hindrance, come close to starving Britain into defeat.

In early 1943 Hitler at last gave full priority to submarine construction, but the necessary elements of a successful counter by the Allies to the U-boats were now in place. Escort carriers and long-range B24 bombers were now made available for the Atlantic battle, as were improved radar and depth charges. By April 1943 Allied losses were halved, and in April and May forty-five U-boats were destroyed. On 23 May Doenitz withdrew his submarines from the North Atlantic, while British Coastal Command aircraft waged a fierce campaign against U-boat bases. Between June and August 1943 seventy-four U-boats were sunk, and only fifty-eight Allied merchant ships.

The Battle of the Atlantic was now decided. Although submarine warfare continued until the end of the war, the German effort to paralyze the British war effort had failed. A total of 47,000 British and Commonwealth seamen and 30,000 merchant sailors died in the war with Germany, the majority in the Battle of the Atlantic, making a crucial and not always fully appreciated contribution to the defeat of Hitler.

Related entries: Doenitz, Karl; Navy; U-boats

Atlantic Charter

The joint declaration of peace aims signed by Franklin Delano Roosevelt and Winston Churchill in August 1941 enshrined the common principles on which a world after Hitler was to be built. There were eight such basic principles: no territorial aggrandizement; no territorial changes without the free consent of the indigenous peoples; self-government for all nations; international economic cooperation for equal access to the world's raw materials and trade opportunities; improved labor standards, economic advancement and social security; freedom from tyranny, fear, and want; freedom of navigation on the seas and oceans; and a general disarmament preceding the abandonment of the use of force and the establishment of a permanent system of general security. The principles were later endorsed in the United Nations Declaration, signed by representatives of twenty-six

countries at the White House on 1 January 1942.

Related entries: Churchill, Winston Leonard Spencer; Roosevelt, Franklin Delano

Auschwitz

The largest of the extermination camps, the very name of which has become synonymous with the Holocaust, was located at Oswiecim (Auschwitz in German), not far from Kraków, Poland. A concentration camp, initially for Polish prisoners of war, was built in spring 1940 around a core of former military barracks to be used as a transit camp toward the east. This was the base camp, where Polish inmates formed a majority of the prisoners until the autumn of 1941, to which were added the industrial complex of Auschwitz-Monowitz and the killing center of Auschwitz-Birkenau, built in November 1941. The mass transports of Jews began arriving in March 1942.

Rudolf Hoess, the commandant of Auschwitz until November 1943, said: "Our system is so terrible that no-one in the world will believe it to be possible. . . . If someone should succeed in escaping from Auschwitz and in telling the world, the world will brand him as a fantastic liar" (Breitman 1991, p. 4). At Auschwitz-Monowitz, German industry, including the IG Farben synthetic rubber and oil factories, exploited the labor of inmates who were forced to work until they died. Up to 100,000 could be housed at Birkenau, which served both to house slave labor and as an extermination camp. The first gas chambers were constructed in January and June 1942 but were replaced by technologically advanced crematoria, which solved the problems of mass burials and the incineration of corpses in the open air. Even so, camp staff did have difficulty in disposing of

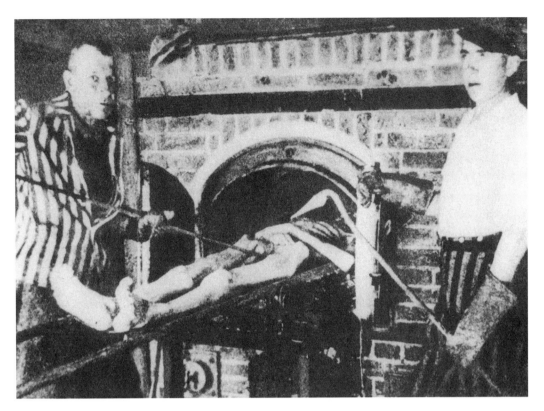

Two inmates of Auschwitz push the body of a dead prisoner into a crematorium oven. At the height of the camp's operation it has been estimated that over 6,000 corpses were being "processed" in this manner every day. (Deutsche Presse/Archive Photos)

corpses fast enough. By 1944 four cremato-ria were in use, with the gas chambers dis-guised as shower rooms.

Transports carrying Jews from all over Europe began arriving in spring 1942. The great majority, judged incapable of work, were sent directly to the gas chambers; the rest were registered, tattooed, given prison clothing, and set to work. SS doctors selected victims for their grotesque medical experi-ments. A part of the Birkenau camp was cor-doned off to house Gypsies, where before it was liquidated in August 1943 more than 100,000 were killed. The last large group to be murdered were Hungarian Jews: more than 400,000 were deported to Auschwitz between March and July 1944.

The total number of victims killed be-tween January 1942 and November 1944 is impossible to calculate exactly. Documentary evidence was destroyed on Heinrich Himm-ler's orders before the Red Army liberated Auschwitz in January 1945. Both Hoess at the Nuremberg trials and the Soviet govern-ment gave exaggerated figures. Reality lies somewhere between 1 million and 2 mil-lion. Even the smaller estimate constitutes the largest toll of any of the extermination camps. Thousands more died from exhaus-tion, starvation, and cold in the winter of 1944–1945, when all remaining inmates ca-pable of walking were marched to Germany to elude the advancing Soviet armies.

Related entries: Extermination Camps; Hoess, Rudolf; Holocaust

Suggestions for further reading:
Breitman, Richard. 1991. *The Architect of Genocide: Himmler and the Final Solution.* London: Bodley Head.

Gutman, Yisrael, and Michael Berenbaum, eds. 1994. *Anatomy of the Auschwitz Death Camp.* Bloomington: Indiana University Press.

Austria

Hitler was Austrian by birth but in his years in Vienna came to despise the multinational Habsburg Empire for whose sake, he thought, Germany was to go to war and make enormous sacrifices in 1914–1918. The Pan-German movement in Austria, calling for union with Germany, was a strong influence on the development of his political views. The union remained a high priority not only for Hitler but for many Austrians and Germans as well. In March 1919 the majority of German Austrians had voted for union, but the Allies vetoed a move that would have strengthened Germany too much. The rump state of Austria was forced to keep its independence. In March 1931 Chancellor Heinrich Brüning's proposal for a customs union between Germany and Austria was vetoed by the French. But the Austrian Nazi Party was gaining strength alongside its German counterpart, and agitation for union continued.

Hitler's accession to power in 1933 changed many Austrians' minds. The majority still probably favored union in principle, but only a minority wanted fusion with a National Socialist Germany. The two largest political parties in Austria, the Social Democrats and the Catholic-based Christian Social Party, both of which had supported Anschluss with a democratic Germany, now opposed it fiercely. The Christian Social Party chancellor Engelbert Dollfuss turned to Benito Mussolini for support. With the Italian dictator's approval, in 1934 he used labor unrest as a pretext for crushing the Social Democrats, depriving Hitler of any excuse to intervene to save the country from "bolshevism." Hundreds of lives were lost as heavy artillery blasted the workers'

apartment blocks, which formed the bastions of "Red Vienna."

The Social Democratic and Nazi Parties were both banned by Dollfuss's quasi-fascist government. In July 1934 the underground Austrian Nazis, with Hitler's support, made an armed bid for power. Dollfuss was assassinated, but the Austrian army remained loyal to the government, and the coup ended in ignominious failure. Mussolini, deeply disturbed by the thought of Anschluss, had moved a number of Italian divisions to the Austrian border. The monarchist Kurt von Schuschnigg succeeded Dollfuss and stabilized the authoritarian but independent regime. Hitler was forced to play a waiting game until 1938.

The Führer was unwilling to let the Austrian question upset his good relations with Mussolini. At their meeting in Venice in June 1934 he had assured the Duce that Austria would not be annexed. The prospects for Anschluss only improved with Mussolini's growing subservience to Hitler and his involvement in Abyssinia. Mussolini took back his guarantee of Austrian independence in January 1936 in return for Hitler's support for his Abyssinian adventure. In July of the same year Hitler signed a new agreement with Schuschnigg under which, in return for a German pledge of nonintervention, the Austrian chancellor promised to pursue a policy "based always on the principle that Austria acknowledged herself to be a German state" (Craig 1978, p. 694) and to grant a greater role in Austrian affairs to the "national opposition," that is, those who favored Anschluss.

Hitler finally bullied Schuschnigg into accepting Anschluss in 1938, and Austria became the Ostmark of the Greater German Reich. After the war Austria was, at the insistence of the Americans and British, declared the "first victim nation" of Nazi aggression, an extremely dubious assertion that owed more to the desire to keep the Russians out than to historical fact. It ignored the enthusiasm of many (probably most) Austrians for the Anschluss and Austria's enthusiastic participation in the war effort and the persecution of the Jews.

Related entries: Anschluss; Dollfuss, Engelbert; Foreign Policy; Italy; Linz; Mussolini, Benito; National Socialism; Pan-Germanism; Schuschnigg, Kurt von; Vienna

Suggestions for further reading:
Craig, Gordon A. 1978. *Germany, 1871–1945*. New York: Oxford University Press.
Pauley, Bruce F. 1981. *Hitler and the Forgotten Nazis: A History of Austrian National Socialism*. Chapel Hill: University of North Carolina Press.
Rich, Norman. 1973. *Hitler's War Aims: Vol. 1: Ideology, the Nazi State, and the Course of Expansion*. New York: Norton.

Autobahnen

Limited-access highways exclusively for automobile traffic were not new in the 1930s, having already been constructed in the United States and Italy, but were carried forward by the Nazis on an unprecedented scale. The autobahnen, or autobahns, became one of the most important public works projects of the Third Reich and one of the regime's few positive achievements. They formed part of the Nazi strategy for the "motorization" of Germany to help the recovery of the motor industry. But they were also to be a form of propaganda in its broadest sense, a symbol of the new Germany, uniting the *Volk* under Hitler's leadership. "The mission of the Reich Autobahn," it was stated, "is to become Adolf Hitler's road . . . to honor him, not only today, but for generations to come." Fritz Todt compared their construction to the building of the pyramids or the roads of the Roman Empire.

Hitler personally inaugurated the building of the first autobahn at Frankfurt on 23 September 1933, and the first completed stretch between Frankfurt and Darmstadt was opened on 13 May 1935. By early 1939 just over 3,000 kilometers of the projected 14,000 were completed, with another 1,500 kilometers under construction and another 2,400 authorized. They represented a highly advanced engineering venture, with a large-scale use of concrete and the latest techniques in surface construction and finish. But they were also to be aesthetic objects, blending harmoniously into the landscape. "The German road," said Todt, "must be an expression of its landscape and an expression of the German essence." The bridges in particular, mostly made with hewn natural stone, were to be works of art and "symbols of eternity."

The principal purposes of the autobahn project were to help absorb unemployment and aid internal trade. Thousands of jobless men were sent to the construction sites, and refusal meant a loss of unemployment support. The employment effects were exaggerated by Nazi propaganda. Wages were low, and much of the hardest work was done by concentration camp prisoners and foreign workers, but the program did bring unskilled workers back into the economy and stimulated supply industries. Including associated work in subcontracting and administration, a maximum of 250,000 men were employed at any one time. The Supreme Reich Authority under Todt could operate outside ministerial jurisdictions and devise mechanisms to speed up road building and coordinate public and private enterprise. With workers living apart from their families in paramilitary-style barracks, the origins of the Todt Organization may be seen in autobahn construction.

The early autobahns connected Germany's major ports and ran principally between the north and the south, thereby in theory helping to bind the Reich together economically. The question of their military application was more controversial. They were useful for short-term troop movements in the annexation of Austria and the Sudetenland, but the north-south orientation of the network shows that military strategy was not the most important factor in its planning, and the army chiefs generally preferred to use rail transport.

The autobahns were not seen as a priority in the war economy, and a total ban on all work was decreed by Albert Speer in 1942, despite the fact that Hitler saw them as one of his pet projects, along with party buildings and the reconstruction of Berlin. The requisition of trucks for the army and shortages of fuel and rubber meant that during the war the autobahns were largely deserted. Part of the network was also destroyed by Allied bombing. Nevertheless, the remainder continued in use in postwar Germany, as the one positive monument of the Third Reich.

Related entries: Economic Policy; Labor Service; Todt, Fritz; Unemployment

Suggestions for further reading:
Freeman, Michael. 1995. *Atlas of Nazi Germany: A Political, Economic and Social Anatomy of the Third Reich.* 2nd ed. London and New York: Longman.
Overy, Richard J. 1973. "Transportation and Rearmament in the Third Reich," *Historical Journal* 16, pp. 389–409.

Aviation

One of Hitler's first acts on becoming chancellor of Germany was the creation of the Air Ministry under Hermann Goering. Hitler's "flights over Germany" during election campaigns had spread his message personally in a way that had never been seen in Germany or anywhere outside the United States. In the third flight in July 1932, with the slogan "the Führer over Germany," he had spoken in fifty-three towns and cities. This had helped to create a progressive image for the Nazis, in tune with the air-crazy spirit of the age, which they tried to boost when in power. "The German people," declared Goering in September 1934, "must become a nation of aviators" (Bramsted 1965, p. 153). The image is encapsulated memorably at the opening of Leni Riefenstahl's *Triumph of the Will,* when Hitler arrives at the Nuremberg rally like a god descending from the clouds.

The Treaty of Versailles had forbidden the construction of military aircraft in Germany, but the Weimar Republic encouraged the production of civil aircraft and research that could eventually have military implications. From the mid-1920s civil air services were a monopoly of Deutsche Lufthansa, which under the Nazis received 50 percent of its revenue from direct state subsidy. On a more popular level, in 1929 the German Union of Sporting Flying boasted 50,000 members. Hundreds of gliders piloted by "sportsmen" prepared for the future air force, the Luftwaffe, created by Hitler in 1935.

Under Hitler, research and development in aviation was geared to the future war. Prototypes of helicopters and jet planes were produced, but the war came too soon for them to have any practical applications. Among the test pilots was Hanna Reitsch, a champion glider pilot who became Germany's own female air ace, the Nazis' answer to Amelia Earhart or Amy Johnson. Personally devoted to Hitler, Reitsch was one of the privileged few allowed access to the Führer's bunker and as a fighter pilot became the only woman to receive the Iron Cross during Hitler's war.

Related entries: Goering, Hermann; Luftwaffe

Suggestions for further reading:
Bramsted, Ernest K. 1965. *Goebbels and National Socialist Propaganda 1925–1945.* East Lansing: Michigan State University Press.

Axis

Benito Mussolini first referred to the Rome-Berlin Axis, "around which all those European states which are animated by a desire for collaboration and peace may work together" (Hiden 1977, p. 150), on 1 November 1936. During a visit to Berlin by Count Galeazzo Ciano in October of that year, the Italian foreign minister had talked at length with Hitler and signed a nine-point protocol covering various aspects of German-Italian cooperation. The Axis represented a delineation of spheres of interest between Hitler and Mussolini, with Italy to dominate the Mediterranean and Germany to dominate eastern Europe. It showed the two dictators' determination to pursue their plans for expansion despite the opposition of Britain and France and provided Hitler with the assurance needed for the pursuit of rearmament. The common interests of Nazism and fascism were, in a way, institutionalized. It was not in itself a detailed pact or plan, nor did it overcome the mutual suspicion between the two countries, most particularly over Austria and southeastern Europe. But as a "joint declaration of war on the *status quo*" (Hiden 1977, p. 150), the public affirmation of the Axis had immense propaganda value, paving the way for Italy's adherence to the Anti-Comintern Pact in November 1937 and the "Pact of Steel" in May 1939.

Related entries: Anti-Comintern Pact; Ciano, Galeazzo, Count; Foreign Policy; Italy; Mussolini, Benito; Pact of Steel

Suggestions for further reading:
Hiden, John. 1977. *Germany and Europe 1919–1939.* New York: Longman.

Bagration, Operation

The Soviet offensive, launched on 22 June 1944, the third anniversary of Hitler's launch of Operation Barbarossa, carried the Russians 300 miles westward from Belorussia to the banks of the Vistula River outside Warsaw. Some 350,000 German soldiers were killed, wounded or captured in a catastrophic month for Hitler. Germany's strategic position on the Eastern Front was destroyed, with the remnants of Army Group Center pushed back to a position less than 400 miles from Berlin. Politically, the Tripartite Pact, laboriously constructed by Hitler in 1940–1941, began to unwind. Romania and Bulgaria were quick to change sides, and Finland rapidly reconsidered its position. Unfortunately, however, the advance of the Red Army also sparked the tragedy of the Warsaw Rising.

Related entries: Eastern Front; Tripartite Pact; Warsaw Rising

Suggestions for further reading:
Overy, Richard. 1998. *Russia's War.* New York: Allen Lane Penguin Press.

Baltic States

The republics of Lithuania, Latvia, and Estonia emerged as independent states from World War I and the Russian Revolution. All contained German minorities, the Baltic Germans, and by the mid-1930s all were ruled by authoritarian regimes. In the Nazi-Soviet Pact of August 1939 Hitler consigned all three countries to the Soviet sphere of influence, and they were all occupied by the Red Army in June 1940. The Baltic Germans were resettled in the Reich. When the Germans invaded in June 1941, the three Baltic states were incorporated into the Reich Commissariat Ostland.

The nationalists who welcomed Hitler's invasion were swiftly disillusioned. The Nazis' policy was to "Germanize" the "racially suitable" members of the indigenous population; to deport or exterminate "undesirables," first of all the Jews; and to promote extensive German colonization. The many Latvians and Estonians who joined the Waffen SS and participated in the persecution of the Jews and as soldiers on the Eastern Front expected political concessions but inevitably got nothing. The Baltic states were reoccupied by the Russians between July and October 1944, and they became republics within the Union of Soviet Socialist Republics.

Related entries: Barbarossa, Operation; Eastern Front; Foreign Policy; Holocaust; Memel; Nazi-Soviet Pact; Soviet Union; *Volksdeutsche;* Waffen SS

Suggestions for further reading:
Hiden, John, and Patrick Salmon. 1994. *The Baltic Nations and Europe: Estonia, Latvia and*

Lithuania in the Twentieth Century. Rev. ed. London and New York: Longman.

Barbarossa, Operation

For Hitler, the invasion and destruction of the Soviet Union was the fulfillment of his life's mission. The Nazi-Soviet Pact had been a temporary expedient, a necessary postponement of the final reckoning with "Jewish bolshevism." On the eve of the attack he wrote to Mussolini: "Since I struggled through to this decision, I again feel spiritually free. The partnership with the Soviet Union . . . seemed to me a break with my whole origin, my concepts and my former obligations. I am happy now to be relieved of these mental agonies" (Bullock 1991, p. 767). In addition, there was the economic factor: the raw materials and resources of the Urals, Siberia, and the Ukraine would sustain the prosperity and expansion of the Reich. With Russia's "immeasurable riches," Hitler thought, "Germany will have the means for waging war even against continents at some future date. Nobody will then be able to defeat her any more. If this operation is carried out, Europe will hold its breath" (Bullock 1991, p. 783).

The timing of the attack, however, was a practical decision and not determined by ideology. Hitler believed that the defeat of the Soviet Union would allow Germany thereafter to mobilize all her forces against Britain. Plans for Operation Barbarossa were approved by Hitler in February 1941, based on blitzkrieg tactics and huge tank drives aimed at the elimination of the Red Army in giant encirclements before the onset of the Russian winter. But Germany's commitment to the war in Greece and the Balkans forced postponement from mid-May to late June. Hitler justified his violation of the Nazi-Soviet Pact by stating that the Russians were planning, in collusion with Britain, to attack Germany. Joseph Stalin, however, refused to believe warnings from the British and his own intelligence service that Hitler was about to attack and was totally taken by surprise. His lack of preparation and initial panic did nothing to hinder the initial success of Barbarossa.

On 22 June 1941, without a declaration of war, Barbarossa launched three parallel offensives on a 2,000-mile front with forces of more than 3.5 million men, 2,770 aircraft, and 3,600 tanks. Romania, Hungary, Finland, Slovakia, Croatia, and Italy joined in the attack. Spectacular gains were made within a few weeks. Preliminary air strikes destroyed nearly 3,000 Soviet aircraft. Large bodies of Soviet troops were trapped by pincer movements: by the end of 1941 more than 3 million prisoners were in German hands. Army Group North crossed Lithuania, cleared Latvia and Estonia, and by September was laying siege to Leningrad. Army Group Center, driving toward Moscow, captured Smolensk in August and advanced toward the Soviet capital. Army Group South, under General Karl Rudolf von Rundstedt, captured Kiev, capital of the Ukraine, on 19 September and Kharkov on 24 October. In the autumn of 1941 the collapse of the Soviet Union seemed imminent.

Related entries: Baltic States; Blitzkrieg; Eastern Front; Nazi-Soviet Pact; Red Army; Soviet Union; Stalin, Joseph; Ukraine

Suggestions for further reading:
Bullock, Alan. 1991. *Hitler and Stalin: Parallel Lives.* London: HarperCollins.
Overy, Richard. 1998. *Russia's War.* New York: Allen Lane The Penguin Press.

Bavaria

Hitler's movement grew out of Bavaria, where the political climate proved favorable to the growth of an extreme nationalist movement. But a distinction should be drawn between Munich, the capital of Bavaria, and the province as a whole. Hitler was drawn to enter politics by events in Munich, specifically the creation of the "Councils Republic" and its suppression in April–May 1919. Vladimir Lenin declared on May Day 1919: "The liberated working class is celebrating its anniversary not only in Soviet Russia, but in Soviet Hungary and Soviet Bavaria" (Bullock 1991, p. 77). But Bavaria as a whole was a land of small towns and small-scale industry, predominantly rural and overwhelmingly Catholic, on the face of it an unpromising environment for either Nazism or communism.

Nevertheless, the drama of the "Soviet Republic" in Munich did create a stronger reaction against the Left in Bavaria than elsewhere in Germany. The right-wing government, administration, and legal system proved more hospitable to Nazism than did Left-dominated northern Germany, as was shown in the openly sympathetic attitude of Hitler's judges after the Beer Hall Putsch of 1923. The fervently nationalist political atmosphere, fueled by anti-Prussian resentment, the strong desire to retain Bavaria's special character, and an obsession with saving Germany from its internal enemies, led to the mushroom growth of *völkisch* groups on which the Nazi movement could feed for ideological support.

Government in Bavaria under the Weimar Republic was dominated by the Bavarian People's Party (BVP), whose firm entrenchment in the Catholic countryside was initially a hindrance to Nazism. In free elections Hitler picked up his strongest support among Protestants in the northern Bavarian areas of Upper and Middle Franconia, where he could capitalize on a protest vote against the Catholic-dominated BVP. The larger Catholic areas swung to the Nazis later, massively in the provincial elections of 5 March 1933. Hitler's movement may have been born in Munich, but Bavaria as a whole was never one of the most fervently Nazi areas of Germany, primarily because of the enduring influence of the Catholic Church.

Related entries: Bavarian People's Party; Beer Hall Putsch; Catholic Church; Landsberg-am-Lech; Munich; Nazi Movement

Suggestions for further reading:
Bullock, Alan. 1991. *Hitler and Stalin: Parallel Lives.* London: HarperCollins.
Mitchell, Allen. 1965. *Revolution in Bavaria, 1918–1919: The Eisner Regime and the Soviet Republic.* Princeton: Princeton University Press.
Pridham, Geoffrey. 1973. *The Nazi Movement in Bavaria, 1923–1933.* New York: Harper and Row.

Bavarian People's Party (BVP)

Although it never held an absolute majority in the provincial Landtag, the BVP set the dominant tone of Bavarian politics under the Weimar Republic: extreme conservatism, anti-socialism, patriotism, and "white-blue" Bavarian Catholic values. It was created in 1918, splitting from the Center Party, and in 1922–1923 and again from 1925 to 1932 belonged to national governing coalitions. As a party of "national order," it leant support to Hitler's Beer Hall Putsch of 1923. After losing ground in the Reichstag elections of 3 March 1933, the BVP voted for Hitler's Enabling Act and dissolved itself on 4 July 1933.

Related entries: Bavaria

Bayreuth

Hitler's idolatrous admiration for Richard Wagner found expression in his attendance at and support for the annual festival of Wagner's operas held at Bayreuth in Franconia. The festival, founded in 1876, had always expressed a *völkisch* German nationalism, with undertones of anti-Semitism despite the important contribution Jewish artists had always made to the festival. Winifred Wagner, the composer's English-born daughter-in-law, first met Hitler in 1923 and remained bedazzled by "this German man who, filled with the most ardent love of his Fatherland, sacrifices his life for his ideal of a purified, united national Greater Germany" (Spotts 1994, pp. 141–142) right up to her death in 1980.

Hitler attended the festival as Winifred's guest each summer from 1933 to 1939, even in the final summer of peace, when he was preoccupied with the preparations for the invasion of Poland. During the final scenes of *Götterdämmerung* he would weep and hold hands with Winifred. "The ten days at Bayreuth," he later recalled, "were always my most wonderful time," and the end of the festival was, with vapid banality, "something terribly sad for me, as when a Christmas tree is stripped of its ornaments" (Spotts 1994, p. 168). Albert Speer recalled that Hitler was at his most relaxed at Bayreuth: "As patron of the festival and as the friend of the Wagner family, Hitler was no doubt realizing a dream which even in his youth he perhaps never quite dared to dream" (Speer 1971, p. 219).

Winifred used her friendship with Hitler to protect herself from attacks by other leading Nazis who did not share the Führer's Wagnerian enthusiasm, most notably Hermann Goering, patron of the rival Berlin Opera House. Also, as Jews and foreign visitors deserted Bayreuth, she became dependent on Hitler's financial support. Seeing himself as stepping into the shoes of Wagner's own benefactor, King Ludwig II of Bavaria, Hitler considered state support for Bayreuth as a "national obligation." "I considered it to be a particular joy," he recalled, "to have been able to keep Bayreuth going at a time when it faced economic collapse" (Spotts 1994, p. 169). He even personally intervened in a vain attempt to persuade Arturo Toscanini to con-tinue conducting at Bayreuth. But the "Highly Esteemed Master," as Hitler called him, joined Bruno Walter, Otto Klemperer, Rudolf Sirkin, Artur Schnabel, and other Jewish and non-Jewish artists in boycotting Bayreuth under the Third Reich. The Wagner festival had become a "Hitler festival," with Sturmabteilung men in the streets, swastika banners everywhere, and the street leading to the Opera House rebaptized Adolf Hitler Strasse.

The outbreak of war in 1939 should have put an end to Bayreuth, but Hitler kept it going as a festival reserved for "guests of the Führer." Munitions workers and wounded soldiers from the Eastern Front were dragooned into attending and housed in barrackslike accommodation for the good of their Aryan souls as the festival sank to its moral nadir. SS troops sounded the fanfares announcing performances and even on occasions took the place of the chorus. As the Reich collapsed, Bayreuth was bombed in April 1945. The sacred buildings and grounds were used as a sanctuary for Germans expelled from the Sudetenland and as a billet for U.S. forces, including, much to Winifred Wagner's disgust, black soldiers. Performances of non-Wagnerian operas and even swing music were staged for U.S. troops. The Wagner festival was reestablished in 1951, forced to make great efforts to live down its past.

Related entries: Cultural Policy; Wagner, Richard

Suggestions for further reading:
Speer, Albert. 1971. *Inside the Third Reich.* Paperback ed. London: Sphere Books.
Spotts, Frederic. 1994. *Bayreuth: A History of the Wagner Festival.* New Haven: Yale University Press.

Beck, Ludwig (1880–1944)

As chief of staff of the armed forces from 1935 to 1938, General Ludwig

Beck, despite being a Nazi appointee, came into increasing conflict with Hitler over his war plans and the growth of Nazi Party influence within and over the army. He was to pay for his opposition by losing his position and ultimately his life. A Rhinelander and a Protestant, born near Wiesbaden into an upper-middle-class family, Beck entered the army in 1898, served as a staff officer in World War I, and by 1929 had risen to the post of commander of the 5th Artillery Regiment. At the same time he flirted briefly with Nazism until he became acquainted with the leading Nazis in person. After the seizure of power he was chosen by the chief of the General Staff, General Kurt von Hammerstein-Equord, as his principal assistant and adjutant general in the Reichswehr Ministry. Hammerstein hoped that Beck as his obvious successor would continue the conservative Prussian military tradition, based on professionalism and limited war, to combat Hitler's plans for adventurous wars of conquest.

As chief of staff, Beck was theoretically in charge of overall military planning and preparations, but he met with Hitler only rarely. He favored a steady buildup of German forces and opposed the growth of the SS and the increasing Nazification of the army. But he was humiliated by the successful reoccupation of the Rhineland in 1936, which he had opposed, and after the "Blomberg–Fritsch crisis" in early 1938 became an increasingly isolated figure among Hitler's more pliable generals. Beck was aware of the basic weakness of Germany's strategic position and the ultimate folly of Hitler's policies. He violently opposed Hitler's policy over Czechoslovakia, but his attempt to organize opposition within the General Staff failed miserably. His resignation on 18 August 1938 signaled the final triumph of Nazism over the army, and his departure removed the final obstacle to Hitler's war policy.

Beck retired into obscurity, but with his convictions unchanged. Believing that Hitler was leading Germany into disaster, he became more and more associated with the opposition group, the Wednesday Club (*Mittwochgesellschaft*), whose members were drawn principally from the military. Had the July Plot to assassinate Hitler in 1944 succeeded, Beck would have become German head of state. After the failure of the conspiracy, aware of the fate that awaited him, he committed suicide, blowing his brains out on 20 July 1944.

Related entries: July Plot; Officer Corps; Opposition; Rearmament

Suggestions for further reading:
O'Neill, Robert. 1995. "Fritsch, Beck and the Führer," in Correlli Barnett, ed., *Hitler's Generals.* London: Phoenix, pp. 19–41.

Beer Hall Putsch

Hitler's improvised coup in Munich in November 1923 played a large part in Nazi mythology of the "time of struggle" but was in reality an inglorious and messy affair. In response to left- and right-wing unrest sparked off by hyperinflation, the Bavarian government on 26 September 1923 appointed Gustav Ritter von Kahr as general state commissar, with near-dictatorial powers to defend the state. The following weeks were tense. Rumors of a putsch circulated freely, and Nazi meetings packed the Munich beer halls. As head of the Deutscher Kampfbund, which brought together the National Socialist German Workers' Party and smaller extreme right groups, Hitler was urged by his allies to act decisively.

Kahr, State Police Chief Hans Ritter von Seisser, and the Reichswehr commander Otto Hermann von Lossow had their own plans, formed in conjunction with northern German contacts, for the installation of a nationalist dictatorship in Berlin. But the Kampfbund wanted a direc-

Armed SA men man a barricade outside the Bavarian War Ministry in Ludwigstrasse, Munich, on 9 November 1923 during the Beer Hall Putsch. Heinrich Himmler (center) is carrying the old flag of the German Reich. (Culver Pictures)

torate in Munich to include Hitler and Erich Ludendorff, which would march on Berlin in imitation of Mussolini's "March on Rome." On the evening of 8 November Kahr was addressing a meeting in the Bürgerbräukeller when Hitler burst in with a troop of Sturmabteilung (SA) men, took the stage, quieted the tumult by firing a shot at the ceiling, and declared that the Bavarian government was deposed and a new provisional Reich government was being formed. He forced Kahr, Seisser, and Lossow to accompany him to an adjoining room and to pledge their collaboration in a new government headed by Hitler, with Ludendorff as army commander.

The putsch soon degenerated into a farce. As soon as they were free from SA intimidation, Kahr and the others repudiated the coup. The country was informed by radio in the early hours of the morning, by which time it was also clear that both the Reichswehr and the state police opposed the putsch. Hitler had no idea what to do next, and it was only during the morning of 9 November that he and Ludendorff decided on a march through the city. Around noon a column of about 2,000 men, many armed (including Hitler) marched toward the Odeonsplatz in the center of the city, where the state police were waiting for them. In a brief gun battle fourteen putschists and four policemen were killed; Hitler, taking evasive action, dislocated his left shoulder; and Hermann Goering was among the wounded, shot in the leg. In the panic Hitler was spirited away to Putzi Hanfstaengl's house.

Hitler was arrested two days later. When the trial of the putsch leaders opened on 26 February 1924 Hitler used the courtroom as a stage, denied that he was guilty of high treason, and claimed that the truly guilty were the "criminals of November 1918." The sympathetic court had to find him guilty, but he was sentenced to a scandalously mild five years imprisonment for high treason. The trial, described by one journalist as a "political carnival," had brought Hitler to the attention of the German people for the first time. He was led away to his comfortable imprisonment in Landsberg. The absurd coup attempt, which should have marked the end of Hitler's political career, had the opposite effect thanks to the complicity of his judges. But he had learned a lesson and after his release from jail would pursue the path of "legality" toward power.

Related entries: Bavaria; Ludendorff, Erich; Munich; National Socialist German Workers' Party

Suggestions for further reading:
Dornberg, John. 1982. *The Putsch That Failed: Munich 1923.* London: Weidenfeld and Nicolson.
Gordon, Harold J., Jr. 1972. *Hitler and the Beer Hall Putsch.* Princeton: Princeton University Press.

Belgium

The kingdom of Belgium abandoned its traditional neutrality following the Treaty of Versailles and created a military alliance with France. The Belgian frontiers established at Versailles were guaranteed by the Locarno Pact of 1925. Hitler's assumption of power endangered the previously relaxed German-Belgian relations. The remilitarization of the Rhineland threatened Belgium, and on 14 October 1936 King Leopold III announced a return to neutrality. Hitler professed to welcome this, declaring that the Belgians had freed themselves from Bolshevik plots and influence, but its neutrality did not save Belgium from invasion and occupation in 1940. King Leopold remained in Belgium, a government-in-exile was formed in London, and the country came under direct German rule, aided

by the collaborationist leader Léon Degrelle. During the occupation, which lasted until September–October 1944, about 18,000 Belgians were deported to German concentration camps for resistance activities; more than 24,000 Belgian Jews perished in the Holocaust; and 140,000 Belgians were recruited as forced laborers in the German armaments industry.

Related entries: Blitzkrieg; Foreign Policy; France; Holocaust; Resistance Movements

Belsen

When British troops liberated the concentration camp of Bergen-Belsen in April 1945, the film images and radio commentaries revealed to the world for the first time something of the true horrors of Hitler's regime. The name "Belsen" has therefore become synonymous with Nazi crimes. Located in the Celle district of northwestern Germany, Bergen-Belsen was built between March and July 1943 and was originally intended for less than 10,000 prisoners, mostly Jews intended to be exchanged for German returnees or "sold" into emigration. But less than 3,000 actually left for Switzerland, Palestine, the United States, and North Africa. The rest, some of whom were put to work, were housed in the usual appalling conditions of the camps.

By the end of the war some 70,000 prisoners had arrived in Belsen from other camps. Well over half of them were to die from hunger, infectious disease, and exhaustion. During 1943 sick inmates were brought from other camps to the "convalescent" section of Belsen, where most died in miserable conditions because of lack of medicine, and many seriously ill inmates were killed by injections of phenol. Thousands of sick female prisoners were transferred from Auschwitz in late 1944 and early 1945, and then many thousands of inmates of all categories arrived from camps evacuated as the Allied armies advanced. After February 1945 new inmates were not even registered. When the British troops arrived, thousands of emaciated bodies lay in heaps or uncovered pits, while thousands of survivors, many on the point of death, stumbled around in an advanced state of starvation. The SS guards, whose savagery had contributed to the catastrophe, were set to work cleaning up the camp, while the commandant, Josef Kramer, was arrested, sentenced to death, and executed by the British.

Related entries: Concentration Camps

Beneš, Eduard (1884–1948)

Having served as foreign minister since 1918, Beneš became president of Czechoslovakia in 1935. Pressurized into resigning by Hitler, he went into voluntary exile following the Munich agreement and with the coming of war became president of the Czech government-in-exile, first in Paris and then in London. Beneš was a living symbol of opposition to Hitler and of an independent Czechoslovak state. He returned to Prague with the Soviet-created Czech Corps, and was re-elected president in 1945. But he was as opposed to Soviet domination as he had been to Hitlerian and was forced to resign in 1948 when the Communists seized power in Czechoslovakia.

Related entries: Czechoslovakia; Munich Agreement

Berchtesgarden

Hitler's retreat at Obersalzberg near Berchtesgarden in the Bavarian Alps was where he relaxed and received foreign visitors and his military commanders. He bought his rented home, the Haus Wachenfeld, and enlarged it into the Berghof. Here during the 1930s a succession of visitors ranging from Kurt von Schuschnigg to David Lloyd George, Lord Halifax and Neville Chamberlain, were taken to be impressed and if necessary bullied. Hitler told a journalist in 1936: "Here and here alone I can breathe and think—and live . . . I remember what I was, and what I have yet to do" (Bullock 1991, p. 422). Less romantically, he could do nothing, indulging his natural laziness in an idle routine, surrounded by a small "court" of aides and sycophants. More seriously, at Berchtesgarden Hitler felt on home ground and could dominate his visitors.

Above the Berghof was the "Eagle's Nest," Hitler's mountain house 6,000 feet above Berchtesgarden. It was reached by 10 miles of road cut into the mountainside in hairpin bends up which Hitler would delight in dragging his often unwilling entourage. The final elevator ride provided spectacular Alpine views in a landscape fully in keeping with the Germanic Romanticism of which Nazi kitsch was a tawdry offshoot. The Berghof was burned down by the SS in May 1945, and the Americans demolished the surrounding buildings when they occupied the region.

Suggestions for further reading:
Bullock, Alan. 1991. *Hitler and Stalin: Parallel Lives.* London: HarperCollins.

Berlin

Before coming to power Hitler had mixed feelings about Germany's capital. On leave there in 1916 he had been shocked by the gloomy "unpatriotic" atmosphere, and as an adopted Münchener he shared some of the traditional Bavarian resentment toward Berlin. After 1918 the nationalist Right attacked "Red Berlin" as the cradle of the November Revolution and the Spartacus uprising, the source of the supposed moral and cultural "decadence" of the Weimar Republic, and the home of one-third of Germany's Jews. However, postwar claims that Hitler always disliked Berlin are unconvincing. "I have always been fond of Berlin," he claimed. "If I'm vexed by the fact that some of the things in it are not beautiful, it's precisely because I'm so attached to the city" (Richie 1998, p. 962).

It was Josef Goebbels who was responsible for creating Hitler's new affection for the "truly Germanic" city of Frederick the Great and Bismarck. As *Gauleiter* of Berlin Goebbels created and built up the Nazi organization, which had less than 200 members when he took over, into a dominant force in the city, confronting the Communists and Socialists on the streets and in the meeting halls, penetrating the huge working-class districts as well as middle-class areas. He brought Hitler to speak in Berlin for the first time on 16 November 1928, before 16,000 people in the Sportspalast, the first of many such rallies in years to come. Nevertheless, the Nazi vote in free elections was always lower in Berlin than in Germany as a whole. At the height of their electoral success in 1933, when the Nazis gained 43.9 percent of the national vote, the figure for Berlin was 34.6 percent.

In the early years of the Third Reich Berlin continued its decadent ways as "an island of modernity in a world of Nazi provincialism" (Richie 1998, p. 442). Its opulent hotels, restaurants, and nightclubs provided a suitable setting for the hypocritical corruption of the Nazi elite, in stark contrast to the peasant fantasies they were peddling to the people. Here the elite and rich could dance to "decadent Negro" jazz music, theoretically banned in the Reich, and consume the finest food and wines. But the vibrant avant-garde culture of the Weimar period was destroyed and hundreds of artists imprisoned or driven into exile,

while the persecution of the Jews destroyed a community that had lived, prospered, and made an enormous contribution to the life of Berlin for centuries. Hitler had his own plans for the capital of the Reich.

Hitler reportedly told Albert Speer in 1936: "Berlin is a big city, but not a real metropolis. Look at Paris, the most beautiful city in the world. Or even Vienna. Those are cities with grand style. Berlin is nothing but an unregulated accumulation of buildings. We must surpass Paris and Vienna" (Speer 1971, p. 122). Hence his megalomaniac plans for rebuilding the city. Berlin would become "Germania," the leading city of Europe, filled with monstrous neoclassical buildings and monuments. "His motivating idea," Alexandra Richie writes, "was that everything had to be longer, bigger, wider, taller and more massive than the buildings in any other capital" (Richie 1998, p. 471). The centerpiece, a 3-mile north-south avenue, would stretch from the new central railway station, under a gigantic Triumphal Arch bearing the names of all the Germans who died in World War I, and culminate in the domed Volkshalle, the largest building in the world, seven times greater than the dome of St Peter's in Rome.

Comparatively little was actually built, and few of Hitler's buildings survive today. Berliners, Germans, and the world were meant to be overawed and intimidated by Hitler's new Reich Chancellery, 150 times the size of Bismarck's residence, Hermann Goering's gargantuan Air Ministry, and Goebbels's suitably overpowering Propaganda Ministry. Hitler delighted in scrutinizing the models built by Speer, even down to the last days in the bunker. His real legacy to Berlin, however, was the almost complete destruction of the city by Allied bombing and the final horrendous battle against the Red Army. The broad and grand "East-West Axis," along which the Wehrmacht had marched proudly on Hitler's fiftieth birthday in 1939, became a guiding path for bombers bent on the destruction of Berlin. The capital of the new Reich ended as a divided city, the beleaguered center of Cold War conflict. The Wall separating East and West Berlin, the symbol of Hitler's legacy of Cold War division, was finally demolished by crowds from both sides on 12 November 1989.

Related entries: Architecture; Bombing Campaigns; Goebbels, Paul Josef; National Socialist German Workers' Party; Olympics; Red Army

Suggestions for further reading:
Richie, Alexandra. 1998. *Faust's Metropolis: A History of Berlin*. London: HarperCollins.
Schäche, Wolfgang. 1995. "From Berlin to 'Germania,'" in *Art and Power: Europe under the Dictators 1930–45*. London: Hayward Gallery, pp. 326–329.

Blitzkrieg

The term "blitzkrieg," or "lightning war," has been ascribed to Hitler himself, but it may in fact have been coined by *Time* magazine. Building on tactics developed in 1918 by young officers such as Erwin Rommel, the blitzkrieg had three elements: surprise, the rapid mobility of forces, and the crippling of the enemy by the cutting of supply and control lines. Put into operation for the first time in the Polish campaign of 1939, it was a resounding success—the Polish army was destroyed within a week—and repeated in France and the Low Countries. But the limits of blitzkrieg were exposed in the invasion of Russia. The idea left little margin for the expansion of armaments or buildup of forces: if offensives lost momentum they were doomed. It was vulnerable to competitive struggles within the armed forces and was weakened by the ad hoc methods of arm procurement in operation before the slow move to armament in depth from 1941 onward.

The concept of the blitzkrieg betrays Hitler's limited ideas about war as a lightning blow, a "smash-and-grab" aggression. Even when irrelevant such thoughts domi-

German tanks enter a Polish village during the invasion of Poland in September 1939. Hitler's attack on Poland provided the Wehrmacht with a chance to test the effectiveness of the blitzkrieg technique and marked the beginning of World War II in Europe. (Archive Photos)

nated his mind, often to the dismay of his generals. Hence his unreasonable expectations about counteroffensives such as at Kursk and later the Ardennes. The connection of blitzkrieg to economics is more controversial. Rapid victory would obviate the need for total mobilization and limit the economic burden of the war on the population. It is not certain, however, whether this was the idea from the beginning or an attempt to rationalize Germany's chaotic economic development and the failure to provide armament in depth. In this latter perspective the blitzkrieg, like so much else in Nazi Germany, only looks planned and efficient in retrospect.

Related entries: Barbarossa, Operation; Eastern Front; Guderian, Heinz; Kursk, Battle of; Panzer Divisions; Poland; Wehrmacht

Suggestions for further reading:
Keegan, John. 1989. *The Second World War.* London: Hutchinson.

Blomberg-Fritsch Crisis

The dual intrigue that removed the military heads of the Wehrmacht in January–February 1938 confirmed the power of Hitler and Nazi organizations over the armed forces. Werner von Blomberg, war minister, and Werner von Fritsch, supreme army commander, were maneuvered from office as a result of moral scandals engineered by Hermann Goering, Heinrich Himmler, and Reinhard Heydrich. Both men had supported rearmament and Hitler's actions against the Sturmabteilung, hoping to make the Reichswehr (later Wehrmacht) the sole arms bearer of the nation. But opposition to the pace of the arms buildup and what Hitler saw as pusillanimity about the premature use of force led to the removal of both men from office within a few dramatic weeks.

The excuse for Blomberg's forced resignation was his marriage to Margarethe ("Eva") Gruhn, subsequently revealed to be a former prostitute well-known to the vice squad. Hitler and Goering acted as witnesses at the wedding on 12 January 1938. The whole business was encouraged and may have been engineered by Goering, who had encouraged Blomberg to go ahead with the wedding, arguing that outdated social conventions, that is, opposition to the marriage of an aristocratic army officer to a commoner of obscure origins, should be discarded. Hitler's position as head of state was deemed to have been compromised by the affair, and Blomberg resigned on 4 February.

Fritsch, like Blomberg, was a professional soldier of the old school. He had served in World War I as a General Staff officer and under the Weimar Republic held a succession of posts connected with the stealthy expansion of the Reichswehr. He was appointed chief of army command (later supreme army commander) on 2 May 1935. Fritsch met rarely with Hitler: his relations with the Führer were distant, and Blomberg acted as Fritsch's channel to Hitler. His view of Hitler was encapsulated by his oft-repeated statement: "Hitler is Germany's fate for good and for bad" (O'Neill 1995, p. 25). He was assumed to be the natural successor to Blomberg as war minister, but Goering had other ideas. Fritsch was accused of homosexual relations with a male prostitute by the name of Schmid, a charge he vehemently denied and that was in fact a fabrication set up by the Gestapo and supported by the SS. Nevertheless, he was dismissed on 4 February 1938 and replaced by Walter von Brauchitsch. Fritsch's supposed rehabilitation through a Reich court-martial presided over by Goering was abandoned amid the euphoria surrounding the Anschluss with Austria. He was made an honorary colonel in the artillery and was killed outside Warsaw on 22 September 1939.

The outcome of the "Blomberg-Fritsch crisis" allowed Hitler to assume personal command of the army, working through the new Wehrmacht High Command headed by Wilhelm Keitel. The armed forces were now firmly in Hitler's grip, and any possibility of opposition from the officer corps had been eliminated. Both men had failed to make their dissent effective, partly because they shared some of Hitler's aims, partly through a misplaced trust in the power of persuasion to change his mind.

Related entries: Blomberg, Werner von; Officer Corps; Wehrmacht

Suggestions for further reading:
Görlitz, Walter. 1995. "Blomberg," in Correlli Barnett, ed., *Hitler's Generals.* London: Phoenix, pp. 129–137.
O'Neill, Robert J. 1987. *The German Army and the Nazi Party 1933–1939.* London: Cassell, 1966. Reprint, New York: Heinemann.
———. 1995. "Fritsch, Beck and the Führer," in Correlli Barnett, ed., *Hitler's Generals.* London: Phoenix, pp. 19–41.

Blomberg, Werner von (1878–1946)

Appointed defense minister on 30 January 1933, the aristocratic Blomberg played an important role in Hitler's consolidation of power but in 1938 fell victim to the perpetual power struggle among the top echelons of the Third Reich. Born into a professional military family, Blomberg held various staff appointments on the Western Front during World War I, joined the Reichswehr in 1919, and served as head of the conscription office at the War Office from 1927 to 1929. During this time he visited the Soviet Union and was impressed by what he saw, considering wrongly that the Red Army and the party were the twin independent pillars of the new state. In 1929 Lieutenant-General von Blomberg was made commander of Military District I in

East Prussia but in 1932 was dispatched to Geneva as leader of the German military delegation at the Disarmament Conference.

Intelligent but intellectually volatile and easily impressed, Blomberg was a natural choice as Hitler's defense minister. In an article in the *Völkischer Beobachter* (29 June 1934) he assured Hitler of the army's loyalty and spelled out how he saw party and army as pillars of the Third Reich, echoing his mistaken assumptions about the Soviet Union. He continued to draw a fictitious and ultimately costly distinction between Hitler and the Nazi Party. Speaking later of the army's oath to Hitler, he said: "We swore the oath on the flag to Hitler as Führer of the German people, not as head of the National Socialist Party" (Kershaw 1998, p. 525). In July Blomberg applauded Hitler's crushing of the Sturmabteilung in the "Night of the Long Knives," thanking the Führer on behalf of the cabinet for the "resolute and courageous action through which he had protected the German people from civil war" (Kershaw 1998, p. 518). In 1935 the defense minister became the war minister. In May of that year Blomberg was made commander in chief of the Wehrmacht and as such was closely involved in planning the military reoccupation of the Rhineland. As a reward Hitler ordained him the first field marshal of the new army in 1936.

The conservative aristocratic figure of Blomberg as head of the Wehrmacht may have been reassuring to traditionally minded army officers, but in reality his compliance with Nazi plans was never in doubt. However, his plans for a streamlining reorganization of the top command structure of the armed forces were very much not to the liking of Hermann Goering as head of the air force or Heinrich Himmler as head of the SS, and Blomberg's private life provided them with the means of getting rid of him. A widower since 1932, Blomberg substituted amorous nocturnal adventures for the normal officer's social life, and in the course of them he met the young and attractive Margarethe ("Eva") Gruhn. Goering obligingly removed another suitor for Eva's hand, and on 12 January she and Blomberg were married in the great hall of the War Ministry. Two weeks later it emerged that the new Frau von Blomberg had been a prostitute and had a criminal record for dealing in pornographic pictures. The extent to which Blomberg had been set up by Goering and Himmler is unclear, but he officially resigned on 4 February 1938, was dismissed from the armed forces, and was never reinstated. Blomberg's fall as part of the "Blomberg-Fritsch crisis" removed any possibility of independent action by the military against Hitler, who took over personally as defense minister and supreme commander of the armed forces.

Thereafter it was forbidden to mention Blomberg's name in the Third Reich. He and his wife settled in Bad Wiessee, and his naïve requests for reinstatement were rejected by Hitler. Blomberg was arrested by the Allies in 1945 and died from a heart attack while under U.S. detention on 14 March 1946.

Related entries: Blomberg-Fritsch Crisis; Officer Corps; Wehrmacht

Suggestions for further reading:
Görlitz, Walter. 1995. "Blomberg" in Correlli Barnett, ed., *Hitler's Generals.* London: Phoenix, pp. 129–137.
Kershaw, Ian. 1998. *Hitler 1889–1936: Hubris.* New York: Allen Lane Penguin Press.
O'Neill, Robert J. 1987. *The German Army and the Nazi Party 1933–1939.* London: Cassell, 1966. Reprint, New York: Heinemann.

Blut und Boden

"**B**lood and soil" was one of the most consistent themes and slogans of the Third Reich. It defined the strength of the *Herrenvolk* (master race) as springing from peasant virtues, the Nordic past, warrior heroes, and the sacredness of the German soil. Supposedly Germanic traditions were revived in an attempt to restore a mythical past, which would provide the clean and healthy alternative to the chaos of a present dominated by urban, intellectual, and "Jewish materialist" values. Culture and propaganda were supposed to give form and substance to this racist fantasy by describing pastoral idylls and utopian visions of virtuous rustic life. Such a vague concept could be used as a slogan in all aspects of life: "blood" implied social stability and a degree of egalitarianism among all "pure-blooded Aryans," and German "soil" could not be confined within the arbitrary boundaries imposed by the Treaty of Versailles. But for committed Nazis the superior virtue of rural life and the need for "living space" in the east were articles of faith. A simple catch-phrase like *Blut und Boden* could help force these ideas down the throats of the population.

Related entries: Anti-Semitism; Art; Cinema; Cultural Policy; Propaganda; Racial Theory; *Volksgemeinschaft*

Bombing Campaigns

Allied bombing of Germany began in a small way in May 1940, intensified after U.S. entry into the war and again after D-Day, and continued virtually uninterrupted to the end of the war. In the single month of March 1945, British and U.S. planes dropped on German cities almost twice the bomb tonnage inflicted on Britain during the entire war. The campaign took two forms: the very difficult daytime bombing of military, industrial, and transportation targets, the special preserve of the U.S. Air Force, and the area bombing of industrial and urban centers, carried out at night by Royal Air Force Bomber Command and aimed at damaging civilian morale.

There is no consensus about the effect of the bombing campaigns on the German war effort. It has been argued that they served to convince Hitler of the necessity of mobilizing the entire economy for war under the direction of Albert Speer, thereby increasing German efficiency. However, they were certainly responsible for creating acute shortages in important sectors, especially in fuel oil. In September 1944 bombing brought production of synthetic oil to a temporary standstill. The bombing of the Rhine-Ruhr area was particularly significant because the concentration of industrial and raw material capacity in this region meant that the damage inflicted there affected industrial capacity throughout the Reich.

Total civilian deaths as a result of bombing amount to some 600,000, with 800,000 injured. More than 2 million homes were destroyed and about 7.5 million people made homeless. The head of Bomber Command, Sir Arthur "Bomber" Harris, sincerely believed that the terror bombing of German cities, such as the actions that resulted in the almost complete destruction of Hamburg and Dresden in firestorms, could break morale and significantly shorten the war. Winston Churchill, with the example of Hitler's bombing of London and other British cities in mind, was not so sure, and relations between the two men were not good. In Germany, as in Britain, it was astonishing how normal life could continue to a remarkable degree even under the horrors of mass bombing.

It is doubtful whether the bombing campaigns in themselves did much to contribute to disillusionment with Hitler. Hermann Goering had promised the German people that his Luftwaffe would prevent Allied bombers from ever reaching Germany, and he was made to carry the blame for the emptiness of his boasting. It was a major factor in the decline of his influence. Hitler tried to appear above it all. Unlike Churchill and the British royal family, he never visited the victims of bombing, but Josef Goebbels did, and his propagandists made much of the "barbarity" of Allied actions. Most German civilians were probably aware that retribution for German bombing of Britain was inevitable. Bombing only helped to destroy the "Hitler myth" as one of the signs that after the defeat at Stalingrad, Germany was losing the war.

Related entries: Britain, Battle of; Goering, Hermann; Industry; Luftwaffe; Propaganda; Public Opinion

Suggestions for further reading:
Garrett, Stephen A. 1993. *Ethics and Airpower in World War II: The British Bombing of German Cities.* New York: St. Martin's Press.
Levine, Alan J. 1992. *The Strategic Bombing of Germany, 1940–1945.* Westport and London: Praeger.

Bonhoeffer, Dietrich (1906–1945)

The young evangelical Protestant theologian Bonhoeffer and his family have remained a symbol of German resistance to Hitler. His father, Karl, a psychiatrist, planned to have Hitler declared legally insane, and his elder brother Klaus, a lawyer by profession, was also associated with opposition groups and was shot in 1945. Dietrich Bonhoeffer studied theology in New York from 1930 to 1933 and then became a pastor in London until 1935, when he returned to Germany to work with the anti-Nazi Confessing Church. He met and worked with other anti-Nazis from a similar elevated social background, including Ludwig Beck and Admiral Wilhelm Canaris, and attempted to maintain contacts in Britain and the United States.

Bonhoeffer was banned from preaching by the Gestapo but maintained his opposition contacts, including the Kreisau Circle. Provided with forged papers, he met the English bishop Bell of Chichester in Sweden, but the Allies remained suspicious, and the insistence on the unconditional surrender of Germany rendered his efforts futile. He was arrested by the Sicherheitsdienst in April 1943 as part of the sweep against plotters planning to assassinate Hitler. Bonhoeffer was held in Buchenwald and finally executed in Flossenburg concentration camp in April 1945.

Related entries: Beck, Ludwig; Confessing Church; Kreisau Circle; Opposition; Protestant Churches

Bormann, Martin
(1900–1945?)

The sinister and somewhat mysterious Bormann rose to become the second most important figure in the Third Reich, described by Hitler as his "most loyal Party comrade." Born at Halberstadt in 1900, son of a former Prussian soldier who had become a post office worker, Bormann dropped out of school, served briefly in an artillery regiment during World War I, and subsequently joined the Rossbach Freikorps in Mecklenburg. In March 1924 Bormann was sentenced to one year's imprisonment as an accomplice of Rudolf Hoess in the murder of Bormann's former teacher, Walther Kadow, whom they accused of treason in the French-occupied Ruhr. After his release in 1925 Bormann joined the Nazi Party and began his crawl to the top.

Bormann became manager of the National Socialist German Workers' Party's (NSDAP's, Nazi Party's) regional press office and then business manager in Thuringia. From 1928 to 1930 he was attached to the Sturmabteilung (SA) Supreme Command and in 1933 became a *Reichsleiter* and was elected to the Reichstag. As chief of cabinet to Rudolf Hess from July 1933, he unofficially ranked next to the deputy Führer himself among Hitler's entourage. Bormann stayed close to Hitler and silently occupied a central position in the party apparatus, keeping himself in the background and being only rarely photographed. Diligent and efficient, he ran the "Adolf Hitler Fund," a supply of funds donated by or extorted from businessmen, and administered Hitler's personal finances, including the purchase of the various properties at Berchtesgarden. Bormann's coarseness and his apparent insignificance caused the other leading Nazis to underestimate him until it was too late. The "Brown Eminence" had discovered how to make himself indispensable.

When Hess fled to Britain in May 1941, Bormann effortlessly took over as head of the *Parteikanzlei*. Now he controlled access to Hitler, showing himself a master of political intrigue and strengthening the position of the party against the SS and the Wehrmacht. Bormann's personal insignificance belied both his skill at infighting and the fanaticism of his views. Everyone—Hermann Goering, Josef Goebbels, Albert Speer, even Heinrich Himmler—had to go through him to see Hitler, and he came effectively to control security matters, acts of legislation, and appointments and promotions. Bormann was largely responsible for the resumption of the fight against the Christian churches, which Hitler had wanted to postpone for the duration of the war, and was a consistent advocate of the most extreme measures against Jews, the conquered peoples of the east, and prisoners of war. It was Bormann who signed the decrees effectively authorizing the extermination of the Jews and enslavement of the Slavs.

Bormann displayed a remarkable ability to exploit Hitler's peculiarities for his own gain, organizing party affairs and allowing the Führer to indulge his pretensions to be a great war leader and his more improbable fantasies. He built a wall sealing Hitler off from reality, preventing him from considering sensible proposals from other party members, and reducing all important matters to simple administrative formulae for the Führer's approval. As a reward he enjoyed Hitler's complete trust. As the Reich crumbled in late 1944 and early 1945, Bormann was virtually the secret ruler of Germany but continued his personal intrigues with seemingly as little sense of reality as Hitler.

As a result of Bormann's machinations Goering was dismissed and Himmler's influence greatly reduced. It was Bormann who signed Hitler's political testament, acted as witness to his marriage to Eva Braun, and watched him commit suicide in the Chancellery bunker. Bormann left the bunker on 30 April 1945, and his subsequent fate remains obscure. Various witnesses claimed to have seen his body, but in different places. He was reported as being in a monastery in northern Italy in 1946, the year that his wife died of cancer. He was subsequently rumored to have settled in South America, being allegedly spotted in Argentina, Brazil, and Chile. But he remained as elusive after his (probable) death as he had been during his rise to power. Bormann was sentenced to death in absentia at the Nuremberg trials and formally pronounced dead by a West German court in April 1973.

Related entries: Bureaucracy; Holocaust; National Socialist German Workers' Party

Suggestions for further reading:
Von Lang, Jochen. 1979. *The Secretary Martin Bormann: The Man Who Manipulated Hitler.* New York: Random House.

Bouhler, Philipp (1899–1945)

Subservient, discreet, and hard-working but inwardly ambitious, Bouhler was a Nazi "old fighter" who became the head of chancery in Hitler's personal office but remains one of the most shadowy figures in the Nazi elite. He worked on the *Völkischer*

Beobachter in the early days of the movement, became business manager of the Nazi Party after its rebirth in 1925, and rose rapidly through the ranks. In 1933 he was given the Party rank of *Reichsleiter* and in 1934 succeeded Heinrich Himmler as police president of Munich while simultaneously assuming his role in Hitler's office. Among Bouhler's duties was to chair the censorship committee, which issued lists of approved and condemned books, and in September 1939 Hitler gave him joint responsibility with Karl Brandt in supervising the T4 euthanasia program. Bouhler and his wife committed suicide in 1945 as U.S. troops came to arrest him.

Related entries: Euthanasia; National Socialist German Workers' Party; Reich Chancellery

Brack, Victor (1904–1948)

As head of the T4 office in the Reich Chancellery, and the son of a medical practitioner but having no medical training himself, Brack was principally responsible for the "Euthanasia Action" between December 1939 and August 1941. A friend of Heinrich Himmler and an SS colonel, Brack was appointed to the Department of Health by Philipp Bouhler in 1936 and subsequently became Bouhler's deputy in Hitler's chancery. Brack personally interviewed and selected personnel for the euthanasia program and in 1941 prepared mobile gassing vans to exterminate Jews deemed "unsuitable for work" in Riga and Minsk. He was closely involved in the construction of the extermination camps and sent some of his personnel from the euthanasia program to install gas chambers. Sentenced to death by a U.S. military tribunal in August 1947, Brack was hanged in Landsberg prison on 2 June 1948.

Related entries: Euthanasia; Extermination Camps

Brandt, Karl Rudolf
(1904–1948)

As one of the doctors attached to Hitler's retinue, Karl Brandt was one of the contestants for the role of medical supremo of the Reich, a struggle that had no ultimate winner. An emergency room surgeon by training, Brandt was introduced to Hitler in 1933 and soon gained his confidence. He was made an SS general and a Reich commissioner for health. His position close to Hitler steered Brandt into responsibility for the beginnings of the euthanasia program in September 1939. Along with Philipp Bouhler, he authorized the first killings of handicapped children.

Brandt tried to oppose Theo Morell's influence on Hitler and reduce the Führer's dependence on Morell's drugs and quackery, urging a regime of rest and exercise instead. In 1945, however, Hitler discovered that Brandt was arranging for his family to find safety with the Americans and declared him sentenced to death. He managed to avoid this death sentence but not a second one. Brandt was tried by a U.S. court for having approved the medical "experiments" carried out by SS doctors in concentration camps and was hanged in 1948.

Related entries: Euthanasia; Morell, Theo

Brauchitsch, Walther von
(1881–1948)

As commander in chief of the German army from 1938 to 1941, Walter von Brauchitsch, descendant of an old Prussian military family and a soldier since 1900, made a significant contribution to Hitler's greatest victories. But he is chiefly remembered by historians for his subservience to Hitler and his vacillating attitude toward attempts by other generals to restrain the Führer's megalomaniacal schemes. One goes so far as to call him "an anatomical marvel, a man totally without backbone" (Bell 1997, p. 218), a slightly unfair judgment if he is compared with sycophants like Wilhelm Keitel and Alfred Jodl.

A holder of the Iron Cross (First Class) from World War I, Brauchitsch's career thereafter followed a steady upward path. His elevation to general came when he succeeded the disgraced Werner von Fritsch as commander in chief of the Wehrmacht in February 1938. Brauchitsch, appointed without any prior consultation and not previously known as a Nazi sympathizer, was under a personal obligation to Hitler. He had been separated from his wife for five years, and Hitler now persuaded him to agree to a divorce and paid the financial settlement, well beyond Brauchitsch's means, from Hitler's personal funds. Brauchitsch was now free to marry his second wife, née Charlotte Schmidt, a fanatical Nazi who never ceased to remind him of how much they owed the Führer.

From then on, Brauchitsch swallowed his doubts about Hitler's plans and policies. He refused to back fellow officers in their attempts to curb Hitler's aggression, and when he did express his concerns, he would wilt under the force of Hitler's withering tirades against weak and vacillating generals. The series of startling successes between 1939 and 1941 only served to strengthen Brauchitsch's compliance. Any personal reservations notwithstanding, he loyally supported the Führer in all his actions and was promoted to field marshal on 17 July 1940. Brauchitsch, along with Franz Halder, also had doubts about Hitler's strategy in Operation Barbarossa, urging that priority should be given to attacking Moscow, but was again incapable of standing up to the Führer. As the German campaign in Russia suffered its first setbacks, Brauchitsch lost what little influence he retained and, afflicted by heart disease, was retired on 19 December 1941.

After his dismissal Brauchitsch never met Hitler again. But his subservience survived intact. He was kept informed about the conspiracies against Hitler, but after the failure of the July Plot of 1944 he not only condemned it in the pages of the *Völkischer Beobachter* but personally denounced several of his former comrades. At the end of the war he was arrested by the Allies and imprisoned for a while at Bridgend in South Wales. He was scheduled to be tried by a British military court in 1949, but delays occurred and he died of heart failure in a British military hospital in Hamburg on 18 October 1948. Fatally beholden to Hitler, politically ineffective and lacking in purpose, Brauchitsch's military record may have been excellent, but as commander in chief he showed himself to lack initiative and in personal conduct to have a "tortured but less than heroic character" (Bond 1995, p. 95).

Related entries: Barbarossa, Operation; Blomberg-Fritsch Crisis; July Plot; Officer Corps; Wehrmacht

Suggestions for further reading:
Bell, P. H. M. 1997. *The Origins of the Second World War in Europe.* 2nd ed. London and New York: Longman.
Bond, Brian. 1995. "Brauchitsch," in Correlli Barnett, ed. *Hitler's Generals.* London: Phoenix.

Braun, Eva (1912–1945)

Hitler's mistress from 1932 and his wife on the last day of her life, Eva Braun was twenty-three years younger than the Führer. A Bavarian girl from a middle-class background, she was working as an assistant in the studio of Heinrich Hoffmann when she first met Hitler in 1929. Blonde, slim, and athletic, Eva became Hitler's mistress after the death of Geli Raubal despite opposition from her father, a Catholic schoolteacher. It would appear that her infatuation with Hitler was not reciprocated.

According to Josef Goebbels, Hitler was more fond of his dog Blondi. Heinrich Hoffmann wrote that for Hitler, Braun was "just an attractive little thing, in whom . . . he found the type of relaxation and repose he sought. . . . But never, in voice, look or gesture, did he behave in a way that suggested any deeper interest in her" (Kershaw 1998, p. 352).

Eva lived in Hitler's apartment until, after an abortive suicide attempt in 1935, Hitler bought her a villa in a Munich suburb. In 1936 she moved to the Berghof in Berchtesgarden, where she acted as hostess but was never allowed to appear with Hitler in public. She led a completely isolated life, keeping her distance from Hitler's male associates. Totally loyal to Hitler, she never sought to exploit her position and spent most of her time exercising, reading, watching films, taking care of her appearance, and probably brooding.

In April 1945, as the Russians closed in on Berlin, Eva Braun joined Hitler in his bunker. They were finally married on 29 April. The next day she committed suicide by swallowing poison, just two minutes before Hitler killed himself. On Hitler's orders, both bodies were burned with gasoline in the Reich Chancellery garden, where Eva's charred corpse was later discovered by the Russians.

Suggestions for further reading:
Kershaw, Ian. 1998. *Hitler 1889–1936: Hubris.* New York: Allen Lane The Penguin Press.

Braunau-am-Inn

Hitler was born on 20 April 1889 in the small town of Braunau on the German-Austrian border, where his father Alois was a customs official. The family moved to Passau, Bavaria, in 1892, following Alois's promotion to the position of higher collector of customs, the first of many such moves in Adolf's childhood. Not

An informal photo of Eva Braun with Hitler found among her personal effects. Eva's presence and position in the Führer's entourage was an open secret, but she never appeared with him in public. (Popperfoto/Archive Photos)

surprisingly, therefore, he retained few, if any, memories of his birthplace and eventually came to look upon Linz as his "hometown." This did not prevent Braunau, which had some 5,000 inhabitants in 1934, from assuming a modest role in Nazi mythology. Braunau's position on the border of the two Germanic countries "destined" to unite was portrayed as providential. "For this little town," Hitler wrote in *Mein Kampf,* "lies on the boundary between the two German states which we of the younger generation at least have made it our life work to reunite by every means at our disposal" (Hitler 1992, p.3). In April 1938 Baldur von Schirach declared it a place of pilgrimage for German youth. The Führer's birthplace, the Gasthaus zum Pommer, now houses an organization for the physically handicapped and bears the memorial plaque "Never Again Fascism."

Related entries: Linz

Suggestions for further reading:
Hitler, Adolf. 1992. *Mein Kampf.* Trans. Ralph Manheim. Intro. by D. C. Watt. London: Pimlico.
Smith, Bradley F. 1967. *Adolf Hitler: His Family, Childhood and Youth.* Stanford: Hoover Institution on War, Revolution, and Peace.

Britain, Battle of

*I*n the summer of 1940, with his victorious armies on the Channel coast, Hitler ordered a new kind of conflict against Britain. British capacity to resist was to be broken by air power alone. The battle began in July 1940 with Luftwaffe attacks on Channel ports and shipping. The Royal Air Force (RAF) would not be drawn into a decisive engagement, so Hitler ordered that attacks should be concentrated on RAF airfields and aircraft. "The Führer," Hermann Goering said on 1 August, "has ordered me to crush Britain

with my Luftwaffe. By means of hard blows I plan to have this enemy, who has already suffered a crushing moral defeat, down on his knees in the nearest future, so that an occupation of the island by our troops can proceed without any risk!" (Keegan 1989, p. 91).

The RAF survived the onslaught but at great cost in lives and aircraft. Many airfields were repeatedly put out of action, while weary pilots had to fight against fatigue as well as well as the Germans. Encouraged by Goering's bombastic declarations that the RAF Fighter Command was on the brink of collapse, in late August Hitler rescinded an order forbidding attacks on civilian targets. Day and night air attacks on London began on 7 September, but this diversion of resources and relaxation of pressure on airfields and production centers allowed Fighter Command to recover its vigor. Heavy losses were inflicted on the Luftwaffe in a mass daylight raid on 15 September, and on 17 September Hitler postponed Operation Sealion, the invasion of England, indefinitely.

From this point the principal German onslaught took the form of night attacks on British cities, designed to break civilian morale. Up to 400 bombers raided London virtually every night between mid-September and mid-November. By the end of October, when daylight fighting had almost ceased, the Luftwaffe had lost about 1,800 aircraft and more than 2,500 aircrew, whereas Fighter Command had lost 1,100 aircraft and about 550 pilots. The "Blitz" of London, Coventry, Liverpool, Birmingham, and other British cities continued until May 1941. But despite killing 40,000 people and destroying 2 million homes, it failed to seriously disrupt British industrial production, port operations, or internal communications. The Allied bombing campaigns over Germany were to prove both more damaging and more effective. The raids on Britain eventually died down as

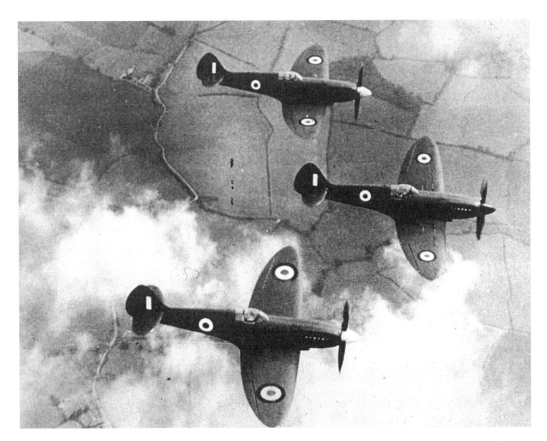

British Spitfire fighters patrol the skies during the Battle of Britain in the summer of 1940. When the battle ended in mid-September the Royal Air Force's resources were almost depleted, but Hitler's invasion of Britain was postponed indefinitely. "Never in the field of human conflict," Churchill told the House of Commons, "has so much been owed by so many to so few." (Archive Photos)

Hitler transferred his bombers east for the invasion of Russia.

Related entries: Bombing Campaigns; Great Britain; Luftwaffe; Sealion, Operation

Suggestions for further reading:
Keegan, John. 1989. *The Second World War.* London: Hutchinson.

British Empire

Hitler expressed a grudging admiration for the British Empire and often referred to the control of the Indian subcontinent by a small number of "Eng- lishmen" as the model for his own vast schemes for the conquest and subjugation of lands and peoples. But "England" (as Hitler always called it) would only hold the empire so long as it retained its pure Aryan racial composition. Hitler's own plans for colonial expansion in Africa and Asia, so far as he had any, were confined to the distant future, after Germany had secured domination of Europe. It was not in Germany's interest for the British Empire to be dismantled "prematurely" because the gainers would be Russia, Japan, and especially the United States.

Hitler's racial ideology prevented him from seriously making common cause with nationalist opponents of British imperialism. He was prepared to collaborate with Subhas Chandra Bose and other nationalist leaders for propaganda purposes. But as he had written in *Mein Kampf:* "As a folkish man, who appraises the value of men on a racial basis, I am prevented by mere knowledge of the racial inferiority of these so-called 'oppressed nations' from linking the destiny of my own people with theirs" (Hitler 1992, p. 602). He continued very long in the illusion that Britain would unite with Germany to prevent the United States from stepping into British shoes as the dominant world imperial power. Hitler's war did indeed play an important role in the end of the British Empire, but not in the way he expected.

Related entries: Foreign Policy; Great Britain

Suggestions for further reading:
Hillgruber, Andreas. 1974, "England's Place in Hitler's Plans for World Dominion," *Journal of Contemporary History* 9, pp. 5–22.
Hitler, Adolf. 1992. *Mein Kampf.* Trans. Ralph Manheim. Intro. by D. C. Watt. London: Pimlico.

Brüning, Heinrich (1885–1970)

A member of the Catholic Center Party, Brüning was made chancellor of Germany in 1930 in the hope that he would help to provide stable, moderate government. He was known for the preparation of financial legislation, but his careful approach did not help in the growing economic crisis. Unable to obtain majority parliamentary support for his financial measures, Brüning prevailed upon President Paul von Hindenburg to allow him to use Article 48 of the Weimar Constitution, enabling him to dispense with majority approval. When the Reichstag reacted strongly, Brüning dismissed parliament in July 1930. He hoped that new elections would strengthen his position, but they only resulted in gains for the Nazis and the Communists. Henceforth until his dismissal on 30 May 1932, Brüning ruled by presidential decree.

His reluctance to explain the logic and aims of his policies, his attempt to be assertive in foreign policy, and the constant intrigues on the Right for a nationalist government that included the Nazis all weakened Brüning's position. In the two years of Brüning's chancellorship, Germany's economic and political crisis did nothing but deepen. His preferred solution of a restoration of the monarchy under one of the sons of the crown prince was rejected by everyone, including Hindenburg and other monarchists. In his memoirs Brüning claimed to have always known exactly what he was doing, but he may also be viewed as a victim of circumstances. Historians' judgments have generally been harsh. One says of Brüning: "His espousal of the art of sabre-rattling on the international scene and the development of authoritarian government during his term of emergency rule made him a key figure in the transition from Stresemann to Hitler, irrespective of his claim that he was trying to defend democracy" (Hiden 1977, p. 36).

In March 1933, as Hitler prepared to pass the Enabling Act, Brüning met with Hitler's Nationalist allies, with a view to inserting a clause into the act guaranteeing civil and political liberties. But both the Nationalists and Brüning's own Center Party had both been bought off by Hitler. In the end he joined with his party in passing the act. As chancellor he had tried to ban both the SS and the Sturmabteilung, and he now realized the danger he was in from an untrammeled Hitler. He escaped to the United States shortly before the Night of the Long Knives, when he would undoubtedly have been killed. Brüning ended his life as a professor at Harvard University and died in Vermont in 1970.

Related entries: Center Party; Enabling Act; Hindenburg, Paul von; Weimar Republic

Suggestions for further reading:
Abraham, David. 1986. *The Collapse of the Weimar Republic: Political Economy and Crisis.* 2nd ed. New York: Holmes and Meier.
Bookbinder, Paul. 1996. *Weimar Germany: The Republic of the Reasonable.* Manchester and New York: Manchester University Press.
Hiden, John. 1977. *Germany and Europe 1919–1939.* New York: Longman.

Buchenwald

Situated in woods outside Weimar, Buchenwald was one of the original concentration camps of the Third Reich. It supplied prisoners as labor for local armaments plants and, when liberated by American forces in April 1945, was found to contain 20,000 starving and exhausted men and boys. The records showed more than 200 deaths per day, some 6,000 a month from starvation, torture, and illness. However, prisoners with experience of several camps declared that it contained more long-term survivors than most.

Related entries: Concentration Camps

Bulgaria

Tsar Boris III of Bulgaria established a "royal dictatorship" in his southeastern European kingdom with the support of the military in 1934–1935 and aligned himself with Germany and Italy. Bulgaria joined the Tripartite Pact in March 1941, securing Hitler's help for its territorial claims against Romania. As a reward for allowing German troops to be deployed in Bulgaria during Hitler's invasion of Yugoslavia and Greece, Boris secured territory lost in 1918, plus Yugoslav Macedonia and the Greek portion of Thrace. He entered the war on Germany's side at the end of 1941, but he refused to participate in Hitler's invasion of the Soviet Union, and the deportation of Bulgarian Jews was opposed by the Bulgarian parliament. Bulgaria was occupied by the Red Army in the fall of 1944. The Communists swiftly secured power and entered the war against Germany on 28 October. Bulgaria remained a Communist country throughout the Cold War era.

Related entries: Foreign Policy; Romania; Tripartite Pact; Yugoslavia

Bulge, Battle of the

The counteroffensive launched in December 1944 through the hilly and wooded region of the Ardennes in northern France and into Belgium was Hitler's last desperate effort to regain the initiative on the Western Front and stave off impending defeat. But the sustained resistance of Allied forces allowed time for General Dwight D. Eisenhower to reorganize his land forces and deploy air forces temporarily grounded by bad weather. By the end of December the offensive was halted well short of its main objective of Antwerp. It took the Allies several weeks to recapture the lost terrain, but the Germans had suffered 100,000 casualties and lost quantities of aircraft and equipment, neither of which they were able to replace.

Bureaucracy

After unification, Germany had developed into a bureaucratic state where about 10 percent of the workforce were civil servants in national, state, or local government. It was a burdensome legacy for the Weimar Republic, which never succeeded in securing the support of its costly and inflexible bureaucratic inheritance. The economic recession reduced the salaries and privileged position of officials, creating discontent that the Nazis exploited to gain support in all levels of the administration. Under Hitler, however, the nature of the bureaucracy changed. While the destruction of democracy and the federal system vastly enlarged the administration, the haphazard growth of new bureaucratic organizations such as the SS, the German Labor Front and the Nazi Party's many associations served to displace or marginalize the traditional bureaucracy. Hitler's regime was highly bureaucratic, but in a different way from earlier systems. The state administration was subordinated to the Nazi Party and its leaders. The function of the bureaucracy was to put the suggestions of the Nazi bigwigs into an appropriate and practical order. In Hitler's "polycracy," bureaucrats were subordinate to the party, a meager reward for the support many of them had given to the Führer.

Related entries: Civil Service

Busch, Ernst (1885–1945)

A professional soldier who never questioned any of Hitler's orders, Busch was representative of those German commanders who hid their disillusion with Hitler's conduct of the war but could not resist his fascination. After participating in the Polish campaign as commander of the 8th Army Corps, Busch was awarded the Knight's Cross in 1940 for his actions in the campaign in France and the Low Countries. He commanded the 16th Army during the invasion of the Soviet Union and was promoted to general field marshal in February 1943. However, Busch was made the scapegoat for the German collapse when the Russians began their offensive in June 1944. He then commanded German forces in Schleswig and Denmark until the end of the war, still showing no signs of disenchantment with the Führer. Busch died in British captivity on 17 July 1945.

Related entries: Barbarossa, Operation; Eastern Front; Officer Corps

C

Casablanca Conference

The meeting between Franklin Delano Roosevelt and Winston Churchill held outside Casablanca, Morocco, in January 1943, which Joseph Stalin foolishly refused to attend, saw heated arguments between the British and Americans over the opening of a second front in Europe. Eventually the invasion of Sicily was resolved, as was an intensification of the bombing campaign over Germany, while the conference also spent much time trying to bring together General Charles de Gaulle and General Henri Giraud as leaders of the Free French in a cosmetic unity. But the most important decision was Roosevelt's casual call for the "unconditional surrender" of Germany. The full horror of Hitler's crimes was becoming apparent to the Allied leaders, and it was evident to Roosevelt in particular that his regime would have to be destroyed utterly and a new Germany rebuilt on fresh foundations.

Related entries: Bombing Campaigns; Churchill, Winston Leonard Spencer; de Gaulle, Charles; Roosevelt, Franklin Delano

Suggestions for further reading:
Kimball, Warren. 1997. *Forged in War: Churchill, Roosevelt and the Second World War.* London: HarperCollins.

Catholic Church

Hitler was born in Catholic Austria and first came to political prominence in Catholic Bavaria. He always retained a respect for and even fear of the power of the Catholic Church as the only body in Germany, with its numerous religious and social organizations and its international dimension, that could retain a hold on the hearts and minds of its adherents apart from and potentially in opposition to National Socialism. He therefore trod carefully in his relations with the Catholic Church, despite the anti-Christian dimensions of Nazi ideology. Any rapprochement between the National Socialist German Workers' Party (NSDAP, Nazi Party) and the church before 1933 was hampered principally by the church's affiliation with the Center Party and, to a lesser extent, by Nazi anti-Semitism and its supposed "socialism" and by the bishops' allegiance to Rome. The church by its very nature was guilty of the sin of "internationalism."

However, the Lateran Treaties of 1929 between the papacy and Benito Mussolini had signaled the church's willingness to enter into agreements with authoritarian but anticommunist regimes. The speedy conclusion of the Concordat of 20 July 1933 showed not only Hitler's desire for accommodation with the church but also the papacy's acquiescence in the liquidation of Catholic political and trade union organizations. But the attitudes of Catholic bishops and ordinary Catholics were more ambiguous. On some issues, such as the display of crucifixes in church schools, allowed to remain open under the Concordat, the Nazis were forced to compromise or give way.

Hitler himself remained aloof from quarrels between Nazis and Catholics, retaining an image of statesmanlike impartiality and moderation. He was rewarded with effusions of fidelity from the majority of the Catholic hierarchy. Cardinal Michael Faulhaber of Munich, for example, was unstinting in his praise of Hitler's "simplicity" and his "modest" life, untainted by the demons of alcohol and nicotine, while at the same time issuing barely veiled attacks on the regime's anti-Semitism. The church was concerned above all to maintain its structures and as far as possible its influence within Germany, but it had to endure close monitoring of sermons, the press, and educational establishments and the suppression of some organizations, such as its sporting association, the German Youth Force. The 1936 papal encyclical "Mit Brennender Sorge" provided a boost to Catholic opponents of Nazi anti-Semitism and attacks on Christianity, but most clergy and laity accepted or approved of Hitler's policies, including the Nuremberg Laws and the cult surrounding Hitler.

The illusion that arrangements could be reached with Nazism should have been exposed by the anti-Christian propaganda, the indoctrination of the Hitler Youth, and the closure of several seminaries. But the failure of fanatical Nazis to replace Christianity altogether with a revived paganism and new festivals showed that the church could survive and still retained its hold on the Catholic faithful. Catholics should have taken note of the fate of the church in Austria after the Anschluss, where the bishops has welcomed Hitler's annexation of their country but the Concordat was not applied.

The outbreak of war exposed these contradictions. Hitler risked open conflict with the church over euthanasia and gave a free hand to petty harassment of the clergy. But the church supported the war effort willingly, even after the Catholics of Poland began to suffer persecution. The church reached the nadir of its acceptance of Hitler in its silence about the Final Solution. Individual clergymen and lay Catholics showed great courage in sheltering and helping Jews, but the official church was concerned as always with self-preservation. This was no straightforward matter: hospital chaplaincies were banned in 1940, as was the distribution of religious literature to soldiers; and candidates for religious orders were restricted, Jesuits discharged from the Wehrmacht, church personnel conscripted for military service, and monasteries and convents expropriated for wartime purposes. The collapse of the Third Reich, however, spared the church from any "final struggle" with National Socialism. Its policy of self-preservation, though often morally reprehensible, was ultimately successful. After 1945 it renewed its position in German life, especially in Bavaria, if anything emerging stronger than it had been before Hitler.

Related entries: Bavaria; Center Party; Concordat; Education; Euthanasia; Middle Classes; Pius XII, Pope; Poland; Trade Unions

Suggestions for further reading:

Conway, John S. 1968. *The Nazi Persecution of the Churches, 1933–1945*. New York: Basic Books.

Helmreich, Ernst Christian. 1979. *The German Churches under Hitler: Background, Struggle and Epilogue*. Detroit: Wayne State University Press.

Lewy, Günter. 1964. *The Catholic Church and Nazi Germany*. New York: McGraw-Hill.

Center Party

The "German Center Party," as it was officially known, was the principal

Catholic political party and the most important governmental party under the Weimar Republic. It formed a necessary component of the "Weimar Coalition" that brought relative stability to the Republic between 1924 and 1929. With a firm foundation in Catholicism, the Center Party enjoyed a stable constituency and in the last years of the Republic lost fewer votes to the Nazis than did the other "bourgeois" parties. However, its leaders were as guilty as other politicians of misjudging and underestimating Hitler. The party chairman, Bishop Ludwig Kaas, had talks with the National Socialist German Workers' Party about participating in a Hitler government as late as autumn 1932, and although the Center Party presented itself as the last bulwark of freedom against Nazism and communism, it lost votes and continued to believe that Hitler could be bought off. When Hitler became chancellor, the Center Party, after much debate, voted to support the Enabling Act of 23 March 1933 and on 5 July dissolved itself under pressure from Hitler.

Related entries: Brüning, Heinrich; Catholic Church; Enabling Act; *Gleichschaltung;* Weimar Republic

Suggestions for further reading:
Bookbinder, Paul. 1996. *Weimar Germany: The Republic of the Reasonable.* Manchester and New York: Manchester University Press.

Chamberlain, Neville (1869–1940)

The name of the British prime minister from 1937 to 1940 is indelibly associated with the policy of appeasement of Hitler. The scion of a distinguished political dynasty, Chamberlain had a long career in local and national politics behind him in 1937, but his lack of knowledge of foreign affairs led him often to ignore the advice of his officials. Whatever defense may be mounted of appeasement, Chamberlain appears to have sincerely believed that Hitler's aggressive appetites could be assuaged by concessions, most notably over the Anschluss and in the Munich Agreement over the Sudetenland and Czechoslovakia in 1938. There is no doubt that Chamberlain's commitment to peace enjoyed overwhelming popular support in both Britain and France.

Following Hitler's occupation of the whole of Czechoslovakia in March 1939, Chamberlain abandoned the policy of appeasement and offered a British guarantee to Poland. The result was Britain's declaration of war against Germany in September 1939. Chamberlain, in failing health and now associated with the failures of the past, lost parliamentary and public confidence in his leadership during the winter of 1940. He resigned as prime minister on 10 May 1940, his Conservative government being replaced by a coalition led by Winston Churchill. Chamberlain continued as a member of the War Cabinet and leader of the Conservative Party until shortly before his death in November 1940.

Related entries: Anschluss; Appeasement; Churchill, Winston Leonard Spencer; Czechoslovakia; Daladier, Edouard; Eden, Anthony; Foreign Policy; Great Britain; Munich Agreement; Poland; Sudetenland

Suggestions for further reading:
McDonough, Frank. 1998. *Neville Chamberlain, Appeasement and Britain's Road to War.* Manchester and New York: Manchester University Press.

Charismatic Domination

Max Weber's concept of "charismatic leadership" has been applied to Hitler by historians and political scientists. The charismatic leader, according to Weber, presents himself as endowed with exceptional personal powers and a heroic or exemplary character. His followers give him personal loyalty and are provided proof of the leader's "calling" by exceptional deeds and notable achievements. The possessor of "charisma" seizes the task for which he is destined and demands that others obey and follow him by virtue of his "mission." Charismatic rule is inherently unstable, an emergency type of rule that is undermined by failure. Weber saw charismatic leadership mainly in "primitive" societies among warlords, chieftains, prophets, and magicians with a following of immediate disciples and agents.

The idea has been used mainly in relation to Hitler and his immediate followers but could be extended to his relationship with the German people in an age of mass communication. There is no doubt that Hitler was presented in Nazi propaganda as a charismatic leader of the type theorized by Weber. His power was wielded and justified in charismatic terms, not as chancellor and head of state but as the Führer of the German *Volk*. Hitler did not merely lead a state but the German nation defined in racial terms. Nor was he a party leader: he was the leader for whom the people had been waiting. The "Hitler Myth," by placing him above the day-to-day realities of life, distanced him from the worst excesses of the regime, making it possible for him to retain his status as a charismatic leader. The charisma only began to wear thin after the defeat of the German army at Stalingrad. As Weber noted, "charismatic domination" could not long outlive such lack of success.

Related entries: Fascism; Führer Principle; Hitler Myth; Nazi Movement; Nuremberg Rallies; Propaganda; Public Opinion

Suggestions for further reading:
Kater, Michael H. 1981. "Hitler in a Social Context," *Central European History* 14, pp. 243–272.
Kershaw, Ian. 1989. *The "Hitler Myth": Image and Reality in the Third Reich.* Paperback ed. New York: Oxford University Press.
Nyomarkay, Joseph. 1967. *Charisma and Factionalism within the Nazi Party.* Minneapolis: University of Minnesota Press.
Weber, Max. 1978. *Economy and Society.* Ed. Guenther Roth and Claus Wittich. Berkeley: University of California Press.
Welch, David. 1993. *The Third Reich: Politics and Propaganda.* London and New York: Routledge.

Churchill, Winston Leonard Spencer (1874–1965)

From the moment he replaced Neville Chamberlain as prime minister of Great Britain in May 1940, Churchill became the living symbol of the struggle of the British and the civilized world against Hitler and what he stood for. His speech to the House of Commons promising nothing but "blood, tears, toil, and sweat" contrasted with Hitler's triumphalism and assurances to the German people that they would remain largely untouched by the war. Cannily appealing to pro-British feeling in the United States, he universalized the fight against Hitler as a struggle for right and justice. He could never accept, however, that it would mark an important stage in the decline of Britain as an imperial and world power.

Churchill already had a long and checkered political career behind him in 1940. His unruly aristocratic spirit had hampered his appointments as first lord of the admiralty during World War I and as chancellor of the exchequer in 1924–1929. During the 1930s Churchill was in the political wilderness, regarded with suspicion by many in the Conservative Party, with which he was at loggerheads over policy toward India, rearmament, and appeasement. But he also took the lead in warning of the threat of Nazism, that Hitler was not a politician with whom one could deal like any other, and that banking on him being overthrown and replaced by someone more reasonable

A formal portrait of Winston Churchill. His portly "British bulldog" demeanor, combined with his loathing of Nazism and concern for efficiency, made him an emblematic figure, symbolizing British determination not to succumb to Hitler. (Express Newspapers/F756/Archive Photos)

make him appear both murderous and ridiculous could not easily survive the turn of the tide of war. Churchill enjoyed a close, though by no means untroubled relationship with President Franklin Delano Roosevelt and attended all the major Allied conferences of the war, including Yalta. On 8 May 1945 Churchill announced the unconditional surrender of Germany.

Defeated in the general election of July 1945, Churchill spent six years as leader of the opposition. In a famous speech at Fulton, Missouri, in 1946 he referred to an "Iron Curtain" across Europe. The two victors of the war against Hitler were the United States and the Soviet Union, and Churchill had to watch over the beginning of the end of the British Empire he had fought to preserve. He again served as prime minister from October 1951 to April 1955 but was ill, with his powers permanently in decline. But Churchill retained the affections of the British people and others throughout the world, who remembered him as an inspirational war leader. His funeral in 1965 was a great national and international ceremony, in suitable contrast to Hitler's miserable end.

Related entries: Appeasement; Atlantic Charter; Bombing Campaigns; British Empire; Casablanca Conference; Chamberlain, Neville; Eden, Anthony; Great Britain; Roosevelt, Franklin Delano; Teheran Conference; Yalta Conference

Suggestions for further reading:
Churchill, Winston S. 1948–1954. *The Second World War.* 6 vols. Boston: Houghton Mifflin.
Gilbert, Martin. 1991. *Churchill: A Life.* London: Heinemann.
Rose, Norman. 1995. *Churchill: The Unruly Giant.* New York: Free Press.

was an illusion. Although, like many other conservatives in several countries, he initially expressed some admiration for Hitler's "patriotic" achievement, Churchill was also quick to characterize the Führer as a "gangster" who fed off "currents of hatred so intense as to sear the souls of those who swim upon them" (Rose 1995, p. 220). He never lost his contempt for "corporal Hitler," though ironically it was Hitler's actions that made him appear to be a prophet.

His inspirational speeches, charismatic presence, and eccentricities, such as the V-sign, adopted as a universal sign not only of victory but as "Up Yours" to Hitler, galvanized the British people and sympathizers worldwide. One German general remarked that he was worth thirty mechanized divisions, and all Josef Goebbels's efforts to

Ciano, Galeazzo, Count (1903–1944)

*I*talian foreign minister from 1936 to 1943, Ciano had a reputation as a playboy and a lightweight. Hitler called him "that disgusting boy" (Mack Smith 1976, p. 141), and what most worried the Germans about him was his lack of discretion. Ciano's inability to keep secrets was one reason why Hitler rarely took Mussolini into his confidence. An early convert to fascism, Ciano gave his career a major fillip in 1930 when he married Mussolini's daughter, Edda. On appointment to the Foreign Ministry he advocated alliance with Germany and cemented the Berlin-Rome Axis in Berlin in October 1936. But he came to realize sooner than his father-in-law that the recognition of Italian power in Europe rested on shaky foundations.

After Hitler invaded Poland without consulting Mussolini (in breach of the Axis agreement) Ciano attempted to extricate Italy from Hitler's fatal embrace but was overtaken by events and Mussolini's ambitions. For all Hitler's successes, the halting of the offensive in Russia and the U.S. declaration of war convinced Ciano of the need to negotiate a separate peace with the Allies. But this only made Mussolini suspicious of his flamboyant son-in-law. Ciano resigned in February 1943 but remained a member of the Fascist Grand Council, thus taking part in the decision to depose Mussolini. Denounced by Marshal Pietro Badoglio's new government in Rome for corruption, Ciano was seized by supporters of Mussolini and shot on 11 January 1944.

Related entries: Axis; Foreign Policy; Italy; Mussolini, Benito; Pact of Steel

Suggestions for further reading:
Mack Smith, Denis. 1976. *Mussolini's Roman Empire.* New York: Longman.

Cinema

I n Hitler's typically crude ideas about art and propaganda, film would merely serve to put across the few simple Nazi ideas that the masses were capable of understanding. He was himself a film addict, viewing his favorites over and over again in his retreat at Berchtesgarden. However, despite the inevitable arguments and petty power struggles within the Nazi hierarchy, the principal responsibility for the Third Reich's movie production lay with Josef Goebbels, whose view of the functions of film were more subtle than Hitler's. "The film of present day Germany," he wrote, "must carry in it the ideology of contemporary Germany, only this ideology must never be allowed to become obtrusive bias. Bias which is detected always fails in its purposes" (Welch 1983a, p. 23). As the most modern means of influencing mass audiences, film production should be orientated toward films "that reflected the ambience of National Socialism rather than those that loudly proclaimed its ideology" (Welch 1983a, p. 46).

Under the Weimar Republic, German cinema had enjoyed a high international reputation but had become increasingly nationalist in orientation, especially after Alfred Hugenberg acquired a controlling interest in the dominant Ufa corporation. After 1933 the industry was "coordinated" while remaining in private hands and subjected to a slow process of creeping state control through a Film Credit Bank and a series of state holding companies. By 1939 these *staatsmittelbar* companies, organized under the umbrella of a reconstituted Ufa headed by Fritz Hippler, had come to dominate film production. The Reich Film Law established a system of precensorship (requiring prior approval of scripts) and prohibition and excluded Jews and left-wingers from the industry. Despite the voluntary or involuntary emigration of many of its most talented figures, the "film world" of Germany and later Austria as a whole submitted willingly to Nazi domination and was happy to profit from the booming production and attendance under the Third Reich.

Audience numbers grew steadily in peace and war. The average German who made four annual visits to the cinema in 1933 was making more than fourteen by 1944, while the Hitler Youth were subjected to regular "film evenings." On the whole, clean-cut entertainment was the order of the day, with direct propaganda being confined to the bombastic newsreels that formed part of every cinema program. But the apparently apolitical nature of most films was only skin deep. Films glorifying the party in the *Kampfzeit* ("time of struggle") were made in the immediate aftermath of the seizure of power. The cheap and rough *SA-Mann Brand* was followed by the more polished *Hans Westmar* (a fictionalized biography of Horst Wessel, pimp, petty criminal, and Nazi martyr) and *Hitlerjunger Quex,* but with the defeat of the Nazis' internal enemies, principally the Communists, such glorification of the past was seen as redundant. It was the new Germany that needed to be celebrated, most notably in Leni Riefenstahl's *Triumph of the Will* (1935) and *Olympiade* (1936), the first glorifying Hitler and the discipline and power of his followers, the second the health and vigor of the Aryan race.

Anti-Semitic films hit the screens in 1940 with the notorious *Jew Süss* and the documentary *Der Ewige Jude (The Eternal Jew),* the latter made by Fritz Hippler, the Reich film manager himself. The euthanasia campaign of 1941 was supported by *Ich Klage an* (I accuse) and the supposed sufferings of Germans in Russia and Poland dramatized by *Friesennot* (1935) and *Heimkehr* (1941). But entertainment films, the bulk of the production, were more popular and more insidious, especially during the war years. "It really seems to me," wrote Goebbels in his diary in 1942, "that we should be producing more films, but above all, lighter and more entertaining films which the people are continually requesting" (Welch 1983a, p. 142). Heroic historical dramas glorified a select band of great Germans of the past, including Bismarck, Frederick Schiller, and Frederick the Great, and operettas, revue films, comedies, war films, and adventure films kept audiences distracted from an ever grimmer reality while instilling the values of self-sacrifice, obedience, submission to destiny, and moral purity. A succession of anti-British and, after 1941, anti-Soviet films sought to arouse hatred for the Anglo-Saxon Jewish Bolshevik enemy. From 1939 on Germans could forget the war for a few hours in front of the cinema screen, but after the defeat at Stalingrad cinema doors were shut during the showing of the newsreel so that they could not see the feature film without enduring the newsreel as well. By 1944 many productions were being abandoned or postponed; yet the lavish *Kolberg,* an almost entirely fictitious account of Prussian resistance to Napoleon, prepared the people for death in the final combat.

Movie actors were among the best-paid artists in the Third Reich. The Nazis were not slow in promoting and exploiting the popularity of stars like Hans Albers, Werner Krauss, or Heinrich George, while the Swedish actress Kristina Söderbaum epitomized faithful, self-sacrificing, blonde German womanhood in, among other films, *Jew Süss* and *Kolberg.* Directors such as Karl Ritter, a specialist in war films, Wolfgang Liebeneiner (*Ich Klage an* and two films about Bismarck), and Veit Harlan (*Jew Süss* and *Kolberg*) willingly prostituted their talents for rewards and prestige, and they were far from being exceptional. Because of Goebbels's special interest in film, his Propaganda Ministry could count it as one of their successes. But the Nazis' relatively sophisticated exploitation of the most important mass medium of the age and their willingness to compromise with the audience's wishes owed everything to Goebbels and very little to Hitler.

Related entries: Cultural Policy; *Gleichschaltung;* Goebbels, Paul Josef; Hugenberg, Alfred; Propaganda; Riefenstahl, Leni

Suggestions for further reading:
Hoffmann, Hilmar. 1996. *The Triumph of Propaganda: Film and National Socialism, 1933–1945*. Providence and Oxford: Berghahn Books.
Phillips, Marcus S. 1971. "The Nazi Control of the German Film Industry," *Journal of European Studies* 1, pp. 37–68.
Welch, David. 1983a. *Propaganda and the German Cinema 1933–1945*. Oxford: Clarendon Press.

Citadel, Operation

After the defeat at Stalingrad and retreat from the Caucasus, Hitler's forces still occupied great swaths of territory in Russia, and the army planned a combined offensive by Army Groups South and Center against the Soviet positions around Kursk, midway between Moscow and the Crimea. In March 1943 Hitler approved Operation Citadel for execution in May. However, events in Italy forced postponement of the transfer of troops, and by the time Citadel was launched on 5 July the Russians had built up their own forces. The final plans were drawn up by Kurt von Zeitzler and the two commanders, Erich von Manstein and Günther von Kluge. Operation Citadel was to lead to the battle of Kursk and German retreat.

Related entries: Kursk, Battle of

Civil Service

Hitler attracted considerable support among civil servants during his rise to power, but under his rule the civil service was to be subordinated to the Nazi Party, and its members swore a personal oath to the Führer. The Civil Service Law of 7 April 1933 made it possible to remove or demote Jewish and politically unreliable civil servants. At first used only against Jews and Communists, it soon came to encompass Social Democrats and any other real or supposed opponents of the regime. In all, some 30,000 people lost their jobs. However, large numbers of civil servants rushed to join the party in 1933: a contemporary joke spoke of them replacing weather vanes on church steeples since they always knew which way the wind was blowing.

The idea of the nonpartisan civil servant, serving all governments impartially and with lifelong tenure, was abolished by the Nazis. All key posts were given to faithful National Socialists, whether of recent vintage or not, and party cells in workplaces ensured political instruction and control. In 1939 civil servants constituted some 28 percent of all Nazi Party members. Yet in Hitler's "polycracy," the civil service, despite its willing acceptance of Nazi rule, remained subsidiary to the numerous organizations in and around the party.

Related entries: Bureaucracy; *Gleichschaltung*

Suggestions for further reading:
Caplan, Jane. 1988. *Government without Administration: State and Civil Service in Weimar and Nazi Germany*. Oxford: Oxford University Press.

Communist Party (KPD)

The Communist Party of Germany (KPD) was the strongest in the world outside the Soviet Union until it was destroyed by Hitler in 1933. It had emerged from radical groups such as the Independent Social Democrats and the Spartakus League (Spartacists) that had split from the Social Democratic Party (SPD) in the later stages of World War I. When the SPD formed the first postwar government, local Marxist groups and soldiers' councils took direct action to take over various towns, and in January 1919 the Spartacists' bid for power in Berlin was brutally put down by the army and Freikorps, and the Spartacist leaders, Karl Liebknecht and Rosa Luxemburg, were murdered. Hitler witnessed and was disgusted by the proclamation of a "Soviet Republic" in Bavaria in April 1919, a short-lived government also destroyed by the Freikorps. The Communist Party itself was founded in 1920 under the inspiration of the newly formed Comintern. At this time the leaders of the Soviet Union were still hoping for an international revolution in which Germany would be the most important element.

The KPD grew rapidly, attracting support among younger workers. The idea of a "national bolshevism" was also appealing to restless intellectuals, including the young Josef Goebbels and Otto Strasser, but they were soon discouraged by the Communists' internationalism. Conservative forces in German society were terrified by the threat of "bolshevism," which partly explains support for Hitler's Beer Hall Putsch and the leniency toward Nazi thuggery shown by legal and political authorities. But while Nazis and Communists fought each other in the streets and beer halls, the KPD's misreading of the nature of Nazism and its subservience to the Comintern led Nazis and Communists to view the Social Democrats as the common enemy, with disastrous consequences.

The KPD, following the Moscow line, saw the Nazis as merely an extreme form of the bourgeois party, the last desperate throe of a doomed capitalism, lacking working-class support. The SPD were declared the real enemy. By the time the Comintern line changed in the mid-1930s, calling for popular fronts against fascism, it was too late for Germany. Local Nazi leaders, of whom Goebbels in Berlin was the most successful, fought the Communists on their own terrain with considerable success, exploiting social discontent and disillusion with the political system and organizing social welfare schemes through the Sturmabteilung. In the presidential election of 1932 the KPD leader, Ernst Thälmann, won 13.2

percent of the vote against Hitler's 30.1 percent. Both Thälmann and the party leader in the Reichstag, Ernst Togeler, along with many other Communists, ended up in concentration camps.

For all its errors and responsibility for the weakening of democracy, the KPD was clearer-eyed than most about the consequences of Hitler's arrival in government in 1933. A Communist proclamation of 30 January declared luridly but largely accurately: "Shameless wage robbery and boundless terror of the brown murderous plague smash the last pitiful rights of the working class. Unrestrained course toward imperialist war. All this lies directly ahead" (Kershaw 1998, p. 432). With its leaders either in concentration camps or in exile in the Soviet Union, the KPD managed for a while to maintain some organization in Germany, producing brochures and pamphlets on secret printing presses and smuggling underground literature into the country under innocent covers. Yet by 1935 the Gestapo was sufficiently organized to carry out mass arrests and trials of both Communists and Socialists.

Communist opposition to Hitler was completely stifled during the period of the Nazi-Soviet Pact. Thereafter, Communists remaining in Germany realized that they could do little to overthrow Hitler and placed their faith in Soviet victory on the battlefield. Only a few, notably the former Reichstag deputy Theodor Neubauer, managed to perpetuate some form of organization, based in Jena. The Rote Kapelle group carried out espionage activities, but their intelligence was not always believed by Joseph Stalin. Under the conditions of the Third Reich, however, mass organization was impossible. Those Communist leaders who were not handed back to Hitler by Stalin during the period of the Nazi-Soviet Pact or who did not disappear into the Gulag as victims of the Soviet leader's paranoid suspiciousness returned in 1945 to support Russian power in the Soviet occupation zone and eventually to establish the German Democratic Republic in eastern Germany.

Related entries: Bavaria; Elections; *Gleichschaltung;* Nazi Movement; Nazi-Soviet Pact; Opposition; Prussia; Public Opinion; Reichstag; Reichstag Fire; Social Democratic Party; Soviet Union; Stalin, Joseph; Trade Unions; Weimar Republic; Working Class

Suggestions for further reading:
Kershaw, Ian. 1998. *Hitler 1889–1936: Hubris.* New York: Allen Lane The Penguin Press.
Kershaw, Ian, and Moshe Lewin, eds. 1997. *Stalinism and Nazism: Dictatorships in Comparison.* Cambridge: Cambridge University Press.
Merson, Allan. 1985. *Communist Resistance in Nazi Germany.* London: Lawrence and Wishart.
Rosenhaft, Eve. 1983. *Beating the Fascists? The German Communists and Political Violence, 1929–1933.* Cambridge: Cambridge University Press.
Weitz, Eric D. 1997. *Creating German Communism, 1890–1990: From Popular Protest to Socialist State.* Princeton: Princeton University Press.

Concentration Camps

*T*he concentration camp system is synonymous with the Nazi regime. The term had first been used during the Boer War to describe camps set up by the British to "concentrate" Boer farming families, but under Hitler they became a network of prisons, reservoirs housing slave labor, and killing sites. In the early years of the Third Reich the camps grew largely as a consequence of the increasingly repressive use of criminal law, but they became the lynchpin of the SS slave empire, used by SS enterprises as penal colonies for political, racial, and social "undesirables."

Immediately on Hitler's coming to power, the Sturmabteilung, acting as auxiliary police, set up "wild camps," some of which were soon closed down, but others of which, including Dachau, became perma-

nent. Although some prisoners were released prior to the handing over of the camps to the SS in 1934, the permanent camps, modeled on Dachau, soon housed thousands of political detainees, freemasons, Jehovah's Witnesses, homosexuals, Jews and anyone deemed to be friendly with them, Gypsies, and any number of other dissenters as well as common criminals. The Concentration Camp Directorate, under Theodor Eicke, the first commandant of Dachau, trained SS men as guards and camp administrators to preside over the growing numbers sentenced to *Schutzhaft* (protective custody). Among the biggest and most notorious camps established in the 1930s were Sachsenhausen-Oranienburg (1936), Flossenbürg and Mauthausen (1938), and Theresienstadt and the women's camp of Ravensbruck (1939).

Before the war began, the number of detainees fluctuated widely. For example, in May 1938 Buchenwald held 3,000 prisoners, rising to 17,000 in December and falling to between 5,000 and 6,000 by mid-1939. At the outbreak of the war there were about 25,000 prisoners in camps, about the same number as in the summer of 1933. War and conquest were to change all that. Many more camps were established in the occupied territories, herding together millions of Jews, political prisoners, Soviet prisoners of war, and Slav slave laborers. The commercial and industrial administration of the SS, the SS-Wirtschafts und Verwaltungshauptamt (WVHA), took over the camps in early 1942. The camps supplied labor to munitions factories and other plants attached to the camps, with satellite labor camps being attached to the new extermination camps. The SS charged companies between 4 and 8 marks per day for the use of prisoners on twelve-hour shifts. The estimated life expectancy of a laborer was taken to be nine months, netting the SS a handy profit, while the commandants of the extermination camps grew rich through legitimized looting.

The extermination camps were founded in the east following the Wannsee Confer-

Human bones near the ovens at the Majdanek Concentration Camp in Poland. Photograph taken during the liberation, April 1945. (Yad Vashem, Jerusalem)

ence in January 1942. While the planned and systematic mass killing took place at Auschwitz, Belzec, Sobibor, Treblinka, and Majdanek, in other camps thousands died from starvation and disease caused by horrific neglect. As the Russian armies moved through Poland, prisoners were evacuated in "death marches," with uncounted numbers dying en route, in a final spasm of lethal barbarity. Only in April 1945 could any relief be given to survivors, and surviving camp records were assembled by the Red Cross at their International Tracing Center at Arolsen. Accurate figures for the numbers of prisoners and their fates are, however, impossible to obtain. The best estimates are that about 6 million Jews and 500,000 Gypsies were killed in the extermination camps and about 1 million (approximately two-thirds of all detainees) in the labor camps.

Related entries: Auschwitz; Belsen; Buchenwald; Dachau; Extermination Camps; Final Solution; Freemasonry; Gypsies; Himmler, Heinrich; Hoess, Rudolf; Holocaust; Jehovah's Witnesses; Jews and Jewish Policy; Law; Poland; Schutzstaffel; Sobibor; Theresienstadt; Totenkopfverbände; Treblinka; War Crimes

Suggestions for further reading:
Sofsky, Wolfgang. 1997. *The Order of Terror: The Concentration Camp.* Princeton: Princeton University Press.

Concordat

The concordat signed by Hitler with the Vatican in July 1933 was designed to gain the loyalty of Germany's millions of Catholics by guaranteeing their religious freedom. Catholic religious education was to be maintained in schools and church property protected; church-run schools were to be expanded and Catholic theological faculties maintained in state universities; and the Holy See kept the right to publish encyclicals in Germany. In return the church was to renounce all political activity and promised to dissolve all its political organizations. Hitler gained international prestige in negotiating the Concordat and an end to political Catholicism in Germany, but it did not prevent future conflicts with the Catholic Church.

Related entries: Catholic Church; Education

Suggestions for further reading:
Lewy, Guenther. 1964. *The Catholic Church and Nazi Germany.* New York: McGraw-Hill.

Condor Legion

The Wehrmacht units sent to aid the Nationalists in the Spanish Civil War gained valuable experience in combat and played an important role in Francisco Franco's victory. The legion included air, communications, and transportation units augmented by tank units, which totaled about 6,000 men, regularly rotated. Hitler's intervention in Spain was kept hidden from the world until the bombing of Guernica in April 1937 by planes of the Condor Legion. Its homecoming was turned into a pompous state celebration: on 6 June 1939 the legion paraded in Berlin, bearing golden tablets inscribed with the names of 300 war dead, as opposed to the actual losses of 420.

Related entries: Franco, Francisco; Spain

Confessing Church

Formed in May 1934, the Confessing Church brought together Protestant clergy and laity opposed to Nazi nationalism and racism. It considered itself the only true evangelical church, dedicated to opposing the official Reich church and the pro-Nazi German Christians. The first organization was the Pastors' Emergency League, formed around Martin Niemöller in September 1933. In the early years of the regime, when Hitler was still consolidating his power, the recalcitrant bishops associated with the Confessing Church could exert a certain influence. When Reich bishop Ludwig Müller, who was supported by the government, used his authority to arrest bishops Theophil Wurm of Württemberg and Hans Meiser of Bavaria, Hitler intervened personally to secure their release. When Hans Kerrl, appointed minister of church affairs in July 1935, attempted to bridge the differences between the "fraternal councils" of the Confessing Church and the German Christians by means of a church commission, the Confessing Church was divided about whether to cooperate.

The split was confirmed in 1936. The "moderates" organized themselves as the Council of the Evangelical Lutheran Church of Germany, whereas the "radicals" adopted a new "provisional" leadership. Hitler, losing all interest in conciliating the Protestants, now gave his subordinates a free hand in harassing the Confessing Church. Recalcitrant pastors were ejected from their posts. Niemöller was arrested and in March 1938 sent to a concentration camp as "the Führer's personal prisoner." Many other pastors followed him, but active conspirators such as Dietrich Bonhoeffer remained a small minority. With the coming of war, a kind of "civil peace" was declared between the Confessing Church and the Nazis. Courageous pastors still risked arrest for confessing the "sole word of God," but the Confessing Church as such remained mostly silent about the genocide of the Jews, a fact recognized in the Stuttgart Confession of Guilt of 19 October 1945.

Related entries: Bonhoeffer, Dietrich; German Christians; Protestant Churches

Suggestions for further reading:
Helmreich, Ernst Christian. 1979. *The German Churches under Hitler: Background, Struggle and Epilogue.* Detroit: Wayne State University Press.

Crystal Night

See Kristallnacht

Cultural Policy

Kulturpolitik had always played an important role in German life, more than in most countries, but the Nazis were the first to attempt systematically to organize and control the entire cultural life of the country. Under Hitler culture was to be a "weapon of the state." He had made clear his idea of culture in *Mein Kampf*: "Theatre, art, literature, cinema, press, posters, and window displays must be cleansed of all manifestations of our rotting world and placed in the service of a moral, political, and cultural idea. . . . In all these things the goal and the road must be determined by concern for the preservation of the health of our people in body and soul. The right of personal freedom recedes before the duty to preserve the race" (Hitler 1992, p. 232). The sole purpose of culture, once it had been "coordinated," was to be an expression of the Aryan race and the new political order, a culture rooted in the people and the *Volksgemeinschaft*. The enemies were "decadent Jewish-Liberal culture" and "cultural bolshevism," associated with modernism and defined conveniently by Alfred Rosenberg as "everything that National Socialism rejects" (*Art and Power* 1995, p. 261).

The controlling body of cultural policy was the Reich Chamber of Culture (RKK), set up by a law of 22 September 1933 to organize the various branches of the cultural professions as public corporations. It was divided into seven separate chambers: the Reich Chamber of Literature; Reich Theater Chamber; Reich Chamber of Music; Reich Film Chamber; Reich Chamber of Fine Arts; Reich Press Chamber; and Reich Radio Chamber.

Each chamber regulated conditions of work in its particular field by keeping a register and issuing work permits. To be refused a permit and membership in the chamber meant professional ruin, but for those willing to comply the new organization provided financial security and possible public recognition.

As minister of propaganda, Josef Goebbels was president of all seven chambers and held the power to exclude anyone considered racially or artistically undesirable. It was hoped that the tight system of control would obviate the need for a system of censorship. Those artists not purged could be relied on to control themselves through self-censorship. But any kind of free criticism was anathema to Nazism. Proclamations in May and November 1936 limited criticism to merely "descriptive" reviews. The press chief of the ministry of propaganda, Alfred Ingemar Berndt, summed up the situation: "Judgement of art work in the National Socialist State can be made only on the basis of the National Socialist viewpoint of culture. Only the Party and the State are in a position to determine artistic values" (Welch 1993, p. 28). Quite evidently, the policy did enormous damage to German culture, producing nothing but a crushing mediocrity.

The cultural domain was the first from which Jews and leftists were expelled in numbers immediately on Hitler's accession to power. Even before the RKK was set up, 10 May 1933 saw the barbarous ceremony of the "burning of the books" on the Franz Joseph Platz in Berlin, when the works of "undesirable and pernicious writers," including Karl Marx, Sigmund Freud, and Thomas Mann, were thrown into a bonfire to the applause of National Socialist students and others. In a radio broadcast Goebbels was ecstatic: "The age of extreme intellectualism is over . . . the past is lying in flames . . . the future will rise from the flames within our hearts. . . . Brightened by these flames our vow shall be: the Reich and the Nation and our Führer Adolf Hitler: Heil! Heil! Heil!" (Welch 1993, p. 28).

A decree on 25 April 1935 confirmed the power of the Reich Chamber of Literature to draw up an "index" of all works deemed to be threatening to "National Socialist cultural aspirations." The works of authors such as Mann, Stefan Zweig, Carl Zuckmayer, and Franz Kafka were banned completely. The nonbanned had at least to pay lip service to the new ideas. All forms of art had to "come from the people" and express the *Volksgemeinschaft*. The preferred literary subgenres were "combat literature" from World War I, historical novels glorifying the German past and *Heimatliteratur,* regional novels celebrating the stolid virtues of rural life as opposed to modern urban "Jewish intellectual" culture. The Reich supervisor of drama, Rainer Schlösser, decided what was acceptable on the stage, and the Reich Chamber of Music kept out all "non-German" music, including the works of Jewish composers from Felix Mendelssohn to Gustav Mahler and Arnold Schoenberg while laying a particular stress of folk music. In general, arts and crafts, controlled by the all-embracing Reich Chamber of Fine Arts, were less directly influenced by Nazi ideology, but even here any craftspeople showing too much independence could be banned from working even in the privacy of their own homes.

The damage done by Hitler and his followers to German culture was immeasurable. The list of writers, artists, scholars, playwrights, musicians, filmmakers, and actors driven into exile for racial or ideological reasons is almost endless: Thomas and Heinrich Mann, Bertolt Brecht, Erwin Panofsky, Walter Gropius, George Grosz, Wassily Kandinsky, Oskar Kokoschka, Max Reinhardt, Bruno Walter, Paul Tillich, Ernst Cassirer, Otto Klemperer, and so on. For every artist who supported Nazism, like Richard Strauss, or came to an accommodation with it, like Wilhelm Furtwängler or Herbert von Karajan, there were many others forced into emigration. The only small consolation from the whole sorry story is that Germany's loss was the rest of the world's gain. While Germany was engulfed by grandiose nonsense, Nazi kitsch, and "blood and soil" populist mysticism, the true beneficiaries of Hitler's cultural policy were the universities and artistic institutions of the United States and the rest of the free world.

Related entries: Architecture; Art; Bayreuth; *Blut und Boden;* Cinema; Education; *Gleichschaltung;* Goebbels, Paul Josef; Press; Propaganda; Racial Theory; Radio; Riefenstahl, Leni; Science and Scientists; Speer, Albert; Universities; *Volksgemeinschaft;* Wagner, Richard

Suggestions for further reading:
Art and Power. 1995. *Art and Power: Europe under the Dictators 1930–45.* London: Hayward Gallery.
Cuomo, Glen R., ed. 1995. *National Socialist Cultural Policy.* New York: St. Martin's Press.
Hitler, Adolf. 1992. *Mein Kampf.* Trans. Ralph Manheim. Intro. by D. C. Watt. London: Pimlico.
Kater, Michael H. 1997. *The Twisted Muse: Musicians and Their Music in the Third Reich.* New York and Oxford: Oxford University Press.
Levi, Erik. 1994. *Music in the Third Reich.* New York: Macmillan.
Ritchie, J. M. 1983. *German Literature under National Socialism.* London: Croom Helm.
Steinweis, Alan E. 1993. *Art, Ideology, and Economics in Nazi Germany: The Reich Chambers of Music, Theater and the Visual Arts.* Chapel Hill: University of North Carolina Press.
Welch, David. 1993. *The Third Reich: Politics and Propaganda.* London and New York: Routledge.

Czechoslovakia

As a democratic Slav state and a creation of the Treaty of Versailles, Czechoslovakia represented much of what Hitler most hated. Only about 50 percent of the population were Czech; 24 percent were German and some 16 percent Slovak. But despite ethnic tensions, under Tomáš Masaryk, president from 1918 to 1935, and then Eduard Beneš the new state attained a remarkable parliamentary and democratic stability, aided by healthy economic development and the readiness of German parties to play their part in government. But the world economic crisis aggravated internal tensions, and whereas under the Weimar Republic Berlin had taken little interest in the German population, especially in the Sudetenland, on coming to power Hitler immediately started encouraging German and Hungarian separatism.

Hitler's clear intention, certainly from 1936 onward, was to "smash" Czechoslovakia, and the Sudeten situation provided the excuse. For its part Czechoslovakia relied principally on alliances with France and the Soviet Union for support in maintaining its territorial integrity. After the Munich Agreement of 1938, what was now called the Second Republic of Czecho-Slovakia lost the Sudetenland and gave autonomy to Slovakia and the Carpathian Ukraine. Hitler was robbed of his chance to destroy Czechoslovakia completely, but his exploitation of nationality problems gained some 5 million new inhabitants for the Reich and increased his popularity. The rump state had to submit to Hitler's will in proceedings against Jews and special legislation against German exiles.

President Emil Hácha yielded to Hitler's threats and blackmail in March 1939. Declarations of independence for Slovakia and the Carpathian Ukraine were drawn up in Berlin, and under the pretext that the state had dissolved itself, the Wehrmacht occupied the "residual Czech state" on 15 March. The next day, Hitler decreed from Prague the creation of the Protectorate of Bohemia and Moravia. Slovakia existed as a puppet state led by Josef Tiso. In international law, however, Czechoslovakia still existed. While the full terror of Nazi rule gripped Bohemia and Moravia, the Czech government-in-exile under Beneš in London was recognized by the Allies, including the Soviet Union, and planned for the nullification of the Munich Agreement and the expulsion of the Sudeten Germans after the war. The Czech Resistance staged an uprising in Prague shortly before the German collapse on 5–7 May 1945. Beneš returned as president of the reborn Czechoslovakia but was unable to prevent the subsequent Communist seizure of power.

Related entries: Beneš, Eduard; Foreign Policy; Munich Agreement; Resistance Movements; Sudetenland; War Crimes

Suggestions for further reading:
Weinburg, Gerhard L. 1980. *The Foreign Policy of Hitler's Germany: Starting World War II, 1937–1939.* Chicago: University of Chicago Press.

Dachau

The first Nazi concentration camp was established in March 1933 on the outskirts of the Bavarian city of Dachau in a former munitions factory. Initially intended for the "protective custody" of political offenders and widely welcomed by the local middle-class population as a reasonable way of dealing with "troublemakers" and "revolutionaries," it was soon used to house Jews, Gypsies, political and religious oppositionists, the handicapped, homosexuals, and criminals. The Dachau camp grew into a complex organization, especially during the war years, supplying a slave labor force to the armaments industry of southern Germany. It became a model for other concentration camps and served as a training center for camp commandants and the SS Totenkopfverbände.

Dachau was not intended to be an extermination camp, but inmates died by the thousand of hunger, disease, and exhaustion; were shot while "trying to escape"; or died under torture or while being subjected to medical experiments. Also by November 1944, more than 3,000 physically and mentally handicapped prisoners had been transferred to the euthanasia facility at Hartheim Castle near Linz and gassed. The camp was liberated by U.S. troops on 29 April 1945, and about 30,000 survivors were released.

Related entries: Concentration Camps; Euthanasia

Daladier, Edouard (1884–1970)

As prime minister of France from April 1938, Radical Party politician Daladier continued the policy of appeasement and was a signatory to the Munich Agreement. As a result, like Neville Chamberlain, he enjoyed great popularity at home and was hailed as a peacemaker. He resigned as premier in March 1940, having failed to unite the people or the parliament behind his cautious approach to mobilization. Interned by Marshal Philippe Pétain's Vichy government, Daladier was tried in February 1942 for betraying his country and deported to Germany, where he was held until the end of the war. He made a reasonably successful return to French politics after 1945 as a pillar of the Radical establishment.

Related entries: Appeasement; France; Munich Agreement

Danzig

The largely German-speaking port city of Danzig at the head of the

"Polish corridor" was declared a free city by the Treaty of Versailles, allowing Poland access to the Baltic Sea. With an autonomous government under the supervision of the League of Nations, Danzig became a symbol of German resentment against the Versailles settlement and a key issue in German-Polish relations. The Nazi Party gained power in Danzig after elections on 28 May 1933 in which it received just over 50 percent of the vote, but *Gauleiter* Albert Forster could not reproduce Hitler's dictatorship in the free city, and the first Nazi president of Danzig, the conservative Hermann Rauschning, followed legal norms and governed with the agreement of Poland and the League.

Rauschning served Hitler's short-term purposes well in facilitating the negotiation of the German-Polish Nonaggression Pact of January 1934, which put the Danzig question on the back burner. But he was forced out of office in November 1934 and replaced by the more dedicated Nazi Arthur Greiser. Electoral fraud and intimidation enabled the Nazis to retain power in 1935, despite economic difficulties in Danzig. All organized opposition had been destroyed by the end of 1937. In 1938 anti-Semitic legislation led to increasing persecution of Danzig's remaining Jewish inhabitants.

Despite downplaying the issue for several years, Hitler was determined to recover Danzig for the Reich and use it as a staging area in the invasion of Poland. On 10 August 1939 Forster made a speech demanding that Danzig be returned "back home to the Reich." When the invasion of Poland began on 1 September, the city was immediately declared part of the Third Reich. Nazi propaganda in France asked whether the French people were ready to "die for Danzig." During the German occupation of Poland, Danzig was capital of the *Gau* of Danzig-West Prussia. With Hitler's defeat, however, the majority German population were driven out, and Danzig became the Polish city of Gdansk.

Related entries: Foreign Policy; Poland; Rauschning, Hermann

Suggestions for further reading:
Levine, Herbert S. 1973. *Hitler's Free City: A History of the Nazi Party in Danzig, 1925–39.* Chicago: University of Chicago Press.

Darlan, Jean François (1881–1942)

The commander in chief of the French navy at the start of the war was equally mistrusted by all sides. Having ordered the French fleet to colonial bases after the fall of France, contrary to assurances he had given to the British, Admiral Darlan became vice premier in the Vichy government in February 1941, collaborating with the Germans while assuring the Americans that he would welcome Allied intervention. In 1942, having been appointed commander in chief of French armed forces and high commissioner in North Africa, Darlan was in Algiers at the time of the Allied landings. He wavered until Hitler occupied Vichy France on 11 November, when he came down on the Allied side. The endorsement of his position as the political head of French North Africa caused public outrage in Britain, stirred up by General Charles de Gaulle. The assassination of Darlan on Christmas Eve 1942 by a young French monarchist spared the Allies further embarrassment.

Related entries: de Gaulle, Charles; France; North Africa

Darré, Richard Walther (1895–1953)

Born into a German merchant family in Belgrano, Argentina, Darré was sent to Germany in 1905 for his education and was preparing to become a colonial farmer when World War I broke out. He served as an artillery officer on the Western Front and then resumed his agricultural studies on demobilization. An early friend of Heinrich Himmler, Darré had briefly been a member of the Berlin Freikorps, and in the late 1920s began to organize farmers in the National Socialist German Workers' Party's Agrarpolitischer Apparat, which infiltrated existing agricultural organizations. He rose rapidly in the Nazi hierarchy after 1930, when his work among the peasants seemed to be paying dividends in increasing rural electoral support, especially in 1932.

Although he was not one of the "old fighters" of the Nazi movement, Darré impressed Hitler with the "blood and soil" ideology he expressed in a series of books, the most important of which was *Das Bauerntum* (The peasantry), published in 1929. Darré's claims that the Nordic race had been the true creators of European culture and that the German peasant as the essence of Germanism and custodian of national integrity was the driving force of history appealed strongly to Hitler's worldview. A happy and prosperous peasantry would serve as the foundation of racial and cultural purity, while a new "Germanic aristocracy of the soil" would dominate the new corporatist state.

Darré was appointed Reich minister for food and agriculture by Hitler on 29 June 1933. Later he became head of the SS Central Office for Race and Resettlement while continuing to pen numerous books on the peasantry, race, and, picking up on his earlier profession as a pig breeder, arcane topics such as the pig in ancient folklore. As minister of agriculture he introduced the largely futile entail farm legislation, seeking to preserve the peasantry as a bulwark against the world of industrial capitalism. But his romantic and backward-looking concepts brought him into conflict with the financial and trade policies of Hjalmar Schacht and the regime's bankers. His poli-

cies failed to halt the flight from the land, and his agrarian ideology fitted badly with Hitler's drive for rearmament. By 1939 he had lost the Führer's confidence, though he remained in office until May 1942, when his failure to ensure efficient provision of food supplies led to his dismissal. Agricultural settlements in the occupied territories were afterward overseen by Himmler.

Captured in 1945, Darré was tried by a U.S. military tribunal at Nuremberg and in 1948 was sentenced to seven years in prison for the confiscation of property from Polish and Jewish farmers and for provoking the starvation of civilians by depriving German Jews of basic foodstuffs. He was released in 1950 and died in Munich of a liver ailment in September 1953. Darré's racism, his anti-Semitism, and his cult of the peasant may have appealed to Hitler, but his backward-looking ideology was not in the end consistent with the Führer's plans for world domination. Claims that he was "not a real Nazi" are debatable in the extreme, but he certainly cut a curious and eventually isolated figure among Hitler's close collaborators.

Related entries: Agriculture; *Blut und Boden;* Economic Policy; Reich Food Estate

Suggestions for further reading:
Bramwell, Anna. 1985. *Blood and Soil: Richard Walther Darré and Hitler's Green Party.* Bourne End: Kensal.

Dawes Plan

The plan for the payment of reparations presented in April 1924 by a committee headed by the U.S. banker Charles G. Dawes took much of the heat out of the reparations issue and therefore out of extreme nationalist politics. It regulated and considerably eased the terms of payments, linking them to Germany's capacity to pay and to the provision of U.S.

loans to aid German economic recovery. Hitler was in jail at Landsberg and the Nazi Party banned at the time, and the provisional settlement represented by the Dawes Plan helped to ensure that the recovery of his political fortunes would be more difficult in the succeeding five years, until the Young Plan of 1929 revived the reparations issue.

Related entries: Reparations; Young Plan

Suggestions for further reading:
Kent, Bruce. 1989. *The Spoils of War: The Politics, Economics and Diplomacy of Reparations, 1918–1932.* Oxford: Clarendon Press.

de Gaulle, Charles (1890–1970)

The controversial leader of Free France first made his mark as a critic of French military doctrine in the 1930s. In his 1934 book *Vers l'Armée de Métier* (rendered in English as *The Army of the Future*), de Gaulle called for the creation of a professional army with mobile armored units and air support, an idea that paralleled the thinking of Heinz Guderian and the "tank school" in Germany. According to Albert Speer, Hitler claimed to have read de Gaulle's book many times and to have learned a great deal from it.

De Gaulle commanded a tank brigade during the early stages of Hitler's invasion of France but was soon drawn into the political sphere. Finding himself in London at the time of the armistice, he made his famous call for resistance over the BBC in June 1940 but was heard by very few people in France at the time. De Gaulle's struggle from then on was to assert his control over the growing but politically diverse resistance movement and to assert his (very dubious) right to speak for France. His haughtiness and punctilious standing on his rights led to difficult relations with the Al-

lies, especially President Franklin Delano Roosevelt. Having outmaneuvered his main rival, General Henri Giraud, de Gaulle formed a provisional government in Algiers in May 1944 and entered Paris to a delirious welcome on 26 August. His later dramatic political career finally saw him as president of the Fifth Republic, presiding over a regime tailored to his requirements, from 1959 to 1969. His extraordinary claim, "Je suis la France" ('I am France'), first made in 1940, his self-confidence, and his identification of his personal ambitions with those of his country turned de Gaulle into a towering symbol of resistance to Hitler in occupied Europe and secured France a place among the victors.

Related entries: France; Resistance Movements

Suggestions for further reading:
Cogan, Charles G. 1996. *Charles de Gaulle: A Brief Biography with Documents.* Boston: Bedford Books.

Denmark

Hitler's forces occupied Denmark in a single day, 9 April 1940, simultaneously with the invasion of Norway. Unlike other European countries, Hitler allowed the Scandinavian kingdom to remain nominally independent under King Christian X. Denmark signed the Anti-Comintern Pact in November 1941. Many Danish diplomats, however, supported the Allies; the Danish territories of Greenland, Iceland, and the Faroe Islands were made available to Allied forces; and the Danish merchant fleet sailed to Allied ports, eventually losing 60 percent of its ships and some 600 sailors to German attacks.

Under German control Denmark began to suffer severe economic problems, and a spirit of resistance grew. In October 1942, therefore, Hitler sent the prominent SS man Werner Best to be German commissioner in Copenhagen, charged with stepping up the exploitation of Danish economic resources. But overt resistance increased rapidly, and in 1943 a Freedom Council organized an effective series of strikes and acts of sabotage. When anti-Semitic legislation was imposed on Denmark in October 1943, the vast majority of the country's 8,000 Jews, aided by the Danish authorities, escaped to Sweden. Uniquely in Europe, the Danish Resistance was not split by factionalism and made plans for full-scale rebellion, which were, however, never implemented. German forces in Denmark capitulated on 5 May 1945.

Related entries: Norway; Resistance Movements; Sweden

Suggestions for further reading:
Oakey, Stewart P. 1972. *A Short History of Denmark*. New York: Praeger.

Doenitz, Karl (1891–1980)

Grand Admiral Doenitz, who briefly succeeded Hitler as Führer in 1945, had been in the navy since 1910. Between 1935 and 1939 he controlled the tactical and technical development of the U-boat fleet but found himself at odds with the naval High Command under Erich Raeder, who opposed the introduction of Doenitz's "wolf-pack" tactics. In 1939 Doenitz went to war against Britain with only thirty-nine U-boats in fully operational condition.

Promoted to rear admiral in 1939, Doenitz led the U-boat arm to shrewd and deadly effect in the early years of the war and during the Battle of the Atlantic. Doenitz made sure that U-boat crews were well-trained and their morale enhanced by his commitment to his commanders. He argued constantly, but for some years in vain, for greater concentration of production and scientific resources on U-boats. In 1942,

however, Hitler was finally convinced by Doenitz's arguments, promoted him to grand admiral, and named him as commander in chief of the navy, replacing Raeder, on 30 January 1943. In his new role Doenitz did his best to maintain a balance between the surface fleet and his favorite, the U-boats. By mid-1943, however, the latter had lost the struggle in the Atlantic, and their deployment was largely defensive.

In early 1945 Doenitz organized the evacuation of troops and German refugees fleeing the Russian advance along the shores of the Baltic. His rise to prominence had always been underpinned by his unequivocal acceptance of Nazi rule in Germany. As the real Nazi leaders scurried for cover in April '1945, Doenitz earned the dubious honor of being Hitler's chosen successor as head of state. He appointed a cabinet of his own choice, not Hitler's, negotiated the surrender of German forces in the west, and was arrested by the Anglo-American forces at Flensburg on 23 May 1945. Convicted at Nuremberg of having planned a war of aggression, Doenitz served ten years in Spandau prison in Berlin.

Related entries: Atlantic, Battle of the; Navy; Raeder, Erich; U-boats

Suggestions for further reading:
Padfield, Peter. 1984. *Dönitz: The Last Führer*. New York: Harper and Row.

Dollfuss, Engelbert (1892–1934)

A jurist and economist from Texing in Lower Austria, the ambitious Dollfuss was appointed chancellor of Austria in May 1932, leading a right-wing coalition with a wafer-thin parliamentary majority. He used authoritarian methods against Left and Right and resisted Anschluss with Germany through the Fatherland Front, which he founded in September 1933. The Nazi and Communist Parties were banned, the Social Democratic workers of Vienna bloodily suppressed, and Austria declared a corporatist state with the Front as the only legal party. The clandestine Austrian Nazis, with Hitler's approval, carried out a campaign of violence against Dollfuss's "Austrofascist" regime and on 25 July 1934 staged an abortive coup in which Dollfuss was murdered. Hitler received the news with undisguised joy while attending the Wagner Festival at Bayreuth. But his hopes for Anschluss were premature as Austrian government forces led by Kurt von Schuschnigg recovered control, and Benito Mussolini mobilized troops on the Austrian border.

Related entries: Anschluss; Austria; Schuschnigg, Kurt von

Drexler, Anton (1884–1942)

As cofounder of the German Workers' Party (DAP), Drexler was a significant figure within the tiny and unruly world of extreme-right politics in post-1918 Munich, but Hitler in his autobiographical writings played down his influence so as to magnify his own role as nascent Führer. A locksmith in a railway workshop, Drexler was declared unfit for military service but found a means of expressing his patriotic and racist sentiments first in the Fatherland Party and his own "Workers' Committee for a Good Peace," designed to stir up support for the war among the Munich working class. In December 1918 he took the initiative in founding the DAP (established on 5 January 1919) with the journalist Karl Harrer. Hitler first attended one of the group's public meetings on 12 September 1919, one of a thin audience of forty-one.

Drexler's ideas contained little that was original. He and Hitler later disputed responsibility for the first program of the Na-

tional Socialist German Workers' Party (NSDAP, Nazi Party), successor to the DAP, the twenty-five theses published in February 1920. The forceful style is Hitler's, but Drexler was probably the principal author. Quasi-socialist elements, including profit-sharing and the breaking of "interest slavery," were combined with intense nationalism, anti-Semitism, and a call for authoritarian government. Hitler had read Drexler's pamphlet, *My Political Awakening (Mein Politisches Erwachen)* and had been impressed with its vision of the German laboring classes as victims of a conspiracy by international Jewish capital. The core of Nazism as an antiliberal, anti-Marxist, and anti-Semitic movement may be seen in Drexler's ideas, but as a politician the naïve and ingenuous Drexler was no match for Hitler. In *Mein Kampf* Hitler disparages Drexler for having never been a soldier and calls him "feeble and uncertain in his whole nature" (Hitler 1992, p. 323). By the summer of 1921 Hitler had established himself as sole leader of the NSDAP. Drexler left the party in 1923 and never again took part in Nazi activity. He died a forgotten figure in Munich on 24 February 1942. On hearing Hitler speak for the first time in September 1919, Drexler reportedly exclaimed: "Goodness, he's got a gob. We could use him" (Kershaw 1998, p. 107). He was not the last mediocre politician to suffer this illusion.

Related entries: Anti-Semitism; German Workers' Party; Munich; National Socialist German Workers' Party

Suggestions for further reading:
Hitler, Adolf. 1992. *Mein Kampf.* Trans. Ralph Manheim. Intro. by D. C. Watt. London: Pimlico.

Dunkirk, Evacuation of

As the German armies swept through the Low Countries and northern France in May 1940, the Allied troops, in-

British troops await evacuation from the beaches of Dunkirk in June 1940. Hitler had been assured that the Luftwaffe would destroy the remnants of the British Expeditionary Force, a fateful mistake that allowed an armada of between 850 and 950 small boats from across the Channel to evacuate over 330,000 British, French, and other Allied troops from the northern French port between 26 May and 3 June, though all their heavy equipment and transport was lost. (Popperfoto/Archive Photos)

cluding the British Expeditionary Force, were allowed to fall back on Dunkirk. His generals blamed Hitler for letting this happen by halting the advance and allowing Hermann Goering to show how his Luftwaffe could destroy the encircled Allies without the help of the army. The resultant evacuation between 26 May and 4 June, in which craft of all shapes and sizes rescued 350,000 men from the beaches, became a symbol of British will to resist Hitler's aggression. The London *Daily Mirror* trumpeted the evacuation as "Bloody Marvellous," but Winston Churchill noted: "Wars are not won by evacuations" (Keegan 1989, p. 81). When German troops finally took Dunkirk, the church bells of Berlin rang for three days, and the victory was announced as "the greatest ever in German history." The British army could be written off as defeated, but as it became clear that Britain would continue the war, the psychological significance of Hitler's blunder became evident.

Suggestions for further reading:
Keegan, John. 1989. *The Second World War.* London: Hutchinson.

E

Eastern Front

On 30 March 1941 Hitler told his generals: "The war against Russia cannot be considered in a knightly fashion; the struggle is one of ideologies and racial differences and will have to be conducted with unprecedented, unmerciful and unrelenting harshness. . . . The commissars are the bearers of ideologies directly opposed to National Socialism. Therefore the commissars will be liquidated. German soldiers guilty of breaking international law . . . will be excused" (Keegan 1989, p. 186). Hitler's war in the east did indeed sink to almost inconceivable levels of barbarity, but his ideological obsessions and prejudices also contributed to his ultimate defeat. For example, instead of encouraging the anti-Soviet feelings of Ukrainians and peasants butchered by Joseph Stalin's collectivization of agriculture, he viewed them purely as Slavic *Untermenschen* to be exploited by the Germans. When the Soviets resorted to partisan warfare, Hitler showed the depths of his mentality: "This partisan war in turn has its advantages: it gives us a chance to exterminate anyone who turns against us" (Bullock 1991, p. 824). The SS Einsatzgruppen needed no such excuse to slaughter Jews, Communists, and anyone else who opposed them.

Hitler had hoped for a swift blitzkrieg victory. But after tremendous advances, the central thrust of Operation Barbarossa ground to a halt in the outskirts of Moscow. Stalin at last pulled himself together and refused to leave the capital. The Soviets managed to mobilize 3 million men, plus the inhabitants, for the defense of Moscow and counterattacked on 5 December 1941. With much of their equipment immobilized by the intense cold and lacking suitable winter clothing, the Germans retreated before stabilizing their line in January 1942 some 90 miles west of Moscow. The war in Russia, it was now clear, would be a long and vicious struggle.

Hitler typically blamed his generals for the setback. He dismissed Walther von Brauchitsch as commander in chief and assumed direct control of operations himself, much to the irritation of the generals in the field. Ensconced in his Wolf's Lair headquarters in East Prussia, he determined day-to-day tactics as well as overall strategy. His belief that the power of the will and natural German superiority could overcome any material or numerical inferiority caused him simply to order his generals never to withdraw. The results were more often than not disastrous. His decisions were, according to General Franz Halder, "the products of a violent nature following its momentary impulses, a nature which acknowledged no bounds to possibility and which made its wish the father of its need" (Bullock 1991, p. 862). But Soviet manpower was practically unlimited and by 1942 they had also organized partisan groups behind German lines.

In 1942 the focus of the fighting switched to the south as Hitler launched a drive through the Caucasus toward the Caspian Sea, with the Grozny and Maikop oilfields, which supplied the Red Army with fuel, as major objectives. The destruction of the German 6th Army at Stalingrad, however, turned out to be the greatest blow to Hitler's war effort in any theater of operations. The front was stabilized in early 1943, but the huge tank battle of Kursk confirmed that the initiative now lay with the Soviets. By the end of the year the Red Army had regained two-thirds of the territory it had lost. The Russians retook Smolensk on 25 September and Kiev on 6 November. Then on 27 January 1944 the siege of Leningrad was lifted after 865 days.

Hitler continued in the face of all common sense to order a strategy of no retreat on the Eastern Front. As Russian success increased, he sacked and replaced generals, blaming everyone but himself. Despite the huge forces involved on both sides, the Russians, with improved equipment and U.S. supplies, could launch their summer offensive of 1944 with little doubt as to the ultimate outcome. Army Group North was pushed back through the Baltic states; Operation Bagration was launched in the Center; and the southern front was pushed toward the Balkans. By February 1945 the Russians had taken Hungary and switched their major thrust toward East Prussia. Marshal Georgi Zhukov's forces advanced 300 miles in two weeks to reach the Oder River and drive through Germany toward Berlin. The final assault on Hitler's capital, involving 2.5 million Soviet soldiers, encircled the city on 25 April, and on 30 April Russian soldiers occupied the Reichstag building. On 2 May Berlin surrendered.

Related entries: Bagration, Operation; Baltic States; Barbarossa, Operation; Brauchitsch, Walther von; Bulgaria; Citadel, Operation; Finland; Holocaust; Hungary; Keitel, Wilhelm; Kursk, Battle of; Manstein, Erich von; Panzer Divisions; Paulus, Friedrich; Poland; Red Army; Romania; Schutzstaffel; Soviet Union; Stalin, Joseph; Stalingrad, Battle of; Ukraine; *Volksdeutsche;* Voroshilov, Klement Efremovich; Waffen SS; War Crimes; Warsaw Rising; Wehrmacht; Zhukov, Georgi Konstantinovich

Suggestions for further reading:
Bullock, Alan. 1991. *Hitler and Stalin: Parallel Lives.* London: HarperCollins.
Erickson, John. 1975. *The Road to Stalingrad.* New York: Harper and Row.
———. 1983. *The Road to Berlin.* Boulder, CO: Westview Press.
Keegan, John. 1989. *The Second World War.* London: Hutchinson.
Overy, Richard J. 1998. *Russia's War.* New York: Allen Lane Penguin Press.

Eckart, Dietrich
(1868–1923)

*I*n the early days of the German Workers' Party and National Socialist German Workers' Party (NSDAP, Nazi Party) in Munich, Hitler looked up to the writer and publisher Eckart as a poet and visionary of anti-Semitism and anti-Marxism. He said of him: "He shone in our eyes like a polar star." Born in Neumarkt into a Catholic family, Eckart trained as a journalist but already before 1914 was blaming his failure as a poet and dramatist on Jews and Marxists, the same forces he later held responsible for Germany's defeat in World War I. Entering politics after the 1918 Revolution in Munich, he founded the anti-Semitic weekly *Auf Gut Deutsch* (In plain German), which featured contributions from Gottfried Feder and Alfred Rosenberg. He invented the battle cry of "Deutschland Erwache!" (Germany awake!) and composed the "Sturm-Lied" (Storming song) for the early Nazis.

Eckart's social and financial connections were of great value for Hitler, at the time merely one beer hall demagogue among others in the small world of extreme right politics. He opened the salons of Munich high society to the young agitator, helping him to improve his social skills and his German. Eckart described Hitler as suffering from a "megalomania halfway between a Messiah complex and Neroism" (Kershaw 1998, p. 182) but nevertheless helped the struggling NSDAP with its finances. Most importantly, he secured the financial backing of the Augsburg chemist and factory owner Dr. Gottfried Grandel, enabling Hitler to buy the *Völkischer Beobachter,* which became the party's own newspaper in December 1920. Eckart edited it briefly before being succeeded by Rosenberg.

By the time of the Beer Hall Putsch in 1923, Eckart was seriously ill, his health weakened by alcoholism and morphine addiction. He took no part in the putsch but was briefly imprisoned, died on 23 December 1923, and was buried at Berchtesgarden. The posthumously published *Bolshevism from Moses to Lenin: A Dialogue between Adolf Hitler and Myself* was in fact entirely Eckart's own work, probably written even without Hitler's knowledge. But its violent anti-Semitism, identifying the Jew as the force of evil in history and bolshevism as the malignant action of the Jew throughout history, gave expression to an apocalyptic anti-Semitism, previously not a fundamental feature of Hitler's agitation but now central to his worldview. Hitler was suitably grateful and dedicated *Mein Kampf* to Eckart along with the comrades killed during the 1923 putsch.

Related entries: Anti-Semitism; Beer Hall Putsch; German Workers' Party; *Mein Kampf;* Munich; National Socialist German Workers' Party; Nazi Movement; *Völkischer Beobachter*

Suggestions for further reading:
Jäckel, Eberhard. 1981. *Hitler's Worldview: A Blueprint for Power.* Cambridge, MA: Harvard University Press.
Kershaw, Ian. 1998. *Hitler 1889–1936: Hubris.* London and New York: Allen Lane The Penguin Press.

Economic Policy

Hitler knew nothing about economics and, apart from a temporary adherence to Gottfried Feder's ideas about "debt slavery," showed little interest in the subject. In the Third Reich, the "primacy of politics," rearmament, an active foreign policy, and the Nazification of Germany meant that in economic policy, ideology was tempered by pragmatism. Hitler benefited from the gradual recovery from the Depression that was already under way when he became chancellor and enjoyed the credit for the decline in unemployment brought about by the introduction of deficit spending and then by the rearmament program.

The economic system of the Third Reich was "a form of capitalism in which the state controlled, organized, and guided production, consumption, and the distribution of income" (Stackelberg 1999, p. 119). The market was highly regulated, and Hitler continued to use the rhetoric of "German socialism" when he thought his audience would appreciate it, but the Nazis never threatened the private ownership of the means of production. Business could enjoy large profits and a considerable degree of freedom so long as it did not impede the political objectives of the regime. There was no attempt to reorganize the economy along fascist corporative lines, and any innovation was meant to inhibit change, not encourage it.

The government's role in the economy was supervisory. When Hjalmar Schacht returned as head of the central bank and then minister of economics from 1935 to 1937 he negotiated trade agreements aimed at boosting German exports and making smaller neighboring countries more dependent on the German market. But Schacht's cautious approach to government spending contradicted Hitler's rearmament plans. When the Four-Year Plan was launched in 1936, the aim was to make

Germany self-sufficient in raw materials and agricultural products. As the economy became geared for war, administrative controls on prices, wages, and labor mobility were strengthened. Fearing the inflationary effects of the Four-Year Plan, Schacht resigned in 1937, to be replaced by Walther Funk.

Under the Four-Year Plan, Germany took on the appearance and to some degree the reality of a centrally planned economy. But private property rights, except those of Jews, were left untouched; industrialists worked closely with the regime and saw their profits rise; and the rivalries and administrative confusion typical of the Third Reich hindered central planning. Employers and managers became the masters of the command economy and workers integrated through the German Labor Front. The Nazi ideal of reversing the disruptive social consequences of industrialization and restoring the traditional agrarian way of German life was in open and flagrant contradiction to the plans for a militarized society, the restoration of German power, and conquest of "living space" in the east. They had to promote heavy industry and advanced technology, hiding the incongruity of their position with cloudy rhetoric about imbuing technology with true Germanic soul and spirit. Hitler, who had always larded his rhetoric with rants against "materialism," whether that of Western capitalists, Jews, or Bolsheviks, was in power as "materialist" and productivist as anyone in his drive for conquest.

Yet Hitler was aware that his popularity rested on economic prosperity and a policy of "guns and butter," rearmament, and the production of consumer goods. The German economy in 1939 was not geared up for a protracted war. As long as German successes continued unhindered, the public could enjoy the spoils of conquest, but from 1942 onward full effort had to be devoted to military production. Under the direction of Albert Speer, industrial capacity was mobilized for the fabrication of armaments. Slave labor from occupied countries was mobilized under the direction of Fritz Sauckel, making up one-fifth of the workforce in agriculture and industry, while the SS made concentration camp prisoners available for industry. Hitler's final economic "system" combined capitalism and slavery, and under Speer's direction it managed to keep the encircled Reich remarkably well supplied even under Allied bombing. It is extremely doubtful, however, whether either earlier implementation of central planning or any alternative economic policy could have staved off the end of the Reich for long.

Related entries: Agriculture; Autobahnen; Concentration Camps; Feder, Gottfried; Four-Year Plan; Funk, Walther; German Labor Front; Goering, Hermann; IG Farben; Industry; Jews and Jewish Policy; Labor Relations; Labor Service; Middle Classes; Rearmament; Reich Food Estate; Reparations; Sauckel, Fritz; Schacht, Hjalmar; Schutzstaffel; Social Policy; Socialism; Speer, Albert; Strength through Joy; Todt, Fritz; Todt Organization; Total War; Trade Policy; Unemployment; Women; Working Class; Youth Policy

Suggestions for further reading:
Barkai, Avraham. 1990. *Nazi Economics: Ideology, Theory, and Policy.* New Haven: Yale University Press.
James, Harold. 1986. *The German Slump: Politics and Economics, 1924–1936.* Oxford: Clarendon Press.
Milward, Alan S. 1965. *The German Economy at War.* London: Athlone Press.
Overy, Richard J. 1994. *War and Economy in the Third Reich.* Oxford: Clarendon Press.
———. 1996. *The Nazi Economic Recovery 1932–1938.* 2nd ed. Cambridge: Cambridge University Press.
Stackelberg, Roderick. 1999. *Hitler's Germany: Origins, Interpretations, Legacies.* London and New York: Routledge.

Eden, Anthony (1897–1977)

As British foreign minister between 1935 and 1938, Anthony Eden met Hitler on several occasions and never had any illusions about him. The dislike was mutual. As minister of League of Nations affairs, Eden had championed Abyssinia against Mussolini's aggression and, as foreign minister, worked increasingly against the flow of appeasement. His attempts to foster collective security, particularly through closer relations with the Soviet Union, foundered on the rocks of mutual suspicion, and he resigned following the Munich Agreement, of which he thoroughly disapproved. Returning as foreign minister in Churchill's war cabinet, Eden undertook numerous delicate missions, championed Charles de Gaulle as the representative of France, and participated in the major Allied conferences. The shadow of appeasement hung over Eden's subsequent political career. Having been actively involved in the establishment of the United Nations, he became prime minister in 1955. He resigned after the debacle of the Suez crisis in 1956, when his identification of President Gamal Abdel Nasser as a new Hitler who could not be appeased fatally affected his judgment.

Related entries: Appeasement; Chamberlain, Neville; Foreign Policy; Great Britain; Munich Agreement

Suggestions for further reading:
Carlton, David. 1981. *Anthony Eden: A Biography.* London: Allen Lane.
Eden, Anthony. 1962. *The Memoirs of Anthony Eden: Facing the Dictators.* Boston: Houghton Mifflin.

Education

Under the Third Reich the federal structure of German education was replaced by a national system. In a directive of 18 December 1934, Hitler's first Reich minister of education, Bernhard Rust, declared: "The principal task of the school is the education of youth in the service of nationhood and state in the National Socialist spirit" (Bullock 1991, p. 361). In lengthy if incoherent thoughts on education in *Mein Kampf,* Hitler sought to define this spirit: "The folkish state must not adjust its entire educational work primarily to the inoculation of mere knowledge, but the breeding of absolutely healthy bodies. The training of mental abilities is only secondary. And here again, first place must be taken by the development of character, especially the promotion of will-power and determination, combined with the training of joy in responsibility, and only in the last place comes scientific schooling" (Hitler 1992, p. 371). The ultimate rationale was racist: "The crown of the folkish state's entire work of education and training must be to burn the racial sense and racial feeling into the instinct and the intellect, the heart and brain of the youth entrusted to it. No boy and no girl must leave school without having been led to an ultimate realization of the necessity and essence of blood purity" (Hitler 1992, p. 389).

The new course in education was begun by purges of teachers and pupils. By the end of 1933 most Jewish teachers had been dismissed, and 97 percent of non-Jews had joined the Nationalsozialistische Lehrerbund, the Nazi organization of teachers. By 1936, 32 percent belonged to the party itself. All teachers had to attend a month-long training course organized by the National Socialist German Workers' Party (NSDAP, Nazi Party). After 1933 pupils of non-Aryan origin were allowed to attend German schools only as a privilege, and by June 1942 Jewish children were excluded entirely.

Changes in the curriculum were more difficult to institute, with thoroughgoing Nazification hampered by rivalries between the Ministry of Education and Rudolf Hess's Central Office. Progress was predictably haphazard, and the censorship of textbooks only brought under central control in 1938. History and geography were recast in accord with racial doctrine, and

German history was studied to the exclusion of any other and supplemented by special courses on the history of the Nazi Party. Literature was categorized to stress blood ties and a sense of racial community, and religious education was replaced by a motley collection of nationalist ideas. Biology was revised to accord with racial doctrines, and those leaving school at fourteen were given a ten-point eugenic plan for life, urging Germans to produce as many children as possible. On girls' education Hitler had been uncharacteristically succinct: "The goal of female education must invariably be the future mother" (Hitler 1992, p. 377). Most girls accordingly learned little but domestic science and left schools with a dead-end qualification known dismissively as the "Pudding Matric."

In accord with Hitler's injunction that "the school in a folkish state must create infinitely more free time for physical training" (Hitler 1992, p. 372), enormous stress was placed on physical education, up to five hours a day, at the expense of academic education. This exacerbated the latent conflict between schools and the Hitler Youth (HJ). School authorities had to be ordered to grant pupils leave to attend HJ functions, and in certain cases special crammers were found to push active members through their exams.

The establishment of specialist or elite schools was similarly hampered by rivalries. The Nationalpolitische Erziehunganstalten (national political educational institutes, or Napolas for short), partly modeled on the old Prussian cadet academies, were created in 1933 by the Education Ministry to produce the next generation of party and army leaders. In 1936 control of the Napolas was handed over to the SS, and by 1942 there were more than forty throughout the Reich. With their emphasis on physical expertise, ideological correctness, and the acquisition of mechanical skills, they were rivals to the equally nonacademic Adolf Hitler Schools as training centers for the future political elite. In fact, the majority of Napola graduates entered the armed forces.

Boys leaving school at the age of eighteen normally then spent three years in the Labor Service or the Wehrmacht and another four years working for a professional qualification. A chosen few then proceeded to one of the four *Ordensburgen* (castles of the order), intended as the Nazi equivalents of West Point or Sandhurst but built in remote and romantic settings, where their bodies rather than their minds were trained in an atmosphere heavy with pseudomedieval chivalry. But once again Nazi ideology ruined any possibility of positive achievement: intellectual standards in the *Ordensburgen* were poor, and many graduates failed even to get a commission in the Wehrmacht.

Related entries: Catholic Church; Eugenics; Hitler Schools; Hitler Youth; Labor Service; Science and Scientists; Universities; Women; Youth Policy

Suggestions for further reading:
Bullock, Alan. 1991. *Hitler and Stalin: Parallel Lives.* London: HarperCollins.
Freeman, Michael. 1995. *Atlas of Nazi Germany: A Political, Economic and Social Anatomy of the Third Reich.* 2nd ed. London and New York: Longman.
Grunberger, Richard. 1971. *A Social History of the Third Reich.* London: Weidenfeld and Nicolson.
Hitler, Adolf. 1992. *Mein Kampf.* Trans. Ralph Manheim. Intro. by D. C. Watt. London: Pimlico.

Eichmann, Adolf (1906–1962)

The man who took primary responsibility for the implementation of the Final Solution in Europe was born in the Rhineland but spent his youth in Hitler's "hometown" of Linz. While working as a traveling salesman, he came under the influence of Ernst Kaltenbrunner and joined the Austrian Nazi Party in 1932. The following year, after losing his job, he crossed the border to Bavaria, where he trained with the exiled Austrian SS legion near Passau and in 1934 at Dachau concentration camp. In September 1934 Eichmann was sent to Berlin and put his bureaucratic talents to work in the head office of the Sicherheitsdienst, joining the newly established Jewish Affairs Department in 1935 and specializing in the Zionist movement. In 1937 he visited Palestine to explore the possibility of Jewish emigration from Germany but opposed the creation of a Jewish state as contrary to German national interest.

Eichmann's big opportunity came with the Anschluss. In August 1938 he was sent to Vienna and put in charge of the Office for Jewish Emigration, swiftly acquiring his ignoble expertise in "forced emigration" and extortion. In March 1939 he moved to Prague to effect the deportation of Czech Jews to Poland. On the creation of the Reich Main Security Office (RSHA) in September 1939, Eichmann took charge of the section of the Gestapo dealing with Jewish affairs and evacuation. His Referat IV B4 was to become the headquarters for the realization of the Final Solution. He took part in the Wannsee Conference of January 1942, where his position as the "Jewish specialist" of the RSHA was confirmed and he was formally entrusted with carrying out the mass extermination of the Jews.

In comparison with Hitler and other Nazis, Eichmann had never appeared to be a fanatical anti–Semite, but he set about his task, arranging and scheduling the transport of Jews to the extermination camps, with bureaucratic zeal and steely determination. He constantly complained of and set about removing all obstacles, loopholes such as the existence of Vichy France, and lack of cooperation from the Italians and other German allies. The desk-murderer came into the open only in early 1944, when he went to Budapest to supervise personally the deportation of half a million Hungarian Jews following the German occupation of its former ally. But the name of Eichmann was still not yet widely known, and though arrested at the end of the war, he managed to escape from a U.S. internment camp in 1946 and eventually fled to Argentina.

Eichmann was tracked down by Israeli secret agents in May 1960, living under an assumed name in a suburb of Buenos Aires. He was secretly abducted to Israel and put on public trial in Jerusalem. The case aroused enormous international interest and some controversy. The sight of the insignificant-looking Eichmann in the dock caused Hannah Arendt to make her famous comment about the "banality of evil." On 2 December 1961 Eichmann was sentenced to death for crimes against the Jewish people and crimes against humanity and was hanged on 31 May 1962. By the nature of his end and the evidence produced at his trial, Eichmann became a symbol of the kind of conscienceless bureaucrat who transformed Hitler's fantasies into horrifying reality.

Related entries: Austria; Extermination Camps; Final Solution; Holocaust; Hungary; Jews and Jewish Policy; Kaltenbrunner, Ernst; Wannsee Conference

Suggestions for further reading:
Arendt, Hannah. 1984. *Eichmann in Jerusalem.* New York: Penguin.
Gilbert, Martin. 1985. *The Holocaust: A History of the Jews during the Second World War.* New York: Holt, Rinehart, and Winston.
Von Lang, Jochen. 1983. *Eichmann Interrogated.* New York: Farrar, Straus and Giroux.

Eisenhower, Dwight David (1890–1969)

Enjoying a unique degree of respect among Allied generals built on an already varied and distinguished career and

General Dwight D. Eisenhower during the liberation of Paris in August 1944. Eisenhower's passion for finding a consensus among his generals often led to friction, but his judgment was more often right than wrong. (Culver Pictures)

on exceptional diplomatic skills, Eisenhower made a singular contribution to the defeat of Hitler. Appointed to command U.S. forces in the European Theater of Operations in June 1942, he created an effective U.S.-British team at Allied Force Headquarters, navigating successfully through a sea of national interests and egoism—British, U.S., and French—in the North African campaign and the early stages of the invasion of Italy. As supreme allied commander of the Allied Expeditionary Force from December 1943, Eisenhower's diplomatic skills were often tested to the uttermost in weaving a heterogeneous bunch of troops and commanders, including such flamboyant and egotistical characters as George Patton and Bernard Montgomery, into an operational entity capable of advancing into Germany. A popular hero in

the United States, after Hitler's defeat Eisenhower was appointed supreme commander of the North Atlantic Treaty Organization and in 1952 and 1956 was elected the 34th president of the United States.

Related entries: Bulge, Battle of the; Normandy Landings; North Africa; United States of America

El Alamein, Battle of

*T*he small coastal town and railway stop of El Alamein, some 50 miles west of Alexandria, Egypt, marked the line of the North African front between June and October 1942. When the British 8th Army under its new commander, General

Troops of the British and Commonwealth 8th Army advance during the first battle of El Alamein, July 1942. Under General Sir Claude Auchinleck, the 8th Army prevented Erwin Rommel's Panzer Army Africa from breaking through toward the Suez Canal and the conquest of Egypt. (Archive Photos)

Bernard Montgomery, enjoying a numerical advantage and intelligence superiority, drove Erwin Rommel's Panzer Group Afrika out of El Alamein and scurrying back toward Tunisia in the first few days of November, it had a huge effect on British morale. Winston Churchill was to write: "Before Alamein we never had a victory. After Alamein we never had a defeat" (Churchill 1948–1954, pp. iv, 603). Taken in conjunction with the battle of Stalingrad, the Allied landings in Morocco and Algeria, and the U.S. victory over the Japanese at Guadalcanal, it showed that the tide of war was at last turning against Hitler and his allies.

Related entries: Montgomery, Bernard Law; North Africa; Rommel, Erwin

Suggestions for further reading:
Churchill, Winston S. 1948–1954. *The Second World War.* 6 vols. Boston: Houghton Mifflin.

Elections

Hitler never won a majority in any free election. At the peak of his fortunes before coming to power, just over one-third of German voters supported the Nazis. Before 1929 the National Socialist German Workers' Party (NSDAP, Nazi Party) was a fringe party, winning 3 percent of the votes in the Reichstag elections of 1924, when Hitler was in prison, and 2.6 percent in 1928. Hitler's breakthrough came in the elections of September 1930: the number of Nazi votes rose from 800,000 to 6.4 million, their percentage vote from 2.6 percent to 18.3 percent, and seats in the Reichstag from twelve to 107. The trend continued in provincial elections in 1931, reaching a peak of 37.2 percent in Oldenburg.

Five major elections were held in 1932. In the first ballot of the presidential elections on 13 March, Hitler won 31.1 percent of the vote and 36.8 percent in the second ballot of 10 April. In May the Nazis won 36.6 percent in the Prussian election and reached 37.3 percent in the Reichstag election on 31 July, the highest percentage they ever won in a free election. They were now the largest group in parliament, with 230 seats. But in the election of 6 November 1932 the vote fell to 33.1 percent and the number of seats to 196. They were still the strongest party, but nearly 2 million people had either abandoned the Nazis or not voted. It was against this background that Hitler came to power.

Reasons for changing electoral fortunes are largely a matter of guesswork. When the Nazis made their breakthrough in 1930 the big losers were the right-wing "bourgeois" parties, but Hitler probably attracted as much, if not more, support from former nonvoters and young first-time voters. In 1932 the new Nazi votes must have come from the other right-wing and center parties. Disillusioned Social Democrats turned rather to the Communists, the other great gainers in the elections. The analysis of the regional geography of the elections by Richard F. Hamilton (1982) suggests that while the Nazis drew support from all social classes, they gained their highest vote among the middle classes rather than the working class or the unemployed.

The simultaneous rise in support for Hitler and in unemployment does not mean that the impoverished came to support the Nazis. They were more likely to turn to the Communists or remain loyal to the Social Democratic Party (SPD). It would appear, rather, that economic crisis, fear of impoverishment, and the continuing advance of the Communist Party drove more and more middle-class voters into Hitler's embrace. This may have been offset by distrust of the NSDAP's socialist tendencies, but the party's program remained vague, and it was above all Hitler's personal party. It was in all probability the figure of the Führer himself, promising strong and charismatic leadership, that caused people freely to give their vote to the Nazis.

Related entries: Berlin; Center Party; Communist Party; German Democratic Party; German National People's Party; German People's Party; Harzburg Front; Middle Classes; National Socialist German Workers' Party; Nazi Movement; Propaganda; Reichstag; Social Democratic Party; Socialism; Weimar Republic; Working Class

Suggestions for further reading:
Childers, Thomas. 1983. *The Nazi Voter: The Social Foundations of Fascism in Germany, 1919–1933.* Chapel Hill: University of North Carolina Press.
Hamilton, Richard F. 1982. *Who Voted for Hitler?* Princeton: Princeton University Press.

Elser, Georg (1903–1945)

The Saxon carpenter Elser came nearer to assassinating Hitler than anyone before the July Plot of 1944. Remarkably, acting entirely alone, Elser succeeded in spending thirty or more nights in the beer hall in Munich where Hitler celebrated the anniversary of the 1923 putsch every November, inserting a powerful explosive device in a hollowed-out stone pillar. Hitler's life was saved only because he decided to leave the meeting earlier than usual. On 8 November 1939 the bomb went off seven minutes after he had left, killing eight people and injuring sixty. Elser was arrested immediately, but the Gestapo wasted time trying to connect him to an opposition network or foreign secret service. He was sent to Dachau concentration camp, where the interrogation continued, but for some unknown reason he was not executed until near the end of the war.

Related entries: Opposition

Enabling Act

The "Act for the Removal of Distress from People and Reich," or Enabling Act of March 1933, set the seal on National Socialist power, ended the influence of the Reichstag, and was the beginning of the end for the other political parties. The election of 5 March had not provided the Nazis with the necessary two-thirds majority to change the constitution. The Communist deputies were in prison, but Hitler still needed the support of the nationalist German National People's Party and the Center Party. Still believing that Hitler's onslaught was directed solely against the Left, the deputies of the Right did not realize that they would be next.

In the face of Hitler's bullying and ranks of Sturmabteilung men filling the Reichstag with chants of "We want the Enabling Act, or there'll be hell to pay," only members of the Social Democratic Party (SPD) summoned up the courage to oppose the passage of the act. A speech by the SPD chairman, Otto Wels, provoked Hitler to a furious riposte: "I can only tell you: I do not want you to vote for it. Germany shall be free, but not through you!" (Bullock 1991, p. 353). The act was passed by 441 votes to 94.

The Enabling Act gave the government power to alter the constitution, authorized the cabinet to enact laws, bestowed the right to draft legislation on the chancellor, and gave the cabinet the power to implement treaties with foreign states. The act, limited initially to four years, was renewed without discussion in 1937 and 1939 and by Führer decree in 1943. Hitler was still far from possessing the absolute power he craved but was no longer dependent on votes in the Reichstag, and his right-wing partners had ignominiously voted for their own destruction.

Related entries: Center Party; German National People's Party; *Gleichschaltung;* Reichstag; Social Democratic Party

Suggestions for further reading:
Bullock, Alan. 1991. *Hitler and Stalin: Parallel Lives.* London: HarperCollins.

Eugenics

The term "eugenics," meaning the science of "fine breeding," had been coined in the late nineteenth century by Francis Galton, a cousin of Charles Darwin. During its long and complex history in Germany, Europe, and the United States, its scientific and "progressive" nature appealed to people across the political spectrum, and it was associated as much with socialism and left-wing social movements as with the extreme Right. Hitler's enthusiasm for "racial hygiene," therefore, had nothing to do with his fondness for quackery and "alternative" medicine but was put into practice by respectable mainstream scientists inspired by international examples. Even the most notorious Nazi doctors, such as Josef Mengele, had won international reputations before the war.

Positive eugenics encouraged reproduction by the physically and mentally "healthy," whereas negative eugenics sought to curb the fertility of the "unfit" through voluntarily or compulsory sterilization. Various U.S. states, including California, introduced eugenic legislation that gave Hitler food for thought. "I have studied with great interest," he declared, "the laws of several American states concerning prevention of reproduction by people whose progeny would, in all probability, be of no value or be injurious to the racial stock" (Burleigh 1997, p. 158). His reading of eugenic literature even allowed him to present his ideas in a humanitarian or progressive light, writing in *Mein Kampf:* "The demand that defective people be prevented from propagating equally defective offspring is a demand of the clearest reason and if systematically executed represents the most human act of mankind. . . . The passing pain of a century can and will redeem millenniums from suffering" (Hitler 1992, p. 232). His "contribution" was to associate eugenics permanently with racism and anti-Semitism and to introduce genetic legislation of unprecedented extent to ensure the "victory of the better and stronger." He turned eugenics into a prelude to euthanasia and eventually racial extermination.

Walther Darré expressed the purpose of Nazi legislation: "We shall gather together the best blood. Just as we are now breeding our Hanover horse from the few remaining pure-blooded male and female stock, so we shall see the same type of breeding over the next generation of the pure type of Nordic German" (Welch 1993, p. 67). A variety of eugenic laws put policy into practice. The Law for the Prevention of Genetically Diseased Offspring of July 1933 made sterilization compulsory for persons with hereditary diseases, habitual criminals, the mentally retarded, and the mentally ill. So-called Hereditary Health Courts decided who should be sterilized, while the Interior Ministry drew up elaborate charts demonstrating that the state could not afford to let "asocials" such as beggars and vagrants to reproduce. A Law for the Protection of Hereditary Health in 1935 ordered the registration of individuals deemed to be of "lesser racial value" and banned marriage between people burdened with "genetic infirmities." Between 360,000 and 400,000 German citizens said to be suffering from hereditary complaints, including "feeblemindedness," al-

coholism, epilepsy, and manic depression, were forcibly sterilized under the Third Reich, mostly before 1939.

The obsession with "racial hygiene" pervaded public policy, affecting women, workers, and farmers as well as Jews, Gypsies, and other racial "undesirables." Social problems were reduced to biology, in a conscious reversal of the "Marxist" emphasis on environmental factors. "Aryan" women were urged to produce as many children as possible and given generous financial rewards. The SS forced its members to marry women of proven Aryan stock, while its Lebensborn organization took care of illegitimate but racially pure children. Eugenics and racial biology were incorporated into the national curriculum at all levels of education; "racial hygiene" formed one of the bases of medical training; and racial hygiene institutes were established in almost half the universities of Germany. The finale of the film *The Eternal Jew* summed it up: "The eternal law of nature, to keep the race pure, is the legacy which the National Socialist movement bequeaths to the German people in perpetuity. It is in this spirit that the nation of German people marches into the future" (Welch 1993, p. 80). The real legacy of the horrors of Hitler's regime, however, was to discredit eugenics permanently. The Nazi analogy continues to inform (or as often misinform) debates about genetic engineering and medical ethics.

Related entries: *Blut und Boden;* Education; Euthanasia; Nuremberg Laws; Racial Theory; Schutzstaffel; Science and Scientists; Universities; *Volksgemeinschaft;* Women

Suggestions for further reading:
Aly, Götz, Peter Chroust, and Christian Pross. 1994. *Cleansing the Fatherland: Nazi Medicine and Racial Hygiene.* Baltimore, MD: Johns Hopkins University Press.
Burleigh, Michael. 1997. *Ethics and Extermination: Reflections on Nazi Genocide.* Cambridge: Cambridge University Press.
Hitler, Adolf. 1992. *Mein Kampf.* Trans. Ralph Manheim. Intro. by D. C. Watt. London: Pimlico.

Kühl, Stefan. 1994. *The Nazi Connection: Eugenics, American Racism, and German National Socialism.* New York: Oxford University Press.

Proctor, Robert N. 1988. *Racial Hygiene: Medicine under the Nazis.* Cambridge, MA: Harvard University Press.

Weindlung, Paul. 1989. *Health, Race and German Politics between National Unification and Nazism, 1870–1945.* Cambridge: Cambridge University Press.

Welch, David. 1993. *The Third Reich: Politics and Propaganda.* London and New York: Routledge.

Euthanasia

The Nazis were not the only proponents of euthanasia in interwar Germany, but when war broke out they put theory into practice as the first step in a process culminating in mass murder on an unprecedented scale. Hitler had advocated sterilization of the mentally ill, the "degenerate" and the "racially unfit" in *Mein Kampf,* and the first sterilization law was passed in July 1933. In 1935 Hitler announced that, in the event of war, euthanasia would be ordained for certain categories of the mentally ill, and the case for "mercy killing" was shown in the film *Ich Klage an* (I accuse, 1941).

Registration of malformed children was made compulsory in August 1939, and in September a circular sent out to all asylums and clinics in Germany ordered the registration of patients unfit for employment. Then by a secret decree of October 1939, Hitler ordered the medical killing of "life unworthy of life," children as well as adults. Known as T4, the euthanasia program was run from an anonymous villa in the Tiergarten area of Berlin, with Philipp Bouhler in charge overall. Selection for extermination was arbitrary. Some doctors refused to take part, which was accepted so long as they did not criticize the program publicly, but many others participated for reasons of professional advancement.

When the program began in the autumn of 1939, killing by carbon monoxide gas was chosen as the preferred method, and the first Nazi gas chamber was designed by Christian Wurth of the SS Criminal Police. Several asylums were equipped with chambers; the first mass killings took place in Pomerania and East Prussia; and while fake death certificates were sent to the families of those killed, their bodies were removed by SS men and burnt in ovens. Elaborate procedures were instituted to keep the killings secret, but news of the sudden deaths of handicapped children and relatives began to spread from family to family. By 1941 T4's work had become an open secret and provoked opposition led by church leaders, both Protestant and Catholic. In August 1941 the Catholic bishop of Münster, Cardinal August von Galen, preached a famous sermon invoking the wrath of God on those who were killing the innocent. Galen's courageous act, which reflected widespread public feeling openly expressed, particularly by Catholics, led to the official suspension of the program before the month was out.

Between October 1939 and August 1941, T4 killed more than 70,000 people. The halting of the euthanasia program is a unique case of the Nazi regime giving in to public opinion, led by the churches. From now on mass killing would be perpetrated outside the boundaries of the old Reich. But aspects of the program did continue on the initiative of particular institutions and doctors. Killing by drugs or starvation disposed of such "useless eaters" as mentally ill children, "insubordinate" psychiatric patients, and, it was strongly rumored, badly wounded soldiers.

The T4 program had a direct bearing on the mass murder of the Holocaust. The gas chamber had been invented, and doctors had been involved in secret procedures tortuously justified as "healing work," merciful to the individual and in the interests of the eugenic health of the community. The treatment of Jewish patients indicates the link. The normal criteria for killing were incurable disease, mental deficiency, schizophrenia, and length of hospitalization. But from April 1940 all Jewish inmates of German mental hospitals were put to death merely because they were Jews and so carriers of a racial infection that had to be eliminated.

Related entries: Bouhler, Philipp; Brack, Viktor; Brandt, Karl Rudolf; Catholic Church; Eugenics; Final Solution; Protestant Churches; Public Opinion; War Crimes

Suggestions for further reading:
Burleigh, Michael R. 1994. *Death and Deliverance: "Euthanasia" in Germany 1900–1945.* Cambridge: Cambridge University Press.
Sereny, Gita. 1974. *Into That Darkness: From Mercy Killing to Mass Murder.* London: Deutsch.

Extermination Camps

*T*he infamous death camps applied the technology of killing tested in the T4 euthanasia campaign to the creation of an efficient system of mass murder and extermination of the Jews. The slaughter of Soviet Jews by shooting was inefficient and had a psychologically debilitating effect on the perpetrators. Even Heinrich Himmler had become physically sick after witnessing SS actions at Minsk in 1941, and alcoholism and psychological problems were widespread among the killing units. In the late summer of 1941, therefore, experiments with poison gas were conducted by the SS at several locations in occupied eastern Europe. Mobile gas vans, using carbon monoxide, were first used in October 1941 to kill the wives and children of Jewish hostages in Serbia and in December went into systematic operation at Chelmno, 40 miles northwest of Lodz.

More than 150,000 Jews, mostly from the Lodz ghetto, were gassed at Chelmno in 1942. A different kind of gas, a powerful pesticide known as Zyklon-B, was first used on 900 Soviet prisoners of war at Auschwitz on 3 September 1941. Four other extermination camps went into operation in 1942: Sobibor; Treblinka; Belzec, where 600,000 Jews were killed using carbon monoxide before it was dismantled at the end of 1942; and Majdanek, originally a prisoner of war camp on the outskirts of Lublin, where both Zyklon-B and carbon monoxide were used in the murder of some 200,000 people, including at least 60,000 Jews, between the summer of 1942 and July 1944, when it was liberated by the Red Army.

Related entries: Auschwitz; Final Solution; Holocaust; Sobibor; Treblinka

Suggestions for further reading:
Cesarani, David, ed. 1994. *The Final Solution: Origins and Implementation.* London: Routledge.

Fascism

Hitler's relationship to fascism is difficult to characterize in a definitive manner. Was Nazism the German version of the broader international phenomenon of "fascism," or was it unique, a specifically German and Hitlerian creation unbeholden to foreign examples? It is difficult to arrive at any exact definition of fascism. Part of the broad appeal of Benito Mussolini's movement in Italy was that it contained so many contradictory elements, including ideas from Left and Right, radical and conservative. Until the introduction of the anti-Semitic Racial Laws in 1938, a sign of Mussolini's growing dependence on Hitler, many Italians could find whatever they were looking for in fascism. Movements imitating Italian fascism grew up all over Europe in the 1920s and 1930s, most strongly in Spain, Portugal, Romania, and Hungary. In Spain the fascist Falange became one of the pillars of General Francisco Franco's authoritarian regime. All had national characteristics of their own. In the case of Nazism it can be argued that these characteristics were so strong as to make it a unique kind of movement.

The basic features of fascism are extreme nationalism, antidemocratic authoritarianism, anti-Marxism and anti-socialism, militarism and devotion to the martial virtues, and an attachment to the "national community" transcending class differences. Fascism had no economic theories and plundered ideas from Right and Left for its rather woolly notion of the "corporate state." To attain power, Mussolini, like Hitler after him, could exploit a frustrated nationalism and sense of national injustice; a perceived threat from the Marxist Left; and economic difficulties, the post-1918 crisis in Italy for Mussolini, the Depression for Hitler. Both men could appeal across all classes, but especially to the traditional middle classes, squeezed between big capitalism and organized labor.

"The novelty of Fascism," says a recent historian, "lay in the military organization of a political party" (Lyttelton 1987, p. 52). Hitler certainly learned from this. He recruited former soldiers for the Sturmabteilung as Mussolini had for his *squadristi* and used them for similar violent purposes in clearing his opponents from the streets. Mussolini had shown how to gain power through a mixture of force and constitutional means. The Fascist seizure of power told Hitler that anything was possible and provided a lesson in how to win over conservatives before ousting them. But Hitler was too arrogant to be a slavish imitator, and the failure of the Beer Hall Putsch in 1923 taught him the dangers of being derivative. There could be no March on Berlin as there had been a March on Rome, itself an event mythologized by fascist ideology. So Hitler thereafter built up a political machine vastly superior to the Italian Fascist Party or any fascist movement, which enabled him to carry through a "revolution from above" far more swiftly and thoroughly than Mussolini.

Mussolini declared in 1933: "The victory of Hitler is also our victory" (Mack Smith 1981, p. 181). The two dictators were also to an extent competitors, and Hitler could not admit too great a debt to fascism. The Nazis did not take part in the ephemeral Fascist International of 1934. In anti-German moments Mussolini could claim that the two movements had nothing in common and that Hitler was "an ideologue who talks more than he governs" (Mack Smith 1981, p. 183). Italian fascism, though xenophobic, was not fundamentally anti-Semitic until 1938, even if racism was undoubtedly a logical consequence of fascist nationalism. Nazism can be seen as a "variety of fascism," but a very special variety. The centrality of anti-Semitism in Hitler's worldview set him apart from Italian fascism and closer to other nonfascist traditions and groups. And the overweening ambitions of his German nationalism would not be acceptable to people otherwise sympathetic to his anti-Marxism and racial worldview. Some French fascists joined the anti-German Resistance after 1940. In the world of extreme right political movements and ideas, Hitler occupies a place uniquely his own.

Related entries: Charismatic Domination; Economic Policy; Führer Principle; Italy; Middle Classes; Mussolini, Benito; Nazi Movement; Socialism; Spain; *Volksgemeinschaft*

Suggestions for further reading:
Bessel, Richard, ed. 1996. *Fascist Italy and Nazi Germany: Comparisons and Contrasts.* Cambridge: Cambridge University Press.
de Grand, Alexander J. 1995. *Fascist Italy and Nazi Germany: The "Fascist" Style of Rule.* London and New York: Routledge.
Knox, MacGregor. 1984. "Conquest, Foreign and Domestic, in Fascist Italy and Nazi Germany," *Journal of Modern History* 56, pp. 1–57.
Laqueur, Walter, ed. 1976. *Fascism: A Reader's Guide.* Berkeley: University of California Press.
Lyttelton, Adrian. 1987. *The Seizure of Power: Fascism in Italy 1919–1929.* 2nd ed. London: Weidenfeld and Nicolson.
Mack Smith, Denis. 1981. *Mussolini.* London: Weidenfeld and Nicolson.
Turner, Henry Ashby, Jr., ed. 1975. *Reappraisals of Fascism.* New York: New Viewpoints.
Woolf, Stuart J., ed. 1969. *The Nature of Fascism.* New York: Random House.
———. 1981. *Fascism in Europe.* London: Methuen.

Feder, Gottfried (1883–1941)

The ideas of the engineer and economist Feder, born in Würzburg on 27 January 1883, had a great if short-lived influence on Hitler during the early years of the Nazi movement. Feder's notion of "interest slavery," blaming international finance for Germany's postwar economic chaos, was incorporated into the original National Socialist German Workers' Party platform of 1920. His peculiar and eclectic form of socialism had been developed in the German Workers' Party, and for several years Hitler continued to look upon him as a guide in economic matters. As the Nazi movement grew Feder became a leader of its populist and anti-industrial wing, and as a deputy in the Reichstag in 1924 he called for the expropriation of Jewish property and large landed estates as well as a freeze on interest rates.

Feder's quasi-socialist ideas, however, jeopardized the potential support for Hitler among big industrialists. Both Hjalmar Schacht and Walther Funk warned Hitler that his schemes would ruin the German economy. Along with the rest of the Nazi "Left," Feder had little future in a Germany dominated by Hitler. On Hitler's accession to power, therefore, he was given the insignificant post of undersecretary in the Ministry of Economic Affairs and exerted little influence. Dismissed in December

1934, he retired into private life and died in Murnau in January 1941.

Related entries: German Workers' Party; Nazi Movement; Socialism

Final Solution

Plans for the total extermination of all the Jews of Europe took shape during the summer of 1941, but the precise nature of the process and Hitler's role in it will always be obscure and have given rise to different interpretations by historians. There is no single document signed by Hitler ordering the "final solution" of the Jewish question, but that was not how the Nazi system operated. Hitler had "prophesied" in 1939 that a new war would lead to "the destruction of the Jewish race in Europe," but there is only indirect evidence as to exactly how and when the decision to adopt a policy of extermination was taken.

Broadly speaking, two different interpretations are possible: either Hitler had always planned the annihilation of the Jews, and the Final Solution was merely a question of timing and opportunity; or the Final Solution was the end product of a cumulative process of radicalization shown in the massacres of Jews in eastern Europe. What is not in doubt is that the decision to attack the Soviet Union marked the most significant turning point in policy toward the Jews. Hitler's plans for eastern Europe involved its resettlement by millions of Germans, with the Slav population reduced to the position of slave laborers and no place for Jews. The extinction of the Jewish population, by whatever method, was an essential component of Hitler's racist imperialism.

By the summer of 1941 Hitler had decided upon the destruction of European Jews. Adolf Eichmann told his Israeli interrogators in 1960 that during that summer,

Reinhard Heydrich told him: "The Führer has ordered the physical extermination of the Jews" (Bullock 1991, p. 841). In August Heinrich Himmler approved a general plan involving the use of gas chambers in extermination camps, which were under construction by October. The Final Solution was thus set in motion before serious anxieties set in about military defeat and was uninfluenced by practical considerations about the use of resources. Those like Eichmann who needed to know that the orders were approved by Hitler were told personally in secret, but Hitler signaled his personal involvement to the Nazi faithful by making frequent public references to his "prophecy" of 1939. The Final Solution was to be implemented not in Germany but in Poland and Russia, from where news could be tightly controlled. The industrialization of mass murder was set in motion within the space of a few months, and the problems of scale settled at the Wannsee Conference in January 1942.

Only Hitler could have conceived of such a bizarre, grandiose, and vile scheme as the Final Solution. His approval cut through the conflicting interests of the SS and party bosses in eastern Europe and legitimized the actions of his subordinates. Only his determination in the service of his twisted imagination could ensure that the fantasy would be translated into reality. Important as it is to try to establish the exact course of events despite gaps in the documentation, arguments about the precise degree of his responsibility are almost inconsequential in view of the subsequent horrors of the Holocaust. Hiding in his bunker amid the ruins of his hopes in 1945, he found a kind of consolation in the thought that the "Jewish problem" had been solved and that he had been responsible for the solution.

Related entries: Anti-Semitism; Auschwitz; Extermination Camps; Holocaust; Jews and Jewish Policy; Wannsee Conference

Suggestions for further reading:
Breitman, Richard. 1991. *The Architect of Genocide: Himmler and the Final Solution.* London: Bodley Head.
Browning, Christopher. 1992. *Paths to Genocide: Essays on Launching the Final Solution.* Cambridge: Cambridge University Press.
Bullock, Alan. 1991. *Hitler and Stalin: Parallel Lives.* London: HarperCollins.
Fleming, Gerald. 1984. *Hitler and the "Final Solution."* Berkeley: University of California Press.
Friedlander, Henry. 1995. *The Origins of Nazi Genocide: From Euthanasia to the Final Solution.* Chapel Hill: University of North Carolina Press.

Finland

Having secured its independence from Russia after World War I and recognized by the Soviet Union in 1920 after a bitter civil war, Finland remained largely isolated in foreign policy during the 1920s and 1930s. The Nazi-Soviet Pact of August 1939 included a secret protocol attaching Finland to the Soviet sphere of interest. Stalin provoked the Winter War of 1939–1940, during which Hitler refused to support Finland but which confirmed his view of the incompetence of the Red Army, held at bay by the comparatively tiny Finnish forces. Totally isolated from the western Allies and threatened by Joseph Stalin, Finland in 1940–1941 moved closer to Germany. During Hitler's invasion of the Soviet Union, Finland pursued its own virtually autonomous war in the north. It joined the Anti-Comintern Pact in November 1941. It was forced to sign a cease-fire with Moscow on 19 September 1944, ceding territory and paying war reparations to the Soviet Union. Finnish independence was secured but was dependent on neutrality and friendly relations with Moscow.

Related entries: Anti-Comintern Pact; Foreign Policy; Mannerheim, Carl Gustav; Nazi-Soviet Pact; Soviet Union

Foreign Policy

Debates about Hitler's foreign policy revolve around three principal overlapping questions. How far did it represent a continuation of traditional Prussian-German policy as opposed to a specifically National Socialist policy? To what extent may it be seen as the working out of a predetermined "program" as opposed to an opportunist reaction to events? And how far was it governed by internal considerations, "domestic policy projected outward," with the aim of stabilizing the regime and providing it with legitimacy and popularity among the people? There is no simple answer to these questions. Power politics, economics, and Hitler's worldview, or ideology, all contributed to giving his foreign policy its peculiar dynamism, but behind them all is aggressive territorial expansion backed by racist justifications.

Proponents of different positions all agree that foreign policy bore Hitler's personal stamp even more than domestic policy and that he considered foreign affairs his special domain and area of expertise. His talent for bluff, bullying, and brinkmanship was given full rein in foreign affairs. Nor is it convincing to argue for a radical change in policy: peaceful and revisionist until 1938, militarist and expansionist thereafter. The fact that his revisionist aims regarding the Treaty of Versailles were shared in the nationalist Right and beyond and enjoyed considerable sympathy in other countries allowed Hitler to pose as a traditional statesman and then pursue his policy without restraints. But his foreign policy was all of one piece and a natural expansion of his worldview. "Foreign policy," he wrote in *Mein Kampf,* "is only a means to an end, and the end is solely the promotion of our own nationality. . . . Partisan, religious, humanitarian, and all other criteria in general, are completely irrelevant" (Hitler 1992, p. 556).

Hitler's success in foreign policy and its popularity up to 1942, despite the bureaucratic chaos of the Nazi regime and the competing agencies and individuals within it, was due to the aura of invincibility imparted by the "Hitler myth" and to a relatively long-lasting consensus about revision of Versailles, restoration of Germany's great-power status in Europe, and antibolshevism. That his aims went beyond peaceful revisionism is shown by the scale of the rearmament program and the efforts to keep it secret, but he had to tread carefully in asserting Germany's position in Europe. The result was a policy based on bilateral agreements to meet immediate objectives, to be broken as soon as it suited Hitler: hence the Concordat with the Vatican (1933); the Nonaggression Pact with Poland (1934); the Anglo-German Naval Agreement (1935); the Berlin-Rome Axis (1936); the Anti-Comintern Pact (1936); the "Pact of Steel" (1939); and the Nazi-Soviet Pact (1939). All these agreements allowed Hitler to take the initiative and become the dominant figure in European politics, but represented necessary tactical and temporary departures from his overall program.

Hitler set himself ever-tighter time pressures for the realization of his goals in foreign policy. The increasingly obvious strains on German economic resources, including raw materials, foreign currency reserves, and labor, imposed by the scale of rearmament also determined the growing overt aggression from 1938 onward. The Anschluss with Austria and then the destruction of Czechoslovakia and Poland were to provide the launching pad for Hitler's grander schemes. What differentiated Hitler's policy from that of earlier German leaders is summed up by John Hiden: "The First World War leaders followed an expansionist policy in the east primarily to help them preserve a conservative reactionary *status quo,* not a racially driven revolution of German then European and, ultimately, world society" (Hiden 1977, p. 161).

The result of such an ideologically driven policy could only be war in the east, though Hitler persisted in thinking that a war on two fronts, east and west, could be avoided. The war he wanted was not the one he got. He was forced in 1938–1939 to exploit the "window of opportunity" provided by the military unpreparedness of Britain and France to pursue "lightning-like" raids against the countries of the east with economic resources and "racially inferior" populations. "For oppressed territories are led back to the bosom of a common Reich, not by flaming protests, but by a mighty sword" (Hitler 1992, p. 558). The ultimate aims were German hegemony in Europe, the destruction of the Soviet Union, and a racial empire in the east. Any remaining calculations in terms of power politics were destroyed by the attack on the Soviet Union. Racist politics triumphed, and any hopes for separate peace settlements were pure illusion. The ultimate result of Hitler's foreign policy, had it been followed to its logical conclusion, would have been the total destruction and collective suicide of the German *Volk.*

Related entries: Anschluss; Anti-Comintern Pact; Appeasement; Austria; Axis; Belgium; Chamberlain, Neville; Churchill, Winston Leonard Spencer; Ciano, Galeazzo, Count; Concordat; Czechoslovakia; Daladier, Edouard; Danzig; Economic Policy; Eden, Anthony; Finland; France; Great Britain; Hossbach Memorandum; Hungary; Italy; Japan; League of Nations; Memel; Middle East; Munich Agreement; Mussolini, Benito; Nationalists; Navy; Nazi-Soviet Pact; Neurath, Konstantin von; Pact of Steel; Poland; Rearmament; Rhineland; Ribbentrop, Joachim von; Romania; Roosevelt, Franklin Delano; Soviet Union; Spain; Stalin, Joseph; Sudetenland; Trade Policy; Tripartite Pact; Turkey; Ukraine; United States of America; Versailles, Treaty of; *Volksdeutsche;* Wehrmacht; Yugoslavia

Suggestions for further reading:

Carr, William. 1972. *Arms, Autarky and Aggression: A Study in German Foreign Policy, 1933–1939.* London: Edward Arnold.
Hiden, John. 1977. *Germany and Europe 1919–1939.* New York: Longman.
Hildebrand, Klaus. 1973. *The Foreign Policy of the Third Reich.* London: Batsford.

Hitler, Adolf. 1992. *Mein Kampf.* Trans. Ralph Manheim. Intro. by D. C. Watt. London: Pimlico.

Weinberg, Gerhard L. 1970. *The Foreign Policy of Hitler's Germany: Diplomatic Revolution in Europe, 1933–1936.* Chicago: University of Chicago Press.

———. 1980. *The Foreign Policy of Hitler's Germany: Starting World War II, 1937–1939.* Chicago: University of Chicago Press.

Four-Year Plan

Announced by Hitler at Nuremberg in 1936, the aim of the Four-Year Plan was to create a "war economy in peacetime," promoting the race for rearmament. The immediate impetus was a crisis in the supply of foodstuffs, raw materials, and fuel during the summer of 1936. Strict controls were imposed on production in an effort to procure products important for rearmament while preventing a fall in the standard of living. The "permanent solution" to such shortages, Hitler declared, lay in autarchy, that is, complete economic self-sufficiency, and he demanded that the German army and the German economy must be ready for war in four years. The economy was to be mobilized for the fulfillment of his aggressive and expansionist policies.

Hermann Goering, although he knew little about economics, was given overall control as "Deputy for the Four-Year Plan." But the plan soon spawned its own bureaucracy, adding one more element into the competing jurisdictions of the Third Reich, and Goering ran into frequent conflict with more orthodox experts, especially Hjalmar Schacht. The supposedly coordinated plan became in reality a series of separate measures and partial planning, hampered by bureaucracy and corruption, with the result that investments lagged some 40 percent behind the declared goals. However, it did achieve a shift in the economy toward the production goods industries, where investment rose to unprecedented levels by 1939.

Although the Four-Year Plan was meant to be comprehensive, it never created a true planned economy. Not only Goering and his cronies but the giant IG Farben concern gained ever more influence within its somewhat confused organization. The failure of the blitzkrieg tactic and subsequent shortage of materials during the invasion of the Soviet Union revealed its weaknesses graphically. In the new economy geared to "total war," planning had once again to be centralized, this time under the direction of Albert Speer.

Related entries: Agriculture; Economic Policy; Goering, Hermann; IG Farben; Industry; Rearmament; Schacht, Hjalmar; Trade Policy

Suggestions for further reading:
Barkai, Avraham. 1990. *Nazi Economics: Ideology, Theory, and Policy.* New Haven: Yale University Press.
Overy, Richard J. 1996. *The Nazi Economic Recovery 1932–1938.* 2nd ed. Cambridge: Cambridge University Press.

France

In Hitler's view, there was no doubt that France was the eternal enemy of the German *Volk.* He wrote in *Mein Kampf:* "The inexorable mortal enemy of the German people is and remains France. It matters not at all who ruled or will rule in France, whether Bourbons or Jacobins, Bonapartists or bourgeois democrats, Clerical republicans or Red Bolshevists: the final goal of their activity in foreign affairs will always be an attempt to seize possession of the Rhine border and to secure the watercourse for France by means of a dismembered and shattered Germany" (Hitler 1992, p. 565). But France was racially degenerate. The spectacle of the African troops stationed by France in the occupied Ruhr and Rhineland fed Hitler's fantasies: "This people, which is basically becoming more and more negrified, constitutes in its tie with the aims of Jewish world domination a menace for the existence of the white race in Europe" (Hitler 1992, p. 569). A new war against France "must and will occur" (p. 615) because of the French aim of dismembering Germany.

It followed that while Hitler could admire the "Anglo-Saxon" British, he only despised the French. The policy of French governments, in turn, was to defend the Versailles settlement in Europe and take a hard line on reparations and revision of the treaty. This made France appear vengeful in its attitude toward Germany, leading to anti-French feeling that could be exploited by the Nazis and other nationalists. With Hitler in power, however, France became the "junior partner" in British appeasement of the Führer. André François-Poncet, French ambassador in Berlin between 1931 and 1938, dedicated himself resolutely to improving Franco-German understanding, earning Hitler's appreciation. Despite these overtures, Hitler could exploit government instability and the defensive mentality of French military leaders. When the feared French reaction to the occupation of the Rhineland in 1936 failed to materialize, Hitler's contempt for the French leadership was confirmed.

Hitler was convinced that French guarantees to the countries of eastern Europe, which France had tried to bind together in the "little entente," would in the end prove worthless. He did not want war with France until he had secured expansion in the east, while the "Maginot mentality" in France encouraged the illusion that the country was safe from his threats. France's pretensions to world-power status seemed belied by impotence over the Spanish Civil War, economic crisis, and an internal political weakness that appeared worse than it actually was. The once dominant power in Europe was simply not asserting itself on the international scene. France was a signatory to the Munich Agreement of 1938 but joined with Britain in giving its guarantee to Poland against Hitler's aggression. In September 1939 Hitler found himself "prematurely" at war.

When Hitler launched his oft-postponed invasion of France in May 1940, the outdated defensive thinking of the French military was cruelly exposed, and his armies swept to an astonishingly easy victory. When the armistice was signed at Compiègne in the same railway carriage in which the French generals had accepted the German surrender in 1918, it was one of the greatest days in Hitler's life. France was shattered and divided. Alsace, Lorraine, and the industrial regions of the extreme north were annexed directly to the Reich, and the rest divided between an occupied zone and the new regime of Marshal Philippe Pétain, with its capital at Vichy. Nice and Savoy came under relatively benign Italian occupation.

Pétain's Vichy regime proclaimed an authoritarian "National Revolution," sweeping away the supposedly "decadent" democracy of the Third Republic, and pursued a policy of collaboration with Hitler. The populations of both zones were divided between two minorities of collaborators and resisters and a majority whose priority was to survive the grave difficulties imposed by the occupation regimes. For Hitler, France was to be used as a reservoir of forced labor and an economic milk cow for the Reich. Thousands of French workers served either voluntarily (in exchange for the release of prisoners of war) or involuntarily in German industry. In 1942, following the Allied landings in French North Africa, Hitler's troops moved into the unoccupied zone, and Vichy became a phantom government totally at Hitler's bidding. French Jews were rounded up by the French authorities in advance of Hitler's orders and dispatched en masse to the extermination camps. But the conscription of young Frenchmen for compulsory labor service in Germany contributed greatly to the growth of an internal Resistance, matching General Charles de Gaulle's external Free French movement.

France, apart from its Jewish inhabitants, did not suffer the same kind of agonies imposed by Hitler on the countries of eastern Europe. But its subordination to German needs led to severe food shortages, and with the growth of Resistance the population suffered bloody reprisals, including such crimes as the destruction of the village of Oradour-sur-Glane by the SS division "Das Reich." Pétain, initially very popular for having saved France from destruction, became widely despised. When de Gaulle and the Free French entered Paris in August 1944, they received an ecstatic welcome. As elsewhere, the long-term gainers from Hitler's policy were the restored democracy of the Fourth Republic and the French Communist Party, dubbed the "party of the Resistance."

Related entries: Alsace-Lorraine; Appeasement; Blitzkrieg; Daladier, Edouard; Darlan, Jean François; de Gaulle, Charles; Dunkirk, Evacuation of; Foreign Policy; Great Britain; Holocaust; Laval, Pierre; Maginot Line; Munich Agreement; Normandy Landings; North Africa; Pétain, Philippe; Phony War; Resistance Movements; Rhineland; Ruhr; Spain; Todt Organization; Versailles, Treaty of; War Crimes

Suggestions for further reading:
Hiden, John. 1977. *Germany and Europe 1919–1939.* New York: Longman.
Hitler, Adolf. 1992. *Mein Kampf.* Trans. Ralph Manheim. Intro. by D. C. Watt. London: Pimlico.
Paxton, Robert O. 1982. *Vichy France: Old Guard and New Order, 1940–1944.* New York: Columbia University Press.

Franco, Francisco (1892–1975)

Francisco Franco Bahamonde was born in El Ferrol, Galicia, in 1892 and was always intended for a military career. He made his reputation as a soldier in leading native troops and the Spanish Foreign Legion in fighting against Rifian

Francisco Franco as leader of the military revolt in Spain in 1936. Franco was to defeat the forces of the Popular Front with German and Italian help but kept his country out of World War II despite Hitler's personal intervention during their meeting at Hendaye in October 1940. (Archive Photos)

rebels in Spanish Morocco. Imbued with authoritarian military values, Franco nevertheless remained aloof from active politics while making no secret of his antidemocratic views and hatred of liberals and Socialists. In 1934, shortly after being promoted to full general, the youngest in Europe, he organized brutally repressive operations against revolutionary strikers in Asturias and Catalonia. When the left-wing Popular Front won the general election of 16 February 1936, Franco was posted into semiexile on the Canary Isles.

As a result Franco was not directly involved in the beginnings of the military rebellion that became the Spanish Civil War. But it was he who, through members of the German business community in Morocco, made a direct appeal to Hitler for planes to carry troops from the colony to Spain. By September 1936 Franco was generalissimo of the Nationalist Armed Forces and head of government of the nationalist state opposed to the republic. While gratefully accepting German and Italian help in winning the civil war, he fought the war in his own way and tolerated no interference from foreigners. His relations with Hitler would never be easy.

When war broke out in Europe, Franco made his pro-Axis sympathies obvious, but he was concerned not to back the losing side, and his policy was always centered on Spain. Franco had little interest in Hitler's plans for eastern Europe; his concern was to further his own expansionist aims in North Africa, against French Morocco and Algeria. Spain's initial stance was neutrality, modified in June 1940 to "nonbelligerence." He would enter the war once Hitler recognized his claims in North Africa and provided Spain with the economic and military aid to place the Spanish army on a war footing. Hitler was exasperated by Franco's seeming ingratitude and pretensions in making conditions for entry into the war. When the two dictators met at Hendaye on the Franco-Spanish border on 23 October 1940, Hitler declared that he would "rather have three or four teeth extracted than go through that again" (Keegan 1989, p. 131). The only result of the meeting was a secret protocol confirming Spain's intention to enter the war on the Axis side, but only when Franco thought the time was ripe.

Hitler came to accept that Spanish "nonbelligerence," modified in July 1941 to the meaningless "moral belligerence," was preferable to Spanish adherence to the Axis. Franco for his part played a double game. He had to mollify those of his supporters who would have been unhappy at joining with the Nazis: pro-Allied monarchists and military men and the immensely influential Catholic Church. He preferred talking and trading with both sides, and the Allies were prepared to put up with his duplicity. Hitler's ambitions were European or global in scope; Franco's were confined to Spain. He sent the Spanish "Blue Legion" of volunteers to fight on the Eastern Front, but he was interested in killing Spanish Communists, not Russians. After the Italian collapse in 1943, Spain returned to "neutral" status in October.

On 24 May 1944 Churchill, speaking in the House of Commons, publicly thanked Franco for not closing the Strait of Gibraltar during the war and in his history of the war paid ironic tribute to the "duplicity and ingratitude of his dealings with Hitler and Mussolini" (Churchill 1948–1954, pp. ii, 530), but the victorious Allies had no illusions about the nature of his regime. Francoist propaganda praising the caudillo's skill in keeping Spain out of the war was dishonest in glossing over Franco's real sympathies. It was not Franco's attitude toward Hitler but the onset of the Cold War that changed U.S. and Allied attitudes toward Franco, transforming him into the "sentinel of the West" during the 1950s. Franco remained in power until his death in 1975, the last authoritarian right-wing dictator in Europe. Totally lacking Hitler's charisma, the two dictators shared many of the same values. Franco continued ranting about the "Judeo-Masonic-communist" conspiracy into the 1960s, but was forced to preside over the political and economic modernization of Spain during the same period. When he died, Spain achieved the transition to a democratic constitutional monarchy with remarkable speed and ease. Ironically, Franco's ultimate legacy may be similar to Hitler's. Spain today, like Germany, is a stable liberal democracy.

Related entries: Condor Legion; Foreign Policy; Spain

Suggestions for further reading:
Churchill, Winston S. 1948–1954. *The Second World War.* 6 vols. Boston: Houghton Mifflin.

Ellwood, Sheelagh. 1994. *Franco.* London and
New York: Longman.
Keegan, John. 1989. *The Second World War.*
London: Hutchinson.
Preston, Paul. 1993. *Franco: A Biography.* London:
HarperCollins.

Frank, Hans (1900–1946)

The Nazi Party's leading jurist, Frank became one of the chief criminals in the reign of terror in Poland during World War II. Born in Karlsruhe, the son of a lawyer, he was studying political economy and law when in 1923 he joined the Sturmabteilung and the National Socialist German Workers' Party (NSDAP, Nazi Party). He took part in the Beer Hall Putsch but in 1926, having temporarily quit the party, qualified as a barrister and began practicing law in Munich. Having rejoined the party in 1927 or 1928, Frank defended NSDAP members, including Hitler, in many legal battles. These cases provided Hitler with numerous opportunities to declare publicly and under oath his strict adherence to legality. A degree of trust developed between Hitler and his personal lawyer, but the Nazi leader never took seriously Frank's ideas of "a renewal of German justice according to the ideas of National Socialist philosophy."

After the Nazi seizure of power in 1933, Frank never became a member of Hitler's inner circle but did accumulate a series of grand-sounding titles: Bavarian minister of justice, Reich leader of the NSDAP (head of the party law division), president of the Academy of German Law, and in 1934 Reich minister without portfolio. Any serious ideas he may have had about reviving German popular law were soon abandoned, and in his numerous speeches to lawyers and students he declared: "The constitutional law of the Third Reich is the legal formulation of the historic intentions of the Führer" (Kershaw 1989, p. 70). For all his status as an "old comrade," Frank's activities as a jurist were peripheral in a state that destroyed the rule of law.

His second, even more barbarous career started when Frank was named head of the Generalgouvernement, the area of central Poland under a separate German administration, in October 1939, an appointment probably best seen as a reward for a loyal party veteran. He was described by Ulrich von Hassell, the former German ambassador in Rome, as "behaving like a megalomaniac pasha." The Poles were treated as slaves of the Greater Reich, to be eliminated as a national entity. Frank ruled from the old royal palace in Kraków, where he lived in extravagant luxury among Poland's ransacked art treasures while the Poles starved. "If I put up a poster for every seven Poles shot," he boasted, "the forests of Poland would not be sufficient to manufacture the paper for such posters." And toward the Jews he was even more brutal. "I ask nothing of the Jews except that they should disappear," he declared in December 1941, adding that "we must destroy the Jews wherever we meet them and whenever opportunity offers" (Wistrich 1982, p. 78).

Frank's rule in Poland, however, was undermined by his constant conflicts with rival authorities, especially Heinrich Himmler's SS. He sought to imitate his beloved Hitler in Poland but seems never to have fully grasped the nature of the system he served with such barbarity. Thus he complained that the extermination policy was robbing his jurisdiction of much-needed labor power, and in July 1942, after the execution for embezzlement of his friend Dr. Carl Lasch of the Academy of German Law, he called for a return to constitutional rule in a series of lectures in German universities. The result was that Frank was stripped of his party honors and legal offices but remained as governor-general of Poland. His criticism of Nazi policy had more to do with asserting his own power than with justice or morality.

Frank's diary for the years 1939 to 1945, published in thirty-eight volumes, shows his desire to model himself on Hitler and his struggle with the SS and the army. Brought to trial at Nuremberg, the "slayer of Poles" admitted his guilt from the beginning, pleading abjectly that "a thousand years will pass and the guilt of Germany will not be erased." He had time to be reconciled to the Catholic Church before being executed as a war criminal in Nuremberg prison on 16 October 1946. Frank was not among the most truly powerful figures of the Third Reich but bears much of the responsibility for the reign of terror in Poland. His pretensions to a refined cultural sensibility only make his cruelty and cynicism as the "butcher of the Poles" even more macabre.

Related entries: Generalgouvernement; Holocaust; Judiciary; Law; Nazi Movement; Nuremberg Trials; Poland; War Crimes

Suggestions for further reading:
Fest, Joachim. 1970. *The Face of the Third Reich: Portraits of the Nazi Leadership.* London: Weidenfeld and Nicolson.
Kershaw, Ian. 1989. *The "Hitler Myth": Image and Reality in the Third Reich.* Paperback ed. New York: Oxford University Press.

Freemasonry

Like other nationalist and *völkisch* critics, Hitler attacked Freemasonry as one of the "cosmopolitan powers" importing "alien" influences into German culture, intimately bound with the Jews. Alfred Rosenberg published *The Crime of Freemasonry* in 1922, and Hitler attacked the institution in *Mein Kampf* as an instrument of the Jewish conspiracy: "To this end he [the Jew] fights with all the tenacity innate in him for religious tolerance—and in Freemasonry, which has succumbed to him completely, he has an excellent instrument with which to fight for his aims and put them across. The government circles and the higher strata of the po-

litical and economic bourgeoisie are brought into his nets by the strings of Freemasonry, and never need to suspect what is happening" (Hitler 1992, p. 285). As a tool of "the Jew," therefore, Freemasonry played the same role in the bourgeoisie as Marxism did among the workers.

There were only about 76,000 freemasons in Germany in 1933, but the nature of Freemasonry was seen as incompatible with the Nazi "folk community" and a betrayal of "racial thinking." By the middle of 1935 most lodges had been harassed into dissolving themselves, and using the Reichstag Fire Decree, the regime closed all remaining Masonic organizations and confiscated lodge property. Masons in public service who had only withdrawn from lodges after 30 January 1933 were excluded from permanent employment, and a Freemasonry Desk was established in the Reich Main Security Office. "Stubborn" adherents of Freemasonry were either sent to concentration camps or conscripted into the army for "frontline testing." Similar measures against Freemasonry were taken in lands occupied during the war.

Suggestions for further reading:
Hitler, Adolf. 1992. *Mein Kampf.* Trans. Ralph Manheim. Intro. by D. C. Watt. London: Pimlico.

Freikorps

Volunteer units known as Free Corps were formed all over Germany by nationalist officers in the aftermath of the defeat of 1918. The Freikorps played a leading role in crushing the Spartacist revolt in Berlin in January 1919 and in overthrowing left-wing governments in the Rhineland and Saxony as well as the "Red" republic in Bavaria. Although paid by the government and acting with its blessing, the ideology of the Freikorps was of a piece with that of the extreme right-wing milieu out of which Hitler emerged. They were disbanded under Allied pressure in 1921 but provided many recruits for Hitler's Sturmabteilung in the early 1920s.

Related entries: Bavaria; Sturmabteilung

Suggestions for further reading:
Waite, Robert G. L. 1952. *Vanguard of Nazism: The Free Corps Movement in Postwar Germany, 1918–1923.* Cambridge, MA: Harvard University Press.

Frick, Wilhelm (1877–1946)

One of Hitler's closest long-term associates and minister of the interior from 1933 to 1943, Frick was born in Alsenz in the Palatinate. After law studies, from 1904 to 1924 he worked as an official in the Munich police, becoming head of the political police section in 1919. As such, he acted as Hitler's liaison at Munich police headquarters. Frick took part in the Beer Hall Putsch in 1923, was arrested, and was sentenced to fifteen months' imprisonment. In 1924, his sentence suspended, he was elected as a National Socialist deputy to the Reichstag.

In January 1930 Frick became the first Nazi to hold ministerial office in a provincial government as minister of the interior, including responsibility for education, in Thuringia. Here his actions gave an early foretaste of what Hitler's rule would mean for Germany. Nazi sympathizers were illegally favored for all state posts, including the police; a special chair created for the Nazi racial theorist, Hans Günther, at the University of Jena; anti-Semitic and militaristic propaganda allowed to flourish; and special "freedom prayers" denouncing "traitors" and "destroyers" introduced in Thuringian schools.

On Hitler's coming to power, Frick was appointed to the key position of minister of the interior, where he was directly responsible for the measures taken against Jews and political opponents of the regime. Frick signed the "coordination" laws abolishing political parties, trade unions, and provincial legislatures and used his legal training to disguise Hitler's crimes in a fog of pseudolegalistic verbiage. He drafted and administered anti-Jewish legislation, including the Nuremberg Laws, as well as the extraordinary law that declared Hitler's actions on the Night of the Long Knives to have been legal and "statesmanlike." Although nominally superior to Heinrich Himmler, he never interfered or placed any serious limits on the activities of the Gestapo and the SS. His oft-repeated dictum that "right is what benefits the German people, wrong is whatever harms them" coincided perfectly with Hitler's own view of his misdeeds.

Frick's function was to provide a mask of legality for *Gleichschaltung,* anti-Jewish policy, and the creation of the police state, ensuring that Hitler's power was consolidated in due legal form. Once this was achieved his importance diminished, and with the coming of war his power was further reduced. However, his bureaucratic skills and legal implementation of even Hitler's most ruthless policies earned him appointment as *Reichsprotektor* of Bohemia and Moravia in August 1943. He held this post until the end of the war, though real power lay with his nominal subordinate Karl-Hermann Frank. At the Nuremberg trials, Frick the legal brain refused to testify but was found guilty of war crimes and crimes against humanity committed in the concentration camps of his protectorate. He was hanged at Nuremberg on 16 October 1946.

Related entries: Beer Hall Putsch; *Gleichschaltung;* Jews and Jewish Policy; Law; Night of the Long Knives; Nuremberg Laws; Nuremberg Trials

Führer Principle (Führerprinzip)

The word *Führer* (leader) had no special meaning in the earliest years of the Nazi Party: all political parties had leaders, and the National Socialist German Workers' Party (NSDAP, Nazi Party) had several. Hitler and Anton Drexler were both referred to as "our Führer." But as Hitler asserted his personal control over the party and with the example of Benito Mussolini as a partial model, personal fidelity to the chosen leader of the future Germany became a defining feature of Nazism. The "German greeting" of "Heil Hitler!" became compulsory within the movement in 1926, and the idea of National Socialism and the person of Hitler became indelibly inseparable. Even those like Gregor Strasser, who retained a certain critical distance from Hitler, saw that the *Führerprinzip* was what held the movement together. "In this ancient German relationship [of leader to companions]," he wrote in 1927, "lies the essence of the structure of the NSDAP" (Kershaw 1998, p. 294).

Once in power, the Hitler cult and its attendant leader principle became the very foundation of the new Germany, and the *Führerprinzip* permeated all levels of government and bureaucracy. The country became a "Führer state" with the "German greeting" as its outward sign. The idea initially designed to instill discipline, stability, and energy into a minority movement was extended into the whole of society. Orthodox systems of administration and control were bypassed or replaced by fidelity to a leader in a new hierarchy stretching upward from *Gauleiters* and Hitler Youth leaders to the Führer himself. The SS, as a state within the state, was based on the same notion.

In essence, the Führer principle replaced bureaucratic structures with individual persons as the final authority. Within the ever more complex organizations of the new state, Nazi leaders could interfere at every level, on the most trivial of pretexts and at their individual whim. Responsibility became confused and blurred; leaders at all levels became corrupt and power hungry; and the resulting chaos made it easier for

the unassailable Hitler both to divide and rule and to distance himself from the innumerable misdeeds of his followers. Behind the façade of a theoretically rigid administrative hierarchy, *Gauleiters* could exploit their regional bases to an extent quite unacceptable in any reasonably based administrative system. Appointed personally by Hitler, the *Gauleiters* were his direct agents in the field, but other Nazi leaders tried to assert their own power and built their own petty empires. While Hitler represented the ultimate and untouchable embodiment of the Führer principle, surrogate personalized leadership permeated the Third Reich. It epitomized the style of Hitler's dictatorship: improvised, confused, open to exploitation by anyone with authority, and built on patronage, not principle.

Related entries: Bureaucracy; Charismatic Domination; Civil Service; Education; Fascism; *Gauleiters;* Hitler Myth; Hitler Youth; Law; Local Government; National Socialism; National Socialist German Workers' Party; Nazi Movement; Nuremberg Rallies; Propaganda; Schutzstaffel; Third Reich

Suggestions for further reading:
Broszat, Martin. 1981. *The Hitler State.* New York: Longman.
Kershaw, Ian. 1993. *The Nazi Dictatorship: Problems and Perspectives of Interpretation.* 3rd ed. London: Edward Arnold.
———. 1998. *Hitler 1889–1936: Hubris.* New York: Allen Lane Penguin Press.

Funk, Walther (1890–1960)

Hitler's minister of economic affairs from 1937 to 1945 was born in East Prussia but made his name as a financial journalist in Berlin during the 1920s. A fervent anti-Marxist and nationalist, Funk joined the Nazi Party and became Hitler's personal economic adviser in 1931. He introduced Hitler to leading industrialists, bankers, and insurance company executives, who saw him as a moderating procapitalist influence within Nazism, and Funk provided a channel through which they could provide finance for the National Socialist German Workers' Party (NSDAP, Nazi Party). In return, he constantly impressed upon Hitler the importance of private initiative and free enterprise. With Funk as chief of the Office for Economic Policy in the party leadership, the voice of heavy industry would never be far from the Führer's ear.

In January 1933 Funk the former journalist was appointed press chief of the Reich government, and in March he became secretary of state in the Ministry of Propaganda and chairman of the board of directors of the Reich Broadcasting Company. He helped Josef Goebbels in creating the Reich Chamber of Culture, of which he became vice president. In November 1937 Funk succeeded Hjalmar Schacht as minister of economics and in January 1939 as president of the Reichsbank. Despite accumulating these many posts, however, and helping to bring some sort of financial order to the early years of the Third Reich, from 1938 onward Funk carried little weight in the higher circles of the Nazi Party. His overt homosexuality and heavy drinking did not help his position, but more important he had no real economic program of his own. By 1944 the real decisions were being taken by Albert Speer.

Indicted at Nuremberg in 1945, Funk protested his innocence, claiming that he had merely been an official carrying out the orders of the Nazi leaders. However, it emerged that he had enriched himself with gold, jewels, and other valuables taken from Jews murdered in the extermination camps and that he was fully aware of their origin. On 1 October 1946 he was sentenced to life imprisonment for war crimes, crimes against peace, and crimes against humanity. Released from Spandau prison on health grounds in 1957, Funk died in Düsseldorf on 31 May 1960.

Related entries: Economic Policy; Industry; Nuremberg Trials; Propaganda; Schacht, Hjalmar; Speer, Albert; Trade Policy; War Crimes

Suggestions for further reading:

Barkai, Avraham. 1990. *Nazi Economics: Ideology, Theory, and Policy.* New Haven: Yale University Press.
Overy, Richard J. 1996. *The Nazi Economic Recovery 1932–1938.* 2nd ed. Cambridge: Cambridge University Press.

G

Gauleiters

The old German term *Gau,* meaning a political or tribal division, survives in many place-names and after 1933 was revived to designate the administrative region defined as the highest "sovereign territory" below the national level of the Reich. Each *Gau* was directed by a *Gauleiter;* its subdivisions were the *Kreis* (district), *Ortsgruppe* (local group), *Zelle* (cell), and *Block.* The thirty-two *Gaue* of Germany became forty with the inclusion of Austria and those parts of Czechoslovakia and Poland integrated directly into Greater Germany. As the "sovereignty bearers" of the Nazi Party in their regions, *Gauleiters* were directly responsible to Hitler. They were often appointed as Reich governors or provincial presidents in order to promote the fusion of the state and the party. Of generally modest social origins and lacking in educational attainment, many of the most notorious *Gauleiters,* such as the extravagant Josef Bürckel of the Westmark, a "party comrade" since 1921, and Adolf Wagner of Munich–Upper Bavaria, probably the most powerful *Gauleiter* of the Third Reich, used their direct contacts with Hitler to exert tyrannical rule in their regions.

Related entries: Local Government; National Socialist German Workers' Party

Generalgouvernement

Established after the Polish campaign, the "Generalgouvernement for the occupied Polish territories," or after July 1940 simply Generalgouvernement, was administered directly by the German government with only very limited Polish participation in administration at the lower levels. Generalgouverneur Hans Frank ruled over the four districts of Kraków, Warsaw, Radom, and Lublin, each with a district governor. Eastern Galicia with Lvov was annexed as the "Galicia District" in August 1941. Frank's fiefdom acted as the reservoir for Polish slave laborers and a dumping ground for Poles displaced from territories annexed to the Reich. After 1942 it was the principal scene for the implementation of the Final Solution. Its industrial and agricultural production was plundered for Hitler's war effort.

The long-term plan was for the majority of Poles to be expelled from the Generalgouvernement and be replaced by German rural settlers. The reality was that while Frank and the civil government tried intermittently and unsuccessfully and for purely practical reasons to mitigate the worst excesses of the occupation policy, the SS and police instigated a reign of terror, and the exploitation of the region resulted in untold misery and brutality. Resistance was organized, but the Warsaw Rising of August 1944 was brutally put down.

Related entries: Frank, Hans; Holocaust; Poland; Resistance Movements; Schutzstaffel; Warsaw Rising

Suggestions for further reading:
Gross, Jan Tomasz. 1979. *Polish Society under German Occupation: The Generalgouvernement.* Princeton: Princeton University Press.

German Christians

Originally an umbrella term used to denote groups sympathetic to Nazism within the Lutheran Evangelical Church, "German Christians" came specifically to refer to the "Faith Movement of German Christians," organized by Wilhelm Kube, *Gauleiter* of the Ostmark. The aim of the German Christians was to create an evangelical Reich church, organized according to the Führer principle and on the basis of race and *Volk*. Before 1933 they were a minority within the Lutheran churches, but the importance attached by Hitler to church affairs in the early years of his rule is shown by his efforts to impose German Christian leadership upon the Lutherans.

In April 1933 Hitler made Ludwig Müller, the chaplain of the Königsberg army corps district who favored the German Christians, his adviser on Protestant church affairs and tried to impose him as the first Reich bishop of the evangelical church. But the representatives of the regional churches instead elected the anti-Nazi Friedrich von Bodelschwingh. However, by use of procedural tricks Bodelschwingh was maneuvered into resigning. Due to Hitler's intervention, new church elections in July 1933 resulted in a victory for the German Christians, and on 27 September Müller was unanimously elected Reich bishop.

Regional churches, however, were not so keen on being "coordinated." The first resist-

ance came in the form of the Pastors' Emergency League, founded by Martin Niemöller. The German Christians reacted with a huge rally at the Berlin Sportspalast. By a vote of 20,000 to 1 they resolved that the German "*Volk* church" had to free itself from "the Old Testament and its Jewish money morality"; that it should present a "heroic image of Jesus"; and that it should exclude non-Aryans from its ranks. German Christian "thinkers" had proved to their own satisfaction that Jesus had not been a Jew but a pure Aryan.

The result of this nonsense was the development of the anti-Nazi Confessing Church, and the German Christians began losing members. Hitler, who had never numbered theology among his principal interests, began to lose interest in them. For all the efforts of the German Christians to ingratiate themselves, he dealt with the churches through negotiation, confrontation, and repression. After 1938 they called themselves "Luther Germans" but were beset by splinter groups and by the hostility of the most anti-Christian of the leading Nazis, most importantly Heinrich Himmler, Martin Bormann, and Alfred Rosenberg. The movement and its publications remained anti-Semitic and nationalist, celebrating the divine rules of *Volk*, state, race, and family. The German Christians ended up as noisy but marginal. With the collapse of the Reich, the movement was banned by the Allies.

Related entries: Anti-Semitism; Confessing Church; *Gleichschaltung;* Protestant Churches

Suggestions for further reading:
Bergen, Doris L. 1996. *Twisted Cross: The German Christian Movement in the Third Reich.* Chapel Hill: University of North Carolina Press.

German Democratic Party (DDP)

Founded in 1918 as a left-liberal "bourgeois" party, the DDP was the third largest party in the early years of the Weimar Republic but constantly lost votes to the German People's Party (DVP) and the Left. By 1928 it had only twenty-five seats in the Reichstag but retained support in the liberal press. Its decline continued, and on 23 March 1933 the last five DDP delegates in parliament voted for Hitler's Enabling Act. The party dissolved itself on 28 June 1933.

Related entries: Enabling Act; Weimar Republic

German Labor Front (DAF)

Before the seizure of power, the Nazi organization for the industrial working class, the Nationalsozialistische Betriebzellenorganisation (National Socialist Factory Cell Organization, or NSBO) had failed to attract significant support away from the well-established socialist and religious trade unions. After the seizure of power, the unions were replaced by the Deutsche Arbeitsfront (German Labor Front, or DAF) under the leadership of Robert Ley. Improvised in structure and ill-defined in function, the DAF, like all such Nazi organisms, was prey to the disputes and rivalries typical of the Third Reich and probably never succeeded in winning workers' hearts and minds in anything other than a superficial fashion.

The DAF was an arm of the National Socialist German Workers' Party, not of the state. Ley was the staff leader of the party's political organization as well as of the DAF, the two posts constituting his power base within the Nazi leadership. The DAF was endowed with a large central office and a pyramidal structure comprising thirteen territorial divisions, divided into *Kreise* (circles), themselves made up of local groups. These factory organizations, the *Betriebsgemeinschaften,* were required to follow the standards set from above by the DAF center. At its largest it had more than 25 million compulsory members and received vast amounts of funds from membership dues, but it never represented its forced adherents in a trade union sense. Despite Ley's efforts, the DAF never won the right to negotiate wages; this power rested with the trustees of labor *(Treuhänder der Arbeit),* state officials appointed by Hitler in June 1933. With any threat of independent trade unionism removed, employers were willingly incorporated into the DAF within a year of Hitler's assumption of power as part of the "coordination" of German society.

The ethos of the DAF rested on replacing class conflict with the "folk community," the *Volksgemeinschaft*. The factory was to be a partnership, dedicated to raising productivity and generating pride in collective achievement. The ideology was in essence little different from that of a modern managerial regime. In pursuit of this goal the DAF created the "Strength through Joy" organization and a department of "Beauty of Work" to enhance the aesthetic appearance of work and create a healthy work environment, the most notable achievement of which was the plan for the Volkswagen. In its various ramifications the DAF became the largest organization in the Third Reich, with a bureaucracy of more than 40,000 employees. Ley was provided with a solid personal base, but on a regional level DAF leaders vied for power and influence with the *Gauleiters* and *Kreisleiters*. Like all Nazi officials, they had to struggle constantly to maintain their position.

Membership in the DAF undoubtedly conferred some benefits, at least for its more enthusiastic adherents. Its holiday schemes were vital for the prosperity of the tourist industry, and in 1936–1937 it became involved in vocational training. But it could not subdue traditional working-class consciousness, especially during the years of labor shortage from 1936 onward, when the normal mechanisms of labor relations were revealed as still operating, with the advantage on the workers' side. Its very existence also got in the way of the state's attempts to direct the labor market. The DAF is one instance of the gap between ideal and reality in Hitler's attempt to combine corporate state, "folk community," and authoritarian government.

Related entries: Bureaucracy; *Gleichschaltung;* Labor Relations; Ley, Robert; National Socialist Factory Cell Organization; National Socialist German Workers' Party; Social Policy; "Strength through Joy"; Trade Unions; Volkswagen; Working Class

Suggestions for further reading:
Mason, Tim. 1993. *Social Policy in the Third Reich: The Working Class and the "National Community."* Providence and Oxford: Berg.
Smelser, Ronald M. 1988. *Robert Ley: Hitler's Labor Front Leader.* Oxford/New York/Hamburg: Berg.

German National People's Party (DNVP)

Organized in November 1918 as a consolidation of various right-wing groups opposed to the Weimar Republic, the DNVP eventually compromised and participated in government between 1924 and 1928, when it held over 100 seats in the Reichstag. The election of Alfred Hugenberg as chairman in 1928 placed the most reactionary elements in control of the party organization and led the DNVP into Hitler's embrace. Authoritarian, anti-Semitic, opposed to the Treaty of Versailles, and assiduously cultivating the "stab in the back" legend, the DNVP had only ever given lukewarm support to the Weimar Republic, and the radical leadership under Hugenberg saw Hitler as a natural ally.

The National Socialist German Workers' Party (NSDAP, Nazi Party) and DNVP joined forces to oppose the Young Plan in 1929, but the publicity surrounding the re-

sultant plebiscite brought far more benefit for Hitler than for his supposedly senior partners. The DNVP lost both moderate support on the one side and radical nationalist support to Hitler on the other. It steadily lost seats in the Reichstag, down to only thirty-seven seats in 1932, while Hugenberg sought unsuccessfully to influence Hitler. The attempt to create the united Harzburg Front in 1931 failed because Hitler wanted a coalition only on his terms and under his control. Hugenberg joined Hitler's "Cabinet of National Concentration" in January 1933, but in the March elections the DNVP joined with other non-Nazi nationalists in the "Battle Front: Black-White-Red." The fifty-two deputies thus elected secured Hitler a majority in the Reichstag and supported the Enabling Act. Having helped to make possible Hitler's first cabinet and having played a significant role in his accession to power, the DNVP disbanded itself on 27 June 1933.

Related entries: Enabling Act; Harzburg Front; Hugenberg, Alfred; Nationalists; Weimar Republic; Young Plan

Suggestions for further reading:
Leopold, John A. 1977. *Alfred Hugenberg: The Radical Nationalist Campaign against the Weimar Republic.* New Haven: Yale University Press.

German People's Party (DVP)

One of the leading political parties of the Weimar Republic, the DVP was founded in December 1918 as a liberal party to the right of the German Democratic Party and was known as the party of Gustav Stresemann, probably the best-known politician of the republic. Under Stresemann as the majority party in the "Weimar Coalition," the DVP adopted a moderate revisionist approach to the Versailles settlement, earning accusations of treachery from Hitler and the rest of the nationalist Right. In the nationalistic climate following Stresemann's death in 1929 the DVP lost votes rapidly, including many to the Nazis. By March 1933 it possessed only two deputies in the Reichstag and dissolved itself on 4 July in the process of *Gleichschaltung.*

Related entries: Weimar Republic

German Workers' Party (DAP)

Founded in January 1919 in Munich by Anton Drexler and the sports journalist Karl Harrer, the DAP, though small, was still the most significant of the nationalist and anti-Semitic parties of the Bavarian capital. But it remained in essence a beer-hall debating society, lacking a political program but promulgating platitudes about recreating the "folk community," breaking "interest slavery," and blaming Germany's problems on Jews and Bolsheviks. It became historically significant only as the precursor to the National Socialist Party and in providing the first springboard for Hitler's political career.

On 12 September 1919, under orders from his army superior, Captain Karl Mayr, Hitler attended a DAP meeting at the Sternecker Beer Hall in Munich. Within days he had joined the party. He wrote in *Mein Kampf* that this was "the most decisive resolve of my life. From here there was and could be no turning back" (Hitler 1992, p. 204). As a member of the executive committee responsible for party propaganda, Hitler focused on combating the Versailles treaty and Jewish influence in German life. At a public meeting on 16 October 1919 Hitler discovered his oratorical skills for the first time. "I could speak," he later exclaimed about the experience. Together with Drexler, he drew up a new party program, still with a strong socialist influence alongside the predictable anti-Semitism and

anti-Marxism. At the end of February 1920 the DAP became the National Socialist German Workers' Party, of which Hitler was to become chairman in June 1921.

Related entries: Anti-Semitism; Drexler, Anton; Feder, Gottfried; Munich; National Socialist German Workers' Party

Suggestions for further reading:
Hitler, Adolf. 1992. *Mein Kampf.* Trans. Ralph Manheim. Intro. by D. C. Watt. London: Pimlico.

Gestapo (Geheime Staatspolizei)

Described by the historian Karl Dietrich Bracher as "the institutional basis of [the] innermost reality of the Third Reich" (Gellately 1990, p. 3), the Secret Security Police was the branch of the Security Police (Sicherheitspolizei, or SIPO) charged with investigating and combating all activities deemed hostile to the National Socialist state. As such, it operated outside all the traditional constraints of law, policing, and administration in dealing with opponents and "political" criminals and in the enforcement of racial policy. Using the so-called Protective Custody Orders, the Gestapo dispatched thousands of real and supposed political enemies to concentration camps and other confinement facilities and created a climate of insecurity backed by terror to attain power over the population. Fear of falling into the hands of the Gestapo was enough to induce silence and effectively cow potential opposition.

Political policing was nothing new in Germany: such forces had existed in most of the federal states before 1933. The first organization specifically called a Secret Police State Office (Geheimes Staatspolizeiamt, or Gestapa) was created in Prussia in early 1933 by Hermann Goering in his capacity as Prussian minister of the interior. Following the Reichstag fire and Enabling Act and augmented by Sturmabteilung and SS personnel, it began placing opponents under "protective custody" in large numbers. But Goering lost the struggle for overall control of political police forces to Heinrich Himmler, and his protégé Rudolf Diels was replaced as head of the Gestapo by Reinhard Heydrich. A separate Prussian force ceased to exist in 1934, and on 17 June 1936 Himmler was named chief of the German police. For the first time in German history the police, including the secret branches, were centralized, and although the usual administrative disarray of the Nazi regime persisted to a degree, the Gestapo was able to act independently of the rest of the administration and for most intents and purposes itself decide what was the law, enforce it, and ignore all objections.

The majority of Gestapo personnel were career policemen rather than fanatical Nazi "old fighters." It provided a career ladder for the ambitious, opportunists, and those anxious to "clean up" the state and impose authoritarian order, first against left-wing organizations and then against Jews and other racial enemies, homosexuals, freemasons, and the generally disaffected who dared to grumble too publicly about Hitler's policies. Almost any sign of nonconformity was seen to be "political" if the Gestapo so decided. In Catholic regions, using the traditional greeting "Grüss Gott" instead of "Heil Hitler!" was denounced as politically subversive. The number of full-time Gestapo officials was remarkably small. For example, in 1937 Düsseldorf and Essen, both cities with more than 400,000 inhabitants, had only 126 and forty-three, respectively. And the extent of its spy network (about which little information survives) was exaggerated by public opinion and by émigré opponents of the regime such as the Sopade. The fact that almost anyone *could* be a Gestapo spy, coupled with the arbitrary and lawless nature of Gestapo actions, was enough to render opposition ineffective.

To a large extent, therefore, the Gestapo relied for its effectiveness on denunciations by ordinary citizens. For example, in Würzburg and Lower Franconia, studied in detail by Robert Gellately, the majority of cases of "friendship with Jews" were initiated by such actions. Hitler himself was moved to complain in May 1933 that "we are living at present in a sea of denunciations and human meanness" (Gellately 1990, p. 139), but such sordid servility was one of the foundations of his rule. Many denunciations were inspired by pure malice, but all were investigated. Husbands denounced wives they wanted to be rid of; neighbors denounced each other; businesspeople denounced rivals. With such help, friendly personal, sexual, and business relations between Jews and non-Jews that had existed for generations were destroyed; the mildly unconventional received the dreaded summons to Gestapo headquarters; and any German woman who had sexual relations with a Polish farmworker or laborer was exposed to public humiliation and her lover to summary execution or a concentration camp. The Gestapo's terror created a kind of self-policing system in German society that, intensifying during the war years, was essential in maintaining Hitler's power to the bitter end.

Related entries: Heydrich, Reinhard; Himmler, Heinrich; Jews and Jewish Policy; Law; Local Government; Opposition; Public Opinion; Racial Theory

Suggestions for further reading:
Gellately, Robert. 1988. "The Gestapo and German Society: Political Denunciations in the Gestapo Case Files," *Journal of Modern History* 60, pp. 654–694.
———. 1990. *The Gestapo and German Society: Enforcing Racial Policy 1933–1945.* Oxford: Clarendon Press.

Gleichschaltung

The "coordination" of German state and society by the Nazis in 1933–

1934 established Hitler's power with remarkable speed and ease. In March 1933, when Hitler had been in power for less than two months, Victor Klemperer noted: "A complete revolution and party dictatorship. And all opposing forces as if vanished from the face of the earth" (Klemperer 1998, p. 5). The term *Gleichschaltung,* borrowed from electrical engineering, means literally "shifting into the same gear, line, or current." In practice it was to produce a uniform *Volksgemeinschaft* based on racial and cultural harmony, all in the name of national reconciliation and reconstruction. In other words, total subordination to Nazi ideology and policy.

The term was first used in laws of 31 March and 7 April 1933 replacing the elected governments of the German states with governors appointed by President Hindenburg on Hitler's recommendation. State parliaments were soon abolished and authority transferred to the Reich Interior Ministry. By a law of 30 January 1934 state governments became mere administrative subdivisions of the central government. Other aspects of *Gleichschaltung* included a huge purge of the civil service, involving the summary dismissal of Jews, Communists, Social Democrats, and anyone else displaying a negative attitude toward National Socialism.

The same process was swiftly applied to schools and universities, professional associations, the judicial system, and the medical profession. Labor unions were replaced by the German Labor Front. Political parties were either suppressed for "treasonable" activities, as with the Communists and Social Democrats, or dissolved themselves under government pressure, as did the German National People's Party (DNVP), the German Democratic Party (DDP), the German People's Party (DVP), and the Catholic Center Party. Cultural activities were brought under control by Josef Goebbels and the Reich Chamber of Culture. *Gleichschaltung* of the army was hardly necessary because the interests of the Reichswehr coincided almost exactly with those of the Nazis. The "Night of the Long Knives," 30 June 1934, which destroyed the independent power of the Sturmabteilung, can be seen as the final bloody act of *Gleichschaltung.* Hitler's conservative supporters could rest assured that Nazi "coordination" did not involve revolutionary disorder.

The remarkably smooth process of *Gleichschaltung* involved more accommodation than upheaval. There was very little resistance, especially not in areas such as the civil service or the judiciary, where the democracy of the Weimar Republic had never been properly accepted. Hans Bernd Gisevius, a member of the Gestapo in 1933, later recalled: "There was, to be sure, a tremendous amount of bitterness and distrust, and frequently open revolt appeared. But there was at least an equal amount of enthusiasm and devotion, not to say fanaticism. Seldom had a nation so readily surrendered all its rights and liberties as did ours in those first hopeful, intoxicated months of the new millennium" (Gellately 1990, p. 11). Individual *Gleichschaltung,* a more or less enthusiastic personal acceptance of the new order, aided and abetted collective *Gleichschaltung.* It meant submission to a new aggressive and militant spirit, backed by a very real threat of dispatch to the new concentration camps. Bernhard Rust, a Reich commissioner in the Prussian Culture Ministry, summed up in May 1933: "Our *Gleichschaltung* means that the new German view of the world [*Weltanschauung*], simply by dint of the fact that it has the force of law, takes precedence over any other view" (Hoffmann 1996, p. 90).

Related entries: Bureaucracy; Civil Service; Cultural Policy; Education; Enabling Act; Frick, Wilhelm; German Labor Front; Judiciary; Labor Relations; Local Government; Middle Classes; National Socialist German Workers' Party; Night of the Long Knives; Public Opinion; Reichstag; Science and Scientists; Social Policy; Trade Unions; Universities; Women; Working Class; Youth Policy

Suggestions for further reading:

Allen, William Sheridan. 1984. *The Nazi Seizure of Power: The Experience of a Single German Town*. Rev. ed. New York: Franklin, Watts.

Broszat, Martin. 1981. *The Hitler State: The Foundation and Development of the Internal Structure of the Third Reich*. New York: Longman.

Gellately, Robert. 1990. *The Gestapo and German Society: Enforcing Racial Policy 1933–1945*. Oxford: Clarendon Press.

Hoffmann, Hilmar. 1996. *The Triumph of Propaganda: Film and National Socialism, 1933–1945*. Providence and Oxford: Berghahn Books.

Klemperer, Victor. 1998. *I Shall Bear Witness: The Diaries of Victor Klemperer, 1933–41*. London: Weidenfeld and Nicolson.

Goebbels, Paul Josef (1897–1945)

Hitler's master propagandist was born into a strict Catholic lower-middle-class family in Rheydt, a small industrial town in the Rhineland. Educated at a Catholic school, he then did the round of eight German universities, ending at Heidelberg as a student of Friedrich Gundolf, a renowned Jewish literary historian. Goebbels had been rejected for service in World War I because of his crippled left leg, the result of infantile paralysis in early childhood. A sense of physical inadequacy tormented Goebbels throughout his life. Small, swarthy, narrow-chested, and limping, he was even further from the ideal of the Nordic *Herrenmensch* than were Hitler and the other Nazi leaders. He was also fearful of being regarded as an intellectual by the anti-intellectual Nazi movement. Highly intelligent but consumed by self-hatred, Goebbels's inferiority complex gave rise to his cynicism, his contempt for the human race in general and Jews in particular (his anti-Semitism was genuine, not opportunistic), and his delight in letting loose the forces of hatred and destruction.

Goebbels's imagination first found expression in a bohemian life, and he even wrote a novel, the thinly disguised autobiographical fantasy, *Michael: A German Destiny* (1926). But his energy, oratorical gifts, opportunism, and radicalism blossomed in the National Socialist German Workers' Party (NSDAP, Nazi Party) where, after some initial doubts, he became totally devoted to Hitler. The moody and cynical Goebbels found comfort in Hitler's simplicity. He wrote in his diary in 1926: "Adolf Hitler, I love you, because you are great and uncomplicated at the same time" (Bramsted 1965, p. 13). However, as business manager of the party in the Ruhr district, Goebbels was closely associated with the anticapitalist radicalism of Gregor and Otto Strasser until he definitively switched to Hitler's side in 1926.

Goebbels's reward for his new loyalty and his big opportunity came from his appointment as *Gauleiter* of Berlin-Brandenburg. Dominating the small conflict-ridden Nazi organization, he soon succeeded in undermining the dominance of the Strasser brothers in northern Germany; in 1927 founded and edited his own weekly newspaper, *Der Angriff* (the attack); and became the best-known agitator and demagogue in the capital, playing on the hopes and fears of the people and employing a combination of propaganda and force to take the Nazi message into the working-class districts of Berlin. He transformed the pimp and occasional student, Horst Wessel, into a martyr of the struggle against bolshevism. By 1929 he had transformed the insignificant Berlin section into a powerful organization. Goebbels's use of slogans, images, myths, slander, venom, and insinuation, all backed by the threat of force, showed how he had found his true vocation as a master of lies and manipulation.

Deeply impressed by Goebbels's success, Hitler made him Reich propaganda leader of the NSDAP in 1929. He thus became the true creator of the "Hitler myth." He sold Hitler to the people, orchestrating the mass meetings and "flights over Germany"

Josef Goebbels speaking at a street meeting during the Nazi Kampfzeit. *An effective and trenchant orator, Goebbels delivered his tirades and took the Nazi message into the toughest of working-class "Red" neighborhoods in Berlin. Brutal SA men, seen protecting him here, ensured that the Nazis came out on top in brawls with Communists and Socialists. (Culver Pictures)*

and staging the pseudoreligious cult of the Führer in such a way as to give the best scope to Hitler's own talents as an orator and demagogue. By 1932 Goebbels had put Hitler at the center of the political stage. On the Nazi accession to power in 1933, he duly became Reich minister for people's enlightenment and propaganda, a new and unique position in German history. Enjoying total control over all communications media and cultural life, Goebbels carried through their "coordination" in remarkably little time. On 10 May 1933 he set the cultural tone for the next decade at the ritual "burning of the books" in Berlin.

Goebbels reveled in his position of power, fought his corner against the other leading Nazis with the necessary viciousness, and enjoyed the good life, especially the company of young actresses wishing to make their way into films. The Hitler myth created by Goebbels grew ever stronger and more influential, but he also showed his skill in back-pedaling on anti-Semitism and Hitler's aggressive plans for both foreign and internal consumption. Hitler admired his political judgment as well as his administrative and propagandist expertise. Goebbels, his wife Magda, and their six children were frequent and welcome guests at Berchtesgarden. When Magda threatened divorce in 1938 over Goebbels's affairs with actresses, Hitler intervened personally to sort out the situation.

Relations between Hitler and Goebbels were made even closer by the war, especially when it began to turn against Germany. He became an ever more prominent public figure as he urged the people to make ever greater efforts. While Hitler became more remote, Goebbels became more visible: he visited the victims of Allied bombing while Hitler skulked; and on 18 February 1943 Goebbels made the famous speech at the Sportspalast announcing "total war," whipping up his audience to a pitch of unbridled emotion. He finally achieved his ambition to be the warlord on the home front in July 1944, when his prompt actions played a large part in foiling the July Plot and were rewarded with the inflated title of general plenipotentiary for total war. He could now lord it over colorless bureaucrats like Martin Bormann and Hans-Heinrich Lammers, whom he had always envied and despised.

To do justice to Goebbels, unlike other leading Nazis he never lost his nerve or tried to jump the sinking Hitlerian ship. Although aware that his propaganda was becoming ever more desperate and unrealistic, he did his best to maintain belief in the Führer's invincibility. But even with his new powers to direct the civil population and obtain more manpower when it was needed, Germany was already too close to collapse, and Goebbels's intervention could only cause even more disruption and confusion. Similarly, his hopes to stir up disunion among the Allies were doomed to failure. Even his skillful exploitation of the Katyn massacre of Polish officers by the Soviets, while it could frighten people on the home front, could do nothing to save Germany.

While other Nazis panicked, tried to negotiate with the Allies, or scuttled away, Goebbels remained Hitler's most loyal follower and seemed genuinely fascinated by the idea of a Nazi Götterdämmerung. Hitler's political testament appointed Goebbels as Reich chancellor, but Goebbels disregarded the order and decided to follow the Führer into suicide. He wrote as an appendix to the testament: "In the delirium of treachery which surrounds the Führer in these most critical days of the war, there must be someone at least who will stay with him unconditionally until death" (Bramsted 1965, p. 373). On 1 May 1945 Goebbels had his six children poisoned by lethal injection and then himself and Magda shot by an SS orderly. Egomaniac and propagandist to the end, he was thinking of how he would be viewed by the future and was determined to be seen as a symbol and exemplar of Nazi fidelity.

Related entries: Berlin; Cinema; Cultural Policy; *Gleichschaltung;* Hitler Myth; Jews and Jewish Policy; July Plot; Press; Propaganda; Public Opinion; Radio; Strasser, Gregor; Strasser, Otto

Suggestions for further reading:
Bramsted, Ernest K. 1965. *Goebbels and National Socialist Propaganda 1925–1945.* East Lansing: Michigan State University Press.
Reuth, Ralf Georg. 1993. *Goebbels.* London: Constable.

Goerdeler, Carl (1884–1945)

A notable civil servant and lord mayor of Leipzig from 1930 to 1937, Goerdeler became the leader of conservative, nationalist opposition to Hitler. The devoutly Protestant Goerdeler remained a monarchist at heart but served as an economic adviser to government in the last years of the Weimar Republic and the first years of the Third Reich. Appointed to the watchdog position of Reich commissioner of prices in November 1934, he resigned in 1935 in protest of the Nazi rearmament program, their rejection of economic liberalism, and their anti-Semitism. His resignation as mayor of Leipzig in 1937 was occasioned by the removal of a bust of Felix Mendelssohn from the front of the city hall.

Goerdeler used his contacts abroad, created through his work for the Bosch company, to warn influential people in Britain, France, and the United States about the Nazi threat and, within Germany, tried to foment opposition to Hitler among army officers. But during the war his nationalist outlook weakened his efforts. In a peace plan of 1943 he envisaged a Greater Germany without Hitler but including Austria, Prussian and Silesian territory in Poland, and the Sudetenland, which he took for granted should be German. Goerdeler's opposition was to a war with apparently un-

limited objectives. He hoped to lure Britain and the United States into separate peace negotiations, so creating a strong Germany as a bulwark against communism, and was bitterly disillusioned by the Allied demand for unconditional surrender.

Goerdeler's political and social attitudes were also old-fashioned, and he was convinced that he could win the support of the German people merely by confronting them with evidence of Nazi crimes. He was designated to succeed Hitler as chancellor of Germany by the July plotters of 1944, and after the failure of the plot the Gestapo found a host of documents implicating Goerdeler and other members of the Resistance, including a list of members of his future cabinet. Goerdeler's mania for drawing up memoranda and plans for a post-Hitler Germany proved his downfall. Arrested and sentenced to death on 8 September 1944, his execution was delayed by the crumbling of the Reich, specifically Himmler's attempt to put out his own peace feelers. Goerdeler was finally hanged in the Prinz Albrechtstrasse prison in Berlin on 2 February 1945.

Related entries: July Plot; Opposition

Suggestions for further reading:
Ritter, Gerhard. 1958. *The German Resistance: Carl Goerdeler's Struggle against Tyranny.* London: George Allen and Unwin.

Goering, Hermann (1893–1946)

B orn in Rosenheim in Bavaria, the son of a judge who had been resident minister plenipotentiary in South-West Africa, Goering joined the army before 1914 and during World War I transferred to the air force, rising by 1918 to command the renowned Richtofen Squadron. He ended the war as a hero, invested with the

Hermann Goering (center) confers with Hitler (right) and Mussolini (left) over the Eastern Front. The Reichsmarschal seems to be still in Hitler's good graces here, but the failure of his Luftwaffe to drop supplies at Stalingrad, despite his fervent promises, was to lead to a permanent loss of influence. (Archive Photos)

aura of an ace fighter pilot. Unable to settle down to civilian life, Goering worked as a show flier and pilot in Denmark and Sweden, marrying his first wife, the Swedish baroness Karin von Fock-Kantzow, in February 1922. When he joined the infant National Socialist German Workers' Party (NSDAP, Nazi Party), Hitler saw him as a prize recruit and gave him command of the Sturmabteilung (SA) in December 1922. Nazism was to offer the swashbuckling but power-hungry and infinitely corruptible Goering a life of action, adventure, greed, and profit.

Goering was wounded during the Beer Hall Putsch of November 1923 and forced into exile for four years. During his wanderings, while in a mental asylum in Sweden in September 1925, he was prescribed morphine to aid his recovery and became an addict for life. On his return to Germany in 1927 he rejoined the NSDAP

and was elected to the Reichstag a year later. Goering used his contacts with traditional conservative circles, big business, and army officers to smooth the path for their acceptance of Hitler. The Nazi success in the elections of July 1932 brought Goering the presidency of the Reichstag. When Hitler became chancellor, Goering was made Prussian minister of the interior, commander in chief of the Prussian police and Gestapo, and commissioner for aviation.

Goering, together with Heinrich Himmler and Reinhard Heydrich, was responsible for the creation of the Gestapo, the setting up of the first concentration camps, the "cleansing" of Prussia, and the implementation of the emergency legislation that destroyed the remnants of civil rights in Germany following the Reichstag fire. He also directed operations against his rival Ernst Röhm and other SA leaders in the Night of the Long Knives. But he soon relinquished his police responsibilities to Himmler, and from 1935 onward devoted himself to building up the Luftwaffe. Goering's power was extended further in 1936 when Hitler gave him overall charge of the Four-Year Plan, with virtually dictatorial powers over the economy. His economic management was greased by bribes at every level, and Goering amassed a huge fortune through the giant industrial conglomerate, the Reichswerke Hermann Goering, and from directorships and shareholdings in many enterprises, including Benz, BMW, newspapers, and aircraft companies.

Goering's luxurious lifestyle became the epitome of corruption as the ruling principle of the Third Reich. His second wedding to the actress Emily Sonnermann in April 1935 (his first wife had died in 1931) was a quasi-royal affair, as was the christening of his daughter Edda, with Hitler as godfather, in 1937. He may have cut a ridiculous and increasingly rotund figure with his extravagant uniforms, feasting, hunts, jewelry, and obvious enjoyment of the trappings of power, but he remained genuinely popular with the German people. He was seen as more accessible, extroverted, and human than the ascetic Hitler. But he also retained the necessary brutality and ambition to help in engineering the "Blomberg–Fritsch crisis" of 1938 in the mistaken hope that he could thereby secure control of the army as well as the air force. Also, after Kristallnacht in November 1938, it was Goering who ordered the elimination of Jews from the German economy and the "Aryanization" of their property and businesses.

Goering fully shared Hitler's territorial ambitions, but his advice to be prudent in foreign affairs until Germany was fully armed was generally ignored by the Führer. Appointed Reich council chairman for national defense on 30 August 1939 and officially designated as Hitler's successor on 1 September, when war broke out Goering was in overall charge of the war economy and in command of the Luftwaffe. The two tasks together were beyond him. The economy was bedeviled by lack of central control and political infighting, and the failure of the air force in the Battle of Britain and its inability to prevent Allied bombing of Germany exposed Goering's incompetence as its supreme commander and the emptiness of his bombast. The Reichsmarshal (a unique title bestowed on Goering alone) sank into lethargy and illusion. Hitler grew to despise his increasingly discredited and isolated dauphin, blaming him for Germany's defeats in the skies and in Russia.

Stripped of most of his economic responsibilities in 1942, Goering was undermined further by the intrigues of Martin Bormann and overtaken in influence by Himmler, Josef Goebbels, and Albert Speer. His personality, weakened by years of drug dependence, began to disintegrate totally. When Hitler declared that he would remain in his Berlin bunker to the end, Goering asked that he be allowed to take over at once. This misinterpretation of Hitler's intentions, which he had seen as an abdication, led to his ignominious dismissal from his posts, expulsion from the party, and arrest. He was arrested again by the U.S. 7th Army and put on trial at Nuremberg in 1946 where, taken off drugs and slimmed down by a prison diet, he defended himself aggressively and skillfully, standing out as the dominant personality among the defendants. He was, however, found guilty of conspiracy to wage war, crimes against peace, war crimes, and crimes against humanity and was sentenced to death. During the night of 14–15 October 1946, two hours before his execution was due to take place, Goering committed suicide in his cell, swallowing poison he had managed to conceal from his guards.

Related entries: Aviation; Beer Hall Putsch; Blomberg-Fritsch Crisis; Bombing Campaigns; Britain, Battle of; Dunkirk, Evacuation of; Economic Policy; Four-Year Plan; Gestapo; Industry; Kristallnacht; Luftwaffe; National

Socialist German Workers' Party; Nazi Movement; Night of the Long Knives; Nuremberg Trials; Rearmament; Reichstag Fire; Stalingrad, Battle of; War Crimes

Suggestions for further reading:
Hoyt, Edwin P. 1990. *Goering's War.* London: Robert Hale.
Overy, Richard J. 1984. *Goering: The "Iron Man."* London: Routledge.

Great Britain

Hitler considered that pre-1914 Germany had been wrong to indulge in an arms race with Britain and to seek to challenge the global position of the British Empire. The natural enemies of the German *Volk* were France and Russia, not the Anglo-Saxon "English," as he always called the peoples of the United Kingdom. It was true that Britain suffered from the nefarious plotting of "the Jew," but British national interests, not necessarily opposed to those of Germany, would prevail: "In this country of the 'freest democracy,' the Jew exerts an almost unlimited dictatorship indirectly through public opinion. And yet, even there an incessant struggle is taking place between the advocates of British state interests and the proponents of a Jewish world dictatorship" (Hitler 1992, p. 582). He at first rejected the conventional (but true) idea that Britain was automatically opposed to domination of continental Europe by one power, and he continued even after war was declared in 1939 to believe that he could reach a separate peace with Britain, the natural racial ally of Germany.

Britain did indeed pursue a relatively moderate policy over reparations and revision of the Treaty of Versailles, often diverging from the more vengeful French. But the policy of bringing Germany back into the community of nations through a system of collective security was exposed and undermined by Hitler's accession to power. With Germany's withdrawal from disarmament negotiations and the remilitarization of the Rhineland in March 1936, it was evident that Hitler posed the major threat to Britain's security. The British response was a dual policy of arms limitation and appeasement.

Hitler's announcement of German rearmament in March 1935 and his vain boast that the Luftwaffe was already the equal of the Royal Air Force (RAF) encouraged the government of Stanley Baldwin to negotiate the Anglo-German Naval Agreement of 18 June 1935, which Hitler, though he had no intention of honoring it, could present as a triumph for his diplomacy and which divided Britain from France. In December 1937 Britain announced a limited program of rearmament while making it clear that it would not oppose peaceful changes in Austria and Czechoslovakia to Germany's benefit. Neville Chamberlain's government wanted to avoid unrestrained rearmament, which would distort the British economy and mean the loss of exports. Unfortunately, Hitler had no such qualms about the German economy. By the time of the crisis over the Sudetenland in 1938, British military weakness and general lack of interest in the affairs of eastern Europe led to the Munich Agreement, the culmination of appeasement.

Chamberlain's return from Munich with "peace in our time" was greeted with broad popular relief. But Hitler's occupation of the rest of Czechoslovakia in March 1939 showed that he would not be deterred by British policy. The change was shown by British guarantees to Poland and Romania, the imposition of conscription in April 1939, and belated development of joint military planning with France. When Hitler invaded Poland in September, an unprepared Britain was forced to commit itself to a war in defense of France, the European balance of power, and, ultimately, freedom and democracy.

It was not the war that Hitler expected or wanted. The British people entered it in a mood of somber determination, far removed from the xenophobic excesses of

1914. The pacifist minority remained vocal during the "phony war," but the struggle for national survival in the Battle of Britain and the gradual mobilization of national and imperial resources soon united the vast majority of the British people behind the inspirational leadership of Winston Churchill. Hitler's hopes for a separate peace, though they were taken seriously for a while by some British politicians, were quickly revealed as an illusion. All the rantings of Hitler and Josef Goebbels against "the Jew Churchill" and his "warmongering clique" made no difference. The British armed forces, the heroism of the merchant marine, the human and material resources of the British Empire, the intelligence and code-breaking services, and the determination of the British people all made decisive contributions to Hitler's defeat. But the price was high. At the end of the war, Britain's role as a global power was permanently weakened. The United States was the new world power, and the writing was on the wall for the British Empire.

Related entries: Appeasement; Atlantic, Battle of the; Bombing Campaigns; Britain, Battle of; British Empire; Casablanca Conference; Chamberlain, Neville; Churchill, Winston Leonard Spencer; Dunkirk, Evacuation of; Eden, Anthony; El Alamein, Battle of; Foreign Policy; Hess, Rudolf; Malta; Middle East; Montgomery, Bernard Law; Munich Agreement; Navy; Normandy Landings; North Africa; Phony War; Poland; Rearmament; Reparations; Rhineland; Ribbentrop, Joachim von; Sealion, Operation; Teheran Conference; Tobruk, Battles of; United States of America; Vergeltungswaffe; Versailles, Treaty of; Yalta Conference

Suggestions for further reading:
Hiden, John. 1977. *Germany and Europe 1919–1939.* New York: Longman.
Hillgruber, Andreas. 1974. "England's Place in Hitler's Plans for World Dominion," *Journal of Contemporary History* 9, pp. 5–22.
Hitler, Adolf. 1992. *Mein Kampf.* Trans. Ralph Manheim. Intro. by D. C. Watt. London: Pimlico.
McDonough, Frank. 1998. *Neville Chamberlain, Appeasement and the British Road to War.* Manchester and New York: Manchester University Press.

Weinberg, Gerhard L. 1970. *The Foreign Policy of Hitler's Germany: Diplomatic Revolution in Europe, 1933–1936.* Chicago: University of Chicago Press.
———. 1980. *The Foreign Policy of Hitler's Germany; Starting World War II, 1937–1939.* Chicago: University of Chicago Press.

Great Patriotic War

The Soviet Union's war against Hitler became known as the "Great Patriotic War" or "Great Fatherland War." Hitler's policies and his conception of the kind of war he was fighting played their part in allowing Joseph Stalin to appeal to traditional Russian patriotism in the struggle against the invader. Possibly if the Nazis had encouraged Ukrainian nationalism or the anticommunist feeling of the Soviet peasantry, they could have gained greater or more permanent support. But this was incompatible with Hitler's racist and imperialist war against the inferior Slavs. Conversely, Stalin evoked the memories of victorious Russian military leaders from Alexander Nevsky to Mikhail Kutuzov, who vanquished Napoleon, and arranged a reconciliation with the Orthodox church. Hitler's mistakes and lunatic schemes helped the elevation of his fellow tyrant into a heroic figure of legendary proportions.

Related entries: Bagration, Operation; Barbarossa, Operation; Eastern Front; Kursk, Battle of; Red Army; Soviet Union; Stalin, Joseph; Stalingrad, Battle of; Ukraine

Suggestions for further reading:
Overy, Richard. 1998. *Russia's War.* New York: Allen Lane Penguin Press.

Greece

Hitler was dragged into the invasion of Greece by the incompetence of Benito Mussolini's ambitions in the Balkans.

The dictatorship of General Ioannis Metaxas after 1936, despite owing more than a little to Hitler's and Mussolini's examples, continued the longstanding Greek foreign policy of compromise, neutrality, and bilateral agreements with neighboring states. An Anglo-French guarantee of 13 April 1939 protected Greek independence but was rendered irrelevant when Mussolini joined the war. The Italian attack on Greece in October–November 1940 was repulsed by valiant resistance from the Greek army, but Hitler secured one of the swiftest victories of the war in conquering the Greek mainland between 6 and 21 April 1941, followed by Crete between 20 May and 1 July. King George II and his government fled to Egypt under British protection, Greece was occupied by German and Italian troops, and the region of Thrace given to Bulgaria. The occupation was marked by shootings of hostages, mass executions, starvation, and pogroms against Jews, 65,000 of whom perished in the Holocaust. The Greek Resistance was bitterly divided between republican nationalists and Communists, who continued their fighting after Hitler's death in a bloody civil war lasting until mid-1949, when the pro-Western forces prevailed with British and U.S. aid.

Related entries: Holocaust; Mussolini, Benito; Resistance Movements

Guderian, Heinz (1888–1954)

*T*he great German pioneer of tank warfare, Guderian was given the chance to put his theories into practice by Hitler and, despite being unafraid to contradict the Führer to his face, served the Nazi regime well. Born into a military family in Kulm (Chelmno), Guderian served as a staff officer in World War I and in the 1920s headed the "tank school" of young military strategists, whose ideas were opposed by conservative military chiefs until Hitler came to power, as well as showing a forward-looking interest in military communications. Radio contacts between groups of tanks would allow the coordinated fast movements of Panzer divisions with air support in the blitzkriegs against Poland and France.

In 1934 Hitler sanctioned the creation of the first tank battalion of the Wehrmacht, and Guderian was made chief of Panzer Troops Command. Named chief of mobile troops in 1938, Guderian proved his theories in the invasion of Poland and then in France, where his troops swept across the north of the country with astonishing speed. The vast spaces of the Soviet Union, however, proved another matter. Guderian, at the head of the 2nd Panzer Group, swept through Belorussia into the Ukraine, but by December 1941 the Russian winter and effective Soviet counterattacks brought Guderian's series of spectacular successes to a halt. After carrying out a withdrawal against Hitler's commands, he was dismissed from his command on Christmas Day 1941.

Recalled to be inspector general of Panzer troops in March 1943, after the defeat at Stalingrad, Guderian did his best to keep the Panzer divisions supplied and equipped during the dreadful fighting on the Eastern Front in 1943 and 1944. Fully aware of the July Plot against Hitler's life, Guderian refused to take part, citing his personal oath of loyalty to the Führer. He did, however, avoid telling Hitler about it by the simple expedient of taking a hunting trip at the opportune movement. Appointed to succeed Kurt von Zeitzler as chief of the army general staff on 21 July 1944, Guderian argued openly with Hitler about the conduct of the war in the west and was dismissed for the second time on 28 March 1945. Though he could be blunt and outspoken, Guderian always saw himself as a model soldier, "more Prussian than the Prussians," which meant honoring his oath to Hitler even when it led to disaster.

Related entries: Barbarossa, Operation; Blitzkrieg; Eastern Front; July Plot; Kursk, Battle of; Panzer Divisions; Wehrmacht

Suggestions for further reading:
Macksey, Kenneth. 1975. *Guderian: Panzer General*. London: Macdonald and Jane's.

Gürtner, Franz (1881–1941)

The son of a locomotive engineer from Regensburg, Gürtner played a significant supporting role in facilitating Hitler's rise to power and served uncomfortably as Reich minister of justice from 1932 until his death in 1941. After service in World War I, Gürtner established a successful legal career in Munich and was appointed Bavarian minister of justice in November 1922. He never joined the National Socialist German Workers' Party (NSDAP, Nazi Party) but was sympathetic to Hitler and other right-wing extremists. He was instrumental in ensuring that Hitler received only a light sentence following the Beer Hall Putsch and was allowed to use the trial to publicize his views at length. Gürtner then obtained Hitler's early release from prison and persuaded the Bavarian government to legalize the Nazi Party and allow Hitler to speak again in public.

Gürtner was made Reich minister of justice by Franz von Papen in June 1932. Hitler retained him in his post in 1933, finding it useful to give a non-Nazi conservative responsibility for "coordinating" the judiciary in the Third Reich. At first Gürtner tried to preserve a degree of independence for the judges, especially against the Sturmabteilung (SA). But when he secured the arrest and condemnation of SA leaders and camp guards for ill-treatment of prisoners in concentration camps, Hitler pardoned the culprits. Nor were his complaints about the methods of the Gestapo and the SS of any avail with the Führer. Gürtner was genuinely disgusted by what was happening in the concentration camps but instead of resigning stayed in office in the vain hope of "preventing the worst." However, he found himself providing legal sanction for the summary "justice" meted out to Poles and Jews in the occupied territories and the decrees that opened the way for the Final Solution. Gürtner died in Berlin on 29 January 1941. The full extent of Nazi crimes was not yet apparent, but Gürtner cannot be absolved from his part in making them possible.

Related entries: Beer Hall Putsch; *Gleichschaltung;* Judiciary; Law

Gypsies

The Gypsies (Sinti and Roma) were the only people other than the Jews marked down for extermination in Hitler's racial fantasies. They were persecuted by the Nazi regime as racially "alien" as well as for supposed antisocial behavior. Gypsies had long been harassed by regional discriminatory legislation in Germany, but persecution was centralized by the Nazis in the Reich Central Office for the Fight against the Gypsy Nuisance, established in 1936. They were effectively subjected to the Nuremberg Laws prohibiting marriage between Germans and "racial aliens"; race experts set about the registration of Sinti and Roma; and local authorities frequently took the initiative in herding them into ad hoc camps, thereby responding to popular complaints about Gypsies and evading their obligations to provide health care, schooling, and basic utilities.

By the time their fate was legally equated with that of the Jews in 1942, many thousands had already been deported. Special wagons were frequently attached to trains carrying Jews to Poland, while in the occupied areas of the Soviet Union, SS and police killing units massacred Gypsies, showing the same alacrity with which they murdered Jews. A special section of the Auschwitz–Birkenau complex was cordoned off for Gypsies and operated until August 1943. In all up to half a million Gypsies perished in their own Holocaust, including more than 100,000 at Auschwitz.

Related entries: Auschwitz; Racial Theory

Suggestions for further reading:
Burleigh, Michael, and Wolfgang Wippermann. 1991. *The Racial State: Germany 1933–1945*. Cambridge: Cambridge University Press.

H

Halder, Franz (1884–1972)

Born into an old Bavarian military family, Franz Halder rose through the ranks to replace the disgraced Ludwig Beck as chief of the General Staff in 1938 and overcame his distaste for Nazism to such good effect that he helped Hitler to win some of his most spectacular victories. He later dated his opposition to National Socialism to the 1920s and in 1938 was frequently heard to refer to Hitler as a "madman," but he could never bring himself to participate in Hitler's removal and subsequently sacrificed honor and dignity in the name of service and loyalty to country. Hitler, knowing his monarchist sympathies and wrongly assuming him to be a Catholic, was dubious about Halder's appointment, but Halder was too concerned with preserving the status of the General Staff and with his own position in history to mount a serious threat to the Führer's plans.

Halder gave encouragement to the army officers who conspired to remove Hitler in 1938 but feared the consequences of leading the officer corps into open revolt, being convinced that the bulk of the army would remain loyal to its oath to the Führer. After opposition had collapsed following the Munich Agreement, Halder confined his reservations to his private journal and supported Hitler's policies for as long as they brought success. He took rather too much credit for the triumphant campaign in France and contributed substantially to the initial advances in Russia in 1941. However, he came to disagree strongly with Hitler's Russian strategy, openly clashing with him by urging an advance on Moscow, the capture of which, he was convinced, would shatter Soviet morale. Finally, when he opposed Hitler's decision to divert forces from the center to take Stalingrad, Halder was dismissed from office on 24 September 1942, becoming one of the scapegoats for the German disaster in Russia.

Halder was arrested by the Gestapo after the July Plot of 1944, narrowly avoiding execution for lack of evidence of his involvement or about his earlier anti-Nazism. Dismissed from the army in January 1945, he was imprisoned briefly in Flossenburg and Dachau concentration camps before being arrested by Allied troops on 5 May 1945. Released in June 1947, Halder was fortunate that his earlier opposition to Hitler was deemed to be sufficient to absolve him from responsibility for his subsequent exploits. He served with the U.S. Army Historical Division from 1948 to 1961, when he was awarded the Meritorious Civilian Service Award of the USA. He died in Aschau, Upper Bavaria, on 2 April 1972.

In his best-selling *Hitler als Feldherr,* translated as *Hitler as Warlord* (1950), Halder showed considerable writing talent in criticizing Hitler's martial abilities. He portrayed his erstwhile Führer as a fanatic who believed willpower to be more important than military expertise. Hitler's ideas of strategy, he wrote, were disastrous; he wasted lives and material and was utterly indifferent to the welfare of his troops; and he was responsible for Germany's defeat by removing professional generals from control of operations. Halder did not explain how he, one of the professional generals in question, had come to betray his principles by serving Hitler for so long.

Related entries: Barbarossa, Operation; Eastern Front; July Plot; Officer Corps; Opposition; Stalingrad, Battle of; Wehrmacht

Suggestions for further reading:
Halder, Franz. 1950. *Hitler as Warlord*. London: Putnam.
Leach, Barry A. 1995. "Halder," in Correlli Barnett, ed., *Hitler's Generals*. London: Phoenix.

Hanfstaengl, Ernst Franz Sedgwick (1887–1975)

Generally known as "Putzi," the wealthy and cultivated Hanfstaengl was Hitler's companion and social contact in the early days of the Nazi movement in Munich and became head of the Foreign Press department of the National Socialist German Workers' Party (NSDAP, Nazi Party). Hanfstaengl's parents owned an art-publishing business in Munich, and his American mother was descended from a family that had included two distinguished Civil War generals. Ernst graduated from Harvard University in 1909 and spent two years in the United States before returning to Munich after World War I. He attended one of Hitler's political meetings in 1921 and was instantly converted. Hanfstaengl's support was instrumental in opening the doors of Munich high society to Hitler, and he also loaned the party $1,000, which facilitated the purchase of the *Völkischer Beobachter*. He took part in the Beer Hall Putsch, and Hitler was arrested two days after its failure in Hanfstaengl's country house at Uffling.

As well as giving him financial support, Hanfstaengl provided Hitler with relaxation and entertainment in the salons of Munich. A virtuoso pianist, eccentric and witty, naturally given to clowning about and playing practical jokes, he provided the NSDAP leader with much needed light relief both before and after he became chancellor. He was appointed Foreign Press chief of the Nazi Party in 1931, and it was hoped that he could use his international contacts to improve the image of the Nazi movement and later regime. According to the distinguished U.S. correspondent, William L. Shirer, Hanfstaengl was popular with foreign journalists despite his "clownish stupidity."

By the mid-1930s, however, Hanfstaengl's position was weakened by his relatively moderate political views and his expressing his sardonically frank opinions about some of the top Nazi leaders. In turn, Josef Goebbels and others who resented his closeness to Hitler cast aspersions on Hanfstaengl's character and dependability. Hitler himself came particularly to resent Hanfstaengl's lining of his own pockets and lack of political steeliness. Seeing how the wind was blowing, in March 1937 Hanfstaengl fled to Britain and thence the United States. He spent part of World War II as an "adviser" on the Third Reich to the U.S. government, providing juicily scandalous but not necessarily accurate information about Hitler's sexual habits and such matters. Briefly interned after the war, he soon returned to Germany, published a memoir translated into English as *Hitler: The Missing Years* in 1957, and died in Munich on 6 November 1975.

Related entries: Beer Hall Putsch; Munich; Press

Suggestions for further reading:
Hanfstaengl, Ernst. 1957. *Hitler: The Missing Years.* London: Eyre and Spottiswoode.

Harzburg Front

The ephemeral association of the "National Opposition" groups in a rally at Bad Harzburg on 11 October 1931 prefigured the coalition that was to bring Hitler to power in 1933. Following the campaign against the Young Plan, Alfred Hugenberg brought together leading right-wing personalities, including Hitler and Hjalmar Schacht, to show the strength of the National Opposition. Hitler was ill at ease and angry among the forces of "reaction," and when the Stahlhelm turned up in much greater numbers than the Sturmabteilung for a march past, he left the platform in a marked manner and refused to attend a joint lunch with the other nationalist leaders. The National Opposition collapsed before it had been formed, and Hitler, the one leader who could claim substantial popular support, was confirmed in his intention to follow his own path toward power.

Related entries: German National People's Party; Hugenberg, Alfred; Nationalists; Schacht, Hjalmar; Stahlhelm; Young Plan

Henlein, Konrad (1898–1945)

The pro-Nazi leader of the Sudeten Germans was born near Reichenberg in Bohemia of a German father and Czech mother. A bank clerk by profession, he founded the Sudetendeutsche Heimatfront, a surrogate for the banned Nazi Party, in October 1933. In elections in 1935, under the name of the Sudetendeutsche

Partei (SDP), it won forty-four seats on a platform of demanding autonomy for the Sudeten German minority within the Czechoslovak state. The SDP secretly received subsidies from the Third Reich, acting in effect as Hitler's fifth column and allowing him to manipulate the dispute between the Sudeten Germans and the Prague government. For international consumption Henlein continued to pretend that he had no connection with Hitler or the Reich, but by 1937 his party was openly pro-Nazi and anti-Semitic. At a secret meeting with Hitler on 28 March 1938, the two men agreed on a common strategy based on demanding so much that they could never be satisfied. Henlein returned to Czechoslovakia only after it had been occupied by Hitler's troops. On 1 May 1939 he was appointed head of the Civil Administration in the Sudetenland and *Gauleiter* of the region, positions he held until the end of the war. Captured by the Americans, Henlein committed suicide in an Allied prisoner of war camp in May 1945.

Related entries: Sudetenland

Hess, Rudolf (1894–1987)

Hitler's colorless but devoted deputy Führer was born in Alexandria, Egypt, in 1894. He served as a volunteer in the army and air force in World War I, joined a Freikorps unit in 1919; and, while a student at the University of Munich in January 1920, heard Hitler speak and joined the National Socialist German Workers' Party (NSDAP, Nazi Party). Arrested and imprisoned for taking part in the Beer Hall Putsch, Hess wrote down Hitler's dictation to compose *Mein Kampf* in Landsberg prison. His only original contribution was to introduce Hitler to the idea of lebensraum, a crude version of the geopolitical theories he had encountered in his university studies in political science. Hess held no official post in the NSDAP before 1932 but acted as Hitler's private secretary and confidant. The shy, introverted, naïve, and deeply insecure Hess seemed to need to hide himself in his Führer's shadow.

Hitler made Hess chairman of the Central Political Commission of the NSDAP in January 1932, and on 21 April 1933 named him as deputy Führer. His duties lay in complete subordination to Hitler, and he was in any case incapable of taking any initiatives of his own. The previously unknown Hess became familiar to the public by warming up the audience at Hitler's meetings and announcing the arrival of the Führer with wild-eyed and frenzied enthusiasm. His sycophantic loyalty to Hitler was excessive even by Nazi standards as he called on the population to follow him in extinguishing their own personalities in uncritical surrender to the man he called "pure reason in human form" and "the greatest son whom my nation has brought forth in the thousand years of its history" (Wistrich 1982, p. 131).

His fidelity was rewarded with a series of high appointments in which he could be relied upon to act as his master's voice. He reached the pinnacle of his career in 1939 when he was made successor-designate as Führer to Hitler and Hermann Goering, but he brought his career to an end in the most bizarre and absurd fashion. On 10 May 1941 Hess secretly piloted a Messerschmitt 110 fighter plane from Germany to Scotland, bailing out close to the home of the Duke of Hamilton, whom he had met briefly at the Berlin Olympics. His self-appointed mission was to use the duke as an intermediary in persuading the British that Hitler had no wish to destroy a fellow-Nordic nation and that if Britain rid itself of the Churchill government, an understanding could easily be reached. To his considerable surprise, Hess was arrested and treated as a prisoner of war. It was a great propaganda coup for the British. Hitler was predictably enraged and declared Hess to be insane, a deranged idealist suffering from hallucinations traceable to injuries received in World War I.

The captive Hess appeared to go to pieces completely. Those charged with examining him discovered only neurosis and paranoia. His behavior at the Nuremberg trials, during which he claimed to be suffering from total amnesia and stared vacantly into space, raised further doubts about his sanity. He was nonetheless found guilty of crimes against peace and conspiracy to commit other crimes and was sentenced to life imprisonment. Hess spent the rest of his life in Spandau prison in Berlin. That he was never released was due largely to the Soviet Union's animosity toward him, despite humanitarian campaigns in the West and the fear that he might become a martyr for neo-Nazis. He died in 1987, still the object of considerable speculation among historians and psychologists.

Related entries: Hitler Myth; Lebensraum; *Mein Kampf;* Nazi Movement; Nuremberg Trials

Suggestions for further reading:
Padfield, Peter. 1991. *Hess: Flight for the Führer.* London: Weidenfeld and Nicolson.
Wistrich, Robert. 1982. *Who's Who in Nazi Germany.* London: Weidenfeld and Nicolson.

Heydrich, Reinhard (1904–1942)

Hitler described his head of the Reich Main Security Office and a leading architect of the Final Solution as "the man with an iron heart" (Bullock 1991, p. 723). The son of a Dresden music teacher, Heydrich was exposed to *völkisch* racial fanaticism in his early years and joined a Freikorps unit in 1919, at the age of fifteen. He joined the navy in 1922, gaining experience in intelligence work, but was forced to resign by Admiral Erich Raeder in 1931 for "conduct unbecoming to an officer and a gentleman" involving a shipyard director's daughter. Heydrich immediately joined the Nazi Party and the SS, rising rapidly through the ranks due to the personal patronage of Heinrich Himmler. He became chief of the Sicherheitsdienst (SD) in July 1932 and played a typically murderous role in the Night of the Long Knives.

Heydrich was now Himmler's right-hand man. Tall, blond, athletic, disciplined, and ice-cool, he epitomized the "Nordic-Aryan" type of Nazi mythology far more than did Himmler or any of the other leading Nazis. He assisted Himmler in gaining control of the Bavarian police after Hitler's accession to power and then ensured the "coordination'" of political police forces throughout Germany. Heydrich's invaluable services and talent for intrigue soon made him chief of the Berlin Gestapo. By 1936 he was in command of the security police throughout the Reich. In 1939 he was appointed to head the Reich Main Security Office (RSHA), incorporating the Gestapo, the SD, and the criminal police. Methodical, calculating, seeing intrigue and treachery everywhere, Heydrich made himself indispensable to Hitler and the leaders of the Reich. He created dossiers on all real and potential "enemies of the state," including his own colleagues, and supplemented terror and persecution with any number of dirty tricks, as in the Blomberg-Fritsch affair or the mock attack on the Gleiwitz radio transmitter that provided Hitler's excuse for the invasion of Poland.

Heydrich also concentrated the overall direction of Jewish affairs in his hands. Following the Anschluss, he sent Adolf Eichmann to Vienna to organize a "Center for Jewish Emigration" and then created a similar office in Berlin. Heydrich and Eichmann together would organize and coordinate the measures implementing the Final Solution, but while Eichmann remained largely unknown, the exhibitionist Hey-

drich was the public face of mass murder. At the Wannsee Conference of January 1942 he spoke in relatively blunt terms about the true aims of the "Final Solution of the Jewish Question in Europe." Operation Reinhard, the code-word for the extermination of Polish Jewry, was appropriately named after him.

On 23 September 1941 Heydrich was appointed deputy Reich protector of Bohemia and Moravia and took up residence in Prague. Convinced of his success in "pacifying" the Czechs, he drove about in an open car without an armed escort. On 27 May 1942 he was seriously wounded in a gun and bomb attack by Czech Resistance agents trained in England and died on 4 June. Along with Himmler and Admiral Wilhelm Canaris, Heydrich's old mentor and rival in military intelligence, Hitler eulogized him at his funeral. The reprisals were terrible, including the destruction of the village of Lidice, one of the most notorious of Nazi war crimes. And while Heydrich had been largely responsible for setting the Final Solution in motion, his assassination did nothing to stop it.

Related entries: Blomberg-Fritsch Crisis; Eichmann, Adolf; Final Solution; Gestapo; *Gleichschaltung;* Himmler, Heinrich; Holocaust; Jews and Jewish Policy; Kristallnacht; Night of the Long Knives; Raeder, Erich; Sicherheitsdienst; Wannsee Conference; War Crimes

Suggestions for further reading:
Bullock, Alan. 1991. *Hitler and Stalin: Parallel Lives.* London: HarperCollins.
Deschner, Günther. 1981. *Heydrich: The Pursuit of Total Power.* London: Orbis.

Himmler, Heinrich (1900–1945)

Second only to Hitler in the power structure of the Third Reich, Himmler was born into a pious Catholic family in

A formal portrait of Heinrich Himmler in SS uniform in the 1930s. Himmler built the SS into a "state within a state," taking Hitler's ideas and fantasies on race and nationalism to their logical conclusion and putting them into horrifying practice. (Popperfoto/Archive Photos)

Munich, the son of a schoolmaster. He served as an officer cadet toward the end of World War I and then studied agriculture in Munich from 1918 to 1922. Himmler took part in the Beer Hall Putsch and then acted as secretary to Gregor Strasser and was acting propaganda leader of the National Socialist German Workers' Party (NSDAP, Nazi Party) from 1926 to 1930. After his marriage in 1927 he returned briefly to chicken farming but failed miserably. In January 1929 he became head of the Schutzstaffel (SS), at that time Hitler's personal bodyguard with only 200 members. Himmler was to build it into his personal empire within the Third Reich.

Himmler concentrated on building up the SS and securing its independence from Ernst Röhm's Sturmabteilung (SA). On Hitler's accession to power Himmler, together with Reinhard Heydrich, organized the Sicherheitsdienst (SD) as the security service of the Third Reich. Himmler was appointed police president of Munich and then commander of the political police for Bavaria. But the greatest step up in his career came with the smashing of the power of the SA in the Night of the Long Knives. Himmler could now establish the SS as an independent organization and dynamic spearhead of Nazi racism. By June 1936 Himmler, as head of the Gestapo and *Reichsführer* of the SS, had won complete control of the political and criminal police throughout the Reich.

Himmler's racial fanaticism, his cranky mysticism, and his obsessions with the occult and "alternative" medicine went beyond even Hitler's. His "contribution" was to turn the negative concept of anti-Semitism into a plan for creating a new society based on racial superiority. Himmler's ideal of a new Nordic aristocracy of blond, blue-eyed warriors, created by selective breeding, stood in considerable contrast to his own unprepossessing appearance. The failed chicken farmer looked more like a bank clerk than a police dictator, let alone a Wagnerian hero. One *Gauleiter* remarked: "If I looked like him, I would not speak of race at all" (Breitman 1991, p. 4). And one English observer noted that "nobody I met in Germany is more normal" (Wistrich 1982, p. 140). Yet Himmler was a bundle of neuroses and contradictions: romantic and ludicrous but also coldly efficient and without conscience in pursuit of his freakish but unspeakably murderous dreams. He could not abide cruelty to animals and did not exploit his enormous power for personal profit. Immeasurably cruel and indifferent to the fate of millions of human beings, he also suffered from psychosomatic illness and severe headaches and almost fainted at the sight of 100 Jews being executed for his benefit on the Russian front. As a result, he ordered the "more humane means" of poison gas to be used in future.

Himmler's success was in indoctrinating the SS with his own perverted "idealism," which rationalized mass murder in the name of honor and duty beyond guilt or responsibility. By 1941 he held all the necessary levers of power to put Nazi racial fantasies into practice: the Reich Main Security Office, run by Reinhard Heydrich and then Ernst Kaltenbrunner; the criminal police; the Foreign Political Intelligence Service; and the Gestapo. He controlled the concentration camps and the extermination camps and in the Waffen SS possessed a powerful private army. Himmler controlled the political administration of the occupied territories, and in August 1943 Hitler made him minister of the interior, giving him control of the courts and the civil service. Under his orders, at Hitler's command, millions of Jews and other "inferior" peoples were murdered; the eastern peoples became slave labor for the Reich; entire ethnic groups were sterilized; and appalling scientific experiments were carried out on human guinea pigs—Jews, Gypsies, criminals, prisoners of war, and others.

Himmler accumulated still more power after the July Plot of 1944, when Hitler forced the Wehrmacht to accept him as commander in chief of the Reserve Army. Yet the man Hitler thought he could trust tried to approach the Allies for peace negotiations, using Count Folke Bernadotte, the head of the Swedish Red Cross, as intermediary. He ordered the mass slaughter of Jews to be halted and proposed that the German armies in the West should surrender while continuing to fight in the East. Himmler appears to have genuinely believed that the Western allies would consider him an acceptable leader for a post–Hitler Germany. Hitler was irate at the treachery of his loyal disciple, stripped him of all his offices, and repudiated him in his political testament. After the German surrender, Himmler assumed a false identity and tried to escape but was unmasked and arrested by British troops. Before he could be brought to trial, Himmler killed himself by swallowing a poison capsule concealed in his mouth at Lüneberg on 23 May 1945.

Related entries: Beer Hall Putsch; Concentration Camps; Eastern Front; Euthanasia; Extermination Camps; Final Solution; Gestapo; Heydrich, Reinhard; Holocaust; Jews and Jewish Policy; Kaltenbrunner, Ernst; Nazi Movement; Night of the Long Knives; Poland; Racial Theory; Schutzstaffel; Sicherheitsdienst; Strasser, Gregor; Totenkopfverbände; Waffen SS; War Crimes

Suggestions for further reading:
Breitman, Richard. 1991. *The Architect of Genocide: Himmler and the Final Solution.* London: Bodley Head.
Wistrich, Robert. 1982. *Who's Who in Nazi Germany.* London: Weidenfeld and Nicolson.

Hindenburg, Paul von (1847–1934)

By the time he was elected president of Germany in 1925, Field Marshal von Hindenburg was not so much a man as a national monument. Retired from the army in 1911, he had been recalled early in World War I. As supreme commander of all German armies in the latter stages of the war, he was virtual dictator of Germany together with General Erich Ludendorff, his chief of staff. After defeat and the abdication of Kaiser Wilhelm II, Hindenburg retired to his estate of Neudeck in East Prussia.

Hindenburg was persuaded to run for president in 1925 by a coalition of nationalists and other conservative groups. Until 1930, whatever his private views, he upheld the constitution of the Weimar Republic, but he appointed Heinrich Brüning as chancellor with powers to rule by decree. In April 1932 Hindenburg was reelected president, convincingly beating Hitler. A leak from the presidential palace in October 1931 had let it be known that Hindenburg thought "the Bohemian corporal a queer fellow who might make a Minister of Posts, but certainly not Chancellor" (Bullock 1991, p. 263). His appointments of Franz von Papen and then Kurt von Schleicher as chancellor were meant to contain Hitler, but to no avail.

In private Hitler was contemptuous of the increasingly senile Hindenburg but in public was always respectful of the great war hero. He told the president at a meeting in August 1932 that he would accept nothing less than "unequivocal leadership of the government," a demand Hindenburg at first resisted. But under the influence of his son Oskar, von Papen, and his Reich chancellery chief, Otto Meissner, Hindenburg was finally persuaded to appoint Hitler as chancellor on 30 January 1933. Hitler continued to pay lip service to Hindenburg's waning authority and to exploit his status as a folk hero to give a veneer of respectability to his consolidation of power. Hindenburg died at Neudeck on 2 August 1934, by which time the Third Reich was firmly in place. A suitably solemn Hitler attended Hindenburg's state funeral, but by the end of August the presidential functions had been transferred by plebiscite to the Führer and chancellor, Adolf Hitler.

Related entries: Brüning, Heinrich; Elections; Papen, Franz von; Schleicher, Kurt von; Weimar Republic

Suggestions for further reading:
Bullock, Alan. 1991. *Hitler and Stalin: Parallel Lives.* London: HarperCollins.
Dorpalen, Andreas. 1964. *Hindenburg and the Weimar Republic.* Princeton: Princeton University Press.

Historikerstreit

Historical controversy about the unique nature of the Holocaust and Nazi crimes became a matter of public ar-

gument in Germany in the late 1980s, but the "historians' debate" rapidly deteriorated into bitter personal attacks between contending groups. The question is whether the Holocaust is unique or can be compared with the crimes committed by other nations, specifically in the name of communism. The debate intensified in the 1980s as West Germany shifted to the right with the electoral successes of Helmut Kohl, and the ideological temperature in Europe was raised by President Ronald Reagan's "Star Wars" program. Some ill-judged remarks by Reagan to the effect that Germany had put its past behind it once and for all were aggravated by a visit he made with Chancellor Kohl to Bitburg cemetery, where Waffen SS men are buried.

The debate was sparked off by Ernst Nolte in an article in the *Frankfurter Allgemeine Zeitung* (6 June 1986) in which he argued that the mass murder of the Jews should be looked at in broad historical context and that the Holocaust might be seen as an "Asiatic deed" modeled on the crimes of the Bolsheviks, to which the Nazis had "only" added the technology of gassing. Nolte's arguments were refuted by Jürgen Habermas in *Die Zeit,* and an ill-tempered hubbub arose over whether the Final Solution could legitimately be compared with other "national" crimes, in particular those of Stalinism.

The attempt to shift the moral opprobrium from Nazi Germany to the Soviet Union led to some unfortunate arguments being put forward, such as the idea that the Final Solution could have been, in Hitler's mind at least, an act of preventive warfare against the Jewish-Communist conspiracy. Nolte and the British historian David Irving also claimed that a declaration by Chaim Weizmann in September 1939 that Jews would fight alongside the British against Germany meant that Jews could plausibly be treated as "prisoners of war." This was rebutted by the Israeli historian Saul Friedländer, who pointed out that this claim derived from a pamphlet cited by Josef Goebbels.

The *Historikerstreit* generated more heat than light. It also sadly obscured valuable developments in German historical writing, such as the growth of the social history of the Third Reich, the staging of historical exhibitions, and positive political gestures such as Willy Brandt's bowing to the Warsaw Ghetto Rising memorial, Kohl's visit to Israel in 1984, and President Richard von Weizsacker's speech in May 1985 on the fortieth anniversary of the end of the war in Europe. As for the uniqueness of the Holocaust, the definitive summary has (one hopes) been made by Eberhard Jäckel: "Never before had a state with the authority of its responsible leader decided and announced that a specific human group, including its aged, its women, its children and infants, would be killed as quickly as possible, and then carried through the resolution using every possible means of state power" (Breitman 1991, p. 21).

Related entries: Final Solution; Holocaust

Suggestions for further reading:
Breitman, Richard. 1991. *The Architect of Genocide: Himmler and the Final Solution.* London: Bodley Head.
Evans, Richard J. 1989. *In Hitler's Shadow: West German Historians and the Attempt to Escape from the Nazi Past.* New York: Pantheon.
Maier, Charles S. 1988. *The Unmasterable Past: History, Holocaust, and German National Identity.* Cambridge, MA: Harvard University Press.

Hitler Myth

Hitler's personal popularity, as opposed to the mostly bad image of the Nazi Party, and the conscious and powerful creation of a heroic image of the Führer at complete variance with the coarse reality were essential to the success of National Socialism as a movement and in government. Josef Goebbels claimed it as his greatest propaganda achievement, but it was also to an extent created by the German people in answer to their beliefs and prejudices. The "Hitler Myth" invented Hitler as the personification of the nation and the "national community," the architect of economic recovery, the upholder of "law and order" and public morality, a sincere man who could not be held responsible for the unpopular actions of his supporters, a statesman of genius upholding Germany's rights in international affairs, a bulwark against Marxism and to a lesser extent the Jews, and finally a great military leader.

The myth originated in the Nazi movement under the Weimar Republic, once Hitler had decided that he was not the "drummer" for a future leader but was himself "the Leader of the coming Germany." Once in power, he was the "symbol of the nation," the "People's Chancellor," not a dictator but the "executor of the people's will," tackling Communists and parasites and leading a "national rebirth" by his many-sided genius. Any improvements, however small, in local economic life were attributed to Hitler personally, exploiting the general feeling in the early years of the regime that things were getting better.

According to the myth Hitler was personally simple and modest, his sincerity standing in stark contrast to the luxurious lies and corruption of the other Nazi bigwigs. He had, it was believed, sacrificed happiness and his private life for the service of the people. A Sopade report of May–June 1934 recorded the attitude of "the easy-going Munich petit-bourgeois man in the street": "Oh yes, our little Adolf, he is alright, but the cronies around him, they're nothing but rogues" (Kershaw 1983, pp. 122–123). Like a medieval king or tsar of Russia surrounded by evil counselors, the mythological Hitler was the defender of the "little man" against the "big shots," the popularity of the "Führer without sin" helping to compensate for the unpopularity of the "little Hitlers" with their corruption, brutality, and petty empire building. "If only the Führer knew," things would turn out all right. The suppression of Ernst Röhm and the Sturmabteilung in the Night of the Long Knives was overwhelmingly popular, and this aspect of the myth took a strong hold on public consciousness. A coalminer's wife in Bavaria stated in 1937: "Hitler means well, but those behind him commit many misdeeds. And he can't be responsible for everything. He knows what he wants and he has always succeeded up to now" (Kershaw 1983, p. 94). Hitler was even disassociated from violence against Jews. A Sopade report after Kristallnacht summed up opinion in Bavaria: "Hitler certainly wants the Jews to disappear from Germany, but he does not want them to be beaten to death and treated in such fashion" (Kershaw 1983, p. 273). Anti-Semitism may have played a minor role in creating the Hitler Myth, but his popularity helped to engender acceptance of Nazi Jewish policy and indifference toward the fate of German Jews.

If Hitler could be disassociated from the questions of everyday life in which his party played such a negative role, it was because he was preoccupied with the great issues of defense, war, and peace. An official report from the Aachen area in 1935 declared that even the most alienated sectors of the population "agreed with the Führer almost without exception in questions of foreign policy" (Kershaw 1989, p. 126). His initial string of foreign policy successes, rectifying the perceived injustices of the Versailles settlement without bloodshed, allowed Hitler to pose as a "man of peace." The military reoccupation of the Rhineland in 1936 was greeted with great enthusiasm and attributed to Hitler alone. "Never," boasted Goebbels, "in the history of all time has one man united in his own person as he has the trust and feeling of belonging to an entire people" (Kershaw 1989, p. 79). This was probably when Hitler himself became a complete believer in his

own myth. The high point of his prestige and popularity came with the Anschluss with Austria in 1938. Again war had been averted by the Führer's genius. "An elemental frenzy of enthusiasm" (Kershaw 1989, p. 131) was reported in border areas, and the Sopade reports recognized that "the country is now fully prepared for the fact that the 'Führer' can do anything he wants to" (Kershaw 1989, p. 132). The longer crisis over the Sudetenland posed the first threat to the myth, but Hitler's prestige was fully restored by the Munich Agreement.

In 1939, then, the population was prepared to follow Hitler, now personally identified with Germany, into a war for which he was not held to blame. Young people, who could not remember World War I and had been fully "socialized" under the Third Reich, were especially susceptible. The victorious western campaign of 1940 added "military genius" to Hitler's list of attributes, and it was difficult for anyone to criticize the generally jubilant popular mood. The war was to lead to the steady decline in the Hitler Myth, but doubts and worries would initially be glossed over by faith in his person. The Sicherheitsdienst reported in March 1941 that "the words of the Führer are gospel for the people" (Kershaw 1989, p. 159). The party was still not popular, but Hitler now associated himself with the army, always appearing in field-gray military uniform, and the myth of "evil counselors" persisted. After Rudolf Hess's flight to Britain, it was reported from Leipzig that people were "convinced that the Führer no longer hears at all about the actual mood and situation of the Reich itself and that most things are kept from him" (Kershaw 1989, p. 167).

The myth only began to crumble during the first winter of the Russian campaign in 1941–1942. But after years of indoctrination, the continuation and extension of the war could still be blamed on external enemies—Bolsheviks, Jews, British, and Americans; scapegoats for failure could be found among the military; and the fear of what defeat would mean for Germany began to grip the people. During the new attack on the Catholic Church and the "crucifix crisis" of 1941 in Bavaria, some voices were raised against Hitler, but most still believed that unpopular measures were instigated without his knowledge. From 1942 onward Hitler became an ever more remote figure, making fewer major speeches: a warlord, still heroic but out of touch with the problems of ordinary people suffering from material hardship and Allied bombing.

The floodgates of criticism were opened by the defeat at Stalingrad. The lies of the propaganda machine were exposed, and Hitler was directly implicated. The war, it was increasingly clear, could not end with either victory or an honorable peace. Ulrich von Hassell noted in his diary: "For the first time Hitler was not able to get out from under the responsibility; for the first time the critical rumours were aimed straight at him. There has been exposed for all eyes to see the lack of military ability of 'the most brilliant strategist of all time,' that is, our megalomaniac corporal" (Kershaw 1989, p. 193). Jokes and rumors began to circulate about Hitler's health and mental condition, and the images of Führer and party were blurred as never before, leading not to rebellion but to apathy. A report from Kitzingen, Franconia, in May 1943 stated: "Even the Führer has lost much sympathy among the people because he has apparently let himself be taken in by his Party people and does not seem to notice what things are like in the State today" (Kershaw 1989, p. 199).

Between 1943 and 1945 a key aspect of Hitler's image, that of military strength, was revealed as an illusion. The Allies were supreme over the skies of Germany, and the "text of leaflets, accusing Hitler of having started the war with every country, was approved, and the Führer cursed and damned" (Kershaw 1989, p. 204). "In the bunker, people cursed the Führer" (Kershaw 1989, p. 207). The Hitler Myth, though declining, remained relatively strong among the young, soldiers, and Nazi activists, but the overwhelming desire for an end to the war made people sullen and silent about Hitler. In the last months of the war he sank from sight, becoming a distant, shadowy figure, and by August 1944 only a tiny proportion of the people believed in victory. An inhabitant of Berchtesgarden complained in March 1945: "If we'd imagined in 1933 how things would turn out, we'd never have voted for Hitler" (Kershaw 1989, p. 223). The realization had been rather late in coming.

Related entries: Charismatic Domination; Führer Principle; Goebbels, Paul Josef; National Socialist German Workers' Party; Nazi Movement; Propaganda; Public Opinion

Suggestions for further reading:
Kershaw, Ian. 1983. *Popular Opinion and Political Dissent in the Third Reich: Bavaria 1933–1945.* Oxford: Clarendon Press.
———. 1989. *The "Hitler Myth": Image and Reality in the Third Reich.* Paperback ed. New York: Oxford University Press.

Hitler Schools

The Adolf Hitler Schools for twelve- to eighteen-year-olds, established from 1937 onward, were operated and financed exclusively by the Nazi Party and were therefore outside the control of the Education Ministry. They were intended as training schools for future Nazi leaders, but only a dozen were ever opened or planned. Selected graduates entered one of the four Ordensburgen (order castles) to continue their political, racial, and biological education and their physical training. Hitler himself, however, perversely seemed to favor the rival national political educational institutes (Napolas), organized by the Education Ministry with the help of the Sturmabteilung and SS.

Related entries: Education; Youth Policy

Hitler Youth

The Nazi organization for young people had its origins in the Jungsturm Adolf Hitler, a Sturmabteilung (SA) organization for the recruitment of future members, founded in Munich in 1922. It became the Hitler Youth (HJ) in December 1926, with Baldur von Schirach at its head. When Schirach became Reich youth leader of the National Socialist German Workers' Party (NSDAP, Nazi Party) in 1931, he made the Hitler Youth, the League of German Girls (BDM), and the party's other youth organizations independent of the directives of the SA and party offices. The HJ began to grow rapidly after the Reich Youth Congress held at Potsdam on 2 October 1932, and on Hitler's accession to power the Reich Youth Leadership under Schirach became a "supreme Reich office," indicating the importance attached to it by Hitler.

The entire HJ encompassed the Jungvolk for ten- to fourteen-year-old boys and the Jungmädel for the same age group of girls, as well as the BDM, and the HJ proper for fifteen- to eighteen-year-old boys. They were organized into forty regions, subdivided into groups known as bands, tribes, followerships, troops, and comradeships. The jurisdiction of the HJ covered everything concerned with young people outside school, including youth hostels, youth homes, vocational education, and youth functionaries in schools and workplaces. All rival organizations were banned, and in 1936 it was granted the status of Supreme Reich Authority, meaning that Schirach was answerable only to Hitler

Hitler inspects a group of Hitler Youth in Thuringia in 1936. The HJ gradually took control of the cultural activities of youth in the Reich, abolishing the distinction between school and training camp and habituating all young people to Nazi ritual and discipline. (Culver Pictures)

and largely outside party and ministerial jurisdiction.

From December 1938 all young Germans were required to be members, and by early 1939 membership totaled 7.25 million. The public face of the HJ emphasized the virtues of community and partnership in the service of the German people and working toward the birth of a new German empire. The reality was of an increasingly militaristic organization, with "special formations" developing militarily useful skills. It was in constant competition with the schools: the time given to HJ activities and the anti-intellectual stress on physical hardening contributed considerably to the decline in educational standards under the Third Reich. Bernhard Rust, the minister of education, succeeded in limiting its direct influence in schools, but in keeping with Hitler's crude philosophy of life, the stress in both was on the physical over the intellectual. It has been claimed that the HJ and the BDM appealed to adolescents because of the opportunities they provided for individual self-assertion. In organizations run largely by their memberships, young people could affirm themselves outside the authority of parents and teachers. The price they paid for this supposed freedom, however, was acceptance of the "Führer principle," a culture of denunciation, the acceptance of a racist and anachronistic worldview, militarism, and a blind adulation of Hitler.

Related entries: Education; Schirach, Baldur von; Youth Policy

Suggestions for further reading:
Horn, Daniel. 1976. "The Hitler Youth and Educational Decline in the Third Reich," *History of Education Quarterly* 16, pp. 425–447.
Koch, Hansjoachim. 1975. *The Hitler Youth: Origins and Development, 1922–45.* London: Macdonald and Jane's.
Rempel, Gerhard. 1989. *Hitler's Children: The Hitler Youth and the SS.* Chapel Hill: University of North Carolina Press.

Hoess, Rudolf (1900–1947)

Commandant of the Auschwitz extermination camp from 1940 to 1944, Hoess has been described as "the Nazis' ultimate technocrat of death" (Freeman 1995, pp. 193–194). He fought in World War I and was a member of the Freikorps and a Nazi from early days, especially closely associated with Martin Bormann in Thuringia. Hoess joined the SS in 1934 and worked at the camps of Dachau and Sachsenhausen before being transferred to Auschwitz. Here he advocated and was the first to use Zyklon-B crystals (hydrogen cyanide) as a quicker and more efficient way of gassing the Nazis' victims en masse. His brutal efficiency in running Auschwitz earned him promotion as deputy inspector general of concentration camps for the SS. Hoess avoided arrest in 1945 but was eventually tracked down. He was hanged by the Poles in Auschwitz in 1947 after writing an account of his bestial career.

Related entries: Auschwitz; Extermination Camps; Holocaust

Suggestions for further reading:
Freeman, Michael. 1995. *Atlas of Nazi Germany: A Political, Economic and Social Anatomy of the Third Reich.* 2nd ed. London and New York: Longman.
Gutman, Yisrael, and Michael Berenbaum, eds. 1994. *Anatomy of the Auschwitz Death Camp.* Bloomington: Indiana University Press.

Hoffmann, Heinrich (1885–1957)

Hitler's official photographer had learned his trade working in his father's photography shop in Fürth before 1914. He served as a photographer in the Bavarian army during World War I and first met Hitler in 1919. It was the beginning of a close relationship. Hoffmann joined the National Socialist German Workers' Party in 1920 and soon became a member of Hitler's inner circle. Hitler enjoyed relaxing at the Hoffmanns' house in Munich, and it was through him that Hitler first met Eva Braun, who worked in Hoffmann's shop. Hoffmann was the only person allowed to photograph Hitler and went with him everywhere, even to the front during the war. In all he took some 2.5 million photographs of the Führer and became a rich man as a result. Hoffmann also had the remarkable idea that Hitler should receive royalties for every picture of himself that appeared on a postage stamp, earning the Führer vast amounts of money.

Hoffmann's several books of photographs of Hitler sold well in the 1930s. His greatest success, *Hitler, wie ihn keiner kennt* (*The Hitler Nobody Knows*), published in 1933, showed a relaxed and friendly Führer and helped greatly in building his image with the public. Hoffmann's privileged position was not based on politics but on his artistic and business connection with Hitler. He knew Hitler's tastes in art and selected paintings for the annual Grand Art Show. Hoffmann enjoyed his place in the sun and, according to Albert Speer, was one of "the alcoholic members of [Hitler's] entourage" (Speer 1971, p. 263). Hoffmann was tried as a Nazi profiteer in 1947 and sentenced to ten years' imprisonment, later reduced to three and raised again to five, and nearly all his personal fortune was confiscated. He died in Munich on 16 December 1957.

Related entries: Art; Hitler Myth

Suggestions for further reading:
Hoffmann, Heinrich. 1955. *Hitler Was My Friend*. London: Burke.
Speer, Albert. 1971. *Inside the Third Reich*. Paperback ed. London: Sphere Books.

Holocaust

The attempted extermination of the Jews of Europe by industrialized mass killing is a unique event in the annals of genocide. Arguments have opposed "intentionalist" interpretations, according to which the Holocaust was the result of the implementation of Hitler's preconceived plans for the Jews, to "functionalist" interpretations, which see it as the result of increasingly radical efforts by different Nazi agencies to solve the "Jewish problem" in the context of the war. Although both kinds of interpretation need to be taken into account, it cannot be denied that Hitler, the central figure in the racial state of the Third Reich whose worldview was based on anti-Semitism, bears the greatest responsibility.

Attempts to portray the Holocaust as an economically rational offshoot of "modernization" or as the product of scientific rationality have little to recommend them. The perpetrators of the Final Solution used irrational "racial science" to justify their actions. At the height of the war the Nazis diverted valuable resources from military uses to the destruction of the Jews. Even when the victims were set to work, they were worked to death, and the death marches across Europe as the Allied armies closed in and liberated the extermination camps show that the goal of the total destruction of the Jews remained fundamental until the end. Hitler ruled over an ideologically motivated regime, and neither extreme "intentionalism," laying all the blame on one man, nor extreme "functionalism," tempering the evil bases of Nazi ideology, should be allowed to complicate overmuch the moral responsibility of the perpetrators. The eagerness with which even the tiny Jewish communities in the Greek islands were tracked down gives the lie to any economic or "modernizing" rationale.

The Holocaust was the culmination of Nazi Jewish policy, following from the 1930s, ghettoization, resettlement plans, the murderous actions of the SS and others in Poland and the Soviet Union, and the decision for a "Final Solution." The mere recital of facts and figures does little to communicate the true horror of the Holocaust, an event made up of millions of individual experiences and tragedies accompanied by unimaginable brutality and psychopathic sadism. The goal of a "Final Solution" may not have been achieved, but approximately 6 million Jews perished, two-thirds of the prewar Jewish population of Europe and one-third of world Jewry. Approximately half the victims died in the death camps; about 1.5 million at the hands of SS Einsatzgruppen and other killing units; and about 1.5 million of disease, starvation, and ill treatment in the ghettos and concentration camps. The death toll encompasses at least 2.7 million Polish Jews; 2.2 million Soviet Jews; half a million Hungarian Jews; 230,000 German and Austrian Jews; 140,000 from Czechoslovakia; more than 100,000 from the Netherlands; 60,000 each from Yugoslavia and Greece; more than 30,000 French Jews; and smaller numbers from Belgium, Albania, Norway, Bulgaria, and Luxemburg. At least 200,000 were killed in Romania at the hands of Hitler's Romanian allies. By contrast, most Danish Jews escaped to Sweden, and in Italy about 85 percent of those still in the country after the German occupation survived.

Related entries: Alsace-Lorraine; Anti-Semitism; Auschwitz; Baltic States; Belgium; Belsen; Buchenwald; Bulgaria; Concentration Camps; Czechoslovakia; Dachau; Denmark; Eastern Front; Eichmann, Adolf; Euthanasia; Extermination Camps; Final Solution; France; Generalgouvernement; Greece; Gypsies; Heydrich, Reinhard; Himmler, Heinrich; *Historikerstreit;* Hoess, Rudolf; Hungary; Italy; Jews and Jewish Policy; Kaltenbrunner, Ernst; National Socialism; Netherlands; Norway; Poland; Racial Theory; Romania; Rosenberg, Alfred; Schutzstaffel; Sobibor; Soviet Union; Treblinka; Ukraine; Wannsee Conference; War Crimes; Warsaw Ghetto; Yugoslavia

Suggestions for further reading:
Burleigh, Michael. 1997. *Ethics and Extermination: Reflections on Nazi Genocide.* New York: Cambridge University Press.
Dawidowicz, Lucy S. 1975. *The War against the Jews, 1933–1945.* New York: Holt, Rinehart and Winston.
Fein, Helen. 1979. *Accounting for Genocide: National Responses and Jewish Victimization during the Holocaust.* Chicago: University of Chicago Press.
Gilbert, Martin. 1985. *The Holocaust: A History of the Jews of Europe during the Second World War.* New York: Holt, Rinehart and Winston.
Hilberg, Raul. 1985. *The Destruction of the European Jews.* Rev. ed. New York: Holmes and Meier.
Levin, Nora. 1973. *The Holocaust: The Destruction of the European Jews.* New York: New Viewpoints.
Marrus, Michael R. 1987. *The Holocaust in History.* New York: Meridian.
Marrus, Michael R., and Robert O. Paxton. 1981. *Vichy France and the Jews.* New York: Basic Books.
Zuccotti, Susan. 1987. *The Italians and the Holocaust: Persecution, Rescue and Survival.* New York: Basic Books.

Horthy, Miklós (1868–1957)

Rear Admiral Horthy, who had led the "National Army" against the Communist regime of Béla Kun in Hungary in 1919, was elected "regent" by the Hungarian National Assembly in 1920. He gradually secured his near-dictatorial power and sought close cooperation with Benito Mussolini and Hitler. His reward was Hitler's backing for Hungarian territorial claims against Czechoslovakia and Romania in 1939–1940, but the price was that Horthy was dragged into support for Hitler's war policies and aims in eastern Europe. As the war in the east turned against Germany, Horthy attempted to make contact with the Allies, but immediately after beginning armistice negotiations with Moscow, he was arrested by SS units on 16 October 1944 and interned in Hansee Palace in Bavaria. Hitler's troops occupied Hungary. After the end of the war Horthy went into exile, first in Switzerland and later in Portugal.

Related entries: Hungary

Hossbach, Friedrich (1894–1980)

Hitler's Wehrmacht adjutant from 1934 to 1938, Hossbach, a soldier since 1913, is chiefly remembered for his careful note taking of the "Hossbach Memorandum." His full account of the meeting of 5 November 1937 was revealed at the Nuremberg trials, providing proof of Hitler's long-term objectives in foreign policy. Hossbach himself was dismissed from his post as adjutant during the "Blomberg-Fritsch crisis" of 1938 but was restored to the General Staff in 1939. During the war, promoted to general of infantry, he commanded the 16th Panzer Corps. He spent two years on the Eastern Front and took over as commander of the 4th Army on 28 January 1945, only to be dismissed two days later for withdrawing his troops in East Prussia against Hitler's orders.

Related entries: Eastern Front; Hossbach Memorandum

Hossbach Memorandum

The account drawn up by Friedrich Hossbach of a small select meeting held on 5 November 1937 is one of the more controversial documents relating to Hitler's foreign policy. Speaking to Hermann Goering, Foreign Minister Konstantin von Neurath, and the commanders in chief of the three armed forces, Hitler made clear his intention to use force in the pursuit of lebensraum in eastern Europe and face the consequent dangers. He stressed the need for Germany to take advantage of its progress in rearmament and that it could not wait longer than 1943–1945 to solve its foreign problems. Action against Austria and Czechoslovakia could probably be undertaken without active resistance from Britain or France, and the outbreak of the Spanish Civil War offered the opportunity for freer actions in the east.

Few would see in the memorandum a meticulously prepared blueprint for aggression. It is a typical monologue such as Hitler frequently inflicted upon his subordinates and cannot be taken as a definite plan for military action. But it does show Hitler prepared to take risks to exploit the instability of European affairs, somewhat to the alarm of his military chiefs. If Britain and France are occupied elsewhere, Hitler is prepared to fall on Austria or Czechoslovakia immediately, even if Germany is not fully prepared. Disagreement centers on whether this marks a turning point in Hitler's view of Britain and the abandonment of any hope of a deal with the British. But whether or not Hitler continued seriously to hope for an alliance between 1937 and 1939, he does appear to have been ready to try his luck in eastern Europe without British approval.

Related entries: Foreign Policy; Great Britain; Hossbach, Friedrich

Suggestions for further reading:
Robertson, Esmonde M, ed. 1971. *The Origins of the Second World War: Historical Interpretations.* London: Macmillan.

Hugenberg, Alfred (1865–1951)

The press and film magnate Hugenberg was typical of the conservative nationalist forces who thought they could control and use Hitler for their own ends. As such, he became one of the principal gravediggers of democracy in Germany. During the 1920s, taking advantage of the inflation of the time, the former director of the Krupp concern and cofounder of the Pan-German League created a great chain of newspapers and news agencies and obtained a controlling interest in Universum Film AG (UFA), the almost monopolistic producer of German films and newsreels. Hugenberg used his concentration of power in the Berlin and provincial presses, advertising, and the cinema to support ultranationalism and robustly oppose pacifism, democracy, and socialism.

Hugenberg became chairman of the German National People's Party (DNVP) in October 1928 and in 1929 joined forces with the rest of the "National Opposition," including Hitler, in the campaign against the Young Plan. Hitler was in theory a junior partner in the alliance, but Hugenberg's propaganda machine had effectively been put at his disposal, and for the first time the name of the Nazi Führer became widely known to the German people. Hugenberg, however, still thought he could constrain Hitler, who still needed DNVP support to gain a majority in the Reichstag in January 1933. In reality he was merely providing the new chancellor with a veneer of respectability and Prussian tradition.

Hugenberg was made minister of economics and agriculture in Hitler's first cabinet. But his electoral support was fading away, the Sturmabteilung harassed his supporters, and the Nazi press attacked his economic ideas as reactionary. He was pressured into resigning on 27 June 1933, and the DNVP dissolved itself two days later. Removed from politics and forced to sell some of his businesses to the Nazi Party, Hugenberg nevertheless retained control of most of his newspapers and publishing empire until 1943. He retained this property after Hitler's downfall: in 1949 a de-Nazification court classified him as a "fellow-traveler," and he was not penalized for his role in levering Hitler into power. Hugenberg died in Kukenbruch bei Rinteln on 12 March 1951.

Related entries: Cinema; German National People's Party; Nationalists; Press; Weimar Republic

Suggestions for further reading:
Jones, Larry Eugene. 1992. "'The Greatest Stupidity of My Life': Alfred Hugenberg and the Formation of the Hitler Cabinet, January 1933," *Journal of Contemporary History* 27, pp. 63–87.
Leopold, John A. 1977. *Alfred Hugenberg: The Radical Nationalist Campaign against the Weimar Republic.* New Haven: Yale University Press.

Hungary

From 1920 onward Hungary was a kingdom with a vacant throne under the "regency" of Admiral Miklós Horthy, and between 1922 and 1931 it pursued a campaign for the revision of the Treaty of Versailles in accordance with its territorial claims against Czechoslovakia, Romania, and Yugoslavia. Under Prime Minister Gyula Gömbös from 1932 to 1936, Hungary opposed the French-backed "little entente," which brought together its three rival countries, and sought closer ties with Hitler's Germany and Benito Mussolini's Italy. Ideological sympathy with the dictators went hand in hand with Hungary's increasing economic dependence on Germany. Hitler financially supported the small "National Socialist Party" of Hungary, generally known as the Arrow Cross, founded by Ferenc Szálasi in 1937.

The near-dictator Horthy, however, was the dominant personality in Hungarian politics. Under his direction Hungary joined the Anti-Comintern Pact in February 1939 and the Tripartite Pact in November 1940. It declared war on the Soviet Union and Great Britain on 27 June 1941. Horthy attempted to maintain independence from Hitler in domestic policy and to protect Hungarian Jews, who made up about 6 percent of the population. But when he attempted to reach an armistice with Moscow, German troops occupied Hungary on 19 March 1944. Horthy was arrested and taken to Germany, while Szálasi became head of state, slavishly carrying out Hitler's policies, including the deportation of Jews to the death camps. But the approach of the Red Army could not be halted. On 1 January 1945 the Soviet Union concluded an armistice with Hungary and swiftly established a Communist regime under Mátyás Rákosi.

Related entries: Anti-Comintern Pact; Czechoslovakia; Holocaust; Horthy, Miklós; Romania; Tripartite Pact; Yugoslavia

I

IG Farben (IG Farbenindustrie AG)

Formed in 1925 by a merger of eight companies, IG Farben was the largest private enterprise in Germany during the Weimar and Nazi periods and the leading exporter, manufacturing products from pharmaceuticals to light metals and monopolizing production of coal-based substitutes for key raw materials, including nitrogen, fuel, and rubber. Its power was indispensable to Hitler's attempts at expansion through conquest.

IG Farben did not back Hitler before his accession to power but after 1933 made the Third Reich's economic aims its own and enthusiastically adhered to Nazi policies, including the extermination of the Jews. The company's activities were effectively militarized, and it provided two-thirds of the staff of the Reich Office for Economic Expansion. During the labor shortage of the late 1930s it recruited Polish workers and handed undisciplined employees over to the Gestapo. And during the war, while its profits increased by 150 percent, it grabbed property in the Greater Reich and employed slave labor, most notoriously at a factory attached to the Auschwitz extermination camp. A subsidiary of IG Farben manufactured the notorious Zyklon-B gas, used in the murder of hundreds of thousands of Jews and others.

By the end of the war, IG Farben employed 333,000 people, just under half of whom were foreign laborers, and made huge profits. It provided 25 percent of German output of synthetic fibers, 33 percent of fuel, 100 percent of synthetic rubbers and stabilizers for explosives, and between one-third and one-half of all German chemical production. In 1947–1948, twenty-three of the company's principal managers were tried for war crimes at Nuremberg, and thirteen were convicted.

Related entries: Auschwitz; Economic Policy; Final Solution; Four-Year Plan; Industry; Rearmament; Trade Policy; War Crimes

Suggestions for further reading:
Hayes, Peter. 1987. *Industry and Ideology: IG Farben in the Nazi Era.* New York: Cambridge University Press.

Industry

The attitude of German business under the Third Reich has been likened to the conductor of a runaway bus who has no control over the actions of the driver but keeps collecting fares right up to the final crash. The Depression saw a dramatic decline in German industrial production of some 70 percent between 1929 and 1931. Hitler's first preoccupation, taking advantage of the signs of recovery al-

Alfried Krupp is taken from his estate in the back of a jeep after being taken prisoner by the Americans in April 1945. At the Krupp Trial held by US Military Court III at Nuremberg in 1947–1948, Krupp and other high-level executives of the Krupp firm were found guilty of crimes against humanity for the employment of slave laborers and prisoners of war in the company's factories and for the plundering of economic resources from occupied countries. (Express Newspapers/Archive Photos)

ready made under the Brüning government, was to restore industrial capacity and investment before launching his major rearmament drive. Hjalmar Schacht, as president of the Reichsbank and minister of economics, was the dominant figure. Having helped rally industrialists to Hitler, he now devised the strategy for financing rearmament while insisting on orthodox financial stringency.

Industry was "coordinated" by the Industrial Group of the Reich Economic Chamber. Industrial concerns realized the importance of direct links to government in an economy geared to rearmament, and directorships fell into the capacious laps of senior Nazi Party leaders. After Schacht's resignation and his replacement by Walther Funk, SS and Gestapo directors became common in German boardrooms. With the quickening pace of rearmament and the introduction of the Four-Year Plan in 1936, industry settled into a subordinate but profitable position in Hitler's state. Industrial concentration proceeded apace, and the power of the large cartels was strengthened. The 9,500 joint stock companies in Germany in 1932 had become 5,400 by 1941.

The great concerns like IG Farben and Krupp reaped healthy profits and expanded enormously during the last years of peace and the first years of the war. In the late 1930s Germany was second only to the United States as a producer of iron and steel and was the largest producer of rubber in continental Europe. Dependence on imported raw materials, especially iron ore and natural rubber, was partly solved by conquest in Europe, which also provided slave labor for the big companies. Reservations about Hitler were correspondingly slow to develop among industrialists, even as the course of war turned to disaster. Only one, Ewald Löser, a director of Krupp, is known to have been involved in the July Plot. From 1942 onward, Albert Speer, as the virtual dictator of German industry, used committees of manufacturers to achieve miracles of arms production over the heads of the Nazi satraps. But for all its ruthless methods and exploitation of subject lands and peoples, German industry could not stand up indefinitely against the combined economic power of the Allies.

By 1944 Allied bombing was being directed more specifically toward industrial targets. The largest businesses, even Krupp's, began to demand compensation for war damage and repayment of debts from the Reich. Investment in new plants became virtually impossible. As the Allies advanced, Hitler issued his infamous "Nero order": in theory a scorched-earth policy but also an act of vengeful nihilism calling for the destruction of the entire infrastructure of German industry. Working with industrialists and some of the *Gauleiters,* Speer successfully thwarted Hitler's apocalyptic folly.

At the last moment, enough of Germany's industrial base was saved to provide a basis for the postwar "economic miracle."

Related entries: Bombing Campaigns; Economic Policy; Four-Year Plan; Funk, Walther; German Labor Front; Goering, Hermann; IG Farben; Krupp, Alfried; Krupp, Gustav; Labor Relations; Labor Service; Ley, Robert; Rearmament; Ruhr; Saarland; Schacht, Hjalmar; Socialism; Speer, Albert; Thyssen, Fritz; Todt, Fritz; Todt Organization; Total War; Trade Policy; Unemployment; Working Class

Suggestions for further reading:
James, Harold. 1986. *The German Slump: Politics and Economics, 1924–1936.* Oxford: Clarendon Press.
Milward, Alan S. 1965. *The German Economy at War.* London: Athlone Press.
Overy, Richard J. 1994. *War and Economy in the Third Reich.* Oxford: Clarendon Press.
———. 1996. *The Nazi Economic Recovery.* 2nd ed. Cambridge: Cambridge University Press.

Italy

Hitler never expressed anything but contempt for the Italians as a people. It was part of the racist nationalist mythology to which he fully subscribed that the Germans had never been subdued by the Roman Empire. Only after Italy's entry into World War II were the Italians briefly awarded honorary Aryan status. But the triumph of fascism in Italy meant that relations between the two dictatorships would be different in kind from normal state relations. Hitler was inspired by Benito Mussolini's example, and whatever the difficulties of their relationship they were bound together by a common contempt for democracy, anti-Marxism, and aggressive nationalism.

During the Weimar period and into the early years of the Third Reich, Italy pursued a generally moderate and careful foreign policy exemplified by the Locarno Pact of 1925 and the Lateran Treaties with the Vatican of 1929. The most thorny question between Germany and Italy was the status of Austria. A united Greater Reich posed a potential threat to Italian security in the north, and Italy mobilized forces on the Austrian border following the murder of Engelbert Dollfuss. But with the adoption of a policy of imperial conquest, shown in the invasion of Abyssinia in October 1935 and the occupation of Albania in April 1939, Italy was drawn into ever greater dependency on the Third Reich. The closer relationship was shown in the Berlin-Rome Axis, created in late October 1936; common intervention in the Spanish Civil War; the Anti-Comintern Pact of November 1937; Italian acquiescence in the Anschluss; and the "Pact of Steel" of 22 May 1939. Italy was also a signatory to the Munich Agreement, consecrating Hitler's aggression in Czechoslovakia.

Italy adopted a position of "nonbelligerence" at the beginning of the war, but its entry into the conflict on 10 June 1940 essentially made it a satellite of the Reich. The Italian economy was not geared to the needs of war, as Italian industry retained a greater independence from the regime than in Germany. Nor were the Italian people overly enthusiastic about fighting either for Hitler or Mussolini's "new Roman Empire." Hitler was forced to come to the rescue of the Italians in the Balkans and in North Africa, thereby overstretching German resources. Military cooperation never worked as it should have, with the Italians bridling at Nazi arrogance and the German awareness of their position as senior partners.

When Mussolini was deposed in July 1943, the new prime minister, Marshal Pietro Badoglio, with the support of King Victor Emmanuel III, concluded a cease-fire with the Allies on 8 September. As the Allied troops began their laborious and difficult conquest of Italy from the south, Badoglio's new government had the status of "co-belligerence" with the British and Americans. German troops occupied northern Italy; Mussolini, now completely Hitler's puppet, was installed as head of the "Italian Social Republic" at Salò on Lake Garda; and the north became embroiled in a bloody civil war opposing Fascists and Germans against an antifascist partisan movement, itself divided between Communist and other groups.

The German capitulation in Italy was formally announced on 2 May 1945, three days after Hitler's suicide. Mussolini was killed by partisans on 28 April. After the war, a referendum rejected the monarchy, and Italy became a democratic republic, propped up by the United States to prevent a communist takeover and dominated by the Christian Democratic Party. The alliance with Hitler had resulted in Italy becoming a theater of war and the downfall of fascism and the Italian monarchy in a conflict that had turned Italian against Italian.

Related entries: Anti-Comintern Pact; Austria; Axis; Ciano, Galeazzo, Count; Fascism; Foreign Policy; France; Greece; Holocaust; Munich Agreement; Mussolini, Benito; North Africa; Pact of Steel; Resistance Movements; Spain; Tripartite Pact; Versailles, Treaty of; Yugoslavia

Suggestions for further reading:

Deakin, F. W. 1962. *The Brutal Friendship: Mussolini, Hitler and the Fall of Italian Fascism.* London: Weidenfeld and Nicolson.

J

Japan

The increasingly militaristic empire of Japan, ruled by the remote and divine Emperor Hirohito, displayed a spirit of aggressive nationalism similar to that of Hitler's Germany and Benito Mussolini's Italy. But the "hollow alliance" between Germany and Japan was a marriage of convenience more than an ideological convergence, and Japan pursued its own aims in a part of the world in which Hitler showed little interest. As in Germany, the roots of Japanese expansionism lay in resentment at the post-1918 settlement, "Japan's Versailles." The Japanese felt that they had been denied equal status with the Western Allies as a victor in World War I and that their claims in China had been unjustly rejected.

The powerful Japanese army, built partly on the Prussian model, proclaimed Japan's "national rebirth" through the conquest of "living space" on the Asian mainland, while Japanese business, supported by politicians, court circles, and the navy, sought markets and raw materials through expansion to the south. Expansion began with the invasion of Manchuria in 1931, followed by withdrawal from the League of Nations in 1933 and war with China in 1937. Japan sought Hitler's support through the Anti-Comintern Pact of 1936 and the Tripartite Pact of 1940. Hitler could claim to be the dominant figure in an antidemocratic and anti-Marxist alliance spanning Europe and Asia. And Japan's proclaimed crusade against the "white" empires of Britain, France, and the Netherlands in Asia could be useful to Hitler even though he had no interest in the liberation of colonial subject peoples.

In 1940–1941 Japan established its position in China and French Indochina, but faced economic sanctions by the United States, the protector of China and the Dutch East Indies. The cabinet of General Hideki Tojo chose the path of "forward escape" with the attack on Pearl Harbor on 7 December 1941. Protected by a nonaggression pact with the Soviet Union, Japan enjoyed a phase of quick victories and great expansion against the British, French, and Americans. But following the turning point of the Battle of Midway of 4–7 June 1942, Japan's limited resources became strained. Heavy naval losses, U.S. bombing raids, and finally the dropping of atomic bombs on Hiroshima and Nagasaki led to Japan's surrender on 2 September 1945. Japan's war had been a separate affair from Germany's: the advantage to Hitler lay in the diversion of British and especially U.S. resources and in divisions within the U.S. military as to whether priority should be given to the struggle with Japan or with Germany, a constant source of friction among the Allies.

Related entries: Anti-Comintern Pact; Tripartite Pact; United States of America

Japanese troops landing in Malaya in December 1941. The first phase of World War II saw victories beyond Japanese expectations in China, French Indochina, British Malaya, Singapore, and the Netherlands East Indies. (Archive Photos)

Suggestions for further reading:
Meskill, Johanna M. 1966. *Hitler and Japan: The Hollow Alliance.* New York: Atherton Press.

Jehovah's Witnesses

The Jehovah's Witnesses, or "earnest Bible students," attracted the particular attention of the Nazis after Hitler's accession to power for their radical pacifism, their international nature as a religious community, and their rejection of the trappings of the Führer principle, such as the oath to the Führer and the "Heil Hitler!" German greeting. The obligation laid on Witnesses to "bear witness" and recruit for the movement ensured conflict with the Gestapo. Denounced as "advance agents of world bolshevism," they were banned in mid-1933. Nearly all of the 6,000 or so German Witnesses were arrested and sent to concentration camps, where more than 2,000 died. They aroused admiration, even from Heinrich Himmler, for their steadfast-

ness in the face of harsh mistreatment from the guards and were considered among the most obdurate and incorruptible of camp inmates.

Related entries: Concentration Camps

Jews and Jewish Policy

At the time of Hitler's accession to power there were approximately 500,000 Jews in Germany, making up only 0.75 percent of the population. Three years of economic depression had exacerbated anti-Semitic feeling, especially among the lower middle classes, but the vast majority of German Jews had no experience of racist aggression and by accepting some discrimination and keeping out of trouble could easily feel "at home" in Germany. The great majority had been successfully assimilated for generations. Only about 20 percent still wore distinctive Jewish garb, and these "eastern Jews" were concentrated into particular quarters of larger cities such as Berlin, Frankfurt, or Breslau. Only a minority of the non-Jewish population ever encountered Jews, which probably helped to make Nazi claims about their exaggerated but hidden influence more credible. In certain professions there was a higher proportion of Jews than non-Jews, but nowhere near the extent claimed by the Nazis: just under 17 percent of lawyers were Jewish (but almost no judges), as were 17 percent of bankers (less than in the late nineteenth century) and almost 11 percent of doctors. The Jewish presence was also pronounced in the clothing and retail trades, with several large department stores created and owned by Jews. This increased the anti-Semitic resentment of small shopkeepers. But the Hitlerian notion of the "Jewish Republic," identifying Jewish influence with cultural and economic decline, was an asinine myth appealing to the gullible, the opportunistic, and the envious and frustrated.

After receiving full legislative powers through the Enabling Act in March 1933, Hitler set about removing the Jews from German public life. This was one election promise Hitler meant to keep. But the actual path of the anti-Jewish policy was far from straightforward, due to differences within the Nazi leadership as to its ultimate purpose and the need to manage national and international opinion. Many Jews and non-Nazis clung for several years to the idea that Hitler's worldview was so preposterous that its implied policies could never be put into practice. In the course of *Gleichschaltung* Jews were removed from the civil service, education, entertainment, the arts, journalism, and the stock exchange. Restrictions were imposed on the practices of Jewish doctors and dentists, and Jews were forbidden to own farmland or deal in livestock, though this last provision remained ignored in Bavaria and Franconia. At the same time, restrictions were placed on Jewish entry into secondary schools and universities. A Nazi-sponsored boycott of Jew-

"Jews Forbidden! to enter the Palace Park by order of the Police Department, June 24, 1938." Nazi policy between 1933 and 1939 was based on the total separation of Jews from the rest of society and their exclusion from the economy. Signs such as this one proliferated in public places throughout Germany. (Archive Photos)

ish businesses on 1 April 1933, however, was abandoned after one day. The economy would be disrupted by the boycott, and accompanying thuggery by the Sturmabteilung (SA) did not evoke the hoped-for popular enthusiasm.

The Nuremberg Laws of September 1935 represented the preliminary culmination of anti-Jewish legislation and policy. They introduced a system of segregation and spawned a variety of discriminatory measures at local and regional levels. Municipal and district authorities could ban Jews from parks, cinemas, public swimming pools, or other recreational facilities while initiating local boycotts of Jewish stores. Towns and villages erected signs proclaiming "Jews are not wanted here." Jews were condemned to a kind of "social death" but could still survive as an alien minority in segregated institutions. The Jewish community still operated its own schools, newspapers, health services, and cultural institutions, and for a while random physical violence against Jews died down, not least during the Olympic year of 1936.

The anti-Jewish campaign was stepped up again after the Olympics. Among other measures, Jews were banned from taking degrees at German universities in April 1937. The intensification of the persecution in 1938 may have been linked to preparations for war. The purpose was to force Jews to emigrate and to identify and segregate those who remained. In July 1938 Jewish physicians and lawyers were forced to close their practices, and in August 1938 the Interior Ministry ordered all Jews without obviously Jewish first names to add "Sara" or "Israel" to their names. All Jews were now required to carry special identification cards, and the letter "J" was stamped in their passports from October 1938.

Instrumental in trying to force Jews to emigrate was the "Aryanization" of Jewish businesses. The immediate exclusion of Jews from economic life at the time of *Gleichschaltung* would have had disastrous consequences. Hence no decree ordering enterprises to dismiss Jewish employees was issued until 1938. Similarly, the regime opted for a gradual transfer of Jewish-owned businesses into "Aryan" hands. The process remained officially voluntary until after the Kristallnacht pogrom of 9–10 November 1938. But even before Aryanization was made compulsory, threats, blackmail, and open violence were used to compel Jews to sell their businesses, houses, and belongings at a fraction of their market value.

A flurry of decrees after Kristallnacht not only enforced Aryanization but also completed the total separation of Jews from German public life. They were prohibited from entering German parks, forests, theaters, concerts, or cultural exhibitions. On 15 November 1938 Jews were barred from German schools and in December 1938 from owning automobiles. Forced emigration was now official policy: Jews were to be removed completely from the Reich. In 1939 the remaining independence of the Jewish community was suppressed. Jewish publications were banned, and Jewish community organizations placed under the direct control of the Gestapo. Jewish life in Germany was to be extinguished.

Although Hitler was obviously the inspiration for anti-Jewish policy, he let his subordinates argue over its precise direction and managed to distance himself in the public eye from the most visible excesses. Whereas one faction, typified by Julius Streicher and the SA, advocated (and practiced when allowed) the most violent methods to eject Jews from society, others such as Hjalmar Schacht and even Hermann Goering in his capacity as head of the Four-Year Plan were worried about the adverse economic effects. The SS also considered the activities of the SA and Nazi Party hooligans to be crude and inefficient.

The biggest obstacles facing Jews wishing to leave Germany were restrictions on immigration erected by other countries and the strict limits imposed by the Nazis on the amount of German currency, foreign exchange, and personal belongings that could be taken out of the country. The obvious reluctance of foreign countries to accept refugees may have encouraged the Nazis in their persecution and their desire to export anti-Semitism. France and Belgium made it difficult for foreigners to earn a living, while the United States and Australia, traditional havens for immigrants, only guaranteed entry for those with proof of employment or assured financial support. An international conference called by President Franklin Delano Roosevelt at Evian-les-Bains in July 1938 produced minimal results. After Kristallnacht, however, U.S. restrictions were eased. Ultimately the United States took in more than 130,000 German and Austrian Jews, while Britain was the most important refuge in Europe, accepting more than 50,000 by the start of the war, including a special children's transport after Kristallnacht.

The principal refuge for the persecuted was Palestine, ruled by Britain under a League of Nations mandate. But in 1937, under severe Arab pressure, the British reversed their earlier support for Zionism and restricted Jewish immigration. Zionists were in the minority among German Jews, but the Nazis favored them, sharing their central assumption that Jews made up a separate national and ethnic group. In August 1933 the Economics Ministry signed the Ha'avara Agreement with the Jewish Agency in Palestine, allowing emigrating German Jews to use a portion of their assets to purchase German products for export to Palestine, while the SS supported illegal immigration. Between 1933 and 1941 about 47,000 Jews found refuge legally in Palestine, and several thousands did so illegally.

By the eve of the war, the SS had taken over emigration policy from the Interior Ministry. After the Anschluss with Austria in 1938, their chief "expert" on the "Jewish question," Adolf Eichmann, established the Reich Central Emigration Bureau in Vienna. Levies on wealthier Jews and funds from foreign Jewish organizations were used to facilitate the emigration of poorer Jews, and the threat of the concentration camp encouraged the reluctant to leave. By November 1938 some 50,000 of Austria's 200,000-strong Jewish community had been forced to emigrate, and similar centers for forced emigration were later established in Berlin and Prague. But the Nazis' policies of confiscation, punitive taxation, and stringent restrictions on what emigrants could take with them impeded emigration. Jews were forced to surrender jewelry and valuables at a fraction of their true value. By the start of the war, about half of German and Austrian Jews had emigrated, but many only to neighboring countries where they would soon fall once again into the hands of the Nazis.

War and conquest removed the constraints on anti-Jewish persecution. The invasion of Poland, through which almost 2 million Polish Jews fell into German hands, changed the nature of the "Jewish problem." During the invasion, SS Einsatzgruppen set about liquidating Polish elites, many of them Jewish, and on 21 September 1939 Reinhard Heydrich, chief of the Sicherheitsdienst (SD), ordered the concentration of all Polish Jews in towns with railway connections to facilitate rapid population transfers to as-yet-undecided destinations. Ghettos were created in every city in Poland, while German officials in the occupied country vied with each other in enthusiasm to rid "their" territories of Jews. The original plan for the establishment of a "Jewish reservation" in the Generalgouvernement was successfully opposed by Governor Hans Frank. The ghettos in the "incorporated territories," the largest in Lódz, became semipermanent.

As conditions in the ghettos deteriorated horrendously, their Jewish councils, responsible for food, housing, health, and welfare, found themselves in a humiliating and impossible position. The Warsaw ghetto was walled in during November 1940, while others were sealed with barbed wire. The populations of the ghettos swelled, and the inhabitants became ever more isolated. Poverty, hunger, and disease killed an estimated 800,000 Jews in the ghettos of eastern Europe. Yet schools, hospitals, and social organizations continued to function in a remarkable manner until the residents began to be transported to the extermination camps in 1942.

The fictions of "resettlement" was maintained, the most remarkable and absurd concerning the establishment of a Jewish settlement under German supervision on the French colonial island of Madagascar.

But in the course of 1941, as it became clear that the war would not end soon, the Nazis turned toward a policy of physical annihilation of the Jews. Such a policy had been inherent in the logic of National Socialism from the start. As the SS and increasingly also the Wehrmacht spread anti-Jewish terror in eastern Europe, the plans were gradually if obscurely put together for a "Final Solution." The Wannsee Conference of January 1942 set in train the process of the Holocaust.

Related entries: Anti-Semitism; Baltic States; Belgium; Berlin; Concentration Camps; Cultural Policy; Eichmann, Adolf; Enabling Act; Eugenics; Extermination Camps; Final Solution; France; Frank, Hans; Generalgouvernement; Gestapo; *Gleichschaltung;* Heydrich, Reinhard; Himmler, Heinrich; Holocaust; Kaltenbrunner, Ernst; Kristallnacht; Law; National Socialism; Netherlands; Nuremberg Laws; Poland; Public Opinion; Racial Theory; Röhm, Ernst; Rosenberg, Alfred; Schutzstaffel; Sicherheitsdienst; Soviet Union; Streicher, Julius; Sturmabteilung; *Stürmer, Der;* Theresienstadt; Ukraine; Universities; Wannsee Conference; War Crimes; Warsaw Ghetto

Suggestions for further reading:
Bankier, David. 1988. "Hitler and the Policy-Making Process on the Jewish Question," *Holocaust and Genocide Studies* 3, pp. 1–20.
Barkai, Avraham. 1989. *From Boycott to Annihilation: The Economic Struggle of German Jews, 1933–1943.* Hanover, NH: University Press of New England.
Bauer, Jehuda. 1994. *Jews for Sale? Nazi-Jewish Negotiations 1933–1945.* New Haven: Yale University Press.
Burrin, Philippe. 1994. *Hitler and the Jews: The Genesis of the Holocaust.* London: Edward Arnold.
Dawidowicz, Lucy. 1975. *The War against the Jews 1933–1945.* New York: Holt, Rinehart and Winston.
Friedländer, Saul. 1997. *Nazi Germany and the Jews. Vol. 1: The Years of Persecution, 1933–1939.* New York: HarperCollins.
Gordon, Sarah. 1984. *Hitler, Germans, and the "Jewish Question."* Princeton: Princeton University Press.
Kaplan, Marion A. 1998. *Between Dignity and Despair: Jewish Life in Nazi Germany.* New York: Oxford University Press.
Klemperer, Victor. 1998. *I Shall Bear Witness: The Diaries of Victor Klemperer, 1933–41.* London: Weidenfeld and Nicolson.
Schleunes, Karl A. 1970. *The Twisted Road to Auschwitz: Nazi Policy toward German Jews.* Urbana: University of Illinois Press.

Jodl, Alfred (1890–1946)

As chief of the Operations Staff of the High Command of the Armed Forces (OKW) from 1939 to 1945, Jodl was Hitler's closest military adviser and, along with Wilhelm Keitel, one of the Führer's most subservient generals. A professional officer who had seen frontline service in World War I, Jodl had known Hitler since 1923 and rose rapidly under the Third Reich. In his new capacity after 1939 he officially directed all the German campaigns except that against the Soviet Union but very rarely contradicted Hitler. He was capable of diplomatically steering Hitler's decisions but retained a fanatical belief in the Führer's genius. In his diary he recorded his criticism of the General Staff's caution in 1938: "The vigour of the soul is lacking, because in the end they do not believe in the genius of the Führer" (Bullock 1991, p. 638). For Jodl Hitler was simply "the greatest statesman since Bismarck" (Bullock 1991, p. 641).

In the later stages of the war, as Hitler effectively took over Jodl's job for himself, Jodl had to assume a more independent role and even issued instructions to front commanders without Hitler's approval. Not without intellectual ability, Jodl's advice was nevertheless not always sound, especially over Stalingrad and the Ardennes offensive of 1944. But he retained Hitler's confidence until the end and was promoted to full general in January 1944. More than any other general, he concerned himself purely with the conduct of the war and prudently avoided all talk of politics. After Hitler's death, it was Jodl, representing Admiral Karl Doenitz, who signed the surrender of the German army to the Allies at Reims on 7 May 1945.

Tried at Nuremberg as a war criminal, Jodl defended himself in sober fashion, claiming that it had not been his function to judge Hitler, his supreme commander. But his involvement in Hitler's criminal schemes was found to be sufficient for him to be found guilty of war crimes and crimes against humanity. Jodl was hanged at Nuremberg on 16 October 1946. It was later adjudged by a de-Nazification court that Jodl had in fact confined himself to operational matters, and he was posthumously exonerated in February 1953.

Related entries: Eastern Front; Nuremberg Trials; Officer Corps; War Crimes; Wehrmacht

Suggestions for further reading:
Bartov, Omer. 1991. *Hitler's Army: Soldiers, Nazis and War in the Third Reich.* New York: Oxford University Press.
Bullock, Alan. 1991. *Hitler and Stalin: Parallel Lives.* London: HarperCollins.

Judiciary

Although the fiction of an independent judiciary was maintained under the Nazi regime, Hitler had no problems in obtaining what he wanted from German judges. The German Federation of Judges had long been dominated by conservatives and nationalists, who showed considerable indulgence toward Nazis (including Hitler himself after the Beer Hall Putsch) and other right-wing extremists while being extremely harsh on left-wing "troublemakers." In 1933, not surprisingly, it was one of the first professional organizations to pledge allegiance to the new regime and be willingly "coordinated."

All Jewish judges, public prosecutors, and district attorneys were removed from office in April 1933, while regional and national federations of judges, prosecutors, and lawyers voluntarily merged into the Federation of National Socialist Jurists. At the first national convention of jurists in Leipzig in October 1933, more than 10,000 lawyers took an oath pledging their allegiance to Hitler. Thereafter the career jurists in the special courts and People's Court willingly collaborated in the mockery of all due process and the use of the courts as instruments of judicial murder. National Socialism and justice were defined as one and the same thing, so that there was no distinction between judges and state prosecutors, the two together sending thousands to their deaths. The special courts were criminal courts established in 1933 for the removal of political opponents and thereafter executed summary justice of real or imagined opponents of the regime; the People's Court was originally one of the special courts, created in Berlin for the Reichstag Fire Trial, and became in effect an instrument of terror against political opponents.

Related entries: Gürtner, Franz; Law

Suggestions for further reading:
Müller, Ingo. 1991. *Hitler's Justice: The Courts of the Third Reich.* Cambridge, MA: Harvard University Press.

July Plot

The attempt to assassinate Hitler on 20 July 1944 was the work of conservative army officers for whom Hitler was leading Germany to ruin. Colonel Claus von Stauffenberg, faced with the evasive reactions of more senior officers, assumed the leading role and began plotting Hitler's downfall in late 1943. The military takeover, code-named "Operation Valkyrie," was to involve the killing of Hitler and seizure of the state at its center in Berlin. General Ludwig Beck was to become head of state of the post-Nazi German state, with Carl Goerdeler as chancellor of a still authoritarian Germany that would retain its 1938 boundaries. Stauffenberg drew up plans for the capture of Berlin, involving a mobilization of army and police forces against the SS. He could rely on the support of the police and some army officers, but the attitude of General Friedrich Fromm, commander of the Home Army, remained ambiguous.

The key was to kill Hitler. Stauffenberg's appointment as Fromm's chief of staff gave him regular access to Hitler at his "Wolf's Lair" headquarters in East Prussia. At the meeting on 20 July Stauffenberg placed his briefcase containing a primed time-bomb as close as possible to Hitler, resting it against the leg of the oak map table that dominated the room. This same table, however, saved Hitler's life. The bomb exploded at 12:42 P.M., killing four and leaving Hitler badly shaken but with only minor injuries. An astonished Stauffenberg only learned that Hitler had survived when he reached Berlin after 4 P.M. His fellow conspirators had delayed setting "Operation Valkyrie" in motion until his return, by which time telephone lines to Hitler's headquarters had been reopened. The conspiracy then quickly fell apart.

Josef Goebbels, the highest-ranking Nazi official in Berlin, acted quickly and effectively. He convinced the officer sent to arrest him that Hitler was still alive and won over the wavering Fromm. Stauffenberg and Beck were shot on the night of 20 July, and months of vengeance followed. Thousands of suspects were arrested, tortured, and sent to concentration camps, including members of the conspirators' families and others only loosely connected to the opposition. Nearly 200 death sentences were passed by the People's Court in humiliating show trials. The guilty were executed by firing squads or hanged in a particularly gruesome fashion with piano wire on meat hooks. It is said that Hitler watched "home movies" of the deaths of the principal conspirators. The plot not only failed abjectly but backfired. The vast majority of high-ranking officers had remained faithful to the regime, and Goebbels orchestrated a propaganda campaign against the "traitors" that expressed a genuine popular relief at Hitler's survival and helped in a temporary revival of the fading myth of his invincibility.

Related entries: Beck, Ludwig; Goerdeler, Carl; Officer Corps; Opposition; Stauffenberg, Claus Schenk, Graf von

Suggestions for further reading:

Hoffmann, Peter. 1988. *German Resistance to Hitler.* Cambridge, MA: Harvard University Press.

Large, David Clay, ed. 1992. *Contending with Hitler: Varieties of German Resistance in the Third Reich.* Cambridge: Cambridge University Press.

Kaltenbrunner, Ernst
(1903–1946)

Born in the valley of the Inn River, not far from Hitler's birthplace of Braunau, Kaltenbrunner studied law at the University of Graz before setting up a legal practice at Linz in 1926. Long active in extreme Right organizations, he joined the Austrian Nazi Party in 1932, bringing with him his childhood friend, Adolf Eichmann. He became a spokesman for the party in Upper Austria and provided legal advice to Nazi members and sympathizers. Twice arrested and struck from the bar for his political activities, Kaltenbrunner was appointed commander of the Austrian SS early in 1935.

In recognition of his subversive activities, after the Anschluss in 1938 Kaltenbrunner was made minister for state security in Austria and promoted to SS Gruppenführer. During the succeeding few years Kaltenbrunner continued his rise as commander in chief of the SS and the police in the regions of Vienna and the Upper and Lower Danube and in April 1941 as lieutenant-general of police, in which posts he built up an impressive intelligence network in Austria. Nevertheless, it was a surprise when in January 1943 Heinrich Himmler recommended him to succeed the assassinated Reinhard Heydrich as head of the Reich Main Security Office in Berlin.

Kaltenbrunner thus came to control the Gestapo, the concentration camp system, and the administrative apparatus charged with implementing the "Final Solution of the Jewish Question."

A fanatical Nazi, nearly 7 feet tall, and bearing deep scars from his student dueling days, Kaltenbrunner set about his tasks with brutal enthusiasm and took a personal interest in the mechanisms of extermination, especially the gas chambers. Under his zealous supervision, several million Jews were hunted down for extermination, and he was also responsible for the murder of Allied prisoners of war. In February 1944 Kaltenbrunner, maintaining his passion for intelligence work and counterespionage, also succeeded in swallowing up the foreign and counterintelligence department of the armed forces, previously governed by Admiral Wilhelm Canaris. But seeing how the wind was blowing, in late 1944 Kaltenbrunner tried to emulate and surpass Himmler in making contact with the Allies through the International Red Cross. These efforts predictably came to nothing, and Kaltenbrunner fled to the Tyrol, removing his headquarters to Alt-Aussee. Captured by a U.S. patrol, he was tried at Nuremberg for war crimes and crimes against humanity and hanged in Nuremberg prison on 16 October 1946.

Related entries: Austria; Concentration Camps; Eichmann, Adolf; Extermination Camps; Final

Solution; Gestapo; Himmler, Heinrich; Nuremberg Trials; Schutzstaffel; War Crimes

Suggestions for further reading:
Black, Peter R. 1984. *Ernst Kaltenbrunner: Ideological Soldier of the Third Reich.* Princeton: Princeton University Press.

Keitel, Wilhelm (1882–1946)

Born into a landowning family in 1883, Wilhelm Keitel joined the army in 1901, served as an artillery officer in World War I, and under the Weimar Republic rose through hard work and organizational ability to become head of the Army Organization Department within the Truppenamt, the disguised General Staff. Having previously shown little or no interest in politics, his first meeting with Hitler at a conference in 1933 impressed him deeply and began the process that transformed the diligent "desk general" into a sycophant nicknamed *Lakeitel* (lackey) in army circles. From October 1935 to February 1938 he served as chief of the Armed Forces Office at the War Ministry before succeeding Werner von Blomberg as chief of staff of the High Command of the Armed Forces *(Chef des Oberkommando der Wehrmacht),* a post he held until the fall of the Third Reich. Keitel was made a field marshal in July 1940 after the victory in France, where he personally conducted the armistice negotiations at Compiègne.

Keitel was Hitler's closest right-hand man within the High Command. He expressed none of the reservations of other high-ranking officers about Hitler's policies between the Anschluss and the invasion of France. His much-quoted and much-mocked description of Hitler as "the greatest commander of all times," though apocryphal, encapsulates his servility to and flattery of the Führer. Like all Hitler's military advisers, he was initially opposed to the invasion of the Soviet Union but

swiftly swallowed his doubts. Although in no way responsible for initiating the barbaric policies of the Nazis in eastern Europe, he willingly signed all the necessary orders, actions that were to lead to his execution at Nuremberg.

Keitel remained faithful to Hitler during and after the July Plot of 1944, personally intervening to prevent commanders of the Reserve Army from supporting the coup. He lacked both the genuine conservative convictions of the plotters and the independence of mind to oppose Hitler. Albert Speer, not without a touch of his usual self-serving guile, said of Keitel: "Constantly in Hitler's presence, he had completely succumbed to his influence. From an honorable, solidly respectable general he had developed in the course of years into a servile flatterer with all the wrong instincts" (Speer 1971, p. 338). He was arrested by the British military police on 13 May 1945 and tried at Nuremberg as a principal war criminal. Here Keitel accepted responsibility for carrying out the orders issued by Hitler but pleaded "not guilty." Such a defense was incomprehensible to his lawyer and unacceptable to the tribunal. Found guilty of war crimes and crimes against humanity, Keitel was hanged at dawn on 16 October 1946.

Related entries: Barbarossa, Operation; Eastern Front; July Plot; Nuremberg Trials; Officer Corps; War Crimes; Wehrmacht

Suggestions for further reading:
Gölitz, Walter. 1995. "Keitel, Jodl and Warlimont," in Correlli Barnett, ed., *Hitler's Generals.* London: Phoenix.
Speer, Albert. 1971. *Inside the Third Reich.* Paperback ed. London: Sphere Books.

Kesselring, Albert (1885–1960)

One of Hitler's most able military commanders, the career of Field Marshal Kesselring testifies to the rigid sense of duty that kept most German soldiers loyal to the Führer, even when they regarded his interventions as wrongheaded. The Bavarian-born Kesselring had been an administrative staff officer under the Weimar Republic. In 1933 he was transferred to the Air Ministry and in 1936 appointed chief of staff of the newly created Luftwaffe. He led the First Air Fleet in the invasion of Poland and commanded combined land-air operations during the invasion of the Low Countries and air operations over Dunkirk. As commander of the Second Air Fleet, he directed air raids on English airfields during the Battle of Britain, always insisting that the good work of his pilots had been undone by Hermann Goering's decision to redirect the Luftwaffe to bomb London.

In 1941, after briefly leading his Second Air Fleet on the Eastern Front, Kesselring was appointed Axis commander in chief in the Mediterranean. As such he became embroiled in difficult German-Italian political relations, and while he officially directed the campaign in North Africa jointly with Erwin Rommel, it was Rommel who enjoyed Hitler's confidence. Kesselring's greatest achievement as a soldier, however, was in the defensive campaign in Italy in 1943–1944, where he had again to persuade Hitler of the difficulties in holding up the advance of the superior Allied forces. Kesselring had secretly opened negotiations with the Americans for a separate surrender when in 1945 Hitler transferred him to replace Karl Rudolf von Rundstedt as commander in chief in the west, where not even his excellent generalship could stem the Allied advance toward Germany.

Kesselring surrendered to U.S. forces on 7 May 1945. He was charged with war crimes, and in 1947 a British military court found him guilty of ordering the massacre of 335 Italian civilians in the Ardeatine caves in March 1944 and other similar reprisals, but the conviction was considered unsafe by many people, including Winston Churchill, for whom the responsibility lay firmly with the SS. Reprieved from the original death sentence, Kesselring began a term of life imprisonment, but still suffering from serious injuries incurred in a road accident during the Italian campaign, he was released as an "act of clemency" in 1952. In his *Memoirs,* published in 1953 (London: William Kimber), Kesselring refrained from criticizing Hitler, still showing the obsessive loyalty he considered a soldier's duty, saving his venom for his chief rival, Rommel.

Related entries: Britain, Battle of; Dunkirk, Evacuation of; Goering, Hermann; Italy; Luftwaffe; North Africa; Officer Corps; Rommel, Erwin; War Crimes

Suggestions for further reading:
Bidwell, Shelford. 1995. "Kesselring," in Correlli Barnett, ed., *Hitler's Generals.* Paperback ed. London: Phoenix, pp. 265–289.

Kirdorf, Emil (1847–1938)

One of the "coal kings" of the Ruhr mining district, Kirdorf was the first figure of any significance in the business world to join the Nazi Party. An extreme authoritarian, ruthless employer, and hater of trade unions, Kirdorf had been instrumental in the creation of the Rhine-Westphalian Coal Syndicate and the United Steel Works, both powerful cartels. In 1927 the octogenarian Kirdorf joined the National Socialist German Workers' Party (NSDAP). He left a year later, distrustful of the radicalism of the Nazi "Left," but maintained friendly relations with Hitler, persuading him to reassure industrialists that the "socialism" of the NSDAP need not be taken seriously. There is no hard evidence that Kirdorf, having retired from active business life, was a heavy financial contributor to the Nazis, as has been claimed, but he was a fellow traveler, attracted by Hitler's anti-Marxism and extreme nationalism. Kirdorf rejoined the party in 1934 and was feted by Hitler's regime as a respectable supporter from the business world. He died in Mühlheim an der Ruhr on 13 July 1938.

Related entries: Industry

Kluge, Hans Günther von (1882–1944)

*T*he Prussian aristocrat Kluge was one of Hitler's most successful generals, but his ambivalent, chameleonlike attitude toward the Führer had ultimately tragic consequences. A soldier since 1908 and imaginative battlefront general, Kluge commanded the successful 4th Army in the invasions of Poland in 1939 and France in 1940, where he promoted and worked with the dynamic Erwin Rommel. Promoted to field marshal in July 1940, he led the 4th Army again in Operation Barbarossa, this time with Heinz Guderian under his command, during the thrust toward Moscow but was irritated by Hitler's diversion of forces toward the south.

After he succeeded field marshal Fedor von Bock as commander of Army Group Center in July 1941, Kluge was exasperated by Hitler's lack of understanding of the difficulties and sufferings of German troops on the Eastern Front and gravitated toward the oppositional group of officers around Baron Henning von Treschkow. But his critical faculties seemed to desert him whenever he was summoned to Hitler's presence, and he cooperated loyally during the desperate offensive of the battle of Kursk. After a serious car crash on 12 October 1943, Kluge went on prolonged sick leave until June 1944.

In July 1944 Hitler appointed Kluge to succeed Karl von Rundstedt as commander in chief of the Western Front. After a stay of several days at Berchtesgarden, Kluge once again became "the Führer's man," berating Rommel for his pessimism. Then he rapidly

changed again. Convinced that the war was lost, Kluge was fully aware of the plans to assassinate Hitler that became the July Plot, but he only agreed to cooperate with the plotters once Hitler was dead. He still thought that Hitler could be made to change his mind and end the war. After the failure of the plot Kluge was dismissed by Hitler on 17 August. Aware that his connections with the plotters had been revealed and that Hitler would blame him for not revealing the conspiracy, Kluge committed suicide on 19 August 1944 while on his way back to Germany.

Related entries: Barbarossa, Operation; Citadel, Operation; Eastern Front; France; July Plot; Kursk, Battle of; Opposition; Rommel, Erwin; Wehrmacht

Suggestions for further reading:
Lamb, Richard. 1995. "Kluge," in Correlli Barnett, ed., *Hitler's Generals.* Paperback ed. London: Phoenix, pp. 395–409.

Kreisau Circle

*T*he group brought together by Graf Helmuth von Moltke on his estate at Kreisau in Silesia to discuss Germany after Hitler included some of the most distinguished names in the opposition to Hitler. At conferences held in 1942 and 1943, representatives of a cross-section of German society discussed the economic, social, and religious bases of a post-Nazi Germany, including decentralization of the state; the redevelopment of political parties and trade unions; church-state relations; and the reestablishment of the rule of law, including war crimes trials. The group included Protestant and Catholic conservatives and liberals, three Jesuit priests, landowners, and Socialists. The society they envisaged was to a large extent a resurrection of the old Germany. They opposed a coup against Hitler but held meetings with more active oppositionists, including Ludwig Beck, Carl Goerdeler, and Ulrich von Hassell. Some of the members of the circle supported the July Plot of 1944 on an individual basis, and in the repression that followed it three leading members were executed: Moltke, Adam von Trott zu Solz, and Peter, Count Yorck von Wartenburg.

Related entries: July Plot; Opposition

Suggestions for further reading:
Large, David Clay, ed. 1992. *Contending with Hitler: Varieties of German Resistance in the Third Reich.* Cambridge: Cambridge University Press.
Nicosia, Francis R., and Laurence D. Stokes, eds. 1992. *Germans against Nazism.* Oxford: Berg.

Kristallnacht

The attacks on Jews, synagogues, and Jewish shops and businesses throughout much of Germany on the night of 9–10 November 1938 was euphemistically given the name of "Kristallnacht," or "Crystal Night," because of the broken glass littering the streets the next morning. The pogrom coincided with the campaign of the Four-Year Plan to "Aryanize" the economy but needed a spark to produce an explosion. This was provided by the assassination in Paris of the German diplomat Ernst vom Rath by the seventeen-year-old Polish Jewish refugee, Herschel Grynszpan. Josef Goebbels instructed newspaper editors to splash the murder across the front pages and to make it clear that it would have serious consequences for the Jewish population.

Hitler, in Munich for the celebrations of the anniversary of the 1923 putsch, talked with Goebbels and made it clear that as head of state he was not to be held responsible for what followed. As Goebbels left the meeting, he was heard to remark: "The SA must be given their fling" (Bullock 1991, p. 654). It was decided that the party should not organize demonstrations but

that "spontaneous" hooliganism by the Sturmabteilung (SA) and Nazi mobs should not be discouraged. The SA, given the "freedom of the streets" they had not enjoyed since 1934, briefly came into their own again in a night of terror. While the police stood by and watched, some 200 synagogues were burnt down; an unknown number, but probably running into the thousands, of shops and businesses were looted and destroyed; and up to ninety Jews murdered. The SS got involved in turn by arresting between 20,000 and 26,000 better-off Jews and herding them into concentration camps.

Kristallnacht caused outrage in the Western world at Germany's relapse into barbarism, and the U.S. ambassador was recalled on 14 November. More striking was the manifest disapproval of the majority of the German public, who may have had no love for Jews but disapproved of the violence, disorder, and wanton destruction of property. Many supported Hitler because he promised to bring order, not turbulence and thuggery. The Nazi leadership was also divided: Hermann Goering deplored the economic damage of the destruction, while Heinrich Himmler's policy of getting rid of the Jews by forced emigration was threatened. Hitler remained in the middle: he did not disassociate himself from what had happened but agreed that there should be no repetition.

To pay for the destruction, a huge fine of 1 billion marks was imposed on the Jewish community, and Jews were required to surrender their property to the state in return for meager compensation. New restrictions, making life for Jews in Germany nearly impossible, were to follow shortly. The ultimate effect of Kristallnacht and the reactions to it was to shift the regime's anti-Jewish policy away from violent demonstrations and "spontaneous" street actions toward the more bureaucratic, ordered, and partly secret procedures preferred by Goering and Himmler.

Berlin women gather outside the broken windows of a Jewish shop after Kristallnacht, 9–10 November 1938. About 7,500 businesses were destroyed in an orgy of destruction led by the SA and the SS. The public in general played only a limited role in the pogrom, even if Nazi propaganda mendaciously stressed the "spontaneous" nature of the outbreak of hostility toward Jews. (Anthony Potter Collection/Archive Photos)

Related entries: Anti-Semitism; Jews and Jewish Policy

Suggestions for further reading:
Bullock, Alan. 1991. *Hitler and Stalin: Parallel Lives.* London: HarperCollins.
Kochan, Lionel. 1957. *Pogrom: 10 November 1938.* London: Andre Deutsch.
Loewenberg, Peter. 1987. "The Kristallnacht as a Public Degradation Ritual," *Leo Baeck Institute Yearbook* 32, pp. 309–323.
Thalmann, Rita, and Emmanuel Feinermann. 1974. *Crystal Night: 9–10 November 1938.* London: Thames and Hudson.

Krupp, Alfried (1907–1967)

The son of Gustav Krupp, Alfried took over sole control of the Krupp industrial empire in 1943 and was made *Wehrwirtschaftführer,* charged with mobilizing the resources of the German armaments industry. As head of the mining and armaments division of Krupps, he supervised the takeover of the iron and steel industry of the Ukraine and was responsible for the employment of slave labor, including Jews from Auschwitz and Soviet prisoners of war, in appalling conditions in mines and steelworks. Alongside Albert Speer, he was the dominant figure in the German economy in the final stages of the war. But as Allied bombing inflicted serious damage on the Krupp empire, the hitherto loyal follower of Hitler began to press for compensation and recovery of debts from the state. Sentenced to twelve years' imprisonment as a war criminal at Nuremberg, Krupp was released from Landsberg prison in 1951 as part of the general amnesty for German industrialists, and his huge personal fortune and confiscated corporate property was returned to him.

Related entries: Industry; Krupp, Gustav; Speer, Albert; Total War; War Crimes

Suggestions for further reading:
Overy, Richard J. 1994. *War and Economy in the Third Reich*. Oxford: Clarendon Press.

Krupp, Gustav (1870–1950)

*T*he "king of the munitions makers," head of the biggest armaments firm in Germany and Europe, strongly opposed Hitler prior to the Führer's accession to power but changed his tune under the Third Reich and became, according to Fritz Thyssen, a "super Nazi." A former diplomat, from 1906 onward Krupp had gradually taken over the Friedrich Krupp Works in Essen, Kiel, Magdeburg, and Berlin, which played a key role in World War I. On 29 January 1933 Krupp warned President Paul von Hindenburg about the folly of appointing Hitler as chancellor. But at a meeting hosted by Hjalmar Schacht on 20 February, Hitler promised Krupp and other leading industrialists that he would eliminate Nazi radicals and restore Germany's armed forces, a promise of particular interest to Krupp as the largest producer of guns, tanks, and ammunition.

Hitler kept his promises, and Krupp benefited immensely from rearmament and the destruction of working-class organizations. In May 1933 he became chairman of the Adolf Hitler Spende, a fund administered by Martin Bormann through which industrialists contributed to the National Socialist German Workers' Party (NSDAP, Nazi Party) in return for special favors. The Krupp family contributed more than 10 million marks annually to the NSDAP and additional amounts to the "Circle of Friends of Heinrich Himmler," which financed "special tasks of the SS." Krupp benefited hugely from Hitler's conquests in eastern Europe, employing hundreds of thousands of slave laborers in his Essen works. Between 70,000 and 80,000 are estimated to have died in conditions not far removed from those in the death camps. Krupps also operated a fuse factory at Auschwitz, where Jews were worked to exhaustion and later murdered.

In the later years of the war, Krupp's operation was largely taken over by his son Alfried. Nevertheless, the elder Krupp was regarded by the Allies as a major war criminal and indicted at Nuremberg. He did not stand trial because a medical panel concluded that he was suffering from senility following a stroke and would be unable to follow the proceedings. Gustav Krupp died in Blühnbach bei Salzburg on 16 January 1950.

Related entries: Economic Policy; Industry; Krupp, Alfried; Rearmament

Suggestions for further reading:
Carroll, Bernice A. 1968. *Design for Total War: Arms and Economics in the Third Reich*. The Hague: Mouton.
Milward, Alan S. 1965. *The German Economy at War*. London: Athlone Press.
Overy, Richard J. 1994. *War and Economy in the Third Reich*. Oxford: Clarendon Press.
———. 1996. *The Nazi Economic Recovery*. 2nd ed. Cambridge: Cambridge University Press.

Kursk, Battle of

*I*n February 1943 Soviet forces recaptured the city of Kursk in the central sector of the Eastern Front and established a salient stretching nearly 120 miles westward. Hitler saw this bulge in the front as providing an opportunity to cut off the extended Red Army and inflict heavy losses. However, by the time Operation Citadel was launched in July 1943 Marshal Georgi Zhukov had reinforced the salient, preparing for a counterattack. The resulting battle of Kursk, the greatest tank battle in history, pitched awesome forces (the exact numbers are not clear) against each other. The Germans inflicted the heavier damage but were pushed back to their first positions, and Hitler, his hand forced by the faulty strategy of Field Marshal Erich von Manstein and by the need to retain armored forces for the Italian campaign, canceled the offensive at the end of July. Hitler's armies in the east were as yet far from defeated, but the Russians now moved onto the offensive along the entire front.

Related entries: Citadel, Operation; Eastern Front; Manstein, Erich von

Suggestions for further reading:
Glantz, David, and Jonathan M. House. 1995. *When Titans Clashed: How the Red Army Stopped Hitler.* Lawrence: University Press of Kansas.
Overy, Richard J. 1998. *Russia's War.* New York: Allen Lane Penguin Press.

L

Labor Relations

From the beginning of the Third Reich, Hitler presented himself as an "honest broker" in relations between workers and employers: "I have no personal interests; I am dependent neither on the state nor on public office, nor am I beholden to business or industry or any union. I am impartial" (Mason 1993, pp. 101–102). In reality, the power to negotiate wages after the destruction of the trade unions rested with the Trustees of Labor, state officials appointed by Hitler in mid-June 1933. But their numbers and expertise remained inadequate. Wage rates were largely determined by market forces, and individual factory "communities" could set their own rates. The Nazi system precluded rational planning in this area. Whatever efforts were made to ensure workers' loyalty to the Third Reich, Hitler's "neutrality" meant that while wages were kept down in order to restrict consumption, workers could vote with their feet, leaving agriculture and the stagnant consumer goods industries for the booming metal, engineering, and building trades stimulated by the rearmament drive. Shortages of labor from 1936 onward increased workers' bargaining power, and wages spiraled as employers competed for workers. The regime's attempts at direction of labor were largely ignored by the working population. During the war the relatively privileged position of German workers in the armaments sector was maintained by the use of imported cheap or slave labor from the occupied territories, but by that time many workers had found themselves conscripted into the Wehrmacht.

Related entries: Rearmament; Unemployment; Working Class

Suggestions for further reading:
Mason, Timothy W. 1993. *Social Policy in the Third Reich: The Working Class and the "National Community."* Providence and Oxford: Berg.

Labor Service

Established by a law of 26 June 1935, the Reich Labor Service (RAD) compelled all healthy males between the ages of eighteen and twenty-five to perform "socially useful tasks" in self-contained units. Hitler saw it as a means of combating unemployment, a vehicle for the "alignment" of young men, a "service of honour to the German *Volk*," and a way of providing basic paramilitary training for the Wehrmacht. Its head, the retired colonel Konstantin Hierl, was appointed by Hitler, but only in 1943 did the RAD become a Supreme Reich Authority, directly responsible to the Führer.

In 1936 a women's labor service, based on voluntary enlistment, was joined to the RAD, and it became compulsory in 1939. On the eve of the war the yearly participants in the RAD numbered 350,000. It was particularly active in farm labor and used in the building of autobahns and the Siegfried Line. With the outbreak of the war, the RAD came under the control of the Wehrmacht. Labor service men were set to work all over occupied Europe, manned antiaircraft guns, built firing ramps for the Vergeltungswaffe weapons, and in 1944–1945 were assigned to the Volkssturm. The RAD was effective in preparing young German people for war, but Hitler's hope that its political schooling would turn them all into committed National Socialists was weakened by a lack of suitable leaders.

Related entries: Education; Unemployment; Volkssturm; Youth Policy

Lammers, Hans-Heinrich (1879–1962)

The head of the Reich Chancellery throughout the Third Reich was a lawyer who had served as an adviser in the Ministry of the Interior under the Weimar Republic. Hitler valued his legal expertise and his industrious, if unimaginative, work in running chancellery business, making him a minister without portfolio in 1937 and ministerial councilor for Reich defense in 1939. Albert Speer described him as "a government official without initiative or imagination whose hair stood on end at the thought of disregard for the sacred bureaucratic procedures" (Speer 1971, p. 353). From January 1943 onward, Lammers together with Martin Bormann controlled access to the Führer, and all orders to be signed by Hitler had to be cleared by a triumvirate of Lammers, Bormann, and Field Marshal

Wilhelm Keitel. Bormann's intrigues against him led to an order for Lammers's arrest just before Hitler's suicide. Interned by the Allies, Lammers stood trial in 1949, accused of formulating and giving legal authority to the measures leading to the Final Solution, but he denied all involvement in the execution of Hitler's orders to Reinhard Heydrich and others. Initially sentenced to twenty years' imprisonment, his sentence was halved by the U.S. High Commissioner and, after another reduction, he was released from Landsberg on 16 December 1951. He died in Düsseldorf on 4 January 1962.

Related entries: Law; Reich Chancellery

Suggestions for further reading:
Speer, Albert. 1971. *Inside the Third Reich.* Paperback ed. London: Sphere Books.

Landsberg-am-Lech

The scene of Hitler's imprisonment after the failure of the Beer Hall Putsch in November 1923 is a picturesque little town some 40 miles west of Munich. He was installed in the fortress in conditions "more akin to those of a hotel than a penitentiary" (Kershaw 1998, p. 217). Treated with respect by his jailers and fawned upon by Rudolf Hess and his fellow Nazi prisoners, Hitler could relax and answer correspondence at the desk in his large, well-furnished room, which afforded a broad view of the attractive countryside. He even received visits from supporters but discouraged them for fear of jeopardizing his chances of parole.

Above all, in Landsberg Hitler read and wrote. Articles were smuggled out for a clandestine Nazi journal, but the main result of his enforced idleness was the ordering of his thoughts into *Mein Kampf.* "Landsberg," he told Hans Frank, was his "university paid for by the state" (Kershaw

1998, p. 240). He claimed to have read voluminously, taking in Friedrich Nietzsche, Karl Marx, Houston Stewart Chamberlain, Leopold von Ranke, Otto von Bismarck, German and Allied war memoirs, and much more, but the depth of his reading is another matter. He read in order to find confirmation of his own preconceptions and prejudices. As he told Frank, through his reading, "I recognized the correctness of my views" (Kershaw 1998, p. 240).

When the time came for Hitler's parole hearing, the sympathetic court could read a eulogy of his most famous prisoner by the governor of Landsberg, Otto Leybold. Hitler, Leybold said, was "a man of order, of discipline . . . contented, modest and accommodating." He was "without personal vanity," did not smoke or drink, was not "drawn to the female sex," was always polite, and kept himself busy with writing his book. "He will be no agitator against the government," the unobservant or mendacious Leybold said, "no enemy of other parties with a nationalist leaning. He emphasizes how convinced he is that a state cannot exist without firm internal order and firm government" (Kershaw 1998, p. 235). This encomium failed to convince either the police or the state prosecutor's office, but the judges of the Bavarian Supreme Court took a different view, and Hitler was released from Landsberg on 20 December 1924. The sympathetic prison staff bade their charge a fond farewell, and he paused to be photographed by Heinrich Hoffmann before hurrying back to Munich. The state prosecution office calculated that he had three years, 333 days, twenty-one hours, and fifty minutes of his sentence still to serve. The world would have been a better place had he been forced to serve it.

Related entries: Bavaria; Beer Hall Putsch; *Mein Kampf*

Suggestions for further reading:
Kershaw, Ian. 1998. *Hitler 1889–1936: Hubris.* New York: Allen Lane The Penguin Press.

Laval, Pierre (1883–1945)

One of the most controversial and detested figures in French politics, the versatile and wily Laval is best known for his coauthorship of the Hoare-Laval Pact of 1935, which sought to appease Benito Mussolini by recognizing his occupation of Abyssinia, and for his collaboration with Hitler after the fall of France. Laval described his seeming opportunism as "practical nationalism." As deputy to Marshal Philippe Pétain from June to December 1940, he persuaded the Vichy government to ratify the armistice. Recalled as prime minister after two years out of favor in April 1942, he continued collaboration, his most controversial policy being to supply French workers for German factories, a major factor in driving young men to join the Resistance. Taken to Germany and then Austria in 1945, Laval escaped to Spain but was returned to France, tried for treason, and executed by firing squad on 15 October 1945.

Related entries: France; Pétain, Philippe

Suggestions for further reading:
Warner, Geoffrey. 1968. *Pierre Laval and the Eclipse of France, 1931–1945.* New York: Macmillan.

Law

The historian Alan Bullock observes: "Hitler's hostility to the idea of law and due process, and his scorn for lawyers were more of a break with German tradition than his attack on democracy" (Bullock 1991, p. 480). Democracy was a recent import, but the concept of the *Rechtsstaat,* the state based on law, had been fundamental in Germany since the Enlightenment. By being made into a mere emanation of the "will of the Führer," the law lost its traditional independence as the third branch of the state. Under the banner of "the power of the Führer," legal norms were subverted along with the liberal principles that had protected individual rights under the Weimar Republic and that Hitler had been willing enough to exploit for propaganda and image building.

Few changes were made to civil law, but all laws were to be interpreted in accord with National Socialist philosophy, and a mass of eugenic and racial legislation served to uphold a system that was by any civilized standards lawless. Executive action by the SS and the police upheld an authoritarian notion of "law and order" that was welcomed by conservatives within the judiciary and supported or at least tolerated by most ordinary Germans. This erosion of the rule of law began immediately after the Reichstag fire, when the Decree for the Protection of the People and the State retrospectively imposed the death penalty on Marinus van der Lubbe for arson, not a capital offense at the time of the crime. This Reichstag Fire Decree was used for the arrest and internment without trial of anyone judged to be an opponent of Nazism. More than 11,000 cases of high treason were heard in 1933 alone.

A new system of Special Courts, operating without juries, was introduced by Minister of Justice Franz Gürtner in March 1933, and the old system further undermined by the establishment of the People's Court (Volksgerichtshof), set up to deal with cases of treason in April 1934. With five judges, only two of whom needed to be lawyers, and juries made up of party officials, the People's Court robbed defendants of all rights, including the right of appeal. Nazi ideologists portrayed the People's Court as the expression of a popular völkisch justice, but even this was less important in practice than the arbitrary power of the SS and the Gestapo, which dispensed with any framework of law altogether in imposing the "will of the Führer."

Law under the Nazis was, in the words of the constitutional lawyer Carl Schmidt,

"a spontaneous emanation of the Führer's will." As leader of the German Reich for life, Hitler embodied the supreme power of the state and, as the delegate of the German people, decided the outward form and structure of the Reich. No law or written constitution was necessary: the Reich was not a *Rechtsstaat* but the racially defined German nation, and Hitler as custodian of the people's will could not be tied down by legal norms. The legal system had no reason to question the decisions of the Führer: laws and decrees issued in Hitler's name simply provided a façade of "normality" for the sake of scrupulous middle-class Germans and foreign observers. It could be violated by anyone claiming to embody any part of the Führer's power, in practice meaning the SS and the police.

As the expression of the will of the *Volk* the law was used for the separation or elimination of those unworthy to be members of the race. Hence the use of racial laws to gradually force the Jews and other racial "undesirables" out of public life, forbid mixing of the races, and eliminate the mentally ill and others deemed "unworthy of life." Law, racial theory, and eugenics worked hand in glove in the task of "cleansing the body of the race" in the name of popular hygiene. The law in all areas was based on punishing the criminal, not the crime, since criminals were by definition "aliens" not worthy of membership in the *Volk*. The healthy, pure, and hygienic nation would deliver itself of all inferior types by using a thin façade of pseudolegality flowing out of Hitler's ubiquitous "will."

Related entries: Concentration Camps; Enabling Act; Eugenics; Euthanasia; Frank, Hans; Frick, Wilhelm; Gestapo; Gürtner, Franz; Jews and Jewish Policy; Judiciary; Nuremberg Laws; Reichstag Fire; Schutzstaffel; Sicherheitsdienst; Thierack, Otto

Suggestions for further reading:
Bullock, Alan. 1991. *Hitler and Stalin: Parallel Lives.* London: HarperCollins.

Müller, Ingo. 1991. *Hitler's Justice: The Courts of the Third Reich*. Cambridge, MA: Harvard University Press.

League of Nations

Established in January 1920, the League of Nations was designed to keep international peace and act as an arbitrating body in disputes. Germany joined the league following the Locarno Pact of 1925, but nationalists, including Hitler, continued to view it as an organ of the victors of 1918, enforcing the unjust territorial settlements of the Treaty of Versailles. It was also responsible for supervising the administration of the Saarland and the Free City of Danzig. Hitler took Germany out of the league on 14 October 1933 using the pretext of demanding immediate parity in armaments. The league could do nothing to prevent Hitler's rearmament program or Benito Mussolini's attack on Abyssinia, but it did help to restrain the ruling Nazis in Danzig.

Related entries: Danzig; Foreign Policy; Saarland

Suggestions for further reading:
Weinberg, Gerhard L. 1970. *The Foreign Policy of Hitler's Germany: Diplomatic Revolution in Europe 1933–36*. Chicago: University of Chicago Press.

Lebensraum

The conquest of "living space" for a supposedly overpopulated Germany had been a slogan used in demands for a German colonial empire before World War I. Hitler believed that Germany not only needed more farmland to support itself but had a historical right to expand in the east in the wake of the migrations of the Middle Ages. "The National Socialist movement," he wrote in *Mein Kampf*, "must strive to eliminate the disproportion between our population and our area . . . between our historical past and the hopelessness of our present impotence" (Hitler 1992, p. 590). In so doing, "the new Reich must again set itself on the march along the road of the Teutonic Knights of old, to obtain by the German sword sod for the German plough and daily bread for the nation" (pp. 128–129). The highest aim of all foreign policy is "to bring the soil into harmony with the population" (p. 593). The inferior Slav peoples would have to give up the land to the superior German warriors. Thus two completely false notions—that the German population was too large for the resources of the country and that Germany was historically engaged in a "drive to the east"— served to justify the imposition of Nazi rule in eastern Europe.

Related entries: Foreign Policy; Racial Theory

Suggestions for further reading:
Hitler, Adolf. 1992. *Mein Kampf*. Trans. Ralph Manheim. Intro. by D. C. Watt. London: Pimlico.

Ley, Robert (1890–1945)

One of Hitler's most devoted and fanatical personal followers, Ley was born in Niederbreidenbach in the Rhineland into a solid farming family that was plunged into poverty when his father was convicted of insurance fraud and jailed. He studied chemistry before joining the air corps during World War I, when he was shot down and spent more than a year in French captivity. After the war he found profitable employment with IG Farben but in 1924 forsook "bourgeois" life to join the National Socialist German Workers' Party (NSDAP). The coarse, eccentric, and crudely anti-Semitic Ley was adept at street brawling and rose quickly to become

Gauleiter of his native Rhineland, a post he held from 1925 to 1931. Despite his heavy drinking, habitually poor judgment, and chronic social insecurity, Hitler approved of Ley and made him Reich organization leader in November 1932.

Ley's real opportunity came in 1933 when Hitler chose him to lead the German Labor Front (DAF), the monolithic labor organization designed to replace the "coordinated" trade unions. Also rejoicing in the title of *Reichsorganisationsleiter* (national organization leader) of the NSDAP, Ley could indulge his thirst for power and make a considerable personal fortune under the cloak of his party activities. His stated ambitions for the DAF were gigantic and gained some kind of realization in the front's 25 million members and the "Strength through Joy" organization, but his dream of a totalitarian society with unlimited social mobility and social security from the cradle to the grave was opposed by the most powerful forces in party, business, and state and of secondary interest to Hitler.

The war brought more titles and jobs for Ley. In 1941 he was charged with formulating the Nazis' postwar social vision, and in 1942 Hitler gave him the task of replacing the housing stock being destroyed by bombing. Ley attacked his new tasks with great enthusiasm and equal ineptitude, but the first was irrelevant and the second hopeless. At the end of the war he was captured by U.S. troops in the mountains near Berchtesgarden. On 24 October 1945 he committed suicide in his prison cell while awaiting trail at Nuremberg.

Despite his origins, Ley had been the prototype of the plebeian Nazi, fanatically and sycophantically devoted to Hitler and mixing rabid anti-Semitism with vague anticapitalism in lurid rhetoric. He was also personally unstable and an alcoholic. But he was the kind of follower Hitler appreciated, one whose enthusiasm and grandiose ambitions far exceeded his competence and good sense.

Related entries: German Labor Front; Industry; Labor Relations; Nazi Movement; Social Policy; "Strength through Joy"; *Volksgemeinschaft;* Working Class

Suggestions for further reading:
Smelser, Ronald. 1988. *Robert Ley: Hitler's Labor Front Leader.* New York and Oxford: Berg.

Linz

The young Hitler moved with his family to Linz, the capital of Upper Austria some 95 miles (153 kilometers) west of Vienna, in November 1898, and he always looked upon it as his "hometown." It reminded him of the carefree days of his indolent youth; was associated with his mother, probably the only human being he ever truly loved; and was considered the most "German" town in the Habsburg Empire. "Those were my happiest days," he later recalled (Bukey 1986, p. 1). He attended the local secondary school, where he failed to stand out in any way, being inspired only by the tales of heroism in the German past recounted by his history teacher, a certain Dr. Leonard Pötsch. Linz was a center of German nationalist feeling, and here Hitler was exposed to the ideas of Georg Ritter von Schönerer.

However, Hitler's assertion in *Mein Kampf* that his pan-Germanism and anti-Semitism were already fully formed during his years in Linz should be treated with suspicion. The account of his life in Linz by his one real friend there, August Kubizek, though it should also be handled with care, paints a very different picture. Kubizek, a dreamy youth with ambitions to be a musician, was clearly dominated by his willful and cocky friend and portrays Hitler as a dandified adolescent with strong opinions about everything. But the friends' greatest interests were artistic. Hitler was already under the spell of Richard Wagner, but his main obsession was with great art and architecture. He would be a great artist and Kubizek a great musician.

The young Hitler already made plans for rebuilding Linz, and the passage of time only increased his attachment to the city he contrasted with "cosmopolitan" Vienna, the ungrateful Austrian capital that had treated him so badly after he had moved there from Linz in 1908. After the Anschluss in 1938 Hitler busied himself with his "favorite project" of making Linz the cultural capital of Europe, home to the largest art gallery in the world. An elegant avenue would lead to the "Hitler Center," and the monumental gallery standing next to this would house paintings donated by German museums or "acquired" elsewhere in conquered Europe. His projects never went beyond the planning stage, but he was still occupied with them in 1945, as he was holed up in his bunker and the Red Army was at the gates of Linz.

Related entries: Architecture; Austria; Schönerer, Georg Ritter von; Vienna

Suggestions for further reading:
Bukey, Evan Burr. 1986. *Hitler's Hometown: Linz, Austria, 1908–1945*. Bloomington: Indiana University Press.
Kershaw, Ian. 1998. *Hitler 1889–1936: Hubris.* New York: Allen Lane The Penguin Press.
Smith, Bradley F. 1967. *Adolf Hitler: His Family, Childhood and Youth*. Stanford: Hoover Institution for War, Revolution, and Peace.

Local Government

The Third Reich effectively abolished local government as it is generally understood, replacing it with Nazi Party rule. The federal structure of the Weimar Republic was abolished, and the positions of Reich governors of the former *Länder* and their equivalent in the Prussian provinces, the *Oberpräsidenten,* were largely filled by existing *Gauleiters*. The German Municipal Charter Law of 1935 introduced a unified system of town government,

which meant in practice rule by Nazi councilors. How far regional and local officials were responsible to the Ministry of the Interior or to Hitler personally was never resolved and added to the administrative pluralism and chaos of the regime. Plans for comprehensive administrative reform drawn up at various times by Rudolf Hess and Wilhelm Frick came to nothing because of too many conflicting views and Hitler's lack of interest in the subject.

Related entries: *Gauleiters;* National Socialist German Workers' Party

Ludendorff, Erich (1865–1937)

Writing in the *Völkischer Beobachter* of 26 February 1925, Hitler called Ludendorff "the most loyal and self-less friend" (Kershaw 1998, p. 267) of the National Socialist movement. But the former war hero was also a potential rival to the Führer, and his views in his later years were bizarre and paranoid even by Nazi standards. Ludendorff had been an army officer since 1881. In the early months of World War I, as chief of staff of Paul von Hindenburg's 8th Army, he demonstrated his strategic skill in the victories over the Russians at the battles of Tannenberg and the Masurian Lakes. Working closely with Hindenburg, he maintained German supremacy on the Eastern Front until the autumn of 1916 and helped to alleviate the increasingly difficult situation on the Western Front. The two men became the virtual dictators of Germany during the last two years of the war.

Dismissed from his post after the failure of the final German offensive in the summer of 1918, Ludendorff moved to Sweden to write his war memoirs. Convinced that Germany's defeat had been caused by the "treachery" of the politicians, Ludendorff

von Hindenburg   Ludendorff

Germany's two heroes of World War I, von Hindenburg and Ludendorff, photographed on the Eastern Front. Both men were to play crucial but different roles in Hitler's rise to power. (Culver Pictures)

158

nourished the legend of the "stab in the back." Returning to Munich in 1919, he gravitated into extreme *völkisch* circles and was assiduously cultivated by Hitler. He participated in the Beer Hall Putsch in November 1923, using his name in the attempt to rally the army and showing a foolhardy heroism in marching straight into police rifle fire, an example not followed by the other putschists. Had the coup succeeded, Ludendorff would have been made chief of the armed forces.

Acquitted of high treason in the trial that led to Hitler's imprisonment, Ludendorff helped keep the Nazi movement alive as the National Socialist Freedom Movement and served as a deputy in the Reichstag from 1924 to 1928. But as surrogate candidate for the imprisoned Hitler in the elections of 1925 he did poorly, winning only 1.1 percent of the vote. Hitler was not displeased. "That's all right," he said, "now we've finally finished him" (Kershaw 1998, p. 269). The nationalist Right had preferred to support Ludendorff's erstwhile superior, Hindenburg. Officially Ludendorff continued to be revered by the Nazis for his part in the Beer Hall Putsch, but his relations with Hitler deteriorated irrevocably. Influenced by his second wife, Mathilde von Kemnitz, Ludendorff founded the *Tannenbergbund* in 1926, disseminating innumerable pamphlets and books denouncing the "supranational" conspiracies of Jews, Freemasons, and Jesuits, a literature "so harebrained in its persecution paranoia that even Nazi ideologues rejected it" (Kershaw 1998, p. 269).

Now too eccentric and zany, Ludendorff was an embarrassment to Hitler, who in 1927 claimed he was a Freemason himself, a charge that was never answered. In 1933 Ludendorff warned President von Hindenburg that "this sinister individual [Hitler] will lead our country into the abyss and our nation to an unprecedented catastrophe" (Wistrich 1982, p. 200). Despite his strange behavior, after his death in Tutzing, Bavaria,

on 20 December 1937, Ludendorff was given a state funeral by the Third Reich and eulogized as a "great patriot."

Related entries: Beer Hall Putsch; Hindenburg, Paul von; Munich; Nationalists; Nazi Movement; World War I

Suggestions for further reading:
Goodspeed, D. J. 1966. *Ludendorff: Soldier, Dictator, Revolutionary.* London: Hart-Davis.
Kershaw, Ian. 1998. *Hitler 1889–1936: Hubris.* New York: Allen Lane The Penguin Press.
Wistrich, Robert. 1982. *Who's Who in Nazi Germany.* London: Weidenfeld and Nicolson.

Lueger, Karl (1844–1910)

At the time of Hitler's arrival in Vienna in 1908, the city's politics were dominated by Lueger, the "King" or "Lord God of Vienna," from whom Hitler learned the political effectiveness of anti-Semitism. He was to refer to Lueger as "the greatest German mayor of all time" (Hitler 1992, p. 51). A lawyer by training, Lueger molded his Christian Social movement into a mass party, dedicated among other things to "liberating the Christian people from the domination of Jewry" (Kershaw 1998, p. 35). His election as mayor of Vienna, the most important elective position in Austria, in 1895 was finally recognized by a reluctant Emperor Franz Joseph in 1897.

Lueger's success was based on using populist rabble-rousing to mobilize a coalition of the lower-middle-class and artisan "little men" of the growing Viennese suburbs against the bourgeois liberals who had previously controlled city government. His vitriolic oratory, using slang and affecting a strong Viennese accent, impressed Hitler by its appeal to the "psychological instincts" of the masses. But Lueger was not a mere agitator; he showed how power could be used. His anti-Semitism and anti-socialism were combined with genuine achievements in a spirit of municipal socialism. As mayor he built hospitals and schools, founded an employment exchange and savings bank, and endowed Vienna with municipally controlled supplies of energy and water. His anti-Semitism, based on arousing resentment against both Jewish financiers and back-street peddlers competing with suburban artisans, was sublimated into a program of social reform.

But unlike Hitler's other early inspiration, Georg Ritter von Schönerer, Lueger was not a German nationalist. Instead he exploited popular Catholicism to fuse social reform and anti-Semitism with loyalty to the Habsburg dynasty. His Catholicism and pro-Habsburg stance had little appeal to Hitler, who would also criticize the "superficiality" of his anti-Semitism, which was more economic and political than racial. He tolerated and manipulated the most vicious anti-Semitism among his followers but was himself more opportunistic. When criticized for his frequent dining with wealthy Jews, he declared: "I decide who is a Jew." Hitler's anti-Semitism was becoming both more visceral and doctrinal. Yet he was among the mourning thousands who watched Lueger's funeral cortege in 1910 and learned an enduring lesson from the creation of the Christian Social movement by the man described by the socialist *Neue Zeit* as "the first bourgeois politician who recognized the importance of the masses in politics."

Related entries: Anti-Semitism; Schönerer, Georg Ritter von; Vienna

Suggestions for further reading:
Boyer, John W. 1981. *Political Radicalism in Late Imperial Vienna: Origins of the Christian Social Movement, 1848–1897*. Chicago: University of Chicago Press.
———. 1995. *Culture and Political Crisis in Vienna: Christian Socialism in Power, 1897–1918*. Chicago: University of Chicago Press.
Hitler, Adolf. 1992. *Mein Kampf*. Trans. Ralph Manheim. Intro. by D. C. Watt. London: Pimlico.
Kershaw, Ian. 1998. *Hitler 1889–1936: Hubris*. New York: Allen Lane Penguin Press.
Pulzer, Peter. 1988. *The Rise of Political Anti-Semitism in Germany and Austria*. Rev. ed. Cambridge, MA: Harvard University Press.
Schorske, Carl E. 1980. *Fin-de-Siècle Vienna: Politics and Culture*. New York: Alfred A. Knopf.

Luftwaffe

Under Hermann Goering, but owing more to the efforts of his deputy, Erhard Milch, by 1939 Hitler possessed the most powerful air force in the world. Although forbidden by the Treaty of Versailles to build military aircraft, Germany under the Weimar Republic had used civil aviation as a cover for constructing aircraft capable of being easily adapted for military use. The Lipetsk flying school, secretly leased from the Soviet Union in 1923, was used for the covert training of Lufthansa personnel as aircrew. On Hitler's accession to power, therefore, Goering and the able Milch already possessed a basis for the overt creation of a military air force.

The establishment of the Luftwaffe was formally announced by Hitler in March 1935. The first chief of staff, General Wever, a leading advocate of long-range strategic bombing, was killed in an air accident in 1936. Subsequently, the development of heavy bombers was neglected in favor of medium-range bombers and dive-bombers, and the Luftwaffe prepared for a sophisticated army support role. The new Heinkel and Dornier bombers, Junkers Stuka dive-bombers, and Messerschmitt fighters demonstrated their effectiveness to horrific effect during the Spanish Civil War, while pilots gained combat experience by being sent to Spain on rotation.

The Luftwaffe command had planned for European war in 1942 or 1943, but nevertheless German aircraft swept all before them supporting armored forces in the invasions of Poland, Norway, the Low Countries, and France. They established air supremacy, sowed chaos in their opponents' military and civil infrastructure, and bombed cities virtually unopposed. By June 1940 the Luftwaffe had gained a fearsome reputation. However, the Battle of Britain showed its limitations: the more modern Royal Air Force (RAF) fighters inflicted heavy losses, and the medium-range bombers, while capable of causing great damage, could not independently deliver a knockout blow on a major power. A new generation of warplanes was needed, but under the incompetent administration of Goering's longtime friend and fellow flying ace and socialite, Ernst Udet, the Luftwaffe technical directorate descended into chaos. A despairing Udet shot himself in November 1941, and Milch took over. Industrial output of aircraft revived, but designs remained outdated, and Milch was unable to persuade Hitler of the importance of fighter aircraft for home defense.

Meanwhile, the Luftwaffe inflicted heavy losses on British shipping in the Mediterranean and almost destroyed the Red Air Force in the invasion of the Soviet Union before Russian production revived remarkably quickly. In 1943 Allied bombing disrupted German aircraft production and forced the Luftwaffe to commit itself increasingly to home defense. It did cause heavy losses among Allied bombers, but resources had to be diverted from other theaters of operation. These were stretched further after the Allied landings in Normandy. By late 1944 large-scale production of new machines was made impossible by Allied bombing. Though now inferior to Allied air forces in men and machines, morale in the Luftwaffe remained surprisingly high until the end. The remaining force of 1,500 aircraft fought on until defeated by lack of fuel.

Related entries: Aviation; Blitzkrieg; Bombing Campaigns; Britain, Battle of; Condor Legion; Eastern Front; Goering, Hermann; Rearmament; Stalingrad, Battle of

M

Maginot Line

Built between 1930 and 1935, in which latter year it absorbed one-fifth of France's military budget, the line of concrete and steel defenses named after the war minister, André Maginot, was meant to be a "Western Front in concrete," an impregnable barrier against German invasion. A remarkable feat of military engineering, the line was effective along the Franco-German border, but left 250 miles of undefended border with Belgium. When Hitler launched his invasion of France, his forces simply went around the Maginot Line, where many of France's best soldiers were kept immobilized. Just as seriously perhaps, its existence had contributed to a "Maginot mentality," the illusion that France was secure from Hitler's threats.

Related entries: France

Malta

As Britain's only military base in the central Mediterranean, the island of Malta was the object of almost continuous bombing attacks by the Luftwaffe from 1941, but Hitler's plans for taking it were never put into effect. In March and April 1942, twice the tonnage of bombs was dropped on Malta as on London during the Blitz; supplies were virtually cut off; and the starving inhabitants were forced to live in caves. Operation Hercules, the planned German airborne invasion of the island, for which the bombing was intended as a prelude, would almost certainly have succeeded, but Hitler's enthusiasm for paratroop operations had been dampened by the heavy losses in Crete in 1941 and by the need for the Luftwaffe to support Erwin Rommel's offensive toward Suez. Supplies finally reached Malta in August 1942. After the defeat of Axis forces in Tunisia in May 1943, Malta became an important forward base for operations in southern Europe. The surrender of the Italian fleet to the Allies took place in the Grand Harbor of Valetta in September 1943.

Related entries: North Africa

Mannerheim, Carl Gustav (1867–1951)

The dominant figure in Finnish politics in the age of Hitler was of noble Swedish ancestry, served in the Imperial Russian Army, and led the White Guard against the Bolshevik-sponsored Red Guard in the brief civil war that followed

Finland's declaration of independence in October 1917. Recalled to politics in 1931 to reorganize the Finnish army, the marshal constructed the Mannerheim Line along the southeastern frontier and led the defense of Finland against the Soviets in the Winter War of 1939–1940. Mannerheim cooperated with Hitler in the invasion of the Soviet Union but was essentially fighting a parallel but separate conflict, known to Finns as the "Continuation War." In 1944 he succeeded in getting favorable terms from a separately negotiated peace settlement with Joseph Stalin. Mannerheim was made president of Finland in recognition of his contribution to preserving national independence but retired in 1946.

Related entries: Finland; Soviet Union

Manstein, Erich von (1887–1973)

Born in Berlin into an old and distinguished military family, Manstein is generally considered to have been the most able military strategist of the Third Reich but one whose effectiveness was hampered by his constant differences of opinion with Hitler. As chief of staff to Karl Rudolf von Rundstedt, he conceived the spectacularly successful plan for the invasion of France that is usually referred to as the "Manstein Plan" and that he personally presented to Hitler against the wishes of Franz Halder and Walther von Brauchitsch. Then in Operation Barbarossa he commanded the 56th Panzer Corps in the advance on Leningrad and later commanded the 11th Army, which completed the conquest of the Crimea.

Promoted to field marshal in July 1942, Manstein was appointed commander of Army Group Don in November, but as the tide of war turned against the Germans he disagreed with Hitler about the aims of fighting in Russia, ignoring the Führer's ultimate political and economic goals. He tried unsuccessfully to relieve Friedrich Paulus's 6th Army at Stalingrad, and his strategy at the battle of Kursk led to heavy losses for no purpose. Manstein had a low opinion of Hitler's understanding of military affairs and refusal to ever retreat. The persistent disagreements led to his dismissal in March 1944. However, he refused to take part in the July Plot against Hitler.

Manstein surrendered to the British in May 1945 and was tried by a British military court on war crimes charges. Though acquitted of many of them, his conception of soldierly duty had led him to acquiesce in the murderous actions of the SS in the Crimea and other areas where he was in command. Manstein's mastery of detail had made him a formidable opponent, and he had always followed Hitler's orders, even while disagreeing strongly with them. He was sentenced to eighteen years' imprisonment, later reduced to twelve, but released in 1953. His war memoirs, translated as *Lost Victories,* were published in 1958 (London: Methuen).

Related entries: Barbarossa, Operation; Citadel, Operation; Eastern Front; France; Kursk, Battle of; Stalingrad, Battle of; War Crimes; Wehrmacht

Suggestions for further reading:
Carver, Field Marshal Lord. 1995. "Manstein," in Correlli Barnett, ed., *Hitler's Generals.* Paperback ed. London: Phoenix.
Manstein, Erich von. 1958. *Lost Victories.* London: Methuen.

Mein Kampf

An essential introduction to Hitler's mentality and political "philosophy," *Mein Kampf,* first published in 1925, was his only major written work. The draft of a second work, known as *Hitler's Secret Book* or *Second Book,* dictated by Hitler to the publisher Max Amann in 1928, was never published during his lifetime. The bulk of *Mein Kampf* was dictated by Hitler to Rudolf Hess and the future Sturmabteilung (SA) man Emil Maurice during his imprisonment at Landsberg. As such it reads like his speeches—clumsy and longwinded when set down in cold print—proving by default that Hitler's true medium was the spoken word. According to the writer Leon Feuchtwanger, *Mein Kampf* is a collection of 164,000 offenses against German grammar and syntax, while Benito Mussolini called it "a boring tome that I have never been able to read" and "little more than commonplace clichés" (Mack Smith 1981, p. 172).

For all its lack of artistic or intellectual merit, under the Third Reich it became necessary for the ambitious to possess a copy of *Mein Kampf*, if not necessarily to read it. From Amann's original print run of 10,000 copies of the first volume, its success grew with Hitler's rise to notoriety and then power, and total sales in his lifetime probably numbered between 8 and 9 million. It was required reading for schoolchildren, and in April 1936 the Ministry of the Interior recommended that every bridal couple should be presented with a copy. English-language versions were published in Britain and the United States in 1939, and it was translated into thirteen other languages, from Japanese in 1928 to Tamil in 1944.

Mein Kampf is divided into two volumes: "A Reckoning," a sort of autobiography liberally interlarded with Hitler's reflections on the political events of his times and any other subject that crossed his mind; and "The National Socialist Movement," intermixing the short history of the movement with an account of its policies. Although the structure seems logical, in fact within each chapter Hitler's views pour out in an unselective manner as if all were equally important. Hitler's opinions about education, Wagner, boxing, art and architecture, eugenics, prostitution and venereal disease, the dress of the young, and anything else that occurs to him are integrated in arbitrary and paranoid fashion into his overriding obsessions with Jewish conspiracy, the iniquities of democracy and the parliamentary system, and the criminal follies of Germany's leaders. The autobiographical sections have been shown to be inaccurate and self-serving, and the whole is excruciatingly egotistic and saturated with Hitler's self-importance. All opinions other than his own are mad or "cowardly," and the people have been "seduced" into believing them by Marxists and Jews, essentially the same people. The result is confused, repetitive, verbose, rambling, and unbearably tedious to read.

The basis of the ideas in *Mein Kampf* is a crude Social Darwinism allied with a racial view of history. Human beings operate according to the laws of the "eternal fight and upward struggle" of nature in a universe where "force alone forever masters weakness, compelling it to be an obedient slave or else crushing it" (Hitler 1992, p. 233). "The racial question gives the key not only to world history, but to all human culture" (p. 308); politics is therefore not determined by economics but by race; and the state exists for "the preservation and intensification of the race, this fundamental condition of all human cultural development" (p. 355). Furthermore, "the German Reich as a state embraces all Germans and has the task, not only of assembling and preserving the most valuable stocks of basic racial elements in this people, but slowly and surely of raising them to a dominant position" (p. 362).

Hitler's paranoia will admit of nothing happening by chance. Germany's defeat in World War I, the revolution of 1918, and the acceptance by politicians of the Treaty of Versailles all show that "conscious purpose is destroying our nation," all "in the service of the Jewish idea and struggle for world conquest" (p. 611). "And so the Jew today is the great agitator for the complete destruction of Germany" (p. 568). "The

Jew" and "Jewish bolshevism" represent the negation of the principle of nationality and are the instigators of Germany's ruin. The simple purpose of the National Socialist movement is to destroy them. Hitler makes clear his contempt for "the masses" and "the bourgeoisie." By a process of natural selection a new Aryan elite will emerge to lead the German people to world power.

Mein Kampf contains no blueprint for the seizure of power or for Nazi foreign policy. But it does make obvious where Germany's destiny lies in Hitler's mind. Expansion to the east and the destruction of the Soviet Union and the other states of eastern Europe will acquire the necessary "living space" for the German people: "And the end of Jewish rule in Russia will also be the end of Russia as a state" (p. 598). In Hitler's fantastic conception of history, Russia was the creation of German "racial elements," and the destruction of "Jewish-Bolshevik" Russia, ruled by the "scum of the earth," will open up the lands of the east for conquest and settlement by German farmers. The sections in Part 2 of *Mein Kampf* dealing with foreign policy should have dispelled any illusions that Hitler's sole aim was to revise the perceived injustices of the Treaty of Versailles.

Readers of *Mein Kampf* at the time of its publication might possibly be forgiven for refusing to believe that a serious politician would put such claptrap into practice. But they underestimated Hitler's consistency and the earnestness with which he took up his own ideas. His aims are set out as the destruction of democracy, the creation of a racial state, the removal of the Jews from Germany, and an aggressive foreign policy leading ultimately to expansion into eastern Europe. With his egotism, paranoia, extraordinary ragbag of a worldview, and sense of his own destiny, it should have been clear that Hitler was not a "normal" politician, a breed for which he showed nothing but hatred and contempt. His book, dreadful as it is in every sense of the word, should above all have acted as a warning to those conservative politicians who thought they could control him or buy him off.

Related entries: Anti-Semitism; Foreign Policy; Landsberg-am-Lech; Lebensraum; National Socialist German Workers' Party; Nazi Movement; Racial Theory; Soviet Union

Suggestions for further reading:
Hitler, Adolf. 1992. *Mein Kampf.* Trans. Ralph Manheim. Intro. by D. C. Watt. London: Pimlico.
Mack Smith, Denis. 1981. *Mussolini.* London: Weidenfeld and Nicolson.

Memel

*T*he area in and around the Baltic port city of Memel in East Prussia was taken from the German Reich in 1918 and annexed by Lithuania in January 1923. A local Nazi Party was founded and flourished among the majority German population and demanded to rejoin Germany. After his successful seizure of the Sudetenland in 1938 Hitler demanded the return of Memel. A treaty was forced upon Lithuania, and on 23 March 1939 German troops marched into Memel, which was incorporated into the German Reich. With the advance of the Red Army through the Baltic states in 1944, most of the German population left the area. It was incorporated into the Lithuanian Soviet Socialist Republic in January 1945.

Related entries: Baltic States

Michael, King of Romania (b. 1921)

*S*on of King Carol II, Prince Michael became regent of Romania when his father was forced to abdicate in September

1940. He was obliged to follow the pro-German policy of Ion Antonescu. In August 1944, however, faced with the serious possibility that Hitler would seize power directly in Romania and with the Russians already invading Romanian soil, Michael took the lead in the overthrow of Antonescu. Michael sued for peace with the Allies, and the Romanian armed forces changed sides. Amid the resultant confusion the Red Army swept across Romania, and armistice with the Soviet Union was signed on 12 September 1944. King Michael was forced to abdicate on 30 December 1947 to make way for a Communist regime.

Related entries: Antonescu, Ion; Romania

Middle Classes

*I*n older historiography, up to the 1970s, the lower middle classes of Germany were forced to take almost all the blame for the rise of Hitler. Squeezed between the big battalions of large-scale capitalism and organized labor, small shopkeepers, self-employed artisans, clerks, and lower civil servants, hit by economic recession and fearful of "proletarianization," found an answer to their psychological disarray in the backward-looking "national community" promised by Nazism. It is now accepted that Hitler's appeal was broader than implied in this model, even if it was often superficial. The National Socialist German Workers' Party (NSDAP, Nazi Party) produced propaganda specially tailored for each social group and even attracted a degree of working-class support. Hitler's promises were deliberately vague but included something for everyone.

Nevertheless, he remained heavily reliant on middle-class support. The Nazis, like other nationalists, used the term *Mittelstand* to denote an "estate" of independent artisans, retail merchants, shopkeepers, and the like, as differentiated from a "new" *Mittelstand* of white-collar employees and civil servants. They promised the "old" group economic protection from the threat posed by department stores and mass production and relief from the tax burden imposed by the Weimar Republic. They also promised better recognition for the professions—doctors, lawyers, teachers, civil servants—and of course the reconstruction of the "national community" after the destruction wreaked by Marxism.

Before 1933 middle-class support for Hitler was weakened somewhat by the apparent social radicalism of Nazism and its hooligan element, both embodied in the Sturmabteilung (SA). But after the seizure of power and especially following the Night of the Long Knives, middle-class *Beamte* (white-collar employees, civil servants, and teachers) rushed to join the Nazi Party, and party activists and functionaries at all levels were predominately of middle-class origin. But Hitler did not deliver a middle-class utopia. Economic reality remained largely unchanged; small businesses suffered declining profit margins; insecurity still existed; and disillusion was strengthened by the regulations and demands of the regime, the corruption and rapacity of "little Hitlers," continuing violence, and attacks on the churches. But Hitler himself remained popular with the middle classes, especially in sectors where the regime boosted the economy, such as building, metal-working, and tourism, and among the *Beamte* in the swollen party and state bureaucracies.

The widely varying economic experiences and religious commitments of the middle classes make generalization impossible, but sectional grievances were perfectly compatible with support for the regime and especially for Hitler. For example, the promises of higher status for teachers were not kept, yet they still provided the backbone of many a local party cell. And grumbling did not become opposition: resignation, fatalism,

and a lack of alternatives were more preva-
lent middle-class attitudes. Their identification with Hitler's ideological aims may not
always have been profound, but it was broad.

Related entries: Civil Service; Economic
Policy; Education; Fascism; *Gleichschaltung;* Hitler
Myth; Industry; Judiciary; Nazi Movement;
Opposition; Public Opinion; Social Policy;
Women; Working Class

Suggestions for further reading:
Childers, Thomas. 1991. "The Middle Classes and
National Socialism," in David Blackbourn
and Richard J. Evans, eds., *The German
Bourgeoisie.* London and New York:
Routledge, pp. 318–337.

Middle East

itler showed little interest in reviving pre-1914 German ambitions in
the Middle East, dominated by Britain and
France as mandated powers of the League of
Nations. Any aggressive intentions he may
have had toward the region would have to
wait until he had secured German control
of eastern Europe and the Caucasus.
Friendly relations with neutral Turkey were
maintained until 1943, but German support
for the Arab revolt against the British mandate in Palestine remained purely verbal, and
during the war, aid for the pro-German
leader in Iraq, Rashid Ali, was limited and
late. During the 1930s the Third Reich favored Jewish emigration to Palestine but
opposed the creation of a Jewish state. In
August 1933 the Economics Ministry
signed the Ha'avara Agreement with the
Jewish Agency in Palestine, permitting emigrating German Jews to use a portion of
their assets to buy German products for export to Palestine. The SS supported Zionist
leaders in Germany in arranging illegal immigration into Palestine as a way of simultaneously ridding Germany of Jews and creating problems for the British mandate.

Related entries: Jews and Jewish Policy; Turkey

Mihajlović, Draža (1893–1946)

he strongly monarchist and Serbian
nationalist soldier Mihajlović formed
the Chetnik resistance group with other Yugoslav officers following Hitler's invasion in
April 1941. But his aims and ideology were
incompatible with those of Josip Tito's
Communist partisans, and he soon began
cooperating with the Germans and Italians
against the common enemy. Mihajlović
nevertheless retained contact with the
British and the post of war minister in the
government-in-exile. In November 1943
London warned him to stop Chetnik collaboration with the occupier, and he was
excluded from the agreement of June 1944
between Tito and the government of King
Peter. After the defeat of the Axis, Mihajlović hid in the mountains until he was captured on 13 March 1946 and executed as a
collaborator in July. In exculpation Mihajlović claimed that his aim had been to limit
civilian casualties and prevent the destruction of Yugoslavia. "I wanted much," he said,
"I began much, but the gale of the world
swept away me and my work" (Keegan
1989, p. 494).

Related entries: Resistance Movements; Tito,
Josip Broz; Yugoslavia

Suggestions for further reading:
Keegan, John. 1989. *The Second World War.*
London: Hutchinson.

Molotov, Vyacheslav Mikhailovich (1890–1986)

ery much one of Joseph Stalin's
creatures, Molotov became Soviet
commissar for foreign affairs in May 1939
and thus figured prominently in negotiating the Nazi-Soviet Pact. Ruthless and realistic, Molotov could not hide his doubts

about Hitler's ultimate success even while discussing the possibility of a four-power pact among Germany, the Soviet Union, Italy, and Japan in 1940. It was Molotov who announced the news of Hitler's invasion to the Soviet people in June 1941, declaring: "Our cause is just. The enemy will be smashed. The victory will be ours" (Volkogonov 1995, p. 244). Thereafter he helped steer Russian relations with Britain and the United States. He formalized Lend-Lease agreements with the Allies, pressured Winston Churchill for the opening of a second front, and attended the Teheran and Yalta conferences. Molotov's career ended after the war following the arrest of his Jewish wife, and he remained out of favor after Stalin's death, being rehabilitated in 1984 shortly before his own death.

Related entries: Nazi-Soviet Pact; Soviet Union; Teheran Conference; Yalta Conference

Montgomery, Bernard Law (1887–1976)

Controversial and vain, Field Marshal Montgomery nevertheless showed a resilience and commitment to the Allied cause that turned him into one of the most popular commanders in the struggle against Hitler. His attention to troop morale, cautious planning, and careful execution of operations was crucial in turning the tide against the Axis in North Africa. Montgomery's conflicts with General Dwight D. Eisenhower and his obsessive rivalry with the equally flamboyant U.S. General George Patton, both in Italy and in the advance toward Germany in 1945, fortunately had no serious effect in delaying Hitler's defeat.

Related entries: El Alamein, Battle of; North Africa

Field Marshal Sir Bernard Montgomery in typically informal battlefield dress and pose. His ability to communicate with his soldiers inspired total confidence in those who served under him, but his conceit and cockiness infuriated his fellow commanders. (Archive Photos)

Morell, Theo (1886–1948)

Hitler was introduced to Morell, a fashionable doctor with prominent patients, by Heinrich Hoffmann in 1936. He came to trust his new doctor, who diagnosed "intestinal exhaustion" as the cause of the Führer's chronic stomach troubles. For the next nine years he submitted to Morell's treatments, from relatively harmless items such as bulls' testicles to more risky amphetamines and an endless number of injections. Other members of Hitler's court were skeptical, especially his big rival, Karl Brandt, who accused Morell of slowly poisoning Hitler. To Albert Speer, Morell "was not an out-and-out quack—rather a bit of a screwball obsessed with making money" (Speer 1971, pp. 160–161). Hitler the health crank remained dependent on Morell until near the end. How far his treatments contributed to Hitler's condition, which resembled a form of Parkinson's disease, is a matter for conjecture. Morell was one of the last to leave the Führer's bunker on 21 April 1945. He fell into the hands of the Americans, was held and questioned in several internment camps, and died in a U.S. military hospital in May 1948.

Related entries: Brandt, Karl

Suggestions for further reading:
Speer, Albert. 1971. *Inside the Third Reich.* Paperback ed. London: Sphere Books.

Munich

When Hitler moved to the capital city of Bavaria in 1913, it was the most culturally vibrant city in Germany. Hitler ignored such un-German decadence but was glad to be away from cosmopolitan Vienna. He recalled his feelings on being in Munich: "A *German* City! What a difference from Vienna!" (Hitler 1992, p. 116). Although no more naturally disposed than anywhere else to be the center of Hitler's movement, Munich became the springboard for his ambitions. He would profit from the generally benevolent outlook of the local administration and police and found patrons in Munich high society. The experience of the "Red" republic in Bavaria made Munich conservatives more than usually sympathetic to the radicalism of Nazi anti-Marxism and anti-Semitism.

It was in Munich that Hitler joined the German Workers' Party (DAP) and transformed it into the National Socialist German Workers' Party (NSDAP, Nazi Party). Munich was the scene of the Beer Hall Putsch, and the Reich party leadership resided there in the Brown House. As such it played a vital role in Nazi mythology. Every year on 8 November Hitler spoke to the "Old Fighters" at the Bürgerbrau beer hall, which was destroyed in Georg Elser's attempted assassination of the Führer in 1939. In 1935 Hitler honored the city with the title "Capital of the Movement." He directed operations against Ernst Röhm in the Night of the Long Knives from Munich, received Benito Mussolini there on a state visit in September 1937, and in 1938 celebrated foreign policy success in the Munich Agreement.

Munich benefited from Hitler's gratitude in other ways. It held more of the Third Reich's architectural showpieces than any other city. The Academy of German Law was founded there in June 1933, followed by the German Academy for Education. As the "city of German art," it could boast the House of German Art, opened on 16 July 1937, a date commemorated annually as the "Day of German Art." The numerous party buildings included the Führer Building on Königlicher Platz, the SS Main Riding School in Riem, and the Temple of Honor, opened in November 1935. Hitler's regular visits to Berchtesgarden took him through Munich on frequent occasions. During the war, however, Munich became a target for many Allied bombing raids, which destroyed about one-third of all the city's residential buildings. Units of the U.S.

7th Army occupied Munich on 30 April 1945, the day Hitler committed suicide.

Related entries: Architecture; Bavaria; Beer Hall Putsch; Drexler, Anton; Elser, Georg; Frick, Wilhelm; German Workers' Party; Hanfstaengl, Ernst Franz Sedgwick; Munich Agreement; National Socialist German Workers' Party; Nazi Movement; Night of the Long Knives

Suggestions for further reading:
Hitler, Adolf. 1992. *Mein Kampf.* Trans. Ralph Manheim. Intro. by D. C. Watt. London: Pimlico.
Large, David Clay. 1997. *Where Ghosts Walked: Munich's Road to the Third Reich.* New York: Norton.

Munich Agreement

The agreement by which Hitler secured the cession of the Sudetenland to Germany can be seen as the summit of appeasement, and "Munich" has come to symbolize abject surrender to dictatorial demands. The threat of war fabricated by Hitler when he mobilized the German army in August 1938 spurred Neville Chamberlain to make three trips to Germany within two weeks, only to find Hitler upping his demands. Benito Mussolini persuaded Hitler to a further meeting with Chamberlain and Edouard Daladier at Munich on 29 September. Here the British and French leaders agreed to Hitler's demands for the military occupation of the Sudetenland, meaning all territories designated by the German government, to be followed by a plebiscite (never held) to determine the German-Czech frontier.

Defenders of the Munich Agreement argue that the peaceful resolution of the Czech crisis gave the democracies time to improve their military preparedness. Critics point that with the military capacity of the Czechs and the likely involvement of the Soviet Union (which had, however, not been invited to Munich), Hitler would have faced a stronger coalition in 1938 than he did in 1939. There is indeed some evidence that Hitler had been less than overjoyed at the agreement. He had been robbed of a chance to show off his military might, and he did not like to be bound by declarations such as the provision for mutual consultations between Britain and Germany on questions of concern to the two countries, which allowed Chamberlain to claim he had secured "peace for our time."

The peoples of Germany, France, and Britain, breathing a collective sigh of relief that peace had been preserved, gave overwhelming support to the signatories of Munich. Within Germany Hitler's popularity hit new heights. Josef Goebbels trumpeted how the Führer had "once more succeeded in preserving world peace" (Bramsted 1965, p. 176). Victor Klemperer noted the applause at newsreels of Munich: "A burden has been lifted from everyone's soul. It is impossible to say what still threatens the Third Reich internally or externally. Munich is Hitler's Austerlitz" (Klemperer 1998, p. 259). But he would not be satisfied. Czechoslovakia, the last surviving democracy in central Europe, was reduced to the status of a German satellite. Within six months, on 15 March 1939, Hitler's troops would march into Prague.

Related entries: Appeasement; Beneš, Eduard; Chamberlain, Neville; Czechoslovakia; Daladier, Edouard; Foreign Policy; France; Great Britain; Public Opinion; Sudetenland

Suggestions for further reading:
Bramsted, Ernest K. 1965. *Goebbels and National Socialist Propaganda 1925–1945.* East Lansing: Michigan State University Press.
Klemperer, Victor. 1998. *I Shall Bear Witness: The Diaries of Victor Klemperer, 1933–41.* London: Weidenfeld and Nicolson.
Taylor, Telford. 1979. *Munich: The Price of Peace.* Garden City, NY: Doubleday.

Mussolini, Benito (1883–1945)

Mussolini's dictatorship in Italy was a major inspiration for Hitler. In

Mussolini with Hitler during one of the Duce's visits to Germany in which Hitler tried to impress him with German might and Nazi pageantry. Hitler acknowledged his political debt to Italian Fascism but was always keen to assert his dominance in the relationship between the two dictators. (Culver Pictures)

Mein Kampf he wrote of "the great man south of the Alps, who, full of ardent love for his people, made no pacts with the enemies of Italy, but strove for their annihilation by all ways and means. What will rank Mussolini among the great men of this earth is his determination not to share Italy with the Marxists, but to destroy internationalism and save the fatherland from it" (Hitler 1992, p. 622). But the close political relationship between the two dictators, governed by their linked ideologies and aggressive nationalist goals, was also marked by distrust. Hitler, always viewing the world in racial terms, never thought much of Italians and in private would joke about Mussolini's vanity and playacting.

Mussolini came to power, as did Hitler, using a mixture of brute force and legality. Following a restless youth, the future Duce had established himself as a left-wing journalist, becoming editor of the Socialist Party paper, *Avanti,* in 1912, before his support for Italian intervention in World War I caused him to move to the Right. After 1918 he organized the paramilitary group Fasci di Combattimento, out of which emerged the Fascist Party, which in turn exploited fear of communism to attract wide support from nationalists. Mussolini became prime minister of a right-wing coalition in 1922 following the largely mythological March on Rome (in fact, for Mussolini a train journey from Milan). A one-party state in which the functions of a cabinet were taken over by the Fascist Grand Council, dominated by Mussolini, was established in 1929.

Hitler realized that the way to Mussolini's support lay in flattery. A bronze bust of the Duce was placed prominently outside the Nazi Party headquarters in Munich. But their first meeting in 1934 did not go well. Mussolini was piqued by Hitler's pretensions of German racial and cultural superiority and declared in a famous quote: "Thirty centuries of history enable us to look with majestic pity at certain doctrines taught on the other side of the Alps by the descendants of people who were wholly illiterate in the days when Rome boasted a Caesar, a Virgil and an Augustus" (Hiden 1977, pp. 144–145). But the affinities between the two regimes and a common interest in intervention in the Spanish Civil War drove them together. Following the creation of the Axis in 1936, Hitler proclaimed: "Mussolini is the leading statesman in the world, to whom no-one else can be remotely compared" (Mack Smith 1981, p. 208). The Duce was treated to a lavish state visit to Germany in September 1937 and his self-importance duly flattered personally by Hitler, who was now clearly the dominant partner. Count Galeazzo Ciano was to note in 1940: "The Duce is fascinated by Hitler, a fascination which involves something deeply rooted in his make-up" (Bullock 1991, p. 741).

Hitler was especially concerned to flatter Mussolini because of the Duce's long-standing opposition to his plans for the Anschluss with Austria. In 1931 Mussolini had declared: "We can march with Germany on the Rhine but not on the Danube" (Hiden 1977, p. 144). The obvious threat to Italy posed by German expansion encouraged the illusion in the Western democracies that Mussolini could be used as an "honest broker" with Hitler. Hence his participation as a guarantor of the Munich Agreement of 1938. Hitler was less naïve and saw that Mussolini's own imperial pretensions would be useful for his own. "So long as the Duce lives," he said in November 1939, "so long it can be calculated that Italy will seize every opportunity to reach her imperialistic goals" (Mack Smith 1981, pp. 240–41).

He changed his ideas once Mussolini's amateurish and incompetent handling of the war became apparent. In 1939 Italy annexed Albania, and the Axis became the "Pact of Steel." Mussolini watched Hitler's early conquests with undisguised envy and in June 1940, ignoring his military and economic advisers, declared war on the Allies just in time to grab some spoils from Hitler's defeat of France. Mussolini expected that Britain would be swiftly defeated, but the disastrous conduct of the Italian invasions of Egypt, Greece, and East Africa, the defeats suffered by the Italian navy in the Mediterranean, and the failure of Italian heavy industry to adapt to a war economy meant that by early 1941 he was totally dependent on German aid.

As Italy's military and economic position grew ever weaker, Mussolini, trying desperately to appear an equal partner with Hitler, issued military orders totally divorced from reality and made things worse by sending Italian troops to the Eastern Front and declaring war on the United States. By the end of 1941 Mussolini had become a passive but irksome junior partner in the dictators' alliance, but he still retained an extraordinary vainglorious belief in his own destiny. With the Allied victories in North Africa, he continued to issue his usual fantastic battle orders, but his health was failing, and he became an ever more isolated figure.

Hitler endeavored to stand by the crumbling colossus. The two dictators met in July 1943 as the Allies prepared to invade Italy, but on his return Mussolini was presented with a demand for his resignation by the Fascist Grand Council, backed by King Victor Emmanuel III and the armed forces. He was placed under house arrest in the Apennine mountains, but Hitler mounted a daring rescue. German airborne troops led by Major Otto Skorzeny grabbed Mussolini from his captors and took him to Germany.

Mussolini was installed as head of the Salò Republic (Italian Social Republic), a Fascist regime nominally ruling German-occupied northern Italy. The Duce was now merely a puppet of Hitler, installed in headquarters at Gargagno on Lake Garda.

His most notable act was the trial and execution of five of the men who had removed him from power, including his son-in-law Ciano. In April 1945, with Germany collapsing, he attempted to escape to Switzerland with his mistress, Clara Petacci. The pair were captured by Italian partisans on the shore of Lake Como on 27 April. They were shot the next day and the bodies displayed for public degradation in Milan.

Related entries: Anti-Comintern Pact; Austria; Axis; Ciano, Galeazzo, Count; Fascism; Foreign Policy; Greece; Italy; Munich Agreement; North Africa; Pact of Steel; Spain

Suggestions for further reading:

Bullock, Alan. 1991. *Hitler and Stalin: Parallel Lives.* London: HarperCollins.
Deakin, F. W. 1962. *The Brutal Friendship: Mussolini, Hitler and the Fall of Italian Fascism.* London: Weidenfeld and Nicolson.
Hiden, John. 1977. *Germany and Europe 1919–1939.* New York: Longman.
Hitler, Adolf. 1992. *Mein Kampf.* Trans. Ralph Manheim. Intro. by D. C. Watt. London: Pimlico.
Mack Smith, Denis. 1981. *Mussolini.* London: Weidenfeld and Nicolson.

Mutterkreuz

As part of the "war of birth" to provide new Germans for Hitler's expansionism, the Mother's Cross, an equivalent for women of the military Iron Cross, was introduced in 1938 to encourage large families. Mothers of four or five children received a bronze cross, mothers of six or seven children a silver cross, and mothers of eight or more children a gold cross. Such mothers were meant to be suitably grateful at being thus decorated but probably welcomed the generous benefits provided by the regime rather more.

Related entries: Social Policy; Women

N

National Socialism (Nazism)

The term "National Socialism" had first been adopted in the early years of the twentieth century by various political associations in the Habsburg Empire. These groups, which sought to combine German nationalist and socialist agendas, came together in 1904 as the German Workers' Party (DAP), which provided the later Munich-based DAP with its name and symbols, including the swastika. However, the ideology of Nazism as we know it, made up of an often confused amalgam of convictions, authoritarian theories, irrational racial mythology, and pseudoreligious symbolism, was a creation of the "Twenty-five-Point Program" of the National Socialist German Workers' Party (NSDAP, Nazi Party), issued on 24 February 1920, and of Hitler's writings and speeches, most importantly *Mein Kampf.*

Insofar as Nazism constituted a coherent ideology expressing Hitler's worldview, the principal components were antiparliamentarianism and an authoritarian concept of state and society, anti-Marxism and anti-socialism, the Führer principle, aggressive nationalism, a racial concept of the nation, anti-Semitism, and militarism. It was promulgated through popular slogans and clichés but relied very much on the cult of the Führer around Hitler to gain popular support. Nazism in practice meant the destruc-tion of democracy, persecution of the Jews and other "racially inferior" groups, and the preparation of a war of aggression in eastern Europe.

Related entries: Anti-Semitism; *Blut und Boden;* Charismatic Domination; Eugenics; Fascism; Führer Principle; German Workers' Party; Hitler Myth; Lebensraum; *Mein Kampf;* National Socialist German Workers' Party; Nazi Movement; Pan-Germanism; Propaganda; Racial Theory; Socialism; Swastika; Third Reich; *Volksgemeinschaft*

National Socialist Factory Cell Organization (NSBO)

The NSBO was founded on the initiative of Nazi activists, some of them former Communists, as a workers' organization winning over employees to the movement. Groups that had formed in workplaces were finally constituted as the NSBO in 1931. It did not see itself as a trade union but rather as the "SA of the workplace." To Hitler and the other Nazi leaders it was essentially a propaganda organization, not in competition with Social Democratic and Christian trade unions but spreading the anti-Marxist message of the National Socialist German Workers' Party (NSDAP, Nazi Party). Membership grew rapidly, reaching about 100,000 in May

1932 and 730,000 by May 1933, but it lagged far behind the growth of the party as a whole during the same period. It began to behave increasingly like a trade union, supported a series of strikes, and talked of founding a single trade union under its leadership with a role to play in the future Nazi state. This was not Hitler's view. For him strikes and labor activism were only useful as ways of weakening the Weimar Republic: in a National Socialist *völkisch* state, strike action could never be legitimate. After his accession to power the NSBO stood alongside the Sturmabteilung in calling for a "second revolution," but it was effectively quieted by the bloodbath of the Night of the Long Knives. The NSBO consequently lost any influence it had, and in January 1935 it was absorbed into the German Labor Front.

Related entries: German Labor Front; Nazi Movement; Working Class

National Socialist German Workers' Party (NSDAP, Nazi Party)

The German Workers' Party (DAP), which Hitler had joined in September 1919, was renamed the NSDAP on 24 February 1920. On 29 July 1921 Hitler was elected chairman with almost unlimited authority, including the right to select all party functionaries. At the poorly attended first "Reich Party Rally" in Munich in January 1923 Hitler had for the first time gained publicity in the press, and he was aware that without him the party would disappear. By offering to resign, he managed to impose his own terms and be recognized as sole leader. The "Twenty-five-Point Program" of the NSDAP, adopted on 24 February 1920, drawn up by Hitler, Anton Drexler, and Gottfried Feder, with

its mixture of nationalist, *völkisch* and anti-Semitic, militarist, authoritarian and antiparliamentarian, and vaguely anticapitalist elements, remained "immutable" party policy until the end of the Third Reich, but much of it was never followed in practice.

The NSDAP declared itself a "new type" of party, different from the "system parties" of the Weimar Republic. Its centralist and authoritarian structure and organization was entirely oriented toward the "Führer," as Hitler was designated in 1922. He headed the Reich leadership, consisting of individual Reich leaders *(Reichsleiter),* including the deputy or secretary to the Führer, the Reich propaganda leader, treasurer, press chief, and so on. These headed the party's main offices, or *Hauptämter.* Regionally, the NSDAP was organized in *Gaue* (thirty-five in 1935; forty-one in 1940), districts *(Kreise),* local groups *(Ortsgruppen),* cells *(Zelle),* and blocks. Their leaders, the *Gauleiters, Kreisleiters, Ortsgruppenleiters, Zellenleiters,* and *Blockwarte,* together formed the corps of political leaders.

At the time of the Beer Hall Putsch in November 1923, the NSDAP claimed about 55,000 members, but after the failure of the coup it was banned. Though kept alive as the "National Socialist Freedom Party" during Hitler's imprisonment in Landsberg, by the time of his release the party was in ruins. Hitler announced the "refoundation" of the NSDAP in February 1925, and party headquarters were opened in Munich. Over the next two years he tightened his grip on what was still a small party, with 49,000 members in 1926, due partly to Gregor Strasser's Nazi organization in northern Germany. Drexler left the party and tried unsuccessfully to set up a rival one in April 1925. And in an open challenge to Hitler's leadership, Strasser published a new party program replacing the "Twenty-five Points" in December 1925.

In February 1926 Hitler called a party meeting in Bamberg, where he outmaneuvered Strasser and won over Strasser's deputy, Josef Goebbels, and others. In May a general party meeting in Munich resolved that the Munich Party was the leadership of the Nazi movement, and in July the first party rally in Weimar was held. Goebbels was made *Gauleiter* of Berlin in November. The party rally was held for the first time at Nuremberg in August 1927. Party membership passed 100,000 in May 1928; 178,000 in December 1929; and 210,000 in June 1930. In September 1930 it made its big breakthrough in elections to the Reichstag, winning 107 seats, making it the second-largest party behind the Social Democrats. Wilhelm Frick became the first NSDAP member of a state government in Thuringia in January 1930, and it first gained an absolute majority in a state legislature in Oldenburg in May of that year.

By January 1933 the NSDAP had 1 million members. By skillful use of propaganda and the terror tactics of the Sturmabteilung, it attracted the support of thousands who were dissatisfied with things as they were. The anticapitalist aspects of the party program fell into oblivion. Analysis of party membership shows an overrepresentation of the middle classes and underrepresentation of the working class in relation to their numbers in the total population. As the party grew it attracted more civil servants and professional people, who largely took over the leadership after the seizure of power. Within the party the "Old Fighters," or *Alte Kämpfer*, who had marched in the Beer Hall Putsch looked down on the "March Violets" who rushed to join in 1933.

Hitler overcame a final crisis in the NSDAP in late 1932, forcing Strasser's resignation, and it became the largest party in the Reichstag in July 1932. The way was open for Hitler's accession to power. With his nomination as chancellor the NSDAP became the ruling party of Germany, although it never gained an absolute majority in free elections. The law of 14 July 1933 forbidding the creation of parties made it the only legal party, and the one-party state was legalized by the Law to Secure the Unity of Party and State of 1 December 1933. Party membership grew to 2.5 million in 1935 and ultimately to 8.5 million in 1935. Such was the desire to join the NSDAP that stops on recruitment had to be imposed on several occasions.

Hitler had defined the role of his party in *Mein Kampf:* "The NSDAP should not become a constable of public opinion, but must dominate it. It must not become a servant of the masses, but their master!" (Hitler 1992, p. 422). Within the so-called polycracy of the Third Reich its principal function was to channel and mobilize the population for the aims of the regime. The party rallies at Nuremberg and other manifestations and ceremonials played a particularly significant role. But the NSDAP was only one rival authority among others. It dominated local government but was ridden by personal and factional rivalries at all levels. The SS and the Gestapo were more important as instruments of Hitler's authority, and policy was implemented principally by the government bureaucracy. The NSDAP and its member associations were outlawed and dissolved on 10 October 1945 by Law No. 2 of the Allied Control Council.

Related entries: Beer Hall Putsch; Berlin; Bormann, Martin; Civil Service; Drexler, Anton; Elections; Fascism; Feder, Gottfried; Frick, Wilhelm; Führer Principle; *Gauleiters;* German Workers' Party; *Gleichschaltung;* Goebbels, Paul Josef; Goering, Hermann; Hess, Rudolf; Hitler Myth; Middle Classes; Munich; National Socialism; Nazi Movement; Night of the Long Knives; Nuremberg Rallies; Propaganda; Public Opinion; Reichstag; Schutzstaffel; Socialism; Strasser, Gregor; Sturmabteilung; *Völkischer Beobachter;* Working Class

Suggestions for further reading:
Brustein, William. 1996. *The Logic of Evil: The Social Origins of the Nazi Party 1925–1933.* New Haven: Yale University Press.
Hitler, Adolf. 1992. *Mein Kampf.* Trans. Ralph Manheim. Intro. by D. C. Watt. London: Pimlico.

Jablonsky, David. 1989. *The Nazi Party in Dissolution: Hitler and the Verbotszeit 1923–25.* London: Frank Cass.

Kater, Michael H. 1983. *The Nazi Party: A Social Profile of Members and Leaders, 1919–1945.* Cambridge, MA: Harvard University Press.

Noakes, Jeremy. 1971. *The Nazi Party in Lower Saxony, 1921–1933.* Oxford: Oxford University Press.

Orlow, Dietrich. 1969. *The History of the Nazi Party, 1919–1933.* Pittsburgh: University of Pittsburgh Press.

———. 1973. *The History of the Nazi Party, 1933–1945.* Pittsburgh: University of Pittsburgh Press.

Nationalists

Hitler's coming to power can be viewed as the culmination of German nationalism, and he could not have succeeded without the support or passive consent of those nationalists who saw the Weimar Republic as an "un-German" system foisted on the country by foreigners and traitors. The main nationalist party, the German National People's Party (DNVP), was divided between reactionary conservative monarchists, who wished to turn the clock back to the pre-1918 *Kaiserreich,* and more radical *völkisch* and anti-Semitic elements. It also inherited the support of the old Pan-German League, whose nationalism rested on a belief in the inherent superiority of the German people.

The National Socialist German Workers' Party (NSDAP, Nazi Party) and its paramilitary offshoots first appeared as one of a host of small extreme nationalist and anti-Semitic groups, which included the Freikorps and splinter groups from the DNVP. But the tolerance shown toward Hitler and his followers in Bavaria indicates the degree of "passive nationalism" among middle-class groups who never wholeheartedly supported Weimar. Nationalist campaigns fed upon the almost universal revulsion against the Treaty of Versailles and the strength of the "stab-in-the-back" legend. "All Ger-

mans were nationalists," it has been said, "but there was no unity within the nation" (Hughes 1988, p. 194). But while the press, especially with the rising influence of Alfred Hugenberg, peddled extreme nationalist ideas and myths, nationalist politicians remained constantly divided and quarrelsome.

When the DNVP decided to enter government, many grass-roots extremists vehemently opposed "collaboration" with the republic. This eventually created a basis of support for the "Hitler movement." Yet the experience of the Harzburg Front should have persuaded Hugenberg and the DNVP that collaboration with Hitler would only lead to their own destruction. While radical nationalists turned to support for Hitler, conservative nationalists continued to believe that they could "tame" him for their own purposes or buy him off. Hence the intrigues and illusions that brought him to power. The different currents of German nationalism contributed to and collaborated in Hitler's triumph, so ensuring the domination of his particular brand of aggressive, *völkisch,* anti-Semitic nationalism.

Related entries: Anti-Semitism; Bavaria; Freikorps; German National People's Party; Harzburg Front; Hugenberg, Alfred; Pan-Germanism; Stahlhelm; Versailles, Treaty of; Weimar Republic

Suggestions for further reading:
Hughes, Michael. 1988. *Nationalism and Society: Germany 1800–1945.* London and Baltimore: Edward Arnold.

Navy

Under the Treaty of Versailles the German navy had been effectively restricted to coastal capabilities and the use of aircraft and submarines banned. The governments of the Weimar Republic had nevertheless carried out secret research in various domains, and once Hitler came to power naval expansion became an open secret. As the world's greatest naval power, Great Britain responded by trying to place limits on Hitler's program with the Anglo-German Naval Agreement of 1935. Hitler's plan, known as Plan Z, was to build a fleet capable of challenging the British Royal Navy, not in absolute numbers but by concentrating on speedy surface squadrons and a powerful submarine arm to attack Britain's vital trade supply routes.

However, German shipyards were incapable of meeting his demands (none of the major warships ordered in 1935 were ready by 1939), and he failed to take British naval rearmament into account. The war came five years before the navy had planned, and it set about simply sinking as much British shipping as possible, to not inconsiderable effect. Developments in naval aviation were repeatedly blocked by Hermann Goering's Luftwaffe. In the perpetual political game of jockeying for position around Hitler, the aloof Grand Admiral Erich Raeder usually lost out, and Hitler's own intrusions into naval affairs, about which he was almost totally ignorant, served to inhibit initiative and new thinking.

With the exception of the U-boat campaign in the Atlantic and to a lesser extent the superiority established by the light surface force (E-boats) in the Baltic Sea, German naval operations in the war were overshadowed by a marked sense of inferiority. The early loss of the pocket battleship *Graf Spee* at Montevideo in December 1939 and losses sustained during the invasion of Norway induced uncertainty about surface operations. The acquisition of French ports as new bases revived German campaigns in the Atlantic for a while, but the sinking of the *Bismarck* in May 1941 and Royal Air Force bombing of the bases meant that the navy was incapable of raiding in the Atlantic with impunity.

By late 1942 Hitler was unhelpfully pressing for greater action from the surface fleet while forbidding it from taking too many risks. In January 1943 he lost patience completely and ordered the fleet dismantled, prompting the resignation of Raeder. His successor Karl Doenitz succeeded in saving it by persuading Hitler that it served to distract Allied attention from antisubmarine operations. The remaining "big ships," the *Scharnhorst* and the *Tirpitz,* achieved little in the North Sea until both were lost, and by late 1944 only the Baltic remained under German control. The last successful operation of Hitler's navy was the rescue of troops and civilians from the advancing Russians in the eastern Baltic in early 1945. By the end of the war only one battleship and two light cruisers remained afloat.

Related entries: Atlantic, Battle of the; Doenitz, Karl; Raeder, Erich; Rearmament; U-boats

Nazi Movement

Hitler was brought to power not by the Nazi Party alone but by a Nazi movement, extending its tentacles far beyond the confines of conventional politics. In *Mein Kampf* he wrote of "the young movement" in quasi-religious terms: "It is not meant to constitute an organization of the contented and satisfied, but to embrace those tormented by suffering, those without peace, the unhappy and discontented, and above all it must not swim on the surface of a national body, but strike roots deep within it" (Hitler 1992, pp. 300–301). The defining features of Nazism under the Weimar Republic were "youth" and "movement": "The party's rationale was constant movement: movement for its own sake, movement that served as a perpetual confirmation of the party's onward march" (Peukert 1991, p. 236).

The Nazi movement, then, comprised not only the National Socialist German Workers' Party (NSDAP, Nazi Party) but also its paramilitary associations, the Sturmabteilung (SA) and SS; the Hitler Youth; the National Socialist Factory Cell Organization (NSBO);

the National Socialist Motor Corps (NSKK), a separate division at the side of the SA; the National Socialist Flyers' Corps (NSFK), which trained young people in gliding and motorized flight; the National Socialist German Students' League (NSDStB), the "shock troops" of Nazism in universities and professional schools; and numerous professional organizations such as the National Socialist German Physicians' League (NSDÄB). All run according to the Führer principle, they imparted a far-reaching dynamism to the "Hitler movement" and then the "Hitler state." Under the Third Reich, membership in such groups would become obligatory for any ambitious individual.

But the groups most significant in bringing Hitler to power were the SA and other street fighters. While mass rallies and meetings secured publicity for the Nazis, making them appear more powerful than they were, they made their point equally through violence. Hitler wrote in *Mein Kampf:* "What we needed and still need were and are not a hundred or two hundred reckless conspirators, but a hundred thousand and a second hundred thousand fighters for our philosophy of life. We should not work in secret conventicles, but in mighty mass demonstrations, and it is not by dagger and poison and pistol that the road can be cleared for the movement, but by the conquest of the streets. We must teach the Marxists that the future master of the streets is National Socialism, just as it will some day be the master of the state" (Hitler 1992, p. 494). Conspiracy was to be replaced by publicity and the cult of action.

About 400 Nazis were killed in street fights up to 1933 and became the honored martyrs of the cause. The pimp Horst Wessel, killed by Communists in February 1930, was transformed into the defender of decent values against the decadent thugs who opposed the pure, new, youthful "Hitler movement." Borrowing tactics and symbols from the Communists and especially the Italian Fascists, the SA brawled

and broke up left-wing meetings, imposing themselves by force and swaggering around the streets as if they owned them, regardless of who controlled the state. The Nazi movement allowed Hitler, by legitimate and illegitimate means, to become a national figure even before the NSDAP's electoral breakthrough in 1930 and represented a threat standing behind him as he bluffed and negotiated his way to dictatorial power.

Related entries: Berlin, Hitler Youth; National Socialist Factory Cell Organization; National Socialist German Workers' Party; Reichsbanner; Sturmabteilung

Suggestions for further reading:
Fischer, Conan. 1995. *The Rise of the Nazis.* Manchester and New York: Manchester University Press.
Hitler, Adolf. 1992. *Mein Kampf.* Trans. Ralph Manheim. Intro. by D. C. Watt. London: Pimlico.
Merkl, Peter. 1975. *Political Violence under the Swastika: 581 Early Nazis.* Princeton: Princeton University Press.
Mühlberger, Detlev. 1991. *Hitler's Followers: Studies in the Sociology of the Nazi Movement.* London: Routledge.
Peukert, Detlev J. K. 1991. *The Weimar Republic: The Crisis of Classical Modernity.* New York: Allen Lane Penguin Press.
Stachura, Peter D. 1975. *Nazi Youth in the Weimar Republic.* Santa Barbara and Oxford: Clio Books.

Nazi-Soviet Pact

The nonaggression agreement between Germany and the Soviet Union, signed in Moscow on 23 August 1939, cleared the way for Hitler's attack on Poland and thus determined the nature of the first two years of World War II. The initiative for the pact came from Germany, whereas on the Soviet side disillusion with the attitude of Britain and France, the failure to create a system of collective security, and the possibility of extending Russian power in eastern Europe overcame any possible ideological misgivings. Not only was the Soviet Union kept out of the war, but by secret protocols Joseph Stalin could invade and annex eastern Poland, including western Belorussia and the western Ukraine, and Bessarabia, with a sphere of influence extending over Finland, Estonia, Latvia, and Lithuania. When Hitler was informed of the signing of the pact by Vyacheslav Molotov and Joachim von Ribbentrop, he is said to have exclaimed "Now Europe is mine!" (Overy 1998, p. 49). Seven days later German armies invaded Poland.

The pact enabled Hitler to defeat Poland and then occupy Norway and Denmark and launch his crucial campaign in the west without facing the threat of war on two fronts. On Stalin's side, he could create a security zone in eastern Europe, which within a year extended from Finland to the Black Sea. He may have had no illusions about Hitler's ultimate intention of attacking the Soviet Union, and he had kept Russia out of the war, but he was hoodwinked by Hitler about how long the pact would last and was genuinely taken by surprise when the attack came in 1941.

Related entries: Baltic States; Foreign Policy; Molotov, Vyacheslav Mikhailovich; Poland; Ribbentrop, Joachim von; Soviet Union; Stalin, Joseph; Ukraine

Suggestions for further reading:
Overy, Richard J. 1998. *Russia's War.* New York: Allen Lane Penguin Press.
Watt, Donald Cameron. 1989. *How War Came: The Immediate Origins of the Second World War, 1938–1939.* New York: Pantheon.

Netherlands

The kingdom of the Netherlands had enjoyed an untroubled relationship with Germany during the Weimar period, but Hitler's accession to power changed all that immediately. Fears for the country's neutrality and economic difficulties were not helped by the creation of the National Socialist Movement under Anton Mussert.

The fear was justified. Hitler's armies invaded the Netherlands on 10 May 1940 without a declaration of war and in violation of Dutch neutrality. While the royal family, headed by Queen Wilhelmina, and the government fled to London, a Reich Commissariat for the Netherlands was established under Arthur Seyss-Inquart.

The Netherlands was treated as a "species-related Germanic country" by its Nazi occupiers. It was to be Nazified and plundered economically, with Dutch forced laborers sent to Germany. The direct occupation left comparatively little scope for collaboration except by Mussert's movement, even if the "Leader of the Dutch People," as he was named, annoyed Hitler by insisting that the Dutch rather than the Germans were the original "true Aryans." The massive Amsterdam pogrom of 1941 marked the beginning of the virtual annihilation of Dutch Jewry, but the harshness of the occupation also provoked movements of solidarity with the Jews and strike movements supported by clandestine left-wing parties and the churches. The worst suffering for the Dutch people occurred between September 1944 and the German surrender on 5 May 1945, when the defense of "Fortress Holland" north of the Rhine delta brought famine, intensified repression, increasing sabotage and resistance, and widespread destruction, including the opening of sluices flooding large areas of land. Queen Wilhelmina and the government-in-exile returned to the Netherlands on 28 June 1945. Mussert was arrested and executed on 7 May 1946.

Related entries: Holocaust; Resistance Movements

Neurath, Konstantin von (1873–1956)

The aristocratic Neurath, son of a court official of the king of Württemberg, served as German foreign minister between 1932 and 1938, but increasingly in a purely decorative capacity. He had already served as ambassador in Copenhagen, Rome, and London before being appointed foreign minister by Franz von Papen on 2 June 1932. The very epitome of the kind of frock-coated diplomat that Hitler detested, he nevertheless served to give a façade of respectability to foreign policy during the early years of the Third Reich. Real decisions and initiatives were taken either by Hitler himself or in Joachim von Ribbentrop's Party Foreign Office.

Neurath was dismissed as foreign minister on 4 February 1938 after expressing his alarm about Hitler's intentions of annexing Austria and Czechoslovakia. From 1938 to 1945 he was Reich minister without portfolio and a member of the Reich Defense Council, but his influence on foreign policy was negligible. In March 1939 he was appointed Reich protector of Bohemia and Moravia, an attempt to reassure foreign opinion about Hitler's policies in the former Czechoslovakia. "Von Neurath was the only man for the job," Albert Speer wrote. "In the Anglo-Saxon world he is considered a man of distinction" (Speer 1971, p. 216). His imposition of Nazi rule in the protectorate, though draconian, was not considered strict enough by Hitler. Neurath wished to resign but was allowed to go on leave instead, being replaced by Reinhard Heydrich and officially succeeded by Wilhelm Frick in August 1943.

Neurath, a Nazi Party member since 1937, now played a passive role in the clandestine opposition to Hitler but could not compensate for his compromised career. At the Nuremberg trials he was found guilty of war crimes, crimes against peace, and crimes against humanity and sentenced to fifteen years' imprisonment. Released from Spandau prison on health grounds in 1954, Neurath died at Enzweihingen on 15 August 1956.

Related entries: Foreign Policy

Night of the Broken Glass

See Kristallnacht

Night of the Long Knives

*T*he massacre of the Sturmabteilung (SA) leadership beginning on the night of 30 June 1934 marked Hitler's final break with the radical elements in the Nazi Party, ensured the support of the army and conservative forces in the state, and served to strengthen the consolidation of his personal power. Hitler was aware that public support for his government had waned during the first half of 1934 and that the repellent and loutish disturbances caused by the SA were profoundly offensive to middle-class German believers in law and order and upright standards of public behavior. While the SA chief, Ernst Röhm, did not hide his contempt for Hitler's compromises with the established order, a powerful coalition of the SS, the army, the *Gauleiters,* Hermann Goering, Heinrich Himmler, and the conservative elites urged him to cut the Stormtroopers down to size.

At first Hitler attempted to force the SA to accept a reduced role with minor military functions and a responsibility in the political education of the nation. But by June 1934 an atmosphere of crisis around the Brownshirts was felt throughout Germany. While their power remained intact, the SA posed the permanent threat of a new putsch hanging over Hitler's head. As he gradually worked himself into a fury against their supposed "treason" (although in fact no real coup was ever planned), Hitler summoned the SA leaders to meet him at Bad Wiessee, some 50 miles southeast of Munich. Arriving without warning at the Hotel Hanselbauer at 6.30 A.M. on 30 June, Hitler, pistol in hand, with members of his entourage and a number of policemen, burst into the rooms of the sleeping SA men and ordered their immediate arrest and transport to Munich.

Hitler hesitated about murdering Röhm, his old right-hand man, but once he had ordered the execution of the SA leaders, a spasm of bloodlust spread throughout Germany. The precise number of victims is unknown but was probably between 150 and 200. As the SA commanders were liquidated, personal scores were settled, and official orders were unnecessary for revenge killings and a settling of old accounts. Many of the victims had nothing to do with the SA. Among them were Gregor Strasser, shot by the Gestapo; former chancellor General Kurt von Schleicher and his wife; his associate, General Ferdinand von Bredow; the conservative intellectual Edgar Jung; the head of "Catholic Action," Erich Klausener; and Gustov Ritter von Kahr, Hitler's old adversary from the days of the Beer Hall Putsch, found hacked to death near Dachau. Heinrich Brüning left the country in the nick of time. Hitler ordered an end to the "cleansing action" on 2 July, and a purge of the mass membership of the SA began, reducing its size by about 40 percent within a year.

International opinion was horrified by the gangster methods employed by the new leaders of Germany, but inside the country it was a different matter. The people as a whole had little or no idea of the background to the slaughter but approved of Hitler's actions. He played on this sense of relief expertly, stressing how internal order and security had been maintained and emphasizing the immorality, specifically the homosexuality, of the SA leadership. Defense Minister Werner von Blomberg congratulated Hitler on behalf of the army, praising the Führer's "soldierly determination and exemplary courage" and assuring him of the armed forces' "devotion and loyalty" (Kershaw 1998, p. 517). The German people, it was genuinely felt, had been rescued from a great danger. But the real winners were neither the army nor the people, but Hitler himself, the SS, Himmler, and Reinhard Heydrich.

Related entries: Public Opinion; Röhm, Ernst; Sturmabteilung

Suggestions for further reading:
Kershaw, Ian. 1998. *Hitler 1889–1936: Hubris.* New York: Allen Lane The Penguin Press.

Normandy Landings

Operation Overlord, the landing of U.S., British, and Canadian troops in Normandy on D-Day, 6 June 1944, opened up the second front in Europe, marking the beginning of the end of Hitler's domination of western Europe. A remarkable feat of secret planning, the landings on the Norman coast managed to fool Hitler, who was convinced by Allied deception, including the assembly of a fictitious U.S. army in the county of Kent, that the attack would come further north in the Pas de Calais. Even after the invasion had begun, Hitler denied the Western Front commander, Karl Rudolf von Rundstedt, reinforcements of two Panzer divisions and the 15th Army, waiting pointlessly in the Pas de Calais. Despite the heavy casualties inflicted on the Americans at Omaha beach, approximately 150,000 men were landed on the first day of the operation. Hitler was at Berchtesgarden, preparing for bed, when the news came through, and he was only presented with firm evidence of the invasion at his regular noon conference, six hours after the landings had begun. His slow reactions and refusal to admit that he could ever be wrong allowed the deception, Winston Churchill's "bodyguard of lies," to succeed brilliantly.

Related entries: Rundstedt, Karl Rudolf Gerd von

North Africa

In a recent work the historian Norman J. W. Gola (1998) puts forward the

Allied troops go ashore during the Normandy landings. Altogether 75,215 British and Canadian troops and 57,500 U.S. troops were landed on D–Day, 6 June 1944. There were about 6,000 U.S. casualties and 4,300 British and Canadian casualties. (Culver Pictures)

controversial thesis that Hitler's policy in northwestern Africa represented a first step toward the projected conquest of the Americas. However, the more likely, if more conventional view is that Hitler never saw the significance of North Africa for the overall course of the war against the Allies and treated it as a sideshow. He was drawn into an African campaign by the failure of Benito Mussolini's campaign against the British in Libya in 1940. He responded to an Italian request for help in January 1941, and on 2 February Erwin Rommel took command of the Afrika Korps and, contrary to Hitler's delaying tactics, went on the offensive.

The rest of 1941 saw an Axis offensive and British counteroffensive across the Libyan desert, and in January 1942, after

heavy losses on both sides, Rommel stood approximately where he had started. In a surprise offensive between January and June 1942 Rommel pushed eastward toward Egypt, capturing the key town of Tobruk on 21 June. But his attempted breakthrough into Egypt was halted in the decisive battle of El Alamein. In October and November an attack by the British 8th Army under General Bernard Montgomery broke through the German lines around Tobruk. The deputy for the absent Rommel, General Georg Stumme, was killed.

At the same time British and U.S. troops landed in Morocco and Algeria on 7–8 November, encountering only minimal resistance from Vichy French forces. Hitler responded by occupying Vichy France. Rommel abandoned Libya to concentrate his forces in Tunisia. The Italian colony of Libya was lost permanently with the surrender of Tripoli on 23 January 1943. On 9 March Rommel was forced by illness to turn over command of the Afrika Korps to General Hans-Jürgen von Arnim. Hitler, true to form, ordered his forces to stand firm, thereby rejecting an opportunity to evacuate up to 130,000 German and 120,000 Italian troops. Arnim was forced to surrender on 13 May 1943.

Related entries: Afrika Korps; Darlan, Jean François; El Alamein, Battle of; France; Italy; Malta; Montgomery, Bernard Law; Mussolini, Benito; Rommel, Erwin; Tobruk, Battles of

Suggestions for further reading:
Gola, Norman J. W. 1998. *Tomorrow the World: Hitler, Northwest Africa and the Path toward America*. College Station: Texas A & M University Press.
Keegan, John. 1989. *The Second World War*. London: Hutchinson.

Norway

During the interwar years Norway adhered to a policy of neutrality and support for the League of Nations. But in 1935 it annoyed Hitler by awarding the Nobel Peace Prize to Carl von Ossietzky, the pacifist journalist whose writings were banned by the regime and who had spent time in a concentration camp. Norway came to Hitler's attention more forcibly during the Soviet-Finnish Winter War of 1939–1940. About 40 percent of Germany's imports of Swedish iron ore went through the Norwegian port of Narvik, giving it a crucial strategic importance. On 8 April 1940 Allied ships mined Norwegian waters; the next day Hitler invaded Norway. By 10 June the conquest was complete. A government-in-exile under King Haakon was set up in London.

On 24 April 1940 Josef Terboren, *Gauleiter* of Essen, was named Reich commissioner for the Occupied Norwegian Territories. The puppet government of Vidkun Quisling and his National Union Party, established in February 1942, enjoyed little popular support. The growing Resistance movement benefited from easier and more continual contact with Britain than most of its counterparts elsewhere. Beginning in 1943 mass arrests led to some 40,000 Norwegians being sent to concentration camps and many being executed. The majority of Norway's small Jewish community were deported and murdered. German forces in Norway surrendered without a fight on 4 May 1945, and the king and government-in-exile returned on 31 May.

Related entries: Blitzkrieg; Holocaust; Quisling, Vidkun; Sweden

Nuremberg Laws

These notorious measures of September 1935 mark an important stage in the development of the Third Reich's Jewish policy while seeking to demonstrate that Hitler was committed to a "legal" solution of the "Jewish question" and to a reduction in the random anti-Jewish violence that had marked the summer of 1935. Racial laws had long been contemplated but were drawn up in typically confused and hurried fashion (there was as yet no legal definition of who was or was not a Jew) in the days leading to their announcement by Hitler at a special meeting of the Reichstag on 15 September, following the final parade of the annual party congress at Nuremberg.

The first law, the Reich Flag Law, proclaimed the swastika flag as the new national flag of Germany. Black, red, and white were henceforth the national colors of the Reich.

The Citizenship Law established a distinction between "citizens of the Reich," who would enjoy full political and civic rights, and "subjects" to be deprived of those rights. Citizenship was reserved for people of "German or related blood," meaning effectively that Jews now had a status analogous to that of foreigners.

The third law, the Law for the Defense of German Blood and Honor, prohibited marriages and extramarital relations between Jews and citizens of German blood. Marriages contracted in disregard of the law, even outside Germany, were considered invalid. In addition, Jews were forbidden to employ in their households German women under forty-five years of age and were not allowed to hoist the German flag.

In his speech Hitler made it clear that the laws were intended to prevent anti-Jewish "defensive action" by an "outraged population." They would provide "a framework within which the German *Volk* would be in a position to establish tolerable relations with the Jewish people," but further action was threatened if "international Jewish agitation," such as an economic boycott of Germany in the United States, continued. Hitler had taken a major step toward his ideological goals while still tactically refraining from the most extreme measures being urged by many of his followers. Jews were to be separated from the main "Aryan" body of the nation, and "more vigorous emigration" was necessary. But the preamble to the third law represented a racial peril to "the purity of German blood" that was "the condition for the survival of the German *Volk*." Further supplementary decrees defining Jewishness and ordering the dismissal of Jews from public posts and the professions would follow swiftly on the heels of the Nuremberg Laws.

Related entries: Anti-Semitism; Jews and Jewish Policy; Racial Theory; Swastika

Suggestions for further reading:
Bankier, David. 1988. "Hitler and the Policy-Making Process on the Jewish Question," *Holocaust and Genocide Studies* 3, pp. 1–20.
Friedländer, Saul. 1997. *Nazi Germany and the Jews. Vol. 1: The Years of Persecution, 1933–1939.* London: Weidenfeld and Nicolson.

Nuremberg Rallies

The party rallies at Nuremberg, "half semireligious pageant, half threatening mass demonstration" (Bramsted 1965, p. 215), began with two parades in January and August 1923, grew in scale in 1926, 1927, and 1928, and in 1933 celebrated Hitler's accession to power. Each annual rally, centered around the figure of Hitler, grew more spectacular. Speeches, marches, parades, and music were combined with spectacular use of torchlight and floodlights. The great auditorium designed by Albert Speer, in use from 1934, saw Hitler moving along the special "Road of the Führer" before standing in silence in front of the *Blutfahne,* the party banner said to be stained with the blood of the Nazis killed during the Beer Hall Putsch of 1923. As he shouted "Heil My Men!," thousands roared back "Heil My Führer!."

Eugen Hadamovsky, later the national broadcasting director, summed up the rationale: "All the power one has, even more than one has, must be demonstrated. One hundred speeches, five hundred newspaper articles, radio talks, films, and plays are unable to produce the same effect as a procession of gigantic masses of people taking place with discipline and mass participation" (Welch 1983a, p. 149). The 1934 rally was shown to the German people and the world in Leni Riefenstahl's film *The Triumph of the Will,* and the Nuremberg Laws were proclaimed at the 1935 event, while Hitler used the last great rally in 1938 to heighten tension during the Munich crisis. As a demonstration of the real and virtual

Hitler reviews a march by members of the Reich Labor Service at the Nuremberg Rally of 1936. Endless marching columns of SA, SS, Hitler Youth, and other Party organizations marked the unchanging ritual of the Reich Party Days on the Zeppelin Field designed by Albert Speer. The setting was calculated for propaganda effect and recorded by the newsreel cameras clearly visible here in strategic locations. (Imperial War Museum / Archive Photos)

power of Hitler and his Reich, the Nuremberg rallies were almost irresistible. The English observer E. Amy Butler wrote: "It was at times a struggle to remain rational in a horde so surcharged with tense emotionalism" (Welch 1983a, p. 155). The combination of showmanship and the paramilitary parading of half a million people was instrumental in making Hitler and his movement seem invincible.

Related entries: Architecture; Charismatic Domination; Cinema; Hitler Myth; Nuremberg Laws; Propaganda; Riefenstahl, Leni; Speer, Albert

Suggestions for further reading:
Burden, H. T. 1967. *The Nuremberg Party Rallies, 1923–39.* London: Pall Mall Press.
Welch, David. 1983a. *Propaganda and the German Cinema 1933–1945.* Oxford: Clarendon Press.

Nuremberg Trials

The United Nations War Crimes Commission had been established by British, U.S., and Soviet delegates in 1943, and by May 1945 an international tribunal had been agreed upon. Hitler cheated justice by committing suicide, as did Josef Goebbels, but twenty-one senior Nazis were tried for crimes against peace, war crimes, crimes against humanity (covering racial persecution), and conspiracy. Death sentences were decreed upon Hermann Goering, Hans Frank, Wilhelm Frick, Alfred Jodl, Ernst Kaltenbrunner, Wilhelm Keitel, Joachim von Ribbentrop, Alfred Rosenberg, Fritz Sauckel, Arthur Seyss-Inquart, and Julius Streicher; life imprisonment for Walther Funk, Rudolf Hess, and

Defendants in the dock at the Nuremberg trials. They include on the front row, left to right, Hans Frank (partly hidden by a standing Wilhelm Frick), Kaltenbrunner, Keitel, Ribbentrop, Hess, and Goering; back row, left to right, von Papen, Jodl, Sauckel, Schirach, Raeder, and Doenitz. (Culver Pictures)

Erich Raeder; twenty years for Baldur von Schirach and Albert Speer; fifteen years for Konstantin von Neurath; and ten years for Karl Doenitz. Werner Freiherr von Fritsch, Franz von Papen, and Hjalmar Schacht were found not guilty.

Related entries: Holocaust; War Crimes

Suggestions for further reading:
Conot, Robert E. 1983. *Justice at Nuremberg.* New York: Harper and Row.
Smith, Bradley F. 1977. *Reaching Judgment at Nuremberg.* New York: Basic Books.

O

Obersalzburg

See Berchtesgarden

Officer Corps

One of the principal reasons why Hitler was able to establish his control over the armed forces and later keep a tight grip on the conduct of the war was that the officer corps was bound to him by an oath of personal loyalty, first extracted in August 1936 after the death of President Paul von Hindenburg. The officer corps numbered some 3,000 in 1933 but increased fourfold in four years. In the course of rearmament some 25,000 new officers, mostly from the younger generation more sympathetic to Nazism, received their commissions. This process diluted the cohesion and traditional conservatism of German officers, making them less able to resist Hitler even if they wanted to. Hitler never ceased to remind the officer corps of their inward-looking nature and weak understanding of strategy. This made it easier for him to pose as a strategic thinker and impose his own strategy, right or wrong.

Related entries: Wehrmacht

Olympics

The success of the Olympic games of 1936 was one of the Nazis' greatest propaganda victories. The staging of the games, awarded to Germany in 1931, was threatened by Hitler's seizure of power. The Nazis, it was well known, disliked internationalism and the participation of Jews and blacks in "healthy" sporting competition. But Hitler placed the anticipated diplomatic benefits and propaganda display above ideology. The German people would see how the world accepted and admired Nazi government. In June 1933 he informed the International Olympic Committee that Germany would adhere to its rules, and Jews would be allowed to compete. The threat of boycott increased after the passage of the Nuremberg Laws in September 1935, especially in the United States, but was headed off by the International Olympic Committee and Avery Brundage, chairman of the U.S. National Olympic Committee.

In the event, the weeks of the Olympics provided a brief respite for Germany's Jews. Signs forbidding access to Jews were removed from Olympic areas and sites likely to be visited by tourists. But the games were used as a pretext for the rounding up of hundreds of Gypsies in Berlin and their transfer to a de facto concentration camp at

Jesse Owens at the 1936 Olympics. Owens's four gold medals provoked Hitler's anger, but for propaganda purposes a positive view was presented of this great achievement by a member of an "inferior race." It was made more palatable by the fact that German athletes won more medals than those of any other nation. (Culver Pictures)

Marzahn. The American liberal periodical *The Nation* (1 August 1936) reported that one "sees no Jewish heads being chopped off, or even roundly cudgeled. . . . The people smile, are polite and sing with gusto in beer gardens. Board and lodging are good, cheap, and abundant, and no-one is swindled by grasping hotel and shop proprietors.

Everything is terrifyingly clean and the visitor likes it all." But behind the scenes the Jewish high jumper Gretel Bergmann was excluded from the German team on a technical pretext, along with the part-Jewish fencing champion Helene Mayer. Only one Jew, the ice hockey player Rudi Ball, was allowed to compete for Germany.

The Winter Games were held at Garmisch-Partenkirchen from 6 to 16 February, with 756 competitors from twenty-eight countries; the Summer Games in Berlin from 1 to 16 August with 4,069 competitors from forty-nine countries. This represented the largest number of participants up to then, and the Winter Games broke all attendance records. The huge Olympic Stadium was completed in the nick of time, and Olympic rituals now considered "traditional," such as the lighting of the flame and the carrying of the torch from Greece to the host city, were invented in keeping with the Nazis' sense of pageantry.

German athletes were more successful than expected, winning more medals than either the United States or Italy. Hitler appeared almost daily as the patron of the games, rejoicing at German victories but ostentatiously ignoring black American winners, most famously Jesse Owens. Otherwise quite rational observers thought that whenever Hitler appeared, Germany won: the London *Sunday Times* reported on 9 August 1936 that "it is uncanny how often Adolf Hitler's entrance coincides with a German win" (Welch 1983a, p. 118). For all the superficiality of the Nazis' tolerant pose, the propaganda risk paid off, and Leni Riefenstahl's visually adventurous film of the Olympiad provided a notable expression of Nazi ideals.

Related entries: Berlin; Cinema; Gypsies; Jews and Jewish Policy; Propaganda; Public Opinion; Racial Theory; Riefenstahl, Leni

Suggestions for further reading:
Graham, Cooper C. 1986. *Leni Riefenstahl and Olympia*. Metuchen, NJ: Scarecrow Press.
Hart-Davis, Duff. 1986. *Hitler's Games: The 1936 Olympics*. London: Century.
Mandell, Richard D. 1987. *The Nazi Olympics*. Urbana: University of Chicago Press.
Welch, David. 1983a. *Propaganda and the German Cinema 1933–1945*. Oxford: Clarendon Press.

Opposition

Assessing opposition to Hitler and the Third Reich raises difficult conceptual problems. Overt "resistance" was very rare and almost entirely the work of Communists, but "opposition" could develop among groups who shared some of the regime's aims. And in an authoritarian police state such as Hitler's, even mildly unconventional behavior could be defined as "opposition," and mere expressions of dissatisfaction were severely punished. Individuals denounced to the Gestapo might have said or done little or nothing but could still end up in prison or concentration camp. Active Catholics or Protestants who withdrew from church organizations or were especially assiduous in church attendance could also be defined as "oppositionists." Likewise, Gypsies, homosexuals, and others defined as "asocials" or "work-shy" met with repression from the regime and indifference from the population. Only on the issue of euthanasia did spontaneous opposition emerge, backed by the churches. Otherwise the gamut from resistance to nonconformity was wide but by its very nature could not be united.

Organized left-wing resistance was enfeebled by their initial unrealistic interpretations of Nazism. Communists offered the earliest and most extensive opposition but believed that Hitler was the last gasp of a desperate capitalism and could not last. By the time the Community Party's (KPD's) exiled leadership adopted new organizational structures in 1935, Hitler's regime was firmly established. After the hiatus of the Nazi-Soviet Pact, during which Communists faithfully followed Moscow's line, Hitler's attack on the Soviet Union in 1941 stimulated the formation of Communist opposition groups independent of the exiled KPD leadership. The former Reichstag deputy Theodor Neubauer maintained an organization in Jena until 1944, while the more formidable "Red orchestra," or *Rote Kapelle,* combined opposition with espionage for the Soviet Union, but under the conditions of the Third Reich such groups were unable to attract any degree of mass support.

Social Democrats and trade unionists similarly misjudged the radicalism of Hitler's plans. Their loyalty to constitutional government made it more difficult for them to adjust to illegality. The exiled SPD, the Sopade, concentrated on disseminating pamphlets, flyers, and magazines within Germany and smuggling out reports for use abroad. Small Social Democratic opposition groups have been documented in some forty cities, but their actions were largely confined to the distribution of anti-Nazi propaganda. Trade unions were destroyed in May 1933, but working-class opposition showed itself when the majority of workers refused to participate in the elections for workplace delegates in 1933, 1934, and 1935. Such elections were not held again. Former union functionaries organized an illegal Reich directorate, bringing together Social Democratic, Christian, and liberal groups. They finally made contacts with conservative opposition groups in preparation for the July Plot of 1944. This cost many of them their lives.

Christian opposition was in a different position, since many in both the Protestant and Catholic churches thought that under Hitler they could maintain or even improve their position in state and society. The internal opposition within Protestantism, which coalesced into the Confessing Church, saw itself more as the guardian of Christian values than an organ of political opposition. Only a minority wished to pursue active opposition to Nazi ideology. Protestants who joined groups such as the Kreisau Circle out of Christian conviction did so as individuals. The Catholic Church behaved in a more unified fashion but combined its battle for self-preservation with loyalty to the Reich. However, Episcopal pastoral letters did protest the elimination of elementary human rights during the war years, and a campaign by Catholic clergy and laity led by Cardinal Clemens von Galen was instrumental in ending the euthanasia program in 1941.

The most direct threat to Hitler came from conservative military circles who shared many of the goals of National Socialism both in domestic and foreign policy. Active military resistance began in early 1942 and assumed an active conspiratorial nature in 1943, as more conservatives became convinced that without suitable safeguards Hitler's death could lead to revolution. But the failure of the July Plot in 1944 led to a reign of terror in which most of them perished. At the other extreme of opposition, young people withdrew from Hitler's *Volksgemeinschaft* by engaging in provocative nonconformist behavior. This became violent protest in the case of the group known as the Edelweiss Pirates and organized opposition with the White Rose group in Munich. Both groups paid with their lives for their principles.

Hitler, then, never faced a united opposition, and his regime was never in danger from internal revolt. A spectrum of behavior only became opposition in particular circumstances, and Hitler was able to conciliate much potential opposition by keeping a constant close eye on public opinion. The problems of opposition are exemplified in the case of the Jews. A homogeneous Jewry existed only in anti-Semitic fantasies and could not mount a collective opposition to Nazi Jewish policy. Jews displayed the whole spectrum of opposition and refusal, were represented in various opposi-

tion groups according to their political outlook, and mounted opposition in concentration camps and outside Germany in
ghettos and Resistance movements. The
opposition as a whole, never united, "could
at times prevent Hitler from doing certain
things, but it could not force a course of action upon him" (Jäckel 1984, p. 32).

Related entries: Bonhoeffer, Dietrich; Catholic
Church; Communist Party; Confessing Church;
Elser, Georg; Euthanasia; Goerdeler, Carl;
Jehovah's Witnesses; Jews and Jewish Policy; July
Plot; Kreisau Circle; Protestant Churches; Public
Opinion; Resistance Movements; Social
Democratic Party; Sopade; Stauffenberg, Claus
Schenk, Graf von; Trade Unions; Working Class;
Youth Policy

Suggestions for further reading:
Fest, Joachim. 1996. *Plotting Hitler's Death: The
German Resistance to Hitler 1933–1945.*
London: Weidenfeld and Nicolson.

Graml, Hermann, et al. 1970. *The German
Resistance to Hitler.* Berkeley: University of
California Press.
Jäckel, Eberhard. 1984. *Hitler in History.* Hanover:
University Press of New England.
Klemperer, Klemens von. 1992. *German Resistance
against Hitler: The Search for Allies Abroad.*
Oxford: Clarendon Press.
Large, David Clay, ed. 1992. *Contending with
Hitler: Varieties of German Resistance in the Third
Reich.* New York: Cambridge University
Press.
Nicosia, Francis R., and Lawrence D. Stokes,
eds. 1992. *Germans against Nazism.* Oxford:
Berg.
Peukert, Detlev J. K. 1987. *Inside Nazi Germany:
Conformity, Opposition and Racism in Everyday
Life.* New Haven: Yale University Press.

Overlord, Operation

See Normandy Landings

Pact of Steel

The treaty between Germany and Italy signed on 22 May 1939 was given the name of "Pact of Steel" by Benito Mussolini. The Italian dictator had been enraged by Hitler's destruction of Czechoslovakia but was mollified by personal reassurances from Hitler that Germany would not meddle in Italy's sphere of expansion in the Mediterranean and the Adriatic. He thought he had outmaneuvered Hitler and secured the Führer's blessing for his expansionist schemes, first of which was the invasion of Albania that he launched in April 1939 without telling Hitler. But the terms of the alliance were drawn up by Hitler: they bound each country to come to the other's aid immediately if either was involved in war and to conclude any armistice only in complete agreement with the other. It was made clear, however, that neither side wanted genuine military cooperation or a unified command. The official Italian press declared that "the two strongest powers in Europe have now bound themselves to each other for peace and war" (Mack Smith 1976, p. 165), though the Italian public were less enthusiastic. For his part, Hitler, convinced that the effect of the treaty would be to weaken British and French resolve to come to the aid of Poland, within hours of the signing ordered his generals to draw up plans for attacking that country, making sure that Mussolini knew nothing about it.

Related entries: Axis; Italy; Mussolini, Benito

Suggestions for further reading:
Mack Smith, Denis. 1976. *Mussolini's Roman Empire.* New York: Longman.
Watt, Donald Cameron. 1989. *How War Came: The Immediate Origins of the Second World War, 1938–1939.* New York: Pantheon.

Pan-Germanism

Pan-Germanism, especially the Austrian variety, strongly influenced the young Hitler, and he learned valuable lessons from its failure. He was attracted to the Pan-German movement of Georg Ritter von Schönerer, with its rejection of the multinational Habsburg Empire and call for union between Austria and Germany. In Germany the Pan-German League, with its *völkisch* nationalism and anti-Semitism, was influential beyond its small numbers before 1914, anticipated a great deal of Hitler's worldview, and fed into the nationalist agitation of 1918 out of which Hitler's movement was to grow. In *Mein Kampf* Hitler gave the reasons for the failure of Austrian Pan-Germanism as the failure to create a mass movement, parliamentarianism, and its attacks on the Catholic Church. "Once again a promising political movement for the salvation of the German nation had gone to the dogs because it had not been led with the necessary cold ruthlessness, but had lost itself in fields which could only lead to disintegration" (Hitler 1992, p. 107). Hitler was to show all the "necessary ruthlessness" in achieving the Pan-German dream by the Anschluss of 1938.

Related entries: Schönerer, Georg Ritter von

Suggestions for further reading:
Hitler, Adolf. 1992. *Mein Kampf.* Trans. Ralph Manheim. Intro. by D. C. Watt. London: Pimlico.

Panzer Divisions

Hitler's rearmament drive of the 1930s neglected the modernization of a large part of the army in favor of the development of a hard core of heavily armed mobile divisions, combining tanks and infantry and operating with coordinated air support. These Panzer divisions swept all before them in the western campaign and the early stages of the war against the Soviet Union. They were designed to win battles swiftly and operated best on flat terrain, less well in built-up areas or mountains. But as the Allied armies modernized and the Soviet forces revived, it became difficult to reequip the Panzers in the face of the kind of losses Hitler had never anticipated. The Führer's insistence on the construction of larger, more technically complex tanks hindered efforts at modernization. Under the command of outstanding generals like Heinz Guderian and Erwin Rommel, the Panzers had spearheaded Hitler's successful blitzkrieg, but the Nazi economy was incapable of sustaining the effort needed to keep them effective as offensive divisions. The depleted divisions fought doggedly against the invaders from

Panzer tanks supported by armored cars and support vehicles during the invasion of Poland in September 1939. (Archive Photos)

east and west in 1944–1945, making good use of the mobile tactics learned in earlier successes, but could not compensate for the numbers of mass-produced smaller tanks produced by the United States and the Soviet Union and the adoption by the Allies of a suitably modified version of the Panzers' own driving tactics.

Related entries: Afrika Korps; Barbarossa, Operation; Blitzkrieg; Guderian, Heinz; Kursk, Battle of; Rearmament; Rommel, Erwin; Waffen SS

Papen, Franz von (1879–1969)

Born into a Catholic noble family in Westphalia, Papen entered politics after World War I and represented the Center Party in the Prussian state legislature from 1920 to 1932. Of no importance politically, he was identified with the authoritarian and antirepublican right wing of the Catholic party, but he did have connections with business circles and in the armed forces. It came as a great surprise when, thanks to the support of Kurt von Schleicher, he was named chancellor of Germany on 1 June 1932 in succession to Heinrich Brüning. Papen was supported by President Paul von Hindenburg and big business, but according to the French ambassador at the time of his appointment, he was "taken seriously by neither his friends nor his enemies" (Bullock 1991, p. 272).

On coming to power, Papen set about appeasing Hitler and the nationalist Right. He lifted the ban on the Sturmabteilung; dismissed republican high officials and state governors; and unconstitutionally deposed the Social Democratic government of Prussia, making himself Reich Commissioner of Prussia. But he had no mandate for his authoritarian actions either in the Reichstag or the nation as a whole. Papen and his en-

tire cabinet resigned on 17 November, and Hindenburg replaced him with Schleicher on 2 December. He then began his catastrophic machinations, which brought Hitler to power.

After meeting secretly with Hitler at the house of the Cologne banker, Kurt von Schroeder, Schleicher succeeded in persuading Hindenburg to sanction a new government with Hitler as chancellor and Papen as vice chancellor. He remained until 3 July 1934, helping to provide the façade of legality for *Gleichschaltung* and Hitler's consolidation in power. Outmaneuvered by Hitler, Papen voiced conservative fears in a speech to students at the University of Marburg on 17 June 1934, calling for greater freedom, a more democratic state, and a renewal of national life through Christian conservative values. An enraged Hitler, for whom Papen represented the frock-coated conservatives he used but despised, called him a "worm" and a "ridiculous pygmy attacking the gigantic renewal of German life" (Wistrich 1982, p. 231). Papen narrowly escaped with his life during the Night of the Long Knives, and resigned as vice chancellor shortly afterwards. Nonetheless, he continued to serve Hitler's regime, first as minister extraordinary in Vienna, becoming ambassador to Austria in 1936, and then as ambassador to Turkey from 1939 to 1944.

Papen was tried and acquitted at Nuremberg in 1946. But in February 1947 a German de-Nazification court reclassified him as a "major offender" and sentenced him to eight years in a labor camp. Following an appeal, he was released in January 1949. Papen's memoirs, published in 1952, were "chiefly notable for revealing his insatiable self-importance and astonishing complacency" (Wistrich 1982, p. 232). He died at Obersasbach on 2 May 1969.

Related entries: Austria; Brüning, Heinrich; Center Party; Hindenburg, Paul von; Night of the Long Knives; Prussia; Schleicher, Kurt von; Turkey; Weimar Republic

Suggestions for further reading:
Bullock, Alan. 1991. *Hitler and Stalin: Parallel Lives.* London: HarperCollins.
Wistrich, Robert. 1982. *Who's Who in Nazi Germany.* London: Weidenfeld and Nicolson.

Paulus, Friedrich (1890–1957)

Paulus's name will forever be associated with the defeat at Stalingrad, but in fact his principal error was in following Hitler's orders unquestioningly. As a staff officer Paulus was involved in the planning of Operation Barbarossa, but he had never assumed a battlefront command of any significance before being appointed commander of the 6th Army in January 1942. In the battle for Stalingrad he followed Hitler's directives to stand firm in anticipation of air support that never materialized, and Hitler cynically appointed him a field marshal with the knowledge that no German field marshal had ever surrendered. After the surrender in late January 1943 Paulus was publicly vilified by Hitler, unable as ever to admit his own mistakes. Kept under close house arrest in Moscow, Paulus, as Hitler had predicted, broadcast for the Russian National Committee for Free Germany and was used by the Soviet Union as a prosecution witness at the Nuremberg trials. He was freed from arrest in 1953 and forced to live in Dresden, East Germany, where he died in 1957.

Related entries: Barbarossa, Operation; Eastern Front; Stalingrad, Battle of

Suggestions for further reading:
Middlebrook, Martin. 1995. "Paulus," in Correlli Barnett, ed., *Hitler's Generals.* Paperback ed. London: Phoenix, pp. 361–373.

Pavelic, Ante (1898–1959)

The Croatian lawyer Pavelic founded the independent movement, the Ustaša, with the help of Fascist Italy in 1929 and engaged in acts of terrorism and agitation against the government of Yugoslavia, most notoriously the murder of King Alexander I in Marseille in 1934. After Hitler's invasion of Yugoslavia in 1941, Pavelic established his "independent state of Croatia" and as head of state followed the examples of Hitler and Mussolini with alacrity. Political opponents were sent to concentration camps, Serbs and Muslims persecuted and "ethnically cleansed," and Jews either killed by the Ustaša or handed over to the SS. Many of Pavelic's followers were killed by Tito's partisans at the end of the war, but Pavelic himself escaped through Austria and Italy to Argentina.

Related entries: Yugoslavia

Pétain, Philippe (1856–1951)

The "victor of Verdun," a popular hero who during World War I had gained a particular reputation for caring about the welfare of his troops, Marshal Pétain became head of the French government after the fall of Paris on 16 June 1940. A symbolic national figure and initially very popular, he concluded a cease-fire with Germany between 22 June and 24 June and on 10 July was appointed chief of the "French state," the unoccupied zone with its capital at Vichy. Pétain's policy was based on limited cooperation with the German occupier, but his meeting with Hitler at Montoire on 24 October 1940, during which he shook the Führer's hand, came to symbolize collaboration and Vichy's subservience to the Nazi state.

Pétain managed to keep France out of Hitler's war plans, but he allowed the shooting of hostages, and Vichy police and officials supervised the deportation of Jews with an enthusiasm that surprised the Germans. Pétain also ordered French troops to resist the Allied landings in North Africa in November 1942. Domestically the "National Revolution" sought to create an authoritarian corporatist state with Pétain as its symbol, but while the marshal himself retained popular affection and support, his governments did not. After the Allied landings in France, Pétain was taken to Sigmaringen in Germany. On 24 April 1945 he presented himself to the new French authorities, though General Charles de Gaulle would have preferred him to go into exile into Switzerland. Pétain was put on trial for treason and sentenced to death on 15 August 1945 but spared the penalty because of his advanced age. He spent his last years confined to the Île d'Yeu off the coast of Brittany.

Related entries: Darlan, Jean François; de Gaulle, Charles; France; Laval, Pierre; Resistance Movements

Suggestions for further reading:
Atkin, Nicholas. 1998. *Pétain.* London and New York: Longman.

Phony War

The period between the crushing of Poland and Hitler's invasion of the Low Countries and France in the spring of 1940 was referred to in Britain as the "phony war," in France as *la drôle de guerre,* and in Germany as the *Sitzkrieg,* or "sitting war." While the French put faith in the Maginot Line and the Allies thought that time was on their side, Hitler offered peace in return for Allied acquiescence in the German occupation of Poland. He also hoped to drive a wedge between Britain and France by offering to guarantee the British Empire. When his offer was summarily rejected, Hitler began to plan his blitzkrieg in the west.

Related entries: France; Great Britain

Pius XII, Pope (1876–1958)

Eugenio Pacelli, elected pope as Pius XII in March 1939, had served as papal nuncio in Berlin from 1920 to 1929 and been a chief adviser to his predecessor, Pius XI, during the negotiation of the Concordat between the Vatican and Hitler's government, signed in July 1933. In November 1939 he assured anti-Nazi Wehrmacht officers that he would act as an intermediary between the British and any new German government, but in the absence of any serious attempt to overthrow Hitler he committed the church to political neutrality in order to safeguard its interests and ensure that Catholics could worship and the church operate freely.

Pius's attitude toward Nazi atrocities in general and the Holocaust in particular has attracted much criticism. Even in his strongly worded Christmas message of 1942 condemning the mistreatment of civilians, he did not mention the Jews specifically, referring instead to "the hundreds of thousands of persons who, without any fault on their part, sometimes only because of nationality or race, have been consigned to death or to a slow decline" (Morley 1980, p. 300). He justified his failure to be more specific on the grounds that it might have made matters even worse for the victims and by his desire to condemn Communist crimes on a level equal to those of the Nazis. Many Catholics, however, believed that the pope's powers of excommunication might have been used to try and disrupt the practical execution of the policy.

There is no doubt that the Vatican was better informed than most, including Allied governments, about the full horror of Nazi crimes. But Pius remained committed to a policy of restraint toward those nations in which the church played an active public role, and he was also influenced by his intransigent anticommunism. Activities by Catholics in the rescue of Jews were the work of courageous priests, monasteries, and convents, not a Vatican too willing to be sympathetic to Hitler.

Related entries: Catholic Church; Concordat

Suggestions for further reading:
Friedländer, Saul. 1966. *Pius XII and the Third Reich: A Documentation.* New York: Alfred A. Knopf.
Morley, John F. 1980. *Vatican Diplomacy and the Jews during the Holocaust 1939–1943.* New York: KTAV Publishing House.

Plebiscites

After banning free elections, Hitler, like Benito Mussolini and other dictators, used plebiscites to grant the appearance of legitimacy to his power and some particularly important policy moves. Through a mixture of genuine popularity, plebiscites called only when he knew he would win, and widespread intimidation and fraud, he could always get the result he wanted. In the Rhineland plebiscite of 1936, the *Gauleiter* of Cologne managed to deliver a "yes" vote of 103 percent: he had provided his men with too many ballot papers. In the first plebiscite, accompanying the Reichstag "election" of 12 November 1933, 95.1 percent of voters supported the decision to leave the League of Nations. A plebiscite of 19 August 1934 produced 89.9 percent support for uniting the positions of head of state and head of government in the person of Hitler. The Saar plebiscite of 13 January 1935, which had to be held in accordance with the Treaty of Versailles, produced 90.8 percent support for incorporation into the Reich. The similar Rhineland plebiscite, held throughout Germany in conjunction with fresh pseudo-elections to the Reichstag, gave 98.9 percent support for Hitler, while the same double procedure after the Anschluss awarded him 99 percent support. This was the last plebiscite and, despite all the fear

and intimidation, marked the high point of Hitler's popularity.

Related entries: Anschluss; Elections; League of Nations; Public Opinion; Rhineland; Saarland

Poland

Hitler always intended the destruction of the new Polish republic created by the Treaty of Versailles. Poland's fate was inevitably closely tied to those of Germany and the Soviet Union. During the 1920s, therefore, it laid claim to leadership of a "Third Europe" between the Baltic and the Adriatic and solidified an alliance with France, initiated in 1921. Under the authoritarian government of Józef Pilsudski and with Józef Beck as foreign minister, Poland tried to pursue an independent policy of balancing between east and west. When Hitler came to power, conscious of Germany's military weakness, he sought a rapprochement with Poland, putting the thorny question of Danzig on the back burner, and signed a German-Polish non-aggression pact on 26 January 1934. Poland put its faith in the irreconcilable differences between Nazism and communism and on its own large but technically backward armed forces.

Hitler turned the screw on Poland in March 1939 by demanding the return of Danzig and abrogating the 1934 pact. After the Nazi-Soviet Pact in August, with its secret protocols for the division of Poland, the country's fate was sealed. The autocratic government of Pilsudski's successor, Ignacy Mościcki, and his prime minister, General Felicjan Slawój-Skladkowski, had refused the suggestion of opposition parties that a government of national unity should be formed. Poles fought desperately against Hitler's invasion in September, but his victory was swift and complete. The Polish state ceased to exist, and the country was partitioned ruthlessly by Hitler and Joseph Stalin.

The western provinces of German-occupied Poland were incorporated directly into the Reich and known as the Wartheland. The remainder, including the cities of Warsaw and Kraków, became the Generalgouvernement, with Hans Frank as governor. Hitler's aim in the Wartheland was to Germanize its inhabitants completely and eradicate all traces of Polish culture. A million Poles considered unsuitable for Germanization were dumped in the Generalgouvernement; those who remained were forbidden to use the Polish language; businesses and property were taken over by ethnic Germans from the Baltic states, eastern Poland, and Romania; and all visible signs of Polish life and culture were erased. The Generalgouvernement was initially seen by Hitler as a reservation for Poles, but here too Nazi policies of economic exploitation and the eradication of Polish culture foresaw the extermination of the Poles as a nation. Some 2 million men and women were deported to the Reich to work in German agriculture and industry, while the rest suffered starvation and relied on the flourishing black market for survival. Especially brutal treatment was reserved for Poland's Jewish population. Herded into ghettos and with their property confiscated, they lived under appalling conditions as food and medicine dwindled.

Following Hitler's invasion of the Soviet Union in June 1941, the whole of Poland came under German rule. The areas formerly occupied by the Soviets became the eastern *Reichkommissariats*. Hitler had decided that the Generalgouvernement would become a German region and 80 percent of its Polish population would be expelled. The Jews were earmarked for extermination: most were to die in the extermination camps, although many thousands died when the ghettos were liquidated. Polish resistance grew into the Home Army, but the collapse of the Warsaw rising in 1944

signaled that Poland's eventual fate depended on Stalin.

The Lublin Committee, formed by the Soviet Union in July 1944, became the Polish provisional government on 1 January 1945 and the Government of National Unity on 28 June. At the Teheran and Yalta Conferences the Western Allies were forced to accept the military reality of the occupation of Poland by the Red Army. By comparison with its 1939 frontiers, Poland "shifted west," losing territory in the east to the Soviet Union and gaining areas formerly in the Reich, including Danzig (Gdánsk). The ethnic German population, whom Hitler had used as an excuse for his aggression and whom he claimed to be protecting, were expelled from the newly acquired territories. Stalin, through sham concessions and rigged elections, prevented the establishment of a democratic government in Poland, and it became a Communist People's Republic.

Related entries: Blitzkrieg; Danzig; Eastern Front; Foreign Policy; Frank, Hans; Generalgouvernement; Holocaust; Nazi-Soviet Pact; Resistance Movements; Soviet Union; Versailles, Treaty of; Warsaw Ghetto; Warsaw Rising; Yalta Conference

Suggestions for further reading:
Lukas, Richard C. 1986. *Forgotten Holocaust: The Poles under German Occupation 1939–1944.* Lexington: University Press of Kentucky.
Weinberg, Gerhard L. 1970. *The Foreign Policy of Hitler's Germany: Diplomatic Revolution in Europe, 1933–1936.* Chicago: University of Chicago Press.
———. 1980. *The Foreign Policy of Hitler's Germany: Starting World War II, 1937–1939.* Chicago: University of Chicago Press.

Press

Hitler was a voracious reader of newspapers but was known to be hostile to the press and journalists. He was convinced that the spoken word was more important and effective than the written word and never forgave the press for its hostility to the Nazi movement before 1933. The "Jewish" press was part of the evil forces opposed to the national revival. In *Mein Kampf* he had declared: "With ruthless determination it [the state] must make sure of this instrument of popular education, and place it in the service of the state and the nation" (Hitler 1992, p. 220). This was not, however, a straightforward task. In 1933 Germany boasted more daily newspapers than Britain, France, and Italy combined, approximately 4,700, reflecting all variety of political and religious opinion and the interests of pressure groups and private companies. Even after "de-Judaizing" and *Gleichschaltung* in 1936 there were still about 2,500 left, all chasing readers.

The Nazi regime adopted a three-pronged approach to bring the press under control: all those involved in the newspaper industry were rigorously vetted and controlled; the Nazi publishing house, the Eher Verlag, gradually acquired the ownership—directly or indirectly—of the great majority of newspapers and periodicals; and the Ministry of Propaganda controlled press content through the state-controlled press agency, the *Deutsches Nachrichtenbüro,* and daily briefings and directives. The press, Josef Goebbels said, should change its style to reflect the new "crusading" spirit and the emotionalism of mass meetings. The party's own *Völkischer Beobachter* was to set the style.

The emergency decree issued after the Reichstag fire on 28 February 1933 gave the government the power to suspend publication and made the spreading of false news and rumors a treasonable offence. This served as a pretext for banning Social Democratic and Communist papers, while Catholic and liberal dailies were soon forced out of business. Goebbels did, however, wish to retain a certain diversity in the press, and some liberal papers, including the most respected, the *Frankfurter Zeitung,* were allowed to continue under strict supervision, maintaining for a while the illusion of a certain degree of freedom. The Reich Press Chamber controlled entry to the newspaper profession and set about training a new generation of Nazi journalists.

But for all Goebbels's efforts, the strict enforcement of government directives, making editors personally responsible if they were ignored, did create a dull uniformity. Large numbers of people in rural areas still read no newspapers. The regime insisted that it was a public duty to read them, and subscriptions to Nazi papers, including the notoriously anti-Semitic *Der Stürmer,* were made compulsory for most institutions. In August 1937 Victor Klemperer noted the insidious way in which Nazi ideology dominated the press: "In the newspaper the relevant supplement is no longer 'The Car' or 'Motor Vehicles' or the like, but 'Motor Vehicles in the Third Reich.' The swastika must be prominent everywhere. Everything has to be related to it and only to it" (Klemperer 1998, p. 224). Hitler was happy with the overall dreariness of the press, even if Goebbels was not. Papers ended up being effectively written by the Ministry of Propaganda, and inventive and questioning journalism was destroyed. Goebbels was moved to write in his diary: "No decent journalist with any feeling of honour in his bones can stand the way he is handled by the press department of the Reich government. . . . Any man who still has a residue of honour will be very careful not to become a journalist" (Welch 1983a, p. 39).

Related entries: Cultural Policy; *Gleichschaltung;* Goebbels, Paul Josef; Hugenberg, Alfred; Propaganda; *Stürmer, Der; Völkischer Beobachter*

Suggestions for further reading:
Bramsted, Ernest K. 1965. *Goebbels and National Socialist Propaganda 1925–1945.* East Lansing: Michigan State University Press.
Hale, Oron J. 1964. *The Captive Press in the Third Reich.* Princeton: Princeton University Press.

Hitler, Adolf. 1992. *Mein Kampf.* Trans. Ralph Manheim. Intro. by D. C. Watt. London: Pimlico.

Klemperer, Victor. 1998. *I Shall Bear Witness: The Diaries of Victor Klemperer, 1933–41.* London: Weidenfeld and Nicolson.

Welch, David. 1983a. *Propaganda and the German Cinema 1933–1945.* Oxford: Clarendon Press.

Propaganda

The Nazis are considered to have been the masters of propaganda, exploiting the media of the press, cinema, and especially radio to attract support and create a consensus around their regime. But the credit for the success lies with Josef Goebbels rather than Hitler. Nor was it sustained until the end. Goebbels realized that propaganda needed political and military successes to keep it plausible.

Hitler had much to say on the subject in *Mein Kampf* and allowed his contempt for the intelligence of "the masses" to color his ideas overmuch. "The art of propaganda," he wrote, "lies in understanding the emotional ideas of the great masses and finding, through a psychologically correct form, the way to the attention and thence to the heart of the broad masses" (Hitler 1992, p. 165). He continued: "The receptivity of the great masses is very limited, their intelligence is small, but their power of forgetting is enormous. In consequence of these facts, all effective propaganda must be limited to a very few points and must harp on these in slogans until the last member of the public understands what you want him to understand by your slogan" (Hitler 1992, p. 165). The spoken word was the most effective form of propaganda, since "the broad mass of the people can be moved only by the power of speech" (Hitler 1992, p. 98). The same few points should be repeated over and over, and persistence would bring success.

For Hitler, then, propaganda meant putting across a few essential ideas through stereotyped formulas. It was important when party membership was small but would decline in significance with the attainment of power, when it would be replaced by organization. For Hitler there was no art of propaganda, and propaganda had nothing to do with art. Fortunately for him, Goebbels was more subtle. "The moment a person is conscious of propaganda," he said, "propaganda becomes ineffective" (Welch 1983a, p. 45). Goebbels realized that successful propaganda should build upon and reinforce opinions, feelings, and prejudices that people already held. The "lie indirect," with the pill sugared with entertainment, was more effective than the "lie direct." Light entertainment not only had an anesthetic effect but allowed a particular worldview to be put across with subtlety. Propaganda should be all-pervading but not always obvious. He also realized that propaganda had to be reinforced by displays of power, such as the Nuremberg rallies, and that it was ultimately dependent on political and later military success.

In the period of the *Kampfzeit* before 1933, although antiparliamentarianism and anti-Semitism played their role in Nazi propaganda, real success only came with the onset of the Depression. The two most important ideas allowing the Nazis to exploit and mobilize widespread grievances were the *Volksgemeinschaft* and the savior figure of Hitler himself. Mass rallies, staged with panache and publicized with imagination, allowed the "Hitler movement," as it called itself, to promise a new vision of the national community transcending the party system and class barriers.

In power, propaganda was to play its part in "reeducating" the people. "The essence of propaganda," Goebbels said, "consists in winning people to an idea so sincerely, so vitally, that in the end they succumb to it utterly and can never again escape from it" (Welch 1983a, p. 236). On 13 March 1933 he became head of the new Ministry for People's Enlightenment and Propaganda (RMVP), which "coordinated" all cultural and propaganda activities under its all-embracing wing. The task of the RMVP, Goebbels said, was "establishing a coordination between the Government and the whole people" (Welch 1983, p. 20). Public opinion was to be orchestrated around themes chosen by the National Socialist regime.

All forms of propaganda—press, radio, cinema, mass rallies—were thus organized around the basic ideas of the *Volksgemeinschaft*, the need for racial purity and the anti-Jewish campaign, and the charismatic leadership of the Führer. Its successes are obvious, as are its limitations and its dependence on the public perception of a dynamic movement going from success to success. The constant barrage of images of the new national community aroused enthusiasm, especially among the young and those already committed to the Nazi vision or something like it, but also created a wide degree of political apathy. Anti-Jewish propaganda played effectively on existing prejudice but could not overcome public dislike of the violent thuggery of the Sturmabteilung and the excesses of Kristallnacht. People could spot the contradiction with the Nazi dedication to law and order. The abandonment of the T4 euthanasia program in 1941 showed the limits of propaganda; workers and Catholics were probably less susceptible than the rest of the population. But the outstanding propaganda success was the creation of the "Hitler Myth" around the Führer himself. Hitler was sold as the personification of the revived nation. In 1941 Goebbels could tell his subordinates that the two greatest achievements of his propaganda were, first, "the style and technique of the Party's public ceremonies; the ceremonial of the mass demonstrations, the ritual of the great Party occasion," and second, the "creation of the Führer myth. Hitler had been given the halo of infallibility, with the result that many people who looked askance at the

Party after 1933 had now complete confidence in Hitler" (Welch 1993, pp. 86–87).

The propaganda triumph continued in the early days of the war. The astonishing series of blitzkrieg victories from 1939 to 1941 allowed the propaganda machine to crow triumphantly over invincible German might. The Nazi-Soviet Pact created problems. Hitler had been presented as the savior of Germany from bolshevism, and a propaganda onslaught against the Soviet Union in the 1930s had been aimed at the whole of Europe. Now the supposed common interests of Germany and the Soviet Union had to be invented for the duration of the pact, until Hitler's invasion of the Soviet Union raised anticommunist hysteria to new heights. Hitler was now not only saving Germany from Slav *Untermenschen* but also the whole of Europe from the barbarities of "Jewish bolshevism."

The first German defeats at Stalingrad and in North Africa forced a complete turnaround in propaganda. With the proclamation of total war, Goebbels had for the first time to set about strengthening morale on the home front. The stress was now on the sacrifices necessary to "save Germany," and ironically Goebbels, the master of the "lie indirect," now began to tell the truth: the reality of German reverses was even exaggerated so as to exhort the population to greater efforts, playing on the fear of what would happen to them if the Russians invaded. The discovery of the bodies of thousands of Polish officers murdered by the Soviets in Katyn Forest proved a godsend for German propaganda, fully exploited by Goebbels.

Fear for the fate of Germany under Soviet rule continued to be the most effective propaganda ploy until the end of the war. But the "Hitler Myth" was crumbling and was only briefly revived after the failure of the July Plot in 1944. Propaganda retreated more and more into mythology: the invincible Führer was still planning victory; retaliation and revenge would come from secret weapons and brilliant strategy. But even Goebbels finally realized that the game was up. Hitler had declared: "Propaganda must be adjusted to the broad masses in content and in form, and its soundness is to be measured exclusively by its effective result" (Hitler 1992, p. 311). His master propagandist had succeeded in speaking the language of the people and hence in buttressing his power, but in the end effective propaganda was dependent upon success in the real world, and when that ended so did the hypnotic power of Hitlerian propaganda.

Related entries: Anti-Semitism; Art; *Blut und Boden;* Charismatic Domination; Cinema; Cultural Policy; Education; Euthanasia; *Gleichschaltung;* Goebbels, Paul Josef; Hitler Myth; Jews and Jewish Policy; Kristallnacht; *Mein Kampf;* Nazi Movement; Nuremberg Rallies; Press; Public Opinion; Radio; *Stürmer, Der; Völkischer Beobachter; Volksgemeinschaft*

Suggestions for further reading:
Baird, Jay W. 1974. *The Mythical World of Nazi War Propaganda 1939–1945.* Minneapolis: University of Minnesota Press.
Bramsted, Ernest K. 1965. *Goebbels and National Socialist Propaganda 1925–1945.* East Lansing: Michigan State University Press.
Hitler, Adolf. 1992. *Mein Kampf.* Trans. Ralph Manheim. Intro. by D. C. Watt. London: Pimlico.
Welch, David. 1983a. *Propaganda and the German Cinema 1933–1945.* Oxford: Clarendon Press.
Welch, David, ed. 1983b. *Nazi Propaganda: The Power and the Limitations.* London: Croom Helm.
Welch, David. 1993. *The Third Reich: Politics and Propaganda.* London and New York: Routledge.
Zeman, Z. A. B. 1973. *Nazi Propaganda.* London: Oxford University Press.

Protestant Churches

Hitler received his earliest support more among Protestants than Catholics. Germany's Protestant churches, divided into three denominations— Lutheran, Reformed, and United—and twenty-eight regional churches, lacked the kind of political representation given to Catholics by the Center Party and had no support from Rome. In contrast to his grudging respect for the Catholic Church, Hitler despised the Protestant clergy: "They are insignificant little people, submissive as dogs, and they sweat with embarrassment when you talk to them. They have neither a religion they can take seriously nor a great position to defend like Rome" (Bullock 1991, p. 429). Many theologians, church leaders, and laity had been attracted to nationalistic *völkisch* ideas, making them vulnerable to Hitler's seemingly Christian rhetoric. Those who saw the danger of National Socialism at an early date, like the adherents of Karl Barth's "dialectical theology," remained a minority as Protestant support for Hitler grew.

Brought up a Catholic, Hitler did not understand Protestant pluralism. He tried to impose unity through the German Christian movement, but while many Protestants were attracted by the idea of a Reich church that would bring unity and state protection, others opposed the introduction of the Führer principle into religious life, state control, and the ideological uniformity Hitler was trying to impose. The division was made concrete with the creation of the Confessing Church. The Law for the Protection of the German Evangelical Church of 24 September 1935 sought to restore a unified leadership and ensure control over theological training but ultimately failed and created a vehement controversy over a statement addressed to Hitler by the Confessing Church and published abroad.

Most clergy and practicing laity in the Nazi state approved of or ignored its political measures, including anti-Jewish legislation and actions. Even when growing numbers of anti-Nazi clergy were arrested or forced to leave their congregations, church leaders continued to seek some arrangement with the regime. But as his rule became more firmly established, Hitler showed less interest in religious affairs. He was not concerned about winning whole-hearted church support for his racist and imperialist goals and gave only lukewarm support to the anti-Christian propaganda, harassment, and ceremonials of the more fanatically "pagan" Nazis. The war brought a "civil truce" with the churches, but Hitler's main attention was directed toward Catholics. In the occupied Polish lands the German Lutheran churches suffered the same kind of persecution as the Catholic Church, including mass arrests of clergy, a near total cessation of state support, and prohibitions against contacts with sister churches in Germany.

Very few Protestant clergy raised their voices against the Final Solution insofar as they were aware of it. Whether Hitler would have stepped up antichurch actions if he had been victorious in the war is unknown. He expressed the view that in the event of a "final victory" they would rot away "like a gangrenous limb." The timidity of most of the forces of church opposition may have been made more courageous by a major onslaught from the state. In any case, brave and martyred individuals like Dietrich Bonhoeffer kept the honor of German Protestantism alive under the Third Reich.

Related entries: Bonhoeffer, Dietrich; Catholic Church; Confessing Church; German Christians; Opposition

Suggestions for further reading:
Bullock, Alan. 1991. *Hitler and Stalin: Parallel Lives*. London: HarperCollins.
Conway, John S. 1968. *The Nazi Persecution of the Churches, 1933–1945*. New York: Basic Books.
Helmreich, Ernst Christian. 1979. *The German Churches under Hitler: Background, Struggle, and Epilogue*. Detroit: Wayne State University Press.

man national unity was under the Weimar Republic, Germany's strongest bastion of democracy and "the citadel of the Republic" (Hughes 1988, p. 199). It no longer dominated Germany as it had under the Kaiser but was still influential by virtue of its territory and population. Prussian government was dominated by the Social Democrats under Minister-President Otto Braun, who opposed attempts at greater federal control. However, on 20 July 1932 the government of Franz von Papen, using the threat to public security posed by street fighting between Nazis and Communists as a pretext, deposed Braun's coalition government and subjected the state to direct federal administration. The Prussian coup was Papen's advance concession to Hitler, hoping to secure his support for the minority cabinet. But in destroying democratic government in the largest of the German states, he was clearing the way for Hitler's accession to power. Prussia continued to exist in name under the Third Reich but had no influence as such. Nazi propaganda worked to establish a continuum between Hitler and illustrious figures from Prussian history, most particularly Frederick the Great. This helped spread the idea that Nazism was the culmination of "Prussianism," a dubious proposition but one that was shared by the victorious Allies. The state of Prussia was abolished by an order of the Allied Control Council in February 1947.

Related entries: Berlin; Papen, Franz von; Social Democratic Party

Suggestions for further reading:
Hughes, Michael. 1988. *Nationalism and Society: Germany 1800–1945*. London and Baltimore: Edward Arnold.

Prussia

The largest of the German federal states and historical center of Ger-

Public Opinion

Strictly speaking, no "public opinion" could exist in a regime like the Third

Reich, where opinions could not be openly and freely expressed. But a "popular opinion" did continue to exist, shown in attitudes and responses to government actions, including those defined as "political" because the Nazis said they were. Our view of popular opinion is bound to be impressionistic, but Hitler was fully aware of the importance of keeping a close eye on popular attitudes and of not imposing too great a burden on the population. The Sicherheitsdienst (SD) produced extremely detailed reports on the popular mood, and other agencies of the regime, including the Gestapo, put a great effort into recording it.

They found the peasantry difficult to mobilize, resentful of state intervention and the "coercive economy," and indifferent to matters not directly affecting their interests. A similar apathy was discernible among other sectors of the population. The middle classes showed the highest degree of ideological identification with Nazism, but this did not prevent widespread grumbling, especially against local Nazi officials. Hitler stood above this, riding a tide of personal popularity created by the "Hitler Myth." A 1938 Sopade report related that "the people curse, stand there, and are dazzled" (Kershaw 1983, p. 151). Victor Klemperer recorded this in June 1937: "The never-ending alarms, the never-ending phrases, the never-ending handing out of flags, now in triumph, now in mourning—it all produces apathy. And everyone feels helpless, and everyone knows he is being lied to, and everyone is told what he has to believe. Whether one gets a quarter pound of butter tomorrow or not, is much more important than all the problems of Spain and the Vatican. And probably no one expects war any more; people have got used to the foreign powers putting up with everything."

Hitler's foreign policy initiatives were overwhelmingly popular, reaching their highest point with the Munich Agreement of 1938. But in the crucial areas to his worldview—foreign policy and Jewish policy—Hitler did not demand enthusiasm, only acceptance. The widespread apathy over the "Jewish question" created the context in which Nazi fanatics could pursue their violent anti-Semitism. "The road to Auschwitz was built by hate, but paved with indifference" (Kershaw 1983, p. 277). The ending of the "euthanasia action" in 1941 provides a unique example of the regime succumbing to popular opinion. For the most part, Hitler was content to keep it under surveillance, secure in the belief that the mechanisms of indoctrination imposed upon the young would ensure that the coming generation would be pure believers in National Socialism.

The coming of the war was greeted with resignation rather than enthusiasm by the bulk of the population, but the successes of its early stages seemed to confirm Hitler's invincibility and hence his popularity. His sensitivity to popular attitudes was shown in the desire to spare the German people from the burdens of war for as long as possible. Even as the war turned against Germany, the SD continued to produce full and remarkably honest reports on the popular mood, but Martin Bormann shielded Hitler from the most negative assessments. Nazi propaganda was successful in sowing fear about the fate of Germany in the event of defeat, but talk of victory was greeted with growing skepticism. By the time the end came the German people were more concerned with their own fate than Hitler's.

Related entries: Anschluss; Charismatic Domination; Euthanasia; Gestapo; Goebbels, Paul Josef; Hitler Myth; Jews and Jewish Policy; Middle Classes; Munich Agreement; Night of the Long Knives; Nuremberg Rallies; Opposition; Plebiscites; Press; Propaganda; Radio; Rhineland; Sicherheitsdienst; Total War;

Volksgemeinschaft; Women; Working Class; Youth Policy

Suggestions for further reading:

Bankier, David. 1992. *The Germans and the Final Solution: Public Opinion under Nazism.* Oxford: Blackwell.

Kershaw, Ian. 1983. *Popular Opinion and Political Dissent in the Third Reich: Bavaria 1933–1945.* Oxford: Clarendon Press.

Steinert, Marlis G. 1977. *Hitler's War and the Germans: Public Mood and Attitude during the Second World War.* Athens: Ohio University Press.

Q

Quisling, Vidkun (1887–1945)

The former Norwegian defense minister and founder of the Norwegian
Fascist Party, whose name became a syn-
onym for abject collaboration, formed a
pro-German government after the German
invasion of Norway in April 1940. An ineffective leader, Quisling was removed from
office and then reinstated by Hitler in 1942,
but real power was wielded in Norway by
the German Reich commissioner, Josef Terboren. Quisling surrendered to the restored
Norwegian government in 1945, was tried,
and was executed as a traitor.

Related entries: Norway

*Norwegian traitor Vidkun Quisling is brought in
1945 to Trandum Forest in Norway, where bodies of
patriots who were murdered by Nazis and Quisling's
government were buried in mass graves. Quisling
(carrying overcoat) looks at the graves.
(Bettmann/Corbis)*

R

Racial Theory

The distinguishing feature of the Nazi dictatorship, setting it apart from Benito Mussolini's Italy or Joseph Stalin's Russia, was the central importance of the obsession with race. The preservation and strengthening of the racially pure *Volk* was the pivotal purpose of Hitler's politics, and his primordial and primitive hatred of Jews was subsumed into a tradition of racial theorizing dating back to the nineteenth century, which was by no means confined to Germany and Austria but had attained a particular cultural and political influence in the Germanic lands. Hitler believed firmly in the existence of "higher" and "lesser" races, the highest being "Aryans," beings bestowed with fanciful Nordic origins, descended according to some Nazi theorists from the original inhabitants of the Arctic, who had spread higher culture and racial values among the lesser races. The biological purity of this superior race, Hitler explained, had to be preserved against its subversion by Jews, prostitutes, and the "planting" of black soldiers by the French in the occupied Rhineland.

The idea that inequalities between the races was the driving force of history had been proposed in the nineteenth century by the French aristocrat, Count Joseph-Arthur de Gobineau, and developed by a host of other theorists, the most influential of whom in Germany was probably Richard Wagner's English-born son-in-law, Houston Stewart Chamberlain, whom Hitler had met in the 1920s. The term "Aryan" had originally been coined by the Sanskrit scholar, Friedrich Max Müller, who understood it in linguistic rather than racial terms. The exact nature of the "Aryan" race was difficult to assess and its application under the Nazis capable of wide extension. Gobineau (naturally) had believed the French to be Aryans, whereas Hitler included the British and northern Italians. The SS, the prime guardians of racial purity in the Third Reich, promoted the Croats to Aryan status in their search for recruits in occupied eastern Europe.

The Nordic Aryan "type" was described by one racial theorist as "blond, tall, long-skulled, with narrow faces, pronounced chins, narrow noses with high bridges, soft fair hair, widely spaced pale-coloured eyes, pinky-white skin" (Welch 1993, p. 67). Any resemblance between this ideal and Hitler and other Nazi leaders was purely coincidental. Nevertheless, a whole industry of "racial science" developed under the Nazis, with institutes attached to universities where chairs were filled by reliable Nazi theorists and the "science" incorporated into the school curriculum. The masters of Hitler's Aryan kingdom were thus prepared for battle against "inferior" Jews and Slavs. There is no evidence that Hitler had read

Gobineau, Chamberlain, and the others in any depth, nor is it clear how far other Nazis like Josef Goebbels and Hermann Goering fully believed in the pernicious nonsense peddled by the regime. But Heinrich Himmler and the SS were true believers, conducting extensive research into "Aryan origins" and searching the globe for the homelands of the original master race. The SS Ahnenerbe (ancestral heritage) organization carried out historical, archaeological, and anthropological research to establish the hierarchy of races and prove theories of "Aryan" origins and the value of "Aryan" blood. In Hitler's equally warped mind, however, all details of racial theory and the promotion of "racial purity" were rendered trivial by comparison with his all-consuming hatred of the Jews.

Related entries: Anti-Semitism; Eugenics; Gypsies; Himmler, Heinrich; Jews and Jewish Policy; *Mein Kampf;* Rosenberg, Alfred; Schutzstaffel; Science and Scientists; *Volksgemeinschaft*

Suggestions for further reading:
Burleigh, Michael, and Wolfgang Wippermann. 1991. *The Racial State: Germany 1933–1945.* Cambridge: Cambridge University Press.
Field, Geoffrey G. 1981. *Evangelist of Race: The Germanic Vision of Houston Stewart Chamberlain.* New York: Columbia University Press.
Welch, David. 1993. *The Third Reich: Politics and Propaganda.* London and New York: Routledge.

Radio

*I*f Hitler's chosen mode of expression was the spoken word, then the radio was the means of bringing his words to the masses. Josef Goebbels realized that radio was "the most modern and the most important instrument of mass influence that exists anywhere" (Welch 1993, p. 30), and the Nazis used it to create a mass listening public in a manner far in advance of Fascist Italy or the Soviet Union. Broadcasting had been a state monopoly since 1925, but program content was largely decided by the nine regional broadcasting companies. In 1933, however, radio was "coordinated" into the Reich Chamber of Radio in liaison with the Ministry of Propaganda, and the medium was mobilized as the "voice of the nation" with remarkable results.

The mass production of cheap receivers was an early priority of the regime, with the aim of installing a radio set in every household in Germany. The "people's receiver" *(Volksempfänger),* one of the cheapest wireless sets in Europe, was advertised with the slogan: "All Germany listens to the Führer with the People's Radio." The number of households with access to a receiver rose from 4.5 million in 1933 to 16 million by the middle of the war, the densest coverage in the world. A veritable army of National Socialist radio workers *(Funkwarte)* set up loudspeakers in public squares, factories, offices, schools, and even restaurants whenever an important announcement was to be made. During the war these wardens became notorious for reporting Germans found listening to foreign broadcasts.

By 1935 Hitler's speeches were reaching an estimated audience of more than 56 million through the radio. Radio propaganda had played an important role in the Saarland plebiscite of 1934 and then brought the 1936 Olympics to a German and international audience with an immediacy never heard before. Radio was "the towering herald of National Socialism," theoretically creating one united public opinion devoted to the Führer. The spirit of opposition, thought Goebbels confidently, had been destroyed by radio.

For all the Nazis' success in their innovative use of radio, it did have its limitations. It was discovered that Hitler alone in a radio station, away from the audience of public meetings, was an ineffective speaker. After October 1933 he only spoke in public rallies, often staged especially for the purpose. He needed direct contact with an audience to work on that public and radio listeners at the same time. In 1933 alone more than fifty speeches by Hitler were transmitted, a monotonous diet unless important announcements were to be made. In 1942 radio wardens reported that bored listeners were turning off the relentless flow of politics. Goebbels therefore decided that up to 70 percent of transmissions should be devoted to light music, thereby grabbing the audience for political broadcasts. His policy of mixing entertainment and propaganda came late to radio. Nevertheless, the creation of a mass listening public was a remarkable achievement and a significant one in creating support for the Nazis and impressing doubters with the all-pervading power of the Reich.

Related entries: Cultural Policy; *Gleichschaltung;* Goebbels, Paul Josef; Propaganda; Public Opinion

Suggestions for further reading:
Bergmeier, Horst J. P., and Rainer E. Lotz. 1997. *Hitler's Airwaves: The Inside Story of Nazi Radio Broadcasting and Propaganda Swing.* New Haven: Yale University Press.
Bramsted, Ernest K. 1965. *Goebbels and National Socialist Propaganda 1925–1945.* East Lansing: Michigan State University Press.
Welch, David. 1993. *The Third Reich: Politics and Propaganda.* London and New York: Routledge.

Raeder, Erich (1876–1960)

As commander in chief of the navy from 1935, Grand Admiral Raeder oversaw its growth into a powerful modern fleet. The professional and somewhat aloof Raeder, whose relationship with the Nazi leadership was not always good, preferred the construction of big warships, and when he failed to prevent Atlantic convoys from reaching Britain an infuriated Hitler forced him to retire and replaced him with Karl Doenitz. Captured by the Russians in Berlin in 1945, Raeder was tried at Nu-

remberg and found guilty of planning the war and issuing orders to kill prisoners. He was sentenced to life imprisonment but released in 1955.

Related entries: Atlantic, Battle of the; Navy

Raubal, Geli (1908–1931)

Hitler's niece, the daughter of his half-sister Angela, was probably the only woman, apart from his mother, whom Hitler loved and became emotionally dependent upon. The exact nature of their relationship, however, is obscured by hearsay and the scandal of Geli's tragic end.

In 1928 Hitler invited his sister to be the housekeeper at the house he rented on the Obersalzburg above Berchtesgarden, and she brought her two daughters, Friedl and Angela, known as "Geli," with her. By early 1929 the seventeen-year-old Geli was Hitler's constant companion in Munich and the mountains, though whether their relationship was explicitly sexual is one of several mysteries surrounding it. Geli was by all accounts vivacious, extroverted, and attractive, and Hitler enjoyed showing her off. But the stories of deviant sexuality put about by Otto Strasser should be seen as the work of a political enemy.

When Hitler took an apartment in Munich, the Raubal family moved in with him. He became pathologically jealous about Geli. There were arguments about her future career—Hitler paid for her to have singing lessons, which bored her—and about her numerous other admirers, including Emil Maurice, Hitler's chauffeur. Geli enjoyed being seen with her increasingly well-known uncle during his rise to political notoriety between 1929 and 1931 but at the same time bitterly resented his possessiveness, which turned her into a virtual prisoner, her every move shepherded and controlled. "My uncle is a monster," she is supposed to have said. "No-one can imagine what he demands of me" (Kershaw 1998, p. 353).

By mid-September 1931 Geli had had enough and announced her intention to return to Vienna, leading to a scene between her and Hitler on 17 September. The next morning she was found dead, shot through the heart. A coroner's investigation recorded a verdict of suicide. Rumors and stories abounded, pounced upon by a gleeful press. Hitler himself was in Nuremberg when Geli died, so the accusation of murder was untenable, but the Nazi Party's line that her death was an accident was equally preposterous. The full truth will never be known, but suicide driven by desperation at Hitler's grasping possessiveness and clinging jealousy remains the most likely explanation.

There is no doubt that Hitler was devastated by Geli's death, and his initial reaction was near-hysterical. He spoke of giving up politics and seemed on the verge of a nervous breakdown. But the scandal and the allegations in the press—stories of physical violence, mixed with sexual innuendo—were probably as significant here as personal grief. Within a few days of Geli's funeral in the Central Cemetery of Vienna, he was able to snap out of his depression and, though still visibly strained, take up his public speaking again. The responses he was able to arouse in a mass audience substituted for the emptiness of his private life.

The idea that Geli might have exerted a restraining influence on Hitler seems farfetched. Their relationship was too one-sided; as long as Hitler was around she was allowed no existence of her own. Eva Braun, it turned out, would accept this control in a way Geli manifestly could not. Ian Kershaw's conclusion is sad but probably true: "History would have been no different had Geli Raubal survived" (Kershaw 1998, p. 355).

Suggestions for further reading:
Kershaw, Ian. 1998. *Hitler 1889–1936: Hubris.* New York: Allen Lane The Penguin Press.

Rauschning, Hermann (1887–1982)

The former president of the Danzig Senate became an early and valuable, though unfortunately unreliable, anti-Nazi writer. Forced to resign his position by the Danzig Nazis in 1934, he stood unsuccessfully against them in the 1935 elections and then fled to Switzerland. In 1940 he moved to Britain and then to the United States, where he took U.S. citizenship. Rauschning's book *Hitler Speaks,* published in 1939, was a timely piece of anti-Hitler propaganda, showing the Führer ranting about world domination and repeating clichés not inconsistent with his character and opinions as recorded elsewhere. However, Rauschning's contacts with Hitler were much less than he implied, and historians today do not use his work as a reliable source.

Related entries: Danzig

Rearmament

By the Treaty of Versailles the German army had been limited to 100,000 officers and soldiers, and compulsory military service was abolished. Successive governments of the Weimar Republic had found ways of circumventing the ban, including secret joint training and weapons experiments with the Soviet Union and a pilot-training school run by Lufthansa. Hitler, however, was determined to make rearmament a priority and to proclaim renewed German military might openly to the world. Rearmament was also a key feature in the increase in industrial production. In 1932 Germany spent 1 percent of the gross national product (GNP) on defense and armaments; by 1939 this had risen to nearly 25 percent.

Rearmament cemented Hitler's alliance with Germany's military leadership.

In March 1935 he announced the reintroduction of universal military training and the expansion of the Wehrmacht to thirty-six divisions, more than three times the number permitted by the Versailles settlement. The creation of the Luftwaffe, secretly under way for years, was openly acknowledged at the same time. Hitler justified his actions by pointing out that the Allies had failed to disarm as stipulated by Versailles and by the need to match the growing Soviet army of nearly 1 million soldiers.

Hitler rightly foresaw that the other powers would do nothing serious to stop his rearmament drive, despite condemnation from the League of Nations. Calls by France for sanctions were opposed by Britain, which instead negotiated a new Anglo-German Naval Agreement, signed in June 1935. An attempt to prevent a new naval arms race, such as had occurred before World War I, it allowed Germany to build up its navy to 35 percent of the size of the British navy and gave Germany full parity in submarine tonnage. Hailed in Britain as a guarantee of British naval predominance, the agreement signaled Britain's final abandonment of the provisions of Versailles. For Hitler the "man of peace," it was a triumph.

Rearmament placed a heavy demand on Germany's productive capacity, especially in the steel industry. Investment in the defense sector, concentrated in the north and west of the country, rose from 1 billion marks in 1933 to 13.6 billion marks in 1938. But extensive credit was made available by the Reichsbank for firms with armaments contracts. Even though Hitler was planning for a war to begin only in 1944, he managed to mobilize ninety-eight divisions on the eve of the attack on Poland and 2.5 million soldiers for the 1940 offensive in the west. Success was, however, dependent on swift victory. Events from 1942 onward were to show that he had not had enough time for full rearmament.

Related entries: Economic Policy; Foreign Policy; Industry; Luftwaffe; Navy; Officer Corps; Wehrmacht

Suggestions for further reading:
Carroll, Bernice A. 1968. *Design for Total War: Arms and Economics in the Third Reich*. The Hague: Mouton.
Overy, Richard J. 1996. *The Nazi Economic Recovery 1932–1938*. 2nd ed. Cambridge: Cambridge University Press.

Red Army

Hitler made the fatal mistake of underestimating the Red Army, but in this he was far from alone. During the interwar period the Soviet armed forces were considered by informed foreign services to have inherited the faults of their tsarist predecessors, including an incompetent officer corps, an unwieldy command structure, and ramshackle supply and communication systems, and to have added the faults of control through commissars, accompanied by secret police, overseeing field command at all levels. From the mid-1930s all the top appointments were made personally by Joseph Stalin. It was recognized that the Soviet Union possessed enormous resources in manpower, but Stalin's purge of the army had destroyed nearly all its competent commanders, removing up to 45 percent of army and navy command and political staff, replacing them with mediocre yes-men and leaving important gaps in the organizational structure. "The Russian Armed Forces," Hitler opined, "are like a headless colossus with feet of clay" (Burleigh 1997, p. 42).

The Red Army's dismal performance against the Finns in the Winter War of 1939–1940 seemed to confirm all Hitler's racial and political prejudices. He was expecting an easy and swift victory over inferior Slavs and Jewish Bolsheviks, and in the early months of Operation Barbarossa that is what he got. It took more than a year for the Red Army to be rebuilt and gain expe-

Red Army soldiers raise the Soviet flag over the Reichstag on 30 April 1945. This famous image, specially staged for the photographer, came to symbolize the victory of the despised "barbarians" from the East over Hitler's master race. (Archive Photos)

rience. In the summer of 1941 about 75 percent of officers had been in their posts for less than a year. Command was concentrated in the hands of Stalin, who at first issued volatile and unrealistic orders in a manner worthy of Hitler but gradually came to grant more initiative to his more competent commanders, even returning some to favor and releasing them from prison. Helped by the removal of industry beyond the Urals and substantial aid from the United States and Britain, the quality of equipment was improved, organization made somewhat more flexible, and a massive tank arm constructed.

The more cohesive force that gradually took shape, backed by powerful air support and seemingly unlimited resources, and despite the persistence of organizational weaknesses, the terrifying omnipresence of Stalin and his agents, and a lack of concern over the scale of losses matched only by Hitler

itself, took firm military control over eastern Europe as the Third Reich dwindled. Hitler's defeat meant that the Red Army, renamed the Soviet Army in 1946, would loom like a threatening shadow over the politics of postwar Europe. How many of the millions of men and women mobilized by the Red Army paid with their lives in battle and in German captivity remains a matter of conjecture but undoubtedly puts the losses of other Allied nations in the shade.

Related entries: Bagration, Operation; Barbarossa, Operation; Citadel, Operation; Eastern Front; Finland; Kursk, Battle of; Soviet Union; Stalin, Joseph; Stalingrad, Battle of; Voroshilov, Klement Efremovich; Zhukov, Georgi Konstantinovich

Suggestions for further reading:
Burleigh, Michael R. 1997. *Ethics and Extermination: Reflections on Nazi Genocide.* New York: Cambridge University Press.

Glantz, David, and Jonathan House. 1995. *When Titans Clashed: How the Red Army Stopped Hitler.* Lawrence: University of Kansas Press.

Reich Chancellery

As head of state Hitler bore the titles of Führer and Reich chancellor. The Reich Chancellery, headed by Hans-Heinrich Lammers, was thus both his office as head of government and his official headquarters. Until January 1939 Hitler resided in the Old Reich Chancellery on the Wilhelmstrasse in Berlin, but he was uncomfortable in a building he did not consider worthy of his new Reich. On 12 January 1939 he moved to the New Reich Chancellery designed by Albert Speer on Vossstrasse. Meant to intimidate and impress visitors, it contained Hitler's huge personal office and an array of other offices and meeting rooms. It was largely destroyed in the fighting for Berlin in 1945 and the building blocks used to build the monument to the Red Army in Berlin-Treptow.

Related entries: Architecture; Berlin; Lammers, Hans-Heinrich; Speer, Albert

Reich Defense Council

The Ministerial Council for the Defense of the Reich was created by Hitler's decree on 30 August 1939, the day before the invasion of Poland. During the war it enabled him to decree ordinances without regard for legal niceties. Under the chairmanship of Hermann Goering, it brought together officials from the party, the Reich Chancellery, and the Wehrmacht. Reich defense commissioners, the organizers of civil defense, served under the Defense Council's authority, working together with commanders of the military districts.

Related entries: Goering, Hermann

Reich Food Estate

Established by law on 19 March 1933, the Reich Food Estate included all persons and businesses involved in agriculture. Membership was compulsory. Headed by Richard Walther Darré, it provided a framework for National Socialist agricultural policy through a strictly hierarchical structure with local peasant unions at the base. However, such a rigid organization failed to realize any of Hitler's proclaimed goals: the Hereditary Farm Law was patchily implemented; the flight from the land was not halted; and autarchic self-sufficiency was not achieved.

Related entries: Agriculture; Darré, Richard Walther

Reichsbanner

The Reichsbanner Schwarz-Rot-Gold was founded in 1924 by Otto Hirsing, the Social Democrat provincial governor of Magdeburg, as a paramilitary force to protect German democracy. As such it became the principal rival of the Nazi movement for control of the streets, responding in kind to the thuggery of the Sturmabteilung. With branches even in the most remote areas and more than 1 million members within a year of its foundation, the Reichsbanner endeavored to teach the population to celebrate the Weimar Republic and honor its flag and constitution. In the violent world of street politics it showed that Republicans could put on uniform, march, and fight with as much gusto as the Nazis.

Related entries: *Sturmabteilung*

Reichstag

Under the extremely democratic constitution of the Weimar Republic, the lower house of the legislature, the Reichstag, was elected on the basis of universal suffrage using a complex proportional voting system. The chancellor, appointed by the president, could be interrogated by the Reichstag and removed by a vote of no confidence. But the president had the power to dissolve the Reichstag and govern for a time by emergency decree under Article 48. Parties with only minimal support could gain representation in the Reichstag, and the Nazis took full advantage of this, but Hitler's contempt for democratic "talking-shops" was an essential component of Nazi ideology. In September 1927, writing in his paper *Der Angriff,* Josef Goebbels declared that "he who joins parliament will perish in it" and that the Nazis would enter the Reichstag "like the wolf who breaks into a flock of sheep" (Bramsted 1965, p. 38).

After 1930 the Reichstag was increasingly bypassed as President Paul von Hindenburg and his government used emergency decrees to impose legislation. Once Hitler became chancellor and following the last elections on 5 March 1933, under Nazi bullying and threats the Reichstag relinquished its authority by passing the Enabling Act. It survived formally as a one-party legislature in the Third Reich, the last session being held in 1942, but served mainly as a stage for Hitler's policy pronouncements. Following the Reichstag fire it met at the Kroll Opera House in Berlin.

Related entries: Center Party; Communist Party; Elections; Enabling Act; German Democratic Party; German National People's Party; German People's Party; National Socialist German Workers' Party; Reichstag Fire; Social Democratic Party; Weimar Republic

Suggestions for further reading:
Bramsted, Ernest K. 1965. *Goebbels and National Socialist Propaganda 1925–1945.* East Lansing: Michigan State University Press.

Reichstag Fire

The fire that destroyed the Reichstag building on the night of 27 February 1933 provided Hitler, chancellor since 30 January, with the excuse to intensify the crackdown on his opponents. The obvious boon it gave Hitler inevitably created the suspicion that the Nazis themselves were responsible, but the evidence suggests that it was one of those lucky accidents or coincidences that Hitler could exploit ruthlessly. The arsonist was Marinus van der Lubbe, a Dutch former Communist at the time unconnected with any political group, who wished to make a spectacular protest against the new government. In this he succeeded, but the consequences were terrible.

Under police interrogation van der Lubbe readily confessed his guilt but insisted he had acted alone. Hitler and the Nazi leadership were convinced or convinced themselves that the fire marked the signal for a Communist uprising. When the interrogator, Rudolf Diels, later the first head of the Prussian Gestapo, tried to reassure Hitler that the fire was the work of a "madman" he found the new chancellor in a state of near hysteria. When he calmed down, he consulted with Hermann Goering and Josef Goebbels on an order for the mass arrest of Communists, Socialists, and other opponents of the government.

The Sturmabteilung were let loose on the streets, and a reign of terror ensued. Opponents of the Nazis were arrested, savagely beaten, tortured, and in some cases murdered. By April some 25,000 people were in "protective custody" in Prussia alone. Once his initial panic subsided, Hitler moved quickly, brutally, and remorselessly. He told Papen: "This is a God-given signal, Herr Vice-Chancellor! If this fire, as I believe, is the work of the Communists, then we must crush out this murderous pest with an iron fist!" (Kershaw 1998, p. 458). The Reichstag Fire Decrees

The Reichstag building ablaze on 27 February 1933. The fire, blamed by the Nazis on Communists, was used as an excuse for mass arrests of Communists and Social Democrats, employing lists drawn up in advance, and on the following day for the Reichstag Fire Decree abrogating fundamental rights. (Culver Pictures)

of 28 February abolished all personal liberties and legitimized the terror, marking the beginning of the process of *Gleichschaltung*. The repression was widely popular because many people were convinced by the story of an incipient Communist rising put about by Hitler and Goering. The Reichstag fire therefore marks a major step in the erection of the dictatorship, seemingly handed to Hitler by providence.

Related entries: *Gleichschaltung*

Suggestions for further reading:
Kershaw, Ian. 1998. *Hitler 1889–1936: Hubris.* New York: Allen Lane Penguin Press.
Tobias, Fritz. 1964. *The Reichstag Fire.* New York: Putnam.

Reparations

Hitler joined with all other nationalist and many moderate German politicians in opposing the payment of war reparations by Germany as decided under the Versailles settlement of 1919. Reparations implied German war guilt, which was unacceptable not only to fanatics like Hitler. Also there was an element of vengeance, especially in France, which had suffered the most physical devastation and saw reparations as a way of retarding German recovery. When Germany defaulted on reparations payments in 1923, French and Belgian forces occupied the Ruhr in an action that impressed and was exploited by Hitler and other agitators, but the situation was defused by the Dawes Plan of 1924. Payment of reparations was modified again by the Young Plan of 1929, the nationalist campaign that brought Hitler to the attention of the public on a national scale for the first time. Eventually, worldwide depression did what Hitler and those like him could not: as part of the limited international cooperation induced by recession, reparations payments were cancelled by the Lausanne Convention of July 1932.

Related entries: Dawes Plan; Ruhr; Young Plan

Suggestions for further reading:
Kent, Bruce. 1989. *The Spoils of War: The Politics, Economics and Diplomacy of Reparations, 1918–1932.* Oxford: Clarendon Press.

Resistance Movements

At first collaborators outnumbered resisters in the countries of occupied Europe, but the changing fortunes of war, especially after Hitler's invasion of the Soviet Union, eventually brought thousands into Resistance movements. The most significant among them in Hitler's defeat were Josip Tito's guerrillas in Yugoslavia, who tied down a number of German divisions throughout the war and beat the Red Army to liberate Belgrade. However, the attempt by the Polish Home Army, controlled by the Polish government-in-exile in London, to liberate their capital before the Soviets ended in the tragedy of the Warsaw Rising.

Everywhere in Europe the Resistance was divided between Communists and others representing a broad range of political opinions, but either noncommunist or anticommunist. In Yugoslavia and Greece the factions clashed, with bloody results. Elsewhere they cooperated more or less easily against the common enemy. The Communists were strongest in eastern Europe, aided by proximity to the Soviet Union and distance from London, home to noncommunist governments-in-exile. In Albania resistance was dominated by the Communist Workers' Party of Enver Hoxha, and in Bulgaria the Communists dominated the Fatherland Front, founded in 1943. In France General Charles de Gaulle's emissary Jean Moulin succeeded in uniting the Resistance, and a similar temporary solidarity was created in Czechoslovakia and Belgium.

Military historians are generally skeptical about the military effectiveness of the Resistance, but none deny the inspirational courage of resisters. Their most direct contribution to Hitler's defeat, outside Yugoslavia and leaving Soviet partisans aside as a special case, lay in providing intelligence and carrying out acts of sabotage in the vanguard of invading Allied armies. Above all, perhaps, Resistance movements were important in retaining a sense of national existence and national honor in countries that had succumbed to the Nazi jackboot and where Hitler and his gang had found too many eager supporters. They gave the lie to Hitler's view of "inferior" peoples and the human race in general. In reality, most people in occupied Europe were neither collaborators nor resisters: they simply wanted to survive.

What is not in doubt is the draconian nature and viciousness of Nazi reprisals. The notorious "Night and Fog" decrees of July 1941 authorized the arrest and deportation to Germany of any person suspected of anti-German activity. Hostages were executed by the hundreds and entire villages destroyed in retaliation for acts of resistance, no matter how small. The most notorious episodes, though by no means the only ones, included the destruction of the Czech village of Lidice and the murder of all its male inhabitants following the assassination of Reinhard Heydrich in May 1942 and the massacre of 335 Italian prisoners in the caves of the Via Ardeatina near Rome in March 1944 in retaliation for an ambush of German troops by Italian partisans. The most abhorrent among many such barbarous actions occurred on 10 June 1944, four days after the Normandy landings, when a unit of the SS tank division "Das Reich" murdered all 642 inhabitants of the French village of Oradour-sur-Glane, including 207 children.

Related entries: Belgium; Bulgaria; Czechoslovakia; de Gaulle, Charles; Eastern Front; France; Greece; Italy; Mihajlović, Draža; Netherlands; Norway; Opposition; Poland; Soviet Union; Tito, Josip Broz; Ukraine; War Crimes; Warsaw Ghetto; Warsaw Rising; Yugoslavia

Rhineland

Hitler's decision in March 1936 to destroy what was left of the Treaty of Versailles and the Locarno Pact of 1925 by reoccupying the demilitarized Rhineland was one of his biggest gambles. The demilitarization of the left bank of the Rhine and a strip 31 miles wide on the right bank was seen as "the single most important guarantee of peace in Europe" (Weinberg 1970, p. 239), rendering impossible a German attack on France or Belgium. The forty-eight hours following the entry of German troops into this area on 7 March 1936 were, Hitler later claimed, the most tense and worrying in his life. He had not intended to seize the Rhineland before the spring of 1937 but was spurred into action by a combination of favorable international circumstances coinciding with the need to bolster the Nazi regime's flagging popularity within Germany. Hitler, Konstantin von Neurath said, "felt the deterioration of mood in favour of the regime and was looking for a new national slogan to fire the masses again" (Kershaw 1998, p. 581). It was Benito Mussolini who provided the opportunity.

The Italian dictator's invasion of Abyssinia broke the fragile agreement known as the Stresa Front among Italy, Britain, and France and pushed Hitler and Mussolini closer together. Anglo-French relations were thrown into confusion, and war threatened in the Mediterranean. Hitler could take advantage of renewed freedom of action in Europe to declare the Locarno Pact dead, using as an excuse the pending ratification of a pact between France and the Soviet Union. In a speech to the Reichstag, relayed to millions of radio listeners, Hitler declared: "In the interest of the primitive rights of a people to the security of its borders and safeguarding of its defence capability, the German Reich government has therefore from today restored the full and unrestricted sovereignty of the Reich in the demilitarized zone of the

Rhineland" (Kershaw 1998, p. 587). Resistance, even by one French division, could have prevented the German troops from marching in, but the French military, misled by intelligence reports grossly exaggerating the numbers of German forces in the region, had ruled it out in advance.

The Western democracies, lacking the will or unity to intervene, handed Hitler a priceless victory. He could now look forward to the prospect of properly defended western borders, an essential precondition for expansion into eastern Europe, where France's system of alliances lay in tatters. Condemnation by the League of Nations was irrelevant, and the crisis ended in a matter of days with complete success for Hitler. He made a triumphant visit to Cologne at the end of the month, remarking to Hans Frank: "Am I happy, my God am I happy that it has gone so smoothly" (Kershaw 1998, p. 589).

The reoccupation of the Rhineland raised Hitler's popularity to new heights and endowed him more than ever with a sense of his own greatness and infallibility. He had overcome the doubts and fears of the conservative forces in the army and the Foreign Office and rode the wave of popular euphoria that extended far beyond committed supporters of the Nazis. The problems created by the unstable economic situation and relations with the Catholic Church were forgotten. Close observers noted that his egomania and belief in his destiny were stronger than ever. As he told a meeting in Munich on 14 March: "I go with the certainty of a sleepwalker along the path laid out for me by Providence" (Kershaw 1998, p. 591).

Related entries: Appeasement; Foreign Policy; France; Great Britain; Hitler Myth; Italy; League of Nations

Suggestions for further reading:
Emmerson, James T. 1977. *The Rhineland Crisis, 7 March 1936: A Study in Multicultural Diplomacy.* London: Temple Smith.

Kershaw, Ian. 1998. *Hitler 1889–1936: Hubris.* New York: Allen Lane Penguin Press.
Weinberg, Gerhard L. 1970. *The Foreign Policy of Hitler's Germany: Diplomatic Revolution in Europe, 1933–36.* Chicago: University of Chicago Press.

Ribbentrop, Joachim von (1893–1946)

Born in Wesel on 30 April 1893, the son of an officer, Ribbentrop fought in World War I, reaching the rank of lieutenant. After the war, his marriage to Anneliese Henckel, daughter of the largest champagne merchant in Germany, established him in international business and introduced him into high society. Ribbentrop was first introduced to Hitler as someone who could translate the foreign press, but he did not join the Nazi Party until May 1932. Within a year he had become a Reichstag deputy and Hitler's adviser on foreign affairs, setting up his own office, the Dientstelle Ribbentrop, in direct competition with the Foreign Ministry.

Hitler, almost completely ignorant of the outside world, accepted the arrogant and vain von Ribbentrop (as he called himself) as a man of the world who understood foreign countries. Ribbentrop in turn flatteringly confirmed Hitler in his ignorance. Other leading Nazis hated Ribbentrop. Josef Goebbels remarked that: "He bought his name, he married his money, and he swindled his way into office" (Bullock 1991, p. 372). Hitler, however, would never hear a word against him, even once calling him "greater than Bismarck." And his successes could be dramatic. Primarily concerned with questions of disarmament until 1935, he negotiated the Anglo-German Naval Agreement of June 1935 and was appointed ambassador to Great Britain on 2 August 1936. Ribbentrop's two-year tenure in London was disastrous. He wasted time cultivating the high society aristocrats and "fellow-travelers of the Right" whom he thought ran the country, but was offended by social rejection. Ribbentrop became convinced that hostility between Germany and Britain was inevitable but also persuaded Hitler that the British would not oppose violent expansion by the Third Reich into eastern Europe.

Ribbentrop's endeavors produced the Anti-Comintern Pact with Japan of 1936, later to expand into the Berlin-Rome-Tokyo Axis. He reached the peak of his career with his appointment as foreign minister on 4 February 1938, his biggest achievement being the negotiation of the Nazi-Soviet Pact, which he signed in Moscow on 23 August 1939. This paved the way for Hitler's invasion of Poland and therefore, ironically, for the waning of Ribbentrop's influence. Having done what he could to frustrate last-minute peace moves, Ribbentrop faded into the background as the importance of diplomatic activity declined. By 1945 he had lost all influence, even with Hitler. On trial at Nuremberg Ribbentrop cut a pathetic figure, spineless and apparently still dependent on the dead Hitler. He was hanged as a war criminal on 16 October 1946.

Related entries: Anti-Comintern Pact; Axis; Foreign Policy; Great Britain; Munich Agreement; Nazi-Soviet Pact; Pact of Steel

Suggestions for further reading:
Bloch, Michael. 1992. *Ribbentrop.* London: Bantam.
Bullock, Alan. 1964. 1991. *Hitler and Stalin: Parallel Lives.* London: HarperCollins.

Riefenstahl, Leni (b. 1902)

After an early career as a dancer, Leni Riefenstahl gained fame in the 1920s as an actress in the popular "mountain films," eventually turning director with *The Blue Light* (1932), a mystical mountain tale much admired by Hitler. They first met on Hitler's initiative in 1932, and Riefenstahl, immediately falling under his spell, remained close to the Führer until 1939, though she saw little of him during the war years. For a public who knew little of Eva Braun, Riefenstahl was "Hitler's Pet" or "Hitler's Girlfriend," and he undoubtedly benefited from his perceived association with the popular and attractive actress who was also a talented film director.

Riefenstahl was chosen by Hitler to direct a film of the 1933 Nuremberg rally, followed by the grander *Triumph of the Will,* a record of the 1934 rally and the apotheosis of Hitler as demigod descending from the skies. The "triumph" shown by Riefenstahl is that of a strong Germany united by the will of its Führer. In *Olympiade,* her film of the 1936 Olympics, Riefenstahl produced a then unprecedented and innovative picture of a sporting event that was also a hymn to the perfect Aryan human body. Both films, widely praised and given prizes throughout the world, advertised the achievements of the new Germany and may certainly be regarded as the highest aesthetic products of the Nazi regime.

Leni Riefenstahl was never a member of the Nazi Party, nor did she enjoy any real influence with Hitler, and the idea that she was his mistress, though often repeated, is false. But she was ambitious, opportunistic, self-centered, and extremely determined. She had an enemy in Josef Goebbels, who resented her independence from his control, but she could always appeal directly to Hitler. Hitler's championing of Riefenstahl against Goebbels is a rare example of the Führer's artistic judgment proving superior to that of his propaganda minister.

Riefenstahl avoided involvement in filming war propaganda apart from a brief trip to Poland during the invasion of 1939. After the war she was cleared of any punishable offense by U.S. and German de-Nazification courts, but her close association with Hitler meant that her career as a filmmaker was over. Riefenstahl has remained a controversial figure, having both defenders and detractors. Her personal devotion to Hitler is unquestionable, and she did not help her case by pseudonaïve assertions that she had made not propaganda but merely a record of reality. In fact, along with her archenemy Goebbels, she was Hitler's greatest propagandist, producing works of great power that, seen today, provide a unique insight into the emotional appeal of the Nazi movement.

Related entries: Cinema; Olympics; Propaganda

Suggestions for further reading:
Welch, David. 1983a. *Propaganda and the German Cinema 1933–1945*. Oxford: Clarendon Press.

Röhm, Ernst (1887–1934)

*B*orn into a family of civil servants in Munich, Röhm pursued a military career and served with distinction in World War I, being wounded three times. After 1918, contemptuous of the hypocrisy and servility of civilian "bourgeois" society, Captain Röhm doubled as an army staff officer and paramilitary freebooter, acting as a link between the authorities in Bavaria and the extreme right-wing nationalist leagues. Röhm's connection and friendship with Hitler began in 1919: he brought many new recruits and organizational ability to the infant National Socialist German Workers' Party (NSDAP, Nazi Party) and Sturmabteilung (SA). He escaped imprisonment for his part in the Beer Hall Putsch of 1923 but was dismissed from the army. After taking and leaving a series of temporary jobs and with his homosexual affairs public knowledge, in 1928 Röhm set off for Bolivia, where he spent two years as a military instructor.

Röhm was recalled by Hitler after the Nazi electoral success of September 1930

to take command of the SA and defuse the tension between the paramilitary Stormtroopers and a Nazi Party pursuing the "legal" path to power. Under Röhm's leadership the SA expanded enormously, won the battle of the streets against the Communists, and intimidated potential opposition. Röhm presided over the violent elimination of political opponents in early 1933, but the SA's continuing violence, its ideology of permanent activism with socialistic elements, and Röhm's ambitions to replace the regular army with a national people's militia with himself as generalissimo were to lead to his downfall and death.

Röhm enjoyed considerable power as SA chief of staff, minister without portfolio, and above all as one of Hitler's oldest comrades and one of the few people to whom the Führer felt any gratitude and warmth. But his continuing talk about a revolutionary conquest of the state and the "socialist" elements in the SA alienated the conservatives and industrialists whose support Hitler still needed, his military ambitions alarmed the armed forces, and uncontrolled SA violence risked alienating the respectable middle classes. Nevertheless, it took considerable pressure from Hermann Goering and Heinrich Himmler before Hitler could bring himself to get rid of Röhm by the most drastic means, using the SS and the Gestapo. Röhm suspected nothing of what became the Night of the Long Knives in June 1934. He was seized by a detachment of SS troops under Hitler's personal command and taken to Stadelheim prison where, after refusing to take his own life, he was executed. Röhm was posthumously branded a traitor, accused with having plotted to overthrow the government. Hitler and other Nazis also professed to be scandalized by his homosexuality, although it had been known publicly and tolerated for years. The real reason for his death, aside from the usual rivalries of the squabbling Nazi elite, was expressed in the charge that he and his followers had wanted "revolution for the sake of revolution."

Related entries: Beer Hall Putsch; Nazi Movement; Night of the Long Knives; Sturmabteilung

Suggestions for further reading:
Fischer, Conan. 1993. "Ernst Julius Röhm: Chief of Staff of the SA and Indispensable Outsider," in Ronald Smelser and Rainer Zitelmann, eds., *The Nazi Elite.* New York: New York University Press, pp. 173–182.

Romania

From 1918 to 1938 Romania was a constitutional monarchy; from February 1938 to September 1940 it had a monarchical dictatorship under King Carol II; and from September 1940 to August 1944 the authoritarian regime of Ion Antonescu ruled the country. The fascist and anti-Semitic Iron Guard, outlawed under Carol II, joined Antonescu's government but was never supported by Hitler and was suppressed with German help in January 1941. Romania was able to achieve a balance in foreign policy until 1940, despite economic and political instability and weakness, but during the 1930s it grew ever more dependent economically on the German market for its oil and wheat.

Romania signed an economic treaty with Germany in March 1939 and an oil pact on 27 May 1940. Hitler's principal interest in Romania was always its oilfields. The country was pulled into the Axis camp by Hitler's victories in eastern and western Europe and by the Soviet Union's annexation of Bessarabia and northern Bukovina under the terms of the Nazi-Soviet Pact. Antonescu's government joined the Tripartite Pact on 23 November 1940 and the Anti-Comintern Pact on 25 November. He proclaimed a "holy war" against the Soviet Union on 24 June 1941. Romanian troops fought alongside the Germans on the Eastern Front and suffered heavy losses in the battle of Stalingrad. The Soviet advance toward Romania in 1944 led to Antonescu's arrest on 23 August, a declaration of war against Germany on 28 August, and a cease-fire with the Soviet Union on 12 September. In the ensuing period, under constant Soviet pressure, the monarchy was overthrown and a Communist regime installed in Romania.

Related entries: Anti-Comintern Pact; Antonescu, Ion; Bulgaria; Eastern Front; Foreign Policy; Holocaust; Hungary; Michael, King of Romania; Soviet Union; Stalingrad, Battle of; Tripartite Pact

Rommel, Erwin (1891–1944)

The most charismatic German battlefield commander of World War II, a popular hero in Germany and accorded legendary status by his opponents, Rommel at first enjoyed a close relationship with Hitler but later became thoroughly disillusioned. He had a distinguished military career in World War I but was languishing in relative obscurity as an instructor in the War College in Potsdam, when on the outbreak of the war Hitler made him commander of his personal headquarters. At that point Rommel admired Hitler, if not the other leading Nazis, while Hitler probably preferred the middle-class Rommel to snooty aristocratic Prussian officers. Rommel then acquired his popular reputation by leading from the front, commanding the so-called Ghost Panzer division in the invasion of Belgium and France.

In February 1941 Rommel arrived in Tripoli as commander of the Afrika Korps, sent to aid the Italians in Libya. Ignoring his orders to mount a defensive campaign, he went immediately onto the offensive, bewildering the British commanders and maintaining the upper hand over the ever-growing British forces for eighteen

Erwin Rommel rides an armored car during the North African campaign of 1942, during which he was promoted to become Germany's youngest field marshal. (Archive Photos)

months. Leading a charmed life, driving his troops from the front, Rommel's rise to hero status was encouraged by Hitler who, following the capture of Tobruk in June 1942, made him the youngest field marshal in Germany. But his relations with the other German commanders, Albert Kesselring and Hans-Jürgen von Arnim, were strained at best, and he was criticized for ignoring the needs and demands of the Italian High Command.

After being forced to retreat by the overwhelming strength of the Allied forces in late 1942, Rommel, suffering from ill health, became convinced that North Africa should be evacuated. He was recalled by Hitler in March 1943, and despite his many decorations, his pessimism was now evident. He was convinced that once the Allies set foot in Italy Benito Mussolini was doomed, but his realistic view of affairs found no favor with Hitler. Charged in January 1944 with defending France from the expected Allied invasion, following the Normandy landings both he and Karl von Rundstedt urged Hitler to withdraw, but to no avail. Nevertheless, he attempted to carry out his orders with typically aggressive intent until 17 July 1944, when his staff car was strafed by a British fighter and Rommel suffered a fractured skull.

Thus Rommel was convalescing at home at the time of the July Plot against Hitler's life, but he had had contacts with the plotters, and one of them, Karl Heinrich von Stülpnagel, mentioned his name under interrogation. As far as can be ascertained, Rommel was against killing Hitler but in favor of his arrest and confinement. Given the choice of committing suicide (in which case his wife and family would be spared) or standing trial for high treason, Rommel took poison on 14 October 1944. His body was incinerated, but he was given a state funeral and his death attributed to his wounds.

Related entries: Afrika Korps; El Alamein, Battle of; July Plot; Kesselring, Albert; Normandy Landings; North Africa

Suggestions for further reading:
Blumenson, Martin. 1995. "Rommel," in Correlli Barnett, ed., *Hitler's Generals.* Paperback ed. London: Phoenix, pp. 293–316.

Roosevelt, Franklin Delano (1882–1945)

Elected as thirty-second president of the United States in 1932 and re-elected in 1936, 1940, and 1944, Roosevelt pursued a policy of flexible neutrality during the 1930s but as a war leader committed himself to the primary aim of destroying Hitler even when urged to concentrate U.S. resources against Japan. Hitler, obsessed with the number of Jews in the U.S. government, believed that he had proof of Roosevelt's "Jewish ancestry" and saw him as, at best, a rich dilettante surrounded by Jews.

Roosevelt's policy was never capable of containing Japan's expansionist schemes and by 1940 he had come to realize the necessity of aiding Britain in a war that could leave Hitler's Germany dominant in Europe and the Atlantic. Faced with the powerful isolationist lobby, in 1940 he fought a presidential campaign promising to keep the United States out of the European war while ordering an unprecedented expansion of all arms of the U.S. military. Within months of his reelection he pushed through the Lend-Lease Act, signaling long-term support for the European Allies.

The Japanese attack on Pearl Harbor on 7 December 1941 dissolved isolationism overnight, and Roosevelt was spared any further complications by Hitler's reckless

President Roosevelt addresses the country during World War II. Roosevelt used all his skills to bring the United States through the war in a mood to take a major role in overseas affairs and banish the dominant isolationism of the interwar years. (Culver Pictures)

declaration of war. The Führer's peculiar misinterpretation of Roosevelt and the United States is evident. Hitler told a Spanish diplomat in August 1941: "The arch-culprit for the war is Roosevelt, with freemasons, Jews and general Jewish-Bolshevism" (Keegan 1989, p. 537). And in his speech to the Reichstag on 11 December 1941 declaring war he called Roosevelt "the main culprit of this war. . . . I consider him mad" (Kimball 1997, p. 123). With Winston Churchill and Joseph Stalin, Roosevelt became one of the "big three" who would successfully bring about Hitler's downfall.

Roosevelt's relations with the other leaders were not straightforward. Stalin was not exactly fighting for Roosevelt's vision of a democratic world, but he nevertheless assured the provision of vast quantities of war and industrial supplies to the Soviet Union. At the Allied conferences at Teheran and Yalta, Roosevelt always tried to mollify and neutralize Stalin's paranoia. Churchill's commitment to the British Empire clashed with Roosevelt's determined anti-imperialism. The two "Anglo-Saxon" leaders played a game of diplomatic cat-and-mouse about strategy and the shape of the postwar world, but one based on mutual respect and the overriding determination to rid the world of Hitler.

Immediately before and during the war Roosevelt presided over a massive expansion of the U.S. economy and recruitment for the armed forces unequalled before or since. It was Roosevelt who decided on the development of the atomic bomb in the Manhattan Project, though it fell to his successor, Harry S. Truman, to decide on its use. Roosevelt died in April 1945, giving Hitler very briefly a straw at which to grasp as his Reich collapsed. Roosevelt's judgment on matters of world politics will always be controversial because of his attitude toward the Soviet Union and his anti-isolationism, but he was supremely effective in marshaling the vast resources of the U.S. for the defeat of Hitler.

Related entries: Atlantic Charter; Casablanca Conference; Churchill, Winston Leonard Spencer; Foreign Policy; Stalin, Joseph; Teheran Conference; United States of America; Yalta Conference

Suggestions for further reading:
Keegan, John. 1989. *The Second World War.* London: Hutchinson.
Kimball, Warren F. 1997. *Forged in War: Churchill, Roosevelt and the Second World War.* London: HarperCollins.

Rosenberg, Alfred (1893–1946)

*T*he semiofficial "philosopher" of National Socialism was born in Tallinn, Estonia; studied in Riga and Moscow; and fled to Paris and then Munich after the Russian Revolution of 1917. Already active in the extreme nationalist Thule Society, Rosenberg joined the National Socialist German Workers' Party (NSDAP, Nazi Party) in 1919 and was introduced to Hitler by Dietrich Eckart. Hitler was impressed by Rosenberg's "learning," meaning principally his virulent antibolshevism and anti-Semitism and belief in a Judeo-Masonic conspiracy that had been responsible for the outbreak of World War I and the Russian Revolution. With such a neurotic and paranoid outlook, Rosenberg was ideally suited to be Hitler's adviser on foreign affairs during the "time of struggle." He even assumed the party chairmanship during Hitler's imprisonment. But the cold, introverted, plodding but insufferably arrogant Baltic German "foreigner" Rosenberg was not suited to political leadership.

Rosenberg founded the "Fighting League for German Culture" to combat "degenerate art" in 1929 and in 1930 published his major work, *The Myth of the Twentieth Century.* Dismissed by Hermann Goering as "junk" and by Josef Goebbels as "an ideological belch" (Bullock 1991, p. 91), it nevertheless sold over a million copies by 1942. Baldur von

Schirach remarked that Rosenberg had "sold more copies of a book no one ever read than any other author" (Wistrich 1982, p. 257). Nor was this merely the usual Nazi rivalry. A mishmash of abstruse race theory and neo-paganism, the book attacked Catholics as well as Jews and Freemasons, claiming Judaism and Christianity were the mortal enemies of the Aryan race and the Teutonic soul and would be replaced by a new Germanic faith based on blood and race.

Although the *Myth* was required reading for party members, Hitler admitted to finding it obscure, and its neopagan mysticism contradicted his policy of avoiding open confrontation with the churches. Cardinal Michael von Faulhaber of Munich attacked it in 1934, undermining any credibility it might have gained among Catholics. Robbed of the position of cultural dictator of the Third Reich by Goebbels, in 1934 Rosenberg became "The Führer's Delegate for the Entire Intellectual and Philosophical Education and Instruction of the National Socialist Party." As head of the Party Foreign Affairs Department, Rosenberg was nominally responsible for Nazi parties in other countries, but he was passed over for the post of foreign minister in 1933 and again in 1938. Rosenberg's practical incompetence and racial dreaming made even Joachim von Ribbentrop preferable for any post requiring diplomacy and political sense.

In 1939 Rosenberg established the "Institute for the Investigation of the Jewish Question" in Frankfurt. Under his direction the institute looted Jewish libraries, archives, and art collections for "scientific and cultural research" and sequestered "ownerless Jewish property" in France, Belgium, and the Netherlands. In such actions Rosenberg was adequately efficient, but Hitler's appointment of him as minister for the occupied eastern territories in July 1941 showed up his incompetence and rather pathetic ineffectiveness against his more power-obsessed rivals. He had long preached the inferiority of the Slavs and supported the brutal Germanization of the Baltic states but had not envisaged his ideas leading to extermination. When he wrote outraged reports about conditions in the Ukraine and the barbarous treatment of Soviet prisoners of war, he received no response from an indifferent Hitler.

Whatever his title, Rosenberg was in too weak a position to determine policy in the occupied east. His authority was overridden by his rivals such as Heinrich Himmler, Goering, and Martin Bormann as well as by SS and army commanders. Rosenberg may have been the philosopher of National Socialism, his works raided for bombastic slogans and the mystical veneer of genocidal dictatorship, but he was just not taken seriously by the real power politicians. For Himmler, the nearest to him in the ability to take pseudomystical nonsense seriously, "working with or even under Rosenberg is the most difficult thing there is in the Nazi Party" (Breitman 1991, p. 160). Put on trial at Nuremberg, Rosenberg blamed his more successful adversaries for the degeneration of the National Socialist "idea." Found guilty of war crimes, he was hanged at Nuremberg on 16 October 1946.

Related entries: Anti-Semitism; Art; Beer Hall Putsch; Cultural Policy; National Socialism; National Socialist German Workers' Party; Racial Theory; Ukraine; *Völkischer Beobachter;* War Crimes

Suggestions for further reading:
Breitman, Richard. 1991. *The Architect of Genocide: Himmler and the Final Solution.* London: Bodley Head.
Bullock, Alan. 1991. *Hitler and Stalin: Parallel Lives.* London: HarperCollins.
Cecil, Robert. 1974. *The Myth of the Master Race: Alfred Rosenberg and Nazi Ideology.* London: Batsford.
Wistrich, Robert. 1982. *Who's Who in Nazi Germany.* London: Weidenfeld and Nicolson.

Ruhr

*T*he unilateral French military occupation of the Ruhr in January 1923

in response to Germany's alleged tardiness in deliveries of coal as part of war reparations had the paradoxical effect of weakening the infant National Socialist German Workers' Party's attacks on the Reich government. The French action created a spirit of national unity, and the firm official German attitude, which secured the evacuation of the Ruhr in July–August 1925, made Hitler's calls for radical action as expressed to General Hans von Seckt, chief of the army command, seem irrelevant and dangerous. Memories of the Ruhr occupation, however, continued to be evoked by Hitler throughout his career. It strengthened his desire, expressed in *Mein Kampf*, for an alliance with Britain and furthered his plans for a war of revenge against France. The sight of black African troops of the French army occupying German territory was particularly offensive to his racial prejudices. In private rants in the 1930s he blamed the Jews for the birth of mixed-race children to German women. The highly industrialized Ruhr itself was one of the areas most resistant to Nazi penetration, giving most political support to the Social Democratic, Communist, and Center Parties.

Related entries: Reparations

Suggestions for further reading:
Kent, Bruce. 1989. *The Spoils of War: The Politics, Economics and Diplomacy of Reparations, 1918–1932.* Oxford: Clarendon Press.

Rundstedt, Karl Rudolf Gerd von (1875–1953)

A punctilious Prussian officer of the "old school," Gerd von Rundstedt (as he preferred to be known) came from old Junker stock and began active military service in 1892. Always claiming to be a "nonpolitical" soldier, Rundstedt brought his qualities as a highly competent military technician to the service of both the Weimar Republic and Hitler with the same solid, even blind loyalty. By 1938 he had risen to be commander in chief of the 2nd Army when he was briefly retired following the "Blomberg-Fritsch crisis." He was recalled to arms for the planning and execution of the invasion of Poland in August 1939 and then led the invasion of France as commander of Army Group A. It was on Rundstedt's orders (though not, as he claimed, by his wishes) that German forces halted behind Dunkirk, thereby providing the opportunity for the British evacuation.

Promoted to field marshal in July 1940, Rundstedt commanded Army Group South in the invasion of the Soviet Union but incurred Hitler's wrath for ordering a tactical retreat at Rostov and was demoted to a reserve command. He was reinstated to become commander in chief in France in March 1942, supervised the occupation of Vichy France in 1943, and remained to command the forces facing the Allied landings of June 1944. Both sides of Rundstedt's character were shown in the events surrounding the July Plot against Hitler's life. Having once again been removed from command for suggesting that the war should be ended, he nevertheless presided over the Court of Honor overseeing the purging of army officers implicated in the plot. Rundstedt was reinstated once again to direct the retreat to the Rhine and the offensive of the Battle of the Bulge in the Ardennes before being permanently retired from active service in March 1945.

Both Dwight D. Eisenhower and Bernard Montgomery thought that Rundstedt was the best of the German commanders they faced, but when he was arrested by the Americans on 1 May 1945 the extent of his responsibility for war crimes was unclear. At best he had shown no concern over the killing of Jews and Soviet prisoners on the Eastern Front, always main-

taining that he had followed his oath of loyalty to Hitler and obeyed his orders with
exactitude. After prolonged discussions it
was decided not to make the seventy-year-
old Rundstedt face trial. Released from
prisoner-of-war status in 1949, he died at
Celle, in the British zone of occupied Germany, on 24 February 1953.

Related entries: Barbarossa, Operation;
Blomberg-Fritsch Crisis; Bulge, Battle of the;
Dunkirk, Evacuation of; Eastern Front; France;
July Plot; Normandy Landings; Rommel, Erwin;
War Crimes; Wehrmacht

Suggestions for further reading:
Ziemke, Earl F. 1995. "Rundstedt," in Correlli
    Barnett, ed., *Hitler's Generals.* Paperback ed.
    London: Phoenix, pp. 174–207.

Saarland

The territory of the Saar on the east bank of the Rhine, covering some 1,000 square miles, had been removed from Germany by the 1919 Treaty of Versailles and placed under League of Nations control for fifteen years, giving France the right to exploit its rich resources of coal and iron. After this period its inhabitants would vote to decide whether or not to return to Germany. Resentment at their fate smoldered implacably within the population, and as the new head of state Hitler could look forward to a major propaganda success from the plebiscite fixed for 13 January 1935.

The Saarland was overwhelmingly Catholic and contained a large industrial working class, the two groups that had been least supportive of Nazism in Germany. But as the day of the vote approached Josef Goebbels unleashed a massive propaganda barrage, raising awareness about the issue throughout the country. In the event just over 90 percent of the voters chose reunion with a Germany under Nazi dictatorship. Any doubts about Hitler's popularity among the German people were dispelled in resounding fashion, and he milked his overwhelming victory for all it was worth. He assured France that he had no further territorial demands, so seeming to renounce Alsace-Lorraine, but his real intentions were very different, and all Europe was aware that his hand had been strengthened. Meanwhile, although the result had never been in doubt, Hitler could present it to the German people as a victory for the new Reich in breaking the shackles of Versailles. On 1 March 1935, the day of the formal incorporation of the Saarland into the Reich, he spoke in Saarbrücken of his supreme joy on "this day of happiness for the entire nation" and "for the whole of Europe" (Kershaw 1998, p. 547).

Related entries: Foreign Policy; France; Plebiscites

Suggestions for further reading:
Kershaw, Ian. 1998. *Hitler 1889–1936: Hubris.* New York: Allen Lane The Penguin Press.
Weinberg, Gerhard L. 1970. *The Foreign Policy of Hitler's Germany: Diplomatic Revolution in Europe, 1933–1936.* Chicago: University of Chicago Press.

Sauckel, Fritz (1894–1946)

A former merchant seaman and factory worker born in Hassfort am Main in Lower Franconia, Sauckel joined the National Socialist German Workers' Party (NSDAP, Nazi Party) in 1923 and held a series of party posts, including *Gauleiter* of Thuringia in 1927. After the seizure of power he became governor of the same province. As plenipotentiary-general for labor mobilization, Sauckel was responsible for mobilizing foreign workers for the Third Reich's war effort and became Hitler's slave-labor boss. Under his direction millions were deported from their homes in the occupied territories and ruthlessly exploited, worked to death amid terror and mistreatment. Proudly Sauckel presented his record-breaking recruitment statistics to Hitler. At the Nuremberg trials he claimed to be innocent of war crimes, even though he was directly responsible for the extermination of thousands of Jewish workers in Poland. Sauckel was hanged for war crimes and crimes against humanity on 16 October 1946.

Related entries: Economic Policy; Poland; Total War; War Crimes

Schacht, Hjalmar (1877–1970)

Hjalmar Horace Greely Schacht was born into a family of Danish origin in Schleswig-Holstein but brought up in the United States. Having returned to Germany to complete his studies in economics, he pursued a highly successful career in banking and in 1923 was made Reich currency commissioner, successfully bringing an end to the astronomical hyperinflation and stabilizing the mark. Schacht served as head of the Reichsbank from December 1923 to 1930. As head of the German delegation at the reparations conference he took part in the negotiation of the Dawes Plan of 1924 and later the Young Plan of 1929. But he resigned as president of the Reichsbank in protest against the provisions of the Young Plan and the country's increasing foreign debt, an act that brought him fatefully closer to Hitler.

Schacht had been one of the founders of the German Democratic Party in 1918 but during the 1920s had steadily become more conservative and nationalist. Declaring that in order to create a strong Germany he would make an alliance with the devil, he joined with Hitler and conservative nationalists in the ephemeral Harzburg Front of October 1931. Schacht played a decisive role in bringing Hitler closer to his friends in banking and industry; he was one of the group urging President Paul von Hindenburg to appoint Hitler as chancellor; and he encouraged industrial giants such as Krupp and IG Farben to support the Nazis as well as other parties in elections in 1932–1933. Hitler reappointed Schacht as Reichsbank president in March 1933 and then as minister of economics in 1934.

In the early years of the Third Reich Schacht essentially made economic policy as he pleased. A firm believer in the free market, he kept business free from party control and succeeded in making Germany financially sound. He was given almost unlimited powers in 1935 as plenipotentiary-general for the war economy and made Hitler's rearmament plans financially possible. Schacht had become indispensable to Hitler, but the Führer never completely trusted this last representative of the conservative bourgeoisie in his government. His policy of stimulating private enterprise and firmly controlling inflation while seeking to finance rearmament soon ran into trouble with the Nazi Party leadership. He resigned his posts in November 1937 but retained a cabinet position as minister without portfolio until January 1943 and once more became president of the Reichsbank in March 1938. In that post he lasted only until January 1939 following new policy disagreements as Hitler sped toward war.

Schacht, disturbed by anti-Jewish violence and the removal of top generals, did not believe that Germany could economically sustain a long war. He renewed old contacts with the conservative opposition around Carl Goerdeler without wholeheartedly committing himself to resistance. Nevertheless, although not directly involved in the conspiracy, he was arrested after the July Plot and sent to Ravensbrück and then Flossenbürg concentration camps. Liberated by U.S. troops in April 1945, he appeared at the Nuremberg trials, charged with organizing Germany for war. Following much confusion over whether his actions constituted criminal activity, he was finally cleared of all charges in November 1950 and began a new career as a financial adviser to developing countries, which lasted until his death in Munich in 1970 at the age of ninety-three.

Related entries: Dawes Plan; Economic Policy; Four-Year Plan; German Democratic Party; Harzburg Front; Industry; Opposition; Rearmament; Unemployment; Young Plan

Suggestions for further reading:
Beck, Earl R. 1955. *Verdict on Schacht.* Tallahassee: Florida State University.
Peterson, Edward N. 1954. *Hjalmar Schacht: For and against Hitler.* Boston: Christopher Publishing House.
Schacht, Hjalmar. 1965. *My First Seventy-Six Years.* London: Wingate.

Schirach, Baldur von (1907–1974)

The future Reich youth leader and wartime governor of Vienna was born in Berlin on 9 March 1907, the son of an aristocratic theater director and his American wife. He joined the National Socialist German Workers' Party (NSDAP, Nazi Party) while studying at Munich University in 1924 and in 1927 dedicated himself to building up the National Socialist German Students' League. Schirach soon proved himself an outstanding organizer and propagandist among secondary school and university students. As Reich youth leader of the NSDAP from 1930 he took control of the Hitler Youth and its as-

sociated organizations. Schirach expressed blind devotion to and hero worship of Hitler in sycophantic verses and sayings such as "loyalty is everything and everything is the love of Adolf Hitler" (Wistrich 1982, p. 272). This naturally appealed to Hitler, as did Schirach's opposition to traditional education.

Schirach was named Youth Führer of the German Reich on 18 June 1933. Aged only twenty-six, he fitted in with Hitler's idea that "youth must be led by youth." A convinced anti-Semite, he was also opposed to Christianity and tried to infuse Hitler Youth members with a romantic mixture of paganism, militarism, blind patriotism, and the conviction of the superiority of German blood. By his own account, Schirach was both an "officer in National Socialist service" and a "priest of the National Socialist faith." In numerous writings, songs, and poems he invoked the heroic warrior ideals that would mold the Hitler Youth into a new race of "supermen." Schirach himself was rather fat and mocked as "effeminate," but that did not prevent his idealization of hard, tough Hitler Youth.

Schirach had less success as a politician among the Nazi elite than he did as a leader among youth. In 1940 the intrigues of Martin Bormann and other enemies resulted in his being replaced as Reich Youth Führer by Arthur Axmann. After a brief spell of frontline service, Schirach was appointed *Gauleiter* and governor of Vienna in August 1940. He lost his remaining influence with Hitler when during a visit to Berchtesgarden in 1943, he and his wife criticized German occupation policies in eastern Europe and the conditions under which Jews were being deported. At the same time, however, he shared responsibility for the deportation of 185,000 Jews from Austria to Poland. On trial at Nuremberg in 1946 he admitted to approving this "resettlement" and to having trained German youth "for millionfold murder" but denied knowledge of the extermination camps. He served twenty years in Spandau prison for crimes against humanity. His memoirs *Ich glaubte an Hitler* (I believed in Hitler), published in 1967, a year after his release, tried to explain the fatal fascination of Hitler and how a generation of youth had been misled. From 1966 until his death, peacefully in his sleep, in 1974 Schirach lived a secluded life in southwestern Germany.

Related entries: Hitler Youth; Universities; Youth Policy

Suggestions for further reading:
Rempel, Gerhard. 1989. *Hitler's Children: The Hitler Youth and the SS.* Chapel Hill: University of North Carolina Press.
Wistrich, Robert. 1982. *Who's Who in Nazi Germany.* London: Weidenfeld and Nicolson.

Schleicher, Kurt von (1882–1934)

The last chancellor of the Weimar Republic was a professional army officer from Brandenburg who in 1929 was made head of the Ministry Bureau in the Reichswehr Ministry, responsible for the political and press affairs of the armed forces. In this role Schleicher became a significant figure behind the scenes of power, being largely responsible for both the appointment and dismissal of Heinrich Brüning as chancellor before playing a similar role in the intrigues surrounding Franz von Papen. On becoming chancellor himself on 2 December 1932, General von Schleicher ruled by presidential decree. He sought to divide the Nazis by offering to appoint Gregor Strasser as vice chancellor and prime minister of Prussia and trying to make a deal with Ernst Röhm, but Hitler managed to put an end to his crude machinations. Schleicher never enjoyed a majority in the Reichstag and was distrusted by industrial interests and the propertied classes. He was abruptly dismissed by Presi-dent Paul von Hindenburg on 28 January 1933 after the complicated intrigues that brought Hitler the chancellorship. Schleicher and his wife were brutally murdered in their home on 30 June 1934 during the Night of the Long Knives.

Related entries: Brüning, Heinrich; Hindenburg, Paul von; Night of the Long Knives; Papen, Franz von; Weimar Republic

Schmidt, Paul Otto (1899–1970)

As chief interpreter in the German Foreign Office, which he had joined in 1924, Schmidt accompanied Hitler at important diplomatic meetings, his role being essential because of the Führer's complete lack of knowledge of foreign languages. He also acted as interpreter during the meetings for the Munich Agreement in 1938. Schmidt was constantly near the center of power but did not join the National Socialist German Workers' Party until 1943. His memoirs, published in Germany in 1948 but never translated into English, were criticized as superficial.

Schönerer, Georg Ritter von (1842–1921)

Along with Karl Lueger, the fiercely nationalist and anti-Semitic Schön-erer was one of the young Hitler's principal inspirations and models during his years in Vienna from 1908–1913. Born to wealthy parents and educated in Germany, Schön-erer was initially a liberal and modernizing landowner in the Waldviertel region, which he represented in the Reich Council in Vi-enna between 1873 and 1888, but soon shifted to pan-German ultranationalism and anti-Semitism. In 1882 he helped to formulate the Linz Program of the German nationalist movement in Austria, and his influence can be seen in the twelfth point, added in 1885, demanding the exclusion of Jews from the economy and politics.

A prison term in 1888 briefly cost Schönerer his seat on the Reich Council, but he returned as a "fighter for an all-German state" representing Eger until failing to be reelected in 1907. Ultimately Schönerer was a political failure, and by the time Hitler arrived in Vienna his star was waning. He had mobilized anti-Semitism as a significant force in Austrian life but never attempted to create a mass movement, believing that change would come through the activities of an elite. Hitler was to criticize Schönerer for this as well for his extreme anti-Catholicism (he had converted to Protestantism because of the Catholic clergy's alleged pro-Slav attitudes). But, unlike Lueger, he incorporated a "blood and soil" mysticism into a worldview with anti-Semitism at its center.

Hitler criticized Schönerer's willingness to participate in unprofitable parliamentarianism, but in *Mein Kampf* wrote approvingly of his program, an early brand of "national socialism" combining German nationalism, social reform, and anti-Semitism. His legacy to the Nazi Party included the "Heil" greeting, the title of Führer (which he had bestowed upon himself), and the rigorous repression of any democratic decisionmaking in the movement.

Related entries: Anti-Semitism; Lueger, Karl; Pan-Germanism; Vienna

Suggestions for further reading:
Carsten, F. L. 1977. *Fascist Movements in Austria, from Schönerer to Hitler.* London: Sage.
Pulzer, Peter. 1988. *The Rise of Political Anti-Semitism in Germany and Austria.* Rev. ed. Cambridge, MA: Harvard University Press.
Whiteside, Andrew G. 1975. *The Socialism of Fools: Georg Ritter von Schönerer and Austrian Pan-Germanism.* Berkeley: University of California Press.

Schuschnigg, Kurt von (1897–1977)

The Austrian chancellor bullied by Hitler into accepting the Anschluss in 1938 was a lawyer and prominent member of the Catholic conservative Christian Social Party who succeeded the assassinated Engelbert Dollfuss as federal chancellor on 25 July 1934. Schuschnigg upheld the authoritarian principles of his predecessor through the Fatherland Front and sought a friendly relationship with Hitler's Germany as a way of preserving Austrian sovereignty and independence. On 11 July 1936 he concluded the so-called July Agreement, undertaking to maintain a friendly attitude toward the Third Reich and defining Austria as a German state. Although no Nazi himself, he further sought to placate Hitler by releasing several thousand Austrian Nazis from prison and including several in the cabinet. But Schuschnigg's policy of concessions was severely undermined in 1936 by the creation of the Axis and Benito Mussolini's withdrawal of support for Austrian independence.

Schuschnigg's government lacked broad popular support, and he could not rally Austrians against the growing pressure from Hitler. At a meeting at Berchtesgarden on 12 February 1938 he was browbeaten by the Führer into accepting the appointment of the Nazi Arthur Seyss-Inquart as minister of the interior and into legalizing the Nazi Party. The obvious threat to Austria's independence forced Schuschnigg into the desperate gamble of announcing a plebiscite in which the Austrian people would be asked to vote for an Austria "free and German, independent and social, Christian and united." But German troops massed on the Austrian border, the plebiscite was abandoned, and a furious Hitler insisted on Schuschnigg's resignation and his replacement by Seyss-Inquart.

Following the Anschluss, Schuschnigg was interned under Gestapo surveillance in a Vienna hotel. In 1941 he was arrested and sent to Dachau, spending the rest of the war in various concentration camps. Liberated by U.S. troops in 1945, he emigrated to the United States in 1947 and became professor of government at the University of St. Louis in 1948 and a naturalized U.S. citizen in 1956. Schuschnigg's memoirs were translated as *Austrian Requiem* (1947) and *The Brutal Takeover* (1971). He returned to Austria in 1967 and settled in the Tyrol.

Related entries: Anschluss; Austria

Schutzstaffel (SS)

The origins of the SS (literally, defense or protection squads) lie in the "Staff Guard" created by Hitler in 1923 in Munich under the leadership of Josef Berchtold. Banned after the Beer Hall Putsch, it was reestablished in 1925 under Julius Schreck. The main task of these new *Schutzstaffeln* was to protect leaders of the National Socialist German Workers' Party (NSDAP, Nazi Party), provide security at meetings, and conduct recruitment for the party. Hitler could count on their absolute loyalty to his person, something he could not rely on from the unruly Sturmabteilung (SA). But the real history of the SS begins with the appointment of Heinrich Himmler as Reichsführer-SS in February 1929 and its establishment as the "party police" of the NSDAP, clamping down on internal dissent and creating the nucleus of the future Sicherheitsdienst (SD). Membership grew from a few hundred to about 52,000 by the end of 1932. The establishment of the "Race and Settlement Office" in 1931 showed Himmler's ambition to create a leadership order on the basis of "biological selection."

After Hitler's accession to power, the SS rose within fifteen months to be the chief instrument of political policing in Ger-

Massed ranks of the SS at the Nuremberg Rally of 1934. Hitler's most fanatical and disciplined followers, they were to carry out even his most extreme policies with a ruthless efficiency untypical of the Third Reich as a whole. (Imperial War Museum / Archive Photos)

many. As such, its actions were no longer defined by the usual norms of justice and law but only by the "will of the Führer." It proved its worth to Hitler in the liquidation of the SA leadership in the Night of the Long Knives and on 20 July 1934 was upgraded into an autonomous organization within the Nazi Party. With Himmler as "Reich Führer of the SS and chief of the German police," the SS and the police were inextricably enmeshed; the SD was expanded; and the concentration camps handed over to the SS, resulting in more effective exploitation of camp labor and their deliberate isolation from the jurisdiction of the Justice and Interior Ministries.

Himmler's ambitions to establish the SS as a military organization encountered stiff resistance from the Wehrmacht. The first volunteer unit outside army control was the Leibstandarte-SS "Adolf Hitler," organized at Hitler's behest in March 1933. The military role of the SS leadership schools, founded in 1934–1935, was recognized by Hitler in a decree of 17 August 1938. Thus the Wehrmacht no longer enjoyed a monopoly on arms. But Himmler conceived of the SS as more even than a police force and military corps. In imitation of old orders of nobility and knighthood, it was to be a leadership elite for the whole of society, restoring the *Volk* to its supposedly original pagan and racial ideological principles. A spiritual center for the order was created at the Wewelsburg in Westphalia and a pseudoreligious complexion bestowed on the SS by rituals and dedication ceremonies, symbols, and cult objects such as the honorary dagger and the death's-head ring.

These cults and symbols bestowed unity on the ever expanding and more diverse SS "state within the state," which included the Race and Settlement Main Office (RSHA), the national political educational institutes, the Lebensborn organization for the raising of illegitimate but "racially pure" children, and the concentration camps and economic enterprises. More than forty different enterprises, with 150 factories and plants, were developed from the workshops that had always existed in the concentration camps, which were transformed into centers of forced labor. Once the war began, the SS acquired enormous wealth by taking over Jewish and Polish firms in the occupied territories. Jewish concentration camp inmates were exploited ruthlessly until the mass extermination measures began in 1942.

With the war, although the goals of the SS did not change, its direction did. The Waffen SS, formed in the autumn of 1939, rapidly increased in importance and scope. And in conquered lands the SS strove to become the prime force of the Nazi "New Order" over and above the military and civil authorities by controlling and exploiting the populations. Through programs of population transfer, displacement, and colonization, the new territories were to be "Germanized" with the most extreme ruthlessness. The purpose of the SS was no longer merely to protect Hitler's regime but also to segregate and "cull out" entire groups of the population—Jews, Slavs, Gypsies—and exploit their labor by "extermination through work." The SS did not devise the Final Solution of the "Jewish question" but carried it out with all the necessary coldhearted efficiency and fanatical racial zeal. It proved itself the unconditionally loyal "executive organ of the Führer" and entertained the hope that it would administer the "cleansed eastern space" after the end of the war. From being Hitler's bodyguard, the SS had become the biggest and most fanatical of Nazi organizations dedicated to the racist ideological will to domination. For all its independent power, its main point of reference was always personal loyalty to Hitler. At the Nuremberg trials it was classified as a "criminal organization." Its crimes were all in Hitler's name.

Related entries: Auschwitz; Concentration Camps; Dachau; Eastern Front; Eugenics; Extermination Camps; Himmler, Heinrich; Nazi Movement; Poland; Racial Theory; Sicherheitsdienst; Totenkopfverbände; Waffen SS; War Crimes

Suggestions for further reading:
Koehl, Robert L. 1983. *The Black Corps: The Structure and Power Struggles of the Nazi SS.* Madison: University of Wisconsin Press.
Krausnick, Helmut, and Martin Broszat. 1970. *Anatomy of the SS State.* New York: Walker and Company.

Science and Scientists

Hitler was totally ignorant about science. Albert Speer referred to his "love of amateurishness and his lack of understanding of fundamental scientific research" (Speer 1971, p. 317). Hitler may have used scientific rhetoric, principally a crude form of Social Darwinism, to justify his racist and imperialist policies, but National Socialism was a political movement, not a scientific one, and did enormous, though fortunately not irreparable damage to the great German tradition of scientific research. Nazism gained the support of many scientists and medical men and women who were products of German universities that had been dominated by extreme right-wing politics under the Weimar Republic, but they found themselves having to defend scientific reason against Nazi irrationalism.

Biology under Hitler was transmuted into racial theory and eugenics, but even in the physical sciences the Nazis separated the "Aryan" from the "Jewish," championing a supposedly "commonsense" view of the universe against the abstruse and difficult concepts underlying modern physics. Einstein's theory of relativity joined atonal discordant music, modern art, and experimental or socially critical literature as a manifestation of evil Jewish influence on healthy German minds. "Jewish physics," claimed Nazi ideologues, was both a manifestation of all-pervading "materialism" and an attempt to bamboozle good sense with obscure theory. By explaining all reality through the interaction of material forces, it ignored the spiritual dimension, the higher truths toward which the German soul was deemed to aspire. Time and space were absolute concepts, rooted in intuition and not to be questioned or made relative.

"Aryan physics" contradicted Enlightenment thinking because it was based on unshakable truths not subject to rational scrutiny and was well-suited to reinforcing authoritarian politics. The true Aryan saw physical reality as it was and strived toward perfection, needing neither Einsteinian physics nor cubist art to strip the veil from his perceptions. The empirical physicists Philipp Lenard and Johannes Stark, both Nobel Prize winners and Nazis well before 1933, led the campaign against "Jewish science," theoretical physics, and relativity theory. When Hitler came to power, Jews and those who dissented from the Aryan line were dismissed from universities and all positions of authority. By 1935 approximately one-quarter of physicists and one-fifth of all scientists had been so expelled. Stark, however, gradually lost influence as war approached. Other physicists, including Max Planck and Werner Heisenberg, discoverer of the uncertainty principle, regained influence by arguing that proper scientific research would be indispensable for the coming war effort. While Nazi biology continued toward its horrific climax, support for "Aryan physics" was discreetly dropped.

Nevertheless, distrust of "Jewish physics" probably contributed to the relatively low priority given to nuclear research during the war. The chief result of German research, led by Heisenberg in Leipzig, was probably to spur the Americans and the British into belated cooperation in 1943. In any case, German scientists had taken a wrong turn in basing their work on heavy water, the chief source of which, the Rjukan nitrates factory in Norway, was destroyed twice, once by saboteurs and once by bombing. Hitler refused to give backing to the diversified research necessary for the development of nuclear weapons. While the more comprehensible rocket technology, led by the dynamic Werner von Braun, received more support, the German nuclear program collapsed in February 1944 when a boat transporting all available supplies of heavy water to Germany was sunk by a Norwegian resistance group. The V-weapons created by rocket research, meanwhile, came mercifully too late to seriously affect the outcome of the war.

Related entries: Cultural Policy; Education; Eugenics; Racial Theory; Universities; Vergeltungswaffe

Suggestions for further reading:

Beyerschen, Alan D. 1977. *Scientists under Hitler: Politics and the Physics Community in the Third Reich.* New Haven: Yale University Press.
Macrakis, Kristie. 1993. *Surviving the Swastika: Scientific Research in Nazi Germany.* New York and Oxford: Oxford University Press.
Powers, Thomas. 1993. *Heisenberg's War: The Secret History of the German Bomb.* New York: Alfred A. Knopf.
Renneberg, Monika, and Mark Walker, eds. 1994. *Science, Technology and National Socialism.* Cambridge: Cambridge University Press.
Speer, Albert. 1971. *Inside the Third Reich.* Paperback ed. London: Sphere Books.
Walker, Mark. 1989. *German National Socialism and the Quest for Nuclear Power, 1939–1949.* Cambridge: Cambridge University Press.

Sealion, Operation

Hitler began giving serious consideration to an invasion of Great Britain in the summer of 1940, after his peace overtures had been unceremoniously rejected. He then ordered preparations for Operation Sealion, a landing along the south coast between Kent and the Isle of Wight, to be completed by mid-August. The army was enthusiastic, but the navy argued successfully for the impossibility of such a large-scale landing. Hitler therefore turned to the Luftwaffe to establish air supremacy by destroying the Royal Air Force, thus allowing an invasion on a smaller scale. The outcome of the Battle of Britain spoiled the plan. On 17 September Hitler effectively abandoned Operation Sealion by postponing it indefinitely.

Related entries: Britain, Battle of

Sicherheitsdienst (SD)

The intelligence and surveillance service of the SS was established in 1931, playing the role of watchdog for both the SS and the National Socialist German Workers' Party (NSDAP, Nazi Party). Headed by Reinhard Heydrich from 1932, after the seizure of power its sections soon came to cover the whole of Germany, with the aim of submitting the entire population to total surveillance. By the summer of 1941 its fifty-seven branches covered the whole of the "new Germany." Estimates of membership cannot be established with any certainty, but it may have had some 3,000 salaried and 30,000 part-time or "honorary" members. These latter were principally responsible for providing the Nazi leadership with accurate assessments of public opinion. The SD evaluated the political reliability of individual "*Volk* comrades," gathered relevant foreign news and established contacts with foreign sympathizers and ethnic Germans. This came to involve the planning of sabotage actions, such as the Gleiwitz radio station incident that provided the excuse for the invasion of Poland.

As was usual under Hitler's rule, however, the precise role of the SD remained ill-defined and confused. In 1939 it was merged with the security police (SIPO) in the Reich Main Security Office (RSHA), making Heydrich (under Heinrich Himmler) technically the head of all the police in Germany. But at the same time it remained a branch of the Nazi Party, receiving its budget from the NSDAP treasury. It retained a separate identity as an instrument of Hitler's power as Führer, above party and state, and as a reinforcement of Himmler's personal power as guard dog of the National Socialist movement. Even many of its own members were confused about their role within the police system, torn between police work with a dash of terror, illegal "dirty work," and surveillance.

Heydrich's attempt in 1937 to delineate a "division of labor" between the Gestapo and the SD only added to the confusion. The SD was to deal with areas of "learning," art, party and state, constitution and administration, foreign lands, Freemasonry and associations, and "all general questions and matters of principle" concerning the churches, pacifism, Jews, right-wing movements, the economy, and the press. Marxism, treason, and emigrants were left to the Gestapo, and the SD was supposed to avoid matters of "state police executive powers," assigned to the Gestapo, and "individual cases" (Gellately 1990, pp. 66–67). Heydrich's own all-powerful position and his subordination to Himmler did not help to clarify affairs.

In practice, the SD's main purpose in peacetime was to report on public opinion and the "general life of the people" through its informers and "honorary members." As with the Gestapo, its very secretiveness and the arbitrary nature of its functions and power helped to instill the atmosphere of apprehension and fear of denunciation essential to Hitler's rule. In the occupied territories during the war, the terroristic functions of the SIPO and SD, directly implementing Hitler's murderous policies, assumed greater importance. The leaders of SS *Einsatzgruppen* were frequently SD functionaries.

Related entries: Gestapo; Heydrich, Reinhard; Himmler, Heinrich; National Socialist German Workers' Party; Public Opinion; Schutzstaffel

Suggestions for further reading:
Browder, George C. 1990. *Foundations of the Nazi Police State: The Foundation of SIPO and SD.* Lexington: University Press of Kentucky.
Gellately, Robert. 1990. *The Gestapo and German Society: Enforcing Racial Policy 1933–1945.* Oxford: Clarendon Press.

Siegfried Line

*T*he 3-mile-deep West Wall, or Siegfried Line, was constructed along Germany's western frontier opposite the French Maginot Line, but its similarly defensive mentality was out of keeping with Hitler's concepts of blitzkrieg and conquest, and the line was still unfinished in 1939. Hitler only ordered its use in desperation in 1944 and early 1945 as the Allied invasion forces advanced toward Germany and against the advice of his commanders, who favored a retreat to the Rhine. It could, however, do little against the Allied superiority in numbers.

Related entries: Todt Organization

Sobibor

*T*he extermination camp of Sobibor, in an isolated area in the east of the Polish Generalgouvernement, went into operation in April 1942 under the command of the Austrian Franz Stangl, who had previously been involved in the euthanasia campaign in Germany and later became commandant of Treblinka. A quarter of a million Jews were exterminated at Sobibor before it ceased operation in 1943 and was transformed into a center for the storage and sorting of captured munitions. The camp was also used to house Soviet prisoners of war.

Related entries: Extermination Camps; Holocaust

Social Democratic Party (SPD)

Formed in 1890 through an amalgamation of socialist parties and associations, the SPD was one of the founding parties of the Weimar Republic, providing the first president, Friedrich Ebert, and four chancellors, mostly heading governments of the so-called Weimar coalition. For Hitler and other extreme nationalists, the SPD represented the "November criminals" of 1918, internationalist "Marxists" who put class and parliamentary politics above nationality. They were "traitors" responsible for Germany's supposed weakness and decadence. Until 1932 the SPD was the strongest party in electoral support and membership. But the collapse in March 1930 of the coalition government led by the Social Democrat Hermann Müller marked the beginning of the crisis of the republic that brought Hitler to power.

Between 1930 and 1932 the SPD lost votes, especially to the Communists, and proved unable to avert the rise of Hitler, either by tolerating the government of Heinrich Brüning or determinedly opposing those of Franz von Papen and Kurt von Schleicher. By adhering to a policy of strict legality it could only mount passive or ineffective resistance, both before and after Hitler's appointment as chancellor. Nevertheless, it was the only party to oppose the Enabling Act of 23 March 1933 as a solid bloc. The courageous speech in the Reichstag by Otto Wels, a member of the SPD executive since 1919, drove Hitler into a rage.

The SPD was banned on 22 June 1933. The Executive Committee of the Exiled SPD, the Sopade, was constituted in Prague, but inside Germany, Social Democratic opposition, mostly from working-class youth groups, was extinguished by Gestapo terror around 1936. Individual Social Democrats were, however, in contact with other opposition groups during the war years. The SPD reemerged after Hitler's death in the summer and autumn of 1945, holding its first party assembly in the western occupation zone in May 1946. In the Soviet zone it was forcibly united with the Communist Party as the Socialist Unity Party.

Related entries: Enabling Act; Opposition; Sopade; Weimar Republic

Suggestions for further reading:
Harsch, Donna. 1993. *German Social Democracy and the Rise of Nazism*. Chapel Hill: University of North Carolina Press.

Social Policy

Before coming to power, Hitler and the National Socialist German Workers' Party (NSDAP, Nazi Party) had at no point developed a coherent economic or social policy. He had been content to rail against the "welfare establishment" of the Weimar Republic while promising a good life for all under a new Reich. Even after 1933 the regime at first avoided any firm position on basic issues of society and social welfare. Hitler had only broad concepts and slogans to offer, the most important of which was the *Volksgemeinschaft*. The demands of the individual were subordinate to the good of the community, and social policy yielded precedence to the goals of the state as the embodiment of that community. Sectional interests were in theory abolished by the Third Reich. Thus after the destruction of the trade unions, the German Labor Front was supposed to represent the interests of workers and employees, but in practice struggles over wages and working conditions persisted.

Hitler linked the overcoming of unemployment with the rearmament drive, with no great concern for the conditions of those on job creation schemes or the remaining unemployed. The numbers of those entitled to state support were systematically reduced and the promised reform of unemployment insurance never implemented. Similarly, the already low level of state pensions was undercut and the conditions for granting pensions made tighter. Not until 1942 were pensions increased, as Hitler kept in mind the social unrest during the later stages of World War I. Reduced state welfare payments were replaced by the voluntary donations of the National Socialist People's Welfare (NSV) agency, which was financed by contributions. But the support provided by the NSV emphasized usefulness to the state over the needs of the individual. Restrictions on wage increases, though threatened by the labor shortage after 1936, limited private consumption to the advantage of arms investments. Surplus cash was supposed to be donated to the Winterhilfe, and a heavier tax burden was imposed on single people and childless couples. Efforts at price control were partly effective and certainly helped to maintain the social peace.

The propaganda of the regime promised classless equality for all "*Volk* comrades," with status dependent not on class or education but on membership in the "German race." Some of the traditions of the workers' movement were retained in modified form in the holidays and mass marches of the Harvest Thanks Festival and the "Day of National Labor." The NSV, the model workplaces of the "Beauty of Work" program, and the "Strength through Joy" organization had their effect, even if participation was compulsory and served the ends of control and war mobilization. In accord with the ideology of the family as the basic cell of the *Volksgemeinschaft* and the idealization of women as wives and mothers, measures were introduced to improve prenatal care, a campaign was mounted against birth control, and a monthly child subsidy was introduced.

Hitler's system promised social order, community, and guaranteed security for the population. The individual experienced improvements in some limited areas of life, but the goals of rearmament and expansion took precedence. He or she was bound to the Third Reich by a combination of force, partial concessions, social welfare measures, and opportunities for identification with the regime. The systematic use of propaganda and mass ceremonials and celebrations were also a part of social policy. Hitler did indeed provide security, but not necessarily much in the way of equality or happiness.

Related entries: Agriculture; Economic Policy; Education; Euthanasia; German Labor Front; Hitler Youth; Industry; Jews and Jewish Policy; Labor Relations; Labor Service; Ley, Robert; Middle Classes; Mutterkreuz; Propaganda; "Strength through Joy"; Todt Organization; Unemployment; *Volksgemeinschaft;* Winterhilfe; Women; Working Class; Youth Policy

Suggestions for further reading:
Mason, Timothy W. 1993. *Social Policy in the Third Reich: The Working Class and the "National Community."* Providence and Oxford: Berg.

Socialism

The destruction of Marxism and "Jewish bolshevism" was one of the fundamental aims of Hitler's political program. Yet the word "socialist" was included in the name of his party. The initial Nazi platform of 1920, which was never changed, included demands for the nationalization of trusts, the sharing of profits from wholesale trade, and the abolition of incomes unearned by labor. While the left wing of the Nazi Party, led by Gregor and Otto Strasser and for a while the young Josef Goebbels, took the socialist elements seriously, for Hitler they were little more than slogans, part of the attempt to include something for everyone. When he spoke to the Düsseldorf Industry Club in January 1932 he ignored the redistributive talk of Nazi radicals. For Hitler the political imperative of a strong expansionist state took priority over any economic system.

In Nazi propaganda class struggle within the nation was replaced by a "class struggle between nations," with Germany as one of the "proletarian nations" opposed by Western plutocracies. In 1930 Hitler explained to Otto Strasser that while he was a socialist and claimed (wrongly) to have once been "an ordinary working man," "What you understand by Socialism is nothing but Marxism. Now look: the great mass of working men want only bread and circuses. They have no understanding for ideals of any sort whatever. . . . There are no revolutions except racial revolutions: there cannot be a political, economic, or social revolution—always and only it is the struggle of the lower stratum of inferior race against the dominant higher race, and if this higher race has forgotten the law of its existence, then it loses the day" (Bullock 1991, p. 190).

Socialism was, therefore, a creation of the Jews in their struggle against superior races. "Nazi collectivism," Harold James writes, "was political, not economic, and left individuals as economic agents" (James 1986, p. 347). "The capitalists," Hitler said, "have worked their way to the top through their capacity, and as the basis of this selection, which again only proves their higher race, they have a right to lead" (Bullock 1991, p. 190). Capitalists had a right to enjoy their profits as long as they served the national interest and the "national community." Workers would be looked after in the factory and through social welfare. In appealing to the middle classes oppressed by big business while leaving capitalist industry free to expand and joining all classes together in a new community, Nazism promised a vague "third way" between socialism and unfettered capitalism.

Related entries: Communist Party; Economic Policy; German Labor Front; Industry; Labor Relations; Labor Service; Middle Classes; National Socialism; Social Democratic Party; Social Policy; Strasser, Gregor; Strasser, Otto; Trade Unions; *Volksgemeinschaft;* Working Class

Suggestions for further reading:
Bullock, Alan. 1991. *Hitler and Stalin: Parallel Lives.* London: HarperCollins.
James, Harold. 1986. *The German Slump: Politics and Economics, 1924–1936.* Oxford: Clarendon.

Sopade

The Social Democratic Party in exile, known as the Sopade, based first in Prague and later in Paris, maintained a network of agents and informants in factories and communities throughout Germany. The remarkable reports delivered by these agents between 1934 and April 1940 and processed into the *Deutschland-Berichte* (Germany reports) provide a wealth of information about the political and social situation and, since their publication in 1980, have proved invaluable for students of public opinion and everyday life under Hitler's regime.

Related entries: Hitler Myth; Public Opinion; Social Democratic Party

Soviet Union

In Hitler's mind the Union of Soviet Socialist Republics (USSR) was always the ultimate enemy. The land where "Jewish Bolsheviks" lorded it over inferior Slavs was bound inevitably to clash sooner or later with a resurgent Germany. He made his view of the Soviet leaders clear in *Mein Kampf:* "The rulers of present-day Russia are common blood-stained criminals . . . the scum of humanity . . . and now for almost ten years have been carrying on the most cruel and tyrannical regime of all time" (Hitler 1992, p. 604). Behind them, of course, stood "the Jew": "In Russian Bolshevism we must see the attempt undertaken by the Jews in the twentieth century to achieve world domination" (Hitler 1992, p. 604). And to defeat this nefarious scheme the regime in Germany would have to be completely opposed to bolshevism: "The fight against Jewish world Bolshevisation requires a clear attitude towards Soviet Russia. You cannot drive out the Devil with Beelzebub" (Hitler 1992, p. 605).

Good relations with Weimar Germany had been important for the Soviet Union in breaking out of international isolation in the 1920s. Joseph Stalin's policy in the first five year plan of building "socialism in one country" (1928–1933) had made the Soviet Union an attractive site for German investments in return for Soviet raw materials and foodstuffs. At the same time the USSR adopted a defensive and isolated security policy toward the rest of the world. All changed with the consolidation of Hitler's regime and especially his nonaggression pact with Poland in 1934. Under Foreign Minister Maxim Litvinov, the Soviet Union forced a strategy of forming popular fronts against fascism on the Communist parties of Europe (perhaps belatedly learning the lesson of the divided opposition to Hitler), joined the League of Nations in September 1934, and opened up to the West, gaining recognition from the United States in 1933 and signing pacts with France and Czechoslovakia in 1935.

This openness was short-lived. The years leading to World War II saw Stalin's bloody purges and the political and diplomatic isolation of the Soviet Union by the Western powers, symbolized by its exclusion from the Munich Agreement of 1938. Litvinov was replaced by Vyacheslav Molotov in May 1939, and after abortive negotiations with London and Paris the Nazi-Soviet Pact was signed on 23 August. The Soviet Union grabbed eastern Poland, the Baltic states, and Bessarabia and northern Bukovina, and Hitler enjoyed deliveries of Soviet raw materials. When Hitler invaded the USSR in June 1941 it came as a great shock to Stalin and a Soviet people lulled into a false sense of security. The attack was, nevertheless, the logical culmination of Hitler's worldview. He told anyone willing to hear of his relief that the "unnatural" alliance with the Soviets was at last finished.

The ultimate effect of Hitler's aggression, however, was the complete opposite of what he intended. The mobilization of national patriotism, the huge number of war victims, the partisan struggle, the brutality of Germany's conduct of the war and occupation policy, and the final victory after enormous sacrifices bestowed mass loyalty, legitimacy, and power on the Stalinist regime. "The resilience of the Soviet people in the face of the German assault and the remorseless demands of their own regime needs a Tolstoy or a Dostoevsky to do it justice" (Overy 1996, p. 190). The victories of the Red Army and the postwar accords, often interpreted unilaterally by Stalin, spread Bolshevik power deep into central and southeastern Europe.

Related entries: Bagration, Operation; Baltic States; Barbarossa, Operation; Citadel, Operation; Communist Party; Eastern Front; Finland; Foreign Policy; Great Patriotic War; Holocaust; Kursk, Battle of; Molotov, Vyacheslav Mikhailovich; Nazi-Soviet Pact; Poland; Red Army; Romania; Stalin, Joseph; Stalingrad, Battle of; Teheran Conference; Ukraine; Voroshilov, Klement Efremovich; War Crimes; Warsaw Rising; Yalta Conference; Zhukov, Georgi Konstantinovich

Suggestions for further reading:
Overy, Richard J. 1998. *Russia's War.* New York: Allen Lane Penguin Press.

Spain

*I*n the early twentieth century, social and economic backwardness and political polarization blocked the development of democracy and modernization in Spain.

The contradictions caused an explosion in 1936 when military revolt sparked a civil war that turned into the first act of the struggle between fascism and democracy in Europe. The conflict pitted nationalist, traditional, fascist, and conservative forces on one side against republican, socialist, communist, and anarchist forces on the other. Between 1936 and 1939 the war, waged with great savagery, cost the lives of more than 500,000 people and polarized international opinion. While thousands of left-wingers from all over the world enrolled on the republican side in the International Brigades and the Soviet Union aided the republicans while trying to establish communist control over the loyalist cause, Hitler and Benito Mussolini aided Francisco Franco's Nationalists.

Hitler was taking few risks in intervening in Spain. France and Britain refused to intervene, leading to increased Soviet support for the republican side, which in turn allowed Hitler to pose as the scourge of bolshevism. He gave less aid to Franco than did Mussolini, channeling it through the Condor Legion. He had several motives and gained several advantages: ideological sympathy for Franco and the Nationalists; improvement of relations with Mussolini; weakening of British and French influence; access to Spanish raw materials, especially tungsten; and the testing of troops and weapons. After Franco's victory in 1939 Hitler did not get all the support he wanted from the new Spanish dictator, but the de facto toleration of his intervention by the Western democracies fortified and encouraged his risk taking in international affairs.

Related entries: Condor Legion; Foreign Policy; Franco, Francisco; Mussolini, Benito

Speer, Albert (1905–1981)

For some observers, people like Albert Speer, highly educated and sophisti-cated, betraying everything they should have stood for, were the real criminals of the Third Reich. Born in Mannheim, the son of a prosperous architect, Speer pursued his own architectural studies in Karlsruhe, Munich, and Berlin. He first heard Hitler speak in 1930 and joined the National Socialist German Workers' Party (NSDAP, Nazi Party) in January 1931. Always somewhat of an outsider within the Nazi Party, Speer was to use his close relationship with Hitler to achieve fame and fortune and realize his architectural ambitions. Possibly also through him, Hitler could vicariously fulfill his own fantasies. Speer wrote: "I have often asked myself whether he was projecting upon me his unfulfilled youthful dream of being a great architect" (Speer 1971, p. 74).

Speer received his first commissions from the NSDAP in 1932, and from 1933 onward was responsible for the designs and decorations used in the great party rallies. His style became the Nazi style, "the monumental liturgy of the movement" (Wistrich 1982, p. 291), the vast public parades illuminated by inventive and impressive effects that he called "architecture in light." Hitler was greatly impressed by Speer's organizing abilities and technological expertise and regarded him as an "architect of genius," largely because he could turn the Führer's monumental concepts into reality. He was given a series of grandiose projects to design, including the new Reich Chancellery and the plans for the rebuilding of Berlin as "Germania." As inspector-general of the Reich, a title he was given in 1937, he would reconstruct German cities in the massive neoclassical style favored by Hitler. He also headed the "Beauty of Work" department of the German Labor Front.

During the war years Speer accumulated several posts but had to fight for his position against the perpetual intrigues of Hermann Goering, Martin Bormann, and other members of Hitler's inner circle. He was general

Hitler (right, with back to camera) with Albert Speer (center) and Fritz Todt (left, back to camera) at Berchtesgarden. Speer and Todt were two of the more efficient among Hitler's leading followers, and after Todt's death in 1942 Speer succeeded him as effective economic overlord of the Reich. (Popperfoto/Imperial War Museum/Archive Photos)

inspector of water and energy; head of the party's main office for technology; and a member of the Central Planning Office. Then in February 1942 he succeeded Fritz Todt as minister of armaments and war production. In his new post Speer performed miracles in expanding production capacity despite Allied bombing. Due to his relentless goading and tireless efficiency, Hitler's military machine was mobilized for "total war." Arguably, his work prolonged the war for up to two years. Speer displayed no scruples in the wholesale exploitation of slave labor in the service of the Führer but became increasingly disillusioned with Hitler's suicidal policy of "victory or annihilation."

By his own account, Speer did contemplate killing Hitler but preferred to combat the illusions of the Führer and his toadies with rational argument. He hid his loyalty to Hitler behind the façade of being a strictly "nonpolitical" specialist. Nevertheless, he did his best to hinder the implementation of Hitler's notorious "Nero order" for the destruction of German industry in the face of the Allied advance. On trial at Nuremberg in 1946, Speer admitted his personal responsibility for the exploitation of slave labor and collaborating with the SS in using concentration camp prisoners in war production.

Speer was found guilty of crimes against humanity, with some mitigation for his behavior in the final stages of the war. Sentenced to twenty years' imprisonment, he served his full term on the insistence of the Soviet Union and was not released from Spandau prison until 1966. His best-selling memoirs, *Inside the Third Reich* (1970), written while he was in prison, provide a fascinating account of life at the top among the Nazi elite but are also a subtle exercise in self-justification, and details always need to be checked against other sources. He had, after all, given loyal and efficient service to Hitler for fifteen years, helping him to accomplish his criminal schemes. Speer died in London on 1 September 1981 during a visit to Great Britain.

Related entries: Architecture; Berlin; Economic Policy; Industry; Nuremberg Rallies; Total War

Suggestions for further reading:
Sereny, Gitta. 1995. *Albert Speer: His Battle with Truth:* New York: Macmillan.
Speer, Albert. 1971. *Inside the Third Reich.* London: Sphere.
Wistrich, Robert. 1982. *Who's Who in Nazi Germany.* London: Weidenfeld and Nicolson.

Stahlhelm

The "Steel Helmet" soldiers' league was founded in 1918 by Franz Seldte to fight against the left-wing risings and bring the "spirit of frontline comradeship" into politics. Nationalist, authoritarian, anti-Semitic, and anti-Catholic, the league had some 400,000 members by 1925. The Stahlhelm collaborated with Hitler in the campaign against the Young Plan in 1929 and in the Harzburg Front, when its numbers (greater than those of the Sturmabteilung [SA]) made Hitler unhappy. It quickly succumbed to his embrace after the seizure of power. Seldte became minister of labor in Hitler's government; the younger members of the Stahlhelm were absorbed into the SA; and the remaining groups, renamed the "National Socialist German Frontline Combatants' League," were dissolved in November 1935.

Related entries: Harzburg Front; Nationalists; Young Plan

Stalin, Joseph (1879–1953)

Born in Gori, Georgia, Iosif Vissarionovich Dzhugashvili adopted the name Stalin ("man of steel") as an underground revolutionary in Tsarist Russia. Having played a secondary role in the Bolshevik Revolution and civil war, during the 1920s and early 1930s Stalin used his position as general secretary of the Communist Party to remove his rivals among the Bolshevik leadership and consolidate his personal dictatorship over party and country. By the time of Hitler's accession to power in 1933 Stalin had imposed a policy of massive industrialization and the disastrous collectivization of agriculture on the Union of Soviet Socialist Republics (USSR). His principal concern during the 1930s, however, was the elimination of all real and imagined opposition to his personal ascendancy, culminating in the great purges of 1937–1938, which saw untold numbers of people executed or sent to the camps of the Gulag.

Stalin had read *Mein Kampf* and had no illusions about Hitler's ultimate aims in eastern Europe. However, while appreciating that the Führer was as ruthless and callous as he was, Stalin still thought that he could predict Hitler's actions. When Britain and France showed no interest in including the Soviet Union in a system of collective security, Stalin signed the Nazi-Soviet Pact in August 1939, using the occasion to extend the USSR's borders in Poland and the Baltic, imposing his reign of terror in the newly acquired regions, but failing to construct adequate defenses. He seems to have believed that Hitler would not attack before he had completely conquered western Europe and would, in the meantime, stick to the terms of their alliance.

Stalin completely ignored all the signs that Hitler was preparing to attack the Soviet Union, including warnings from Britain, his own spies, and German deserters. When Hitler launched Operation Barbarossa in June 1941, the ill-prepared Red Army, the leadership of which had been decimated by Stalin's purges, suffered disastrous reversals. Recovering from his initial disbelief and panic, however, Stalin set about coordinating the Soviet war effort, refused to leave Moscow as the German army advanced to its very outskirts, and learned to listen to the advice of his better military commanders. Like Hitler, Stalin showed a complete disregard for the human cost of victory. Thousands of Red Army soldiers lost their lives as a result of his order never to retreat or surrender. Again like Hitler, he blamed everyone but himself for reverses. Commanders were removed and soldiers of all ranks executed or otherwise sent to their deaths by his direct orders. In his diplomatic dealings with Winston Churchill and Franklin Delano Roosevelt, Stalin extracted considerable military aid from the Allies and pressed consistently for the opening of a second front. All of the "big three" were acutely aware that the Soviet people were making the greatest sacrifices in defeating Nazism. His journeys to Teheran and Potsdam for Allied conferences were the only foreign trips Stalin ever made.

The defeat of Hitler raised Stalin to new heights of power and adulation. His rule continued to be utterly ruthless until his death in 1953, and victory over the Reich brought no new dawn for the Soviet people. Thousands of prisoners of war disappeared permanently into the Gulag following their liberation, and similar numbers of "enemies of the people," guilty of nothing but trying to follow Stalin's orders, were only rehabilitated after his death. Stalin's dictatorship was as callous and immoral as Hitler's but had different origins and aims, and the two dictators were united only in a common inhumanity. Unlike Hitler, Stalin was a poor public speaker and extraordinarily hard-working. His image was like Hitler's in being based on a supposed modesty and simplicity, but he justified his

power by constant reference to his position as Lenin's "heir" and cultivated an iconic picture of himself as the "good tsar" and "father of the people." That such a man should have been genuinely admired, even loved by the people he ruled with tyrannical thoroughness and by others throughout the world was due in no small degree to his part in Hitler's defeat and may be taken as one of the Führer's strangest achievements. He had helped raise a despised Slav and Bolshevik to a pinnacle that reached higher and lasted longer than his own. The Russian people are still living with the consequences.

Related entries: Baltic States; Barbarossa, Operation; Eastern Front; Finland; Foreign Policy; Great Patriotic War; Kursk, Battle of; Molotov, Vyacheslav Mikhailovich; Nazi-Soviet Pact; Poland; Red Army; Romania; Soviet Union; Stalingrad, Battle of; Teheran Conference; Ukraine; Voroshilov, Klement Efremovich; Yugoslavia; Zhukov, Georgi Konstantinovich

Suggestions for further reading:
Bullock, Alan. 1991. *Hitler and Stalin: Parallel Lives.* London: HarperCollins.
Volkogonov, Dmitri. 1995. *Stalin: Triumph and Tragedy.* Paperback ed. London: Weidenfeld and Nicolson.

Stalingrad, Battle of

*I*f any battle deserves to be called the decisive battle of Hitler's war, it was the struggle for Stalingrad between July 1942 and February 1943. The German 6th Army under Friedrich Paulus invested the former Volgograd, now renamed after Stalin, an important industrial and communications center whose very name made its capture an obsession for Hitler. After weeks of ferocious combat in appalling weather, the Germans had advanced street by street almost to the banks of the Volga, until in November the Soviets unexpectedly launched a counterattack to the north and south of the city, rapidly breaking through lines defended by

Soviet troops during the defense of Stalingrad, the turning point of the German–Soviet war, in the winter of 1942–1943. After Stalingrad the idea of the blitzkrieg was dead, and Hitler, on the defensive, would have to fight the war on Stalin's terms. ((Imperial War Museum/Archive Photos)

Romanian troops. By 25 November some 300,000 German troops, lacking fuel, ammunition, and transportation, were surrounded in the devastated city. Efforts to relieve them by air failed utterly, yet Hitler refused Paulus permission to attempt a breakout to the rear.

Intense and desperate fighting continued as the Red Army tightened the noose on the 6th Army. Hitler promoted Paulus to field marshal on 31 January 1943. Two days later he became the first German field marshal ever to surrender in battle. His troops had run out of ammunition and food. Hitler's anger at Paulus was unjustified and rather pathetic. Two-thirds of the 6th Army had died at Stalingrad, many of them starving or freezing to death. Only a handful of the less than 100,000 survivors captured by the Soviets would ever seen Germany again after being displayed in Moscow en route to prison camps.

Albert Speer summed up the significance of the defeat: "For hitherto there had always been a success to offset every setback; hitherto there had been a new triumph to compensate for all losses or at least make everyone forget them. Now for the first time we had suffered a defeat for which there was no compensation" (Speer 1971, p. 351). Heinz Guderian recorded the permanent effect on Hitler: "His left hand trembled, his back was bent, his gaze was fixed, his eyes protruded but lacked their former lustre, his cheeks were flushed with red. He was more excitable, easily lost his composure and was prone to angry outbursts and ill-considered decisions" (Keegan 1989, p. 458). His interference in military affairs became more irrational than ever, but typically he blamed the people for the disaster. "What you are witnessing," he told the *Gauleiters,* "is a catastrophe of unheard-of magnitude. If the German people fails, then it does not deserve that we fight for its future" (Bullock 1991, p. 877).

Related entries: Eastern Front; Paulus, Friedrich

Suggestions for further reading:
Beevor, Antony. 1998. *Stalingrad.* London:Viking.
Bullock, Alan. 1991. *Hitler and Stalin: Parallel Lives.* London: HarperCollins.
Keegan, John. 1989. *The Second World War.* London: Hutchinson.
Overy, Richard J. 1998. *Russia's War.* New York: Allen Lane Penguin Press.
Speer, Albert. 1971. *Inside the Third Reich.* Paperback ed. London: Sphere Books.

Stauffenberg, Claus Schenk, Graf von (1907–1944)

The key figure in the attempted assassination of Hitler on 20 July 1944 was born in Greifenstein Castle, Upper Franconia, into an old military and aristocratic family. Growing up in a cultivated and devoutly Catholic milieu, the young Stauffenberg gravitated toward the romantic nationalism of the circle of the poet Stefan George but opted for a military career. He initially welcomed the creation of the Third Reich with its promise of a new legal order and as late as 1938 was still advocating the removal of Jews from German cultural life. But after his transfer to the Wehrmacht High Command he was sickened by the conduct of the war on the Eastern Front; the treatment of the occupied territories; and the mass murder of Jews, civilians, and prisoners of war.

Well before the July Plot, Stauffenberg was planning the removal of Hitler from power so that the army could take over. Dissatisfied with the conservatism of oppositionists such as Ludwig Beck and Carl Goerdeler, he toyed with the idea of a corporate state along the lines of Fascist Italy but came to support the Social Democrat Julius Leber rather than Carl Goerdeler as

Hitler's replacement. Posted to Tunisia in February 1943 Stauffenberg was badly wounded, losing his left eye, right hand, half of his left hand, and part of his leg. During his convalescence Stauffenberg decided on the removal of Hitler at all costs, determined that the Führer should not be allowed to drag down the Fatherland with him.

Posted back to Berlin as chief of staff to General Friedrich Olbricht, deputy commander of the Reserve Army, Stauffenberg had access to secret information that allowed him to put Operation Valkyrie into practice. Further promotion as chief of staff to General Friedrich Fromm, head of the Reserve Army, gave him an official excuse for visiting Hitler's headquarters and attending staff conferences without being searched. The opportunity arrived on 20 July 1944 with a meeting at Rastenburg in East Prussia. Stauffenberg carried a bomb in his briefcase, which he left under a map table in the meeting room, but unfortunately Hitler suffered only minor injuries.

Stauffenberg was convinced that Hitler was dead, but uncertainty among the other conspirators in Berlin allowed Josef Goebbels to move against them, while General Fromm, Stauffenberg's superior, refused to join in the plot. Stauffenberg was arrested after an exchange of gunfire in which he was wounded. After a drumhead court-martial assembled by Fromm, Stauffenberg and others were hauled into the courtyard of the War Ministry in Berlin, stood up against a wall in the light of a lorry's headlights, and shot. His last words were: "Long live our sacred Germany."

Related entries: July Plot; Opposition

Suggestions for further reading:
Fest, Joachim. 1996. *Plotting Hitler's Death: The German Resistance to Hitler 1933–1945.* London: Weidenfeld and Nicolson.
Hoffmann, Peter. 1988. *German Resistance to Hitler.* Cambridge MA: Harvard University Press.
———. 1995. *Stauffenberg: A Family History, 1905–1944.* Cambridge: Cambridge University Press.

Strasser, Gregor (1892–1934)

Hitler's principal rival in the early years of the Nazi movement was born in Geisenfeld, Lower Bavaria, on 31 May 1892. After service in World War I, he joined a Freikorps unit and was active in other anticommunist paramilitary groups in Munich. Strasser joined the National Socialist German Workers' Party (NSDAP, Nazi Party) and commanded a Sturmabteilung (SA) detachment during the Beer Hall Putsch. Already on bad terms with Hermann Goering and Ernst Röhm, during Hitler's imprisonment in Landsberg the tireless Strasser founded a Nazi organization in northern Germany, independent from the headquarters in Munich, and his own independent party press, the Kampfverlag. He hired the young Goebbels as editor of his fortnightly newsletter, *NS-Briefe*.

Strasser's northern German wing of the Nazi Party was dominated by its leader's socially revolutionary ideas. Until his death Strasser was to attack what he took to be Hitler's abandonment of the "socialist" ideals of the movement and his alliance with big business, conservative politicians, and the reactionary army leadership. He wrote in one of his journals in 1927, "We National Socialists are enemies, deadly enemies, of the present capitalist system with its exploitation of the economically weak . . . and we are resolved under all circumstances to destroy this system" (Bullock 1991, p. 173), and he once defined National Socialism as "the opposite of what exists today" (Wistrich 1982, p. 303). Strasser was taking his own idiosyncratically socialist path toward the creation of a *völkisch* community, and it was not Hitler's.

Strasser was Reich propaganda leader of the NSDAP from 1926 to 1932, but the rift between him and Hitler over economic policy and outlook grew ever wider. After the elections of November 1932, he lost his place in Hitler's inner circle. Strasser privately expressed his opinions of the Führer's entourage: Goering was a "brutal egoist"; Goebbels "from the bottom up devious"; and Röhm "a swine" (Kershaw 1998, p. 398). On 7 December 1932 the new chancellor, Kurt von Schleicher, offered Strasser the post of vice chancellor and prime minister of Prussia. Hitler rejected any compromise with the Schleicher government and insisted that Strasser refuse the offer. Strasser now faced the choice of either rebelling against Hitler in the hope of taking some of the party with him or resigning his offices and retiring from active politics. He chose the latter course, resigning on 8 December. Whatever his bad feelings toward Strasser may have been, Hitler was angry and shaken by his defection. Strasser lived quietly as director of a chemical combine until the Night of the Long Knives, 30 June 1934, when he was arrested and murdered by the Gestapo on Hitler's orders.

Related entries: National Socialist German Workers' Party; Nazi Movement; Socialism; Strasser, Otto

Suggestions for further reading:
Bullock, Alan. 1991. *Hitler and Stalin: Parallel Lives.* London: HarperCollins.
Kershaw, Ian. 1998. *Hitler 1889–1936: Hubris.* New York: Allen Lane The Penguin Press.
Stachura, Peter D. 1983a. *Gregor Strasser and the Rise of Nazism.* London: Allen and Unwin.
Wistrich, Robert. 1982. *Who's Who in Nazi Germany.* London: Weidenfeld and Nicolson.

Strasser, Otto (1897–1974)

The younger brother of Gregor Strasser had briefly been a Social Democrat and took the radical anticapitalist content of the original Nazi program even more seriously than did Gregor. Otto Strasser joined the National Socialist German Workers' Party (NSDAP, Nazi Party) in 1925 and, together with his brother and the young Josef Goebbels, built up the radical wing of the party in northern Germany. As head of the Kampfverlag publishing house he disseminated his anticapitalist views, supported some strikes called by the Social Democratic trade unions, and demanded the nationalization of industry and the big banks. Strasser's views became increasingly embarrassing for Hitler as he attempted to win support from industrialists. The showdown came in 1930 and led to Otto Strasser's expulsion from the party on 4 July.

Hitler called Otto Strasser "an intellectual white Jew, totally incapable of organization, a Marxist of the purest ilk" (Kershaw 1998, p. 327). There was no place for his social radicalism in a Nazi Party dedicated to the "legal" road to power. He and some of his followers, mostly from Berlin, formed the breakaway Union of Revolutionary National Socialists, known as the Black Front, but failed to win significant support away from Hitler. In exile in Prague Strasser published a stream of pamphlets and books attacking Hitler for betraying Nazi ideals. But he remained no less racist and anti-Semitic than his opponents, which weakened his otherwise articulate attacks on the Third Reich.

Related entries: National Socialist German Workers' Party; Nazi Movement; Socialism; Strasser, Gregor

Suggestions for further reading:
Kershaw, Ian. 1998. *Hitler 1889–1936: Hubris.* New York: Allen Lane The Penguin Press.

Streicher, Julius (1885–1946)

The leading Jew-baiter of the Third Reich was a primary school teacher from Bavaria who joined the National Socialist German Workers' Party (NSDAP, Nazi Party) in 1921 and became one of Hitler's closest associates. In 1925 he was made *Gauleiter* of Franconia, with his headquarters in Nuremberg, which he turned into the leading center of violent anti-Semitism in Germany. A tireless speaker and rabble-rouser, Streicher's political influence came largely from the impact of *Der Stürmer,* which he founded in 1923 and continued to edit until 1945. He could reach and influence millions of Germans with his own poisonous hatred and sadism through the crude and pornographic pages of his own journal. Through *Der Stürmer* Streicher provided a focus for anti-Jewish measures, anticipating and instigating acts of state such as the Nuremberg laws.

Hitler was one of Streicher's most avid readers and declared that he would always stand by him, despite his widespread unpopularity and unsavory reputation. He regarded the "primitive methods" of his old "friend and comrade in arms" as useful and effective in addressing the person in the street and fully in tune with his own disdainful view of the mentality of the masses. Declaring that Streicher's repellent newspaper was amusing and cleverly done, Hitler resisted repeated requests to suppress *Der Stürmer* as a "cultural disgrace." The paper made Streicher a rich man: he accumulated positions, including director of the "Central Committee for Defense against Jewish Atrocity and Boycott Propaganda"; enlarged his newspaper business, eventually owning ten papers; and extended his personal fortune by dealing in expropriated Jewish property in Franconia.

Streicher's corruption, dishonesty, sadism, brutality, and sexual peccadilloes were intolerable even to his Nazi colleagues, and by 1939 party officials were constantly complaining about his psychopathic behavior. Even Hitler could not ignore the united front of the Nazi potentates against Streicher. His dismissal from his party posts in 1940, however, was occasioned by his specific allegation that Hermann Goering was impotent and that his daughter had been conceived by artificial insemination. This was more serious than charges of rape and his admitted horsewhipping of political prisoners. A commission sent to Franconia by Goering examined Streicher's business dealings and personal life and led to his downfall. But he continued to edit *Der Stürmer* until the end of the Third Reich. Condemned at Nuremberg for "incitement to murder and extermination," Streicher was hanged on 16 October 1946. He regarded his death sentence as "a triumph for world Jewry" and went to the scaffold proclaiming his eternal loyalty to Hitler.

Related entries: Anti-Semitism; Jews and Jewish Policy; *Stürmer, Der*

"Strength through Joy"

The name of the German Labor Front's recreational organization was said to have originated in a suggestion by Hitler. Based on the Italian Fascist "After Work" organization, "Strength through Joy" (*Kraft durch Freude,* or KDF) presented theater performances and concerts; directed workplace sports for "military fitness training" and "racial improvement"; ran the "Beauty of Work" office, which was concerned with improving working conditions and the aesthetic appearance of the workplace; and organized cheap vacation trips and cruises in Germany and abroad for approximately 10 million people up to 1938. The Volkswagen car was also produced by the KDF. The purpose of KDF activities was to send people back to their workplaces "with new strength and purpose," but the undoubted popularity, especially of the vacations, lay in their fulfilling a desperate need for fun and diversion. It was popularly said that people had lost strength through too much joy. The increased leisure offered to workers did not mean that productivity rose, but it did mean that people could escape the constant political pressure and "let themselves go" for a while before knuckling down to work for Hitler's war plans.

Related entries: German Labor Front; Social Policy; Volkswagen; Working Class

Sturmabteilung (SA)

The SA, popularly known as the Brownshirts, was founded in Munich in 1921 to protect Nazi Party members and their activities, principally at public meetings, but soon began to seek out and create violent confrontation with the left-wing enemies of the National Socialist German Workers' Party (NSDAP, Nazi Party). Ernst Röhm recruited former servicemen and members of the Freikorps, from which they copied their style of uniform and raised-arm salute. Acting under Röhm's orders rather than Hitler's, the SA propelled the Nazis to public attention in Bavaria, where their violence was viewed with complacency by the sympathetic state authorities until the SA was banned after the Beer Hall Putsch of 1923. They remained under the wing of the *Frontbann* organization of former soldiers before re-emerging in 1925 with the reformation of the party.

In November 1926, the north German Pfeffer von Salomon was made chief of the SA, now no longer dominated by Bavarians. In the late 1920s recruitment increased among young people, especially in working-class areas, feeding on the youth discontent fueled by unemployment, and street brawls with Communists and the socialist Reichsbanner became commonplace. Violence served as a virility test and rite of passage for rootless young men to whom membership in the SA gave a sense of belonging, square meals, and an impressive uniform. Statistics about SA membership are unreliable because of the high turnover of members, many of whom were not too active or had joined for opportunistic rather than political reasons. By January 1931 there were probably about 100,000

Hitler with Ernst Röhm (center). Despite their close friendship Röhm's SA was brought to heel and their leader murdered in the Night of the Long Knives on 30 June 1934. (Culver Pictures)

Brownshirts. In that year Röhm was recalled to head the SA, and under his energetic leadership membership grew impressively, and the territorial organization was consolidated. In 1932 the SA had nearly 300,000 members, with an elaborate central command organization and twenty-one regional formations.

As the SA grew so did rivalry with Heinrich Himmler's SS and Röhm's pretensions to turn his organization into a national defense force. The SA leaders saw it as a revolutionary and insurgent body, dedicated to a radical economic as well as political revolution. Hitler, however, wanted to keep it subservient to his leadership, and as Nazi influence grew from 1930 to 1932 the SA was to Hitler a double-edged sword. Street violence was useful, but overhasty action could be disastrous. Hitler walked the tightrope successfully, even at the cost of banning the SA briefly during 1932. "The SA," Alan Bullock writes, "were to be the

shock troops of a revolution that was never to be made" (Bullock 1991, p. 256).

Once Hitler was in power, new members flooded into the SA. In 1934 membership was approaching 3 million, and intimidation and street violence reached new levels, effectively destroying any potential opposition. The SA leadership lived in feverish expectation of revolution, but Hitler was busy consolidating his power with the help of the old conservative elites. It was agreed that the SA, along with the SS and the Stahlhelm, would be subordinated to the Ministry of War, but this only increased Röhm's expectations of a national defense role for his men. Fear of the SA drew the army, the party, and the SS into an alliance urging Hitler to act. After typically hesitating for months, Hitler acted to destroy the SA's power in June 1934 with the bloodletting of the Night of the Long Knives.

After 1934 the SA, under the leadership of Viktor Lutze, became thoroughly subservient to the Führer, decisively stripped of its revolutionary trappings. Party leaders sympathetic to the original SA were removed in purges during 1934 and 1935. The Brownshirts now paraded to order, smashing Jewish shop windows and lording it over the rest of the population. They collected the Winterhilfe, provided part-time military training for future members of the Wehrmacht, and during the war carried our air-raid duties. But as a political elite the SA had lost out definitively to the SS, and the days of SA radicalism had been buried in the blood and murder of 1934.

Related entries: National Socialist German Workers' Party; Nazi Movement; Night of the Long Knives; Röhm, Ernst

Suggestions for further reading:
Bessel, Richard. 1984. *Political Violence and the Rise of Nazism: The Storm Troopers in Eastern Germany 1925–1934.* New Haven: Yale University Press.
Bullock, Alan. 1991. *Hitler and Stalin: Parallel Lives.* London: HarperCollins.
Fischer, Conan. 1983. *Stormtroopers: A Social, Economic, and Ideological Analysis.* London: Allen and Unwin.
Merkl, Peter H. 1980. *The Making of a Stormtrooper.* Princeton: Princeton University Press.

Stürmer, Der

The most notorious of Nazi newspapers was the personal property of Julius Streicher, but up to 1940 it was a most powerful means of imbuing the masses with Hitler's anti-Semitism. After 1933 it was posted in all German cities and villages, proclaiming its message, "The Jews are our misfortune," to all readers, whether they bought it or not. Founded by Streicher in Nuremberg in 1923, it only had a small circulation in its early years, reaching about 20,000 by 1933 and a peak of 600,000 in 1940 before declining during the war years. *Der Stürmer* only had one theme—Jew-baiting—presented in popular format, openly porno-

graphic with stories of sexually rapacious Jews and Jewish ritual murder. Presenting Streicher's pornographic fantasies, even more horrific than Hitler's, *Der Stürmer* represented the most vile degradation of the German mass media under the Third Reich.

Related entries: Jews and Jewish Policy; Press; Streicher, Julius

Sudetenland

The area of western Czechoslovakia bordering Germany known as the Sudetenland was home to a German population of some 3.3 million. Conflicts over demands for Sudeten autonomy had simmered since 1919 but only erupted seriously in 1937–1938 when the flames were fanned by Hitler. In 1933 Hitler told the Sudeten Nazi, Hans Krirsch, that they "should make their own policy; the Reich could not help them for a long time" (Weinberg 1970, p. 109). The Sudeten German Party (SDP), founded by Konrad Henlein in October 1933, therefore, initially fought merely to repair the "injustices done since 1918–1919" and for autonomy within Czechoslovakia. Financed by Berlin, it gained the support of two-thirds of German voters, and its membership rose from 70,000 in October 1934 to 1.3 million in July 1938.

The SDP thus became Hitler's instrument for launching his claims to the Sudetenland in 1938. He encouraged Henlein to make unacceptable demands to the Prague government and propagated half-true reports of excesses against the Sudeten Germans. Hitler was by now determined to destroy Czechoslovakia, using the Sudetenland as his pretext. In a speech on 12 September 1938 he offered military support to the Sudeten Germans, precipitating the crisis that was only ended by the Munich Agreement and the annexation of the Sudetenland.

German troops occupy the Sudetenland in 1938. The reaction of the crowd seems curiously sullen. (Archive Photos).

Related entries: Czechoslovakia; Henlein, Konrad; Munich Agreement

Suggestions for further reading:
Weinberg, Gerhard L. 1970. *The Foreign Policy of Hitler's Germany: Diplomatic Revolution in Europe, 1933–1936.* Chicago: University of Chicago Press.

Swastika

The swastika became the official symbol of the National Socialist German Workers' Party (NSDAP, Nazi Party) and Nazi Germany, chosen personally by Hitler. His "token of freedom" became a symbol of slavery for the whole of Europe. Derived from the Sanskrit *svastika,* meaning "salutary sign," the symmetrical cross with four arms extending at right angles appears with variations in European and Asiatic cultures dating back to the third millen-

nium B.C.E. and more rarely in Africa and Central America. It was traditionally interpreted mainly as a solar symbol and in India and Japan even today promises good luck and protection from disaster. In Greece it was a symbol of the sun, while in Germanic folk tradition it could be Thor's hammer, a sun wheel, a wolf trap, a mill wheel, crossed lightning bolts, or a fertility sign.

The swastika was rediscovered as an "Aryan" symbol in German nationalist circles in the late nineteenth century. It became the official emblem of the German Gymnasts' League, inspired by Friedrich Ludwig Jahn, the "father of gymnastics," as a symbol of their German identity. The way was prepared for its appropriation by racist ideologues by the Munich poet Alfred Schuler in the 1890s and the *völkisch* writer Guido von List in his *The Character of the Aryo-Germans* (1910). In the aftermath of World War I various anti-Semitic

SA men carrying standards and banners with swastika emblems parade through the Brandenburg Gate after the seizure of power in 1933. (Culver Pictures)

organizations and paramilitary Freikorps units used the swastika as their emblem, as did the Austrian National Socialists, so that it was already widely associated with reac-

tion and racism before its adoption by the Nazis.

Hitler became familiar with the swastika principally through the *Ostara,* a series of pamphlets by the racist ideologue Josef Lanz, and the Thule Society, which sought to coordinate nationalist and *völkisch* groups in Bavaria after 1918. He designed the swastika flag, which became the official banner of the NSDAP in 1920, and it was declared the sole national flag of Germany by the Reich Flag Law of September 1935. The swastika, Hitler wrote in *Mein Kampf,* represents "the mission of the struggle for the victory of the Aryan man, and, by the same token, the victory of the idea of creative work, which as such always has been and always will be anti-Semitic" (Hitler 1992, p. 452). The flag appropriated the black, white, and red colors of Prussia and imperial Germany, rejecting the black, red, and gold of the Weimar Republic, which expressed liberal and democratic ideals going back to the 1848 revolution. Introducing the flag law in the Reichstag, Hermann Goering declared: "The swastika has become a sacred symbol for us—the symbol around which all our hopes and dreams revolve, under which we have endured suffering, under which we have fought, sacrificed, and ultimately, for the benefit of the German people, triumphed" (Hoffmann 1996, p. 17).

The swastika symbol, now standardized, and swastika flag became the "true symbol of the race" in Nazi pageantry and propaganda, the object of a quasi-religious cult. Seas of flags overwhelmed the senses at the Nuremberg rallies, and the Hitler Youth anthem, "Unsere Fahne flattert uns voran" (our flag flutters before us), declared that "the flag is greater than death." "To the average Nazi Party member," Hilmar Hoffmann writes, "the swastika flag was equated directly with the Führer who was, as it were, present in every fold. . . . The flag was Hitler's ubiquitous deputy. Identifying with the flag was synonymous to identifying with the Führer" (Hoffmann 1996, p. 19). By his personal appropriation of the swastika, Hitler created a sign still recog-

nized throughout the world as the symbol of anti-Semitic hatred.

Related entries: Anti-Semitism; Architecture; Cinema; Nuremberg Laws; Nuremberg Rallies; Propaganda

Suggestions for further reading:
Hitler, Adolf. 1992. *Mein Kampf.* Trans. Ralph Manheim. Intro. by D. C. Watt. London: Pimlico.
Hoffmann, Hilmar. 1996. *The Triumph of Propaganda: Film and National Socialism, 1933–1945.* Providence and Oxford: Berghahn Books.
Mosse, George L. 1961. "The Mystical Origins of National Socialism," *Journal of the History of Ideas* 22, pp. 81–96.

Sweden

As the leading industrial nation in Scandinavia, Sweden was of considerable importance for Hitler's economic policy and especially for the German war economy. On the outbreak of war Sweden skillfully used delaying tactics to safeguard its neutrality against Hitler's bullying and Allied threats of economic warfare and blockades. Sweden supplied Germany with high-grade iron ore, covering some 30 percent of military needs, ball bearings, machinery, wood, foodstuffs, and ships. It also had economic treaties with Britain and the United States and conducted limited trade with countries other than Germany. After the occupation of Denmark and Norway and Finland's entry into the war as an ally of Germany, Sweden was effectively surrounded by the Third Reich. Cut off from the west between 1940 and 1943, Sweden's independence and neutrality were more precarious than ever. They were preserved at the price of uninterrupted deliveries of war materials to Germany backed by ready extension of credit, as well as guaranteed transit for German military and freight transports through northern Sweden. From 1943 Sweden gradually extricated itself from Hitler's political and commercial stranglehold and also acted as a refuge for Jews from Denmark escaping the Final Solution.

Related entries: Economic Policy; Trade Policy

Switzerland

Hitler had sympathizers in Switzerland, led by a certain Wilhelm Gustloff, but Fascist and Nazi-style movements gained little support. From being a member of the League of Nations, the country reverted to "integral," unconditional neutrality in 1938. After Hitler's invasion of France in 1940 Switzerland was completely isolated and surrounded by the Axis. It adapted to the situation by collaborating to the extent of maintaining press censorship, ignoring violations of strict neutrality, and allowing German and Italian transport of materials using the Gotthard railway. However, a general mobilization of the Swiss citizen army was maintained; the government was a broad alliance of Left and Right for the "spiritual defense of the country"; and a military strategy of deep defense ensured that any attack would be costly and troublesome. Switzerland accepted political refugees, acting as a haven for free speech in the German language, and was the preferred place for secret contacts between the combatants, including preparations for the German surrender in Italy in April 1945. The role of Swiss banks in handling "Nazi gold" and money and belongings looted from Jews in Germany and occupied Europe remains controversial to this day.

T

Teheran Conference

When Franklin Delano Roosevelt, Joseph Stalin, and Winston Churchill met in the capital of Iran in November 1943, they decided that a second front would be opened against Germany by cross-channel invasion in May 1944. The plan for Operation Overlord had been in preparation for several months, and although Churchill was less attracted to the project than were the Americans, he found himself squeezed between the new superpowers. The Teheran meeting was a major success for Stalin: it was evident that the major voices in the postwar settlement in Germany and Europe would be those of the Soviet Union and the United States.

Related entries: Churchill, Winston Leonard Spencer; Roosevelt, Franklin Delano; Stalin, Joseph

Suggestions for further reading:
Kimball, Warren F. 1997. *Forged in War: Churchill, Roosevelt and the Second World War.* London: HarperCollins.

Theresienstadt

The camp established in November 1941 in the town of Theresienstadt (Terezin), some 36 miles north of Prague, was theoretically intended as a ghetto for elderly Jews but in reality served as a transit camp to the death camps. Cleaned up and refurbished for visits by the Red Cross, it was presented to the world as the "acceptable face" of Nazi Jewish policy. In 1944 a propaganda film, *The Führer Makes the Gift of a City to the Jews,* was produced to show Hitler's humane policy. Some inmates were indeed tricked out of money to pay for lifelong care in the "Reich Home for the Elderly" at Theresienstadt. In reality 34,000 died, undernourished and worked to death, in the overcrowded, unsanitary main and satellite camps, and nearly 86,000 were deported to the extermination camps. Nevertheless, Theresienstadt, half-camp, half-ghetto, illustrates the lengths to which Hitler and his Reich would go to hide the reality of the Final Solution from the world.

Related entries: Concentration Camps; Final Solution

Thierack, Otto (1889–1946)

A lawyer who had served as public prosecutor in Leipzig and then Dresden, Thierack was an early member of the National Socialist German Workers' Party (NSDAP, Nazi Party) who became leader of the National Socialist Lawyers' League. In 1936 Hitler chose him to become president of the People's Court in Berlin, providing secret, summary justice without appeal for people accused of crimes against the Reich. Thierack became minister of justice in August 1942 with a brief from Hitler empowering him to disregard existing law in order to establish a "National Socialist administration of justice." He thus provided a pseudolegal cover for the imprisonment and "extermination by labor" of the Reich's conquered subjects, including Jews, Gypsies, Russians, Ukrainians, Poles, and "anti-social" Germans and Czechs. Thierack was quite open about the effects of his policies: the law was making its contribution to the extermination of inferior slave peoples. Even so he was criticized by Hitler for not being tough enough and sticking to legalistic niceties. Arrested at the end of the war, Thierack hanged himself in an internment camp on 26 October 1946 before he could be brought to justice at Nuremberg.

Related entries: Law

Third Reich

The epithet applied by the Nazis to their new German state has come to be used as the standard term to describe Hitler's time in power from 1933 to 1945. The term was borrowed from an eponymous book by Arthur Moeller van den Bruck, published in 1923, one of a number of works looking to a new messianic leader for Germany. Hermann Broch's 1932 novel, *The Sleepwalkers,* called this new messiah "the Healer who by his own actions will give meaning to the incomprehensible events of the age, so that Time will begin anew" (Griffin 1999, p. 43).

Initially, the idea of the Third Reich was meant to establish Hitler's place in the con-

tinuity of German history. The First Reich was the Holy Roman Empire, abolished by Napoleon in 1806; the Second Reich was the Hohenzollern empire, proclaimed in 1871 and destroyed in 1918; the Third Reich was the rule of Hitler, inaugurating a new period of glory for the German people. The Weimar Republic was thus to be expunged from history as a mere interim period of disorder and national humiliation. But the idea of the Third Empire was also linked to the medieval Christian concept, first expressed by the twelfth-century Italian mystic Joachim of Fiore, in which the Third Age of the Spirit would see the foundation of the "earthly Jerusalem," following the ages of the Father (the Law) and the Son (the Church). Hitler would embody the new age when ideas, the ideal Germany, would be reconciled with reality, and the Reich would be not only a territorial empire but also a new realm of the spirit.

The use of Christian imagery was as vague as it was confused. The Third Reich became mixed up with the "Thousand-Year Reich," which would last as long as the reign of Christ after the resurrection of the righteous and under Hitler came to represent the culmination of German history through National Socialism. Both terms risked becoming ridiculous when the realities of Nazi rule became evident. The liturgical pageantry of Nazism, expressed most vividly in the Nuremberg rallies, asserted a new conception of time appealing to Nazi fanatics and those who swallowed whole the messianic vision of Hitler but invited scorn from nonbelievers or those who saw Hitler as a merely human leader, even if they approved of many of his actions. And Nazi propagandists saw the dangers of an overuse of grandiose words and concepts. The idea of a Third Reich was useful during the period of the seizure of power and accumulation of power in Hitler's hands, but in 1939 the Propaganda Ministry prohibited its use in the press. Instead, the term "das Reich" would be used to designate Germany and its new possessions, brought together as a single national unity. The Germans were to refer to it as the British referred to "the Empire," without a number possibly implying that there might be others. Similarly, Hitler himself never referred directly to the "Thousand-Year Reich," though his apocalyptic style of speech making did lead him to declare in 1934 that there would be no more revolutions in Germany for a thousand years and in 1940 that the campaign against France would settle Germany's fate for the next thousand years. He was, however, offering a hostage to fortune with an idea exposed by events as absurd.

Related entries: Hitler Myth; Nuremberg Rallies; Propaganda

Suggestions for further reading:
Griffin, Roger. 1999. "Party Time: The Temporal Revolution of the Third Reich," *History Today* 49 (4), pp. 43–49.

Thyssen, Fritz (1873–1951)

Heir to one of the greatest industrial fortunes in Germany, Fritz Thyssen was the first leading industrialist to back Hitler. An ardent nationalist who had been arrested for organizing passive resistance against the French occupation of the Ruhr in 1923, Thyssen first heard Hitler speak in the same year and became convinced that he was the leader who would save Germany from bolshevism. He became a heavy financial contributor to the Nazi Party and joined it in December 1931. Thyssen brought Hitler into contact with the coal and steel magnates of the Rhineland and Westphalia. He invited him to speak to a meeting of industrialists in Düsseldorf on 27 January 1932, where Hitler defended private property, stressed the need for a powerful state, and assured them that they had nothing to fear from Nazi radicals.

Thyssen accepted various posts after Hitler's accession to power, including that of councilor for life in Prussia. By the late 1930s, however, he had become disillusioned with the regime's rearmament drive, its anti-Catholicism, and the persecution of the Jews. He fled to Switzerland in December 1939, and in a letter to Hitler stated that his doubts about the Third Reich had begun with the dismissal of Franz von Papen, followed by "the persecution of Christianity," and finally Kristallnacht on 9–10 November 1938, which had shocked him profoundly. The Nazi-Soviet Pact followed by the outbreak of war had been the final straw.

Thyssen's appeal for a restoration of "freedom, right, and humanity" cut predictably little ice with Hitler. He was stripped of his German citizenship in absentia, and his property was confiscated. His memoirs, *I Paid Hitler,* appeared in English in 1941 and took the form of an anguished settling of accounts with the regime that "has ruined Germany," but he was less than totally honest about the extent of his financial relationship with the Nazis, to whom he had given over a million marks over a period of fifteen years. Arrested in France by the Vichy police, Thyssen was returned to Germany, where he was imprisoned for the rest of the war. He died in Buenos Aires on 8 February 1951.

Related entries: Industry

Tiso, Josef, Monsignor (1887–1947)

The Catholic priest Tiso, a founder of the Slovak People's Party in 1918, became prime minister of an autonomous Slovakia on 6 October 1938 following the Munich Agreement. When the Prague government declared him deposed on 10 March 1939 he placed Slova-

kia under German protection and pronounced its independence on 14 March.
Tiso became Slovakia's president on 26
October 1939 and proved himself a willing accomplice of Hitler. He took his puppet state into the Tripartite Pact and the
Anti-Comintern Pact and collaborated in
the application of the Final Solution to the
Jews of Slovakia. When the Slovak Resistance rose in August 1944 Tiso supported
its suppression by the SS. He fled to the
West in April 1945 as the Red Army entered Slovakia but was extradited to
Czechoslovakia. Tiso was sentenced to
death for high treason and executed on 18
April 1947.

Related entries: Czechoslovakia; Resistance
Movements

Tito, Josip Broz (1892–1980)

One of the founders of the Yugoslav
Communist Party in 1920, Tito
spent six years in prison between 1928 and
1934, after which he moved to Moscow.
After fighting in the Spanish Civil War, he
returned to Yugoslavia following Hitler's invasion and organized the Communist Partisans against the occupiers. His forces tied
down German divisions in Yugoslavia, significantly hampering Hitler's war effort, but
Tito was equally ruthless in settling accounts with collaborators and rival Resistance leaders. His forces, rather than the invading Soviets, liberated Yugoslavia. After
forming a provisional Yugoslav government
and ousting noncommunists, he became
head of state of the People's Republic of
Yugoslavia. The only Communist to successfully defy both Hitler and Stalin, Tito
was to die in his bed in 1980, still president
of the republic he had founded more than
thirty years earlier.

Related entries: Resistance Movements;
Yugoslavia

Tobruk, Battles of

The Libyan port of Tobruk became a
powerful symbol of Britain's fortunes during the desert war and ultimately
of its resistance against Hitler. During
Erwin Rommel's offensive of 1941 the
British garrison of Tobruk held out against
his siege from April until 4 December. On
24 June 1942, however, Rommel took Tobruk in a single day, forcing the surrender
of 35,000 British troops. When it was abandoned by Rommel on 13 November 1942,
during his retreat after El Alamein, it was a
not particularly important but deeply satis-
fying moment for Hitler's adversaries.

Related entries: El Alamein, Battle of; North
Africa; Rommel, Erwin

Todt, Fritz (1891–1942)

Hitler's road builder and head of the
Todt Organization was working as a
civil engineer when he joined the Nazi
Party in January 1922. An unassuming but
expert technologist, he was made an SS
colonel in 1931 and on Hitler's accession to
power became inspector general of the German road and highway system. Over the
next nine years he accumulated in his hands
responsibility for the construction industry,
including military fortifications and the autobahn system. The Todt Organization, his
own army of workers, was created to complete the building of the West Wall, or
Siegfried Line, before the outbreak of war.

As head of construction within the Four-
Year Plan, Todt clashed frequently with Hermann Goering but was always supported by
Hitler. Made minister of armaments and
munitions in March 1940 and inspector
general of roads, water, and power in 1941
and put in charge of the Head Office for
Technology within the Nazi Party, Todt
managed all the major technical tasks relat-

ing to the war effort. He used a vast army of slave labor and divisions of troops in his organization. By the autumn of 1941, however, Todt had become pessimistic about the military situation. He served Hitler loyally but refused to get involved in Nazi power intrigues. Todt was killed in an air crash at Rastenburg in East Prussia on 8 February 1942. He was buried in the military cemetery in Berlin, and most of his responsibilities were taken over by Albert Speer.

Related entries: Autobahnen; Siegfried Line; Todt Organization

Todt Organization

One of the most important specialized organizations of the Third Reich, the Todt Organization (OT), named after its director, Fritz Todt, was used for the construction of military and related sites, especially in occupied Europe. Labor service "volunteers" and private construction firms were first used by the OT in the building of the Siegfried Line in 1938–1939. During the war hundreds of thousands of foreign civilian workers, prisoners of war, and in places close to concentration camps, Jewish and other slave laborers were used to repair war damage and construct military-related projects. It was one of the few organizations in Hitler's Reich to enjoy extensive administrative autonomy and worked all the more efficiently as a result.

Related entries: Labor Service; Todt, Fritz

Total War

In a huge rally at the Sportspalast in Berlin on 18 February 1943, Josef Goebbels admitted that the Reich faced a severe crisis and announced wide-reaching measures, declaring that "only the supreme effort, the most total war, can and will meet this peril" (Bramsted 1965, p. 264). Hitler had by then disappeared from sight as a public speaker, so it fell to the minister of propaganda to proclaim the new policy. Any pretense of sheltering the German people from the consequences of Nazi aggression was abandoned. With a banner proclaiming "Total War—Shortest War" at his back, Goebbels announced the transfer of men from the civilian sector to the army and a strengthening of the war effort in industry. However, Hitler could never be brought to agree wholeheartedly to the complete mobilization urged and planned for by Goebbels and Albert Speer. The effort was mounted under Speer's orders as much despite Hitler as because of him and was hindered by the infighting among the Nazi leadership. Also, the effort led to resentment among the working class, partly because of the belated mobilization of women in the workforce, and among the lower middle classes when "inessential" shops and businesses were closed. In the final analysis, the popularity of the Führer and his regime was incompatible with the total mobilization of German society, which came far too late in the summer of 1944.

Related entries: Economic Policy; Industry; Propaganda; Public Opinion; Speer, Albert; Volkssturm; Women

Suggestions for further reading:
Bramsted, Ernest K. 1965. *Goebbels and National Socialist Propaganda 1925–1945*. East Lansing: Michigan State University Press.
Hancock, Eleanor. 1991. *National Socialist Leadership and Total War, 1941–1945*. New York: St. Martin's Press.

Totenkopfverbände

The SS "Death Head Units" under SS-Gruppenführer Theodor Eicke guarded the concentration camps, where, "incited against" the prisoners, they were the obedient and ruthless executors of Hitler's "will." The brutalized units, with their special uniforms sporting a skull on the right collar patch, numbered about 9,000 by the end of 1938. In November 1939 they were combined into the Waffen SS, forming the core of the Totenkopf (death's head) Division. Numbering about 24,000 by 1944, they were distinguished, even within the SS, by their extraordinarily inhumane conduct of the war and were involved in a number of major war crimes. The soldierly qualities they undoubtedly showed during the fighting on the Eastern Front fades into insignificance by comparison.

Related entries: Concentration Camps; Dachau; Schutzstaffel; Waffen SS; War Crimes

Trade Policy

German foreign trade declined dramatically during the Depression and continued to stagnate under Hitler. Nor was there any discernible novelty in trade policy, despite the rearmament drive and the proclaimed goal of autarchic self-sufficiency. Germany was perpetually short of foreign exchange for the import of food, textiles, and industrial raw materials, but the prices of most imports fell during the 1930s, a factor of major importance in securing supplies of foodstuffs and expanding the armaments industry. Exports, however, needed subsidy in the face of declining world prices.

The policy of "autarchy" implied import substitution for raw materials and food, but the scale of expansion in the armaments and related industries was well beyond Germany's substitution capacity. The trend, therefore, was for imports of industrial raw materials to increase proportionately against those of foodstuffs, forcing the population to choose "guns or butter." This could not

be sustained indefinitely, and in the last years of peace the gap narrowed. Imports of iron ore, however, especially from Sweden, continued to rise. The drive for rearmament continued to distort German trade patterns and place severe strains on the country's currency reserves right up to the outbreak of war.

Related entries: Agriculture; Economic Policy; Four-Year Plan; Industry; Rearmament

Suggestions for further reading:
Overy, Richard J. 1996. *The Nazi Economic Recovery.* 2nd ed. Cambridge: Cambridge University Press.

Trade Unions

In Hitlerian ideology trade unions were instruments of class struggle, incompatible with the revived national community *(Volksgemeinschaft)*. They had, therefore, to be not merely "coordinated" but destroyed. Under the Weimar Republic there were three separate groups of unions: the free trade unions, the largest group, closely associated with the Social Democratic Party; the Catholic Christian trade unions, linked with the Center Party; and the smaller Hirsch-Dünker unions, traditionally allied with the liberals. The free trade unions were "coordinated" on 2 May 1933; the Hirsch-Dünker unions voluntarily "coordinated" themselves; and after a brief respite while Hitler negotiated the Concordat with the Vatican, the Christian unions were disbanded at the end of June. All workers were now to be members of Robert Ley's German Labor Front, which theoretically took over trade union functions, but in a new spirit of cooperation within the national community.

Related entries: Center Party; Economic Policy; German Labor Front; Industry; Labor Relations; National Socialist Factory Cell Organization; Socialism; Working Class

Treblinka

The extermination camp of Treblinka could claim a death toll second only to that of Auschwitz. Located only 45 miles from Warsaw, this camp was the place where the majority of the Jews from the Warsaw ghetto were killed. During the period of its operation from July 1942 to August 1943, some 900,000 people were murdered, with no selection process as at Auschwitz: victims were taken straight to the gas chambers. The camp was officially dissolved in October 1943, and the barracks and fences were dismantled by the last Jewish inmates before they too were shot. The Ukrainian camp personnel were then lodged in newly built housing on the site.

Related entries: Extermination Camps; Holocaust; Warsaw Ghetto

Tripartite Pact

The agreement among Germany, Italy, and Japan, drawn up by Joachim von Ribbentrop and signed on 27 September 1940, recognized the leadership of Germany and Italy in establishing a new order in Europe and of Japan in creating its new order in greater East Asia. Ribbentrop wanted to extend the pact to include the Soviet Union, establishing a global coalition for the defeat of Britain and partition of the British Empire. This was in effect an alternative policy to Hitler's, and it is surprising that the Führer was persuaded to invite Vyacheslav Molotov to Berlin for discussions. Joseph Stalin, however, saw the Tripartite Pact as directed against the Soviet Union, and Molotov, unimpressed by Hitler's flights of fancy about a division of the globe, insisted on Russia's interests in eastern Europe. Bulgaria, Hungary, Romania, and Slovakia joined the Pact in early 1941, joined briefly by Yugoslavia before the coup against the Axis led by General Dusan Simovic on 26–27 March 1941.

Related entries: Italy; Japan; Ribbentrop, Joachim von

Turkey

During the interwar years the Turkish republic, inspired by its founding president, Kemal Atatürk, modernized rapidly and became a respected member of the concert of European nations. It was potentially a valuable ally for Hitler, who sent Franz von Papen to be German ambassador in Ankara, but up to 1939 it maintained a neutral position, including a treaty of alliance with Great Britain and France signed on 19 October 1939. As Hitler's power grew so did German influence in Turkey, culminating in a treaty of friendship signed on 16 June 1941 but "subject to existing commitments." But as the tide of war turned against Hitler, Turkey moved closer to the Allies. On 1 May 1944 Turkey ceased delivery of its valuable chrome shipments to Germany; on 2 August diplomatic relations were broken off; and on 1 March 1945 Turkey declared war on Germany.

Related entries: Middle East

U

U-boats

German submarines (U-boats) had been horribly effective as commerce raiders in World War I, and Hitler restarted construction in the mid-1930s. By 1939 the fifty-five U-boats constituted a small but highly professional force under the command of Admiral Karl Doenitz. More than 1,000 new boats were built in all, and between 1940 and 1943 they took an enormous toll on Allied shipping in the Atlantic, the Arctic, and to a lesser extent the Mediterranean. From mid-1943 onward, however, Allied antisubmarine warfare outstripped the Germans in tactics, technology, and intelligence, and by the end of the war, although more than 350 U-boats were still in action, they had ceased to be a major threat.

Related entries: Atlantic, Battle of the; Doenitz, Karl; Navy; Rearmament

Ukraine

The rich agricultural lands of the Ukraine suffered terribly under Stalin's reign of terror. As many as one-third of the population had perished in the famine resulting from the forced collectivization of agriculture in the 1930s. Then the western Ukraine, formerly under Polish rule, was taken over by the Russians under the Nazi-Soviet Pact, and more than a million people were deported. Thousands of imprisoned Ukrainian nationalists were massacred by the Soviet People's Commissariat for Internal Affairs (NKVD) as the Germans advanced in 1941. It is little wonder, then, that German troops entering the Ukraine were widely welcomed as liberators. However, Hitler's racist ideology ensured that such goodwill was quickly squandered by Nazi policies. While the Germans did not lack for collaborators, including the notorious Ukrainian SS units who worked in the extermination camps and eventually manned some of the defenses of northern France, the tyrannical occupation policies of *Reichskommissar* Erich Koch, fully backed by Hitler, turned the majority of the population against the invaders.

The Nazi regime had maintained contacts with exiled Ukrainian nationalists, including rival branches of the Organization of Ukrainian Nationalists (OUN), but Hitler despised these émigré circles, and they were banned from even entering the occupied areas. In Hitler's fantastic vision of postwar Europe the Ukraine was to be Germany's "breadbasket" and the population of Slav *Untermenschen* reduced to the level of slaves working for an elite of Aryan settlers. When the branch of the OUN

The launching of a new submarine during the war. During their heyday from 1940 to late 1942 Hitler's U-boats nearly brought Great Britain to its knees through unrestricted submarine warfare against merchant shipping. (Archive Photos)

headed by Stepan Bandera tried to proclaim a Ukrainian state centered on Lvov, Bandera was arrested and sent to Germany.

Koch set up headquarters in the small town of Rivne rather than Kiev in order to dispel any idea of Ukrainian statehood. Food was requisitioned on a massive scale for the German army, and famine returned to the Ukraine as thousands of men were rounded up for labor service in Germany and SS Einsatzgruppen systematically slaughtered Jews, Gypsies, and anyone defined as a partisan. In all under German occupation, some 700 towns and 28,000 villages were destroyed. Nearly 7 million people were killed, including vir-

tually the entire Jewish population. From 1942 onward thousands of peasants joined the Ukrainian Insurgent Army (UPA), fighting a triangular war against both German occupiers and Soviet and Polish partisans. The UPA's struggle did not end with Hitler's defeat but continued as an anti-Soviet revolt until 1953.

Related entries: Eastern Front; Foreign Policy; Holocaust; Nazi–Soviet Pact; Poland; Romania; Soviet Union; Stalin, Joseph

Suggestions for further reading:
Boshyk, Yury, ed. 1986. *Ukraine during World War II.* Edmonton: Canadian Centre of Ukrainian Studies.

Mulligan, Timothy P. 1988. *The Politics of Illusion and Empire: German Occupation Policy in the Soviet Union, 1942–1943.* New York: Praeger.

Unemployment

When Hitler came to power more than one-third of the German working population were unemployed. His success in solving the problem was trumpeted as one of the Nazi regime's great achievements. By 1939 the situation was reversed, and the Reich was suffering from a labor shortage: there were only 74,000 unemployed and more than 1 million job vacancies. In Hitler's eyes the "battle for work" was a political, not an economic problem. He told a cabinet meeting on 8 February 1933 that: "the next five years in Germany had to be devoted to rendering the German people again capable of bearing arms. Every publicly sponsored measure to create employment had to be considered from [this] point of view. . . . This had to be the dominant thought, always and everywhere" (Weinberg 1970, p. 30).

The first step in the process was a "cynical book-keeping manoeuvre" (Welch 1993, p. 59) by which nearly 1 million unemployed were removed from the register by being placed in voluntary or temporary work schemes (a trick often employed by other governments in later years). Public works schemes, one-half of which had been planned by Hitler's predecessors, were

Masses of paper money are carried in sacks and laundry baskets as a payroll is collected at the Reichsbank in Berlin in 1923. Although the mark was stabilized during the central years of the Weimar Republic, the inflation of 1922–1923 was a traumatic experience, especially for the middle classes, and its memory helped to create a climate of fear that favored Nazi agitation during the Depression after 1929. (Culver Pictures)

begun later in 1933. The rearmament drive, conscription, prestige projects such as the autobahns, and the general recovery of the world economy allowed the number of registered unemployed to fall below 2 million in 1935, an improvement that continued steadily until the outbreak of war. Victory in the "battle for work" was won mainly by preparation for real battles, but it did increase business confidence in Hitler's regime and reconcile many of the working class to the regime, despite the longer working hours they had to endure as the price of employment.

Related entries; Autobahnen; Economic Policy; Four-Year Plan; German Labor Front; Industry; Labor Relations; Labor Service; Rearmament; Social Policy; Todt Organization; Working Class; Youth Policy

Suggestions for further reading:
Evans, Richard J., and Dick Geary, eds. 1987. *The German Unemployed*. London: Croom Helm.
Weinberg, Gerhard L. 1970. *The Foreign Policy of Hitler's Germany: Diplomatic Revolution in Europe, 1933–1936*. Chicago: University of Chicago Press.
Welch, David. 1993. *The Third Reich: Politics and Propaganda*. London and New York: Routledge.

United States of America

*T*he historian Gerhard L. Weinberg writes: "No two major powers were on better terms with each other than Germany and the United States before 1933, and the destruction of that relationship must be considered one of the signal events of the 1930s" (Weinberg 1970, p. 133). Hitler could not understand the nature of a "racially mixed" country—according to his worldview, such a nation could produce neither culture nor military ability. His underestimation of U.S. economic and potentially military strength would be one of his biggest mistakes. Anything good in the

United States came from its large population of German origin, but the country was dominated by Jews: "It is Jews who govern the stock exchange forces of the American Union. Every year makes them more and more the controlling masters of the producers in a nation of one hundred and twenty millions; only a single great man, [Henry] Ford, to their fury, still maintains a full independence" (Hitler 1992, p. 583). Even after declaring war on the United States, he was contemptuous: "What is America but millionaires, beauty queens, stupid records and Hollywood?" (Overy 1996, p. 205).

Under President Franklin Delano Roosevelt and Secretary of State Cordell Hull, the U.S. government believed that in order to overcome the international economic crisis and maintain peace it was necessary to rebuild a liberal trade economy based on the principle of the "open door." Hitler saw this as a threat to Germany's autarchic economy and policy of bilateral agreements. In the United States, the neutralist legislation of 1935 and 1937 and ingrained isolationism among the population made it impossible for Roosevelt to steer U.S. policy against the Third Reich, but farsighted Americans were disturbed by Hitler's rearmament drive, militarism, aggressive nationalism, and anti-Semitism. On 10 November 1938 the U.S. ambassador in Berlin was recalled in protest against Kristallnacht. Generally, however, Roosevelt's policy could not go beyond vague warnings toward the aggressor powers, including Hitler, whom he had always seen as a "pure unadulterated devil."

From 1936 onward, the U.S. began to rearm, building up an "arsenal of democracy." A trade agreement was concluded with Britain on 2 November 1938, but it was only after the defeat of France that Roosevelt led the country into an "undeclared war" against the objections of isolationists. The Lend-Lease Act of 11 March

1941 provided U.S. help for Britain, and the Atlantic Charter of 14 August 1941 associated the United States and Britain in their vision of a postwar world. Japan's attack on Pearl Harbor on 7 December 1941 plunged the United States into war against one of Hitler's allies, but he was not obliged to declare war on the United States as he did on 11 December. He now challenged U.S. economic power and growing military power directly. It was a monumental error. The United States may have been in two minds as to the relative priority of the wars against Germany and Japan, but in North Africa and then in Europe U.S. troops played a significant part in Hitler's defeat.

Related entries: Atlantic, Battle of the; Atlantic Charter; Bombing Campaigns; Bulge, Battle of the; Casablanca Conference; Eisenhower, Dwight David; Foreign Policy; Japan; Normandy Landings; North Africa; Roosevelt, Franklin Delano; Teheran Conference; Yalta Conference

Suggestions for further reading:

Compton, James V. 1967. *The Swastika and the Eagle: Hitler, the United States and the Origins of World War II*. Boston: Houghton Mifflin.
Friedländer, Saul. 1967. *Prelude to Downfall: Hitler and the United States 1929–1941*. New York: Alfred A. Knopf.
Hitler, Adolf. 1992. *Mein Kampf*. Trans. Ralph Manheim. Intro. by D. C. Watt. London: Pimlico.
Overy, Richard J. 1996. *The Nazi Economic Recovery 1932–1938*. 2nd ed. Cambridge: Cambridge University Press.
Weinberg, Gerhard L. 1970. *The Foreign Policy of Hitler's Germany: Diplomatic Revolution in Europe, 1933–1936*. Chicago: University of Chicago Press.

Universities

German universities traditionally played a greater role in politics than they did in most other European countries. Student opinion of one decade could easily become the national opinion of the next decade. Anti-Semitism had been a political force in universities in Germany and even more in Austria since the 1870s, and in the years after 1918 the nationalist extreme Right was the strongest influence among German students. Hitler's regime, however, did enormous damage to higher education in Germany. The numbers of students and teachers declined substantially. In 1930 the number of matriculated students reached a postwar peak of almost 130,000; by 1939 it was less than half that figure. In the course of *Gleichschaltung* the universities lost 16 percent of their staff through ejections, the technical institutes about 10 percent, and the law schools 21 percent.

In his inaugural address as rector of Freiburg University in 1933, the philosopher Martin Heidegger declared the new covenant: "No dogmas or ideas will any longer be the laws of your being. The Führer himself, and he alone, is the present and future reality for Germany and its law" (Bullock 1991, p. 362). Hitler's and the Nazis' anti-intellectualism was incompatible with any spirit of free inquiry. Student numbers were cut by law in 1933, officially because of graduate unemployment. Students and many of their teachers participated enthusiastically in the burning of unacceptable books. And people who start by burning books end up burning people. "Non-Aryans" were gradually excluded from higher education: Jewish law students were no longer permitted to take the qualifying examinations in July 1934, and Jewish medical students were excluded in February 1935. Curricula in all spheres were Nazified, and those who could not demonstrate a satisfactory record in the Hitler Youth were ineligible for university admission. Germany under Hitler became an intellectual desert, and the best scholars either conformed, emigrated, or lost their jobs. It was a miserable legacy to a country that had once been the scholarly leader of the world.

Related entries: Cultural Policy; Education; Science and Scientists

Suggestions for further reading:

Bullock, Alan. 1991. *Hitler and Stalin: Parallel Lives.* London: HarperCollins.

Giles, Geoffrey J. 1985. *Students and National Socialism in Germany.* Princeton: Princeton University Press.

Steinberg, Michael H. 1977. *Sabers and Brown Shirts: The German Students' Path to National Socialism 1918–1935.* Princeton: Princeton University Press.

Vergeltungswaffe (V1, V2)

Hitler and the Nazi propaganda machine claimed that V weapons, intended for long-range bombardment, would reverse the course of the war even in its final stages, but they were proved wrong. The V1 was a pilotless jet-propelled aircraft launched from specially constructed ramps and with a maximum flying time of one hour. The V2 was a rocket fueled by liquid oxygen and alcohol, capable of carrying a warhead of up to a ton in weight. In July 1932 Hitler declared that the V2 would be "the decisive weapon of the war" (Keegan 1989, p. 581), but the British were fully aware of German research, and a heavy raid on the development center of Peenemünde on 16–17 August 1943 set back the program seriously. The first V weapons were launched in June 1944, shortly after the Normandy landings, aimed at London and subsequently also at Antwerp. But despite the fear that a new kind of weapon caused, their impact was negligible. They were inaccurate and unreliable, and the launching sites outside Germany, mainly on the Channel coast, were taken by the Allies in late 1944 and early 1945. Albert Speer called the "retaliation weapons": "not only our biggest but our most misguided project" (Speer 1971, p. 318).

Related entries: Science and Scientists

Suggestions for further reading:
Keegan, John. 1989. *The Second World War.* London: Hutchinson.
Speer, Albert. 1971. *Inside the Third Reich.* Paperback ed. London: Sphere Books.

Versailles, Treaty of

The treaty imposed on Germany in 1919 after World War I provided Hitler with one of the most consistent and popular sources of ammunition for his agitation. He called it "this instrument of boundless extortion and abject humiliation" and declared: "In the boundlessness of its oppression, the shamelessness of its demands, lies the greatest propaganda weapon for the reawakening of a nation's dormant spirits to life" (Hitler 1992, p. 577). For this reason, he made it a central theme of *Mein Kampf* as well as his speeches.

The Versailles treaty had been harsher than even the most pessimistic Germans had imagined. Germany lost Alsace and Lorraine to France and the industrial region of Upper Silesia to Poland. France was to occupy the Saarland and Germany west of the Rhine for fifteen years. Danzig became a "free city," and West Prussia turned into the Polish corridor, giving Poland access to the sea and cutting East Prussia off from the rest of Germany. The army was reduced to 100,000 men and the General

A V1 flying bomb about to crash into London in the summer of 1944. About 800 in all crashed on greater London, the most serious single incident being when one landed on the Guards Chapel at Wellington Barracks during a service on 18 June, killing 121 people, including 63 soldiers. (Imperial War Museum / Archive Photos)

Staff disbanded. The humiliating "war guilt" clause saddled Germany with sole responsibility for starting the war. The Social Democratic government forced to sign the treaty was burdened with the epithet of "November criminals," and the legend of the "stab in the back" soon took hold. Germany had not been beaten on the battlefield but betrayed by left-wing politicians, war profiteers, saboteurs, and Jews.

Hitler would doubtless have ranted and raved against Versailles whatever its precise terms had been. So would the nationalist Right as a whole. The real damage it did was to create disillusionment among more moderate people, Left and Right, making it more difficult for them to oppose his fulminations. Revision of the treaty became the basis of the foreign policy of the Weimar Republic, but Hitler's more spectacular success in the early years of the Third Reich

caused his popularity to rise beyond that of any Weimar politician.

Related entries: Alsace-Lorraine; Czechoslovakia; Danzig; Foreign Policy; France; Great Britain; Hitler Myth; League of Nations; Poland; Propaganda; Public Opinion; Rearmament; Reparations; Rhineland; Ruhr; Saarland; Wehrmacht

Suggestions for further reading:
Hiden, John. 1977. *Germany and Europe 1919–1939.* New York: Longman.
Hitler, Adolf. 1992. *Mein Kampf.* Trans. Ralph Manheim. Intro. by D. C. Watt. London: Pimlico.

Vienna

The five years Hitler spent in Vienna from 1908 to 1913 were the most miserable and aimless of his life, and in typ-

The "armistice car" of 1918, preserved at Compiègne. In 1940 Hitler took great delight in accepting the French surrender in the very same railway wagon, for him a symbol of the humiliation of Germany. (Culver Pictures)

ically self-pitying and paranoid fashion he never forgave the Austrian capital he considered had treated him so badly. "Even today," he wrote in *Mein Kampf,* "this city can arouse in me nothing but the most dismal thoughts" (Hitler 1992, p. 20). His own account of his years there is a mixture of self-pity, egotistic fabulation, and genuine feeling about the seamy underside of the great metropolis. Some of his stories are blatantly false: he never worked on a building site, arguing with and besting Social Democratic workers. But he does not hide his poverty and constant struggle, not always successful, to make ends meet.

Having spent the small amount of money he inherited from his family and twice being refused entry to the Academy of Arts, for most of his time in Vienna Hitler lived in hostels and scraped a living selling the postcards he painted of the city. He expressed his admiration for the archi-

tecture of the famous Ringstrasse, and while he still had the money he and his friend August Kubizek attended the Vienna Opera, where he heard and admired Gustav Mahler's interpretations of Wagner. But for the most part Hitler's Vienna was not the avant-garde city of Sigmund Freud, Arnold Schoenberg, Oskar Kokoschka, Arthur Schnitzler, and Ludwig Wittgenstein. It was rather a city of poverty and homelessness, ethnic tension between Germans, Czechs, and Jews, populist politics, the struggle between "national" politicians and internationalist Social Democrats, and dotty theoreticians of race and Aryan supremacy.

Hitler learned a lot about politics in Vienna. Although World War I and the revolution of 1918 were the crucial experiences that turned him to politics, his view from below of the last days of the Habsburg Empire planted the seeds of his future development. He rationalized this later in racial terms: "I was repelled by the conglomeration of races which the capital showed me, repelled by the whole mixture of Czechs, Poles, Hungarians, Ruthenians, Serbs and Croats, and everywhere the eternal mushroom of humanity—Jews and more Jews. To me the giant city seemed the embodiment of racial desecration" (Hitler 1992, p. 113). There is in fact little evidence that Hitler was already a full-fledged anti-Semite in Vienna (his relations with the art dealers and other Jews he encountered seem to have been generally good), but his voracious reading of the burgeoning anti-Semitic and anti-Slav press and pamphlets was undoubtedly crucial in the formation of his worldview. More importantly, perhaps, his admiration for the anti-Semitic mayor of Vienna, Karl Lueger, and the pan-German leader Georg Ritter von Schönerer provided him with political role models from whom he drew valuable lessons. Also, his adventures in the lower depths of society explain the extraordinary amount of space devoted to prostitution and the ravages of syphilis in *Mein Kampf.*

Hitler left Vienna in 1913 to avoid service in the Austro-Hungarian army and to try his luck in the "truly German" city of Munich. He left as a German nationalist, anti-Socialist, antiparliamentarian, antifeminist, and on the way to becoming anti-Semitic. Hitler never overcame his ambivalent feelings about the old Habsburg capital. Even after the Anschluss in 1938, Berlin was to be the undisputed capital of the Greater German Reich, and his hometown of Linz was to be the cultural center of the Ostmark. Vienna was systematically sacked of its treasures. "The Führer," Josef Goebbels wrote, "stressed that even though Vienna is a city with over a million people, its role has to be reduced to one of a provincial city" (Hamann 1999, p. 87).

Despite the ecstatic reception he received there after the Anschluss, Hitler could not stop thinking of Vienna as "un-German." His was not a nostalgic home-coming but a triumphant conquest of the scene of his youthful humiliation. There was to be no investment in Vienna, "otherwise [its] cultural attraction will be too great" (Hamann 1999, p. 87). The population was to be "cleansed," the old multiethnic imperial capital destroyed for good, and the "repulsive" Viennese put in their place once and for all. The significance of Vienna for Hitler was ultimately that it had been a hard school: "In it I obtained the foundations for a philosophy in general and a political view in particular which later I only needed to supplement in detail, but which never left me" (Hamann 1999, p. 404).

Related entries: Anschluss; Anti-Semitism; Lueger, Karl; Schönerer, Georg Ritter von

Suggestions for further reading:
Hamann, Brigitte. 1999. *Hitler's Vienna: A Dictator's Apprenticeship.* New York: Oxford University Press.
Hitler, Adolf. 1992. *Mein Kampf.* Trans. Ralph Manheim. Intro. by D. C. Watt. London: Pimlico.

Völkischer Beobachter

The central organ of the National Socialist German Workers' Party (NSDAP, Nazi Party) was acquired in 1920 and as of 1921 bore the subhead "Militant Paper of the Great-German National Socialist Movement." Apart from rallies and demonstrations, the *Völkischer Beobachter* (VB) was Hitler's most important propaganda medium, presenting his ideology in the popular, easily accessible format of the mass press, and was regarded as the "connecting link between the Führer and his followers." It was published daily by the Eher Press, directed by Max Amann, and the first editor in chief was Dietrich Eckart, replaced in March 1923 by Alfred Rosenberg. The VB was banned after the Beer Hall Putsch and reestablished in February 1925. Hitler himself acted as publisher until

30 April 1933. The circulation of 4,000 in 1925 rose to 126,000 in 1932, including separate Bavarian and Berlin editions.

From 30 January 1933 the VB became a quasi-official organ. It tried to extend its appeal with numerous supplements such as "The German Woman" and "The Film Observer." With Wilhelm Weiss as editor in chief from 1938, a Viennese edition began publication after the Anschluss, and a "Field Post" edition was distributed to the armed forces in 1941. In 1938 some 600,000 copies of the VB were printed daily, though many remained unsold. In 1944 the press run was 1.7 million. The last copy of the north German edition was dated 27 April 1945 and the south German edition, 30 April.

Related entries: Eckart, Dietrich; Hanfstaengl, Ernst Franz Sedgwick; Press; Propaganda; Rosenberg, Alfred

propaganda mill, most notably in the Sudetenland and Poland. Where they could not be used to justify Hitler's aggressive politics, for example in the Italian-ruled South Tirol, their problems were ignored. Following the Nazi-Soviet Pact, Germans from the Baltic states were resettled in the Reich, as were some 900,000 other *Volksdeutsche* in succeeding years. But as the Russians moved into eastern Europe, far more fled or were expelled, and about 1 million lost their lives. The ultimate result of Hitler's racial imperialism for the *Volksdeutsche* was that by 1946 the German population east of the Elbe had been reduced from 17 million to 2,600,000. Centuries-old communities had been destroyed for the sake of Greater Germany.

Related entries: Baltic States; Danzig; Foreign Policy; Memel; Poland; Sudetenland

Volksdeutsche

Also known as *Auslandsdeutsche,* people of German origin living outside Germany, specifically in eastern Europe, were mobilized by the Nazis in support of Hitler's expansionist aims. The most diverse communities were included, including Germans who had lived in southeastern or eastern Europe since the Middle Ages, those who emigrated overseas in the nineteenth century, and those who had become foreign citizens because of boundary changes forced by the Treaty of Versailles. Connections between the Reich and ethnic Germans abroad were maintained by several organizations, most notably the Ethnic German Central Office, established by Rudolf Hess in 1936.

Most ethnic Germans were anxious to maintain good relations with their host states—in 1937 a maximum of 6 percent of Germans outside the Reich were Nazi Party members—but their real and imagined difficulties were grist for the Nazi

Volksgemeinschaft

The concept of the *Volksgemeinschaft,* the national or people's community, was central to Hitler's ideology. Class, religious, and sectional divisions would be sublimated or displaced into a new set of values drawing their strength from an idealized Germanic past. Modern humans, alienated by urban industrial civilization, would be transformed by the sense of belonging to the *Volk,* the united and racially pure "people's community." The Nazis invented the word *Volkwerdung,* "a people becoming itself," to describe the events of 1933. In so doing they were playing on the double meaning of the German *Volk,* which can mean either "the people" in a democratic sense or "the folk" in the racial sense embodied in *völkisch* thought or both. From the second meaning came the idea of the *Volk* community related to the earlier notions of *völkisch* intellectuals who had interpreted Social Darwinism as a struggle between races rather than individuals. The

Volksgemeinschaft was involved in a perpetual battle against other peoples, at first within Germany and then outside.

The lack of a clear definition of *Volksgemeinschaft* increased its appeal. It could slip easily into widely shared aspirations for a national "reawakening" or "resurrection." The example of historians has been used to show how people who, though not adhering to Nazi ideas on race and religion, nevertheless believed in a historical *Volksgemeinschaft* and how this belief worked against the development of oppositional ideas. A constant barrage of propaganda urging the population to "put the community before the individual" and using slogans like "One People! One Reich! One Führer!" sought to create a consensus in which Hitler, the state, and the *Volksgemeinschaft* were all identified one with the other. Social divisions and regional differences were papered over by demagogy.

The spirit of superficial egalitarianism within the *Volk* involved the exclusion of outsiders: the communal expulsion of Jews and other "racial undesirables" as well as "traitors," a category capable of almost indefinite expansion. Physical labor was exalted, while the population was encouraged to drop outward forms of distinction. Almost every institution had the prefix "*Volks*" attached to it, and Hitler himself was the "people's chancellor." The fact that within the Nazi Party and its affiliated organizations hierarchies sprouted in ever greater profusion did not go unnoticed, but the "Hitler Myth" allowed the Führer to appear at least semidetached from this apparent contradiction of the *Volksgemeinschaft*. In fact, the party and its offshoots were sources of upward social mobility for those prepared to subscribe to *völkisch* views, and in the civil service and local government, political qualifications could make up for a lack of academic distinction.

Hitler declared in September 1933: "The conviction will grow that the National Community is not an empty concept, but something really alive" (Kershaw 1983, p. 31). The idea of *Volksgemeinschaft*, inescapable and ubiquitous under his rule, did undoubtedly gain a grip on the German people. But this did not necessarily mean that they would support his policies in their extremism and viciousness; nor could it solve the problem of the antisocial behavior of his subordinates. An intensely practical program of indoctrination and socialization through Nazi ritual, terror, and especially the Hitler Youth and similar organizations was also necessary.

Related entries: Anti-Semitism; *Blut und Boden;* Cultural Policy; Education; *Gleichschaltung;* Hitler Myth; Hitler Youth; Jews and Jewish Policy; Middle Classes; Nuremberg Rallies; Propaganda; Racial Theory; Social Policy; Socialism; Winterhilfe; Women; Working Class; Youth Policy

Suggestions for further reading:
Hermand, Jost. 1993. *Old Dreams of a New Reich: Volkisch Utopias and National Socialism.* Bloomington and Indianapolis: Indiana University Press.
Kershaw, Ian. 1983. *Popular Opinion and Political Dissent in the Third Reich: Bavaria 1933–1945.* Oxford: Clarendon Press.
Lambert, Peter. 1995. "German Historians and Nazi Ideology: the Parameters of the *Volksgemeinschaft* and the Problem of Historical Legitimation, 1930–45," *European History Quarterly* 25, pp. 555–582.
Mosse, George L. 1964. *The Crisis of German Ideology: Intellectual Origins of the Third Reich.* New York: Grosset and Dunlap.

Volkssturm

The new home defense force, the Volkssturm, was formed in February 1943 as a sign of the Nazis' increasing pessimism about a possible invasion of Germany by the Russians. Every man between the ages of sixteen and sixty, whatever his class or occupation, was ordered to join the Volkssturm and defend the homeland. The ragtag army of the adolescent and the aged, poorly equipped and armed, did their best in resisting the Russian attack on Berlin in 1944 but were swept aside by the Red Army. The last known authentic photograph of Hitler shows him inspecting Volkssturm youths in what is intended to be an avuncular fashion.

Related entries: Total War

Volkswagen

Designed by Ferdinand Porsche, the "people's car" was intended to make automobiles available to the German mass public. As such it formed part of the German Labor Front's (DAF's) policy of boosting workers' morale and reconciling the working class to the Hitler regime. It was to be manufactured at a DAF factory at Wolfsburg, and the DAF issued savings certificates of 5 marks per week toward its purchase. More than 300,000 people signed up but were destined to be disappointed. Prototypes were ready in 1936, but as preparation for war took priority the factory was converted to production of military vehicles. The Volkswagen did not become available for civilian use until after the war, to great success.

Related entries: German Labor Front

Voroshilov, Klement Efremovich (1881–1969)

An associate of Joseph Stalin since the days of the Russian Civil War following the October Revolution, Marshal Voroshilov was the epitome of the "political" Soviet soldier who owed his rise more to ideological correctness and suppleness than to military expertise. As commissar for defense between 1925 and 1940 and deputy premier in 1941, he was the kind of Soviet officer who caused Hitler's wrongheaded dismissal of the capacities of the Red Army. Following his failure to check the German advance of Operation Barbarossa, Voroshilov was recalled to Moscow and held staff appointments for the duration of the war. His replacement by Marshal Georgi Zhukov symbolized the reversal in Hitler's fortunes. Voroshilov attended several Allied conferences, including Teheran in November 1943. After the war he became head of the Soviet Control Commission in Hungary and between 1953 and 1960 filled the largely honorific post of president of the Soviet Union.

Related entries: Barbarossa, Operation; Eastern Front; Red Army

Suggestions for further reading:
Overy, Richard J. 1998. *Russia's War.* New York: Allen Lane Penguin Press.

Waffen SS

The military arm of the SS was originally conceived by Heinrich Himmler in the 1930s as a force to be used for internal purposes in Germany, their total commitment to Nazi ideology making them, from Hitler's point of view, more trustworthy than the Wehrmacht. With the beginning of the war they were transformed into a fighting force in the field, totally loyal to the Führer and committed to Hitler's kind of war—an ideological and biological conflict against "racial inferiors." The Waffen SS eventually numbered thirty-nine divisions, and nearly 1 million men of fifteen different nationalities passed through their ranks. They took part in a dozen major battles, mostly in eastern Europe, fighting with a fanaticism and ruthlessness that owed more to the traditions of the Freikorps than those of the Prussian army.

Despite the criticisms of the regular army generals, who did their best to restrict their numbers, the three Waffen SS divisions organized during the phony war spearheaded the German attack on the Netherlands and participated in the battle of France and the invasion of Norway. Four divisions took part in Operation Barbarossa and, permeated with anti-Slav and anti-Semitic ideology, fought furiously in the opening of the Russian campaign, winning Hitler's praise for their "National Socialist qualities." They were not, however, involved in the battle for Stalingrad, the full blame for which fell on the regular army.

Himmler's ideal was to make the Waffen SS an international organization, with "foreign legions" of dedicated racists. Gottlob Berger, in charge of recruitment in the SS Head Office, started by appealing to *Volksdeutsche* in eastern Europe. The reluctance of the Wehrmacht to release enough Germans to fill the ranks spurred on the process, so that by 1945 more than one-third of Waffen SS troops were drawn from all parts of Europe and included Scandinavians, Yugoslavs, Ukrainians, Latvians, Estonians, Albanians, Dutch, Italians, Hungarians, Belgian, Russians, and French. Most were combined in units with ethnic Germans and counted for little in the overall military picture. The original nature of the Waffen SS was diluted somewhat by this expansion, but until the end Hitler viewed them as his Praetorian Guard and praised them for their actions in Poland, Slovakia, and Hungary during the retreat from the east.

The Waffen SS was indicted as a criminal organization at the Nuremberg trials. Wehrmacht officers also on trial claimed that atrocities in combat, especially on the Eastern Front, were committed by the Waffen SS and not by regular army units. This was far from being completely true, but there is no doubt that Himmler's soldiers, imbued with racism and anti-Semitism and thinking of themselves as Nordic supermen, do bear more than their fair share of the blame for the peculiarly barbaric nature of the conflicts in which they were engaged.

Related entries: Barbarossa, Operation; Eastern Front; Himmler, Heinrich; Panzer Divisions; Schutzstaffel; War Crimes

Suggestions for further reading:
Stein, G. H. 1966. *The Waffen SS: Hitler's Elite Guard at War, 1939–45*. Ithaca, NY: Cornell University Press.

Wagner, Richard (1813–1883)

"Whoever wants to understand National Socialist Germany," Hitler said, "must know Wagner." He claimed to have seen *Lohengrin* at the age of twelve and become instantly addicted to Wagner's "heroic-German world-view": "My youthful enthusiasm for the Master of Bayreuth knew no bounds" (Hitler 1992, p. 16). Most people outgrow the uncritical artistic enthusiasms of adolescence, but Wagner's nationalism and anti-Semitism and the quasi-religious cult that surrounded his work even during his lifetime served to justify Hitler's lifelong devotion to "the greatest prophetic figure the German people has ever had." Hitler's dedication was shown by his support for the Bayreuth festival and personal acquaintance with the Wagner family, including the composer's son-in-law, the racist theorist Houston Stewart Chamberlain, whom he first met in 1923.

Born in Leipzig, Wagner spent most of his eventful and turbulent life evading his numerous creditors. He and Hitler may have shared a boundless egotism, but Wagner's extravagant and sybaritic lifestyle was far removed from the Führer's relative austerity. Financial stability was only achieved in 1864 when Wagner received the support of King Ludwig II of Bavaria. The complexities of politics made Ludwig's backing intermit-

tent, even dangerous, nor did the "fairy-tale king" share Wagner's anti-Semitism and half-baked racial theories. Rather, he was captivated by the compelling power of Wagner's music and his romantic medievalism. For Hitler, however, anti-Semitism and the later Wagner's turgid and incoherent racist diatribes were crucial. "Wagner's work," he wrote, "showed me for the first time what is the myth of blood."

In his book *Jewry in Music* (1850) Wagner portrayed "the Jew" as a materialist, impeding the pure idealistic instincts of the German *Volk* in their attempt to create the "art-work of the future," Wagner's "total works of art" *(Gesamtkunstwerke)*. Unlike Hitler, Wagner befriended individual Jews, whom he treated no more shabbily than he did all his acquaintances, but anti-Semitism became an ever more central part of his artistic vision, the exaltation of instinct over reason. Anti-Semitism was a hatred as necessary to him "as gall is to the blood." Like Hitler in *Mein Kampf* he contrasted the materialistic instincts of the Jews with the idealism of the Aryan drive for mastery. Wagner even associated antivivisectionism and vegetarianism (two other interests he shared with Hitler) with anti-Semitism: flesh eating had been invented by the Jews, "former cannibals, educated to be the business leaders of our society." The true German artist, "demonically suffering, god-like," stood opposed to Jewry, racially and ideologically.

The Nazi cult of Wagner as the artistic god of the Third Reich, then, merely carried one aspect of the composer's ideas to its logical conclusion. In the words of Robert W. Gutman: "The art-work was swallowed by its hypotheses." But Hitler could not be accused of willfully distorting the work of an artist whose mediocre intellect fell far short of his outstanding and uncompromising musical talent. Wagner had stipulated that the evil Nibelungs in the *Ring* cycle were to speak a kind of Jewish-German and gesticulate in a "Semitic" manner. His most popular and accessible opera, *Die Meistersinger von Nürnberg* (1867), a celebration of the pure and instinctive artistic genius of the German *Volk,* was staged at Nuremberg to coincide with the Nazi Party rallies. Wagner had seen Nuremberg as an ancient seat of German tradition and was outraged by its synagogue "in purest Oriental style," standing opposite the monument to the opera's hero, Hans Sachs. He would presumably have been delighted at its demolition by the Nazis.

The other leading Nazis did not necessarily share Hitler's enthusiastic embrace of the Wagner cult. In their own materialism and opportunism they yielded nothing to Wagner's paranoid stereotype of the Jew. But Josef Goebbels and his captive press piled cliché upon cliché in praise of Wagner: "the greatest music genius of all time," "the fullest embodiment of the national ideal," "the herald of National Socialism," and so forth. In 1911 Thomas Mann had written: "The Germans should be made to decide between Goethe and Wagner. They cannot have both. But I fear they would choose Wagner." Under Hitler's Reich they had no choice.

Related entries: Anti-Semitism; Bayreuth; Cultural Policy; Racial Theory

Suggestions for further reading:
Gutman, Robert W. 1968. *Richard Wagner: The Man, His Mind and His Music.* London: Secker and Warburg.
Hitler, Adolf. 1992. *Mein Kampf.* Trans. Ralph Manheim. Intro. by D. C. Watt. London: Pimlico.
Rose, Paul Lawrence. 1992. *Wagner, Race and Revolution.* London: Faber.
Weiner, Marc A. 1995. *Richard Wagner and the Anti-Semitic Imagination.* Lincoln: University of Nebraska Press.

Wannsee Conference

Called by Reinhard Heydrich in January 1942, the Wannsee Conference discussed the organizational problems involved in the recently decided "total solution of the Jewish question in Europe." Attended by the bureaucrats concerned, with minutes taken by Adolf Eichmann, it discussed in a sickeningly objective and businesslike fashion questions of selection and possible exceptions and the transportation of hundreds of thousands of people to their deaths. In Eichmann's own words: "In very blunt terms—the talk was of killing, elimination and annihilation." The resultant memo is a horrifying testimony to the way in which the most grotesque acts may be planned in the numbing language of bureaucratic procedure.

Related entries: Final Solution

Suggestions for further reading:
Noakes, Jeremy, and Geoffrey Pridham, eds. 1988. *Nazism 1919–1945: A Documentary Reader. Vol. 3: Foreign Policy, War and Racial Extermination.* Exeter: Exeter University Press.

War Crimes

The Interallied War Crimes Tribunal in 1945 distinguished war crimes, crimes against humanity, and crimes against international peace. Under Hitler's command Germans committed all three. The catalogue of German crimes filled twenty-three volumes of the record of the Nuremberg trials, with documentary evidence taking up another nineteen. In western Europe Hitler had committed clear acts of aggression against Belgium, the Netherlands, Denmark, Norway, and France. There were numerous acts of repression and deportation of Jews and members of Resistance movements, shooting of hostages, and horrific incidents such as the razing of the village of Oradour-sur-Glane in France and the shooting of U.S. prisoners at Malmédy during the Ardennes campaign.

In eastern Europe, however, no holds were barred. On Hitler's specific orders, his forces showed no mercy in Poland and the Soviet Union, and warfare on the Eastern Front sank to atrocious levels of barbarity, with the SS and Waffen SS taking the lead. German soldiers were expressly absolved from any civilized behavior: prisoners were usually not taken in combat; Jews and commissars shot on sight; refugees strafed; hostages executed; and between 3 and 4 million prisoners of war systematically starved to death. Hundreds of villages in Poland, Belorussia, and the Ukraine were razed and their inhabitants massacred. The biggest single crime was the crime against humanity of the Final Solution, but it was all of a piece with Hitler's "war of extermination."

Related entries: Eastern Front; Nuremberg Trials; Resistance Movements; Schutzstaffel; Waffen SS; Warsaw Rising; Wehrmacht

Warsaw Ghetto

Following the German conquest of Poland, the Jewish population was concentrated in urban ghettos, the largest of which was in Warsaw. Some 80,000 Gentile inhabitants of the old Jewish quarter of the Polish capital were removed and replaced with 150,000 Jews from elsewhere in the city. In November 1940 the ghetto was sealed and its twenty-two entrances closed. A Jewish Council (*Judenrat*) did its best to maintain contact with the German authorities. But from 1940 to 1942 an estimated 100,000 Jews died in the ghetto from starvation, disease, or execution. In July 1942 some 300,000 were rounded up and transported, mostly for extermination at Treblinka.

In January 1943 Himmler ordered a swift end to the "resettlement" program with a view to making Warsaw "Jew-free"

A scene from the suppression of the Warsaw ghetto uprising in the early months of 1943. After the final defeat of the revolt in mid-May SS-Brigadeführer Jürgen Stroop reported: "The Jewish quarter of Warsaw no longer exists." (Archive Photos)

by 20 April, Hitler's birthday. Two thousand Waffen SS, supported by sappers and artillery from three army divisions, German and Polish police, some Jewish ghetto police, and Ukrainian and Latvian SS auxiliaries, swept into the ghetto. But the inhabitants were determined to resist. The Farband (Jewish military union), formed in 1939, had links with the Polish Home Army, and a communist "Jewish fighting organization" (ZOB) had been set up in 1942. The Jews, armed with some machine guns, pistols, rifles, and "Molotov cocktails," inflicted heavy casualties on the SS and their auxiliaries on 19 April, the first day of fighting.

For twenty days, Jews fought the Nazis for every inch of the ghetto. But artillery and aircraft gradually reduced the area to ruins. On 16 May the SS commander could report that the former Jewish quarter of Warsaw no longer existed. Some 60,000 Jews had been killed in the month's fighting. A few isolated groups continued resistance into July. It is believed that only about 100 Jews survived the ghetto rising, but it did inspire resistance in other Polish cities and acted as a powerful symbol of Jewish ability to fight back.

Related entries: Poland; Resistance Movements

Warsaw Rising

The insurrection by the Polish Home Army, beginning on 1 August 1944, in an attempt to liberate Warsaw before the arrival of the Red Army, has remained one of the most controversial tragedies of World War II. After some initial successes for the Polish underground fighters, Hitler retaliated in force, and they were savagely decimated by the SS while calling in vain on the Soviet forces to come to their aid. Joseph Stalin saw the rising as an attempt to seize power by the Home Army and called

them "rebels" and even "criminals." The Nazis did Stalin's work for him by destroying the only organized Polish force capable of opposing Soviet occupation. Some historians, however, by no means Soviet apologists, point out that the purpose of the rising was to gain power rather than to help the war against Hitler, that the British and Americans were divided over the question of trying to help the insurgents, and that the German forces were probably sufficient to hold up any Soviet attack, which would have been costly and brought no strategic advantage.

Related entries: Poland; Resistance Movements

Suggestions for further reading:
Glantz, David, and Jonathan House. 1995. *When Titans Clashed: How the Red Army Stopped Hitler.* Lawrence: University of Kansas Press.

Wehrmacht

Following the public announcement of rearmament, Hitler established his new armed forces by the Law for the Creation of the Wehrmacht in 1935. The army, navy, and air force (Luftwaffe) became independent services under the ultimate superiority of Hitler as Führer, and all took a personal oath to him rather than to Germany or the state. Below him, a war minister exercised specific authority over the forces, but his authority and the remaining independence of the armed forces were undermined in a process culminating in the "Blomberg-Fritsch crisis" of 1938. Hitler assumed direct command of the forces, with a Wehrmacht High Command (OKW) under the subservient Wilhelm Keitel acting, in effect, as his personal staff.

The Army High Command (OKH) planned and conducted the campaigns against Poland, France, and the Soviet Union. When Hitler assumed supreme command of the army in December 1941, the OKH assumed the principal responsibility for the Eastern Front, with the Wehrmacht High Command assuming primary authority in western Europe and the Mediterranean. Both bodies, of course, were ultimately controlled by Hitler, who took ever less account of the advice of his commanders. The Wehrmacht became increasingly Nazified at all levels and collaborated thoroughly in Hitler's genocidal war. Wehrmacht atrocities against civilians and prisoners of war played a major role in the barbarization of warfare, especially on the Eastern Front. Attempts to put all the blame on the SS or a handful of fanatical Nazis do not stand up to close scrutiny.

Another consequence of the permeation of the Wehrmacht by Nazi ideology was the stress on willpower and courage, which in Hitler's worldview were supposed to compensate for growing technical and material inferiority. The notion that German heroism, idealism, and steadfastness, guided by the "will of the Führer," could overcome numberless hordes of "racially inferior" enemies only served to increase the savagery of warfare. Nevertheless, the traditional German military virtues of initiative and flexibility, bolstered by Nazi ideology, made the Wehrmacht a formidable opponent. Never have soldiers fought better in a worse cause than did Hitler's. The offensive campaigns of 1939–1941 and the long retreat of 1943–1945 both provide many examples of tactical and operational excellence. Strategic planning, with Hitler interfering constantly, did remain a significant weakness, but the postwar tendency by his commanders to blame Hitler for everything that went wrong is exaggerated and covers up the inability of the three services to achieve the proper degree of cooperation. Internal squabbles and rivalries also played their part in the destruction of the Wehrmacht.

Related entries: Afrika Korps; Arnhem, Battle of; Barbarossa, Operation; Beck,

Ludwig; Blitzkrieg; Blomberg-Fritsch Crisis; Blomberg, Werner von; Brauchitsch, Walther von; Bulge, Battle of the; Busch, Ernst; Citadel, Operation; Condor Legion; Doenitz, Karl; Eastern Front; El Alamein, Battle of; Goering, Hermann; Guderian, Heinz; Halder, Franz; Jodl, Alfred; July Plot; Keitel, Wilhelm; Kesselring, Albert; Kluge, Hans Günther von; Kursk, Battle of; Luftwaffe; Manstein, Erich von; Navy; Normandy Landings; North Africa; Officer Corps; Panzer Divisions; Paulus, Friedrich; Raeder, Erich; Rearmament; Rommel, Erwin; Rundstedt, Karl Rudolf Gerd von; Stalingrad, Battle of; Tobruk, Battles of; War Crimes; Weichs, Maximilian Freiherr von; Zeitzler, Kurt von

Suggestions for further reading:
Bartov, Omer. 1991. *Hitler's Army: Soldiers, Nazis and War in the Third Reich.* New York: Oxford University Press.
Deist, Wilhelm. 1983. *The Wehrmacht and German Rearmament.* Toronto: University of Toronto Press.
O'Neill, Robert J. 1987. *The German Army and the Nazi Party 1933–1939.* New York: Heinemann.

Weichs, Maximilian Freiherr Von (1881–1954)

An experienced professional soldier promoted to general field marshal in 1943, Weichs was one of Hitler's most valuable commanders and one of the few who survived until the end of the war without incurring the Führer's anger and blame. In 1938 he led the 13th Army Corps into Austria and the Sudetenland and in 1940 participated in the French campaign at the head of the 2nd Army. Weichs led the same 2nd Army to success in the invasion of the Balkans in April 1941 and in the early stages of the Russian campaign, until he was given supreme command of Army Group B. After the reverses in the east Weichs commanded the Southeast Army, stationed in Hungary, until the end of the war. He was arrested, but his poor health led to his release in November 1948 before some of the other commanders in the Balkans were brought to trial for war crimes. He died in Cologne in 1954.

Related entries: Barbarossa, Operation; Eastern Front

Weimar Republic

The collapse of Germany's first democratic regime paved the way for Hitler's takeover of power in January 1933. Like others on the extreme Right he had never ceased to campaign against the Weimar Republic since its foundation in 1919. For Hitler Weimar was the regime of the "November criminals," the men who had signed the Treaty of Versailles: it was weak and "un-German," beholden to other countries for its existence, enfeebled by the party system, politically corrupt and culturally decadent, and dominated by Jews and Marxists. The tragedy of the Weimar Republic was that too many people in positions of influence held views differing from Hitler's only in degree and vehemence, not in essence.

The history of the republic may be divided into three periods. From 1919 to 1924 it had to survive economic and political disruption, revolutionary and counter-revolutionary uprisings, hyperinflation, and frequently changing governments. The failure of Hitler's Beer Hall Putsch was one sign that this period was drawing to a close. The rescheduling of reparations payments through the Dawes Plan in 1924 and the signing of the Locarno Pact in 1925 ushered in the second period of relative prosperity and stability from 1925 to 1929. Although governments came and went frequently, the "Weimar Coalition" of Social Democrats, Center Party members, and liberals had steered Germany through difficult times to an apparent position of strength. These were the years of low political fortunes for Hitler, when he was most concerned with establishing his power over the Nazi Party.

The onset of the Great Depression in 1930 opened the final stage of the republic's history, culminating in Hitler's appointment as chancellor. More and more voters began to think that democratic governments were too weak to solve Germany's economic problems; the Nazis made spectacular gains in elections; the Left divided bitterly between Socialists and Communists; hopelessly unrepresentative governments could gain no credibility, even for the sensible aspects of their policies; and conservatives thought they could use Hitler in the installation of a more authoritarian republic. In so doing they made him the gravedigger of democracy. Hitler, it should be noted, came to power legally but without a democratic mandate.

The leaders of the Weimar Republic, including President Paul von Hindenburg, actively connived in its destruction. This does not mean that the structure of the regime was inherently weak. The system of a directly elected president separate from parliament and the cabinet and holding emergency powers is not necessarily unstable, as the example of the French Fifth Republic has shown. The weakness of Weimar lay not in its liberal and democratic constitution but in the attitudes and actions of those who were supposed to uphold it. As the divisions on the Left between Socialists and Communists grew ever more bitter, the Communists on occasions joined with the Nazis in opposition to "bourgeois democracy." More significantly in the longer perspective, conservative forces in important positions had never accepted the legitimacy of the republic. In the civil service, judiciary, police, army, educational system, and parliament itself, too many people remained monarchists or extreme nationalists at heart. Weimar was called a "republic without republicans." It had many solid achievements to its name, and it has become identified with a cultural golden age, but without the solid commitment of the elites and the influential it was vulnerable to maneuvers from within that let in the destructive forces from without.

Related entries: Bavaria; Bavarian People's Party; Beer Hall Putsch; Brüning, Heinrich; Center Party; Communist Party; Dawes Plan; Elections; German Democratic Party; German National People's Party; Harzburg Front; Hindenburg, Paul von; Hitler Myth; Hugenberg, Alfred; *Mein Kampf;* Middle Classes; Munich; National Socialist German Workers' Party; Nationalists; Nazi Movement; Neurath, Konstantin von; Papen, Franz von; Reichstag; Reparations; Ruhr; Schacht, Hjalmar; Schleicher, Kurt von; Social Democratic Party; Versailles, Treaty of; Young Plan

Suggestions for further reading:
Abraham, David. 1986. *The Collapse of the Weimar Republic: Political Economy and Crisis.* 2nd ed. New York: Holmes and Meier.
Bookbinder, Paul. 1996. *Weimar Germany: The Republic of the Reasonable.* Manchester and New York: Manchester University Press.
Broszat, Martin. 1987. *Hitler and the Collapse of Weimar Germany.* Leamington Spa: Berg.
Kolb, Eberhard. 1988. *The Weimar Republic.* London: Unwin Hyman.
Nicholls, A. J. 1991. *Weimar and the Rise of Hitler.* 3rd ed. New York: Macmillan.

West Wall

See Siegfried Line

Winterhilfe

As part of creating a sense of *Volksge-meinschaft* in 1933 Hitler's government initiated the Winterhilfe (winter help) program in which money, food, and clothing were collected from the better-off to be distributed to poor families. Contributions were collected in the streets by Sturmabteilung men, and large sums of money passed through the inevitable Nazi corruption and did reach the needy. In 1937 about 10 million people received money or

parcels. Money was deducted from workers' wages during winter, but for the most part donations in the early years were genuinely voluntary, until with the drop in unemployment, contributions were diverted to pay for welfare measures and rearmament. Giving to the Winterhilfe became a compulsory gesture of conformity and political reliability, a coercive plebiscite for the regime. Talking about the campaign in 1942, Hitler declared: "While others talk about democracy, this is true democracy" (Welch 1993, p. 60).

The gestures associated with Winterhilfe provided Nazi leaders with excellent photo opportunities. Hitler and Goebbels were shown enjoying the *Eintopf* (one-pot) meals, "the meal of sacrifice for the Reich," by which people were exhorted to have only one dish for Sunday lunch during the winter months and donate what they had saved to the collectors who came knocking threateningly at the door. Similarly, on "days of national solidarity," the Nazi top brass would be seen working in soup kitchens or carrying out other such charitable acts. Charity became an expression of the "national community" and proof of loyalty to the Führer, backed by threats of violence and public shame. The last major campaign in 1942, the collection of winter clothing for suffering soldiers on the Eastern Front, was a great success. Fear of Russian invasion encouraged Germans who were not necessarily committed Nazis to make an effort in a vain attempt to save the regime.

Related entries: Social Policy; *Volksgemeinschaft*

Suggestions for further reading:
Welch, David. 1993. *The Third Reich: Politics and Propaganda.* London and New York: Routledge.

Women

For Hitler the role of women in the world was to produce children and hence preserve the species and the race. In Nazi ideology the family household was the foundation of the state, and nature decreed that this was women's special sphere and responsibility. A woman's place was in the home, circumscribed within the traditional limits of *Kinder, Kirche, und Küche* (children, church, and kitchen). The political and social emancipation of women under the Weimar Republic was to be reversed and the public sphere of politics and the professions reserved for men. The National Socialist Women's Union was run by and for women, but they were to hold no positions of leadership in the Nazi Party. Hitler attracted a considerable following among women, probably equal to that among men, but not among the emancipated, the left-wing, or the even remotely feminist. The promise of order, stability, prosperity, and national revival appealed to both sexes, but not on specific gender grounds.

Marriage was women's destiny, but not, Hitler said, as "an end in itself, but must serve the one higher goal, the increase and preservation of the species and the race. This alone is its meaning and its task" (Hitler 1992, p. 229). Motherhood was accordingly rewarded with social esteem and medals, the Mutterkreuz. In the Bund Deutscher Mädel (League of German Girls, or BDM), the girls' equivalent of the Hitler Youth, adolescent girls' minds and bodies were trained for their future role. Though the BDM provided girls with the opportunity to escape their home lives through summer schools, camping trips, and hikes, this was only temporary relief. Women's bodies were not their own but dedicated to the service of the nation and the *Volksgemeinschaft*.

Generous benefits, advice, and support were provided for mothers, except, of course, for Jews and women judged to be "hereditarily inferior." Even single women, if they were good Aryans, were encouraged to have children, helped by the Lebensborn (well of life) agency established by the SS in December 1935. The decision not to have children was made grounds for divorce, while abortion was restricted to women whose lives were medically certified to be in danger. All forms of birth control were condemned, except for Jews. The Nazis blamed Germany's declining birth rate in the early twentieth century on the feminist movement, so women were to be discouraged from entering the professions. The proportion of women admitted to universities was reduced to 10 percent by a decree of December 1933, and women were permitted to enter the civil service only after the age of thirty-five. The government provided marriage loans to women to give up their jobs, loans that could be paid off by bearing children.

Nazi policies succeeded in raising marriage and birth rates, but Hitler's external aggression and the gearing up of society for war worked eventually against the desire to confine women to the home and childbed. The proportion of women in the workforce declined from 37 percent in 1933 to 31 percent in 1937. But the total numbers of working women grew thereafter with the need for workers in war-related industries, the shortage of male workers, conscription, and the desire of women with children to supplement family incomes. The ban on employment for women in receipt of marriage loans was revoked in 1937, and by 1939 there were 7 million women in the blue- and white-collar workforce.

Hitler wanted to keep women at home even during wartime, partly for ideological reasons and partly to enforce the pretense that "normal" life could continue for ordinary women. But grim reality forced changes. By 1944 the number of women working in industry had increased to about 14.5 million. This could not compare with the mobilization of women in Britain or the United States, where the ideological objections were weaker and the sense of emergency not kept hidden for so long, but in the later stages of the war women accounted for some 60 percent of the domestic labor force. For all Hitler's efforts, in 1945 a much higher proportion of German women were in employment than in 1933.

Related entries: Education; Mutterkreuz; Social Policy; Total War; Working Class

Suggestions for further reading:
Bridenthal, Renate, Anita Grossmann, and Marion Kaplan, eds. 1984. *When Biology Became Destiny: Women in Weimar and Nazi Germany.* New York: Monthly Review Press.
Evans, Richard J. 1976. "German Women and the Triumph of Hitler," *Journal of Modern History* 48, pp. 1–53 (demand supplement).
Hitler, Adolf. 1992. *Mein Kampf.* Trans. Ralph Manheim. Intro. by D. C. Watt. London: Pimlico.
Pine, Lisa. 1997. *Nazi Family Policy, 1933–1945.* London: Berg.
———. 1999. "Girls in Uniform," *History Today* 49 (3), pp. 24–29.
Stephenson, Jill. 1975. *Women in Nazi Society.* London: Croom Helm.
———. 1980. *The Nazi Organization of Women.* London: Croom Helm.

Working Class

Hitler's appeals to the working-class electorate under the Weimar Republic amounted to little more than his intermittent anticapitalist rhetoric and the general Nazi strategy of offering something for everyone. He contrasted the idealized figure of "the German worker" with the "criminal functionaries" of the system; promised to abolish unemployment by destroying the Treaty of Versailles, which he alleged was at the root of it; and promised that manual labor would be honored and its value recognized in his new Reich. Working-class support for the National Socialist German Workers' Party (NSDAP, Nazi Party) came mainly from nonorganized workers in sectors and regions where the hold of left-wing parties and trade unions was weak, in small-scale industry, agricul-

ture, public service, transportation, commerce, and private services. In the early 1930s between 26 percent and 32 percent of Nazi Party members described themselves as "workers," a fluid category that probably included many self-employed. Working-class support for Hitler, then, was real but in proportional terms far below that of the middle classes.

The idea that Hitler produced prosperity and contentment for the working class is tenacious but wrong. In 1936 the trustee of labor for Hesse characterized the attitude of workers after three years of Nazi rule not as "real peace" but as "resignation and surrender" (Mason 1993, p. 150). Nazi ideology replaced class conflict with the united "factory community" and more human class and labor relations with social peace guaranteed by the "Führer principle" within the workplace. Yet after the destruction of the trade unions and other working-class organizations, workers probably respected the German Labor Front (DAF) and the "Beauty of Work" campaign less than they did Hitler or the regime as a whole. While the DAF struggled against other organs of the Nazi state to improve workers' lives and ensure their loyalty to the regime, the workers themselves were more concerned with the traditional priorities of higher pay, shorter hours, and longer holidays.

The return to full employment and the competition for labor in industries affected by the rearmament drive improved workers' conditions and bargaining power. Between December 1935 and June 1939 gross average hourly earnings in industry increased by nearly 11 percent and weekly earnings by some 17 percent, though workers in consumer goods industries benefited little and a part of the gains was the result of being forced to work longer hours. Workers' attitudes were marked by apathy and indifference to politics, but Hitler himself seemed to meet with general approval. Attempts to control the jobs market to overcome the severe shortage of skilled workers were halfhearted for fear of alienating workers from the regime. Hitler was unwilling to impose too great a material burden on the working class, even in the cause of massive rearmament, and the resultant economic problems could, in his view, be overcome by suitable exercise of the will. The working class, neutralized as a political force, may not have been converted to Nazism, but Hitler ensured that they would accept it.

Hitler's memories of 1918 and working-class revolution colored his attitudes both before and during the war. His concern not to impose overly strict limits on working-class consumption did not seriously affect the war effort in the period of victory and blitzkrieg, but it did make the mobilization for total war more difficult. The use of forced labor from the occupied territories and the concentration camps to replace Germans conscripted into the armed forces was no substitute for skilled German workers. For all Hitler's intentions, rationing and a fall in consumption hit the German working class ever harder as the war went on, but a combination of terror, respect for Hitler personally, and the relatively privileged position of German workers prevented the growth of serious working-class opposition.

Related entries: Agriculture; Communist Party; Economic Policy; German Labor Front; Industry; Ley, Robert; National Socialist Factory Cell Organization; Opposition; Public Opinion; Social Democratic Party; Social Policy; "Strength through Joy"; Trade Unions; Unemployment; *Volksgemeinschaft;* Women

Suggestions for further reading:
Mason, Timothy W. 1993. *Social Policy in the Third Reich: The Working Class and the "National Community."* Providence and Oxford: Berg.

World War I

As a political figure Hitler was a product of World War I. "Without the experience of war," Ian Kershaw writes, "the humiliation of defeat, and the upheaval of revolution the failed artist and social drop-out would not have discovered what to do with his life by entering politics and finding his métier as a propagandist and beerhall demagogue" (Kershaw 1998, p. 73). Whatever he may have said in *Mein Kampf* about his political ideas being fully formed before 1914, in reality it was the war that gave meaning to his life. His years in uniform, he said in 1924, were "the greatest and most unforgettable time of my earthly existence" (Hitler 1992, p. 150). And without the humiliation of surrender, which provided Hitler with the myth of the "stab in the back" by the "November criminals," his incoherent and hate-filled message would have encountered much greater difficulty in finding a receptive audience.

Hitler had left Vienna to avoid military service in the Austrian army, and the outbreak of the war in August 1914 found him in Munich. A famous photograph taken by Heinrich Hoffmann, later his personal photographer, shows Hitler among the crowd in the Odeonsplatz enthusiastically greeting the news of war. He at once volunteered for service, was accepted by the 16th Bavarian Reserve Infantry Regiment, and in October was fighting in the first battle of Ypres. He remained on the Western Front without applying for home leave until he was wounded in October 1916. There is no doubt that Hitler was a courageous soldier. His work as a regimental runner, carrying messages when other methods of communication broke down, was fraught with danger, and he had many narrow escapes. In all he took part in some forty engagements from 1914 to 1918.

It appears that Hitler could not stand life away from the front, as if he had come to depend on it. In *Mein Kampf* he was to express in a very crude way the *Fronterlebnis,* the unique "front experience" that more talented nationalist writers like Ernst

Hitler (right) with his fellow dispatch messengers Ernst Schmidt and Anton Bachmann and their dog Foxl at Fournes on the Western Front in April 1915. For Hitler, as for many ex-soldiers, the **Fronterlebnis** *("front experience") was central to the development of his political ideas. (Archive Photos)*

Jünger were to turn into a minor branch of literature. Hitler was one of the *Front-kämpfer,* who were to play an important role in the creation of the Nazi Party. His apologia of the violent warrior male found its justification in the intensity of combat amid the horrors of the Western Front. After his return to the front in March 1917, Hitler took part in the German offensives of 1917 and early 1918 with renewed optimism. By the summer of 1918, when he was awarded the Iron Cross, First Class, an exceptional honor for a mere corporal, Hitler was convinced that Germany was in sight of victory.

Caught in a British gas attack in October 1918, Hitler was lying, temporarily blinded, in hospital at Pasewalk when he heard of the insurrection of German workers and soldiers leading to the abdication of the Kaiser, the declaration of the republic, and on 11 November the new government's acceptance of the Allies' armistice terms. His anger at the "shirkers" and "traitors" who had in his eyes betrayed Germany knew no bounds. "If today the graves of Flanders field were to open," he wrote in *Mein Kampf,* "from them would arise the bloody accusers, hundreds of thousands of the best young Germans who, due to the unscrupulousness of these parliamentarian criminals, were driven, poorly trained and half-trained, into the arms of death" (Hitler 1992, p. 247).

The enthusiasm that had marked the beginning of the war had seemed to confirm Hitler's crass racial view of history. "In August 1914" he wrote, "the whole Jewish jabber about international solidarity had vanished at one stroke from the heads of the German working class, and in its stead, only a few weeks later, American shrapnel began to pour down the blessings of brotherhood on the helmets of our marching columns" (Hitler 1992, p. 155). Now Hitler wove his own fantasy about how that spirit had been betrayed. The sacrifices of the German soldiers had been in vain. Hitler could not accept that Germany had been defeated militarily and that unrest and revolution at home was a consequence, not a cause of the exhaustion brought on by years of warfare. It was much easier to blame the enemies of the fatherland: Jews, Marxists, and the "fools, liars and criminals" who had stabbed the nation in the back. This was a potent myth ripe for exploitation by demagogues of the Right. Within a year of the end of the war, Hitler, once again at loose ends, decided to go into politics.

Related entries: *Mein Kampf;* Weimar Republic

Suggestions for further reading:
Hitler, Adolf. 1992. *Mein Kampf.* Trans. Ralph Manheim. Intro. by D. C. Watt. London: Pimlico.
Kershaw, Ian. 1998. *Hitler 1889–1936: Hubris.* New York: Allen Lane The Penguin Press.

Yalta Conference

By the time Winston Churchill, Franklin Delano Roosevelt, and Joseph Stalin met for the second time, at Yalta in the Crimea, from 4 to 11 February 1945, Russian, British, and U.S. troops were all fighting on German soil. Hitler's very last hope—a split between the Allies—was revealed as the final illusion. Roosevelt's primary goal at Yalta was to secure Soviet participation in the war against Japan; Churchill's wish was to continue the "special relationship' with the United States into peacetime and maintain U.S. involvement in European affairs; and Stalin was preoccupied with securing Russian territory and his own dictatorship by extending the frontiers of the Soviet Union and creating a large sphere of influence in Europe and Asia. Most of the discussions, therefore, concerned Poland and southeastern Europe. Stalin argued for the dismemberment of Germany, but any mention of this was kept out of the final communiqué. All Hitler got from Yalta and his hopes of Allied disunity was a communiqué announcing agreement on the defeat and occupation of Germany and a reaffirmation of the demand for unconditional surrender.

Suggestions for further reading:
Kimball, Warren F. 1997. *Forged in War: Churchill, Roosevelt and the Second World War.* London: HarperCollins.

Young Plan

The final plan for German payment of war reparations was drawn up in 1929 by a committee headed by Owen Young, the former vice chairman of the Dawes Committee. Under the plan Germany would continue to pay reparations until 1988, the same year in which France would complete repayment of its war debts to the United States. In return for accepting the Young Plan, Germany would regain complete financial independence, with Allied controls over its railways and banking system abolished. The scheme aroused furious opposition among German nationalists, not so much because of its terms as because it set the seal on Germany's defeat, mortgaged the future for generations, and would weaken German will to undermine the Treaty of Versailles.

Opposition was led by Alfred Hugenberg, who in July 1929 established a committee to campaign for a plebiscite rejecting the plan. The Nazis were invited to participate in the campaign alongside the German National People's Party, the Stahlhelm, and the Pan-German League. Hugenberg thought he could use Hitler's unrestrained attacks on the Weimar system to whip up popular support, while Hitler saw the campaign as "the occasion for a propaganda wave the like of which had never been seen before" (Kershaw 1998, p.

Churchill, Roosevelt, and Stalin at the Yalta Conference, February 1945, assisted by their respective foreign ministers Anthony Eden, Edward R. Stettinius, and Vyacheslav Molotov. (Culver Pictures)

318). He made the decision to take part without consulting other party leaders, but links with the other organizations were supervised by Gregor Strasser. The plan provided the Nazis with much-needed and valuable publicity in the Hugenberg press at a time when the party's electoral fortunes were just beginning to revive, provided them with an aura of respectability, and introduced Hitler to potentially helpful men of wealth and influence.

In the plebiscite of December 1929 the campaign against the Young Plan registered 5.8 million votes, well short of the 21 million needed for success. But it had ensured that acceptance was seen in Germany as an expedient at best, a national humiliation at worst. In any event the plan was rendered irrelevant by the onset of the Depression. Its principal effect in Germany may well have been to increase right-wing illusions

that they could use and control Hitler for their own propagandist ends.

Related entries: Dawes Plan; Hugenberg, Alfred; Propaganda; Reparations

Suggestions for further reading:
Kent, Bruce. 1989. *The Spoils of War: The Politics, Economics and Diplomacy of Reparations, 1918–1932.* Oxford: Clarendon Press.
Kershaw, Ian. 1998. *Hitler 1889–1936: Hubris.* New York: Allen Lane The Penguin Press.

Youth Policy

The Nazis presented their movement as a "young" movement, channeling the rebelliousness of the young against old outmoded institutions, and this strategy paid dividends shown particularly by the support they gained among students. Hitler retained throughout his life a juvenile contempt for formal education and learning, considered that "youth must be led by youth," and insisted that, like himself, young people should learn principally from the hard school of real life. The stress on youth was shown in the importance given to the Reich Youth Leadership, established in 1931 under Baldur von Schirach, which sponsored the Hitler Youth, the National Socialist German Students' League, and the National Socialist School Students' League. It achieved government status in June 1933, when Schirach was appointed "Youth Führer of the German Reich," and became a Supreme Reich Authority in 1936.

The "coordination" of German youth was to be achieved through the Hitler Youth and revolutionary changes in the education system. Youthful supporters of Hitler were made to feel special as Hitler Youth leaders who were granted the privileges of issuing commands, wearing uniforms, and carrying daggers. On 6 November 1933 Hitler warned his adult opponents: "Your child belongs to me already. A people lives forever. What are you? You will pass on. Your descendants, however, now stand in the new camp. In a short time they will know nothing but this new community" (Horn 1976, p. 428). He appealed successfully to the idealistic, anti-industrial spirit of the earlier middle-class Youth Movement, but with disastrous consequences for education in Germany.

The attempt to "capture" German youth, however, was bedeviled by rivalry between the Hitler Youth and the education system. The new Germans may have been disciplined and obedient to the Führer but not toward their teachers, even when Nazis were still seen as on the wrong side of a generational conflict in which the future belonged to the young. Educational standards fell dramatically, which in turn weakened Germany's war effort. Hitler lacked the requisite numbers of trained and educated technicians to back up his mili-

tary victories. Instead, sixteen- to eighteen-year-olds were conscripted to man antiaircraft batteries, sent to military preparedness camps, and beginning in 1943 evacuated from heavily bombed cities. At the same time, the rebellious spirit that had once helped Hitler was turned among circles of working-class young people and secondary school students against the tedious activities of the Hitler Youth and the all-pervading control of the party. Groups such as the "Edelweiss Pirates" moved from superficial nonconformity toward organized opposition, and the White Rose student group in Munich paid with their lives for plotting the destruction of Nazi terror. Hitler's once successful courting of the young ended in numerous executions and the creation of special concentration camps, such as that in Neuweid for young men under the age of twenty.

Related entries: Education; Hitler Youth; Nazi Movement; Opposition; Schirach, Baldur von

Suggestions for further reading:
Horn, Daniel. 1976. "The Hitler Youth and Educational Decline in the Third Reich," *History of Education Quarterly* 16, pp. 425–447.
Stachura, Peter D. 1981. *The German Youth Movement, 1900–1945.* New York: St. Martin's Press.

Yugoslavia

Established as the "Kingdom of the Serbs, Croats, and Slovenes" under the Versailles settlement in 1919, the highly unstable southern Slav state assumed the name Yugoslavia in October 1929. King Alexander I established a "royal dictatorship" by a coup on 6 January 1929. After his assassination in Marseille on 9 October 1934, power lay with a regency council acting for the minor King Peter II. A German-Yugoslav trade agreement, signed on 1 May 1934, increased Yugoslav economic dependence on Germany despite its formally neutral position in foreign policy. The ever-closer Yugoslav dependence on Hitler, deemed necessary because of Benito Mussolini's aggression in neighboring Albania and Greece, culminated in Yugoslavia joining the Tripartite Pact in March 1941.

The alliance with Hitler provoked an anti-German military coup in Yugoslavia, one of the reasons for Hitler's invasion in April 1941 when his armies swept through the Balkans to Greece. On 10 April 1941 an "independent state of Croatia" was proclaimed by Ante Pavelic; Montenegro also became an "independent" puppet state; and the remaining Yugoslav territory was divided among the Greater German Reich, Italy, Hungary, and Bulgaria. The government-in-exile in London, under Peter II, was dropped by the Allies in 1943 in favor of Tito's communist partisan movement. By November 1945, after bitter fighting between communist and noncommunist partisans, the transformation into the Federal People's Republic of Yugoslavia was complete.

Related entries: Bulgaria; Foreign Policy; Greece; Hungary; Italy; Mihajlović, Draža; Pavelic, Ante; Resistance Movements; Tito, Josip Broz

Z

Zeitzler, Kurt von (1893–1963)

A career officer, Zeitzler impressed Hitler by his logistical planning of the western offensive of 1940. He was made chief of staff of the German Army High Command in 1942, replacing Franz Halder, who had been too outspoken in his criticism of Hitler's interference in the Stalingrad campaign. Albert Speer called him "a straightforward, insensitive person who made his reports in a loud voice. He was not the type of military man given to independent thinking and no doubt represented the kind of Chief of Staff Hitler wanted" (Speer 1971, p. 333). Zeitzler supported Hitler in the launching of the battle of Kursk in 1943, but its failure caused him to be removed from playing any further part in the initiation of operations. He then adopted a peculiar line in diplomatic illnesses (feigning illness so as not to attend meetings), effectively ceasing to carry out his duties, and after several unsuccessful attempts to resign was dismissed from the army in July 1944.

Related entries: Wehrmacht

Suggestions for further reading:
Speer, Albert. 1971. *Inside the Third Reich.* Paperback ed. London: Sphere Books.

Zhukov, Georgi Konstantinovich (1896–1974)

Appointed commander in chief of the Red Army in October 1941, Marshal Zhukov played a leading role in Hitler's defeat in the east, but one he was prone to exaggerate to the detriment of other Soviet commanders. His greatest achievement was probably the defense of Moscow in December 1941 and the successful counteroffensive that drove the Germans back from the suburbs of the Russian capital. Zhukov's subsequent counteroffensives at Stalingrad, Kursk, and in the Ukraine showed his tactics of aiming continuous blows along the length of the front without any consideration of the cost in human lives. During this period he spent much time in Moscow advising Joseph Stalin on strategy, allowing his front commanders freedom of action.

Returning to field command in March 1944, Zhukov drove the 1st Ukrainian Front to the Hungarian frontier, directed the advance on Warsaw, and in April 1945 ordered the launch of the final offensive against Berlin. He took the surrender of German forces on 2 May, three days after Hitler's suicide. Zhukov's success and his popularity among his soldiers aroused Stalin's mistrust, and in 1946 he was effectively sidelined by being given command of a relatively small military district. He got his revenge, however, and full recognition for his part in defeating Hitler by becoming Soviet minister of defense after Stalin's death in 1953.

Related entries: Eastern Front; Kursk, Battle of; Stalin, Joseph; Stalingrad, Battle of

Suggestions for further reading:
Overy, Richard J. 1998. *Russia's War.* New York: Allen Lane Penguin Press.

DOCUMENTS

HITLER'S WORLDVIEW

From the confused and repetitive morass of half-baked claptrap that is *Mein Kampf,* the foundations of Hitler's worldview in a racial interpretation of history, anti-Semitism, and anti-Marxism do nevertheless emerge, if not with clarity, then at least with force. In this extract from the section on "Philosophy and Party," his peculiar view of "Jewish bolshevism" is opposed to the "folkish philosophy," and Hitler's fantastic conception of the connections between race and politics is expressed in a typically incoherent but atypically succinct fashion.

Our present political world view, current in Germany, is based in general on the idea that creative, culture-creating force must indeed be attributed to the state, but that it has nothing to do with racial considerations, but is rather a product of economic necessities, or, at best, the natural result of a political urge for power. This underlying view, if logically developed, leads not only to a mistaken conception of basic racial forces, but also to an underestimation of the individual. For a denial of the difference of the various races with regard to their general culture-creating forces must necessarily extend this greatest of all errors to the judgment of the individual. The assumption of the equality of the races then becomes a basis for a similar way of viewing peoples and finally individual men. And hence international Marxism is only the transference, by the Jew, Karl Marx, of a philosophical attitude and conception, which had actually long been in existence, into the form of a definite political creed. Without the subsoil of such generally existing poisoning, the amazing success of this doctrine would never have been possible. Actually Karl Marx was only the one among millions who, with the sure eye of the prophet, recognised in this morass of a slowly decomposing world the most essential poisons, extracted them, and, like a wizard, prepared them into a concentrated solution for the swifter annihilation of the independent existence of free nations on this earth. And all this in the service of his race.

His Marxist doctrine is a brief spiritual extract of the philosophy of life that is generally current today. And for this reason alone any struggle of our so-called bourgeois world against it is impossible, absurd in fact, since this bourgeois world is also essentially infected by these poisons, and worships a view of life which in general is distinguished from the Marxists only by degrees and personalities. The bourgeois world is Marxist, but believes in the possibility of the rule of certain groups of men (bourgeoisie), while Marxism itself systematically plans to hand the world over to the Jews.

In opposition to this, the folkish philosophy finds the importance of mankind in its basic racial elements. In the state it sees on principle only a means to an end and construes its end as the preservation of the racial existence of man. Thus, it by no means believes in an equality of the races, but along with their difference it recognises their higher or lesser value and feels itself obligated, through this knowledge, to promote the victory of the better and stronger, and demand the subordination of the inferior and weaker in accordance with the eternal will that dominates the universe. Thus, in principle, it serves the basic aristocratic idea of Nature and believes in the validity of this law down to the last individual. It sees not only the different value of the races, but also the different value of individuals. From the mass it extracts the importance of the individual personality, and thus, in contrast to disorganising Marxism, it has an organising effect. It believes in the necessity of an idealisation of humanity. But it cannot grant the right to existence even to an ethical idea if this idea represents a danger for the racial life of the bearers of a higher ethics; for in a bastardised and niggerised world all the concepts of the humanly beautiful and sublime, as well as all ideas of an idealised future of our humanity, would be lost forever.

Human culture and civilisation on this continent are inseparably bound up with the presence of the Aryan. If he dies out or declines, the dark veils of an age without culture will again descend on this globe.

The undermining of the existence of human culture by the destruction of its bearer seems in the eyes of a folkish philosophy the most execrable crime. Anyone who dares to lay hands on the highest image of the Lord commits sacrilege against the benevolent creator of this miracle and contributes to the expulsion from paradise.

And so the folkish philosophy of life corresponds to the innermost will of Nature, since it restores that free play of forces which must lead to a continuous mutual higher breeding, until at last the best of humanity, having achieved possession of this earth, will have a free path for activity in domains which will lie partly above it and partly outside it.

We all sense that in the distant future humanity must be faced by problems which only a highest race, become master people and supported by the means and possibilities of an entire globe, will be equipped to overcome. . . .

It is self-evident that so general a statement of the meaningful content of a folkish philosophy can be interpreted in thousands of ways. And actually we find hardly a one of our newer political formations which does not base itself in one way or another on this world view. And, by its very existence in the face of so many others, it shows the difference of its conceptions. And so the Marxist world view, led by a unified top organisation, is opposed by a hodge-podge of views which even as ideas are not very impressive in face of the solid, hostile front. Victories are not gained by such feeble weapons! Not until the international world view—politically led by organised Marxism—is confronted by a folkish world view, organised and led with equal unity, will success, supposing the fighting energy to be equal on both sides, fall to the side of eternal truth.

A philosophy can only be organisationally comprehended on the basis of a definite formulation of that philosophy, and what dogmas represent for religious faith, party principles are for a political party in the making.

Hence an instrument must be created for the folkish world view which enables it to fight, just as the Marxist party organisation creates a free path for internationalism.

This is the goal pursued by the National Socialist German Workers' Party.

Excerpts from *Mein Kampf* by Adolf Hitler, translated by Ralph Manheim. Copyright © 1943, renewed 1971 by Houghton Mifflin Company. Reprinted by permission of Houghton Mifflin Company and The Random House Group Ltd. on behalf of Pimlico. All rights reserved.

THE BEER HALL PUTSCH

Hitler used his trial after the failure of the Beer Hall Putsch in 1923 to address a sympathetic audience about his political ideas and make a plea before "the court of history." At that time he still saw himself as a "drummer," announcing the coming messianic leader who would save Germany, but he spells out his plans with grandiose rhetorical flourishes. The judges, sympathizers with the aims of the putsch, ensured that Hitler was given the minimum sentence of five years' imprisonment and would be released early on probation.

Lossow said here that he had spoken with me in the spring and had not noticed then that I was trying to get something for myself and had thought that I only wanted to be a propagandist and a man who would rouse people.

How petty are the thoughts of small men! You can take my word for it, that I do not consider a ministerial post worth striving for . . .

From the very first I have aimed at something more than becoming a Minister. I have resolved to be the destroyer of Marxism. This I shall achieve and once I've achieved that, I should find the title of "Minister" ridiculous. When I first stood in front of Wagner's grave, my heart overflowed with pride that here lay a man who had forbidden any such inscription as "Here lies State Councillor, Musical Director, His Excellency Richard von Wagner." I was proud that this man and so many others in German history have been content to leave their names to posterity and not their titles. It was not through modesty that I was willing to be a "drummer" at that time for that is the highest task: the rest is nothing. . . .

I am no monarchist, but ultimately a Republican. Pöhner is a monarchist, Ludendorff is devoted to the House of Hohenzollern. Despite our different attitudes we all stood together. The fate of Germany does not lie in the choice between a Republic or a Monarchy, but in the content of the Republic and the Monarchy. What I am contending against is not the form of a state as such, but its ignominious content. We wanted to create in Germany the precondition which alone will make it possible for the iron grip of our enemies to be removed from us. We wanted to create order in the state, throw out the drones, take up the fight against international stock exchange slavery, against our whole economy being cornered by trusts, against the politicising of the trade unions, and above all, for the highest honourable duty which we, as Germans, know should be once more introduced—the duty of bearing arms, military service. And now I ask you: Is what we wanted high treason? . . .

. . . The army which we have formed grows from day to day; it grows more rapidly from hour to hour. Even now I have the proud hope that one day the hour will come when these untrained bands will grow to battalions, the battalions to regiments and the regiments to divisions, when the old cockade will be raised from the mire, when the old banners will once again wave before us: and the reconciliation will come in that eternal last Court of Judgement, the Court of God, before which we are ready to take our stand. Then from our bones, from our graves, will sound the voice of that tribunal which alone has the right to sit in judgement upon us. For, gentlemen, it is not you who pronounce judgement upon us, it is the external Court of History which will make its pronouncement upon the charge which is brought against us. The verdict that you will pass I know. But that Court will not ask of us, "Did you commit high treason or did you not?" That Court will judge us . . .as Germans who wanted the best for their people and their fatherland, who wished to fight and die. You may pronounce us guilty a thousand times, but the Goddess who presides over the Eternal Court of History will with a smile tear in pieces the charge of the Public Prosecutor and the verdict of this court. For she acquits us.

Noakes, Jeremy, and Geoffrey Pridham, eds. 1983. *Nazism 1919–1945: A Documentary Reader. Vol. 1: The Rise to Power 1919–1934*. Exeter: University of Exeter Press, pp. 34–35. Reprinted by permission.

MEIN KAMPF: *LEBENSRAUM AND RUSSIA*

In *Mein Kampf* Hitler made his ultimate expansionist project crystal clear. German power would be built upon racial expansion to the east against an enfeebled Jew-dominated Russia and the acquisition broken by "the German plough." However pragmatic he was forced to be during his early years in power, it would have been evident to anyone who had read Hitler's book that his foreign policy would be inseparable from anti-Marxist ideology and racism.

As opposed to this [the restoration of Germany's 1914 boundaries], we National Socialists must hold unflinchingly to our aim in foreign policy, namely, to secure for the German people the land and soil to which they are entitled on this earth. And this action is the only one which, before God and our German posterity, would

make any sacrifice of blood seem justified: before God, because we have been put on this earth with the mission of eternal struggle for our daily bread, beings who receive nothing as a gift, and who owe their position as lords of the earth only to the genius and courage with which they can conquer and defend it; and before our German posterity in so far as we have shed no citizen's blood out of which a thousand others are not bequeathed to posterity. The soil on which some day German generations of peasants can beget powerful sons will sanction the investment of the sons of today, and will some day acquit the responsible statesmen of blood–guilt and sacrifice of the people, even if they are persecuted by their contemporaries. . . .

Much as all of us today recognise the necessity of a reckoning with France, it would remain ineffectual in the long run if it represented the whole of our aim in foreign policy. It can and will achieve meaning only if it offers the rear cover for an enlargement of our people's living space in Europe. For it is not in colonial acquisitions that we must see the solution of this problem, but exclusively in the acquisition of a territory for settlement, which will enhance the area of the mother country, and hence not only keep the new settlers in the most intimate community with the land of their origin, but secure for the total area those advantages which lie in its unified magnitude. . . .

But we National Socialists must go further. The right to possess soil can become a duty if without extension of its soil a great nation seems doomed to destruction. And most especially when not some little nigger nation or other is involved, but the Germanic mother of life, which has given the world its cultural picture. Germany will either be a world power or there will be no Germany. And for world power she needs that magnitude which will give her the position she needs in the present period, and life to her citizens. . . .

And so we National Socialists consciously draw a line beneath the foreign policy tendency of our pre-War period. We take up where we broke off six hundred years ago. We stop the endless German movement to the south and west, and turn our gaze towards the land in the east. At long last we break off the colonial and commercial policy of the pre-War period and shift to the soil policy of the future.

If we speak of soil in Europe today, we can primarily have in mind only Russia and her vassal border states.

Here Fate itself seems desirous of giving us a sign. By handing Russia to Bolshevism, it robbed the Russian nation of that intelligentsia which previously brought about and guaranteed its existence as a state. For the organisation of a Russian state formation was not the result of the political abilities of the Slavs in Russia, but only a wonderful example of the state-forming efficacy of the German element in an inferior race. Numerous mighty empires on earth have been created in this way. Lower nations led by Germanic organisers and overlords have more than once grown to be mighty state formations and have endured as long as the racial nucleus of the creative state race maintained itself. For centuries Russia drew nourishment from this Germanic nucleus of its upper leading strata. Today it can be regarded as almost totally exterminated and extinguished. It has been replaced by the Jew. Impossible as it is for the Russian by himself to shake off the yoke of the Jew by his own resources, it is equally impossible for the Jew to maintain the mighty empire forever. He himself is no element of organisation, but a ferment of decomposition. The Persian empire in the east is ripe for collapse. And the end of Jewish rule in Russia will also be the end of Russia as a state. We have been chosen by Fate as witness of a catastrophe which will be the mightiest confirmation of the soundness of folkish theory.

Our task, the mission of the National Socialist movement, is to bring our own people to such political insight that they will not see their goal for the future in the breath-taking sensation of a new Alexander's conquest, but in the industrious work of the German plough, to which the sword need only give soil.

Excerpts from *Mein Kampf* by Adolf Hitler, translated by Ralph Manheim. Copyright © 1943, renewed 1971 by Houghton Mifflin Company. Reprinted by permission of Houghton Mifflin Company and The Random House Group Ltd. on behalf of Pimlico. All rights reserved.

HITLER SPEAKS

Hitler's success was based not on the written word but on his skill as an orator, whipping up the fervor of crowds in packed and emotional mass meetings. The impact of Nazi rallies cannot by conveyed through merely reproducing Hitler's words. It is better shown in accounts like that of Frau Luise Solmitz, a Hamburg schoolteacher, of one such meeting in 1932.

The April sun shone hot like in summer and turned everything into a picture of gay expectation. There was immaculate order and discipline, although the police left the whole square to the stewards on the sidelines. Nobody spoke of "Hitler," always just "the Führer," "the Führer says," "the Führer wants," and what he said and wanted seemed right and good. The hours passed, the sun shone, expectations rose. In the background, at the edge of the track there were columns of carriers like ammunition carriers. What they carried were crates of beer. Aeroplanes above us. Testing of the loudspeakers, buzzing of the cine-cameras. It was nearly 3 p.m. "The Führer is coming!" A ripple went through the crowds. Around the speaker's platform one could see hands raised in the Hitler salute. A speaker opened the meeting, abused the "system," nobody listened to him. A second speaker welcomed Hitler and made way for the man who had drawn 120,000 people of all classes and ages. There stood Hitler in a simple black coat and looked over the crowd, waiting—a forest of swastika pennants swished up, the jubilation of this moment was given vent in a roaring salute. Main theme: Out of parties shall grow a nation, the German nation. He censured the "system" ("I want to know what there is left to be ruined in this state!"). "On the way here Socialists confronted me with a poster, 'Turn back, Adolf Hitler.' Thirteen years ago I was a simple unknown soldier. I went my way. I never turned back. Nor shall I turn back now." Otherwise he made no personal attacks, nor any promises, vague or definite. His voice was hoarse after all his speaking during the previous days. When the speech was over, there was roaring enthusiasm and applause. Hitler saluted, gave his thanks, the Horst Wessel song sounded out across the course. Hitler was helped into his coat. Then he went.—How many look up to him with touching faith! As their helper, their saviour, their deliverer from unbearable distress—to him who rescues the Prussian prince, the scholar, the clergyman, the farmer, the worker, the unemployed, who rescues them from the parties back into the nation.

Noakes, Jeremy, and Geoffrey Pridham, eds. 1983. *Nazism 1919–1945: A Documentary Reader. Vol. 1: The Rise to Power 1919–1934.* Exeter: University of Exeter Press, p. 74. Reprinted by permission.

PROCLAMATION OF 1 FEBRUARY 1933

Within twenty-four hours of becoming chancellor, Hitler issued a ringing proclamation to the German people. After blaming Marxism and the spirit of partisanship for the decline and ruin of Germany, Hitler promised economic recovery and the revival of Germany as a world power. German society would become united, with class collaboration replacing class struggle. By its very vagueness Hitler's program promised salvation for almost everyone but made no mention of what would happen to the Jews and anyone who did not fit into the new national community.

Over fourteen years have passed since that unholy day when, deluded by domestic and foreign promises, the German people forgot and thereby lost the highest values of its past, of the Reich.

Since that day of treason the Almighty has withheld His blessing from our people.

Discord and hatred made their entrance. In deep distress millions of the best German men and women from all stations of life saw the unity of the nation break apart and dissolve in a chaos of political and personal opinions, economic interests, and ideological differences. . . .

The heritage we have assumed is of the utmost gravity.

The task which we must solve is the most difficult one that has ever faced German statesmen. Faith in us, however, is unlimited, for we believe in our people and in their imperishable honor. Peasants, workers, and townsmen, all must work together to lay the foundation stones of our new Reich.

The national government sees as its first and foremost task to reestablish the spiritual unity of our people. It will preserve and protect the fundamentals on which our nation rests. It regards Christianity as the basis of our system of morality, the family as the germ cell of the body of the people and the state. It will look beyond ranks and classes in order to bring our people to the consciousness of a national and political unity and the duties which go along with it. To educate German youth it will use as a basis the glory of our great past and pride in our old traditions. In that way it will counter the spiritual, political, and cultural annihilation of a cruel war. Germany should not and will not sink into anarchism and communism.

That government will install a national discipline to replace turbulent instinct as the guiding principle of our lives. Thinking carefully in terms of such adjustments, it will thereby guarantee the energy and vitality of our nation.

The national government will see to the reorganization of the economy of our people through two great Four Year Plans: rescue of the German peasantry as a means of assuring the nourishment and thereby the life of the nation; and salvation of the German worker through a powerful and wide-ranging attack against unemployment.

In fourteen years the November parties have ruined the German agricultural class. In fourteen years they created an army of millions of unemployed.

The national government will, with iron will and tenacious perseverance, accomplish the following plan: Within four years the German farmer must be relieved of his misery. Within four years unemployment will be conquered. At the same time this hypothesis holds for the rest of industry.

The national government will combine the gigantic task of cleansing our economy with the task of accomplishing the cleansing of the Reich, the states, and the local communes in administrative and fiscal matters.

In that way only will the idea of a federated existence of the Reich be implemented.

To the foundation stones of this program belong the ideas of workers' responsibility and the politics of land settlement.

Care to guarantee daily bread will be combined with care for illness and old age.

In the economy of the administration, in the extension of work, in the attitude of the farmer, as well as in the use of initiative by the individual, lie the best guarantees for avoiding those experiments which would endanger our standards.

In its foreign policy, the national government regards it as its highest mission to preserve the right to life and with it the re-establishment of freedom for our people. Because it is dedicated to the task of bringing an end to the chaotic conditions inside Germany, it will work along in common with other nations in the task of fashioning a state of equal value and along with it of equal rights. For that purpose it bears the great responsibility of representing the free and equal people in the goal of winning and maintaining the peace, which all the world needs even more than in the past. Let us hope that all others will cooperate and understand the nature of this deep-felt wish for the benefit of Europe, indeed of all the world.

As great as is our love for our army as bearer of our weapons and as symbol of our great past, we would be happy if the world through its limitation of armaments would make it no longer necessary for us to increase our own weapons.

As Germany experiences this political and economic awakening and scrupulously fulfills its obligations to other nations, one overriding fact emerges: the overcoming of the communist disintegration of Germany.

We men of this government feel ourselves responsible before German history for the reconstruction of an ordered folk community and with it for the definite elimination of that crazy class warfare. We do not represent one class, but all the German people, the millions of farmers, city folk, and workers, who will either together overcome the troubles of these times or succumb to them.

We are determined, true to our oath, and despite the incompetence of the present Reichstag, to accomplish this goal, and to place its implementation where it belongs, on the German people, whom we represent.

Reich President General Field Marshal von Hindenburg has called on us to use our courage to bring about the reconstruction of the nation.

We appeal, therefore, once more to the German people to give its support to this act of conciliation.

The government of the national uprising will work, and you will work. It was not responsible for the fourteen years during which the nation fell apart, but it will lead the nation upward. It is determined to make good within four years all the damage done in fourteen.

All alone it just cannot effect the reconstruction necessitated by the collapse.

The parties of Marxism and their collaborators have had fourteen years to show what they can do. The result has been desolation. Now, German people, give us four years and then judge and try us!

True to the command of the General Field Marshal shall we begin: May Almighty God bless us in our work, maintain our will, bless our judgment, and favor us with the trust of our people. For we desire not to struggle for ourselves alone, but for Germany!

From *Hitler's Third Reich: A Documentary History,* 1st edition, ed. by Louis L. Snyder, © 1981. Chicago: Nelson-Hall, pp. 85–89. Reprinted by permission of Wadsworth, a division of Thompson Learning. Fax 800-730-2215.

RACIAL "SCIENCE"

The elevation of the "study of race" to scientific respectability reached down into the classrooms. The standard work used to indoctrinate German children was Professor Hermann Grauch's *New Foundations of Racial Research,* in which the professor reclassified the animal world into Nordic

men and lower animals, the latter including the other races, notably blacks and Jews.

In non-Nordics, the teeth, corresponding to the snoutlike narrowness of the upper jaw, stand at a more oblique angle than in animals. The grinding motion of chewing in Nordics allows mastication to take place with the mouth closed, whereas men of other races are inclined to make the same smacking noise as animals . . .

The Nordic mouth has further superiorities. Just as the color red has a stirring effect, the bright red mouth of Nordics attracts and provokes kisses and courtship. The Nordic mouth is kiss-capable. On the other hand, the non-Nordic's broad, thick-lipped mouth together with his wide-dilated nostrils display sensual eagerness, a false and malicious sneering expression and a dipping movement indicative of voluptuous self-indulgence.

Talking with the aid of hands and feet is characteristic of non-Nordics, whereas the Nordic man stands calmly, often enough with his hands in his pockets.

Generally speaking, the Nordic race alone can emit sounds of untroubled clearness, whereas among non-Nordics the pronunciation is impure, the individual sounds are more confused and like the noises made by animals, such as barking, sniffing, snoring, squeaking. . . . That birds can learn to talk better than other animals is explained by the fact that their mouths are Nordic in structure—that is to say, high, narrow, and short-tongued. The shape of the Nordic gum allows a superior movement of the tongue, which is the reason why Nordic talking and singing are fuller . . .

If non-Nordics are more closely allied to monkeys and apes than to Nordics, why is it possible for them to mate with Nordics and not with animals? The answer is this: it has not been proved that non-Nordics cannot mate with apes.

From *Hitler's Third Reich: A Documentary History,* 1st edition, ed. by Louis L. Snyder,

© 1981. Chicago: Nelson-Hall, pp. 85–89. Reprinted by permission of Wadsworth, a division of Thompson Learning. Fax 800-730-2215.

LIFE UNDER HITLER

The journal of the novelist and anti-Nazi Hermann Stresau provides a vivid picture of life under Hitler's regime. The reality behind the image of the *Volksgemeinschaft* is revealed as a pervasive atmosphere of fear, where chance or careless remarks could have the most distressing consequences. Stresau also notes the generation gap, how the younger generation who had not experienced World War I were much less concerned about the dangers inherent in Hitler's policies.

The German way or, rather, that which is German sits closer than ever on the body, it constricts one, and at times takes one's breath away. Hitler's rule is no longer the rule of Hitler alone. One could almost think he had become a secondary figure or, even, an advertising poster. But this does not change anything of that pressure.

It is hard to explain what this pressure consists of. Nothing happens to us personally. We hardly notice the party out here as long as we do not leave the forest. But on the way to Berlin one hears and sees many things. These are not always special events, but small, unimportant experiences which keep the feeling of pressure alive. For example, the following little event on a bus: It is evening, just before departure time. A short man sits in front of me. By profession he is a gardener and he has a part-time job as a night-watchman in the settlement. I know him because Jackie once replaced him. He is a timid, rather simple-minded, talkative but completely harmless person. A tall, broad-shouldered chap wearing a black melon-shaped hat entered the bus. He had an unpleasant appearance and looked something like the way a policeman in civilian clothes looks in the movies. He sat down next to the short fellow and greeted him after he had called out a "Heil Hitler!" in a baritone voice to everyone in the bus. They talked about the weather, the frost, and the little gardener observed quite harmlessly: "Strict rulers don't rule for long." This is a popular saying that one can hear in almost every conversation touching on that kind of frosty weather. What did the fat fellow do? He bent forward, cleared his throat, and said with noticeable emphasis: "I don't quite understand what you mean by that, Mr.——." The little fellow obviously did not know how close he came to being thrown into a concentration camp.

Another time a young mother was sitting in the bus with her little girl, who was about four or five. She was standing on the seat and was looking at the world outside her window with great interest. A young SA man was walking up and down in front of the waiting bus. Suddenly the little girl said: "Look Mommy! That man won't come in here, will he?" Horrified, the mother placed her hand on the child's mouth and warned her to be quiet.

This is called the Volk community . . .

To this must be added the turnover in generations: there are more and more people growing up who have had no experience of the war. They are oblivious of the experiences of the older generation and are apt to look upon war as a refreshing adventure or even as an opportunity to develop great virtues. I cannot so easily forget one morning in the library when a colleague and I, working on a catalog, got to talking about the war novels, most of them anti-war, which were at that time being published in great numbers. Without being dramatic, the two of us shared the opinion that war was a "swinish business," since we had taken part in the war and had had a belly full of war once and for all. At this point a little girl employee, who was still on probation, interrupted us and rather insolently asserted that there was something elevating about war. "How's that?" I asked her. The little girl who was not yet twenty, a beautiful, delicately built thing, and on top of this slightly deformed, baffled us. Why? Well, after all, war brings out the best qualities: a sense of sacrifice, comradeship, and courage. What was one supposed to say to this? My colleague grouchily advised her first to live through the whole "swinish business" herself. But one cannot refute the argument of an idealistic young girl this way. She will usually answer with a contemptuous, disparaging facial expression, perhaps even rightly so. I tried to explain to her: in ancient times there were epidemics, such as plagues and cholera, which also provided plenty of opportunities to develop human virtues—readiness to help others, a sense of sacrifice, etc. I asked her whether because of these virtues we ought to regret that we have successfully exterminated these epidemics? The girl had no comment to make on this, but she did not seem to be overly convinced. At least she didn't offer the most stupid of all arguments, which some people have come up with: there have always been wars, therefore we will always have wars. The stupidity of this logic becomes apparent only when millions of people have paid for it with their lives.

Mosse, George L., ed. 1981. *Nazi Culture: Intellectual, Cultural and Social Life in the Third Reich*. New York: Schocken Books, pp. 383–384. Reprinted by permission.

THE FÜHRER AND THE "FÜHRER STATE"

The constant fear and anxiety among the people was a necessary consequence of Hitler's concept of his new state. As he explained in a long speech to 800 local National Socialist German Workers' Party (NSDAP) leaders in April 1937, the German people would only be contented with "strong leadership." In these brief extracts from a two-hour speech, Hitler proclaims the superiority of the "Führer state" over democracy and how true leaders will emerge from the national community and through natural genius achieve whatever is asked of them by the one Leader, "the bearer of the Idea" in the *völkisch* state.

We National Socialists have found a very specific definition for the state, that is, we say the state cannot be all things to all men, it only has meaning if its final mission is yet again the preservation of a living Folkdom [*Volksstum*]. It must not just preserve the life of a Volk, but in so doing it must also be the guardian of the substance, the guardian of the blood of a Volk. Otherwise, in the final analysis, the state has no meaning. To create an organization simply for the sake of the organization is senseless. . . . The state itself has the task of securing the Folkdom as such and thereby guaranteeing it for the future. Therefore we recognize not a state with an indeterminate sense of purpose but one with a clearly defined sense of purpose. We also know that all achievements are only conceivable under the precondition of the existence of this state, i.e., therefore only through the combination of all forces in this organization is it possible to bring about really great, powerful and collective achievements.

For us, then, there is also no possibility of a discussion about the question of, let's say, primacy within the state; that means, therefore, to take a concrete example: we will never tolerate, in a *völkisch* state, that anything should place itself above the authority of this *völkisch* state. No matter who it is, and that includes the Church! [Thunderous applause]. Here too the inviolable principle applies: the authority of the state, that is, of this living national community, stands above everything. Everything must submit itself to this authority. If anyone attempts to take a position against this authority, he will be made to yield to this authority, whatever it takes! [Bravo] Only one authority is conceivable, and that can only be that of the state, again with the proviso that this itself recognizes as its highest purpose only the maintenance, securing and continuation of a particular Folkdom. Such a state is then the source of all achievements . . .

The Idea does not live amongst the broad masses. We must finally recognize this, and that is also quite clear. If every human advance represents a higher achievement than the given, already existing, then it is evident that someone must have led the way. And this one person who will have led the way, he is the bearer of the Idea, and not the broad masses who stand behind him. He is the pioneer, not those who follow. And it is also only too logical and evident that an organization is only sensible if, from the very beginning, it concentrates on seeking to promote the most capable minds from every sphere into a position of leading and decisive influence and then in turn follows them. . . .

In a genuine Führer State, it is now, let's say, the honour of him who leads that he also assumes the responsibility. All the world's really big organizations are based to a degree on such considerations, on such principles. All of them. One person always has to bear the responsibility for a particular decision. And he can't then organize votes. The complete absurdity of this parliamentary democracy always becomes clearest when you come to the simplest of procedures. Just imagine that parliamentary democracy, that is, this select bunch which results from a majority vote, that they then have to make decisions on the greatest of problems. Now let's look at the detail of everyday life. Just for once, let the house that's being built down the road, yes, let it be built by majority voting, let the workers meet together and now let them vote on the plans. Which plan is the right one? Yes, you may laugh, you'll say, of course that's idiotic. Of course it's idiotic! Of course you can't let either the inhabitants or the workers vote on the plan of the house, we all know that. But apparently it is reasonable to let them vote on the construction of, let's say, a state, a Reich, because that's naturally "much easier" to understand. Of course, it's "much easier" to govern a people of 68 million souls . . .

Today, the people are happier in Germany than anywhere else in the world. They only become uncertain if there is no leadership. The moment there is a firm leadership they are happy, for they themselves know very well: "Yes, we don't understand this at all." They are all of the same opinion: "God, we can put our trust in our leadership, it will do things properly." I saw the madness of the belief that the ordinary man does not want any leadership in the first place, I saw this never more starkly than during the war. If a company is faced with a critical situation, the company only has one wish, that is has a decent company commander, and then it will rely on him. And if he's a good chap, a real man, then he has his men behind him. They won't say: "Well, why weren't we asked?" Nobody would think of it! On the contrary, they don't want to be asked at all, they want a commander who gives them instructions and then they follow him. [Shouts of "Heil" and thunderous applause] . . .

Believe me: this current crisis can only be alleviated by a genuine state of leadership and thus a Führer State. At the same time it is quite clear that the purpose of such leadership lies in trying to obtain, from all walks of life, by means of a natural selection, always from the people, those who are suited for such leadership. And that is also the best, and in my view the most Germanic democracy. For what can be better for a people than the knowledge: out of our ranks the most able can attain the highest position regardless of origin or birth or anything else. He only has to have the necessary abilities. We are striving to find able people. What they may have been, what their parents were, what their mummies were, that is completely unimportant. If they are able, all doors are open to them. They then only have to be willing to accept responsibility as well, that means they must really have the stuff of leadership in them. Purely abstract intellectual ability counts for nothing. The person really has to be able to lead as well. If he is placed somewhere, no matter where, he must also have the courage to say: "Yes, that's what must be done now. I can see that." He must consult those of his men who are responsible with him for the implementation of the decision, but in the final analysis he must answer for his ideas and for his decision. He must make the decision.

That is the best type of democracy there is.

Norbert, Frei, *National Socialist Rule in Germany: The Führer State 1933–1945*. English translation by Simon R. Steyne. English edition by Blackwell publishers, 1993. © 1987 Deutscher Taschenbuch Verlag, München.

A WARNING TO THE JEWS

Debates about the origins of the Final Solution center on whether the extermination of the Jews had been Hitler's longstanding intention or whether it arose from the cumulative actions of the Nazis in occupied eastern Europe. In the absence of precise documentation, Hitler's speech to the Reichstag on 30 January 1939, with its chilling prophecy about the Jewish fate in the event of war, is a key piece of evidence. To what extent is it propaganda or rhetoric, how far a genuine statement of intent?

Europe cannot find peace until the Jewish question has been solved. It may well be that sooner or later an agreement may be reached in Europe itself between nations who otherwise would not find it so easy to arrive at an understanding. There still exists sufficient available land on this globe. . . .

One thing I should like to say on this day which may be memorable for others as well as for us Germans. In the course of my life I have very often been a prophet, and have usually been ridiculed for it. During the time of my struggle for power it was in the first instance only the Jewish race that received my prophecies with laughter when I said that I would one day take over the leadership of the State, and with it that of the whole nation, and that I would then among other things settle the Jewish problem. Their laughter was uproarious, but I think that for some time now they have been laughing on the other side of their face. Today I will once more be a prophet: if the international Jewish financiers in and outside Europe should succeed in plunging the nations once more into a world war, then the result will not be the Bolshevizing of the earth, and thus the victory of Jewry, but the annihilation of the Jewish race in Europe!

Noakes, Jeremy, and Geoffrey Pridham, eds. 1991. *Nazism 1919–1945: A Documentary Reader. Vol. 3: Foreign Policy, War and Racial Extermination*. Exeter: Exeter University Press, p. 1049. Reprinted by permission.

DECISION FOR WAR

In the summer of 1939 Hitler was still assuring the world that he was a man of peace, but his private attitude was very different. Talking to his army commanders at Berchtesgarden on 21 August, he made clear his intentions toward Poland. The minutes of this talk, found by U.S. troops toward the end of the war, reveal the extent of Hitler's personal responsibility for its immediate origins.

I have called you together to give you a picture of the political situation, in order that you may have some insight into the individual factors on which I have based my decision to act and in order to strengthen your confidence.

After this we shall discuss military details.

It was clear to me that a conflict with Poland had to come sooner or later. I had already made this decision in the spring, but I thought that I would first turn against the West in a few years, and only after that against the East. . . .

First of all two personal factors:

My own personality and that of Mussolini.

Essentially all depends on me, on my existence, because of my political talents. Furthermore, the fact that probably no one will ever again have the confidence of the whole German people as I have. There will probably never again in the future be a man with more authority than I have. My existence is therefore a factor of great value. But I can be eliminated at any time by a criminal or a lunatic.

The second personal factor is the Duce. His existence is also decisive. If anything happens to him, Italy's loyalty to the alliance will no longer be certain.

The other side presents a negative picture as far as authoritative persons are concerned. There is no outstanding personality in England or France.

It is easy for us to make decisions. We have nothing to lose; we have everything to gain. Because of our restrictions our economic situation is such that we can only hold out for a few more years. Goering can confirm this. We have no other choice, we must act. . . .

All these favorable circumstances will no longer prevail in two or three years' time. No one knows how much longer I shall live. Therefore, better a conflict now . . . The probability is still great that the West will not intervene. We must take the risk with ruthless determination. The politician must take a risk just as much as the general. We are faced with the harsh alternatives of striking or of certain annihilation sooner or later. . . .

We will hold our position in the West until we have conquered Poland. We must bear in mind our great production capacity. It is much greater than in 1914–1918.

The enemy had another hope, that Russia would become our enemy after the conquest of Poland. The enemy did not reckon with my great strength of purpose. Our enemies are small fry. I saw them in Munich.

I was convinced that Stalin would never accept the English offer. Four days ago I took a special step, which led to Russia replying yesterday that she is prepared to sign. Personal contact with Stalin is established. The day after tomorrow von Ribbentrop will conclude the treaty. . . .

I am only afraid that at the last moment some swine or other will yet submit to me a plan for mediation. . . .

The destruction of Poland has priority. The aim is to eliminate active forces, not to reach a definite line. Even if war breaks out in the West, the destruction of Poland remains the priority. A quick decision in view of the season.

I shall give a propagandist reason for starting the war, no matter whether it is plausible or not. The victor will not be asked afterwards whether he hold the truth or not. When starting and waging war it is not right that matters, but victory.

Close your hearts to pity. Act brutally. Eighty million people must obtain what is their right. Their existence must be made secure.

From *Hitler's Third Reich: A Documentary History,* 1st edition, ed. by Louis L. Snyder, © 1981. Chicago: Nelson-Hall, pp. 85–89.

Reprinted by permission of Wadsworth, a division of Thompson Learning. Fax 800-730-2215.

EUTHANASIA: PREPARATION FOR GENOCIDE

The testimony of Dr. August Becker about the gassing of mentally ill "delinquents" at the Brandenburg asylum near Berlin in 1940 disclosed the first use of the technology later used in the extermination camps. The "twisted road to Auschwitz" wound its way through the euthanasia program, with the full cooperation of doctors, the police, and the SS.

I was ordered by Brack to attend the first euthanasia experiment in the Brandenburg asylum near Berlin. I went to the asylum in the first half of January 1940. Additional building work had been carried out especially for the purpose. There was a room similar to a shower room which was approximately 3 metres by 5 metres and 3 metres high and tiled. There were benches round the room and a water pipe about 1" in diameter ran along the wall about 10 cm off the floor. There were small holes in this pipe from which the carbon monoxide gas poured out. The gas cylinders stood outside this room and were already connected up to the pipe. The work on this installation had been carried out by the SS Main Building Office in Berlin. . . . There were already two mobile crematoria in the asylum with which to burn the corpses. There was a rectangular peephole in the entrance door, which was constructed like an air raid shelter door, through which the delinquents could be observed. The first gassing was carried out by Dr Widmann personally. He turned the gas tap and regulated the amount of gas. At the same time, he instructed the asylum doctors, Dr Eberl and Dr Baumhardt, who later took over the extermination in Grafeneck and Hadamar.

As far as I can remember, among the prominent personalities who were there were: the doctors already mentioned, Professor Dr Brandt, the Führer's personal physician, and a detective, Wirth, at that time head of the homicide branch in the Stuttgart police department and later head of the Hartheim asylum near Linz. For this first gassing about 18–20 people were led into this "shower room" by the nursing staff. These men had to undress in an anteroom until they were completely naked. The doors were shut behind them. These people went quietly into the room and showed no signs of being upset. Dr Widmann operated the gas. I could see through the peephole that after about a minute the people had collapsed or lay on the benches. There were no scenes and no disorder. After a further five minutes the room was ventilated. Specially assigned SS people collected the dead on special stretchers and took them to the crematoria. When I say special stretchers I mean stretchers specially constructed for this purpose. They could be placed directly on the ovens and the corpses could be pushed into the oven mechanically by means of a device without the people carrying them coming into contact with the corpse. These ovens and the stretchers were also constructed in Brack's department. . . . Following this successful test, Brack—who was naturally also present and whom I forgot to mention—said a few words. He expressed satisfaction with the test and emphasized once again that this action must only be carried out by doctors according to the motto—"syringes are a matter for doctors." Finally, Dr Brandt spoke and reiterated that doctors alone should carry out this gassing. With that, the start in Brandenburg was considered a success and the thing continued under Dr Eberl.

Noakes, Jeremy, and Geoffrey Pridham, eds. 1991. *Nazism 1919–1945: A Documentary Reader. Vol. 3: Foreign Policy, War and Racial Extermination*. Exeter:

Exeter University Press, pp. 1019–1020. Reprinted by permission.

THE SS AT WAR

In a speech to SS leaders at Posen on 4 October 1943, Heinrich Himmler laid out the role of the SS in eastern Europe and the Nazis' vision for the future. He hinted at rivalry with the Wehrmacht and the Nazi Party but also noted how he could usually count on Hitler to back him up in the brutal application of his millenarian plans.

One basic principle must be the absolute rule for the SS man: we must be honest, decent, loyal, and comradely to members of our own blood and to nobody else. What happens to a Russian or to a Czech does not interest me in the slightest. What the nations can offer in the way of good blood of our type we will take, if necessary by kidnapping their children and raising them here with us. Whether nations live in prosperity or kick the bucket interests me only in so far as we need them as slaves for our Kultur; otherwise, it is of no interest to me. Whether 10,000 Russian females fall down from exhaustion while digging an anti-tank ditch interests me only in so far as the anti-tank ditch for Germany is finished. We shall never be rough and heartless when it is not necessary, that is clear. We Germans, who are the people in the world who have a decent attitude towards animals, will also assume a decent attitude towards these human animals. But it is a crime against our own blood to worry about them and give them ideals, thus causing our sons and grandsons to have a more difficult time with them. When some body comes to me and says, "I cannot use women and children to dig the anti-tank ditch; it is inhuman, it would kill them," then I have to say, "You are a murderer of your own blood because if the anti-tank ditch is not dug, German soldiers will die, and they are sons of German mothers. They are our own blood." That is what I want to instill into the SS and what I believe I have instilled into them as one of the most sacred laws of the future. Our concern, our duty is our people and our blood. It is for them that we must provide and plan, work and fight, nothing else. We can be indifferent to everything else. I wish the SS to adopt this attitude to the problem of all foreign, non-Germanic peoples, especially Russians. All else is vain, false to our own nation, and an obstacle to the early winning of the war. . . .

If the peace is a final one, we shall be able to tackle our great work of the future. We shall colonize. We shall indoctrinate our boys with the laws of the SS. I consider it to be absolutely necessary to the life of our peoples that we should not only impart the meaning of ancestry, grandchildren and future, but feel these to be part of our being. Without there being any talk about it, without our needing to make use of rewards and similar material things, it must be a matter of course that we have children. It must be a matter of course that the most copious breeding should be from this racial elite of the German people. In twenty to thirty years we must really be able to provide the whole of Europe with its ruling class. If the SS together with the farmers . . .then run the colony in the east on a grand scale, without any restraint, without any question of tradition, but with nerve and revolutionary impetus, we shall in twenty years push the national boundary 500 kilometres eastwards.

Today I have asked the Führer that the SS, if we have fulfilled our task and our duty by the end of the war, should have the privilege of holding Germany's most easterly frontier as a defence frontier. I believe this is the only privilege for which we have no competitors. I believe that not a single person will dispute our claim to this privilege. We shall be in a position there to train every young age-group in the use of arms. We shall impose our laws on the east. We shall charge ahead and push our way forward little by little to the Urals. I hope that our generation will successfully bring it about that every age-group has fought in the east, and that every one of our divisions spends a winter in the east every second or third year. Then we shall never grow soft, then we shall never have SS members who come to us only because it is distinguished or because the black coat will naturally be very attractive in peacetime. Everyone will know: "If I join the SS, there is the possibility that I may be killed." He has contracted in writing that every other year he will not dance in Berlin or attend the carnival in Munich, but that he will be posted to the eastern frontier in an ice-cold winter. Then we will have a healthy elite for all time. Thus we will create the necessary conditions for the whole Germanic people and the whole of Europe, controlled, ordered and led by us, for the Germanic people, to be able, in generations to come, to stand the test in her battles of destiny against Asia, which will certainly break out again. We do not known when that will be. Then, when the mass of humanity of 1–1/2 milliards lines up against us, the Germanic people, numbering, I hope, 250–300 millions, and the other European peoples, making a total of 600–700 millions (and with an outpost area stretching as far as the Urals, or in a hundred years beyond the Urals), must stand the test in its vital struggle against Asia. It would be an evil day if the Germanic people did not survive it. It would be the end of beauty and of Kultur, of the creative power of this earth. That is the distant future. It is for that we are fighting, pledged to hand down the heritage of our ancestors.

We see into the distant future, because we know what it will be. That is why we are doing our duty more fanatically than ever, more devoutly than ever, more bravely, more obediently and more thoroughly than ever. We want to be worthy of being permitted to be the first SS-men of the Führer, Adolf Hitler, in the long history of the Germanic people stretching before us.

Now let us remember the Führer, Adolf Hitler, who will create the Germanic Reich and will lead us into the Germanic future.

Our Führer Adolf Hitler
Sieg Heil!
Sieg Heil!
Sieg Heil!

Noakes, Jeremy, and Geoffrey Pridham, eds. 1991. *Nazism 1919–1945: A Documentary Reader. Vol. 3. Foreign Policy, War and Racial Extermination*. Exeter: Exeter University Press, pp. 919–921. Reprinted by permission.

THE REICH FALLS APART

The last surviving report of the Sicherheitsdienst (SD), from the end of March 1945, makes no attempt to gloss over the attitudes of the German people as Hitler's empire collapsed. The end of the "Hitler myth" is revealed in this Section Four of the report: Nazi propaganda no longer grips or convinces the population, and contempt for the Nazi leadership is openly expressed.

During the last few days trust in the leadership has fallen away like an avalanche. Everywhere criticism of the Party, of specific figures in the leadership and of propaganda is rife. With a clean conscience for having done everything possible, the "little man" in particular is assuming the right to speak his mind in the most open manner and with extreme frankness. People are not mincing their words. Up until now it has been said repeatedly that the Führer will make it, but first we want to win the war. But now the passionate, nervous, and in parts rancorous disappointment is breaking out, that

National Socialist reality, in many respects, does not correspond with the idea, nor the development of the war with the official statements.

In contrast to the propaganda commentaries, the realization then slowly dawned that the offensive had run aground prematurely. From then on the feeling has been deepening that we can do no more and that there is nothing more to be done.

Since then there can be less and less talk of a unified formation of public opinion in terms of leadership and propaganda. Everyone develops their own views and opinions independently. A tangled web of reasons, reproaches and accusations is emerging about why the war could not have gone well. A mood is spreading in which the national comrades are now hardly being reached and addressed by the propaganda media. Apart from fear, even the revelation of the disgusting behaviour of the Soviets in the German territory they occupy has caused only sullen indignation that our military leadership has exposed German people to the Soviet terror. It was the leadership which had constantly, and right into the last few weeks, portrayed our enemies in a fashion which under-estimated them. Countless discussions in the air-raid shelters typify how detached the individual is from the leadership, of how much he has regarded himself only as an object and is now proceeding from a position of simply having to participate to one of criticism: "What are 'they' thinking of?"

. . .All the talk in the press of heroic resistance, of the strength of the German heart, of an uprising of the whole Volk, all the pomposity expended in empty phraseology, especially that of the press, is cast aside with anger and scorn. People are instinctively distancing themselves from slogans such as "Walls can break, but not our hearts," or "They can destroy everything we have, but not our faith in victory." Even if they are true, the population has long ceased to want slogans written on walls and the façades of burnt-out buildings. The population has become so circumspect that it will no longer be possible to instigate a popular uprising. People are hardly participating even superficially any more. The production management which previously aided the success of mass meetings at the Sportspalast is no longer functioning, because what it was that once gave those rallies content, life and movement, no longer exists.

Gradually, explanations are being demanded more openly. Disparaging remarks like this from a farmer and Party comrade in Linz are typical: "The big-shots who made the mistakes and who must answer for them deserve a summary court-martial." This applies especially in relation to the Luftwaffe for, according to general opinion, the outcome of the entire war depended on them. Harsh and bitter verdicts are pronounced on the men who made the decisions concerning the Luftwaffe's strategy in both attack and defence and who, as a result of the failures demonstrated throughout the war and right up to the present, have brought so much privation and misery to the German people. This does not occur without unjustified generalizations, for example, in relation to Fighter Command people talk about "useless toy pilots" and "line-shooters." The Front feels that it has been left in the lurch by the Luftwaffe. Anybody coming from the West sadly shrugs their shoulders at the fact that, despite all the valour that has been shown a million times in this war, it is simply impossible to get the better of the carpet bombing, the fighter-bombers and the fighters. In the air-raid shelters of the towns and cities, the Reich Marshal is the object of violent invective and abuse. Of him, who with all his personal attributes once enjoyed the respect of the entire Volk, it is said: "He sat in Karinhall and stuffed his brat with food, instead of keeping the Luftwaffe in the air" (armaments worker), or, "He is to blame that everything we possess now lies in ashes and ruins. If I get hold of the bastard, I'll kill him" (working–class woman).

On the surface, the population is still keeping very calm and although becoming daily more common, such criticism of the leadership and leading figures is only expressed here and there and by individual persons or groups of persons. But this fact should not obscure the real inner disposition of the national community in its attitude towards the leadership. The German Volk is patient like no other. Most people stand by the Idea and the Führer. The German Volk is accustomed to discipline. Since 1933 it has felt itself watched over and supervised from all sides right up to the front door by the many branches of the Party apparatus, its organizations and associations. Traditional respect for the police is a further reason. People swallowed everything they did not like, or moaned and grumbled about this or that phenomenon or person, always good-humouredly, in private. Only the heavy air-raids caused the accumulated anger, since then often blunt and to an extent malicious, to burst out in utterances like: "The pig-heads up there will fight to the last babe in arms." Often it is women who do the talking, for example, in Vienna, in particularly rabble-rousing manner: "Them up there won't stop of their own accord," or, "If two million people are prepared to put up with it, then you can't do a thing," or, "If only someone would have the courage to start."

Norbert, Frei, *National Socialist Rule in Germany: The Führer State 1933–1945*. English translation by Simon R. Steyne. English edition by Blackwell publishers, 1993. © 1987 Deutscher Taschenbuch Verlag, München.

BELSEN

This eyewitness account broadcast on 24 April 1945 by the BBC commentator Patrick Gordon Walker was one of several that revealed the full horror of the concentration camps. But it is also a testimony to the survival of the human spirit among the very worst that Hitler and his followers could do to destroy it.

I went to Belsen. It was a vast area surrounded by barbed wire. The whole thing was being guarded by Hungarian guards. They had been in the German Army and are now immediately and without hesitation serving us. They are saving us a large number of men for the time being. Outside the camp, which is amidst bushes, pines, and heather, all fairly recently planted, were great notices in red letters: DANGER—TYPHUS.

We drove into what turned out to be a great training camp, a sort of Aberdeen, where we found the officers and men of the Oxfordshire Yeomanry. They began to tell us about the concentration camp.

It lies south of the training area and is behind its own barbed wire. The Wehrmacht is not allowed near it. It was entirely guarded by SS men and women. This is what I discovered about the release of the camp that happened about the fifteenth. I got this story from Derek Singleton, political officer, and from officers and men of the Oxfordshire Yeomanry.

Typhus broke out in the camp, and a truce was arranged so that we could take the camp over. The Germans originally had proposed that we should by-pass the camp. In the meanwhile, thousands and thousands of people would have died and been shot. We refused these terms, and demanded the withdrawal of the Germans and the disarmament of the SS guards. Some dozen SS men and women were left behind under the command of Higher Sturmfuehrer Kramer, who had been at Auschwitz. Apparently they had been told all sorts of fairy tales about the troops, that they could go on guarding, and that we would let them free and so forth.

We only had a handful of men so far, and the SS stayed there that night. The first night of liberty, many hundreds of people died of joy.

Next day some men of the Yeomanry arrived. The people crowded around them. Kissing their hands and feet—and dying from weakness. Corpses in every state of decay were lying around, piled up on top of each other in heaps. There were corpses in the compound in flocks. People were falling dead all around, people who were walking skeletons. One woman came up to a soldier who was guarding the milk store and doling the milk out to children, and begged milk for her baby. The man took the baby and saw that it had been dead for days, black in the face and shriveled up. The woman went on begging for milk. So he poured some on the dead lips. The mother then started to croon with joy and carried the baby off in triumph. She stumbled and fell dead in a few yards. I have this story and some others spoken by the men who saw them.

On the sixteenth, Kramer and the SS were arrested. Kramer was taken off and kept in the icebox with some stinking fish of the officers' home. He is now going back to the rear. The rest, men and women, were kept under guard to save them from the inmates. The men were set to work shoveling up the corpses into lorries.

About thirty-five thousand corpses were reckoned, more actually than the living. Of the living, there were about thirty thousand.

The SS men were driven and pushed along and made to ride on top of the loaded corpses and then shovel them into their mass open graves. They were so tired that they fell exhausted amongst the corpses. Jeering crowds collected around them, and they had to be kept under strong guard.

Two men committed suicide in their cells. Two jumped off the lorry and tried to run away and get lost in the crowd. They were shot down. One jumped into a concrete pool of water and was riddled with bullets. The other was brought to the ground, with a shot in the belly.

The SS women were made to cook and carry heavy loads. One of them tried to commit suicide. The inmates said that they were more cruel and brutal than the men. They are all young, in their twenties. One SS woman tried to hide, disguised as a prisoner. She was denounced and arrested.

The camp was so full because people had been brought here from East and West. Some people were brought from Nordhausen, a five-day journey, without food. Many had marched for two or three days. There was no food at all in the camp, a few piles of roots amidst the piles of dead bodies. Some of the dead bodies were of people so hungry that though the roots were guarded by SS men they had tried to storm them and had been shot down then and there. There was no water, nothing but these roots and some boiled stinking carrots, enough for a few hundred people.

Men and women had fought for these raw, uncooked roots. Dead bodies, black and blue and bloated, and skeletons had been used as pillows by sick people. The day after we took after, seven block leaders, mostly Poles, were murdered by the inmates. Some were still beating the people. We arrested one woman who had been beaten by other women with a board. She quite frankly admitted the offense. We are arresting these people.

An enormous buried dump of personal jewelry and belongings was discovered in suitcases. When I went to the camp five days after its liberation, there were still bodies all around. I saw about a thousand.

In one place, hundreds had been shoveled into a mass grave by bulldozers; in another, Hungarian soldiers were putting corpses into a grave that was sixty feet by sixty feet and thirty feet deep. It was almost half full.

Other and similar pits were being dug. Five thousand people had died since we got to the camp. People died before my eyes, scarcely human, moaning skeletons, many of them gone mad. Bodies were just piled up. Many had gashed wounds and bullet marks and terrible sores. One Englishman, who had lived in Ostend, was picked up half dead. It was found that he had a great bullet wound in the back. He could just speak. He had no idea when he had been shot. He must have been lying half unconscious when some SS man shot him as he was crawling about. This was quite common. I walked about the camp. Everywhere was the smell and odor of death. After a few hours you get used to it and don't notice it any more. People have typhus and dysentery.

In one compound I went, I saw women standing up quite naked, washing among themselves. Nearby were piles of corpses. Other women suffering from dysentery were defecating in the open and then staggering back, half dead, to their blocks. Some were lying groaning on the ground. One had reverted to the absolute primitive.

A great job had been done in getting water into the camp. It has been pumped in from the outside and carried by hoses all over the camp with frequent outlet points. There are taps of fresh clean water everywhere. Carts with water move around.

The Royal Army Service Corps has also done a good job in getting food in.

I went into the typhus ward, packed thick with people lying in dirty rags of blankets on the floor, groaning and moaning. By the door sat an English Tommy talking to the people and cheering them up. They couldn't understand what he said, and he was continually ladling milk out of a caldron. I collected together some women who could speak English and German and began to make records. An amazing thing is the number who managed to keep themselves clean and neat. All of them said that in a day or two more, they would have gone under from hunger and weakness.

There are three main classes in the camp: the healthy, who have managed to keep themselves decent, but nearly all of these had typhus; then there were the sick, who were more or less cared for by their friends; then there was the vast underworld that had lost all self-respect, crawling around in rags, living in abominable squalor, defecating in the compound, often mad or half mad. By the other prisoners they are called Mussulmen. It is these who are still dying like flies. They can hardly walk on their legs. Thousands still of these cannot be saved, and if they were, they would be in lunatic asylums for the short remainder of their pitiful lives.

There were a very large number of girls in the camp, mostly Jewesses from Auschwitz. They have to be healthy to survive. Over and over again I was told the same story. The parades at which people were picked out arbitrarily for the gas chambers and the crematorium, where many were burned alive. Only a person in perfect health survived. Life and death was a question of pure chance.

Rich Jews arrived with their belongings and were able to keep some. There were soap and perfume and fountain pens and watches. All amidst the chance of sudden, arbitrary death, amidst work commandos from which the people returned to this tomb so dead beat that they were sure to be picked for the gas chamber at the next parade, amidst the most horrible death, filth, and squalor that could be imagined.

People at Auschwitz were saved by being moved away to work in towns like Hamburg and were then moved back to Belsen as we advanced. At Auschwitz every woman had her hair shaven absolutely bald.

I met pretty young girls whose hair was one inch long. They all had their numbers tattooed on their left arm, a mark of honor they will wear all their lives.

One of the most extraordinary things was the women and men—there were only few—who had kept themselves decent and clean.

On the first day many had on powder and lipstick. It seems the SS stores had been located and looted and boots and clothes had been found. Hundreds of people came up to me with letters, which I have taken and am sending back to London to be posted all over the world. Many have lost all their relatives. "My father and mother were burned. My sister was burned." This is what you hear all the time. The British Army is doing what it can. Units are voluntarily giving up blankets. Fifty thousand arrived while I was there and they are being laundered. Sweets and chocolate and rations have been voluntarily given.

Then we went to the children's hut. The floors had been piled with corpses there had been no time to move. We collected a chorus of Russian girls from twelve to fourteen and Dutch boys and girls from nine to fifteen. They sang songs. The Russian children were very impressive. Clean and quite big children, they had been looked after magnificently amidst starvation. They sang the songs they remembered from before captivity. They looked happy now. The Dutch children had been in camp a long time and were very skinny and pale. We stood with our backs to the corpses, out in the open amidst the pines and the birch trees near the wire fence running around the camp.

Men were hung for hours at a time, suspended by their arms, hands tied behind their back, in Belsen. Beatings in workshops were continuous, and there were many deaths there. Just before I left the camp a crematorium was discovered. A story of Auschwitz was told to me by Helen—and her last name, she didn't remember. She was a Czechoslovak.

When the women were given the chance to go and work elsewhere in the work zones like Hamburg, mothers with children were, in fact, given the choice between their lives and their children's. Children could not be taken along. Many preferred to stay with their children and face certain death. Some decided to leave their children. But it got around amongst the six-year-old children that if they were left there they would be gassed. There were terrible scenes between children and their mothers. One child was so angry that though the mother changed her mind and stayed and died, the child would not talk to her.

That night when I got back at about eleven o'clock very exhausted, I saw the Jewish padre again and talked to him as he was going to bed. Suddenly, he broke down completely and sobbed.

The next morning I left this hellhole, this camp. As I left, I had myself deloused and my recording truck as well. To you at home, this is one camp. There are many more. This is what you are fighting. None of this is propaganda. This is the plain and simple truth.

From *Hitler's Third Reich: A Documentary History,* 1st edition, ed. by Louis L. Snyder, © 1981. Chicago: Nelson-Hall, pp. 85–89. Reprinted by permission of Wadsworth, a division of Thompson Learning. Fax 800-730-2215.

CHRONOLOGY

1889	*20 April* Birth of Adolf Hitler in Braunau-am-Inn, fourth child of Alois Hitler and Klara Hitler, née Pölzl.
1903	*3 January* Death of Alois Hitler.
1907	*21 December* Death of Klara Hitler.
1908–1913	Hitler lives in Vienna, mostly scraping a living as an artist.
1913	*24 May* Hitler moves to Munich.
1914	*August* Outbreak of World War I; Hitler joins the army in an infantry regiment.
1918	*October–November* Temporarily blinded by gas, Hitler hears of revolution in Berlin and Munich, the proclamation of the German Republic (9 November), and the abdication of Kaiser Wilhelm II.
1919	*5 January* Foundation in Munich of the German Workers' Party by Anton Drexler and Karl Harrer.
	April–May Foundation and suppression of the "Councils Republic" in Munich.
	28 June Signing of the Treaty of Versailles.
	12 September Hitler, employed by the army as an informant on subversive organizations, attends a meeting of the German Workers' Party and joins shortly afterward.
1920	*February* The German Workers' Party, renamed the National Socialist German Workers' Party (NSDAP), issues its program.
1921	*29 July* After an internal crisis, during which Hitler had quit the NSDAP, an extraordinary meeting of party members elects him as party chairman with dictatorial powers.
	3 August Foundation of what soon became the Sturmabteilung (SA).
1922	*24–27 July* Hitler briefly imprisoned following disturbances the previous September.
1923	*11 January* Occupation of the Ruhr by French and Belgian troops.
	27–29 January First "Reich Party Rally" of the NSDAP in Munich.
	1 March Hermann Goering becomes commander of the SA, now merged with other Bavarian paramilitary groups.
	8–9 November "Beer Hall Putsch" ends in a march through Munich in which sixteen putschists are killed; Hitler and other putsch leaders are arrested.
1924	*26 February* Hitler's trial for high treason begins.
	1 April Hitler is sentenced to five years' imprisonment and a fine of 200 marks.

20 December Hitler is released from prison in Landsberg-am-Lech.

1925 *26 February* Refoundation of the NSDAP.

9 March Hitler is banned from speaking in Bavaria (until 5 March 1927); ban in Prussia lasts until September 1928.

18 July First volume of *Mein Kampf* is published.

1926 *3–4 July* Second Reich Party Rally, in Weimar.

10 December Second volume of *Mein Kampf* is published.

1927 *19–21 August* Third Reich Party Rally, in Nuremberg.

1928 *16 November* Hitler's first public speech in Berlin.

1929 *23 June* The town of Coburg becomes the first to give the NSDAP a majority in local elections.

1–4 August Fourth Reich Party Rally in Nuremberg.

22 December Plebiscite of Young Plan for reparations; Nazis and their nationalist allies gain 13.8 percent support.

1930 *23 January* Wilhelm Frick becomes minister of the interior in Thuringia, the first Nazi to assume a ministerial post.

30 March Heinrich Brüning forms a minority government.

14 September Reichstag elections; the Nazis gain 18.3 percent of the vote and 107 seats, making NSDAP the second-largest party in the Reichstag.

1931 National economic crisis worsens.

5 January Ernst Röhm becomes SA chief of staff.

18 September Suicide of Geli Raubal, Hitler's niece, in his Munich apartment.

11 October Rally of the "National Opposition," including the Nazis, in Bad Harzburg, creates the short-lived "Harzburg Front."

1932 *25 February* Hitler acquires German citizenship.

13 March Reich presidential election; Hitler gains 30.1 percent of the votes.

10 April Second presidential election; Hitler gets 36.8 percent of the vote; Hindenburg reelected with 53 percent.

24 April State elections leave the NSDAP as the largest party in Prussia, Württemberg, Anhalt, and Hamburg and the second-largest in Bavaria.

1 June Franz von Papen is appointed Reich chancellor following resignation of Brüning.

20 July The "Prussia Putsch"; the Social Democratic government of Prussia is deposed; Papen takes over Prussia as Reich commissar.

31 July Reichstag election; with 37.3 percent of the vote, the Nazis are the largest party.

13 August Hitler rejects offer of post of vice chancellor.

6 November New Reichstag election; the Nazi vote falls, but they remain the largest party.

17 November Von Papen resigns as Reich chancellor.

2 December General Kurt von Schleicher is appointed Reich chancellor.

8 December Gregor Strasser resigns all his offices in the Nazi Party.

1933 *17–29 January* Political maneuvering leads to the agreement that Hitler as chancellor will head a cabinet of conservatives.

30 January Hitler becomes Reich chancellor of a "national government," with Frick and Goering the only other Nazis holding office.

27 February Reichstag building is burned down.

28 February "Reichstag Fire Decree" suspends civil rights and leads to mass arrests.

5 March Reichstag elections; Nazis gain 43.9 percent of the vote.

5–9 March Nazis seize power in provincial Länder.

20 March First concentration camp established at Dachau.

23 March Enabling Act gives Hitler comprehensive legislative powers.

1 April Nationwide boycott of Jewish shops.

2 May Forcible dissolution of trade unions.

10 May Burning of books by "un-German" authors in university cities.

22 June Social Democratic Party banned; the other parties dissolve themselves over the next few weeks, leading to proclamation of a one-party state on 14 July.

20 July Concordat with papacy.

October Germany leaves the League of Nations and the Geneva Disarmament Conference.

12 November New "election" gives NSDAP 92.2 percent of the vote.

1934 *20 January* "Law for the Ordering of National Labor" is passed.

26 January Nonaggression treaty between Germany and Poland.

30 January "Law on the Reconstruction of the Reich" abolishes the sovereignty of the *Länder.*

30 June "Night of the Long Knives"; Röhm and other SA leaders are murdered; the end of the SA as a political force.

2 August Death of President Paul von Hindenburg; offices of president and chancellor are amalgamated; army swears oath of allegiance to Hitler as "Führer and Reich chancellor."

1935 *13 January* Saar plebiscite leads to its incorporation in the Reich on 1 March.

16 March Introduction of conscription.

18 June Under the Anglo-German Naval Agreement, the strength of the German navy is set at 35 percent of that of the British navy.

15 September Nuremberg laws, forming the basis of anti-Semitic measures in following years, are announced at a party rally.

3 October Italian invasion of Abyssinia.

1936 *7 March* Hitler reoccupies the demilitarized Rhineland, breaching the Locarno Pact of 1925.

29 March Hitler gains 99 percent support in Reichstag "election."

July Beginning of Spanish Civil War.

1 August Hitler opens the Olympic Games in Berlin.

9 September Announcement of the "Four Year Plan" for self-sufficiency and preparation for a war economy.

1 November Benito Mussolini announces the "Berlin-Rome Axis."

25 November Anti-Comintern Pact between Germany and Japan.

1 December Hitler Youth declared the state youth organization.

1937 *30 January* Enabling Act renewed for four years.

1 May Lifting of ban on new membership of the NSDAP imposed in May 1933; membership will rise to 5.3 million by 1939.

25–29 September State visit of Mussolini.

5 November "Hossbach meeting" identifies Austria and Czechoslovakia as targets for German expansion.

6 November Italy joins the Anti-Comintern Pact.

1938 *4 February* "Blomberg-Fritsch crisis" leads to dismissal of War Minister Blomberg and head of the army Fritsch; Hitler takes over as supreme commander of the Wehrmacht; von Ribbentrop becomes foreign minister.

12–13 March The Anschluss; German troops march into Austria, which is incorporated into the German Reich.

30 May In a directive to the Wehrmacht Hitler declares his intention of destroying Czechoslovakia.

June–September Anti-Jewish persecution is stepped up; synagogues in Berlin and Nuremberg are destroyed; Jewish doctors and lawyers are banned from practicing.

September Sudetenland crisis; Munich Conference on 29–30 September hands Sudetenland to Germany.

9–10 November Kristallnacht; nationwide pogrom against Jews leads to murders, widespread destruction of Jewish shops and property, burning of synagogues, and arrest and incarceration of thousands of Jews.

1939 *30 January* In a speech to the Reichstag Hitler "prophesies" the destruction of the Jews in the event of war.

14–15 March German troops march into Czechoslovakia; "Reich Protectorate of Bohemia and Moravia" is established; Slovakia becomes "independent" under German patronage.

21 March Hitler demands the return of Danzig and the Polish corridor.

23 March Germany annexes Memel territory from Lithuania.

31 March British and French provide guarantees to Poland.

22 May Germany and Italy form a military alliance, the "Pact of Steel."

23 August Signing of Nazi-Soviet Pact, a nonaggression pact with a secret clause about the division of Poland.

1 September Germany invades Poland.

3 September Great Britain and France declare war on Germany.

October Jews from Austria and Czechoslovakia begin to be deported to Poland.

6 October Conquest of Poland completed.

9 October Hitler sets 12 November as date for attack in the west, but it is repeatedly postponed.

8 November Attempt on Hitler's life in Munich by the Swabian joiner Georg Elser.

1940 *9 April* German invasion of Denmark and Norway.

10 May Beginning of western offensive.

4 June Evacuation of British troops from Dunkirk.

22 June Armistice with France signed in forest of Compiègne.

17 September Hitler's plans for the invasion of Britain are postponed indefinitely.

27 September Tripartite Pact is concluded among Germany, Italy, and Japan.

23 October Hitler meets Franco but cannot persuade him to bring Spain into the war.

1941 *6 April* German invasion of Yugoslavia and Greece.

10 May Hitler's deputy, Rudolf Hess, flies to Britain; Martin Bormann replaces him and receives the title "head of the party chancellery."

22 June Operation Barbarossa; Hitler invades the Soviet Union.

1 September German Jews are compelled to wear the Yellow Star of David.

2 October–5 December German offensive grinds to a halt in the battle for Moscow.

14 October Jews from Reich territory are to be deported to eastern ghettos.

December Mass killings of Jews by gassing begins in Chelmno, Poland.

11 December Hitler declares war on the United States, following the Japanese attack on Pearl Harbor (7 December).

16 December Hitler refuses to allow retreat in face of Soviet counteroffensive; he takes over as head of the army after dismissing Walther von Brauchitsch.

1942 *20 January* Wannsee Conference coordinates the "Final Solution" of the "Jewish Question."

8 February Albert Speer is appointed Reich minister for armaments and munitions; armaments production improves sharply.

March Beginning of the systematic killing of Jews in the extermination camps; first transports from western Europe and Germany to Auschwitz.

26 April Hitler obtains supreme judicial powers to override formal law when necessary.

27 May Assassination attempt on Reinhard Heydrich in Prague; he dies on 4 June; on 10 June the village of Lidice is razed in retaliation.

June Beginning of mass gassings of Jews in Auschwitz.

June–August A new German offensive advances toward Stalingrad.

24 September Kurt von Zeitzler replaces Franz Halder as army chief of staff.

23 October British counteroffensive begins in North Africa.

November 1942–February 1943 Battle of Stalingrad; German 6th Army surrenders on 2 February.

1943 *14–26 January* Allied conference at Casablanca demands "unconditional surrender" of Germany.

18 February Goebbels announces "total war" in a speech at the Sportspalast in Berlin.

March Survivors of eastern ghettos and Dutch Jews are sent to extermination camps.

19 April–16 May Rising in Warsaw ghetto, ruthlessly suppressed by SS and police.

13 May Germans surrender in Tunisia.

5–13 July Massive tank battle at Kursk opens way for Soviet advances in Ukraine.

10 July Allied landing in Sicily.

25 July Mussolini is removed from power in Italy.

24 August Himmler replaces Frick as minister of the interior.

10 September German troops occupy northern Italy after new Italian government concludes armistice with Allies.

15 September Mussolini is rescued by German paratroopers.

28 November–1 December Allied Conference at Teheran decides in principle on postwar division of Germany.

1944 *19 March* German occupation of Hungary.

April–June Greek and Hungarian Jews are deported to Auschwitz.

6 June D-Day; Allied landing in Normandy.

10 June SS division "Das Reich" burn French village of Oradour-sur-Glane as retaliation for activity of French Resistance.

22 June Beginning of major Soviet offensive.

20 July "July Plot" by army officers against Hitler, who is injured by a bomb in his headquarters in East Prussia; Graf von Stauffenberg and many other plotters are executed.

24 July Majdanek extermination camp liberated by Red Army.

31 July U.S. breakthrough near Avranches opens way for rapid liberation of France.

August–October Warsaw rising; Polish Home Army forced to capitulate on 2 October.

25 August U.S. and Free French troops enter Paris.

25 September Formation of the Volkssturm, Hitler's ill-equipped "people's army."

21 October Aachen is the first German town to be occupied by Allied troops.

16 December Hitler begins Ardennes offensive, the "Battle of the Bulge," which enjoys some initial success but rapidly fails.

1945 *27 January* Auschwitz liberated by Red Army.

30 January Hitler's last broadcast speech.

4–11 February Yalta Conference; Franklin Delano Roosevelt, Winston Churchill, and Joseph Stalin settle Germany's postwar fate.

7 March U.S. troops cross the Rhine at Remagen.

19 March Hitler issues the "Nero order" to destroy all German industrial plant to prevent it falling into Allied hands; Speer manages to block its full implementation.

11 April Buchenwald concentration camp is handed over to U.S. troops.

13 April Red Army takes Vienna.

15 April Bergen-Belsen camp is liberated by British troops.

16 April Beginning of battle for Berlin.

25 April U.S. and Soviet troops meet at Torgau on the Elbe.

28 April Mussolini is captured and shot by Italian partisans.

29 April Hitler's will appoints Admiral Doenitz as his successor as head of state and exhorts the German people to continue its "merciless opposition" to "international Jewry."

30 April Hitler and Eva Braun commit suicide in his bunker at the Reich Chancellery in Berlin.

2 May Red Army takes Berlin.

7–9 May German surrender at Reims, repeated in Soviet headquarters in Berlin.

BIBLIOGRAPHY

Abraham, David. 1986. *The Collapse of the Weimar Republic: Political Economy and Crisis.* 2nd ed. New York: Holmes and Meier.

Allen, William Sheridan. 1984. *The Nazi Seizure of Power: The Experience of a Single German Town.* Rev. ed. New York: Franklin, Watts.

Aly, Götz, Peter Chroust, and Christian Pross. 1994. *Cleansing the Fatherland: Nazi Medicine and Racial Hygiene.* Baltimore, MD: Johns Hopkins University Press.

Ambrose, Stephen E. 1994. *D-Day, June 6 1944: The Climactic Battle of World War II.* New York: Simon and Schuster.

Arendt, Hannah. 1984. *Eichmann in Jerusalem.* New York: Penguin.

Art and Power. 1995. *Art and Power: Europe under the Dictators 1930–45.* London: Hayward Gallery.

Atkin, Nicholas. 1998. *Pétain.* London and New York: Longman.

Aycoberry, Pierre. 1981. *The Nazi Question: An Essay on the Interpretation of National Socialism (1922–1975).* New York: Pantheon.

Baird, Jay W. 1974. *The Mythical World of Nazi War Propaganda 1939–1945.* Minneapolis: University of Minnesota Press.

———. 1992. *To Die for Germany: Heroes in the Nazi Pantheon.* Bloomington: Indiana University Press.

Bankier, David. 1988. "Hitler and the Policy-Making Process on the Jewish Question," *Holocaust and Genocide Studies* 3, pp. 1–20.

———. 1992. *The Germans and the Final Solution: Public Opinion under Nazism.* Oxford: Blackwell.

Barkai, Avraham. 1989. *From Boycott to Annihilation: The Economic Struggle of German Jews, 1933–1943.* Hanover, NH: University Press of New England.

———. 1990. *Nazi Economics: Ideology, Theory, and Policy.* New Haven: Yale University Press.

Barnett, Correlli, ed. 1995. *Hitler's Generals.* London: Phoenix.

Barron, Stephanie, ed. 1991. *"Degenerate Art": The Fate of the Avant-Garde in Nazi Germany.* Los Angeles: Los Angeles County Museum of Art.

Bartov, Omer. 1991. *Hitler's Army: Soldiers, Nazis and War in the Third Reich.* New York: Oxford University Press.

Bauer, Jehuda. 1994. *Jews for Sale? Nazi-Jewish Negotiations 1933–1945.* New Haven: Yale University Press.

Baynes, Norman H., ed. 1969. *The Speeches of Adolf Hitler, April 1933–August 1939.* 2 vols. New York: Howard Fertig.

Beck, Earl R. 1955. *Verdict on Schacht.* Tallahassee: Florida State University.

———. 1986. *Under the Bombs: The German Home Front 1942–1945.* Lexington: University Press of Kentucky.

Beevor, Antony. 1998. *Stalingrad.* London: Viking.

Bell, P. H. M. 1997. *The Origins of the Second World War in Europe*. 2nd ed. London and New York: Longman.

Bergen, Doris L. 1996. *Twisted Cross: The German Christian Movement in the Third Reich*. Chapel Hill: University of North Carolina Press.

Bergmeier, Horst J. P., and Rainer E. Lotz. 1997. *Hitler's Airwaves: The Inside Story of Nazi Radio Broadcasting and Propaganda Swing*. New Haven: Yale University Press.

Bessel, Richard. 1984. *Political Violence and the Rise of Nazism: The Storm Troopers in Eastern Germany 1925–1934*. New Haven: Yale University Press.

Bessel, Richard, ed. 1987. *Life in the Third Reich*. Oxford: Oxford University Press.

———. 1996. *Fascist Italy and Nazi Germany: Comparisons and Contrasts*. Cambridge: Cambridge University Press.

Beyerschen, Alan D. 1977. *Scientists under Hitler: Politics and the Physics Community in the Third Reich*. New Haven: Yale University Press.

Binion, Rudolph. 1976. *Hitler among the Germans*. New York and Oxford: Elsevier.

Black, Peter R. 1984. *Ernst Kaltenbrunner: Ideological Soldier of the Third Reich*. Princeton: Princeton University Press.

Bloch, Michael. 1992. *Ribbentrop*. London: Bantam.

Bookbinder, Paul. 1996. *Weimar Germany: The Republic of the Reasonable*. Manchester and New York: Manchester University Press.

Boshyk, Yury, ed. 1986. *Ukraine during World War II*. Edmonton: Canadian Institute of Ukrainian Studies.

Boyer, John W. 1981. *Political Radicalism in Late Imperial Vienna: Origins of the Christian Social Movement, 1848–1897*. Chicago: University of Chicago Press.

———. 1995. *Culture and Political Crisis in Vienna: Christian Socialism in Power, 1897–1918*. Chicago: University of Chicago Press.

Bracher, Karl Dietrich. 1973. *The German Dictatorship: The Origins, Structure and Effects of National Socialism*. New York: Praeger.

Bramsted, Ernest K. 1965. *Goebbels and National Socialist Propaganda 1925–1945*. East Lansing: Michigan State University Press.

Bramwell, Anna. 1985. *Blood and Soil: Richard Walther Darré and Hitler's Green Party*. Bourne End: Kensal.

Breitman, Richard. 1991. *The Architect of Genocide: Himmler and the Final Solution*. London: Bodley Head.

Bridenthal, Renate, Anita Grossmann, and Marion Kaplan, eds. 1984. *When Biology Became Destiny: Women in Weimar and Nazi Germany*. New York: Monthly Review Press.

Broszat, Martin. 1981. *The Hitler State: The Foundation and Development of the Internal Structure of the Third Reich*. New York: Longman.

———. 1987. *Hitler and the Collapse of Weimar Germany*. Leamington Spa: Berg.

Browder, George C. 1990. *Foundations of the Nazi Police State: The Formation of SIPO and SD*. Lexington: University Press of Kentucky.

Browning, Christopher. 1992. *Paths to Genocide: Essays on Launching the Final Solution*. Cambridge: Cambridge University Press.

Brustein, William. 1996. *The Logic of Evil: The Social Origins of the Nazi Party 1925–1933*. New Haven: Yale University Press.

Bukey, Evan Burr. 1986. *Hitler's Hometown: Linz, Austria, 1908–1945*. Bloomington: Indiana University Press.

Bull, Hedley, ed. 1986. *The Challenge of the Third Reich*. Oxford: Clarendon.

Bullock, Alan. 1964. *Hitler: A Study in Tyranny*. Rev. ed. New York: Harper and Row.

———. 1991. *Hitler and Stalin: Parallel Lives*. London: HarperCollins.

Burden, H. T. 1967. *The Nuremberg Rallies: 1923–39*. London: Pall Mall Press.

Burleigh, Michael R. 1994. *Death and Deliverance: "Euthanasia" in Germany 1900–1945*. Cambridge: Cambridge University Press.

———. 1997. *Ethics and Extermination: Reflections on Nazi Genocide*. New York: Cambridge University Press.

Burleigh, Michael, and Wolfgang Wippermann. 1991. *The Racial State: Germany 1933–1945*. Cambridge: Cambridge University Press.

Burrin, Philippe. 1994. *Hitler and the Jews: The Genesis of the Holocaust*. London: Edward Arnold.

Caplan, Jane. 1988. *Government without Administration: State and Civil Service in Weimar and Nazi Germany*. Oxford: Oxford University Press.

Carlton, David. 1981. *Anthony Eden: A Biography*. London: Allen Lane.

Carr, William. 1972. *Arms, Autarky and Aggression: A Study in German Foreign Policy, 1933–1939*. London: Edward Arnold.

————. 1978. *Hitler: A Study in Personality and Politics*. London: Edward Arnold.

————. 1981. "Historians and the Hitler Phenomenon," *German Life and Letters* 34, pp. 260–272.

Carroll, Bernice A. 1968. *Design for Total War: Arms and Economics in the Third Reich*. The Hague: Mouton.

Carsten, F. L. 1977. *Fascist Movements in Austria, from Schönerer to Hitler*. London: Sage.

Cecil, Robert. 1974. *The Myth of the Master Race: Alfred Rosenberg and Nazi Ideology*. London: Batsford.

Cesarani, David, ed. 1994. *The Final Solution: Origins and Implementation*. London: Routledge.

Childers, Thomas. 1983. *The Nazi Voter: The Social Foundations of Fascism in Germany, 1919–1933*. Chapel Hill: University of North Carolina Press.

————. 1991. "The Middle Classes and National Socialism," in David Blackbourn and Richard J. Evans, eds., *The German Bourgeoisie*. London and New York: Routledge, pp. 318–337.

Childers, Thomas, and Jane Caplan, eds. 1993. *Reevaluating the Third Reich*. New York and London: Holmes and Meier.

Churchill, Winston S. 1948–1954. *The Second World War*. 6 vols. Boston: Houghton Mifflin.

Cogan, Charles G. 1996. *Charles de Gaulle: A Brief Biography with Documents*. Boston: Bedford Books.

Compton, James V. 1967. *The Swastika and the Eagle: Hitler, the United States and the Origins of World War II*. Boston: Houghton Mifflin.

Conot, Robert E. 1983. *Justice at Nuremberg*. New York: Harper and Row.

Conrad, Peter. 1998. *Modern Times, Modern Places*. London: Thames and Hudson.

Conway, John S. 1968. *The Nazi Persecution of the Churches, 1933–1945*. New York: Basic Books.

Corni, Gustavo. 1990. *Hitler and the Peasants*. New York, Oxford, and Munich: Berg.

Craig, Gordon A. 1978. *Germany, 1871–1945*. New York: Oxford University Press.

Crew, David F., ed. 1994. *Nazism and German Society, 1933–1945*. London: Routledge.

Cuomo, Glen R., ed. 1995. *National Socialist Cultural Policy*. New York: St. Martin's Press.

Dawidowicz, Lucy S. 1975. *The War against the Jews, 1933–1945*. New York: Holt, Rinehart and Winston.

De Gaulle, Charles. 1972. *The Complete War Memoirs of Charles de Gaulle*. New York: Simon and Schuster.

De Grand, Alexander J. 1995. *Fascist Italy and Nazi Germany: The "Fascist" Style of Rule*. London and New York: Routledge.

Deakin, F. W. 1962. *The Brutal Friendship: Mussolini, Hitler and the Fall of Italian Fascism*. London: Weidenfeld and Nicolson.

Deist, Wilhelm. 1983. *The Wehrmacht and German Rearmament*. Toronto: University of Toronto Press.

Deschner, Günther. 1981. *Heydrich: The Pursuit of Total Power*. London: Orbis.

Dornberg, John. 1982. *The Putsch That Failed: Munich 1923*. London: Weidenfeld and Nicolson.

Dorpalen, Andreas. 1964. *Hindenburg and the Weimar Republic*. Princeton: Princeton University Press.

Düffler, Jost. 1996. *Nazi Germany 1933–1945: Faith and Annihilation*. London: Arnold.

Eden, Anthony. 1962. *The Memoirs of Anthony Eden. Vol. I: Facing the Dictators*. Boston: Houghton Mifflin.

———. 1965. *The Memoirs of Anthony Eden. Vol. 2: The Reckoning*. Boston: Houghton Mifflin.

Eley, Geoff. 1986. *From Unification to Nazism: Reinterpreting the German Past*. Boston: Unwin Hyman.

Ellwood, Sheelagh. 1994. *Franco*. London and New York: Longman.

Emmerson, James T. 1977. *The Rhineland Crisis, 7 March 1936: A Study in Multicultural Diplomacy*. London: Temple Smith.

Engelmann, Bernt. 1986. *In Hitler's Germany: Daily Life in the Third Reich*. New York: Pantheon.

Erickson, John. 1975. *The Road to Stalingrad*. New York: Harper and Row.

———. 1983. *The Road to Berlin*. Boulder, CO: Westview Press.

Evans, Richard J. 1976. "German Women and the Triumph of Hitler," *Journal of Modern History*, 48, pp. 1–53 (on-demand supplement).

———. 1989. *In Hitler's Shadow: West German Historians and the Attempt to Escape from the Nazi Past*. New York: Pantheon.

Evans, Richard J., and Dick Geary, eds. 1987. *The German Unemployed*. London: Croom Helm.

Farquharson, John E. 1976. *The Plough and the Swastika: The NSDAP and Agriculture, 1928–45*. Bloomington: Indiana University Press.

Fein, Helen. 1979. *Accounting for Genocide: National Responses and Jewish Victimization during the Holocaust*. Chicago: University of Chicago Press.

Fest, Joachim. 1970. *The Face of the Third Reich: Portraits of the Nazi Leadership*. New York: Pantheon.

———. 1975. *Hitler*. New York: Vintage Books.

———. 1996. *Plotting Hitler's Death: The German Resistance to Hitler 1933–1945*. London: Weidenfeld and Nicolson.

Field, Geoffrey G. 1981. *Evangelist of Race: The Germanic Vision of Houston Chamberlain*. New York: Columbia University Press.

Finkelstein, Norman G., and Ruth Bettina Birn, eds. 1998. *A Nation on Trial: The Goldhagen Thesis and Historical Truth*. New York: Henry Holt.

Fischer, Conan. 1983. *Stormtroopers: A Social, Economic and Ideological Analysis, 1929–35*. London: Allen and Unwin.

———. 1993. "Ernst Julius Röhm: Chief of Staff of the SA and Indispensable Outsider," in Ronald Smelser and Rainer Zitelmann, eds., *The Nazi Elite*. New York: New York University Press, pp. 173–182.

———. 1995. *The Rise of the Nazis*. Manchester and New York: Manchester University Press.

Fischer, Klaus P. 1995. *Nazi Germany: A New History*. New York: Continuum.

Fleming, Gerald. 1984. *Hitler and the "Final Solution."* Berkeley: University of California Press.

Flood, Charles Bracelen. 1989. *Hitler: The Path to Power*. Boston: Houghton Mifflin.

Freeman, Michael. 1995. *Atlas of Nazi Germany: A Political, Economic and Social Anatomy of the Third Reich*. 2nd ed. London and New York: Longman.

Frei, Norbert. 1993. *National Socialist Rule in Germany: The Führer State 1933–1945*. Oxford: Basil Blackwell.

Friedlander, Henry. 1995. *The Origins of Nazi Genocide: From Euthanasia to the Final Solution*. Chapel Hill: University of North Carolina Press.

Friedländer, Saul. 1966. *Pius XII and the Third Reich: A Documentation*. New York: Alfred A. Knopf.

———. 1967. *Prelude to Downfall: Hitler and the United States 1929–1941*. New York: Alfred A. Knopf.

———. 1984. *Reflections on Nazism: An Essay on Kitsch and Death*. New York: Harper and Row.

———. 1997. *Nazi Germany and the Jews. Vol. 1: The Years of Persecution, 1933–1939.* New York: HarperCollins.

Fritzsche, Peter. 1998. *Germans into Nazis.* Cambridge, MA: Harvard University Press.

Garrett, Stephen A. 1993. *Ethics and Airpower in World War II: The British Bombing of German Cities.* New York: St. Martin's Press.

Gehl, Jürgen. 1963. *Austria, Germany and the Anschluss.* Oxford: Oxford University Press.

Gellately, Robert. 1988. "The Gestapo and German Society: Political Denunciations in the Gestapo Case Files," *Journal of Modern History* 60, pp. 654–694.

———. 1990. *The Gestapo and German Society: Enforcing Racial Policy 1933–1945.* Oxford: Clarendon Press.

Geyer, Michael, and John W. Boyer, eds. 1994. *Resistance against the Third Reich, 1933–1990.* Chicago: University of Chicago Press.

Gilbert, Martin. 1985. *The Holocaust: A History of the Jews of Europe during the Second World War.* New York: Holt, Rinehart and Winston.

———. 1991. *Churchill: A Life.* London: Heinemann.

Giles, Geoffrey J. 1985. *Students and National Socialism in Germany.* Princeton: Princeton University Press.

Glantz, David, and Jonathan House. 1995. *When Titans Clashed: How the Red Army Stopped Hitler.* Lawrence: University of Kansas Press.

Gola, Norman J. W. 1998. *Tomorrow the World: Hitler, Northwest Africa and the Path toward America.* College Station: Texas A & M University Press.

Goldhagen, Daniel Jonah. 1996. *Hitler's Willing Executioners: Ordinary Germans and the Holocaust.* New York: Alfred A. Knopf.

Goodspeed, D. W. 1966. *Ludendorff: Soldier, Dictator, Revolutionary.* London: Hart-Davis.

Gordon, Harold J., Jr. 1972. *Hitler and the Beer Hall Putsch.* Princeton: Princeton University Press.

Gordon, Sarah. 1984. *Hitler, Germans and the "Jewish Question."* Princeton: Princeton University Press.

Görlitz, Walter. 1995. "Blomberg," in Correlli Barnett, ed., *Hitler's Generals.* London: Phoenix, pp. 129–137.

Graham, Cooper C. 1986. *Leni Riefenstahl and Olympia.* Metuchen, NJ: Scarecrow Press.

Graml, Hermann. 1992. *Anti-Semitism in the Third Reich.* Oxford: Blackwell.

Graml, Hermann, et al. 1970. *The German Resistance to Hitler.* Berkeley: University of California Press.

Griffin, Roger. 1999. "Party Time: The Temporal Revolution of the Third Reich," *History Today* 49(4), pp. 43–49.

Gross, Jan Tomasz. 1979. *Polish Society under German Occupation: The Generalgouvernement.* Princeton: Princeton University Press.

Grunberger, Richard. 1971. *A Social History of the Third Reich.* London: Weidenfeld and Nicolson.

Gutman, Robert W. 1968. *Richard Wagner: The Man, His Mind and His Music.* London: Secker and Warburg.

Gutman, Yisrael, and Michael Berenbaum, eds. 1994. *Anatomy of the Auschwitz Death Camp.* Bloomington: Indiana University Press.

Halder, Franz. 1950. *Hitler as Warlord.* London: Putnam.

Hale, Oron J. 1964. *The Captive Press in the Third Reich.* Princeton: Princeton University Press.

Hamann, Brigitte. 1999. *Hitler's Vienna: A Dictator's Apprenticeship.* New York: Oxford University Press.

Hamilton, Richard F. 1982. *Who Voted for Hitler?* Princeton: Princeton University Press.

Hancock, Eleanor. 1991. *National Socialist Leadership and Total War, 1941–1945.* New York: St. Martin's Press.

Hanfstaengl, Ernst. 1957. *Hitler: The Missing Years.* London: Eyre and Spottiswoode.

Harsch, Donna. 1993. *German Social Democracy and the Rise of Nazism.* Chapel Hill: University of North Carolina Press.

Hart-Davis, Duff. 1986. *Hitler's Games: The 1936 Olympics.* London: Century.

Hauner, Milan. 1978. "Did Hitler Want a World Dominion?" *Journal of Contemporary History* 13, pp. 15–32.

Hayes, Peter. 1987. *Industry and Ideology: IG Farben in the Nazi Era.* New York: Cambridge University Press.

Heilbron, John L. 1986. *The Dilemmas of an Upright Man: Max Planck as Spokesman for German Science.* Berkeley: University of California Press.

Helmreich, Ernst Christian. 1979. *The German Churches under Hitler: Background, Struggle, and Epilogue.* Detroit: Wayne State University Press.

Hermand, Jost. 1993. *Old Dreams of a New Reich: Volkisch Utopias and National Socialism.* Bloomington: Indiana University Press.

Hiden, John. 1977. *Germany and Europe 1919–1939.* New York: Longman.

Hiden, John, and John Farquharson. 1983. *Explaining Hitler's Germany: Historians and the Third Reich.* Totowa, NJ: Barnes and Noble.

Hiden, John, and Patrick Salmon. 1994. *The Baltic Nations and Europe: Estonia, Latvia and Lithuania in the Twentieth Century.* Rev. ed. London and New York: Longman.

Hilberg, Raul. 1985. *The Destruction of the European Jews.* Rev. ed. New York: Holmes and Meier.

Hildebrand, Klaus. 1973. *The Foreign Policy of the Third Reich.* London: Batsford.

———. 1984. *The Third Reich.* London: Allen and Unwin.

Hillgruber, Andreas. 1974. "England's Place in Hitler's Plans for World Dominion," *Journal of Contemporary History* 9, pp. 5–22.

Hinz, Berthold. 1979. *Art in the Third Reich.* New York: Pantheon.

Hitler, Adolf. 1992. *Mein Kampf.* Trans. Ralph Manheim. Intro. by D. C. Watt. London: Pimlico.

Hoffmann, Heinrich. 1955. *Hitler Was My Friend.* London: Burke.

Hoffmann, Hilmar. 1996. *The Triumph of Propaganda: Film and National Socialism, 1933–1945.* Providence and Oxford: Berghahn Books.

Hoffmann, Peter. 1988. *German Resistance to Hitler.* Cambridge, MA: Harvard University Press.

———. 1995. *Stauffenberg: A Family History, 1905–1944.* Cambridge: Cambridge University Press.

Holborn, Hajo. 1972. *Republic to Reich: The Making of the Nazi Revolution.* New York: Pantheon.

Horn, Daniel. 1976. "The Hitler Youth and Educational Decline in the Third Reich," *History of Education Quarterly* 16, pp. 425–447.

Hoyt, Edwin P. 1980. *Goering's War.* London: Robert Hale.

Hughes, Michael. 1988. *Nationalism and Society: Germany 1800–1945.* London and Baltimore: Edward Arnold.

Jablonsky, David. 1989. *The Nazi Party in Dissolution: Hitler and the Verbotszeit 1923–25.* London: Frank Cass.

Jäckel, Eberhard. 1981. *Hitler's Worldview: A Blueprint for Power.* Cambridge, MA: Harvard University Press.

———. 1984. *Hitler in History.* Hanover: University Press of New England.

James, Harold. 1986. *The German Slump: Politics and Economics, 1924–1936.* Oxford: Clarendon.

Jones, Larry Eugene. 1992. "'The Greatest Stupidity of My Life': Alfred Hugenberg and the Formation of the Hitler Cabinet, January 1933," *Journal of Contemporary History* 27, pp. 63–87.

Kaplan, Marion A. 1998. *Between Dignity and Despair: Jewish Life in Nazi Germany.* New York: Oxford University Press.

Kater, Michael H. 1981. "Hitler in a Social Context," *Central European History* 14, pp. 243–272.

———. 1983. *The Nazi Party: A Social Profile of Members and Leaders, 1919–1945.* Cambridge, MA: Harvard University Press.

———. 1989. *Doctors under Hitler*. Chapel Hill: University of North Carolina Press.

———. 1997. *The Twisted Muse: Musicians and Their Music in the Third Reich*. New York and Oxford: Oxford University Press.

Kauders, Anthony. 1996. *German Politics and the Jews: Düsseldorf and Nuremberg, 1910–1933*. Oxford: Clarendon Press.

Keegan, John. 1989. *The Second World War*. London: Hutchinson.

Kent, Bruce. 1989. *The Spoils of War: The Politics, Economics and Diplomacy of Reparations, 1918–1932*. Oxford: Clarendon Press.

Kershaw, Ian. 1983. *Popular Opinion and Political Dissent in the Third Reich: Bavaria 1933–1945*. Oxford: Clarendon Press.

———. 1989. *The "Hitler Myth": Image and Reality in the Third Reich*. Paperback ed. New York: Oxford University Press.

———. 1991. *Hitler*. London and New York: Longman.

———. 1993. *The Nazi Dictatorship: Problems and Perspectives of Interpretation*. 3rd ed. London: Edward Arnold.

———. 1998. *Hitler 1889–1936: Hubris*. New York: Allen Lane The Penguin Press.

Kershaw, Ian, and Moshe Lewin, eds. 1997. *Stalinism and Nazism: Dictatorships in Comparison*. Cambridge: Cambridge University Press.

Kimball, Warren F. 1997. *Forged in War: Churchill, Roosevelt and the Second World War*. London: HarperCollins.

Kirk, Timothy. 1994. *The Longman Companion to Nazi Germany*. London and New York: Longman.

Klemperer, Klemens von. 1992. *German Resistance against Hitler: The Search for Allies Abroad*. Oxford: Clarendon Press.

Klemperer, Victor. 1998. *I Shall Bear Witness: The Diaries of Victor Klemperer, 1933–41*. London: Weidenfeld and Nicolson.

Knox, MacGregor. 1984. "Conquest, Foreign and Domestic, in Fascist Italy and Nazi Germany," *Journal of Modern History* 56, pp. 1–57.

Koch, Hansjoachim. 1975. *The Hitler Youth: Origins and Development, 1922–45*. London: Macdonald and Jane's.

Kochan, Lionel. 1957. *Pogrom: 10 November 1938*. London: Andre Deutsch.

Koehl, Robert L. 1983. *The Black Corps: The Structure and Power Struggles of the Nazi SS*. Madison: University of Wisconsin Press.

Kolb, Eberhard. 1988. *The Weimar Republic*. London: Unwin Hyman.

Krausnick, Helmut, and Martin Broszat. 1968. *Anatomy of the SS State*. New York: Walker and Company.

Kühl, Stefan. 1994. *The Nazi Connection: Eugenics, American Racism, and German National Socialism*. New York: Oxford University Press.

Lambert, Peter. 1995. "German Historians and Nazi Ideology: The Parameters of the *Volksgemeinschaft* and the Problem of Historical Legitimation, 1930–45," *European History Quarterly* 25, pp. 555–582.

Langer, Walter C. 1972. *The Mind of Adolf Hitler*. New York: Basic Books.

Laqueur, Walter, ed. 1976. *Fascism: A Reader's Guide*. Berkeley: University of California Press.

Large, David Clay. 1997. *Where Ghosts Walked: Munich's Road to the Third Reich*. New York: Norton.

———, ed. 1992. *Contending with Hitler: Varieties of German Resistance in the Third Reich*. Cambridge: Cambridge University Press.

Leopold, John A. 1977. *Alfred Hugenberg: The Radical Nationalist Campaign against the Weimar Republic*. New Haven: Yale University Press.

Levi, Erik. 1994. *Music in the Third Reich*. New York: Macmillan.

Levin, Nora. 1973. *The Holocaust: The Destruction of the European Jews*. New York: New Viewpoints.

Levine, Alan J. 1992. *The Strategic Bombing of Germany, 1940–1945*. Westport and London: Praeger.

Levine, Herbert S. 1973. *Hitler's Free City: A History of the Nazi Party in Danzig.* Chicago: University of Chicago Press.

Lewin, Ronald. 1977. *The Life and Death of the Afrika Korps.* London: Batsford.

Lewy, Günter. 1964. *The Catholic Church and Nazi Germany.* New York: McGraw-Hill.

Loewenberg, Peter. 1987. "The Kristallnacht as a Public Degradation Ritual," *Leo Baeck Institute Yearbook* 32, pp. 309–323.

Lukacs, John. 1997. *The Hitler of History.* New York: Alfred A. Knopf.

Lukas, Richard C. 1986. *Forgotten Holocaust: The Poles under German Occupation 1939–1944.* Lexington: University Press of Kentucky.

Lyttelton, Adrian. 1987. *The Seizure of Power: Fascism in Italy 1919–1929.* 2nd ed. London: Weidenfeld and Nicolson.

Mack Smith, Denis. 1976. *Mussolini's Roman Empire.* New York: Longman.

———. 1981. *Mussolini.* London: Weidenfeld and Nicolson.

Macksey, Kenneth. 1975. *Guderian: Panzer General.* London: Macdonald and Jane's.

Macrakis, Kristie. 1993. *Surviving the Swastika: Scientific Research in Nazi Germany.* New York and Oxford: Oxford University Press.

Maier, Charles S. 1988. *The Unmasterable Past: History, Holocaust, and German National Identity.* Cambridge, MA: Harvard University Press.

Maier, Charles S., Stanley Hoffmann, and Andrew Gould, eds. 1986. *The Rise of the Nazi Regime: Historical Reassessments.* Boulder, CO: Westview.

Mandell, Richard D. 1987. *The Nazi Olympics.* Urbana: University of Chicago Press.

Manstein, Erich von. 1958. *Lost Victories.* London: Methuen.

Marrus, Michael R. 1987. *The Holocaust in History.* New York: Meridian.

Marrus, Michael R., and Robert O. Paxton. 1981. *Vichy France and the Jews.* New York: Basic Books.

Mason, Tim. 1993. *Social Policy in the Third Reich: The Working Class and the "National Community."* Providence and Oxford: Berg.

McDonough, Frank. 1998. *Neville Chamberlain, Appeasement and Britain's Road to War.* Manchester and New York: Manchester University Press.

Merkl, Peter H. 1975. *Political Violence under the Swastika: 581 Early Nazis.* Princeton: Princeton University Press.

———. 1980. *The Making of a Stormtrooper.* Princeton: Princeton University Press.

Merson, Allan. 1985. *Communist Resistance in Nazi Germany.* London: Lawrence and Wishart.

Meskill, Johanna M. 1966. *Hitler and Japan: The Hollow Alliance.* New York: Atherton Press.

Milward, Alan S. 1965. *The German Economy at War.* London: Athlone Press.

Mitchell, Allen. 1965. *Revolution in Bavaria, 1918–1919: The Eisner Regime and the Soviet Republic.* Princeton: Princeton University Press.

Morley, John F. 1980. *Vatican Diplomacy and the Jews during the Holocaust 1939–1943.* New York: KTAV Publishing House.

Mosse, George L. 1961. "The Mystical Origins of National Socialism," *Journal of the History of Ideas* 22, pp. 81–96.

———. 1964. *The Crisis of German Ideology: Intellectual Origins of the Third Reich.* New York: Grosset and Dunlap.

———, ed. 1981. *Nazi Culture: Intellectual, Cultural and Social Life in the Third Reich.* New York: Schocken Books.

Mühlberger, Detlev. 1991. *Hitler's Followers: Studies in the Sociology of the Nazi Movement.* London: Routledge.

Müller, Ingo. 1991. *Hitler's Justice: The Courts of the Third Reich.* Cambridge, MA: Harvard University Press.

Mulligan, Timothy P. 1988. *The Politics of Illusion and Empire: German Occupation Policy in the Soviet Union, 1942–1943.* New York: Praeger.

Neumann, Franz. 1966. *Behemoth: The Structure and Practice of National Socialism.* 1942. Reprint, New York: Harper and Row.

Nicholls, A. J. 1991. *Weimar and the Rise of Hitler.* 3rd ed. New York: Macmillan.

Nicholls, Anthony, and Erich Matthias, eds. 1971. *German Democracy and the Triumph of Hitler.* London: Allen and Unwin.

Nicosia, Francis R., and Laurence D. Stokes, eds. 1992. *Germans against Nazism.* Oxford: Berg.

Niewyk, Donald L. 1980. *The Jews in Weimar Germany.* Baton Rouge: Louisiana State University Press.

Noakes, Jeremy. 1971. *The Nazi Party in Lower Saxony, 1921–1933.* Oxford: Oxford University Press.

Noakes, Jeremy, and Geoffrey Pridham, eds. 1983–1998. *Nazism 1919–1945: A Documentary Reader.* 4 vols. Exeter: Exeter University Press.

Nyomarkay, Joseph. 1967. *Charisma and Factionalism within the Nazi Party.* Minneapolis: University of Minnesota Press.

Oakey, Stewart P. 1972. *A Short History of Denmark.* New York: Praeger.

O'Neill, Robert J. 1987. *The German Army and the Nazi Party 1933–1939.* London: Cassell, 1966. Reprint, New York: Heinemann.

———. 1995. "Fritsch, Beck and the Führer," in Correlli Barnett, ed., *Hitler's Generals.* London: Phoenix.

Orlow, Dietrich. 1969. *The History of the Nazi Party, 1919–1933.* Pittsburgh: University of Pittsburgh Press.

———. 1973. *The History of the Nazi Party, 1933–1945.* Pittsburgh: University of Pittsburgh Press.

Overy, Richard J. 1973. "Transportation and Re-armament in the Third Reich," *Historical Journal* 16, pp. 389–409.

———. 1984. *Goering: The "Iron Man."* London: Routledge.

———. 1994. *War and Economy in the Third Reich.* Oxford: Clarendon Press.

———. 1995. *Why the Allies Won.* New York and London: Norton.

———. 1996. *The Nazi Economic Recovery 1932–1938.* 2nd ed. Cambridge: Cambridge University Press.

———. 1998. *Russia's War.* New York: Allen Lane The Penguin Press.

Padfield, Peter. 1984. *Dönitz: The Last Führer.* New York: Harper and Row.

———. 1991. *Hess: Flight for the Führer.* London: Weidenfeld and Nicolson.

Parker, R. A. C. 1993. *Chamberlain and Appeasement: British Policy and the Coming of the Second World War.* New York: St. Martin's Press.

Pauley, Bruce F. 1981. *Hitler and the Forgotten Nazis: A History of Austrian National Socialism.* Chapel Hill: University of North Carolina Press.

———. 1992. *From Prejudice to Persecution: A History of Austrian Anti-Semitism.* Chapel Hill: University of North Carolina Press.

Paxton, Robert O. 1982. *Vichy France: Old Guard and New Order, 1940–1944.* New York: Columbia University Press.

Peterson, Edward N. 1954. *Hjalmar Schacht: For and against Hitler.* Boston: Christopher Publishing House.

———. 1969. *The Limits of Hitler's Power.* Princeton: Princeton University Press.

Petropolous, Jonathan. 1996. *Art as Politics in the Third Reich.* Chapel Hill: University of North Carolina Press.

Peukert, Detlev J. K. 1987. *Inside Nazi Germany: Conformity, Opposition and Racism in Everyday Life.* New Haven: Yale University Press.

———. 1991. *The Weimar Republic: The Crisis of Classical Modernity.* New York: Allen Lane The Penguin Press.

Phillips, Marcus S. 1971. "The Nazi Control of the German Film Industry," *Journal of European Studies* 1, pp. 37–68.

Pine, Lisa. 1997. *Nazi Family Policy, 1933–1945.* London: Berg.

————. 1999. "Girls in Uniform," *History Today* 49(3), pp. 24–29.

Powers, Thomas. 1993. *Heisenberg's War: The Secret History of the German Bomb.* New York: Alfred A. Knopf.

Preston, Paul. 1993. *Franco: A Biography.* London: HarperCollins.

Pridham, Geoffrey. 1973. *The Nazi Movement in Bavaria, 1923–1933.* New York: Harper and Row.

Proctor, Robert N. 1988. *Racial Hygiene: Medicine under the Nazis.* Cambridge, MA: Harvard University Press.

Pulzer, Peter. 1988. *The Rise of Political Anti-Semitism in Germany and Austria.* Rev. ed. Cambridge, MA: Harvard University Press.

Read, Anthony, and David Fisher. 1988. *The Deadly Embrace: Hitler, Stalin and the Nazi-Soviet Pact 1939–1941.* London: Joseph.

Rees, Laurence. 1997. *The Nazis: A Warning from History.* London: BBC Books.

Rempel, Gerhard. 1989. *Hitler's Children: The Hitler Youth and the SS.* Chapel Hill: University of North Carolina Press.

Renneberg, Monika, and Mark Walker, eds. 1994. *Science, Technology and National Socialism.* Cambridge: Cambridge University Press.

Reuth, Ralf Georg. 1993. *Goebbels.* London: Constable.

Rich, Norman. 1973–1974. *Hitler's War Aims. Vol. 1: Ideology, the Nazi State and the Course of Expansion; Vol. 2: The Establishment of the New Order.* New York: Norton.

Richie, Alexandra. 1998. *Faust's Metropolis: A History of Berlin.* London: HarperCollins.

Ritchie, J. M. 1983. *German Literature under National Socialism.* London: Croom Helm.

Ritter, Gerhard. 1958. *The German Resistance: Carl Goerdeler's Struggle against Tyranny.* London: Allen and Unwin.

Robertson, Esmonde M. 1967. *Hitler's Pre-War Policy and Military Plans, 1933–1939.* New York: Citadel Press.

————, ed. 1971. *The Origins of the Second World War: Historical Interpretations.* London: Macmillan.

Rose, Norman. 1995. *Churchill: The Unruly Giant.* New York: Free Press.

Rose, Paul Lawrence. 1992. *Wagner, Race and Revolution.* London: Faber.

Rosenhaft, Eve. 1983. *Beating the Fascists? The German Communists and Political Violence, 1929–1933.* Cambridge: Cambridge University Press.

Schäche, Wolfgang. 1995. "From Berlin to 'Germania,'" in *Art and Power: Europe under the Dictators 1930–45.* London: Hayward Gallery.

Schacht, Hjalmar. 1965. *My First Seventy-Six Years.* London: Wingate.

Schleunes, Karl A. 1970. *The Twisted Road to Auschwitz: Nazi Policy toward German Jews.* Urbana: University of Illinois Press.

Schoenbaum, David. 1980. *Hitler's Social Revolution: Class and Status in Nazi Germany, 1933–1939.* 1966. Reprint, New York: Norton.

Schorske, Carl E. 1980. *Fin-de-Siècle Vienna: Politics and Culture.* New York: Alfred A. Knopf.

Scobie, Alex. 1990. *Hitler's State Architecture: The Impact of Classical Antiquity.* University Park: Pennsylvania State University Press.

Sereny, Gita. 1974. *Into That Darkness: From Mercy Killing to Mass Murder.* London: Deutsch.

————. 1995. *Albert Speer: His Battle with Truth.* New York: Macmillan.

Smelser, Ronald M. 1988. *Robert Ley: Hitler's Labor Front Leader.* Oxford/New York/Hamburg: Berg.

Smelser, Ronald, and Rainer Zitelmann, eds. 1993. *The Nazi Elite.* New York: New York University Press.

Smith, Bradley F. 1967. *Adolf Hitler: His Family, Childhood and Youth.* Stanford: Hoover Institution for War, Revolution, and Peace.

————. 1977. *Reaching Judgment at Nuremberg.* New York: Basic Books.

Smith, Woodruff D. 1986. *The Ideological Origins of Nazi Imperialism*. New York: Oxford University Press.

Snyder, Louis L. 1981. *Hitler's Third Reich: A Documentary History*. Chicago: Nelson Hall.

Sofsky, Wolfgang. 1997. *The Order of Terror: The Concentration Camp*. Princeton: Princeton University Press.

Speer, Albert. 1971. *Inside the Third Reich*. Paperback ed. London: Sphere Books.

Spotts, Frederic. 1994. *Bayreuth: A History of the Wagner Festival*. New Haven: Yale University Press.

Stachura, Peter D. 1975. *Nazi Youth in the Weimar Republic*. Santa Barbara and Oxford: Clio Books.

———. 1981. *The German Youth Movement 1900–1945*. New York: St Martin's Press.

———. 1983a. *Gregor Strasser and the Rise of Nazism*. London: Allen and Unwin.

———. 1983b. *The Nazi Machtergreifung*. London: Allen and Unwin.

———, ed. 1978. *The Shaping of the Nazi State*. London: Croom Helm.

Stackelberg, Roderick. 1999. *Hitler's Germany: Origins, Interpretations, Legacies*. London and New York: Routledge.

Stein, George Henry. 1966. *The Waffen SS: Hitler's Elite Guard at War, 1939–45*. Ithaca, NY: Cornell University Press.

Steinberg, Michael H. 1977. *Sabers and Brown Shirts: The German Students' Path to National Socialism 1918–1935*. Princeton: Princeton University Press.

Steinert, Marlis G. 1977. *Hitler's War and the Germans: Public Mood and Attitude during the Second World War*. Athens: Ohio University Press.

Steinweis, Alan E. 1993. *Art, Ideology, and Economics in Nazi Germany: The Reich Chambers of Music, Theater and the Visual Arts*. Chapel Hill: University of North Carolina Press.

Stephenson, Jill. 1975. *Women in Nazi Society*. London: Croom Helm.

———. 1980. *The Nazi Organization of Women*. London: Croom Helm.

Stern, J. P. 1992. *Hitler: The Führer and the People*. Rev. ed. Berkeley: University of California Press.

Stoakes, Geoffrey. 1986. *Hitler and the Quest for World Domination*. Leamington Spa: Berg.

Stone, Norman. 1980. *Hitler*. Boston: Little, Brown.

Taylor, A. J. P. 1961. *The Origins of the Second World War*. Greenwich, CT: Fawcett Publications.

Taylor, Brandon, and Wilfried Van Der Will, eds. 1990. *The Nazification of Art: Art, Design, Music, Architecture and Film in the Third Reich*. Winchester, England: Winchester School of Art Press.

Taylor, Simon. 1985. *Prelude to Genocide: Nazi Ideology and the Struggle for Power*. New York: St. Martin's Press.

Taylor, Telford. 1979. *Munich: The Price of Peace*. Garden City, NY: Doubleday.

Thalmann, Rita, and Emmanuel Feinermann. 1974. *Crystal Night: 9–10 November 1938*. London: Thames and Hudson.

Tobias, Fritz. 1964. *The Reichstag Fire*. New York: Putnam.

Toland, John. 1976. *Adolf Hitler*. Garden City NY: Doubleday.

Trevor-Roper, Hugh. 1971. *The Last Days of Hitler*. 4th ed. London: Macmillan.

———, ed. 1953. *Hitler's Table Talk*. London: Weidenfeld and Nicolson.

Turner, Henry Ashby. 1985. *German Big Business and the Rise of Hitler*. New York: Oxford University Press.

———. 1996. *Hitler's Thirty Days to Power: January 1933*. Reading, MA: Addison-Wesley.

———, ed. 1975. *Reappraisals of Fascism*. New York: New Viewpoints.

Volkogonov, Dmitri. 1991. *Stalin: Triumph and Tragedy*. Paperback ed., 1995. London: Weidenfeld and Nicolson.

Von Lang, Jochen. 1979. *The Secretary Martin Bormann: The Man Who Manipulated Hitler.* New York: Random House.

———. 1983. *Eichmann Interrogated.* New York: Farrar, Strauss and Giroux.

Waite, Robert G. L. 1952. *Vanguard of Nazism: The Free Corps Movement in Postwar Germany, 1918–1923.* Cambridge, MA: Harvard University Press.

———. 1977. *The Psychopathic God: Adolf Hitler.* New York: Basic Books.

Walker, Mark. 1989. *German National Socialism and the Quest for Nuclear Power, 1939–49.* Cambridge: Cambridge University Press.

Warner, Geoffrey. 1968. *Pierre Laval and the Eclipse of France, 1931–1945.* New York: Macmillan.

Watt, Donald Cameron. 1960. "The Rome-Berlin Axis, 1936–1940: Myth and Reality," *Review of Politics* 22, pp. 519–543.

———. 1989. *How War Came: The Immediate Origins of the Second World War, 1938–1939.* New York: Pantheon.

Weber, Max. 1978. *Economy and Society.* Ed. Guenther Roth and Claus Wittich. Berkeley: University of California Press.

Weinberg, Gerhard L. 1970. *The Foreign Policy of Hitler's Germany: Diplomatic Revolution in Europe, 1933–1936.* Chicago: University of Chicago Press.

———. 1980. *The Foreign Policy of Hitler's Germany: Starting World War II, 1937–1939.* Chicago: University of Chicago Press.

———. 1995. *Germany, Hitler, and World War II: Essays in Modern German and World History.* New York: Cambridge University Press.

Weindlung, Paul. 1989. *Health, Race and German Politics between National Unification and Nazism, 1870–1945.* Cambridge: Cambridge University Press.

Weiner, Marc A. 1995. *Richard Wagner and the Anti-Semitic Imagination.* Lincoln: University of Nebraska Press.

Weitz, Eric D. 1997. *Creating German Communism, 1890–1990: From Popular Protest to Socialist State.* Princeton: Princeton University Press.

Welch, David. 1983a. *Propaganda and the German Cinema 1933–1945.* Oxford: Clarendon Press.

———. 1993. *The Third Reich: Politics and Propaganda.* London and New York: Routledge.

———, ed. 1983b. *Nazi Propaganda: The Power and the Limitations.* London: Croom Helm.

Whiteside, Andrew G. 1975. *The Socialism of Fools: Georg Ritter von Schönerer and Austrian Pan-Germanism.* Berkeley: University of California Press.

Wistrich, Robert. 1982. *Who's Who in Nazi Germany.* London: Weidenfeld and Nicolson.

Woolf, Stuart J., ed. 1969. *The Nature of Fascism.* New York: Random House.

———. 1981. *Fascism in Europe.* London: Methuen.

Wunderlich, Frieda. 1961. *Farm Labor in Germany, 1810–1945.* Princeton: Princeton University Press.

Yahil, Leni. 1990. *The Holocaust: The Fate of European Jewry.* New York: Oxford University Press.

Zeman, Z. A. B. 1974. *Nazi Propaganda.* London: Oxford University Press.

Zuccotti, Susan. 1987. *The Italians and the Holocaust: Persecution, Rescue and Survival.* New York: Basic Books.

INDEX

German National People's Party
(DNVP), 77, **98**, 101, 129,
178, 299
German People's Party (DVP), **97**,
101
German Union of Sporting Flyers,
16
German Workers' Party (DAP),
xvii, 64, 68, 82, **99**, 170,
175, 176
German Youth Force, 44
Gestapo, xxiv, 32, 51, 73, 76–77,
92, **99–100**, 105, 106–07,
111, 117, 119, 131, 132,
136, 138, 143, 154, 177,
183, 191, 207, 224, 237–38,
242, 243, 253
Gibraltar, 89
Giraud, Henri, 43, 62
Gisevius, Hans Bernd, 101
Gleichschaltung, xxi, xxii, xxiii, 10,
92, 99, **100–02**, 137, 138,
197, 202, 220, 275
Gleiwitz, 117, 241
Gobineau, Joseph-Arthur de,
211–12
Goebbels, Josef, xix, xxi, xxviii,
xxix, 2, 10, 27, 32, 33, 36,
47, 48–49, 51, 56, 94, 101,
102–05, 107, 109, 114,
120–21, 122, 142, 147, 171,
177, 187, 202, 203–05,
212–13, 218, 222, 223–24,
228, 229, 233, 244, 252,
253, 267, 280, 287, 292
Goebbels, Magda, 104
Goerdeler, Carl, **105**, 141, 147,
234–35, 252
Goering, Edda, 107
Goering, Hermann, xviii, xxi, xxiv,
16, 22, 24, 27, 29, 30, 32,
33, 34, 38, 65, 86, 99,
105–08, 116, 128, 138, 145,
147, 160–61, 179, 182, 187,
212, 217, 218, 224, 228,
229, 247, 253, 254–55, 260,
266, 317, 321–22
Gola, Norman J. W. (historian),
183–84
Goldhagen, Daniel J. (historian), 5
Gömbös, Gyula, 129
Gordon Walker, Patrick, 322–25
Gori (Georgia), 249
Götterdämmerung (Wagner), 22
Graf Spee (battleship), 179
Grafeneck, 318

Grandel, Gottfried, 69
Grauch, Hermann, 312
Graz university, 143
Great Britain, xxiv, xxvi–xvii,
xxix, 6–8, 11–12, 17, 32,
38–39, 45, 64–65, 70–71,
85, 105, **108–09**, 110, 114,
128, 129, 139, 165, 168,
169, 171, 180, 183, 195,
199, 202, 214, 215, 216,
221, 222–23, 241, 247, 249,
260, 269, 274–75, 293–94
Hess's flight to, 33, 122
Great German Art Exhibition, 10
Great Patriotic War, **109**
Greece, 20, 41, **109–10**, 174, 220,
258, 302
Greenland, 62
Greifenstein Castle, 252
Greiner, Josef, 5
Greiser, Arthur, 60
Gropius, Walter, 56
Grosz, George, 56
Grozny, 68
Gruhn, Margarethe, 29, 31
Grynszpan, Herschel, xxvi, 147
Guadalcanal, 75
Guderian, Heinz, xiv, 62, **110–11**,
146, 196, 251
Guernica, 54
Günther, Hans, 92
Gundolf, Friedrich, 102
Gürtner, Franz, **111**, 154
Gustloff, Wilhelm, 261
Gutman, Robert W. (historian),
286
Gypsies, 13, 54, 59, 78, **111–12**,
119, 189–90, 191, 239, 264,
272

Haakon, King of Norway, 185
Ha'avara Agreement, 139, 168
Habermas, Jürgen, 120
Hácha, Emil, 57
Hadamar, 318
Hadamovsky, Eugen, 186
Halberstadt, 33
Halder, Franz, xxvii, 35, 67,
113–14, 164, 303
Halifax, Lord, 26
Hamburg, xx, 32, 36, 309–10
Hamilton, Duke of, 116
Hamilton, Richard F. (historian),
76
Hammerstein-Equord, Kurt von,
23

Hanfstaengl, Ernst "Putzi," xvii,
24, **114–15**
Hans Westmar (film), 49
Harlan, Veit, 49
Harrer, Karl, 64, 99
Harris, Sir Arthur, 32
Hartheim Castle, 59
Harvard University, 40, 114
Harzburg Front, 98, **115**, 178, 234,
249
Hassell, Ulrich von, 90, 123, 147
Hassfort Am Main, 233
Heidegger, Martin, 275
Heidelberg, 102
Heimatliteratur, 56
Heimkehr (film), 49
Heinkel, bomber, 160
Heisenberg, Werner, 240
Henckel, Anneliese, 222
Hendaye, 89
Henlein, Konrad, **115**, 257
Hercules, Operation, 163
Hereditary Farm Law, 217
Hereditary Health Courts, 78
Hess, Rudolf, xviii, 33, 71,
115–16, 122, 152, 157, 165,
187, 281
Hesse, 294
Heydrich, Reinhard, 29, 83, 100,
106, **116–17**, 118, 119, 139,
143, 152, 182, 183, 221,
241–42, 287
Hiden, John (historian), 85
Hierl, Konstantin, 151
Himmler, Heinrich, xxi, xxiv,
xxviii–xxix, 13, 24, 29, 30,
33, 34, 61, 80, 83, 90, 92,
96, 100, 105, 106, 107,
117–19, 136, 147, 182,
183, 212, 224, 229,
238–39, 242, 256, 285,
319–20
Hindenburg, Oskar von, 120
Hindenburg, Paul von, xx, xxi,
xxiii, 40, 101, **119–20**, 149,
157–59, 189, 197, 218, 234,
236, 291, 312
Hippler, Fritz, 48, 49
Hirohito, Emperor of Japan, 135
Hiroshima, 135
Hirsch-Dünker Unions, 268
Hirsing, Otto, 217
Historikerstreit, **120–21**
Hitler, Alois, xvi, 36
Hitler as Warlord (Halder), 113–14
Hitler, Klara, xvi

Rosenheim, 105
Rostov, 230
Rote Kapelle, 51, 192
Royal Air Force, 11, 38–39, 108, 161, 179, 241
  Bomber Command, 31–32
  Fighter Command, 38
Royal Navy (British), 179
Ruhr, 32, 102, 145
  French occupation of xviii, 33, 86, 220, **229–30**, 265
Rundstedt, Karl Rudolf von, 20, 145, 146, 164, 183, 226, **230–31**
Russia, 2, 5, 28, 35, 38, 48, 49, 50, 83, 84, 108, 113, 164,166, 309, 317. *See also* Soviet Union
Russian National Committee for Free Germany, 198
Rust, Bernhard, 71, 101, 125

SA. *See* Sturmabteilung
SA-Mann Brand (film), 49
Saarbrücken, 233
Saarland, xxiii–xxiv, 155, 200, 212, **233**, 277
Sachsenhausen-Oranienburg, 52, 125
Salò, 134
Sauckel, Fritz, 70, 187, **233–34**
Savoy, 87
Saxony, xix, 5, 91
Schacht, Hjalmar, xxi, 61, 69–70, 82, 86, 94, 115, 132, 138, 149, 188, **234–35**
Scharnhorst (battleship), 179
Schiller, Frederick, 49
Schirach, Baldur von, 38, 124–25, 188, 228–29, **235–36**, 301
Schleicher, Kurt von, xxi, 120, 183, 197, **236**, 243, 253
Schleswig, 42
Schleswig-Holstein, 234
Schlösser, Rainer, 56
Schmidt, Carl, 154
Schmidt, Charlotte, 35
Schmidt, Ernst, 296
Schmidt, Paul Otto, **236**
Schnabel, Artur, 22
Schnitzler, Arthur, 279
Schoenberg, Arnold, 56, 279
Schönerer, Georg Ritter von, 5, 156, 160, 195, **236–37**, 280
Schreck, Julius, 238
Schröder, Kurt von, xxi, 197

Schuler, Alfred, 258
Schuschnigg, Kurt von, xxv, 3, 14, 26, 64, **237–38**
Schutzstaffel (SS), xxii, 22, 23, 30, 33, 34, 40, 42, 52–54, 70, 83, 90, 91, 93, 95, 100, 111–12, 117, 118–19, 123, 125, 127, 132, 138, 139, 140, 142, 145, 147, 149, 154, 164, 168, 177, 179, 182–83, 198, 211–12, 224, **238–40**, 241, 248, 256, 266, 288, 289, 318, 319–20, 322–23
  Ahnenerbe, 212
  Austrian, 73, 143
  Central Office for Race and Resettlement, 61, 238, 239
  concentration camp guards, 26
  Criminal Police, 79
  doctors, 13, 35
  Einsatzgruppen, 67, 127, 139, 242, 272
  Lebensborn organization, 78, 239, 293
  Main Riding School, 170
  Panzer Divisions, 9
  Totenkopfverbände, 59, **267–68**
  Wirtschaft und Verwaltungshauptamt (WVHA), 52
  See also Waffen SS
Science and Scientists, **240–41**
Scotland, 116
Sculpture, 10
SD. *See* Sicherheitsdienst
Sealion, Operation, 38, **241**
Seckt, Hans von, 230
Seisser, Hans Ritter von, 23–24
Seldte, Franz, 249
Serbia, 80. *See also* Yugoslavia
Seyss-Inquart, Arthur, xxv, 3, 181, 187, 237
Shirer, William L., 114
Siberia, 20
Sicherheitdienst (SD), xxiv, 2, 33, 117, 118, 122, 139, 207, 238–39, **241–42**, 320–22
  Jewish Affairs Department, 73
Sicherheitspolizei (SIPO), 99, 241–42
Sicily, xxviii, 43
Siegfried Line, 152, **242**, 266, 267
Sigmaringen, 199
Silesia, 146, 277

Simovic, Dusan, 269
Singapore, 136
Sinti. *See* Gypsies
Sirkin, Rudolf, 22
Skorzeny, Otto, 174
Slawój-Skladkowski, Felicjan, 200
Sleepwalkers, The (H. Broch), 264
Slovak People's Party, 265
Slovakia, xxvi, 20, 57, 265–66, 269, 285. *See also* Czechoslovakia
Smolensk, 20, 68
Sobibor, xxvii, 54, 80, **242–43**
Social Darwinism, xiv, 165, 240, 281
Social Democratic Party (SDP), 5, 50, 76, 77, 101, 177, 192, 206, 230, **243**, 245, 268
  Austrian, 14
  and "Weimar coalition," xx, 291
Social Policy, **243–44**. *See also* Winterhilfe; Women
Socialism, **244–45**
Socialist Unity Party, 243
Söderbaum, Kristina, 49
Solmitz, Luise, xxiv, 309–10
Sonnermann, Emily, 107
Sopade, 100, 121, 122, 192, 207, 243, **245**
South Tyrol, 281
Soviet Union, xxvi, xxvii, 4, 19, 20, 30, 41, 42, 47, 51, 57, 58, 67–68, 71, 84, 85, 86, 109, 110, 111–12, 116, 120, 126, 129–30, 135, 140, 144, 160, 161, 164, 167, 168–69, 180–81, 192, 196, 198, 200–01, 204, 214, 220, 221, 225, 230, **245–46**, 247, 248, 249–52, 263, 269, 283, 288, 289, 299. *See also* Belorussia; Russia; Ukraine
Spain, xxx, 54, 81, 87, 88–90, 128, 133, 153, 160, 173, **246–247**, 266
Spanish Civil War. *See* Spain
Spartakus League, 50–51. *See also* Berlin
Speer, Albert, xxviii, xxix, 8–9, 16, 22, 27, 32, 33, 62, 70, 86, 94, 107, 126, 132, 144, 148, 152, 170, 182, 186, 187, 188, 240, **247–49**, 251, 267, 277, 303
Squadristi (Fascist), 81
SS. *See* Schutzstaffel